The Art of Data Recording

John Watkinson

For Chrissie

Focal Press
An imprint of Butterworth-Heinemann Ltd
Linacre House, Jordan Hill, Oxford OX2 8DP

A member of the Reed Elsevier plc group

OXFORD LONDON BOSTON
MUNICH NEW DELHI SINGAPORE SYDNEY
TOKYO TORONTO WELLINGTON

First published 1994

© John Watkinson 1994

British Library Cataloguing in Publication Data
Watkinson, John
    Art of Data Recording
    I. Title
    621.382

ISBN 0 240 51309 6

Library of Congress Cataloguing in Publication Data
Watkinson, John
    The art of data recording/John Watkinson.
    p.   cm.
    Includes bibliographical references and index.
    ISBN 0 240 51309 6
    1. Computer storage devices.   I. Title.
TK7895.M4W38   94–10814
621.382'34–dc20   CIP

Composition by Genesis Typesetting, Rochester, Kent
Printed and bound in Great Britain by Clays Ltd, St Ives plc

Contents

Preface

Data recording is becoming increasingly common. From credit card stripes, bar codes, personal computers and Compact Discs to high-definition digital video recorders working at over a gigabit per second, today's world has come to depend on reliable storage, almost to the point where it is taken for granted. Security, national defence, banking, entertainment, manufacturing and transport systems are now critically dependent on computation and data recording, to the extent that in some cases failures can result in deaths and extensive damage. In my view, this is sufficient justification for a book which explains the whole subject of data recording.

Data is the plural of datum, and is a word which has come to be loosely interchangeable with information. For the purposes of this book, data are symbols which can be represented by some form of binary code. The origin of data recording is in digital computation, which in turn grew out of earlier technologies such as Hollerith's punched cards used for census taking. Digital computation gathered momentum during World War II when applications such as weapons design had high priority. Computation is only practicable if instructions and information can be fed in and out of a processor as required, and so the data-recording requirement is obvious. The processing speed of computers continues to rise as techniques are refined and at the same time the cost continues to fall. There is then a requirement for ever higher performance in data-recording systems, which must match the processor in performance and cost. The requirements of the enormous personal computer market have had a major impact on data recording as the product volume and intensive competition justifies extensive research. As a result, storage capacity and cost improve annually. Much of this book is devoted to techniques which are used to increase performance.

The use of binary or switching logic allows a simplification in circuit design in comparison with analog circuits. The invention of pulse code modulation (PCM) by Reeves was intended to allow analog signals to be carried in switching circuits and systems, thus eliminating the gradual signal degradation experienced in complex analog systems. PCM can be applied to any analog waveform, including signals from transducers such as accelerometers, strain gauges, microphones, etc., and is limited only by the data rate which results from the conversion. Manufacturers of instrumentation, audio recorders and video recorders turned to PCM and developed methods of recording whatever bit rate was necessary. In comparison with most computer applications, the data capacity of such machines was rather high and as a result these formats were often adapted for computer purposes.

The approach of this book is that data are unaware of their purpose, as this depends upon the interpretation at the data sink. All that matters is that there is an appropriate combination of cost, speed and reliability for a given application. As a result the examples given here are deliberately chosen from a wide range of applications and have probably not appeared in the same book before.

One of the fascinations of data-recording technology is the wide range of disciplines which are combined. Disparate subjects such as servos, error correction, transform coding, optical physics, magnetism, tribology, structural analysis and aerodynamics, to name only some, are harnessed in practical equipment. Whilst these subjects may be sciences, the skill required to combine the appropriate measure of each in a practical product can only be described as an art; hence the title of this book.

Whilst each of these disciplines has its own specialist vocabulary, it is hardly appropriate in a wide-ranging book like this to assume that the reader is familiar with all specialist terms in all fields. Similarly it is impossible to design this book for a particular reader. I wanted to make this volume more accessible than that; one consequence of that desire is that mathematics has been ruthlessly eliminated wherever possible. Thus this book defines terms as they are met using plain English and explains each step. The first chapter serves as a tutorial introduction to the rest of the book and is a straighforward treatment of the subject in its own right.

Although this book is designed to be easy to follow, it is not an elementary book and each chapter deals comprehensively with the subject and contains references for further study.

Acknowledgements

This is a multidisciplinary book which has required information to be gathered from a wide variety of sources. Without help from my friends in the audio, video, computer and instrumentation recording industries, the groves of academe and learned societies it would not have been possible at all.

My first acknowledgement must be for the opportunities extended by the Digital Equipment Corporation, Sony and Ampex during my various employments. The publications and conventions of several learned societies have been tremendously useful sources. I would particularly thank the Audio Engineering Society, the Society of Motion Picture and Television Engineers, the Institution of Electrical Engineers and the Institute of Electrical and Electronics Engineers.

Many individuals have given time and encouragement and the discussions I have had with them have helped to make the explanations here clearer. My thanks go to C. Denis Mee, Eric Daniel, John Mallinson, Roger Wood, Arvind Patel, Roger Lagadec, Toshi Doi, John Ajimine, Tony Griffiths, Kees Schouhamer Immink, Eng Tan, Yoshinobu Oba and Steve Owen.

John Watkinson
Burghfield Common, England

Chapter 1

Introduction to data recording

Data recording embraces numerous technologies and principles which are covered in detail elsewhere in this book. This chapter is designed to be a tutorial introduction to the subject and to help put the remaining chapters in perspective.

1.1 Uses of data recording

Data recording is an enabling technology which is essential in a surprisingly large number of different areas. Data are simply bit patterns which only have meaning when decoded at the destination, or *data sink*, by a system which is compatible with the encoder used. For example, an eight bit binary number could represent an ASCII character in a word processor, a pixel in a video recorder, a microprocessor instruction, or half a sample on a CD. In between the source and destination, all data are basically the same, and for many purposes any type of data can in principle be recorded on any type of data recorder.

Figure 1.1 shows that data recording can be combined with other processes to produce a wide range of useful devices. The first, large requirement for data recording was digital computation; the data may be instructions in the form of programs, or information to be processed. Computer aided design (CAD) uses computation in conjunction with graphic images to assist in the rapid design of manufactured items. Computer aided manufacturing (CAM) uses computation to control automated manufacture. Computer graphics may be used as an art form, for the production of animated films, for television captions or for icon-driven computer programs. Computers are often interconnected in communications systems. The conversion of analog signals into data results in digital audio, video and instrumentation recorders. All of these processes have in common the need for reliable storage of data.

As the basic principles of digital recording are independent of the application, it is not uncommon to find recorders designed for one purpose being used for another. The audio, video and film community have embraced the random access of hard disks in order to build so-called non-linear editing equipment. To redress the balance, as it were, the computer industry converted Compact Disc into CD-ROM and RDAT (rotary-head digital audio tape) into DDS (digital data storage). Digital video recorders have also been adapted for computer data storage (e.g. DD-2) and the instrumentation community developed the D-1 DVTR into the MIL-STD 2179 data recorder. Eventually recorder designers may simply

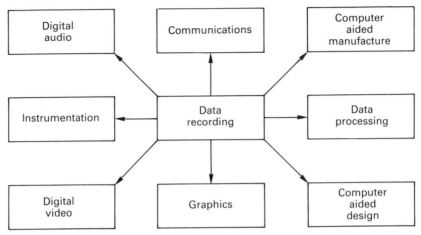

Figure 1.1 Data recording is an enabling technology and is thus found at the centre of this diagram. When combined with one or more of the peripheral technologies, many useful devices can be implemented.

produce generic devices which will be tailored to specific applications by appropriate interfaces and formatting logic.

1.2 Characteristics of source data

Whatever the source, it is possible to categorize data in just a few ways. In some applications, the data must be accepted from the source and returned at a particular rate. Where the direction is immaterial, the term *data transfer* can be used. In digital audio recording, the data rate at the source and sink must be phenomenally stable if audible impairments are to be avoided. Digital audio data are continuous and cannot be interrupted. Digital video data also require a stable timebase at the sink but there are periodic interruptions in the data flow owing to the need for flyback time in the display. These are real-time applications having a constant average transfer rate.

Instrumentation data are harder to categorize. Signals from accelerometers and strain gauges require a constant data rate, but in other cases the data rate may vary. In extreme cases in, for example, radar receivers, instrumentation data may start and stop at random. It is often required to reproduce instrumentation recordings at less than normal speed in order to allow analysis. Telemetry data from satellites may be in this category, as the data gathered during one orbit are sent back during the short time an earth station remains within range.

Most computer data are required by non-real-time processes. Computers can supply and accept data at virtually any rate and generally a dependent process will not begin until all data are received. The data rate simply affects the speed of response. Computers are often available with a range of storage devices of different transfer rate and cost to give users a choice for their intended applications.

Thus an important parameter of source data is the rate, or sometimes the minimum rate, at which it must be transferred. In practical machines, a high peak data rate may be possible, but sometimes this cannot be sustained. Peak and average transfer rates may be used to show the whole picture.

If the source data rate is too great for the recorder envisaged, then some form of data reduction or source coding may be used. Source coding takes advantage of natural redundancy in real signals to reduce the data required to represent them. There are two forms of data reduction. In the first, the data are subsequently recovered bit for bit and there is no loss whatsoever. Such systems are essential for computer use. Alternatively, in audio, video or graphic data, perceptual coding may be used to reduce the data rate by removing signals which humans cannot perceive. Such systems are not fully reversible. Data reduction processes are statistical, and the degree of compression will depend on the input data. Thus the output data rate from a reduction unit may be variable even if the input is constant.

No data recorder is perfect, and another important parameter is the bit error rate (BER) which the data can tolerate. Computer instructions are highly intolerant of bit errors as these are a necessarily concise form of data. A corrupted instruction can crash a processor. In contrast digital audio data can accept a much higher BER, and even if the errors are audible, there is no equivalent of a crash. Errors in digital video are even more tolerable as human vision is quite forgiving. Audio and video data contain a certain amount of redundancy, making it possible to conceal errors. This is, of course, impossible in computer instructions. The requirements of instrumentation recording are too diverse to make any general observations.

1.3 Characteristics of data recorders

Data recorders are classified by a number of parameters which are not specific to the operating principle. It is impossible to say which parameter is most important, as this will depend on the application. One vital parameter is the *cost per bit* which is self explanatory and determines the economic viability of a device.

The *transfer rate* has been mentioned above, and it must equal or exceed the requirements of the application.

The access time, or *latency*, is a vital parameter. This is the time taken from a request for a transaction to the beginning of the data transfer. Devices such as tapes are called serial access stores, whereas disks and RAM are referred to as random access storage devices (in IBM, Direct Access is the term used).

Most practical data recorders have a higher BER than the data allow. The solution is to use an error correction system of appropriate power. The error rate from the storage medium is called the *raw* error rate, but after error correction the *residual* error rate is what matters. A poor medium combined with a powerful error correction system may achieve the same residual BER as a good medium with a less powerful correction system, but the raw BER will be quite different.

Recording media are also classified by practical matters such as *exchange-ability*. This is the ability physically to transfer the medium from one drive to another and reliably to read the data. Often the need for exchangeability will compromise some other parameters. Exchangeable media often have higher cost per bit and slower access.

Some media can only be written once; the recording then becomes permanent. The acronym WORM (write once read many) is applied to such media. In other media the data may be erased and re-recorded a limited or an indefinite number of times. Media also vary in lifetime; some decay more rapidly than others.

1.4 Recording media

Recording requires a physical carrier or medium which is moved with respect to a pickup or head by a transport or drive. The head can selectively make some stable change to the carrier which can be detected at some later time. There are several types of carrier which can be classified as follows:

(1) *Magnetic*. The carrier has a magnetic coating whose magnetization can be altered by the recording head. Magnetic tape, credit cards, hard and floppy disks are in this category. Bubble memories also operate using stored magnetic fields.

(2) *Mechanical*. The carrier is physically deformed by the recording process. Holes can be punched in paper tape, cards or thin metal disks. Barrel organs are programmed by such a carrier, which was also used to control Jacquard looms a century ago. Thin metal punched disks were used in Swiss music boxes. Nowadays the holes are smaller and may be punched by laser in WORM disks. The Compact Disc is mechanical in that the information is carried in a relief structure which can be conveniently duplicated by moulding.

(3) *Optical*. The carrier is recorded by altering its optical characteristics such as reflectivity or transmittivity using, for example, photographic techniques. Bar codes are read in this way.

Random access memory (RAM) is not generally considered to be a recording medium but has many of the attributes of traditional media. Data are stored as the amount of electric charge in a tiny capacitor. Unlike other recording media, RAM is volatile, and loss of power will destroy the recording. There are more recent devices which can retain data without applied power, for example NOVRAM (non-volatile RAM) and these will be used for recording applications whenever their high cost per bit can be justified.

1.5 Readout mechanisms

There are numerous readout or pickup systems, and sometimes the same carrier can be read by more than one readout technique. Magnetic recordings are read by a head which converts flux variations into an electrical signal. Magnetic recordings can also be read optically using the Kerr or Faraday effects in which magnetism rotates the plane of polarization of light. Mechanical recordings having punched holes can be read by light beams or airflow, both of which will be interrupted except where there is a hole. Optical recordings are obviously read by a light beam which can be transmissive or reflective. Variations in the optical characteristics of the carrier affect the light returning from the carrier.

Uniquely, the CD and CD-ROM are mechanical recordings which do not have any variation in the optical characteristics of the carrier. The entire surface of the carrier is metallized and all incident light is always reflected. Deformities out of the plane of the carrier selectively cause incident light to be diffracted outside the aperture of the pickup, causing an apparent contrast known as phase contrast.

1.6 Magnetic tape recording

Magnetic recording relies on the hysteresis of certain magnetic materials. After an applied magnetic field is removed, the material remains magnetized in the same direction. By definition the process is non-linear, and analog magnetic recorders have to use bias to linearize it. Digital recorders are not concerned with the non-linearity, and HF bias is unnecessary.

Figure 1.2 shows the construction of a typical stationary-head magnetic tape transport. The tape is driven by a capstan which determines the speed, and the reel motors are used to control the supply and take-up tension. The tape passes in a curved path across the heads and the tension results in a suitable contact pressure. Figure 1.3 shows a typical digital head, which is not dissimilar in principle to an analog head. Various terms are used to describe heads. The computer community prefers terms such as write head, read head and read/write head, whereas the audio and video community refers to record heads and replay, or reproduce, heads. There seems to be no alternative term for the erase head.

In order to write data, a magnetic circuit carries a coil through which the write current passes and generates flux. A non-magnetic gap forces the flux to leave the magnetic circuit of the head and penetrate the medium. The current through the head must be set to suit the coercivity of the tape. The amplitude of the current is constant, and writing is performed by reversing the direction of the current with respect to time. As the track passes the head, this is converted to the reversal of the magnetic field left on the tape with respect to distance. The magnetic recording is therefore bipolar. Figure 1.4 shows that the recording is actually made just after the trailing pole of the record head where the flux strength from the gap is falling. As in analog recorders, the width of the gap is generally made quite large to ensure that the full thickness of the magnetic coating is recorded, although this cannot be done if the same head is intended to be used for replay. Magnetic reversals on the tape are known as flux changes or transitions.

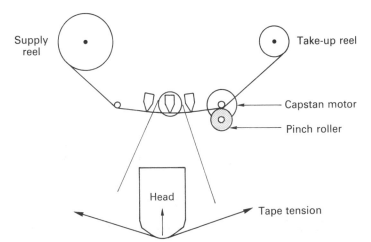

Figure 1.2 Stationary-head tape transport. Capstan provides constant linear tape speed with varying reel contents. Reel motors provide tension needed for head contact.

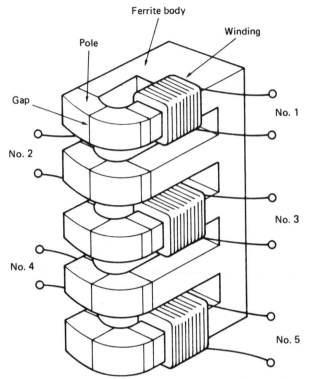

Figure 1.3 A typical ferrite head – windings are placed on alternate sides to save space, but parallel magnetic circuits have high crosstalk.

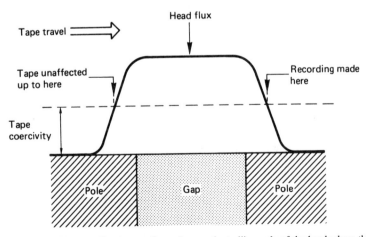

Figure 1.4 The recording is actually made near the trailing pole of the head where the head flux falls below the coercivity of the tape.

1.7 Rotary-head digital recorders

The rotary-head recorder borrows technology from video recorders. Rotary heads have a number of advantages which will be detailed in Chapter 8. One of these is extremely high packing density: the number of data bits which can be recorded in a given space. This results in an extremely low cost per bit.

In a rotary-head recorder, the heads are mounted in a revolving drum and the tape is wrapped around the surface of the drum in a helix as can be seen in Figure 1.5. The helical tape path results in the heads traversing the tape in a series of diagonal or slanting tracks. The space between the tracks is controlled not by head design but by the speed of the tape, and in modern recorders this space is reduced to zero with corresponding improvement in packing density.

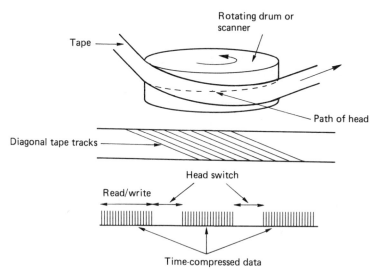

Figure 1.5 In a rotary-head recorder, the helical tape path around a rotating head results in a series of diagonal or slanting tracks across the tape. Time compression is used to create gaps in the recorded data which coincide with the switching between tracks.

The added complexity of the rotating heads and the circuitry necessary to control them is offset by the improvement in density. The discontinuous tracks of the rotary-head recorder are naturally compatible with time-compressed data.

1.8 Magnetic disk recording

Heads designed for use with tape work in actual contact with the magnetic coating. The tape is tensioned to pull it against the head. There will be a wear mechanism and need for periodic cleaning.

Rigid, or hard, magnetic disk drives are designed for rapid access, and they evolved from rotating drum stores. Unlike tape, the entire data surface of a disk is permanently accessible. Data are written in concentric tracks on a revolving disk by a stationary head. In the hard disk, the rotational speed is high in order to reduce rotational latency. In the worst case, where the wanted data have just passed the head, the latency will be the rotational period. The average rotational latency will be half this amount.

As the drive must be capable of staying on line for extended periods, the heads do not contact the disk surface, but are supported on a boundary layer of air. The presence of the air film causes spacing loss, which restricts the wavelengths at which the head can replay. This is the penalty of rapid access.

The spacing loss due to the air film can be minimized by using a small head-to-disk spacing, or flying height, but this raises the precision required, and increases the possibility of a *head crash* in which contamination becomes trapped between head and disk with disastrous consequences. As contamination is most likely to be encountered when disks are exchanged, one solution was to make a drive in which the disk could not be removed. The entire assembly was sealed to exclude dirt, allowing a lower flying height and higher recording density. This is the basis of the Winchester disk drive.

Early disk drives had one fixed head for every data track, but this increases the cost, particularly as the number of tracks rose with density improvements. This led to the development of the moving-head disk drive, in which the tracks on each data surface could be accessed by moving a single head on a positioner.

Clearly the time taken to position the head, the *positioning latency*, has to be added to the *rotational latency* to obtain the overall access time. This led to the development of extremely rapid positioners.

In the case of the floppy disk, rapid access takes second place to low cost. The head is in physical contact with the disk and the situation is more like that of tape recording. In fact floppy disks are punched from wide, thick tape in manufacture. Wear is minimized by retracting the head or stopping the disk unless data transfer is taking place.

The Bernoulli disk is positioned functionally between hard and floppy disks. Whilst the disk itself is floppy, it is spun at high speed adjacent to a fixed flat surface. The resultant air film stabilizes the disk. It is then possible to employ a flying head as in a hard disk drive with corresponding improvements in access time and transfer rate.

1.9 Optical disk recording

The small flying height of magnetic disk drives is a drawback. The advantage of optical recording methods is that light can be focused from a distance on to the medium. No close contact between the pickup and the medium is necessary and the risk of head crashes does not arise. This makes it easy to provide an exchangeable optical disk.

There are many different types of optical disk, but the only ones which can compete in the same applications as the magnetic hard disk are those which are erasable. In the early days of optical disks, claims were often heard that magnetic disks would be superseded. This has not happened, and it is not difficult to see why. Firstly, the development of the optical disk acted as an incentive to improve the performance of magnetic disks. Secondly, there are good physical reasons. The magnetic disk is relatively simple to manufacture, whereas the information layer of an optical disk is complex. The pickup of an optical drive must carry a collection of mirrors, lenses, etc., and this must be larger and heavier than a magnetic head, resulting in slower access time. The size of the optical pickup makes multiplatter drives difficult to construct, whereas the slim magnetic head allows disks to be stacked close together in a compact assembly.

The resolution of disk optics is limited by the wave nature of light, and that limit is reached in current hardware. Improvement can only be obtained by using shorter wavelength lasers. The limits of magnetic physics are still some way off, and ultimately magnetic recording will overtake optical recording in density.

It would appear that optical and magnetic disks will coexist. The speed and density of Winchester disks will be complemented by the exchangeability of optical disks.

1.10 Recording media compared

Despite years of competition no single digital recording technology has dominated the others, leading to the conclusion that no single one is best in all circumstances. It is worth considering why that should be, because this may reveal a fundamental pattern which will hold as a model on which the future may be based. The only factor which might invalidate the model is the sudden discovery of some new recording technique. It will be seen in Figure 1.6 that digital recording only requires some parameter to be maintained in one of two states. The examples given there cover all of the families of physical processes, so something different is unlikely not least because it would have appeared by now if it were simple enough to be economically useful. One learns not to use the

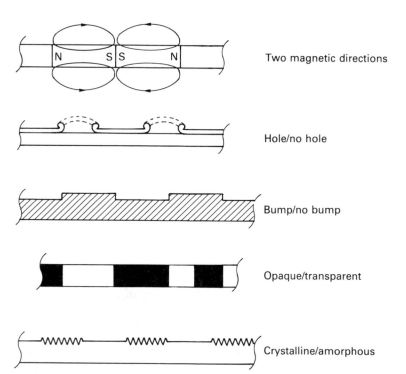

Two magnetic directions

Hole/no hole

Bump/no bump

Opaque/transparent

Crystalline/amorphous

Figure 1.6 The basic physics behind all data recording is no more complicated than leaving the medium in two distinguishable states.

word impossible, and there is still a slim chance that something may come along and turn recording on its head.

Today's data recording takes place on a wide variety of media. These include RAM, magnetic and optical disk, stationary-head tape and rotary-head tape. Media have primarily been compared on three factors: the access time, the cost per bit and the transfer rate. Subsidiary considerations include exchangeability, reliability, and reaction to power loss.

Figure 1.7 contrasts technologies in access time terms. RAM has extremely rapid access time because it has no moving parts (except for electrical charge). Magnetic disks come next because the whole recording area is exposed to a two-dimensional access mechanism (rotation and radial address). Optical disks have the same access principle, but the pickup is heavier and slower. Tape and film come last in this race because they have to be shuttled to expose the wanted area to the pickup.

Fast	Access time	Cost per bit	Low
↑	RAM	Tape	↑
	Disk	Disk	
Slow	Tape	RAM	High

Figure 1.7 The access time of media is contrasted in the left-hand column, whereas the cost per bit is contrasted in the right-hand column. Note the reverse ranking, illustrating that there is no one best medium.

Figure 1.7 also contrasts the cost per bit. Here magnetic tape is supreme because it is such a simple medium to manufacture. Rotary-head tape comes top because it offers higher recording density than stationary heads allow. Magnetic disk drives need an air film between the disk surface and the head to eliminate wear so they can stay on line for years at a time. As stated, this causes a spacing loss and limits the recording density. Also the precision metal disk substrate costs more to make than plastic film. These factors push the cost per bit up.

Erasable optical disks are also expensive to make because of the complex construction. Most expensive is RAM which is extremely intricate, with every bit having its own wiring inside a chip.

It will be seen that the best medium on one scale is the worst on the other! Thus there is no overall best storage technology, and this will continue to be true in the future, because improvements will occur to all media in parallel until physical limits are finally reached.

It is worthwhile exploring these limits. Figure 1.8 shows how the storage density of any technology is determined by the size of the bit which can be individually created. In RAM, the size of the bit is limited by our ability to produce sufficient resolution in the photographic process which precedes the etching of the RAM structure. The same is true of the size of feature which can be resolved on an optical or magneto-optical disk. In fact the disk has an easier job because it scans one bit at a time. The optics of a disk drive only need a very small field of view, whereas the optics needed to expose the track pattern of a chip must have a wide field of view and this is harder to achieve. The only way

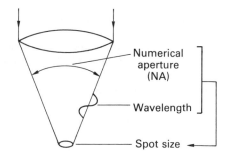

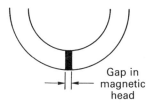

Figure 1.8 All practical media have some fundamental limit to their recording density as shown here.

to increase resolution is to use shorter wavelength light. Any progress in that direction can be employed to increase the capacity of RAM and optical disk, maintaining the relative status quo.

In magnetic recording, the density is determined by the wavelength along the track which can be resolved by the head and the narrowest track which can be followed by the mechanism. A great deal of improvement remains to be made in tracking mechanisms which allow ever narrower tracks to be reliably followed. As the area of the bit gets smaller, noise becomes a problem, and this is opposed by the adoption of higher coercivity media. The coercivity of current media has yet to reach the physical limits, but is instead limited by the availablity of heads which can apply sufficiently powerful fields to media without themselves saturating.

Unlike optical recording, where the wave nature of light sets a limit on density, there is no such limit in contact magnetic recording, and magnetic recording densities in the future may well outstrip those on optical disks. If one considers bits per unit volume rather than bits per unit area, magnetic recording is already ahead. Comparison of the volume of a Compact Disc with the volume of the tape in an RDAT cassette reveals that the RDAT tape has a smaller volume but holds more data.

1.11 Analog and digital

In an analog system, information is carried by infinitely variable parameters which are arranged to change in sympathy with the original information parameter. The vinyl audio disk functions by mimicking the air velocity at the microphone with the transverse velocity of the stylus in a groove. The distance along the groove is a further analog of time. Any waveform is permissible so the unwanted addition of noise or timebase error simply changes one valid signal into another valid signal. As a result analog systems are particularly vulnerable to noise and speed variations. Any lack of linearity in an analog system results in distortion of the waveforms passed.

In contrast a digital system expresses the information as a series of discrete numbers which are supplied at regular intervals. The discrete nature of the time axis means that any unwanted instabilities can be detected and eliminated by the temporary storage of symbols. The effects of noise on a discrete signal are either non-existent or result in the symbol being changed to another discrete value which could be detected by a coding scheme. Such conversion is known as pulse code modulation (PCM) and was first proposed by Reeves.[1,2] In PCM the continuous analog waveforms are sampled, or measured periodically, and then each sample is converted to a discrete value, a process known as quantizing. The wordlength of digital audio samples is commonly sixteen bits, whereas digital video signals are usually represented by eight or ten bit words.

Digital recording can be defined as any technique which allows discrete numbers to be impressed on a medium for subsequent retrieval. All real digital media have analog attributes and digital recording is actually only a way of generating waveforms which, when stored on an analog medium, can be advantageously interpreted as discrete numbers. In other words, whether a medium or a channel is digital or not depends solely on the way in which waveforms passing down it are interpreted. For example, a telephone line can pass speech or connect two modems without modification. Magnetic tape used for analog recording does not differ in any fundamental way from that used for digital recording. Certain video disks store analog video and digital audio in the same waveform.

Data to be recorded are almost always binary numbers of some fixed wordlength. An exception is where data reduction has been used as this may result in variable length words. Wordlength is measured in bits, which is a contraction of 'binary digits'. A word of eight bits is called a byte (although it was originally taken to mean six bits). Words can be computer instructions which are inherently discrete, or they may be samples which result from converting analog signals into data.

1.12 Buffering and time compression

Cases often arise in data recording where there is a mismatch between the timing of the data source/sink and the timing of the medium. In computers, the storage subsystem has to compete with other peripherals for use of the system bus in order to transfer data to or from memory. Other transactions may slow down the transfer rate which can be achieved. Disk drives, however, cannot be slowed down, and if the data rate they require cannot be met, data are lost. The solution is to insert a quantity of memory between the drive and the data source/sink which acts as a buffer.

In applications such as digital audio and certain instrumentation signals, an analog waveform is converted to data. With continuous signals, the ADC must run at a constant clock rate and it outputs an unbroken stream of samples. Time compression allows the sample stream to be broken into blocks for convenient handling.

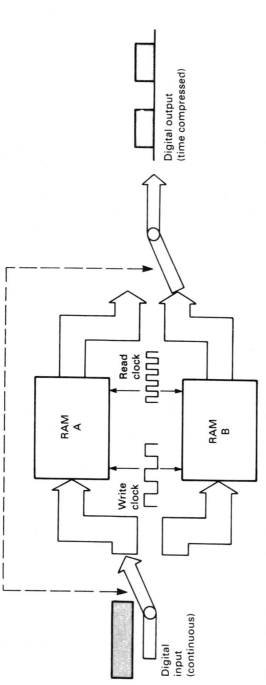

Figure 1.9 In time compression, the unbroken real-time stream of samples from the input is broken up into discrete blocks. This is accomplished by the configuration shown here. Samples are written into one RAM at the sampling rate by the write clock. When the first RAM is full, the switches change over, and writing continues into the second RAM whilst the first is read using a higher-frequency clock. The RAM is read faster than it was written and so all the data will be output before the other RAM is full. This opens spaces in the data flow which are used as described in the text.

Figure 1.9 shows an ADC feeding a pair of RAMs. When one is being written by the ADC, the other can be read, and vice versa. As soon as the first RAM is full, the ADC output switches to the input of the other RAM so that there is no loss of samples. The first RAM can then be read at a higher clock rate than the sampling rate. As a result the RAM is read in less time than it took to write it, and the output from the system then pauses until the second RAM is full. The samples are now time compressed. Instead of being an unbroken stream which is difficult to handle, the samples are now arranged in blocks with convenient pauses in between them. In these pauses numerous processes can take place. A rotary-head recorder might switch heads; a hard disk might move to another track. On all types of recording, the time compression of the data allows space for synchronizing patterns, header and error-correction words to be written.

Subsequently, any time compression can be reversed by time expansion. Samples are written into a RAM at the incoming clock rate, but read out at the standard sampling rate. Unless there is a design fault, time compression is totally indetectable. In a recorder, the time expansion stage can be combined with the timebase correction stage so that speed variations in the medium can be eliminated at the same time. The use of time compression or buffering is universal in data recording. In general the *instantaneous* data rate at the medium is not the same as the data rate at source/sink, although clearly the *average* rate must be the same if the buffer is not to overflow.

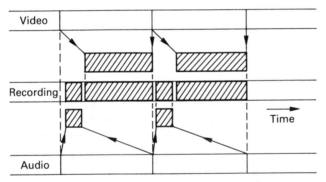

Figure 1.10 Time compression is used to shorten the length of track needed by the video. Heavily time-compressed audio samples can then be recorded on the same track using common circuitry.

Figure 1.10 shows that in digital video recorders both audio and video data are time compressed so that they can share the same heads and tape tracks and much common circuitry.

1.13 Channel coding

In most recorders used for storing digital information, the medium carries a track from which is reproduced a single waveform. Clearly data words contain many bits and so they have to be recorded serially, a bit at a time. Some media, such as CD, only have one track, so it must be totally self contained. Other media, such as tape, have many parallel tracks. At low density, it is possible to arrange a word so that the bits are spread across the tracks, but at high recording densities, physical tolerances cause phase shifts, or relative timing errors, and so it is not possible to read them in parallel. Each track must still be self contained until the replayed signal has been timebase corrected.

Recording data serially is not as simple as connecting the serial output of a shift register to the head. Consider the case where the word to be recorded contains a run of zeros. If a shift register containing zeros is shifted out serially, the output stays at a constant low level, and no feature is recorded on the track. On replay there is nothing to indicate how many zeros were present, or even how fast to move the medium. Clearly, serialized raw data cannot be recorded directly, but must be modulated into a waveform which contains an embedded clock irrespective of the values of the bits in the samples. On replay a circuit called a data separator can lock to the embedded clock and use it to separate strings of identical bits.

The process of modulating serial data to make it self clocking is called channel coding. Channel coding also shapes the spectrum of the serialized waveform to make it more efficient. With a good channel code, more data can be stored on a given medium. Spectrum shaping is used in optical disks to prevent the data from interfering with the focus and tracking servos, and in magnetic recorders to allow the use of azimuth recording and re-recording without erase heads. In rotary-head recorders signals must pass through rotary transformers in order to reach the heads. Such signals cannot contain DC components and channel coding will be used to eliminate them.

All of the techniques of channel coding are covered in detail in Chapter 4.

1.14 Error correction

Although economical, magnetic tape is an imperfect medium. It suffers from noise and dropouts, which in analog recording corrupt the reproduced waveform. In a data recording, a bit is either correct or wrong, with no intermediate stage. Small amounts of noise are rejected but, inevitably, infrequent noise impulses cause some individual bits to be in error. Dropouts cause a larger number of bits in one place to be in error. An error of this kind is called a burst error. Whatever the medium and whatever the nature of the mechanism responsible, data are either recovered correctly, or suffer some combination of bit errors and burst errors. In optical disks, random errors can be caused by imperfections in the manufacturing process, whereas burst errors are due to contamination or scratching of the disk surface.

Real recording media have error rates which are a function of two main factors. The first is the recording principle employed, i.e. the physics of the process. The second is the recording density employed with the process, i.e. the amount of data to be written in a unit area (or volume) of the medium. The error rate of the medium is adapted to the allowable error rate of the application by the use of an error-correction strategy. It is the combination of the medium and the correction strategy which gives the overall quality. It does not really matter from a data reliability standpoint whether we use a grim medium with powerful correction or a wonderful medium with weak correction, although it may matter economically. Error-correction circuitry costs money, but so do high quality media. A Winchester disk cannot be removed from its drive, so only one is necessary; making it of high quality is easier than making all of the tapes which work with one recorder of high quality. As a result, tapes tend to have more powerful correction than disks. Another factor is that the cost of error-correction circuitry falls with time. This year's balance between the medium quality and the correction power could be inappropriate next year.

In binary, a bit has only two states. If it is wrong, it is only necessary to reverse the state and it must be right. Thus the correction process is trivial and perfect. The main difficulty is in identifying the bits which are in error. This is done by coding the data by adding redundant bits. Adding redundancy is not confined to digital technology: airliners have several engines and cars have twin braking systems. Clearly the more failures which have to be handled, the more redundancy is needed. If a four-engined airliner is designed to fly normally with one engine failed, three of the engines must have enough power to reach cruise speed, and the fourth one is redundant. The amount of redundancy is equal to the amount of failure which can be handled. In the case of the failure of two engines, the plane can still fly, but it must slow down; this is graceful degradation. Clearly the chances of a two-engine failure on the same flight are remote.

In data recording, the amount of error which can be corrected is proportional to the amount of redundancy, and it will be shown in Chapter 5 that, within this limit, the symbols are returned to exactly their original value. Consequently *corrected* symbols are indistinguishable from the original. If the amount of error exceeds the amount of redundancy, correction is not possible. In computer data, a retry or a backup recording will be sought, whereas in digital audio and video recording which work in real time, concealment will be used. Concealment is a process where the value of a missing sample is estimated from those nearby. The estimated sample value is not necessarily exactly the same as the original, and so under some circumstances concealment can be detectable, especially if it is

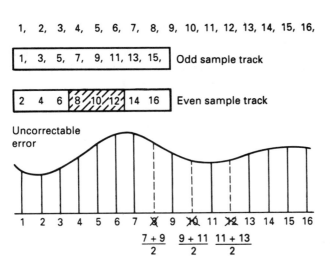

Figure 1.11 In cases where the error correction is inadequate, concealment can be used provided that the samples have been ordered appropriately in the recording. Odd and even samples are recorded in different places as shown here. As a result an uncorrectable error causes incorrect samples to occur singly, between correct samples. In the example shown, sample 8 is incorrect, but samples 7 and 9 are unaffected and an approximation to the value of sample 8 can be made by taking the average value of the two. This interpolated value is substituted for the incorrect value.

frequent. However, in a well-designed system, concealments occur with negligible frequency unless there is an actual fault or problem.

Concealment is made possible by rearranging or shuffling the sample sequence prior to recording. This is shown in Figure 1.11 where odd-numbered samples are separated from even-numbered samples prior to recording. The odd and even sets of samples may be recorded in different places, so that an uncorrectable burst error only affects one set. On replay, the samples are recombined into their natural sequence, and the error is now split up so that it results in every other sample being lost. The waveform is now described half as often, but can still be reproduced with some loss of accuracy. This is better than not being reproduced at all, even if it is not perfect. Almost all digital audio and/or video recorders use such an odd/even shuffle for concealment. Clearly if any errors are fully correctable, the shuffle is superfluous; it is only needed if correction is not possible.

In high-density recorders, more data are lost in a given sized dropout. Adding redundancy equal to the size of a dropout to every code is inefficient. Figure 1.12 shows that the efficiency of the system can be raised using interleaving. Sequential symbols from the source are assembled into codes, but these are not recorded in their natural sequence. A number of sequential codes are assembled along rows in a memory. When the memory is full, it is copied to the medium by reading down columns. On replay, the symbols need to be de-interleaved to return them to their natural sequence. This is done by writing symbols from tape into a memory in columns, and, when it is full, the memory is read in rows. Symbols read from the memory are now in their original sequence so there is no effect on the recording. However, if a burst error occurs on the medium, it will damage sequential symbols in a vertical direction in the de-interleave memory. When the memory is read, a single large error is broken down into a number of small errors whose size is exactly equal to the correcting power of the codes and the correction is performed with maximum efficiency.

The interleave, de-interleave, time compression and timebase correction processes cause delay. In a random access device, this decoding delay must be added to the mechanical latency. This is a further reason why hard disks employ better media and less powerful correction, as suggested above.

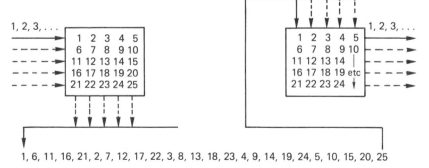

1, 6, 11, 16, 21, 2, 7, 12, 17, 22, 3, 8, 13, 18, 23, 4, 9, 14, 19, 24, 5, 10, 15, 20, 25

Figure 1.12 In interleaving, samples are recorded out of their normal sequence by taking columns from a memory which was filled in rows. On replay the process must be reversed. This puts the samples back in their regular sequence, but breaks up burst errors into many smaller errors which are most efficiently corrected. Interleaving and de-interleaving cause delay.

The presence of an error-correction system means that the data integrity is independent of the medium/head quality within limits. There is no point in trying to assess the health of a machine by studying the output data, as this will not reveal whether the error rate is normal or within a whisker of failure. The only useful procedure is to monitor the frequency with which errors are being corrected, and to compare it with normal figures.

1.15 Outline of a data recorder

Figure 1.13 shows a block diagram of a conceptual data recorder. Each of the stages of processing will be treated in detail in a later chapter, as will the various media and transports. The input may be analog audio, video or instrumentation waveforms, and a suitable analog-to-digital converter is necessary. Alternatively the data may originate in digital form on some standard bus or interface. A buffer may be required if the data source is subject to, for example, bus contention. It may be necessary to distribute the input data over more than one channel. This will be required by stationary-head tape drives, which have many parallel tracks, or in any recorder where the source data rate exceeds the bandwidth of a single channel.

The next stage is to block the data using time compression. This makes space for extra symbols for synchronizing, addressing and error correction. The blocks will be coded by the addition of redundant symbols and may be interleaved to increase resistance to burst errors. The resultant data have no constraints over their bit patterns, and cannot be recorded directly. Instead a channel coding stage is required, which converts data patterns into recordable waveforms which are self clocking and which have a constrained spectrum.

The output of the channel coder is sent to a write head suitable for the medium employed, and a variety of possibilities are available.

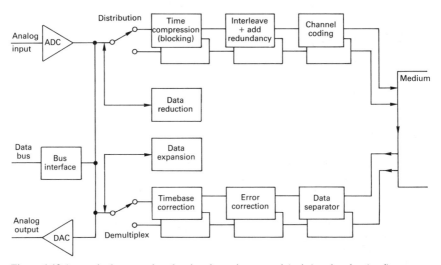

Figure 1.13 A generic data recorder, showing the various record (write) and replay (read) processes used in typical machines.

On reading the medium, the pickup or head reproduces a version of the recorded waveform which may require equalization prior to decoding. The first step in decoding is the data separator which extracts a continuous bit clock from the clock content of the channel-coded data. This clock is used to reverse the channel coding process and to deserialize the data stream in conjunction with the recorded synchronizing patterns.

The data from the data separator will resemble the recorded data except for random errors, burst errors and timebase error. The error correction process will correct random and burst errors, and the timebase error will be removed by buffering. This allows data from several tracks to be combined correctly. Any time compression used during recording may be removed at this stage.

In the case of a computer data recorder, a suitable bus interface will be employed, in which further buffering may be available to accommodate bus contention.

Digital-to-analog converters will be provided for audio, video or instrumentation purposes.

1.16 Practical data recorders

Whilst the basic principles of recording are common, the range of application of data recording is so great that a wide variety of different equipment has been developed. In consumer markets, cost and recording capacity are major concerns, no great operator skill is expected and maintenance is likely to be minimal. In research or in military applications the cost is of less consequence than sheer performance. In compensation, skilled operators are more likely to be available and in large organizations maintenance will be available so that equipment can be made with fewer compromises. Most data recording takes place in an office or laboratory in a moderate environment. In instrumentation recording the environment may be quite the opposite; shock, vibration and extremes of temperature and pressure are quite common. The next few sections of this chapter give outlines of some of the major types of data recorder.

1.17 A disk subsystem

Disk drives are designed for rapid random access to fixed sized blocks of data. Figure 1.14 shows a representative disk subsystem. The disk drive itself contains means to rotate the disk, a positioner to move the heads and generally a channel coder and data separator to convert the data into waveforms suitable for the recording medium and heads. Most disks turn at constant speed and the data circuitry has to lock to the disk rotation. The disk drive will provide timing information which is derived from the disk rotation. One or more disk drives may be connected to a disk controller. The disk controller adapts the characteristics of the disk drive to suit the requirements of the host computer. A disk controller has two main sections; one handles the control of the drives and returns status to the host, the other is concerned with the data transfer itself.

The controller is generally capable of transferring host data by direct memory access rather than tying up the processor. DMA transfers may be interrupted by bus contention with other devices and this conflicts with the constant speed of the disk. A buffer or silo is required to absorb the data rate difference. A DMA transfer will consist of a block of host data of arbitrary size. An essential function

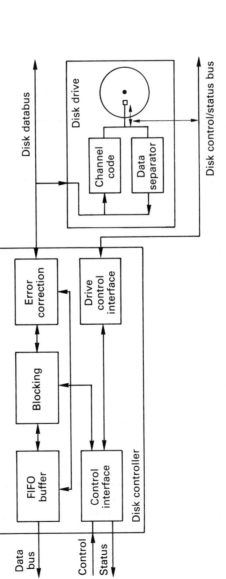

Figure 1.14 A disk subsystem. The drives contain individual channel coding systems, but the disk format is determined by the disk controller which may be shared between several drives.

of the controller is to convert the raw data into fixed sized blocks of formatted data carrying synchronizing patterns and error-correction codes suitable for recording on the disk track.

1.18 Computer tape drives

Tape drives are serial access devices which are often used for archiving or backup of data held on disks. Winchester disks have a particular need for backup because the disk is non-removable and in the case of a failure the data are generally lost. Unlike disks, tape systems frequently operate with data blocks of variable size. Such blocks were not subsequently capable of being rewritten (update in place).

The tape subsystem shown in Figure 1.15 is superficially similar to the disk system of Figure 1.14 except that the control logic is generally called a formatter. As with the disk drive, the tape transport usually contains its own channel coding and data separation system. Many tape formats are designed with quite large gaps between data blocks in which the transport can stop and start. These are known as inter-record gaps (IRG). As a result of this stop–start ability, the amount of data buffering required is reduced.

The formatter is responsible for DMA transfer to and from host memory, and for generation of IRGs, synchronizing patterns and error-correcting codes on the tape track.

In order to speed backup of large, fast Winchester disks, it was necessary to raise the tape speed, but this made it difficult to stop and start within the IRG. The solution was the so-called streamer tape system in which the tape runs continuously at high speed and buffering is used to absorb instantaneous variations in DMA transfer rate. If memory data were not supplied fast enough when writing, the streamer would terminate the block and reverse the tape some way before the end of the recording. Upon data flow resuming, as soon as the buffer began to fill the tape would accelerate and reach operating speed by the end of the previous record. In early streamers the IRGs were retained to allow replay on non-streaming transports. Later formats were designed for streaming only and made the IRGs much smaller to improve packing density.

1.19 RDAT – rotary-head digital audio tape

As its name suggests, the system uses rotary heads, but there is only limited similarity to conventional video recorders. In video recorders, each diagonal tape track stores one television field, and the switch from one track to the next takes place during the vertical interval. In a recorder with two heads, one at each side of the drum, it is necessary to wrap the tape a little more than 180 degrees around the drum so that one head begins a new track just before the previous head finishes. This constraint means that the threading mechanism of VCRs is quite complex. In RDAT, threading is simplified because the digital recording does not need to be continuous. RDAT uses the technique of time compression to squeeze continuous audio samples into intermittent recorded bursts. Blocks of samples to be recorded are written into a memory at the sampling rate, and are read out at a much faster rate when they are to be recorded. In this way, the memory contents can be recorded in less time. Figure 1.5 shows that when the samples are time compressed, recording is no longer continuous, but is interrupted by long pauses.

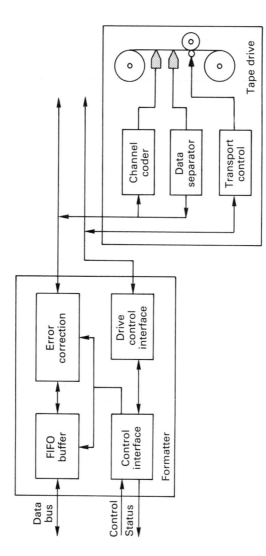

Figure 1.15 A tape subsystem. The general layout is similar to the approach used for disks, but the controller, known as a formatter, has to contend with variable length data blocks and the access process is quite different.

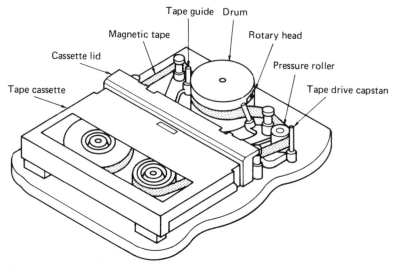

Figure 1.16 The simple mechanism of RDAT. The guides and pressure roller move towards the drum and capstan and threading is complete.

During the pauses in recording, it is not actually necessary for the head to be in contact with the tape, and so the angle of wrap of the tape around the drum can be reduced, which makes threading easier. In RDAT the wrap angle is only 90 degrees on the commonest drum size. As the heads are 180 degrees apart, this means that for half the time neither head is in contact with the tape. Figure 1.16 shows that the partial-wrap concept allows the threading mechanism to be very simple indeed. As the cassette is lowered into the transport, the pinch roller and several guide pins pass behind the tape. These then simply move towards the capstan and drum and threading is complete. A further advantage of partial wrap is that the friction between the tape and drum is reduced, allowing power saving in portable applications, and allowing the tape to be shuttled at high speed without the partial unthreading needed by video cassettes. In this way, the player can read subcode during shuttle to facilitate rapid track access.

The track pattern laid down by the rotary heads is shown in Figure 1.17. The heads rotate at 2000 rev/min in the same direction as tape motion, but because the drum axis is tilted, diagonal tracks 23.5 mm long result at an angle of just over 6 degrees to the edge. The diameter of the scanner needed is not specified, because it is the track pattern geometry which ensures interchange compatibility. For portable machines, a small scanner is desirable, whereas for professional use, a larger scanner allows additional heads to be fitted for confidence replay and editing.

There are two linear tracks, one at each edge of the tape, where they act as protection for the diagonal tracks against edge damage. Owing to the low linear tape speed the use of these edge tracks is somewhat limited.

Figure 1.18 shows a block diagram of a typical RDAT recorder, which will be used to introduce most of the major topics to be described. In order to make a recording, an analog signal is fed to an input ADC, or a direct digital input is taken from an AES/EBU/IEC interface. The incoming samples are subject to

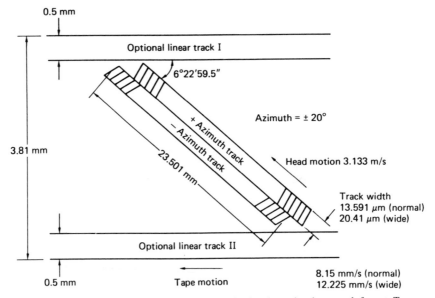

Figure 1.17 The two heads of opposite azimuth angles lay down the above track format. Tape linear speed determines track pitch.

interleaving to reduce the effects of error bursts. Reading the memory at a higher rate than it was written at performs the necessary time compression. Additional bytes of redundancy computed from the samples are added to the data stream to permit subsequent error correction. Subcode information is added, and the parallel byte structure is converted to serial form and fed to the channel encoder, which combines a bit clock with the data and produces a recording signal known as a 8/10 code which is free of DC (see Chapter 4). This signal is fed to the heads via a rotary transformer to make the binary recording, which leaves the tape track with a pattern of transitions between the two magnetic states.

On replay, the transitions on the tape track induce pulses in the head, which are used to re-create the record current waveform. This is fed to the 10/8 decoder which converts it to a serial bit stream and a separate clock. The subcode data are routed to the subcode output, and the audio samples are fed into a de-interleave memory which, in addition to time expanding the recording, functions to remove any wow or flutter due to head-to-tape speed variations. Error correction is performed partially before and partially after de-interleave. The subject of error correction is discussed in Chapter 5. The corrected output samples can be fed to DACs or to a direct digital output.

In order to keep the rotary heads following the very narrow slant tracks, alignment patterns are recorded as well as the data. The automatic track-following system processes the playback signals from these patterns to control the drum and capstan motors. Chapter 6 describes the operation of servos and Chapter 8 describes the tracking system. The subcode and ID information can be used by the control logic to drive the tape to any desired location specified by the user.

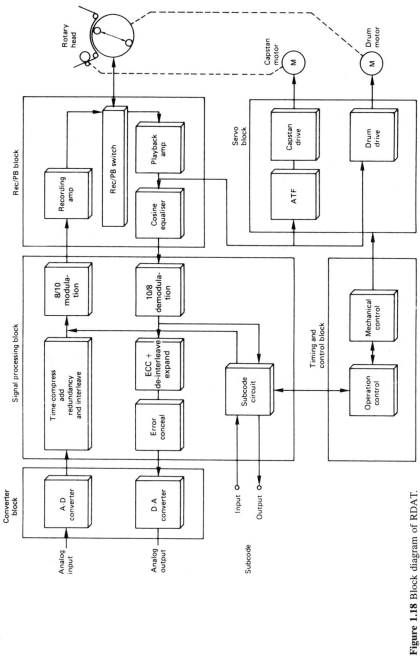

Figure 1.18 Block diagram of RDAT.

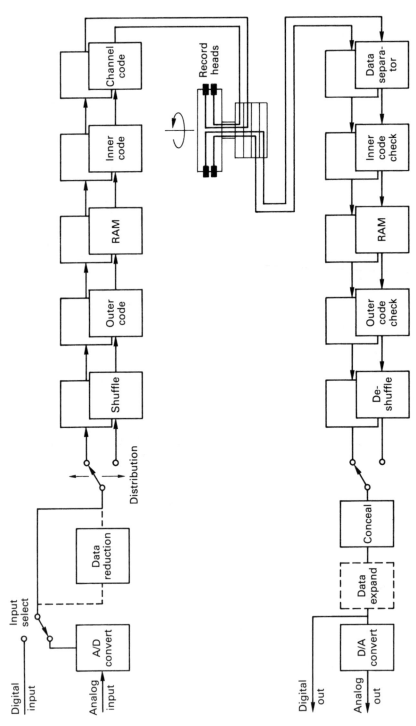

Figure 1.19 Block diagram of a DVTR. Note optional data reduction unit which may be used to allow a common transport to record a variety of formats.

1.20 A digital video recorder

An outline of a composite digital video recorder follows to illustrate the basic principles. Composite video is a single signal where the colour information is conveyed on a modulated subcarrier added to the luminance waveform.

Figure 1.19 shows a representative digital video recorder. Once in digital form, an optional data reduction process may be used. The data are formed into blocks, and the encoding section of the error-correction system supplies additional bits designed to protect the data against errors. These blocks are then converted into some form of channel code which combines the data with clock information in a DC-free waveform.

The coded data are recorded on tape by a rotary head. Upon replaying the recording of the hypothetical machine of Figure 1.19, the errors caused by various mechanisms will be detected, corrected or concealed using the extra bits appended during the encoding process.

In addition to analog video connections, the digital recorder will also have standardized digital inputs and outputs, to allow connection between units of different manufacture.

Chapter 8 details the mechanisms necessary for rotary-head tape recording, and gives some examples, including digital VTRs.

1.21 Instrumentation recorders

Instrumentation recorders have a wide range of duties, but some classifications can be found. Laboratory-based recorders work in a controlled environment and can be of large size. For high bit rate applications such as satellite data, such machines may use large open reels and have many parallel tracks on the tape which moves at high speed. Where huge volumes of data are involved single reels are more space efficient than cassettes which must contain one full reel and one empty one. Many such machines are capable of recording and reproducing at a range of speeds.

Airborne instrumentation recorders must be small, light and resistant to accelerations, yet still offer high capacity. The transverse-scan rotary head is advantageous in this application because it is more compact than helical scan and has lower inertia. Where miniaturization is not paramount, helical-scan recorders

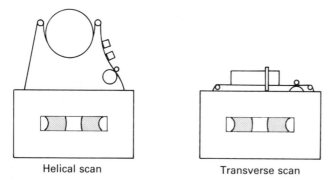

Helical scan   Transverse scan

Figure 1.20 Transverse-scan tape transports can be made much more compact than those using helical scan, making them ideal for airborne applications.

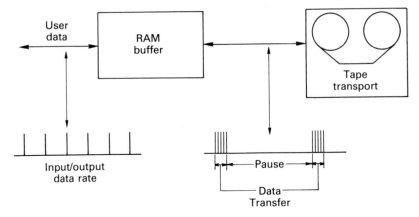

Figure 1.21 Tape transports, particularly those with rotary heads, cannot easily run at a wide range of speeds. The solution is to use RAM buffering, shown here, which allows the transport to run at a single speed incrementally whilst the data source/sink can have any rate up to the maximum.

such as MIL-STD 2179 can be used. Figure 1.20 compares the size of transverse and helical machines.

Rotary-head instrumentation recorders are not easy to operate at variable data rate because the dynamics of the rotating system are quite complex and can only be optimized over a narrow speed range. The solution is to use the principle of incremental operation. Figure 1.21 shows that a large buffer RAM is inserted between the data source/sink and the recorder. The data rate can have any value between zero and maximum, but the transport only runs at one speed or pauses. The RAM buffers the data when the transport pauses. It will be seen in Chapter 8 that a transverse-scan transport is ideally suited to this mode of operation.

1.22 Bibliography

The subject matter of this book is extremely wide ranging and the author is not aware of a similar volume. However, there are a number of definitive works which treat some of the subjects of this book in greater detail. Mallinson[3] forms an excellent introduction to magnetic recording, whereas Bouwhuis et al.[4] is essential reading for those interested in optical recorders. Mee and Daniel[5] is an extremely comprehensive three-volume, multi-author treatment of magnetic recording having copious references. Those requiring a single volume on magnetic recording are referred to Jorgensen.[6] Optical recording is treated in Isailovic.[7] The only comprehensive book on channel coding is the excellent work by Schouhamer Immink.[8]

Error correction is well treated for those with a mathematical bent in Peterson and Weldon,[9] but the chapter by Patel in Mee and Daniel[5] is more relevant to recording.

This book is one of a trilogy, and readers interested in further details of digital audio and video may want to risk more Watkinson.[10,11] RDAT/DDS is treated in a separate volume[12] and a comprehensive treatment of digital video recorder formats is also available in one work.[13]

In this field the majority of documentation is distributed in the form of conference papers and articles in learned journals; numerous references to these will be found in each chapter.

References

1. REEVES, J.H., U.S. Pat. 2,272,070 (1942)
2. CATTERMOLE, K.W., *Principles of pulse code modulation*. London: Iliffe Books Ltd (1969)
3. MALLINSON, J.C., *The foundations of magnetic recording*. London: Academic Press (1987)
4. BOUWHUIS, G. *et al., Principles of optical disc systems*. Bristol: Adam Hilger (1985)
5. MEE, C.D. and DANIEL, E.D. (eds), *Magnetic Recording Vols I–III*. New York: McGraw-Hill
6. JORGENSEN, F., *The complete handbook of magnetic recording*. Blue Ridge Summit, Penn: TAB Books (1980)
7. ISAILOVIC, J., *Videodisc and optical memory systems*. New Jersey: Prentice-Hall (1985)
8. SCHOUHAMER IMMINK, K.A., *Coding techniques for digital recorders*. Hemel Hempstead: Prentice Hall (1991)
9. PETERSON, W.W. and WELDON, E.J., *Error correcting codes*. London: MIT Press (1972)
10. WATKINSON, J.R., *The art of digital audio (second ed.)*. Oxford: Focal Press (1993)
11. WATKINSON, J.R., *The art of digital video (second ed.)*. Oxford: Focal Press (1994)
12. WATKINSON, J.R., *RDAT*. Oxford: Focal Press (1991)
13. WATKINSON, J.R., *The digital video recorder*. Oxford: Focal Press (1994)

Chapter 2

Some essential principles

There are many different types of data recorder, but in virtually all there are common processes and techniques. This chapter brings together all of the common principles to save later repetition.

2.1 Pure binary code

Figure 2.1 shows some binary numbers and their equivalent in decimal. The radix point has the same significance in binary: symbols to the right of it represent one-half, one-quarter and so on. Binary is convenient for electronic circuits, which do not get tired, but numbers expressed in binary become very long, and writing them is tedious and error-prone. The octal and hexadecimal notations are both used for writing binary since conversion is so simple. Figure 2.1 also shows that a binary number is split into groups of three or four digits starting at the least significant end, and the groups are individually converted to octal or hexadecimal digits. Since sixteen different symbols are required in hex, the letters A–F are used for the numbers above nine.

When pulse code modulation is used, there will be a fixed number of bits in each PCM sample. The number of bits determines the size of the quantizing range. For example, in the 16 bit samples used in much digital audio equipment, there are 65 536 different numbers. Each number represents a different analog signal voltage, and care must be taken during conversion to ensure that the signal does not go outside the converter range, or it will be clipped. In Figure 2.2 it will be seen that in a 16 bit pure binary system, the number range goes from 0000 hex, which represents the largest negative voltage, through 7FFF hex, which represents the smallest negative voltage, through 8000 hex, which represents the smallest positive voltage, to FFFF hex, which represents the largest positive voltage. Effectively, the zero voltage level of the audio has been shifted so that the positive and negative voltages in a real audio signal can be expressed by binary numbers which are only positive. This approach is called offset binary, and is perfectly acceptable where the signal has been digitized only for recording or transmission from one place to another, after which it will be converted directly back to analog.

Figure 2.3 shows that the analog signal voltage from many types of transducer, such as microphones and accelerometers, is referred to midrange. The level of the signal is measured by how far the waveform deviates from midrange, and attenuation, gain and adding all take place around that midrange. Such signals

30

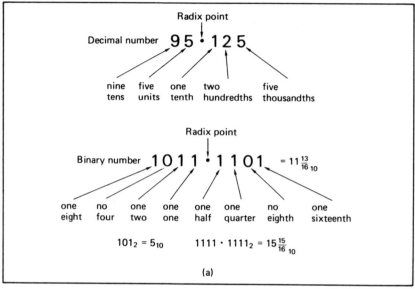

(a)

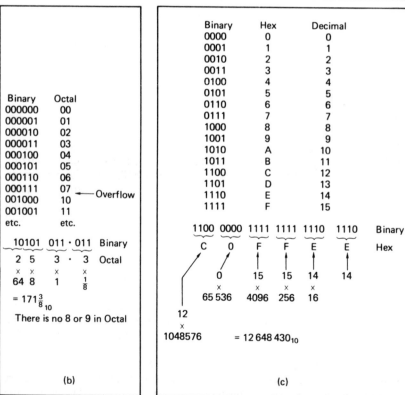

(b)

(c)

Figure 2.1 (a) Binary and decimal. (b) In octal, groups of 3 bits make one symbol 0–7. (c) In hex, groups of 4 bits make one symbol 0–F. Note how much shorter the number is in hex.

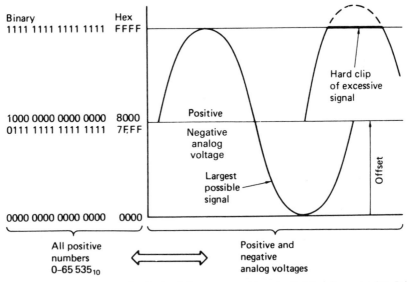

Figure 2.2 Offset binary coding is simple but causes problems in digital audio processing. It is seldom used.

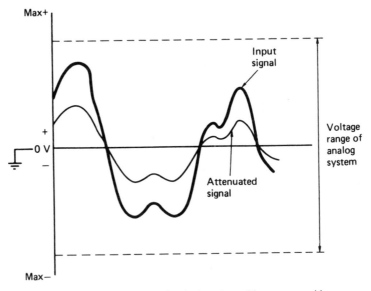

Figure 2.3 Attenuation of an audio signal takes place with respect to midrange.

will also be found in digitally controlled servos, where, for example, a motor or positioner must be capable of being driven in both directions. The motor drive signal may be a function of the difference between some commanded value and the feedback from a sensor and will need to be capable of handling bipolar values.

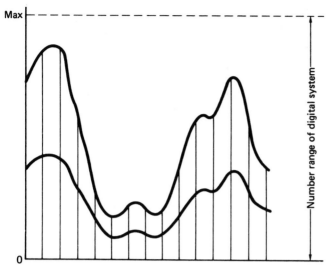

Figure 2.4 The result of an attempted attenuation in pure binary code is an offset. Pure binary cannot be used for digital audio processing.

If two offset binary sample streams are added together in an attempt to perform digital mixing, the result will be that the offsets are also added and this may lead to an overflow. Similarly, if an attempt is made to attenuate by, say, 6.02 dB by dividing all of the sample values by two, Figure 2.4 shows that the offset is also divided and the waveform suffers a shifted baseline. The problem with offset binary is that it works with reference to one end of the range. What is needed in many PCM systems is a numbering system which operates symmetrically with reference to the centre of the range.

2.2 Two's complement

In the two's complement system, the upper half of the pure binary number range has been redefined to represent negative quantities. If a pure binary counter is constantly incremented and allowed to overflow, it will produce all the numbers in the range permitted by the number of available bits, and these are shown for a four bit example drawn around the circle in Figure 2.5. As a circle has no real beginning, it is possible to consider it to start wherever it is convenient. In two's complement, the quantizing range represented by the circle of numbers does not start at zero, but starts on the diametrically opposite side of the circle. Zero is midrange, and all numbers with the MSB (most significant bit) set are considered negative. The MSB is thus the equivalent of a sign bit where 1 = minus. Two's complement notation differs from pure binary in that the most significant bit is inverted in order to achieve the half-circle rotation.

Figure 2.6 shows how a real ADC is configured to produce two's complement output. In (a) an analog offset voltage equal to one-half the quantizing range is added to the bipolar analog signal in order to make it unipolar as in (b). The ADC produces positive-only numbers in (c) which are proportional to the input

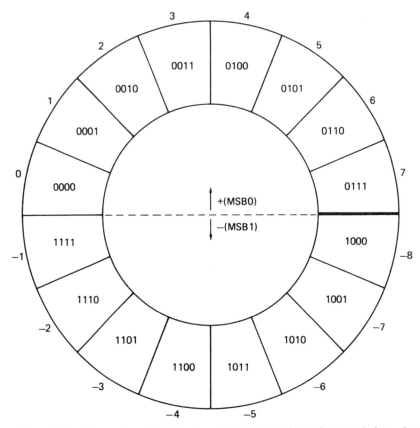

Figure 2.5 In this example of a 4 bit two's complement code, the number range is from −8 to +7. Note that the MSB determines polarity.

voltage. The MSB is then inverted in (d) so that the all-zeros code moves to the centre of the quantizing range. The analog offset is often incorporated in the ADC, as is the MSB inversion. Some converters are designed to be used in either pure binary or two's complement mode. In this case the designer must arrange the appropriate DC conditions at the input. The MSB inversion may be selectable by an external logic level.

The two's complement system allows two sample values to be added and the result will be referred to the system midrange; this is the equivalent of adding analog signals in an operational amplifier.

Figure 2.7 illustrates how adding two's complement samples simulates the analog adding process. The waveform of input A is depicted by solid black samples, and that of B by samples with a solid outline. The result of mixing is the linear sum of the two waveforms obtained by adding pairs of sample values. The dashed lines depict the output values. Beneath each set of samples is the calculation which will be seen to give the correct result. Note that the calculations are pure binary. No special arithmetic is needed to handle two's complement numbers.

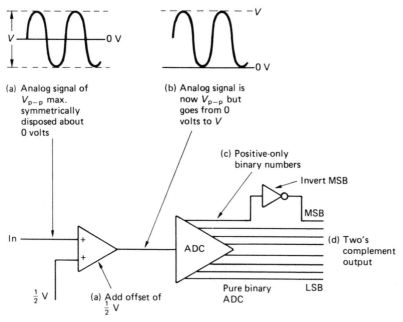

Figure 2.6 A two's complement ADC. In (a) an analog offset voltage equal to one-half the quantizing range is added to the bipolar analog signal in order to make it unipolar as in (b). The ADC produces positive only numbers in (c), but the MSB is then inverted in (d) to give a two's complement output.

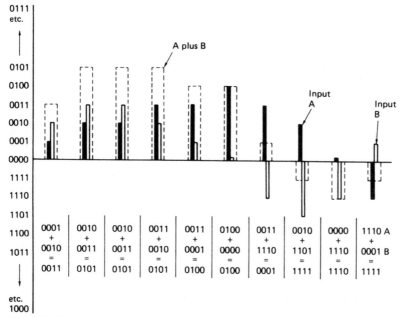

Figure 2.7 Using two's complement arithmetic, single values from two waveforms are added together with respect to midrange to give a correct mixing function.

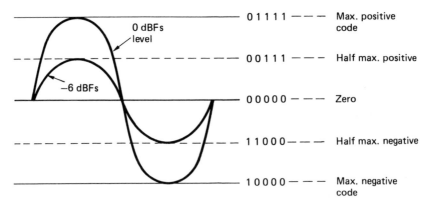

Figure 2.8 0 dBFs is defined as the level of the largest sinusoid which will fit into the quantizing range without clipping.

Figure 2.8 shows some audio waveforms at various levels with respect to the coding values. Where an audio waveform just fits into the quantizing range without clipping it has a level which is defined as 0 dBFs where Fs indicates *full scale*. Reducing the level by 6.02 dB makes the signal half as large and results in the second bit in the sample becoming the same as the sign bit. Reducing the level by a further 6.02 dB to −12 dBFs will make the second and third bits the same as the sign bit and so on. If a signal at −36 dBFs is input to a 16 bit system, only ten bits will be active; the remainder will copy the sign bit. For the best performance, analog inputs to digital systems must have sufficient levels to exercise the whole quantizing range.

It is often necessary to invert a two's complement signal, for example to reverse a servo motor. The process of inversion in two's complement is simple. All bits of the sample value are inverted to form the one's complement, and one is added. This can be checked by mentally inverting some of the values in Figure 2.5. The inversion is transparent and performing a second inversion gives the original sample values.

Using inversion, signal subtraction can be performed using only adding logic. The inverted input is added to perform a subtraction, just as in the analog domain. This permits a significant saving in hardware complexity, since only carry logic is necessary and no borrow mechanism need be supported.

In summary, two's complement notation is the most appropriate scheme for bipolar signals, and allows simple waveform addition in conventional binary logic.

Two's complement numbers can have a radix point and bits below it just as pure binary numbers can. It should, however, be noted that in two's complement, if a radix point exists, numbers to the right of it are added. For example, 1100.1 is not −4.5, it is −4 + 0.5 = −3.5.

2.3 Introduction to digital processes

However complex a digital process, it can be broken down into smaller stages until finally one finds that there are really only two basic types of element in use.

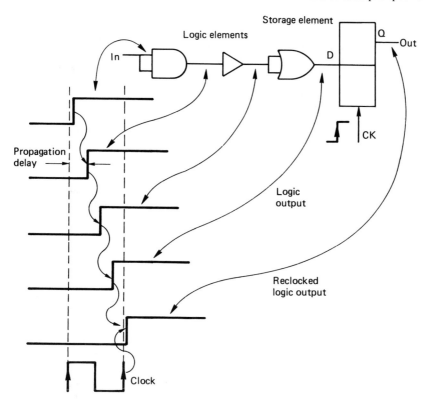

Figure 2.9 Logic elements have a finite propagation delay between input and output and cascading them delays the signal an arbitrary amount. Storage elements sample the input on a clock edge and can return a signal to near coincidence with the system clock. This is known as reclocking. Reclocking eliminates variations in propagation delay in logic elements.

Figure 2.9 shows that the first type is a *logical* element. This produces an output which is a logical function of the input with minimal delay. The second type is a *storage* element which samples the state of the input(s) when clocked and holds or delays that state. The strength of binary logic is that the signal has only two states, and considerable noise and distortion of the binary waveform can be tolerated before the state becomes uncertain. At every logical element, the signal is compared with a threshold, and thus can pass through any number of stages without being degraded. In addition, the use of a storage element at regular locations throughout logic circuits eliminates time variations or jitter. Figure 2.9 shows that if the inputs to a logic element change, the output will not change until the *propagation delay* of the element has elapsed. However, if the output of the logic element forms the input to a storage element, the output of that element will not change until the input is sampled *at the next clock edge*. In this way, the signal edge is aligned to the system clock and the propagation delay of the logic becomes irrelevant. The process is known as reclocking.

2.4 Logic elements

The two states of the signal when measured with an oscilloscope are simply two voltages, usually referred to as high and low. The actual voltage levels will depend on the type of logic family in use, and on the supply voltage used. Within logic, these levels are not of much consequence, and it is only necessary to know them when interfacing between different logic families or when driving external devices. The pure logic designer is not interested at all in these voltages, only in their meaning. Just as the electrical waveform from a microphone represents sound velocity, so the waveform in a logic circuit represents the truth of some statement. As there are only two states, there can only be *true* or *false* meanings. The true state of the signal can be assigned by the designer to either voltage state. When a high voltage represents a true logic condition and a low voltage represents a false condition, the system is known as *positive logic*, or *high true*

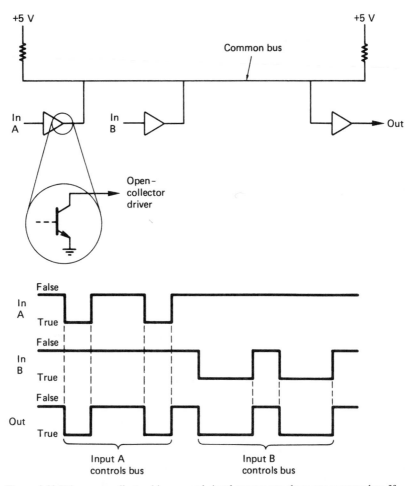

Figure 2.10 Using open-collector drive, several signal sources can share one common bus. If negative logic is used, the bus drivers turn off their output transistors with a false input, allowing another driver to control the bus. This will not happen with positive logic.

logic. This is the usual system, but sometimes the low voltage represents the true condition and the high voltage represents the false condition. This is known as *negative logic* or *low true* logic. Provided that everyone is aware of the logic convention in use, both work equally well.

Negative logic is often found in the TTL (transistor transistor logic) family, because in this technology it is easier to sink current to ground than to source it from the power supply. Figure 2.10 shows that if it is necessary to connect several logic elements to a common bus so that any one can communicate with any other, an open-collector system is used, where high levels are provided by pull-up resistors and the logic elements only pull the common line down. If positive logic were used, when no device was operating the pull-up resistors would cause the common line to take on an absurd true state; whereas if negative

Positive logic name	Boolean expression	Positive logic symbol	Positive logic truth table	Plain English
Inverter or NOT gate	$Q = \overline{A}$	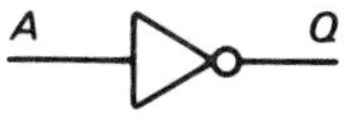	$\begin{array}{c\|c} A & Q \\ \hline 0 & 1 \\ 1 & 0 \end{array}$	Output is opposite of input
AND gate	$Q = A \cdot B$	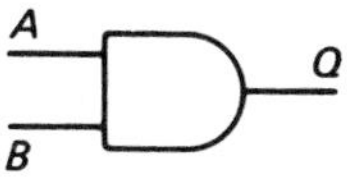	$\begin{array}{cc\|c} A & B & Q \\ \hline 0 & 0 & 0 \\ 0 & 1 & 0 \\ 1 & 0 & 0 \\ 1 & 1 & 1 \end{array}$	Output true when both inputs are true only
NAND (Not AND) gate	$Q = \overline{A \cdot B}$ $= \overline{A} + \overline{B}$	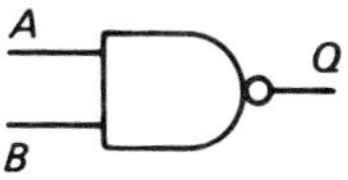	$\begin{array}{cc\|c} A & B & Q \\ \hline 0 & 0 & 1 \\ 0 & 1 & 1 \\ 1 & 0 & 1 \\ 1 & 1 & 0 \end{array}$	Output false when both inputs are true only
OR gate	$Q = A + B$	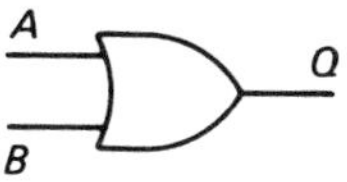	$\begin{array}{cc\|c} A & B & Q \\ \hline 0 & 0 & 0 \\ 0 & 1 & 1 \\ 1 & 0 & 1 \\ 1 & 1 & 1 \end{array}$	Output true if either or both inputs true
NOR (Not OR) gate	$Q = \overline{A + B}$ $= \overline{A} \cdot \overline{B}$	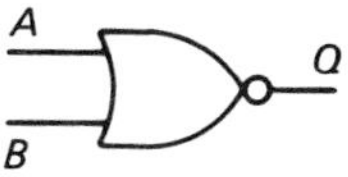	$\begin{array}{cc\|c} A & B & Q \\ \hline 0 & 0 & 1 \\ 0 & 1 & 0 \\ 1 & 0 & 0 \\ 1 & 1 & 0 \end{array}$	Output false if either or both inputs true
Exclusive OR (XOR) gate	$Q = A \oplus B$	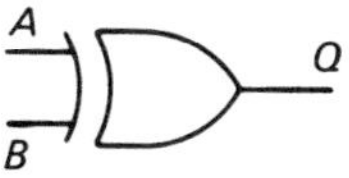	$\begin{array}{cc\|c} A & B & Q \\ \hline 0 & 0 & 0 \\ 0 & 1 & 1 \\ 1 & 0 & 1 \\ 1 & 1 & 0 \end{array}$	Output true if inputs are different

Figure 2.11 The basic logic gates compared.

logic is used, the common line pulls up to a sensible false condition when there is no device using the bus. Whilst the open collector is a simple way of obtaining a shared bus system, it is limited in frequency of operation due to the time constant of the pull-up resistors charging the bus capacitance. In the so-called tri-state bus systems, there are both active pull-up and pull-down devices connected in the so-called totem-pole output configuration. Both devices can be disabled to a third state, where the output assumes a high impedance, allowing some other driver to determine the bus state.

In logic systems, all logical functions, however complex, can be configured from combinations of a few fundamental logic elements or *gates*. It is not profitable to spend too much time debating which are the truly fundamental ones, since most can be made from combinations of others. Figure 2.11 shows the important simple gates and their derivatives, and introduces the logical expressions to describe them, which can be compared with the truth-table notation. The figure also shows the important fact that when negative logic is used, the OR gate function interchanges with that of the AND gate. Sometimes schematics are drawn to reflect which voltage state represents the true condition. In the so-called intentional logic scheme, a negative logic signal always starts and ends at an inverting 'bubble'. If an AND function is required between two negative logic signals, it will be drawn as an AND symbol with bubbles on all the terminals, even though the component used will be a positive logic OR gate. Opinions vary on the merits of intentional logic.

If numerical quantities need to be conveyed down the two-state signal paths described here, then the only appropriate numbering system is binary, which has only two symbols, 0 and 1. Just as positive or negative logic could be used for the truth of a logical binary signal, it can also be used for a numerical binary signal. Normally, a high voltage level will represent a binary 1 and a low voltage will represent a binary 0, described as a 'high for a one' system. Clearly a 'low for a one' system is just as feasible. Decimal numbers have several columns, each of which represents a different power of ten; in binary the column position specifies the power of two.

Several binary digits or bits are needed to express the value of a binary audio sample. These bits can be conveyed at the same time by several signals to form a parallel system, which is most convenient inside equipment because it is fast, or one at a time down a single signal path, which is slower, but convenient for cables between pieces of equipment because the connectors require fewer pins. When a binary system is used to convey numbers in this way, it can be called a digital system.

2.5 Storage elements

The basic memory element in logic circuits is the latch, which is constructed from two gates as shown in Figure 2.12(a), and which can be set or reset. A more useful variant is the D-type latch shown in (b) which remembers the state of the input at the time a separate clock either changes state for an edge-triggered device, or after it goes false for a level-triggered device. D-type latches are commonly available with four or eight latches to the chip. A shift register can be made from a series of latches by connecting the Q output of one latch to the D input of the next and connecting all of the clock inputs in parallel. Data are

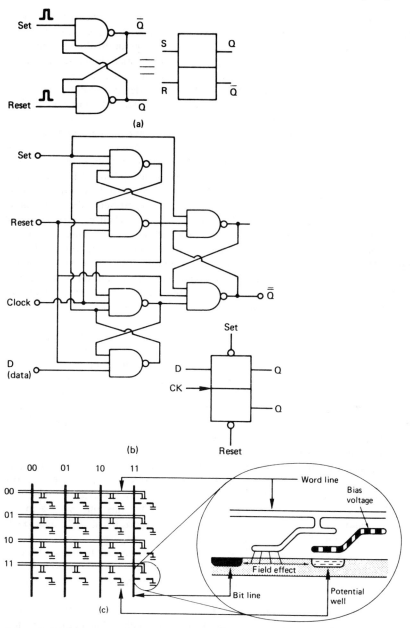

Figure 2.12 Digital semiconductor memory types. In (a), one data bit can be stored in a simple set–reset latch, which has little application because the D-type latch in (b) can store the state of the single data input when the clock occurs. These devices can be implemented with bipolar transistors of FETs, and are called static memories because they can store indefinitiely. They consume a lot of power.

In (c), a bit is stored as the charge in a potential well in the substrate of a chip. It is accessed by connecting the bit line with the field effect from the word line. The single well where the two lines cross can then be written or read. These devices are called dynamic RAMs because the charge decays, and they must be read and rewritten (refreshed) periodically.

delayed by the number of stages in the register. Shift registers are also useful for converting between serial and parallel data transmissions.

Where large numbers of bits are to be stored, cross-coupled latches are less suitable because they are more complicated to fabricate inside integrated circuits than dynamic memory, and consume more current.

In large random access memories (RAMs), the data bits are stored as the presence or absence of charge in a tiny capacitor as shown in Figure 2.12(c). The capacitor is formed by a metal electrode, insulated by a layer of silicon dioxide from a semiconductor substrate, hence the term MOS (metal oxide semi-conductor). The charge will suffer leakage, and the value would become indeterminate after a few milliseconds. Where the delay needed is less than this, decay is of no consequence, as data will be read out before they have had a chance to decay. Where longer delays are necessary, such memories must be refreshed periodically by reading the bit value and writing it back to the same place. Most modern MOS RAM chips have suitable circuitry built in. Large RAMs store thousands of bits, and it is clearly impractical to have a connection to each one. Instead, the desired bit has to be addressed before it can be read or written. The size of the chip package restricts the number of pins available so that large memories use the same address pins more than once. The bits are arranged internally as rows and columns, and the row address and the column address are specified sequentially on the same pins.

2.6 Binary adding

The binary circuitry necessary for adding two's complement numbers is shown in Figure 2.13. Addition in binary requires pairs of bits to be taken from the same position in each word, starting at the least significant bit. Should both be ones, the output is zero, and there is a *carry-out* generated. Such a circuit is called a half adder, shown in Figure 2.13(a), and is suitable for the least-significant bit of the calculation. All higher stages will require a circuit which can accept a carry input as well as two data inputs. This is known as a full adder (Figure 2.13(b)). Multibit full adders are available in chip form, and have carry-in and carry-out terminals to allow them to be cascaded to operate on long wordlengths. Such a device is also convenient for inverting a two's complement number, in conjunction with a set of inverters. The adder chip has one set of inputs grounded, and the carry-in permanently held true, such that it adds one to the one's complement number from the inverter.

When mixing by adding sample values, care has to be taken to ensure that if the sum of the two sample values exceeds the number range the result will be clipping rather than wraparound. In two's complement, the action necessary depends on the polarities of the two signals. Clearly if one positive and one negative number are added, the result cannot exceed the number range. If two positive numbers are added, the symptom of positive overflow is that the most significant bit sets, causing an erroneous negative result, whereas a negative overflow results in the most significant bit clearing. The overflow control circuit will be designed to detect these two conditions, and override the adder output. If the MSB of both inputs is zero, the numbers are both positive, thus if the sum has the MSB set, the output is replaced with the maximum positive code (0111 ...). If the MSB of both inputs is set, the numbers are both negative, and if the sum has no MSB set, the output is replaced with the maximum

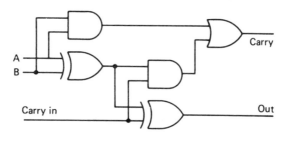

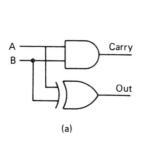

(a)

Data A	Bits B	Carry in	Out	Carry out
0	0	0	0	0
0	0	1	1	0
0	1	0	1	0
0	1	1	0	1
1	0	0	1	0
1	0	1	0	1
1	1	0	0	1
1	1	1	1	1

(b)

(c)

Figure 2.13 (a) Half adder; (b) full-adder circuit and truth table; (c) comparison of sign bits prevents wraparound on adder overflow by substituting clipping level.

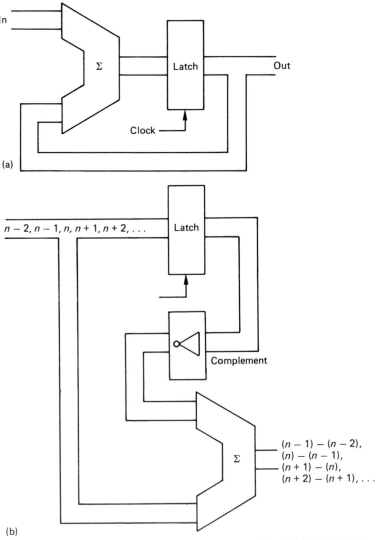

Figure 2.14 Two configurations which are common in processing. In (a) the feedback around the adder adds the previous sum to each input to perform accumulation or digital integration. In (b) an inverter allows the difference between successive inputs to be computed. This is differentiation.

negative code (1000...). These conditions can also be connected to warning indicators. Figure 2.13(c) shows this system in hardware. The resultant clipping on overload is sudden, and sometimes a PROM or software routine is included which translates values around and beyond maximum to soft-clipped values below or equal to maximum.

A storage element can be combined with an adder to obtain a number of useful functional blocks which will crop up frequently in processing equipment. Figure 2.14(a) shows that a latch is connected in a feedback loop around an adder. The latch contents are added to the input each time it is clocked. The configuration is known as an accumulator in computation because it adds up or accumulates values fed into it. In filtering, it is known as a discrete time integrator. If the input is held at some constant value, the output increases by that amount on each clock. The output is thus a sampled ramp.

Figure 2.14(b) shows that the addition of an invertor allows the difference between successive inputs to be obtained. This is digital differentiation. The output is proportional to the slope of the input.

2.7 Modulo-*n* arithmetic

Conventional arithmetic which is in everyday use relates to the real world of counting actual objects, and to obtain correct answers the concepts of borrow and carry are necessary in the calculations.

There is an alternative type of arithmetic which has no borrow or carry which is known as modulo arithmetic. In modulo-*n* no number can exceed $n - 1$. If it does, *n* or whole multiples of *n*, are subtracted until it does not. Thus 25 modulo-16 is 9 and 12 modulo-5 is 2. The count shown in Figure 2.5 is from a four-bit device which overflows when it reaches 1111 because the carry out is ignored. If a number of clock pulses *m* are applied from the zero state, the state of the counter will be given by *m* (mod 16). Thus modulo arithmetic is appropriate to systems in which there is a fixed wordlength and this means that the range of values the system can have is restricted by that wordlength. A number range which is restricted in this way is called a finite field.

Modulo-2 is a numbering scheme which is used frequently in digital processes. Figure 2.15 shows that in modulo-2 the conventional addition and subtraction are replaced by the XOR function such that: A + B (mod 2) = A XOR B. When multibit values are added modulo-2, each column is computed quite independently of any other. This makes modulo-2 circuitry very fast in operation as it is not necessary to wait for the carries from lower-order bits to ripple up to the high-order bits.

Modulo-2 arithmetic is not the same as conventional arithmetic and takes some getting used to. For example, adding something to itself in modulo-2 always gives the answer zero.

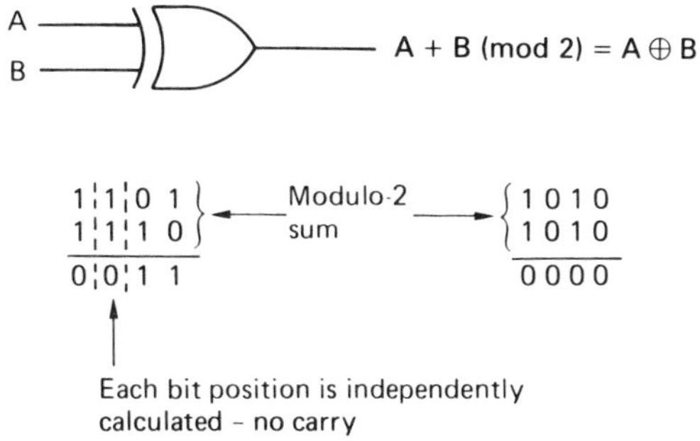

Figure 2.15 In modulo-2 calculations there can be no carry or borrow operations and conventional addition and subtraction become identical. The XOR gate is a modulo-2 adder.

2.8 The Galois field

Figure 2.16 shows a simple circuit consisting of three D-type latches which are clocked simultaneously. They are connected in series to form a shift register. At (a) a feedback connection has been taken from the output to the input and the result is a ring counter where the bits contained will recirculate endlessly. At (b) one XOR gate is added so that the output is fed back to more than one stage. The result is known as a twisted-ring counter and it has some interesting properties. Whenever the circuit is clocked, the left-hand bit moves to the right-hand latch, the centre bit moves to the left-hand latch and the centre latch becomes the XOR of the two outer latches. The figure shows that whatever the starting condition of the three bits in the latches, the same state will always be reached again after seven clocks, except if zero is used. The states of the latches form an endless ring of non-sequential numbers called a Galois field after the French mathematical prodigy Evariste Galois who discovered them. The states of the circuit form a maximum-length sequence because there are as many states as are permitted by the wordlength. As the states of the sequence have many of the characteristics of random numbers, yet are repeatable, the result can also be called a pseudo-random sequence (prs). As the all-zeros case is disallowed, the length of a maximum-length sequence generated by a register of m bits cannot exceed $(2^m - 1)$ states. The Galois field, however, includes the zero term. It is useful to explore the bizarre mathematics of Galois fields which use modulo-2 arithmetic. Familiarity with such manipulations is helpful when studying the error correction, particularly the Reed–Solomon codes used in recorders and treated in Chapter 5. They will also be found in processes which require pseudo-random numbers such as randomized channel codes used in, for example, D-1, D-3 and DDS and discussed in Chapter 4.

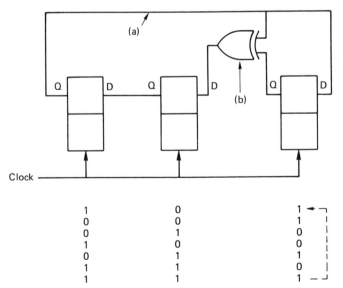

Figure 2.16 The circuit shown is a twisted-ring counter which has an unusual feedback arrangement. Clocking the counter causes it to pass through a series of non-sequential values. See text for details.

The circuit of Figure 2.16 can be considered as a counter and the four points shown will then be representing different powers of 2 from the MSB on the left to the LSB on the right. The feedback connection from the MSB to the other stages means that whenever the MSB becomes 1, two other powers are also forced to one so that the code of 1011 is generated.

Each state of the circuit can be described by combinations of powers of x, such as:

$$x^2 = 100$$

$$x = 010$$

$$x^2 + x = 110, \text{ etc.}$$

The fact that three bits have the same state because they are connected together is represented by the modulo-2 equation:

$$x^3 + x + 1 = 0$$

Let $x = a$, which is a primitive element. Now:

$$a^3 + a + 1 = 0 \tag{2.1}$$

In modulo-2:

$$a + a = a^2 + a^2 = 0$$

$$a = x = 010$$

$$a^2 = x^2 = 100$$

$$a^3 = a + 1 = 011 \text{ from (2.1)}$$

$$a^4 = a \times a^3 = a(a + 1) = a^2 + a = 110$$

$$a^5 = a^2 + a + 1 = 111$$

$$a^6 = a \times a^5 = a(a^2 + a + 1)$$

$$= a^3 + a^2 + a = a + 1 + a^2 + a$$

$$= a^2 + 1 = 101$$

$$a^7 = a(a^2 + 1) = a^3 + a$$

$$= a + 1 + a = 1 = 001$$

In this way it can be seen that the complete set of elements of the Galois field can be expressed by successive powers of the primitive element. Note that the twisted-ring circuit of Figure 2.16 simply raises a to higher and higher powers as it is clocked; thus the seemingly complex multibit changes caused by a single clock of the register become simple to calculate using the correct primitive and the appropriate power.

The numbers produced by the twisted-ring counter are not random; they are completely predictable if the equation is known. However, the sequences produced are sufficiently similar to random numbers that in many cases they will be useful. They are thus referred to as pseudo-random sequences. The feedback connection is chosen such that the expression it implements will not factorize. Otherwise a maximum-length sequence could not be generated because the circuit might sequence around one or other of the factors depending on the initial

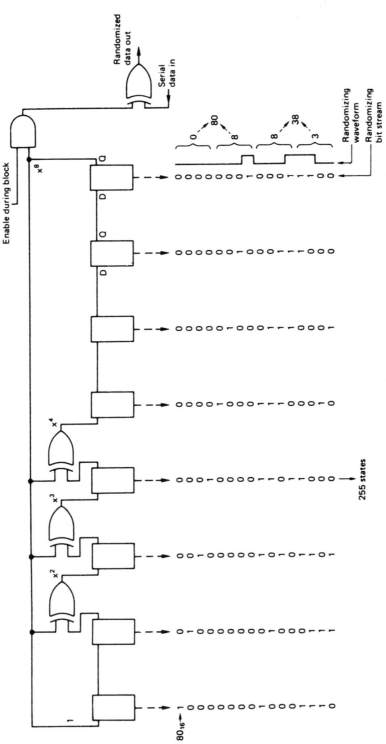

Figure 2.17 The polynomial generator circuit shown here calculates $x^8 + x^4 + x^3 + x^2 + 1$ and is preset to 80_{16} at the beginning of every sync block. When the generator is clocked it will produce a Galois field having 255 states. The right-hand bit of each field element becomes the randomizing bit stream and is fed to an exclusive OR gate in the data stream. Randomizing is disabled during preambles and sync patterns. It is also possible to randomize using a counter working at byte rate which addresses a PROM. Eight exclusive OR gates will then be needed to randomize 1 byte at a time.

condition. A useful analogy is to compare the operation of a pair of meshed gears. If the gears have a number of teeth which are relatively prime, many revolutions are necessary to make the same pair of teeth touch again. If the number of teeth has a common multiple, far fewer turns are needed.

Figure 2.17 shows the pseudo-random sequence generator used in a number of DVTR applications. The sequence length of the circuit shown is 255 because the expression will not factorize.

2.9 Noise and probability

Probability is a useful concept when dealing with processes which are not completely predictable. Thermal noise in electronic components is random, and although under given conditions the noise power in a system may be constant, this value only determines the heat that would be developed in a resistive load. In digital systems, it is the instantaneous voltage of noise which is of interest, since it is a form of interference which could alter the state of a binary signal if it were large enough. Unfortunately the instantaneous voltage cannot be predicted; indeed if it could the interference could not be called noise. Noise can only be quantified statistically, by measuring or predicting the likelihood of a given noise amplitude.

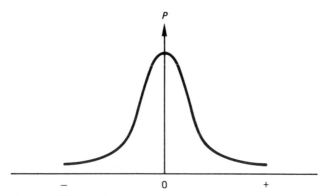

Figure 2.18 White noise in analog circuits generally has the Gaussian amplitude distribution.

Figure 2.18 shows a graph relating the probability of occurrence to the amplitude of noise. The noise amplitude increases away from the origin along the horizontal axis, and for any amplitude of interest, the probability of that noise amplitude occurring can be read from the curve. The shape of the curve is known as a Gaussian distribution, which crops up whenever the overall effect of a large number of independent phenomena is considered. Thermal noise is due to the contributions from countless molecules in the component concerned. Magnetic recording depends on superimposing some average magnetism on vast numbers of magnetic particles.

If it were possible to isolate an individual noise-generating microcosm of a tape or a head on the molecular scale, the noise it could generate would have physical limits because of the finite energy present. The noise distribution might

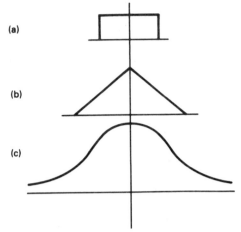

Figure 2.19 In (a) is a rectangular probability: all values are equally likely but between physical limits. In (b) is the sum of two rectangular probabilities, which is triangular, and in (c) is the Gaussian curve which is the sum of an infinite number of rectangular probabilities.

then be rectangular as shown in Figure 2.19(a), where all amplitudes below the physical limit are equally likely. The output of a twisted-ring counter such as that in Figure 2.16 can have a uniform probability. Each value occurs once per sequence. The outputs are positive only but do not include zero, but every value from 1 up to $2^n - 1$ is then equally likely.

The output of a prs generator can be made into the two's complement form by inverting the MSB. This has the effect of exchanging the missing all-zeros value for a missing fully negative value as can be seen by considering the number ring in Figure 2.5. In this example, inverting the MSB causes the code of 1000 representing −8 to become 0000. The result is a four-bit prs generating uniform probability from −7 to +7 as shown in Figure 2.19(a).

If the combined effect of two of these uniform probability processes is considered, clearly the maximum amplitude is now doubled, because the two effects can add, but provided the two effects are uncorrelated, they can also subtract, so the probability is no longer rectangular, but becomes triangular as in Figure 2.19(b). The probability falls to zero at peak amplitude because the chances of two independent mechanisms reaching their peak value with the same polarity at the same time are understandably small.

If the number of mechanisms summed together is now allowed to increase without limit, the result is the Gaussian curve shown in Figure 2.19(c), where it will be seen that the curve has no amplitude limit, because it is just possible that all mechanisms will simultaneously reach their peak value together, although the chances of this happening are incredibly remote. Thus the Gaussian curve is the overall probability of a large number of uncorrelated uniform processes.

2.10 Filters

Filtering is inseparable from digital recording. Analog or digital filters, and sometimes both, are required in the ADCs, DACs, control systems and data channels of digital recorders. Optical systems used in disk recorders also act as filters.[1] There are many parallels between analog, digital and optical filters, which this section treats as a common subject. The main difference between analog and digital filters is that in the digital domain very complex architectures can be constructed at low cost in LSI hardware, or implemented in generic processors using suitable software. Such arithmetic calculations are not subject to component tolerance or drift.

Filtering may modify the frequency response of a system, and/or the phase response. Every combination of frequency and phase response determines the impulse response in the time domain. Figure 2.20 shows that impulse-response testing tells a great deal about a filter. In a perfect filter, all frequencies should experience the same time delay. If some groups of frequencies experience a different delay to others, there is a group-delay error. As an impulse contains an infinite spectrum, a filter suffering from group-delay error will separate the different frequencies of an impulse along the time axis.

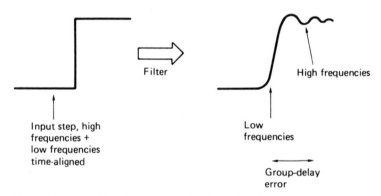

Figure 2.20 Group-delay time-displaces signals as a function of frequency.

A pure delay will cause a phase shift proportional to frequency, and a filter with this characteristic is said to be phase-linear. The impulse response of a phase-linear filter is symmetrical. If a filter suffers from group-delay error it cannot be phase-linear. It is almost impossible to make a perfectly phase-linear analog filter, and many filters have a group-delay equalization stage following them which is often as complex as the filter itself. In the digital domain it is straightforward to make a phase-linear filter, and phase equalization becomes unnecessary.

Because of the sampled nature of the signal, whatever the response at low frequencies may be, all digital channels (and sampled analog channels) act as low-pass filters cutting off at the Nyquist limit, or half the sampling frequency.

Figure 2.21(a) shows a simple RC network and its impulse response. This is the familiar exponential decay due to the capacitor discharging through the

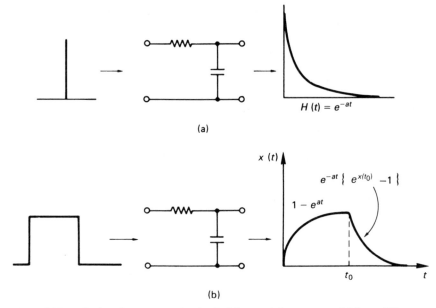

(a)

(b)

Figure 2.21 (a) The impulse response of a simple *RC* network is an exponential decay. This can be used to calculate the response to a square wave, as in (b).

resistor (in series with the source impedance which is assumed here to be negligible). The figure also shows the response to a square wave in (b). These responses can be calculated because the inputs involved are relatively simple. When the input waveform and the impulse response are complex functions, this approach becomes almost impossible.

In any filter, the time domain output waveform represents the convolution of the impulse response with the input waveform. Convolution can be followed by reference to a graphic example in Figure 2.22. Where the impulse response is asymmetrical, the decaying tail occurs *after* the input. As a result, it is necessary to reverse the impulse response in time so that it is mirrored prior to sweeping it through the input waveform. The output voltage is proportional to the shaded area shown where the two impulses overlap.

The same process can be performed in the sampled, or discrete, time domain as shown in Figure 2.23. The impulse and the input are now a set of discrete samples which clearly must have the same sample spacing. The impulse response only has value where impulses coincide. Elsewhere it is zero. The impulse response is therefore stepped through the input one sample period at a time. At each step, the area is still proportional to the output, but as the time steps are of uniform width, the area is proportional to the impulse height and so the output is obtained by adding up the lengths of overlap. In mathematical terms, the output samples represent the convolution of the input and the impulse response by summing the coincident cross products.

As a digital filter works in this way, perhaps it is not a filter at all, but just a mathematical simulation of an analog filter. This approach is quite useful in visualizing what a digital filter does.

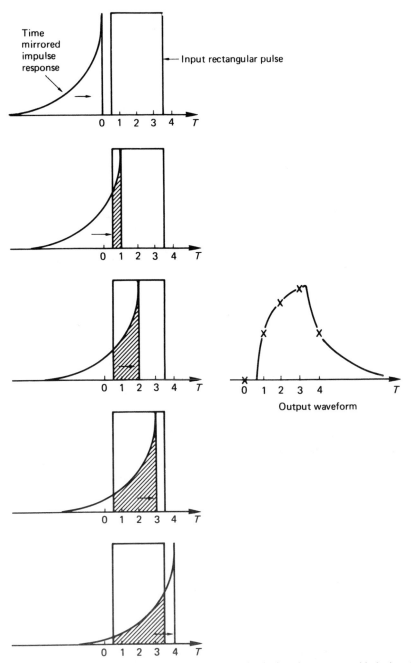

Figure 2.22 In the convolution of two continuous signals (the impulse response with the input), the impulse must be time reversed or mirrored. This is necessary because the impulse will be moved from left to right, and mirroring gives the impulse the correct time-domain response when it is moved past a fixed point. As the impulse response slides continuously through the input waveform, the area where the two overlap determines the instantaneous output amplitude. This is shown for five different times by the crosses on the output waveform.

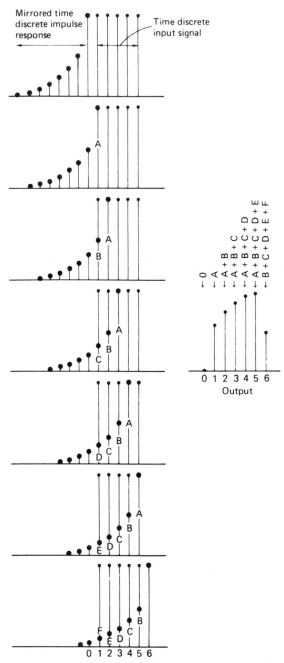

Figure 2.23 In time discrete convolution, the mirrored impulse response is stepped through the input one sample period at a time. At each step, the sum of the cross products is used to form an output value. As the input in this example is a constant-height pulse, the output is simply proportional to the sum of the coincident impulse response samples. This figure should be compared with Figure 2.22.

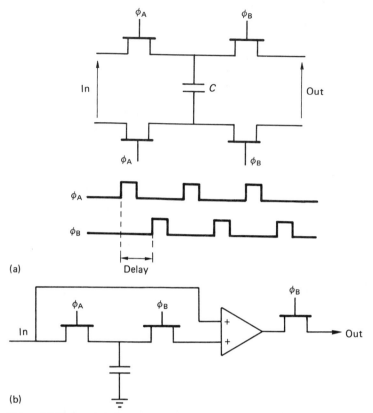

Figure 2.24 In a switched capacitor delay (a), there are two clock phases, and during the first the input voltage is transferred to the capacitor. During the second phase the capacitor voltage is transferred to the output. (b) A simple switched capacitor filter. The delay causes a phase shift which is dependent on frequency and the resultant frequency response is sinusoidal.

Somewhere between the analog filter and the digital filter is the switched capacitor filter. This uses analog quantities, namely the charges on capacitors, but the time axis is discrete because the various charges are routed using electronic switches which close during various phases of the sampling rate clock. Switched capacitor filters have the same characteristics as digital filters with infinite precision. They are often used in preference to continuous time analog filters in integrated circuit converters because they can be implemented with the same integration techniques. Figure 2.24(a) shows a switched capacitor delay. There are two clock phases and during the first the input voltage is transferred to the capacitor. During the second phase the capacitor voltage is transferred to the output. Combining delay with operational amplifier summation allows frequency-dependent circuitry to be realized. Figure 2.24(b) shows a simple switched capacitor filter. The delay causes a phase shift which is dependent on frequency. The frequency response is sinusoidal.

2.11 FIR and IIR filters compared

Filters can be described in two main classes, as shown in Figure 2.25, according to the nature of the impulse response. Finite-impulse response (FIR) filters are always stable and, as their name suggests, respond to an impulse once, as they have only a forward path. In the temporal domain, the time for which the filter responds to an input is finite, fixed and readily established. The same is therefore true about the distance over which an FIR filter responds in the spatial domain. FIR filters can be made perfectly phase linear if required. Most filters used for sampling rate conversion and oversampling fall into this category.

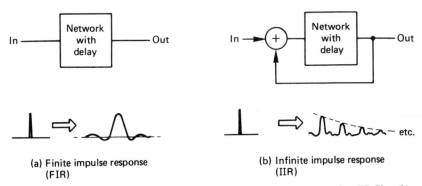

(a) Finite impulse response
(FIR)

(b) Infinite impulse response
(IIR)

Figure 2.25 An FIR filter (a) responds only to an input, whereas the output of an IIR filter (b) continues indefinitely rather like a decaying echo.

Infinite-impulse response (IIR) filters respond to an impulse indefinitely and are not necessarily stable, as they have a return path from the output to the input. For this reason they are also called recursive filters. As the impulse response is not symmetrical, IIR filters are not phase linear.

2.12 FIR filters

An FIR filter works by graphically constructing the impulse response for every input sample. It is first necessary to establish the correct impulse response. Figure 2.26(a) shows an example of a low-pass filter which cuts off at one-quarter of the sampling rate. The impulse response of a perfect low-pass filter is a sin x/x curve, where the time between the two central zero crossings is the reciprocal of the cut-off frequency. According to the mathematics, the waveform has always existed, and carries on for ever. The peak value of the output coincides with the input impulse. This means that the filter is not causal, because the output has changed before the input is known. Thus in all practical applications it is necessary to truncate the extreme ends of the impulse response, which causes an aperture effect, and to introduce a time delay in the filter equal to half the duration of the truncated impulse in order to make the filter causal. As an input impulse is shifted through the series of registers in Figure 2.26(b), the impulse response is created, because at each point it is multiplied by a coefficient as in Figure 2.26(c). These coefficients are simply the result of sampling and quantizing the desired impulse

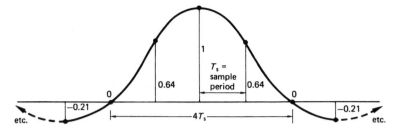

Figure 2.26 (a) The impulse response of an LPF is a sin x/x curve which stretches from −∞ to +∞ in time. The ends of the response must be neglected, and a delay introduced to make the filter causal.

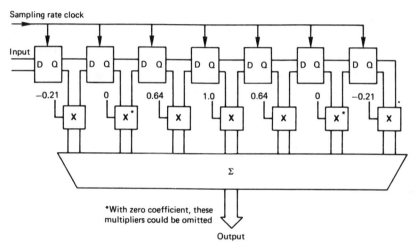

Figure 2.26 (b) The structure of an FIR LPF. Input samples shift across the register and at each point are multiplied by different coefficients.

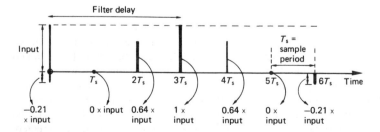

Figure 2.26 (c) When a single unit sample shifts across the circuit of Figure 2.26(b), the impulse response is created at the output as the impulse is multiplied by each coefficient in turn.

response. Clearly the sampling rate used to sample the impulse must be the same as the sampling rate for which the filter is being designed. In practice the coefficients are calculated, rather than attempting to sample an actual impulse response. The coefficient wordlength will be a compromise between cost and performance. Because the input sample shifts across the system registers to create the shape of the impulse response, the configuration is also known as a transversal filter. In operation with real sample streams, there will be several consecutive sample values in the filter registers at any time in order to convolve the input with the impulse response.

Simply truncating the impulse response causes an abrupt transition from input samples which matter and those which do not. Truncating the filter superimposes a rectangular shape on the time-domain impulse response. In the frequency domain the rectangular shape transforms to a $\sin x/x$ characteristic which is superimposed on the desired frequency response as a ripple. One consequence of this is known as Gibb's phenomenon: a tendency for the response to peak just before the cut-off frequency.[2,3] As a result, the length of the impulse which must be considered will depend not only on the frequency response, but also on the amount of ripple which can be tolerated. If the relevant period of the impulse is measured in sample periods, the result will be the number of points or multiplications needed in the filter. Figure 2.27 compares the performance of filters with different numbers of points. A typical digital audio FIR filter may need as many as 96 points, whereas a video filter can be implemented with around 10.

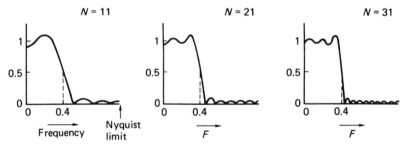

Figure 2.27 The truncation of the impulse in an FIR filter caused by the use of a finite number of points (N) results in ripple in the response. Shown here are three different numbers of points for the same impulse response. The filter is an LPF which rolls off at 0.4 of the fundamental interval. (Courtesy *Philips Technical Review*)

Rather than simply truncate the impulse response in time, it is better to make a smooth transition from samples which do not count to those that do. This can be done by multiplying the coefficients in the filter by a window function which peaks in the centre of the impulse. Figure 2.28 shows some different window functions and their responses. The rectangular window is the case of truncation, and the response is shown in I. A linear reduction in weight from the centre of the window to the edges characterizes the Bartlett window II, which trades ripple for an increase in transition-region width. In III is shown the Hanning window, which is essentially a raised cosine shape. Not shown is the similar Hamming window, which offers a slightly different trade-off between ripple and the width

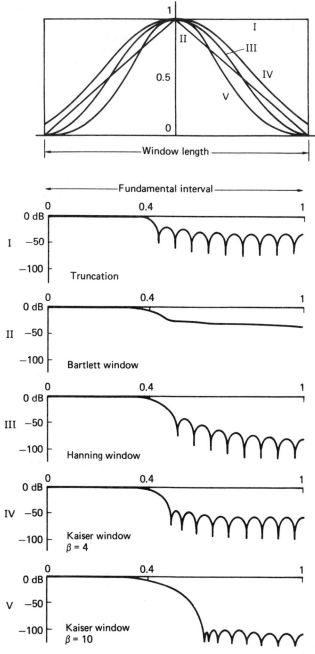

Figure 2.28 The effect of window functions. At top, various window functions are shown in continuous form. Once the number of samples in the window is established, the continuous functions shown here are sampled at the appropriate spacing to obtain window coefficients. These are multiplied by the truncated impulse response coefficients to obtain the actual coefficients used by the filter. The amplitude responses I–V corresond to the window functions illustrated. (Responses courtesy *Philips Technical Review*)

of the main lobe. The Blackman window introduces an extra cosine term into the Hamming window at half the period of the main cosine period, reducing Gibb's phenomenon and ripple level, but increasing the width of the transition region. The Kaiser window is a family of windows based on the Bessel function, allowing various trade-offs between ripple ratio and main lobe width. Two of these are shown in IV and V.

Filter coefficients can be optimized by computer simulation. One of the best-known techniques used is the Remez exchange algorithm, which converges on the optimum coefficients after a number of iterations.

In the example of Figure 2.29, the low-pass filter of Figure 2.26 is shown with a Bartlett window. Acceptable ripple determines the number of significant sample periods embraced by the impulse. This determines in turn both the number of points in the filter, and the filter delay. For the purposes of illustration, the number of points is much smaller than would normally be the case in an audio application. As the impulse is symmetrical, the delay will be half the impulse period. The impulse response is a sin x/x function, and this has been calculated in

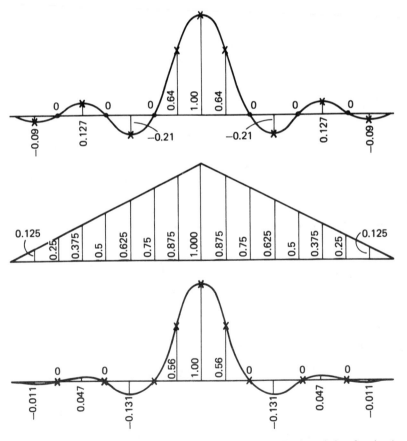

Figure 2.29 A truncated sin x/x impulse (top) is multiplied by a Bartlett window function (centre) to produce the actual coefficients used (bottom).

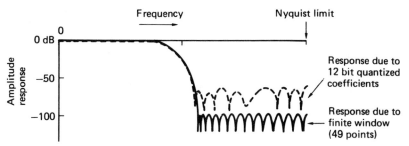

Figure 2.30 Frequency response of a 49 point transversal filter with infinite precision (solid line) shows ripple due to finite window size. Quantizing coefficients to 12 bits reduces attenuation in the stopband. (Responses courtesy *Philips Technical Review*)

the figure. The $\sin x/x$ response is next multiplied by the window function to give the windowed impulse response.

If the coefficients are not quantized finely enough, it will be as if they had been calculated inaccurately, and the performance of the filter will be less than expected. Figure 2.30 shows an example of quantizing coefficients. Conversely, raising the wordlength of the coefficients increases cost.

The FIR structure is inherently phase linear because it is easy to make the impulse response absolutely symmetrical. The individual samples in a digital system do not know in isolation what frequency they represent, and they can only pass through the filter at a rate determined by the clock. Because of this inherent phase-linearity, an FIR filter can be designed for a specific impulse response, and the frequency response will follow.

The frequency response of the filter can be changed at will by changing the coefficients. A programmable filter only requires a series of PROMs to supply the coefficients; the address supplied to the PROMs will select the response. The frequency response of a digital filter will also change if the clock rate is changed, so it is often less ambiguous to specify a frequency of interest in a digital filter in terms of a fraction of the fundamental interval rather than in absolute terms. The configuration shown in Figure 2.26 serves to illustrate the principle. The units used on the diagrams are sample periods and the response is proportional to these periods or spacings, and so it is not necessary to use actual figures.

Where the impulse response is symmetrical, it is often possible to reduce the number of multiplications, because the same product can be used twice, at equal distances before and after the centre of the window. This is known as folding the filter. A folded filter is shown in Figure 2.31.

2.13 Transforms

Convolution is a lengthy process to perform on paper. It is much easier to work in the frequency domain. Figure 2.32 shows that if a signal with a spectrum or frequency content a is passed through a filter with a frequency response b the result will be an output spectrum which is simply the product of the two. If the frequency responses are drawn on logarithmic scales (i.e. calibrated in dB) the two can be simply added because the addition of logarithms is the same as multiplication. Whilst frequency in electrical waveforms has traditionally meant

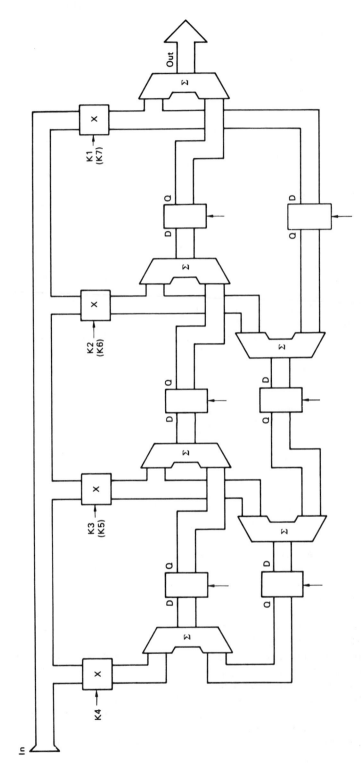

Figure 2.31 A seven-point folded filter for a symmetrical impulse response. In this case K1 and K7 will be identical, and so the input sample can be multiplied once, and the product fed into the output shift system in two different places. The centre coefficient K4 appears once. In an even-numbered filter the centre coefficient would also be used twice.

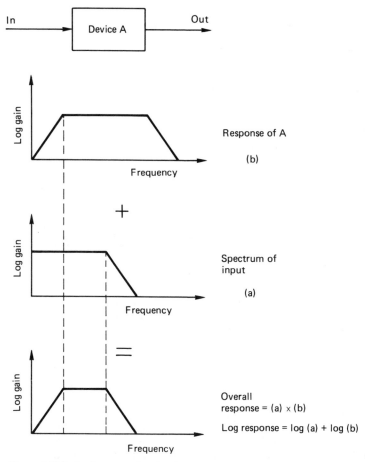

Figure 2.32 In the frequency domain, the response of two series devices is the product of their individual responses at each frequency. On a logarithmic scale the responses are simply added.

temporal frequency measured in Hertz, frequency in optics can also be spatial and measured in lines per millimetre (mm^{-1}). Multiplying the spectra of the responses is a much simpler process than convolution.

   In order to move to the frequency domain or spectrum from the time domain or waveform, it is necessary to use the Fourier transform, or in sampled systems, the discrete Fourier transform (DFT). Fourier analysis holds that any waveform can be reproduced by adding together an arbitrary number of harmonically related sinusoids of various amplitudes and phases. Figure 2.33 shows how a square wave can be built up of harmonics. The spectrum can be drawn by plotting the amplitude of the harmonics against frequency. It will be seen that this gives a spectrum which is a decaying wave. It passes through zero at all even multiples of the fundamental. The shape of the spectrum is a $\sin x/x$ curve. If a square wave has a $\sin x/x$ spectrum, it follows that a filter with a rectangular impulse response will have a $\sin x/x$ spectrum.

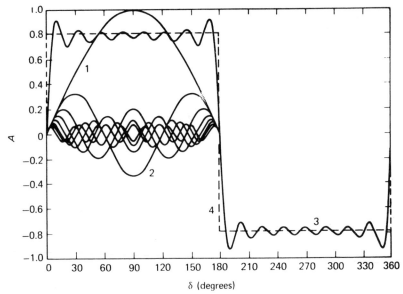

Figure 2.33 Fourier analysis of a square wave into fundamental and harmonics. A, amplitude; δ, phase of fundamental wave in degrees; 1, first harmonic (fundamental); 2, odd harmonics 3–15; 3, sum of harmonics 1–15; 4, ideal square wave.

A low-pass filter has a rectangular spectrum, and this has a $\sin x/x$ impulse response. These characteristics are known as a transform pair. In transform pairs, if one domain has one shape of the pair, the other domain will have the other shape. Thus a square wave has a $\sin x/x$ spectrum and a $\sin x/x$ impulse has a square spectrum. Figure 2.34 shows a number of transform pairs. Note the pulse pair. A time domain pulse of infinitely short duration has a flat spectrum. Thus a flat waveform, i.e. DC, has only zero in its spectrum. Interestingly the transform of a Gaussian response in still Gaussian. The impulse response of the optics of a laser disk has a

$$\left(\frac{\sin x}{x}\right)^2$$

function, and this is responsible for the triangular falling frequency response of the pickup.

The spectrum of a pseudo-random sequence is not flat because it has a finite sequence length. The rate at which the sequence repeats is visible in the spectrum. Where pseudo-random sequences are to be used in sample manipulation, i.e. where their effects can be audible, it is essential that the sequence length should be long enough to prevent the periodicity being audible.

Figure 2.35 shows that the spectrum of a pseudo-random sequence has a $\sin x/x$ characteristic, with nulls at multiples of the clock frequency. A closer inspection of the spectrum shows that it is not continuous, but takes the form of a comb where the spacing is equal to the repetition rate of the sequence.

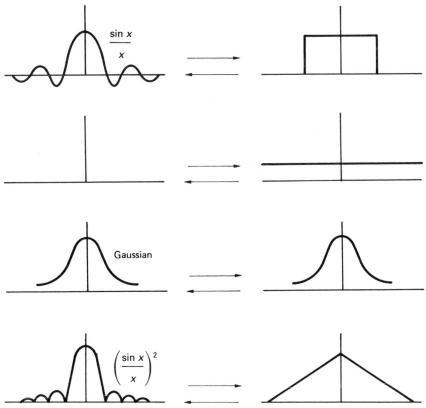

Figure 2.34 The concept of transform pairs illustrates the duality of the frequency (including spatial frequency) and time domains.

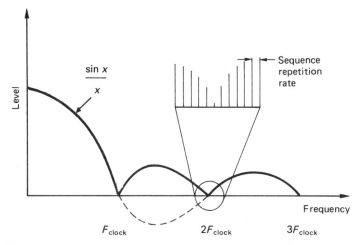

Figure 2.35 The spectrum of a pseudo-random sequence has a sin x/x characteristic, with nulls at multiples of the clock frequency. The spectrum is not continuous, but resembles a comb where the spacing is equal to the repetition rate of the sequence.

2.14 The Fourier transform

The Fourier transform is a processing technique which analyses signals changing with respect to time or distance and expresses them in the form of a temporal or spatial spectrum. Any waveform can be broken down into frequency components. Figure 2.36 shows that if the amplitude and phase of each frequency component is known, linearly adding the resultant components in an inverse transform results in the original waveform.

The Fourier transform may be performed on a continuous analog waveform, in which case a continuous spectrum results. However, in digital systems the waveform is expressed as a number of discrete samples. As a result the Fourier transform analyses the signal into an equal number of discrete frequencies. This is known as a discrete Fourier transform or DFT. The fast Fourier transform is no more than an efficient way of computing the DFT.[4]

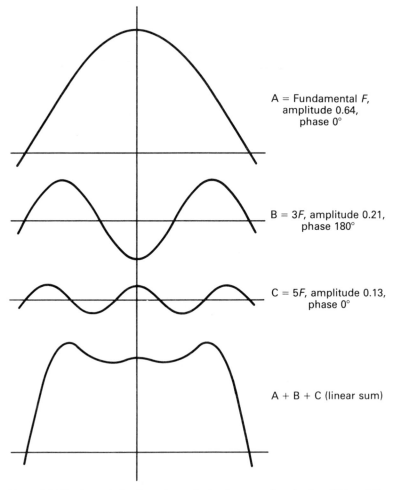

Figure 2.36 Fourier analysis allows the synthesis of any waveform by the addition of discrete frequencies of appropriate amplitude and phase.

It will be evident from Figure 2.36 that the knowledge of the phase of the frequency component is vital, as changing the phase of any component will seriously alter the reconstructed waveform. Thus the DFT must accurately analyse the phase of the signal components.

There are a number of ways of expressing phase. Figure 2.37 shows a point which is rotating about a fixed axis at constant speed. Looked at from the side, the point oscillates up and down at constant frequency. The waveform of that motion is a sine wave, and that is what we would see if the rotating point were to translate along its axis whilst we continued to look from the side.

One way of defining the phase of a waveform is to specify the angle through which the point has rotated at time zero ($T = 0$). If a second point is made to revolve at 90 degrees to the first, it would produce a cosine wave when

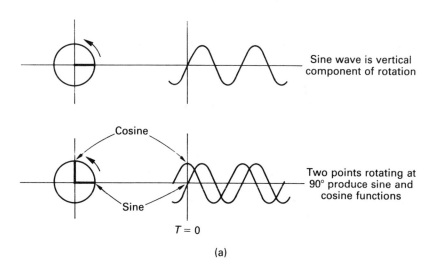

(a)

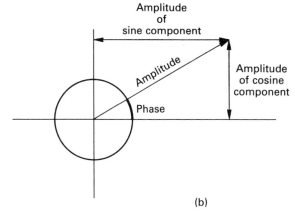

(b)

Figure 2.37 The origin of sine and cosine waves is to take a particular viewpoint of a rotation. Any phase can be synthesized by adding proportions of sine and cosine waves.

translated. It is possible to produce a waveform having arbitrary phase by adding together the sine and cosine wave in various proportions and polarities. For example, adding the sine and cosine waves in equal proportion results in a waveform lagging the sine wave by 45 degrees.

Figure 2.37 shows that the proportions necessary are respectively the sine and the cosine of the phase angle. Thus the two methods of describing phase can be readily interchanged.

The discrete Fourier transform spectrum analyses a block of samples by searching separately for each discrete target frequency. It does this by multiplying the input waveform by a sine wave having the target frequency and

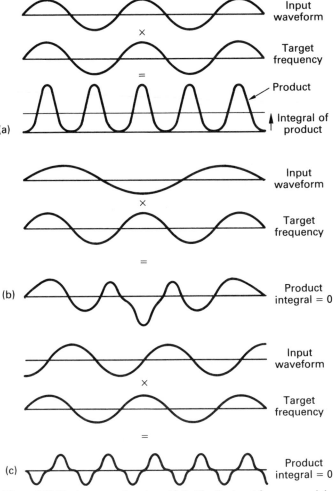

Figure 2.38 The input waveform is multiplied by the target frequency and the result is averaged or integrated. In (a) the target frequency is present and a large integral results. With another input frequency the integral is zero as in (b). The correct frequency will also result in a zero integral shown in (c) if it is at 90° to the phase of the search frequency. This is overcome by making two searches in quadrature.

adding up or integrating the products. Figure 2.38(a) shows that multiplying by the target frequency gives a non-zero integral when the input frequency is the same, whereas Figure 2.38(b) shows that with a different input frequency (in fact all other different frequencies) the integral is zero, showing that no component of the target frequency exists. Thus from a real waveform containing many frequencies all frequencies except the target frequency are excluded. The magnitude of the integral is proportional to the amplitude of the target component.

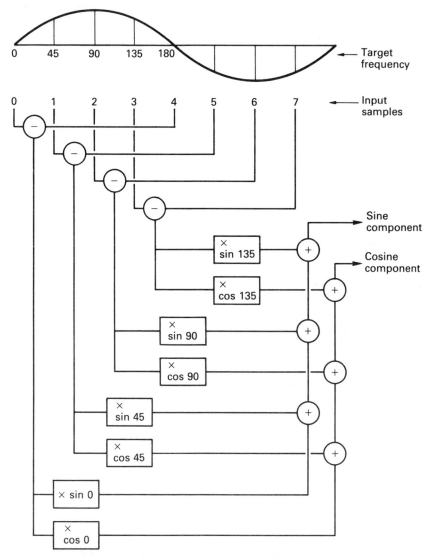

Figure 2.39 An example of a filtering search. Pairs of samples are subtracted and multiplied by sampled sine and cosine waves. The products are added to give the sine and cosine components of the search frequency.

Figure 2.38(c) shows that the target frequency will not be detected if it is phase shifted 90 degrees as the product of quadrature waveforms is always zero. Thus the discrete Fourier transform must make a further search for the target frequency using a cosine wave. It follows from the arguments above that the relative proportions of the sine and cosine integrals reveals the phase of the input component. Thus each discrete frequency in the spectrum must be the result of a pair of quadrature searches.

Searching for one frequency at a time as above will result in a DFT, but only after considerable computation. However, a lot of the calculations are repeated many times over in different searches. The fast Fourier transform gives the same result with less computation by logically gathering together all of the places where the same calculation is needed and making the calculation once.

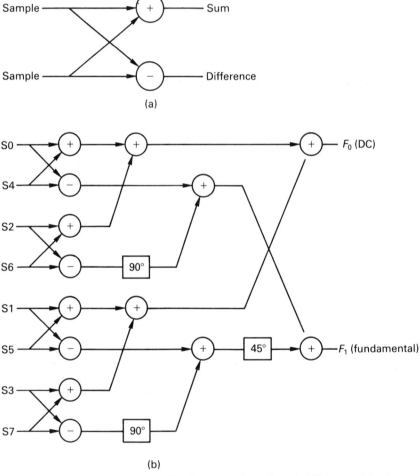

Figure 2.40 The basic element of an FFT is known as a butterfly as in (a) because of the shape of the signal paths in a sum and difference system. The use of butterflies to compute the first two coefficients is shown in (b). An actual example is given in (c) which should be compared with the result of (d) with a quadrature input. In (e) the butterflies for the first two coefficients form the basis of the computation of the third coefficient.

The amount of computation can be reduced by performing the sine and cosine component searches together. Another saving is obtained by noting that every 180 degrees the sine and cosine have the same magnitude but are simply inverted in sign. Instead of performing four multiplications on two samples 180 degrees apart and adding the pairs of products, it is more economical to subtract the sample values and multiply twice, once by a sine value and once by a cosine value.

The first coefficient is the geometric mean, which is the sum of all of the sample values in the block divided by the number of samples. Figure 2.39 shows how the search for the lowest frequency in a block is performed. Pairs of samples are subtracted as shown, and each difference is then multiplied by the sine and the cosine of the search frequency. The process shifts one sample period, and a new sample pair are subtracted and multiplied by new sine and cosine factors.

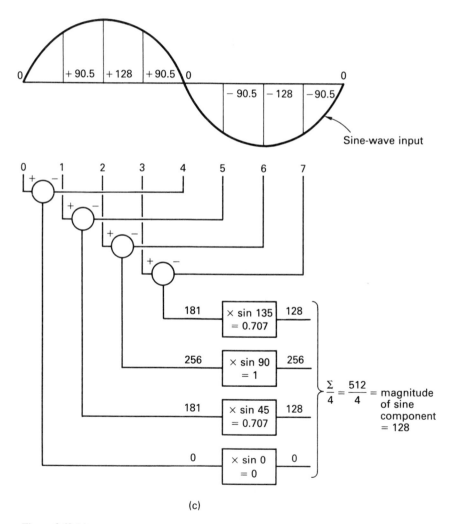

(c)

Figure 2.40 (c)

This is repeated until all of the sample pairs have been multiplied. The sine and cosine products are then added to give the value of the sine and cosine coefficients respectively.

It is possible to combine the calculation of the DC component, which requires the sum of samples, and the calculation of the fundamental, which requires sample differences, by combining stages shown in Figure 2.40(a) which take a pair of samples and add and subtract them. Such a stage is called a butterfly because of the shape of the schematic. Figure 2.40(b) shows how the first two components are calculated. The phase rotation boxes attribute the input to the sine or cosine component outputs according to the phase angle. As shown the box labelled 90 degrees attributes nothing to the sine output, but unity gain to the cosine output. The 45 degree box attributes the input equally to both components.

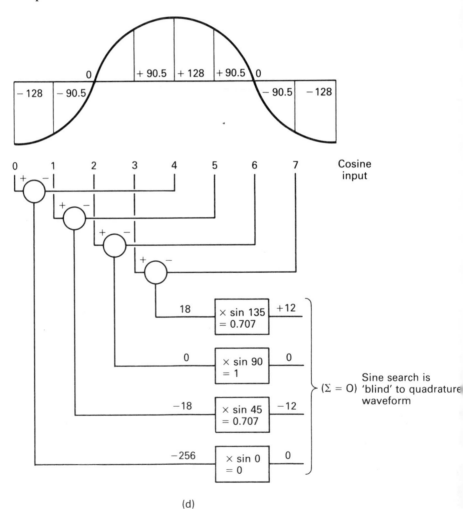

(d)

Figure 2.40 (d)

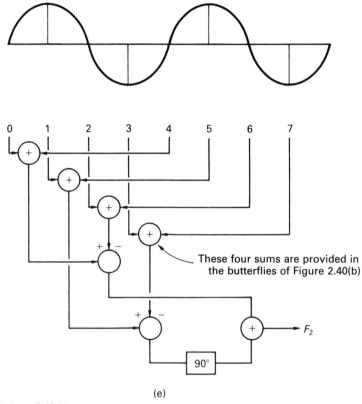

These four sums are provided in
the butterflies of Figure 2.40(b)

90°

F_2

(e)

Figure 2.40 (e)

Figure 2.40(c) shows a numerical example. If a sine wave input is considered where zero degrees coincides with the first sample, this will produce a zero sine coefficient and non-zero cosine coefficient. Figure 2.40(d) shows the same input waveform shifted by 90 degrees. Note how the coefficients change over.

Figure 2.40(e) shows how the next frequency coefficient is computed. Note that exactly the same first stage butterfly outputs are used, reducing the computation needed.

A similar process may be followed to obtain the sine and cosine coefficients of the remaining frequencies. The full FFT diagram is shown in Figure 2.41(a). The spectrum this calculates is shown in Figure 2.41(b). Note that only half of the coefficients are useful in a real band-limited system because the remaining coefficients represent frequencies above one-half of the sampling rate.

The number of frequency coefficients resulting from a DFT is equal to the number of input samples. In the case of digital video, if the input consists of a larger number of samples it must cover a larger area of the screen, but its spectrum will be known more finely. Thus a fundamental characteristic of such transforms is that the more accurately the frequency and phase of a waveform is analysed, the less is known about where such frequencies exist on the screen axis.

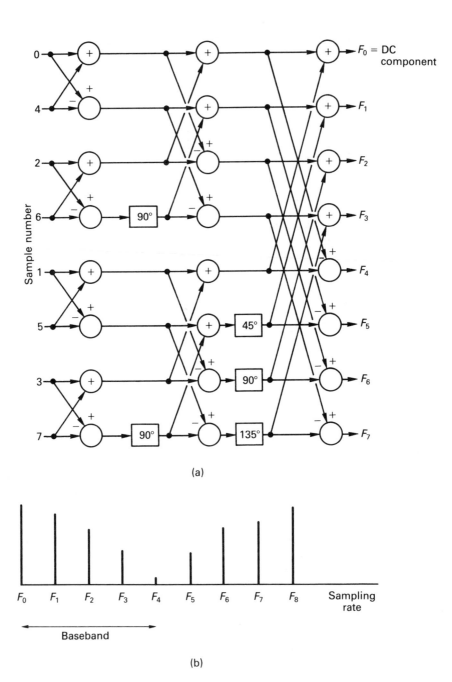

(a)

(b)

Figure 2.41 In (a) is the full butterfly diagram for an FFT. The spectrum this computes is shown in (b).

2.15 The discrete cosine transform (DCT)

The DCT is a special case of a discrete Fourier transform in which the sine components of the coefficients have been eliminated, leaving a single number. This is actually quite easy. Figure 2.42(a) shows the input samples to a transform process. By repeating the samples in a time-reversed order and performing a discrete Fourier transform on the double-length sample set a DCT is obtained. The effect of mirroring the input waveform is to turn it into an even function whose sine coefficients are all zero. The result can be understood by considering the effect of individually transforming the input block and the reversed block. Figure 2.42(b) shows that the phase of all the components of one block are in the opposite sense to those in the other. This means that when the components are added to give the transform of the double-length block all of the sine components cancel out, leaving only the cosine coefficients, hence the name of the transform.[5] In practice the sine component calculation is eliminated. Another

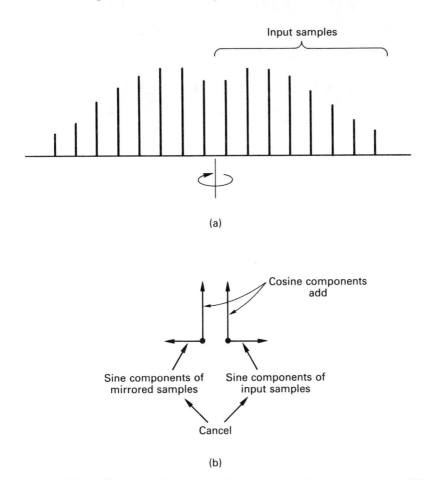

Figure 2.42 The DCT is obtained by mirroring the input block as shown in (a) prior to an FFT. The mirroring cancels out the sine components as in (b), leaving only cosine coefficients.

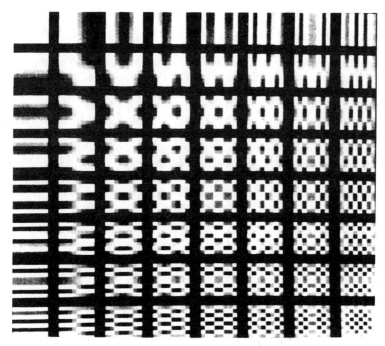

Figure 2.43 The discrete cosine transform breaks up an image area into discrete frequencies in two dimensions. The lowest frequency can be seen here at the top left corner. Horizontal frequency increases to the right and vertical frequency increases downwards.

advantage is that doubling the block length by mirroring doubles the frequency resolution, so that twice as many useful coefficients are produced. In fact a DCT produces as many useful coefficients as input samples.

For image processing two-dimensional transforms are needed. In this case for every horizontal frequency, a search is made for all possible vertical frequencies. A two-dimensional DCT is shown in Figure 2.43. The DCT is separable in that the two-dimensional DCT can be obtained by computing in each dimension separately. Fast DCT algorithms are available.[6]

The DCT is primarily used in data-reduction processing. The DCT itself does not result in any reduction, as there are as many coefficients as samples, but it converts the input video into a form where redundancy can be easily detected and removed.

2.16 Introduction to data reduction

Data reduction will be employed wherever there are practical or economic constraints on recording capacity or throughput. Recording time is increased in proportion to the compression factor used. There are two basic types of data-reduction system. In lossless coders, the original data are restored to bit accuracy so that there is no difference between the input and output data. Such coders are essential for computer programs and other such critical data. The degree of compression possible is limited. However, where the data are the result of

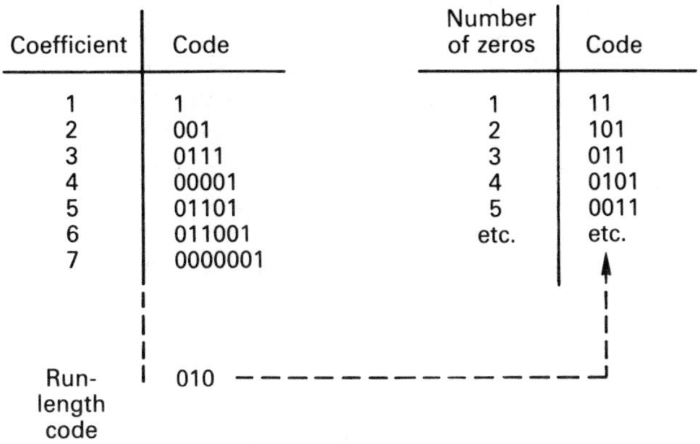

Coefficient	Code	Number of zeros	Code
1	1	1	11
2	001	2	101
3	0111	3	011
4	00001	4	0101
5	01101	5	0011
6	011001	etc.	etc.
7	0000001		
Run-length code	010		

Figure 2.44 In Huffman coding the most probable coefficient values are allocated to the shortest codes. All zero coefficients are coded with run-length coding which counts the number of zeros.

digitizing sound waveforms or images, the required result is the appropriate subjective impression rather than bit accuracy. Such coders exploit the non-uniform perception of human senses to reduce signal resolution in parts of the signal in which it is less detectable. Compressors based on knowledge of human senses are called perceptual coders.

Knowledge of the signal statistics gained from extensive analysis of real material can be used to describe the probability of a given coefficient having a given value. This is the basis of entropy coding, in which coefficients are described not by fixed wordlength numbers, but by variable-length codes. The shorter codes are allocated to the most probable values and the longer codes to the least probable values. This allows a coding gain on typical signals. One of the best known variable-length codes is the Huffman code.[7]

The main difficulty with variable-length codes is separating the symbols when they are serialized. With fixed wordlength, the bit clock is merely divided by the wordlength to obtain a wordclock. With variable-length coding the bitstream coding must be such that the decoder can determine the boundaries between words unaided. Figure 2.44 shows an example of Huffman coding.

2.17 Audio data reduction

The human hearing system comprises not only the physical organs, but also processes taking place within the brain. One of purposes of the subconscious processing is to limit the amount of information presented to the conscious mind, to prevent stress and to make everyday life safer and easier. Auditory masking is a process which selects only the most important frequencies from the spectrum applied to the ear. Data reduction takes advantage of this process to reduce the amount of data needed to carry sound of a given subjective quality. The data-reduction process mimics the operation of the hearing mechanism as there is little point in recording information only for the ear to discard it.

Data reduction can be used to reduce consumption of the medium in consumer recorders such as DCC and MiniDisc. Reduction to around one-quarter or one-fifth of the PCM data rate can be virtually inaudible on high quality data-reduction systems, as the error between the original and the reproduced waveforms can be effectively masked. Greater compression factors inevitably result in quality loss which may be acceptable for certain applications such as communications but not for quality music reproduction.

The output of a data-reduction unit is still binary data, but it is no longer regular PCM, so it cannot be fed to a normal DAC without passing through a matching decoder which provides a conventional PCM output.

There are numerous proprietary data-reduction units, and each needs the appropriate decoder to return to PCM. The combination of a data-reduction unit and a decoder is called a codec. These techniques fall into three basic categories: predictive coding, sub-band coding and transform coding.

Predictive coding uses circuitry which uses a knowledge of previous samples to predict the value of the next. It is then only necessary to send the difference between the prediction and the actual value. The receiver contains an identical predictor to which the transmitted difference is added to give the original value.

Sub-band coding splits the audio spectrum up into many different frequency bands to exploit the fact that most bands will contain lower level signals than the loudest one.

In spectral coding, a Fourier transform of the waveform is computed periodically. Since the transform of an audio signal changes slowly, it need be sent much less often than audio samples. The receiver performs an inverse transform.

Practical data-reduction units will usually use some combination of at least two of these techniques along with non-linear or floating point re-quantizing of sub-band samples or transform coefficients.

The sensitivity of the ear to distortion probably deserves more attention than fidelity of dynamic range or frequency response. All audio data reduction relies to a certain extent on an understanding of the hearing mechanism, particularly the phenomenon of masking, as this determines the audibility of artifacts. Thus data reduction is a form of perceptual coding.[8] The basilar membrane in the ear behaves as a kind of spectrum analyser. The part of the basilar membrane which resonates as a result of an applied sound is a function of the frequency. The high frequencies are detected at the end of the membrane nearest to the eardrum and the low frequencies are detected at the opposite end. The ear analyses with frequency bands, known as critical bands, about 100 Hz wide below 500 Hz and from one-sixth to one-third of an octave wide, proportional to frequency, above this. Critical bands were first described by Fletcher.[9] Later Zwicker experimentally established 24 critical bands,[10] but Moore and Glasberg suggested narrower bands.[11]

In the presence of a complex spectrum, the ear fails to register energy in some bands when there is more energy in a nearby band. The vibration of the membrane in sympathy with a single frequency cannot be localized to an infinitely small area, and nearby areas are forced to vibrate at the same frequency with an amplitude that decreases with distance. Within those areas, other frequencies are excluded unless the amplitude is high enough to dominate the local vibration of the membrane. Thus the membrane has an effective Q factor which is responsible for the phenomenon of auditory masking, defined as the decreased audibility of one sound in the presence of another.

The degree of masking depends upon whether the masking tone is a sinusoid, which gives the least masking, or noise.[12] However, harmonic distortion produces widely spaced frequencies, and these are easily detected even in minute quantities by a part of the basilar membrane which is distant from that part which is responding to the fundamental. The masking effect is asymmetrically disposed around the masking frequency.[13] Above the masking frequency, masking is more pronounced, and its extent increases with acoustic level. Below the masking frequency, the extent of masking drops sharply at as much as 90 dB per octave. Clearly very sharp filters are required if noise at frequencies below the masker is to be confined within the masking threshold.

Owing to the resonant nature of the membrane, it cannot start or stop vibrating rapidly. The spectrum sensed changes slowly even if that of the original sound does not. The reduction in information sent to the brain is considerable; masking can take place even when the masking tone begins after and ceases before the masked sound. This is referred to as forward and backward masking.[14] An example of the slowness of the ear is the Haas effect, in which the direction from which a sound is perceived to have come is determined from the first arriving wavefront. Later echoes simply increase the perceived loudness as they have the same spectrum and increase the existing excitation of the membrane.

A detailed model of the masking properties of the ear is necessary to the design of audio data-reduction systems. Since quantizing distortion results in energy moving from one frequency to another, the masking model is essential to estimate how audible the effect of distortion will be. The greater the degree of reduction required, the more precise the model must be. If the masking model is inaccurate, then equipment based upon it may produce audible artifacts under some circumstances. Artifacts may also result if the model is not properly implemented. As a result, development of data-reduction units requires careful listening tests with a wide range of source material.[15] The presence of artifacts at a given compression factor indicates only that performance is below expectations; it does not distinguish between the implementation and the model. If the implementation is verified, then a more detailed model must be sought.

Properly conducted listening tests are expensive and time consuming, and alternative methods have been developed which can be used to rapidly evaluate the performance of different techniques. The noise-to-masking ratio (NMR) is one such measurement.[16] Figure 2.45 shows how NMR is measured. Input audio signals are fed simultaneously to a data-reduction coder and decoder in tandem (known as a codec) and to a compensating delay. At the output of the delay, the

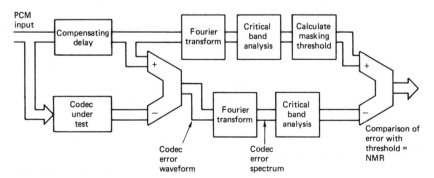

Figure 2.45 The noise-to-masking ratio is derived as shown here.

coding error is obtained by subtracting the codec output from the original. The original signal is spectrum-analysed into critical bands in order to derive the masking threshold of the input audio, and this is compared with the critical band spectrum of the error. The NMR in each critical band is the ratio between the masking threshold and the quantizing error due to the codec. An average NMR for all bands can be computed. A positive NMR in any band indicates that artifacts are potentially audible. Plotting the average NMR against time is a powerful technique, as with an ideal codec the NMR should be stable with different types of program material. NMR excursions can be correlated with the waveform of the audio input to analyse how the extra noise was caused and to redesign the codec to eliminate it.

Practical systems should have a finite NMR in order to give a degree of protection against difficult signals which have not been anticipated and against the use of post-codec equalization or several tandem codecs which could change the masking threshold. There is a strong argument that professional devices should have a greater NMR than consumer or program delivery devices.

There are, of course, limits to all technologies. Eventually artifacts will be heard as the amount of compression is increased which no amount of detailed modelling will remove. The ear is only able to perceive a certain proportion of the information in a given sound. This could be called the perceptual entropy,[17] and all additional sound is redundant or irrelevant. Data reduction works by removing the redundancy, and clearly an ideal system would remove all of it, leaving only the entropy. Once this has been done, the masking capacity of the ear has been reached and the NMR has reached zero over the whole band. Reducing the data rate further must reduce the entropy, because raising noise further at any frequency will render it audible. Thus there is a limit to the degree of data reduction which can be achieved even with an ideal coder. Systems which go beyond that limit are not appropriate for high quality music, but are relevant in telephony and communications where intelligibility of speech is the criterion.

Interestingly, the data rate out of a coder is virtually independent of the input sampling rate unless the sampling rate is very low. This is because the entropy of the sound is in the waveform, not in the number of samples carrying it.

The compression factor of a coder is only part of the story. All codecs cause delay, and in general the greater the compression the longer the delay. In some applications where the original sound may be heard at the same time as sound which has passed through a codec, a short delay is required.[18] In most applications, the compressed channel will have a constant bit rate, and so a constant compression factor is required. In real programme material, the entropy varies and so the NMR will fluctuate. If greater delay can be accepted, as in a recording application, memory buffering can be used to allow the coder to operate at constant NMR and instantaneously variable data rate. The memory absorbs the instantaneous data rate differences of the coder and allows a constant rate in the channel. A higher effective degree of data reduction will then be obtained.

2.18 Sub-band coding

Sub-band data reduction takes advantage of the fact that real sounds do not have uniform spectral energy. The wordlength of PCM audio is based on the dynamic range required and this is generally constant with frequency although any pre-emphasis will affect the situation. When a signal with an uneven spectrum is conveyed by PCM, the whole dynamic range is occupied only by the loudest spectral component, and all of the other components are coded with excessive headroom. In its simplest form, sub-band coding[19] works by splitting the audio signal into a number of frequency bands and companding each band according to its own level. Bands in which there is little energy result in small amplitudes which can be transmitted with short wordlength. Thus each band results in variable length samples, but the sum of all the sample wordlengths is less than that of PCM and so a coding gain can be obtained. Sub-band coding is not restricted to the digital domain; the analog Dolby noise reduction systems use it extensively.

The number of sub-bands to be used depends upon what other reduction technique is to be combined with the sub-band coding. If it is intended to use reduction based on auditory masking, the sub-bands should preferably be narrower than the critical bands of the ear, and therefore a large number will be required; ISO/MPEG and PASC, for example, use 32 sub-bands. Figure 2.46 shows the critical condition where the masking tone is at the top edge of the sub-band. It will be seen that the narrower the sub-band, the higher the requantizing noise that can be masked. The use of an excessive number of sub-bands will, however, raise complexity and the coding delay, as well as risking pre-echo on transients exceeding the temporal masking.

The band-splitting process is complex and requires a lot of computation. One band-splitting method which is useful is quadrature mirror filtering.[20] The QMF is a kind of twin FIR filter which converts a PCM sample stream into two sample streams of half the input sampling rate, so that the output data rate equals the input data rate. The frequencies in the lower half of the audio spectrum are carried in one sample stream, and the frequencies in the upper half of the spectrum are carried in the other. Whilst the lower frequency output is a PCM band-limited representation of the input waveform, the upper frequency output is not. A moment's thought will reveal that it could not be because the sampling rate is not high enough. In fact the upper half of the input spectrum has been heterodyned down to the same frequency band as the lower half by the clever use

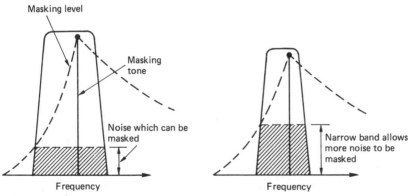

Figure 2.46 In sub-band coding the worst case occurs when the masking tone is at the top edge of the sub-band. The narrower the band, the higher the noise level which can be masked.

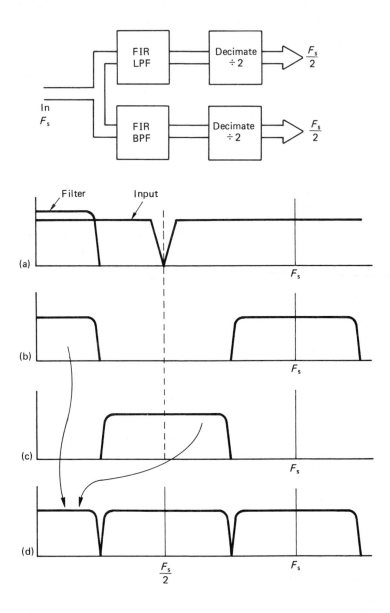

Figure 2.47 The quadrature mirror filter. In (a) the input spectrum has an audio baseband extending up to half the sampling rate. The input is passed through an FIR low-pass filter which cuts off at one-quarter of the sampling rate to give the spectrum shown in (b). The input also passes in parallel through a second FIR filter whose impulse response has been multiplied by a cosinusoidal waveform in order to amplitude-modulate it. The resultant impulse gives the filter a mirror image frequency response shown in (c). The spectra of both (b) and (c) show that both are oversampled by a factor of two because they are half empty. As a result both can be decimated by a factor of two, resulting in (d) in two identical Nyquist-sampled frequency bands of half the original width.

of aliasing. The waveform is unrecognizable, but when heterodyned back to its correct place in the spectrum in an inverse step, the correct waveform will result once more.

Figure 2.47 shows the operation of a simple QMF. In (a) the input spectrum of the PCM audio is shown, having an audio baseband extending up to half the sampling rate and the usual lower sideband extending down from there up to the sampling frequency. The input is passed through an FIR low-pass filter which cuts off at one-quarter of the sampling rate to give the spectrum shown in (b). The input also passes in parallel through a second FIR filter which is physically identical, but the coefficients are different. The impulse response of the FIR LPF is multiplied by a cosinusoidal waveform which amplitude-modulates it. The resultant impulse gives the filter a frequency response shown in (c). This is a mirror image of the LPF response. If certain criteria are met, the overall frequency response of the two filters is flat. The spectra of both (b) and (c) show that both are oversampled by a factor of 2 because they are half empty. As a result, both can be decimated by a factor of two, which is the equivalent of dropping every other sample. In the case of the lower half of the spectrum, nothing remarkable happens. The upper half of the spectrum, however, has been resampled at half the original frequency as shown in (d). The result is that the upper half of the audio spectrum aliases or heterodynes to the lower half.

An inverse QMF will recombine the bands into the original broadband signal. It is a feature of a QMF/inverse QMF pair that any energy near the band edge which appears in both bands due to inadequate selectivity in the filtering reappears at the correct frequency in the inverse filtering process provided that there is uniform quantizing in all of the sub-bands. In practical coders, this criterion is not met, but any residual artifacts are sufficiently small to be masked.

The audio band can be split into as many bands as required by cascading QMFs in a tree. However, each stage can only divide the input spectrum in half. In some coders certain sub-bands will have passed through one splitting stage more than others and will be half their bandwidth.[21] A delay is required in the wider sub-band data for time alignment.

A simple quadrature mirror is computationally intensive because sample values are calculated which are later decimated or discarded, and an alternative is to use polyphase pseudo-QMF filters[22] or wave filters[23] in which the filtering and decimation process is combined. Only wanted sample values are computed. In a polyphase filter a set of samples is shifted into position in the transversal register and then these are multiplied by different sets of coefficients and accumulated in each of several phases to give the value of a number of different samples between input samples. In a polyphase QMF, the same approach is used. Figure 2.48 shows an example of a 32 band polyphase QMF having a 512 sample window. With 32 sub-bands, each band will be decimated to $\frac{1}{32}$ of the input sampling rate. Thus only one sample in 32 will be retained after the combined filter/decimate operation. The polyphase QMF only computes the value of the sample which is to be retained in each sub-band. The filter works in 32 different phases with the same samples in the transversal register. In the first phase, the coefficients will describe the impulse response of a low-pass filter, the so-called prototype filter, and the result of 512 multiplications will be accumulated to give a single sample in the first band. In the second phase the coefficients will be obtained by multiplying the impulse response of the prototype filter by a

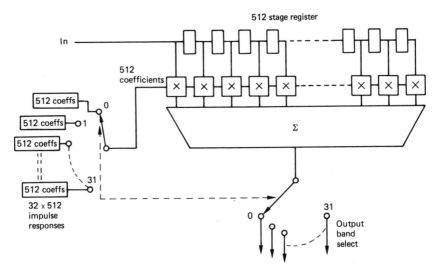

Figure 2.48 In polyphase QMF the same input samples are subject to computation using coefficient sets in many different time-multiplexed phases. The decimation is combined with the filtering so only wanted values are computed.

cosinusoid at the centre frequency of the second band. Once more 512 multiply accumulates will be required to obtain a single sample in the second band. This is repeated for each of the 32 bands, and in each case a different centre frequency is obtained by multiplying the prototype impulse by a different modulating frequency. Following 32 such computations, 32 output samples, one in each band, will have been computed. The transversal register then shifts 32 samples and the process repeats.

The principle of the polyphase QMF is not so different from the techniques used to compute a frequency transform and effectively blurs the distinction between sub-band coding and transform coding.

The QMF technique is restricted to bands of equal width. It might be thought that this is a drawback because the critical bands of the ear are non-uniform. In fact this is only a problem when very large amounts of reduction are required. In all cases it is the masking model of hearing which must have correct critical bands. This model can then be superimposed on bands of any width to determine how much masking and therefore coding gain is possible. Uniform width sub-bands will not be able to obtain as much masking as bands which are matched to critical bands, but for many applications the additional coding gain is not worth the added filter complexity.

2.19 Transform coding

Audio is usually considered to be a time-domain waveform as this is what emerges from a microphone. As has been seen in Section 2.13, Fourier analysis allows any waveform to be represented by a set of harmonically related components of suitable amplitude and phase. In theory it is perfectly possible to decompose an input waveform into its constituent frequencies and phases, and to record or transmit the transform. The transform can then be reversed and the original waveform will be precisely recreated. Although one can think of exceptions, the transform of a typical audio waveform changes relatively slowly. The slow speech of an organ pipe or a violin string, or the slow decay of most musical sounds, allows the rate at which the transform is sampled to be reduced, and a coding gain results. A further coding gain will be achieved if the components which will experience masking are quantized more coarsely.

In practice there are some difficulties. The computational task of transforming an entire recording of perhaps an hour's duration as one waveform is staggering. Even if it were feasible, the coding delay would be at least equal to the length of the recording, which is unacceptable for many purposes.

The solution to this difficulty is to cut the waveform into short segments and then to transform each individually. The delay is reduced, as is the computational task, but there is a possibility of artifacts arising because of the truncation of the waveform into rectangular time windows. A solution is to use window functions, and to overlap the segments as shown in Figure 2.49. Thus every input sample appears in just two transforms, but with variable weighting depending upon its position along the time axis. Although it appears from the diagram that twice as much data will be generated, in fact certain transforms can eliminate the redundancy.

Figure 2.49 Transform coding can only be practically performed on short blocks. These are overlapped using window functions in order to handle continuous waveforms.

The DFT (discrete frequency transform) does not produce a continuous spectrum, but instead produces coefficients at discrete frequencies. The frequency resolution (i.e. the number of different frequency coefficients) is equal to the number of samples in the window. If overlapped windows are used, twice as many coefficients are produced as are theoretically necessary. In addition the DFT requires intensive computation, owing to the requirement to use complex arithmetic to render the phase of the components as well as the amplitude. An alternative is to use discrete cosine transforms (DCT). These are advantageous when used with overlapping windows. In the modified discrete cosine transform (MDCT),[24] windows with 50% overlap are used. Thus twice as many coefficients as necessary are produced. These are subsampled by a factor of two to give a critically sampled transform, which results in potential aliasing in the frequency domain. However, by making a slight change to the transform, the alias products in the second half of a given window are equal in size but of opposite polarity to the alias products in the first half of the next window, and so will be cancelled on reconstruction. This is the principle of time-domain aliasing cancellation (TDAC).

The requantizing in the coder raises the quantizing noise in the frequency bin, but it does so over the entire duration of the block. Figure 2.50 shows that if a transient occurs towards the end of a block, the decoder will reproduce the waveform correctly, but the quantizing noise will start at the beginning of the

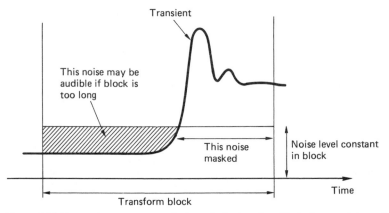

Figure 2.50 If a transient occurs towards the end of a transform block, the quantizing noise will still be present at the beginning of the block and may result in a pre-echo where the noise is audible before the transient.

block and may result in a pre-echo where the noise is audible before the transient.

The solution is to use a variable time window according to the transient content of the audio waveform. When musical transients occur, short blocks are necessary and the frequency resolution and hence the coding gain will be low. At other times the blocks become longer and the frequency resolution of the transform rises, allowing a greater coding gain.

The transform of an audio signal is computed in the main signal path in a transform coder, and has sufficient frequency resolution to drive the masking model directly. However, in certain sub-band coders the frequency resolution of the filter bank is good enough to offer a high coding gain, but not good enough to drive the masking model accurately, particularly in respect of the steep slope on the low-frequency side of the masker. In order to overcome this problem, a transform will often be computed for control purposes in a side chain rather than in the main audio path, and so the accuracy in respects other than frequency resolution need not be so high. This approach also permits the use of equal width sub-bands in the main path.

2.20 A simple sub-band coder

Figure 2.51 shows the block diagram of a simple sub-band coder. At the input, the frequency range is split into sub-bands by a filter bank such as a quadrature mirror filter. The output data rate of the filter bank is no higher than the input rate because each band has been heterodyned to a frequency range from DC upwards. The decomposed sub-band data are then assembled into blocks of fixed size, prior to reduction. Whilst all sub-bands may use blocks of the same length, some coders may use blocks which get longer as the sub-band frequency becomes lower. Sub-band blocks are also referred to as frequency bins.

The coding gain is obtained as the waveform in each band passes through a requantizer. The requantization is achieved by multiplying the sample values by a constant and rounding up or down to the required wordlength. For example, if

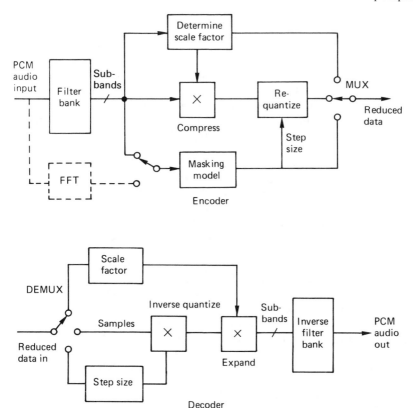

Figure 2.51 A simple sub-band coder. The bit allocation may come from analysis of the sub-band energy, or, for greater reduction, from a spectral analysis in a side chain.

in a given sub-band the waveform is 36 dB down on full scale, there will be at least six bits in each sample which merely replicate the sign bit. Multiplying by 2^6 will bring the high-order bits of the sample into use, allowing bits to be lost at the lower end by rounding to a shorter wordlength. The shorter the wordlength, the greater the coding gain, but the coarser the quantization steps and therefore the level of quantization error.

If a fixed data-reduction factor is employed, the size of the coded output block will be fixed. The requantization wordlengths will have to be such that the sum of the bits from each sub-band equals the size of the coded block. Thus some sub-bands can have long wordlength coding if others have short wordlength coding. The process of determining the requantization step size, and hence the wordlength in each sub-band, is known as bit allocation. The bit allocation may be performed by analysing the power in each sub-band, or by a side chain which performs a spectral analysis or transform of the audio. The complexity of the bit allocation depends upon the degree of compression required. The spectral content is compared with an auditory masking model to determine the degree of masking which is taking place in certain bands as a result of higher levels in other bands. Where masking takes place, the signal is quantized more coarsely until the quantizing noise is raised to just below the masking level. The coarse quantization requires shorter wordlengths and allows a coding gain. The bit allocation may be iterative as adjustments are made to obtain the best NMR within the allowable data rate.

The samples of differing wordlength in each bin are then assembled into the output coded block. Unlike a PCM block, which contains samples of fixed wordlength, a coded block contains many different wordlengths and these can vary from one block to the next. In order to deserialize the block into samples of various wordlength and demultiplex the samples into the appropriate frequency bins, the decoder has to be told what bit allocations were used when it was packed, and some synchronizing means is needed to allow the beginning of the block to be identified. Demultiplexing can be done by including the transform of the block which was used to determine the allocation. If the decoder has the same allocation model, it can determine what the coder must have done from the transform, and demultiplex the block accordingly. Once all of the samples are back in their respective frequency bins, the level of each bin is returned to the original value. This is achieved by reversing the gain increase which was applied before the requantizer in the coder. The degree of gain reduction to use in each bin also comes from the transform. The sub-bands can then be recombined into a continuous audio spectrum in the output filter which produces conventional PCM of the original wordlength.

The degree of compression is determined by the bit allocation system. It is not difficult to change the output block size parameter to obtain a different compression. The bit allocator simply iterates until the new block size is filled. Similarly the decoder need only deserialize the larger block correctly into coded samples and then the expansion process is identical except for the fact that expanded words contain less noise. Thus codecs with varying degrees of compression are available which can perform different bandwidth/performance tasks with the same hardware.

2.21 Video data reduction

Digital video suffers from an extremely high data rate, particularly in high definition, and one approach to the problem is to reduce that rate without affecting the subjective quality of the picture. The human eye is not equally sensitive to all spatial frequencies, so some coding gain can be obtained by quantizing more coarsely the frequencies which are less visible. Video images typically contain a great deal of redundancy where flat areas contain the same pixel value repeated many times. Furthermore, in many cases there is little difference between one field and the next, and inter-field data reduction can be achieved by sending only the differences. Whilst this may achieve considerable reduction, the result is difficult to edit because individual fields can no longer be identified in the data stream. Thus for production purposes, data reduction is restricted to exploiting the redundancy within each field individually. Production DVTRs such as Sony's Digital Betacam and the Ampex DCT use only very mild compression of 2:1. This allows simple algorithms to be used and also permits multiple generations without artifacts being visible.

Clearly a consumer DVTR needs only single-generation operation and has simple editing requirements. A much greater degree of compression can then be used, which also takes advantage of redundancy between fields.

2.22 Intra-field data reduction

This type of data reduction takes each individual field (or frame in progressive scan standards) and treats it in isolation from any other field or frame. The most common algorithms are based on the discrete cosine transform described in Section 2.15.

Figure 2.43 showed an example of the different coefficients of a DCT for an 8×8 pixel block, and adding these together in different proportions will give any original pixel block. The top left coefficient conveys the DC component of the block. This one will be a unipolar (positive only) value in the case of luminance and will typically be the largest value in the block as the spectrum of typical video signals is dominated by the DC component. Moving to the right the coefficients represent increasing horizontal spatial frequencies and moving downwards the coefficients represent increasing vertical spatial frequencies. The bottom right coefficient represents the highest diagonal frequencies in the block. All of these coefficients are bipolar, where the polarity indicates whether the original spatial waveform at that frequency was inverted.

In typical pictures, the coefficients representing the higher two-dimensional spatial frequencies will be zero or of small value in large areas of typical video, due to motion blurring or simply plain undetailed areas before the camera. In general, the further from the top left corner the coefficient is, the smaller will be its magnitude on average. Coding gain (the technical term for reduction in the number of bits needed) is achieved by taking advantage of the zero and low-valued coefficients to cut down on the data necessary. Thus it is not the DCT which compresses the data, it is the subsequent processing. The DCT simply expresses the data in a form which makes the subsequent processing easier. Thus the correct terminology is to say that a compression algorithm is *DCT-based*.

Once transformed, there are various techniques which can be used to reduce the data needed to carry the coefficients. These will be based on a knowledge of the signal statistics and the human vision mechanism and will often be combined in practical systems.[25,26]

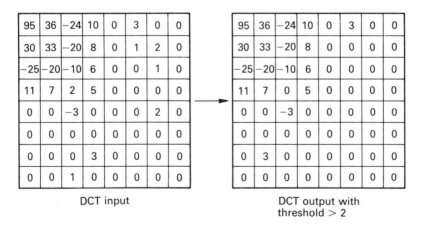

DCT input

95	36	−24	10	0	3	0	0
30	33	−20	8	0	1	2	0
−25	−20	−10	6	0	0	1	0
11	7	2	5	0	0	0	0
0	0	−3	0	0	0	2	0
0	0	0	0	0	0	0	0
0	0	0	3	0	0	0	0
0	0	1	0	0	0	0	0

DCT output with threshold > 2

95	36	−24	10	0	3	0	0
30	33	−20	8	0	0	0	0
−25	−20	−10	6	0	0	0	0
11	7	0	5	0	0	0	0
0	0	−3	0	0	0	0	0
0	0	0	0	0	0	0	0
0	3	0	0	0	0	0	0
0	0	0	0	0	0	0	0

Figure 2.52 After the DCT, a simple way of compressing the data is to transmit only those coefficients which exceed a threshold.

Possibly the simplest reduction method involves setting a threshold magnitude for coefficients. Only coefficients which exceed the threshold are transmitted, as it is assumed that smaller values make a negligible contribution to the picture block. Figure 2.52 shows the result, which is that most coefficients then have a value of zero.

Psycho-visual knowledge may also be used to process the coefficients. Omitting a coefficient means that the appropriate frequency component is missing from the reconstructed block. The difference between original and reconstructed blocks is regarded as noise added to the wanted data. The visibility of such noise is far from uniform. Figure 2.53 shows that the sensitivity of the eye to noise falls with frequency. The maximum sensitivity is at DC and as a result the top left coefficient is often treated as a special case and left unchanged. It may warrant more error protection than other coefficients.

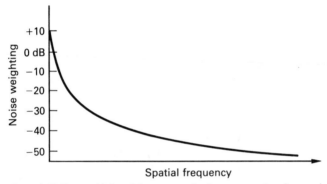

Figure 2.53 The sensitivity of the eye to noise is greatest at low frequencies and drops rapidly with increasing frequency. This can be used to mask quantizing noise caused by the compression process.

Psycho-visual coding takes advantage of the falling sensitivity to noise by multiplying each coefficient by a different weighting constant as a function of its frequency. This has the effect of reducing the magnitude of each coefficient so that fewer bits are needed to represent it. Another way of looking at this process is that the coefficients are individually requantized with step sizes which increase with frequency. The larger step size increases the quantizing noise at frequencies where it is not visible.

When serializing a coefficient block, it is normal to scan in a sequence where the largest coefficient values are scanned first. Clearly such a scan begins in the top left corner and ends in the bottom right corner. Statistical analysis of real program material can be used to determine an optimal scan, but in many cases a regular zig-zag scan shown in Figure 2.54 will be used with slight loss of performance. The advantage of such a scan is that on typical material the scan finishes with coefficients which are zero valued. Instead of transmitting these zeros, a unique 'end of block' symbol is transmitted instead. Just before the last finite coefficient and the EOB symbol it is likely that some zero-value coefficients will be scanned. The coding enters a different mode whereby it simply transmits a unique prefix called a run-length prefix, followed by a code

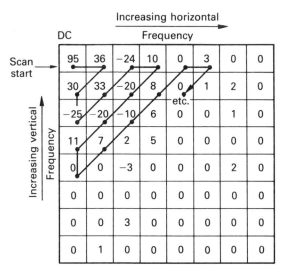

Figure 2.54 The zig-zag scan starting top left orders the coefficients in the best sequence for compression as the later ones will have smaller value.

specifying the number of zeros which follow. This is also shown in Figure 2.44.

Figure 2.55(a) shows a block diagram of a representative image data-reduction unit. The input image is blocked, and the DCT stage transforms the blocks into a form in which redundancy can be identified. Psycho-visual weighting then reduces coefficient values according to the human visual process. Block scanning and variable length/run length coding finish the job. The receiver is shown in Figure 2.55(b). The input bitstream is deserialized into symbols, and the run-length decoder reassembles the runs of zeros. The variable length decoder then converts back to constant wordlength coefficients. The psycho-visual weighting is reversed by a division which cancels the original multiplication. An inverse DCT then reconstructs the blocks.

The compression factor of the system of Figure 2.55 is a function of the input image. A detailed contrasting image will result in more data than a soft image containing self-similar areas. This is not a problem for single-image applications like wirephotos, because the result is that on a fixed rate link the transmission time varies slightly from one image to the next, just as it does in a fax machine.

In a recorder the picture rate is constant and this variable compression is a nuisance because it demands a variable rate recorder. The solution is to make the compression factor constant. This is done by using feedback from the output coder which is given a bit budget. If the bit budget is exceeded, the coefficients are requantized to larger steps. If the bit budget is under-utilized, the quantization steps are made more accurate. This is an iterative process which converges on an optimally filled output block in a variable time. This variability is undesirable in real-time hardware and instead the coefficients may be requantized by all step sizes in turn. At the end of this fixed-time process the best quantization step size is then picked.

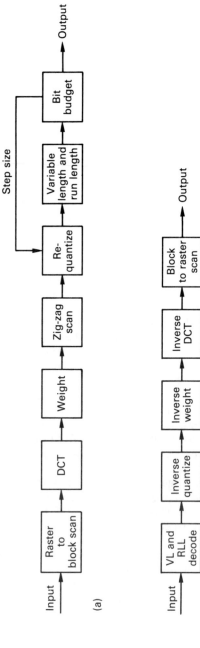

Figure 2.55 (a) An intra-field DCT-based coder; (b) the corresponding decoder.

Variable quantizing results in variable noise, and it is desirable to reduce the visibility of program-sensitive noise. One way in which this can be done is to combine a number of DCT blocks together into an entropy block. The entropy block is then given a bit budget. In this system, one DCT block having high entropy can use up the bit budget made available by other DCT blocks in the entropy block which have low entropy. Coarse quantization is not then necessary and an improvement in signal-to-noise ratio results. The chances of every DCT block in an entropy block having high entropy are not great, but can be reduced further by shuffling the DCT blocks so that an entropy block is made up from blocks which are distributed around the screen.

In practice entropy blocks cannot be made arbitrarily large because only an entire block can be properly decoded owing to the use of variable-length coding. In digital VTRs, the entropy block length is restricted to the track length which can be recovered in shuttle, but a useful noise advantage is still obtained.

2.23 Inter-field data reduction

Higher compression factors are easier to obtain if advantage is taken of redundancy between successive images. Only the difference between images need be sent. Clearly with a still picture, successive images will be identical and the difference will be trivial. In practice, movement reduces the similarity between successive images and the difference data increase. One way of increasing the coding gain is to use motion compensation. If the motion of an object between images is known and transmitted, the decoder can use the motion vector to shift the pixel data describing the object in the previous image to the correct position in the current image. The image difference for the object will then be smaller. The differences between images will be compressed by a DCT-based system as described above.

Figure 2.56 shows a motion-compensated system. Incoming video passes in parallel to the motion estimator and the line-scan to block-scan converter. The motion estimator compares the incoming frame with the previous one in the frame store in order to measure motion, and sends the motion vectors to the motion compensation unit which shifts objects in the frame store output to their estimated positions in the new frame. This results in a predicted frame, which is subtracted from the input frame in order to obtain the frame difference or prediction error. The result of this process is that the temporal or inter-frame redundancy and the entropy have been separated. The redundancy is the predictable part of the image as anything which is predictable carries no information. The prediction error is the entropy, the part which could not be predicted. The frame difference is then processed to remove spatial redundancy. This is done with a combination of DCT, weighting and quantizing as was explained in Section 2.22. The spatially reduced frame difference is combined with the motion vectors in order to produce the system output.

It will be seen from Figure 2.56(a) that there is also a local decoder which consists of an inverse quantizer, inverse weighting stage and an inverse DCT. Adding the locally decoded prediction error (image difference) to the predicted frame must result in the original frame (plus quantizing noise) which updates the frame store. Figure 2.56(b) shows the decoder. The frame store output is shifted by the transmitted motion vectors and the result is the same predicted frame as

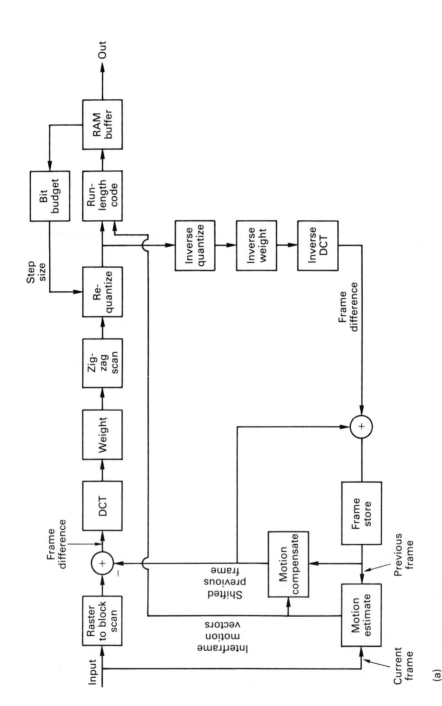

Figure 2.56 (a)

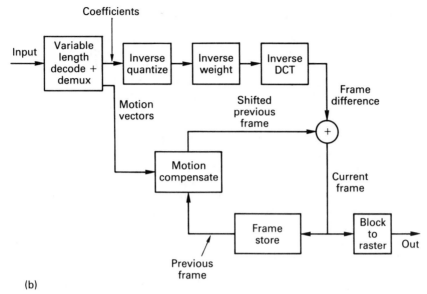

(b)

Figure 2.56 (a) An inter-field motion-compensated coder; (b) the corresponding decoder. See text for details.

was produced in the encoder. The decoded frame error is added to the predicted frame and the original frame results.

The motion estimation process needs to be simple and economical and it does not need to be very accurate as it is inside the error loop. The motion compensator works to pixel accuracy using address mapping only and so there is no point in having sub-pixel accurate vectors. If a motion vector is slightly incorrect, the frame difference will correct for it at the expense of a slight increase in data. Block matching is generally adequate for such a motion estimation application and is widely used.

Whilst a system based purely on inter-field redundancy will work, it has some weaknesses. One of these is the situation where a moving object reveals background area which was concealed in the previous image. This area cannot be predicted and results in a large error. Data from such an area might just as well be coded on an intra-field basis, and this might be more efficient. Another problem is that the current field is based on the history of many previous fields. The system will take some time to produce a picture from a cold start, and if a transmission error occurs, the result will propagate through a large number of future fields. In practical systems, these problems may be overcome by switching between inter-field and inter-frame mode. This may be done on a DCT block basis as required in order to handle obscured and revealed image areas. In addition, a certain proportion of blocks may be forced into intra-field mode in every field. The position of these blocks moves around the field so that within a certain time period, perhaps a second, the entire picture area has been given an absolute reference. This process is known as refreshing, and helps to cut down the effects of error propagation. A further possibility is to transmit a signal structure in which periodically there are fields which are entirely intra-field coded.

2.24 Timebase compression and buffering

One strength of digital technology is the ease with which delay can be provided. Accurate control of delay is the essence of buffering, necessary whenever the instantaneous time of arrival or rate from a data source does not match the destination. In digital audio and certain instrumentation applications, the destination will almost always have perfectly regular timing, namely the sampling rate clock of the final DAC. This application of buffering is known as timebase correction and consists of aligning jittery signals from storage media or transmission channels with that stable reference. In this way, wow and flutter are rendered unmeasurable.

A further function of timebase correction is to reverse the time compression applied prior to recording or transmission. As was shown in Section 1.12, digital recorders compress data into blocks to facilitate error correction as well as to permit head switching between blocks in rotary-head machines. Owing to the spaces between blocks, data arrive in bursts on replay, but must be fed to the output converters in an unbroken stream at the sampling rate. The extreme time compression used in RDAT to reduce the tape wrap is a further example of the use of the principle (see Chapter 8).

In computer hard-disk drives, a converse problem also arises. Data from the disk blocks arrive at a reasonably constant rate, but cannot necessarily be accepted at a steady rate by the logic because of contention for the use of buses and memory by the different parts of the system. In this case, the data must be buffered by a relative of the timebase corrector which is usually referred to as a silo.

Although delay is easily implemented, it is not possible to advance a data stream. Most real machines cause instabilities balanced about the correct timing: the output jitters between too early and too late. Since the information cannot be advanced in the corrector, only delayed, the solution is to run the machine in advance of real time. In this case, correctly timed output signals will need a nominal delay to align them with reference timing. Early output signals will receive more delay, and late output signals will receive less delay.

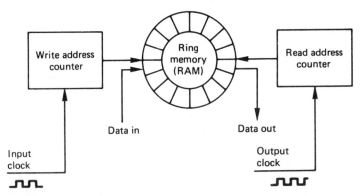

Figure 2.57 If the memory address is arranged to come from a counter which overflows, the memory can be made to appear circular. The write address then rotates endlessly, overwriting previous data once per revolution. The read address can follow the write address by a variable distance (not exceeding one revolution) and so a variable delay takes place between reading and writing.

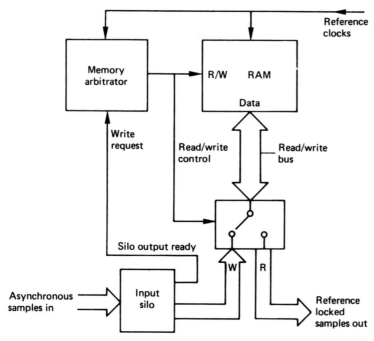

Figure 2.58 In a RAM-based TBC, the RAM is reference synchronous, and an arbitrator decides when it will read and when it will write. During reading, asynchronous input data back up in the input silo, asserting a write request to the arbitrator. Arbitrator will then cause a write cycle between read cycles.

Section 2.5 showed the principles of digital storage elements which can be used for delay purposes. The shift-register approach and the RAM approach to delay are very similar, as a shift register can be thought of as a memory whose address increases automatically when clocked. The data rate and the maximum delay determine the capacity of the RAM required. Figure 2.57 shows that the addressing of the RAM is by a counter that overflows endlessly from the end of the memory back to the beginning, giving the memory a ring-like structure. The write address is determined by the incoming data, and the read address is determined by the outgoing data. This means that the RAM has to be able to read and write at the same time. The switching between read and write involves not only a data multiplexer but also an address multiplexer. In general the arbitration between read and write will be done by signals from the stable side of the TBC as Figure 2.58 shows. In the replay case the stable clock will be on the read side. The stable side of the RAM will read a sample when it demands, and the writing will be locked out for that period. The input data cannot be interrupted in many applications, however, so a small buffer silo is installed before the memory, which fills up as the writing is locked out, and empties again as writing is permitted. Alternatively, the memory will be split into blocks as was shown in Chapter 1, such that when one block is reading a different block will be writing and the problem does not arise.

2.25 FIFO buffering

Figure 2.59 shows the operation of a FIFO (first in first out) chip, colloquially known as a silo because the data are tipped in at the top on delivery and drawn off at the bottom when needed. Each stage of the chip has a data register and a small amount of logic, including a data-valid or V bit. If the input register does not contain data, the first V bit will be reset, and this will cause the chip to assert 'input ready'. If data are presented at the input, and clocked into the first stage, the V bit will set, and the 'input ready' signal will become false. However, the logic associated with the next stage sees the V bit set in the top stage, and if its own V bit is clear, it will clock the data into its own register, set its own V bit, and clear the input V bit, causing 'input ready' to reassert, when another word can be fed in. This process then continues as the word moves down the silo, until

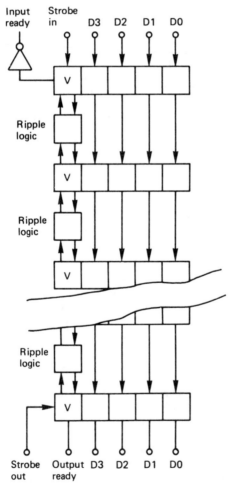

Figure 2.59 Structure of FIFO or silo chip. Ripple logic controls propagation of data down silo.

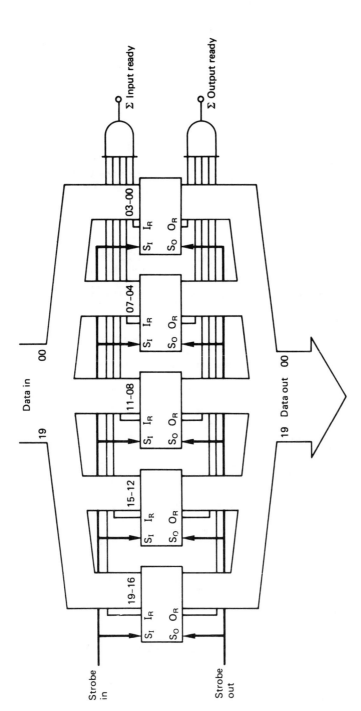

Figure 2.60 In this example, a 20 bit wordlength silo is made from five parallel FIFO chips. The asynchronous ripple action of FIFOs means that it is necessary to 'AND' together the ready signals.

it arrives at the last register in the chip. The V bit of the last stage becomes the 'output ready' signal, telling subsequent circuitry that there are data to be read. If this word is not read, the next word entered will ripple down to the stage above. Words thus stack up at the bottom of the silo. When a word is read out, an external signal must be provided which resets the bottom V bit. The 'output ready' signal now goes false, and the logic associated with the last stage now sees valid data above, and loads down the word when it will become ready again. The last register but one will now have no V bit set, and will see data above itself and bring that down. In this way a reset V bit propagates up the chip whilst the data ripple down, rather like a hole in a semiconductor going the opposite way to the electrons. Silo chips are usually available in 4 bit wordlengths, but can easily be connected in parallel to form longer words. Silo chips are asynchronous, and paralleled chips will not necessarily all work at the same speed. This problem is easily overcome by 'ANDing' together all of the input-ready and output-ready signals and parallel-connecting the strobes. Figure 2.60 shows this mode of operation.

References

1. RAY, S.F., *Applied photographic optics*, Chapter 17. Oxford: Focal Press (1988)
2. VAN DEN ENDEN, A.W.M. and VERHOECKX, N.A.M., Digital signal processing: theoretical background. *Philips Tech. Rev.*, **42**, 110–144 (1985)
3. McCLELLAN, J.H., PARKS, T.W. and RABINER, L.R., A computer program for designing optimum FIR linear-phase digital filters. *IEEE Trans. Audio and Electroacoustics*, **AU-21**, 506–526 (1973)
4. KRANIAUSKAS, P., *Transforms in signals and systems*, Chapter 6. Wokingham: Addison Wesley (1992)
5. AHMED, N., NATARAJAN, T. and RAO, K., Discrete Cosine Transform. *IEEE Trans. Computers*, **C-23**, 90–93 (1974)
6. DE WITH, P.H.N., Data compression techniques for digital video recording. *Ph.D. Thesis*, Technical University of Delft (1992)
7. HUFFMAN, D.A., A method for the construction of minimum redundancy codes. *Proc. IRE*, **40**, 1098–1101 (1952)
8. JOHNSTON, J.D., Transform coding of audio signals using perceptual noise criteria. *IEEE J. Selected Areas in Comms.*, **JSAC-6**, 314–323 (1988)
9. FLETCHER, H., Auditory patterns. *Rev. Modern Physics*, **12**, 47–65 (1940)
10. ZWICKER, E., Subdivision of the audible frequency range into critical bands. *J. Acoust. Soc. Amer.*, **33**, 248 (1961)
11. MOORE, B. AND GLASBERG, B., Formulae describing frequency selectivity as a function of frequency and level, and their use in calculating excitation patterns. *Hearing Research*, **28**, 209–225 (1987)
12. EHMER, R.H., Masking of tones vs. noise bands. *J. Audio Eng. Soc.*, **31**, 1253–1256 (1959)
13. FIELDER, L.D. and DAVIDSON, G.A., AC-2: a family of low complexity transform based music coders. *Proc. 10th Int. Audio Eng. Soc. Conf.*, pp. 57–70. New York: Audio Eng. Soc. (1991)
14. CARTERETTE, E.C. and FRIEDMAN, M.P., *Handbook of Perception*, pp. 305–319. New York: Academic Press (1978)
15. GREWIN, C. and RYDEN, T., Subjective assessments on low bit-rate audio codecs. *Proc. 10th Int. Audio Eng. Soc. Conf.*, pp. 91–102. New York: Audio Eng. Soc. (1991)
16. BRANDENBURG, K. and SEITZER, D., Low bit rate coding of high quality digital audio: algorithms and evaluation of quality. *Proc. 7th Int. Audio Eng. Soc. Conf.*, pp. 201–209. New York: Audio Eng. Soc. (1989)
17. JOHNSTON, J., Estimation of perceptual entropy using noise masking criteria. *ICASSP*, pp. 2524–2527 (1988)
18. GILCHRIST, N.H.C., Delay in broadcasting operations. Presented at 90th Audio Eng. Soc. Conv. (1991), preprint 3033
19. CROCHIERE, R.E., Sub-band coding. *Bell System Tech. J.*, **60**, 1633–1653 (1981)
20. JAYANT, N.S. and NOLL, P., *Digital coding of waveforms: principles and applications to speech and video*. Englewood Cliffs, NJ: Prentice Hall (1984)

21. THEILE, G., STOLL, G. and LINK, M., Low bit rate coding of high quality audio signals: an introduction to the MASCAM system. *EBU Tech. Review*, No. 230, 158–181 (1988)
22. CHU, P.L., Quadrature mirror filter design for an arbitrary number of equal bandwidth channels. *IEEE Trans. ASSP*, **ASSP-33**, 203–218 (1985)
23. FETTWEIS, A., Wave digital filters: Theory and practice. *Proc. IEEE*, **74**, 270–327 (1986)
24. PRINCEN, J.P., JOHNSON, A. and BRADLEY, A.B., Sub-band/transform coding using filter bank designs based on time domain aliasing cancellation. *Proc. ICASSP*, 2161–2164 (1987)
25. CLARKE, R.J., *Transform coding of images*. London: Academic Press (1985)
26. NETRAVALI, A.N. and HASKELL, B.G., *Digital pictures – representation and compression*. New York: Plenum Press (1988)

Chapter 3

Recording principles

Data recording is no more than the process of making more or less permanent changes between a minimum of two states of some carrier or medium. Although the physics of the recording processes are unaffected by the meaning attributed to signals, digital techniques are rather different from those used with analog signals, although often the same phenomenon shows up in a different guise. Recording and transmission have a lot in common as both need to adapt the original data to suit the available channel. One view of a data recorder is that it preserves a transmission waveform on a medium. In this chapter the fundamentals of digital recording are introduced prior to the descriptions of the coding techniques used in the next chapter.

3.1 Introduction to the channel

Communication theory does not distinguish between recording and transmission. The generic term for the path down which the information is sent is the *channel*. In a transmission application, the channel may be no more than a length of cable. In a recording application the channel will include the record head, the medium and the replay head. In analog systems, the characteristics of the channel affect the signal directly, whereas in a data channel this is not the case.

In digital circuitry there is a great deal of noise immunity because the signal has only two states, which are widely separated compared with the amplitude of noise. In both digital recording and transmission this is not always the case. In magnetic recording, noise immunity is a function of track width and reduction of the working SNR of a digital track allows the same information to be carried in a smaller area of the medium, improving economy of operation. This reduction also increases the random error rate, but, as was seen in Chapter 1, an error-correction system may already be necessary in a practical system and it is simply required to work harder.

In real channels, the signal may *originate* with discrete states which change at discrete times, but most real channels will treat it as an analog waveform and so it will not be *received* in the same form. Various loss mechanisms will reduce the amplitude of the signal. These attenuations will not be the same at all frequencies. Many channels, such as magnetic and optical media, are fundamentally non-linear and distort the waveform. Noise will be picked up in the channel as a result of many mechanisms which will be considered here. As a result, the voltage received at the end of the channel will have an infinitely varying state along with a degree of uncertainty due to the noise. Different frequencies can propagate at different speeds in the channel; this is the phenomenon of group delay. An alternative way of considering group delay is that there will be frequency-dependent phase shifts in the signal and these will result in uncertainty in the timing of pulses.

In digital circuitry, the signals are generally accompanied by a separate clock signal which reclocks the data to remove jitter, as was shown in Chapter 1. In contrast, it is generally not feasible to provide a separate clock in recording and transmission applications. In the transmission case, a separate clock line would not only raise cost, but is impractical because at high frequency it is virtually impossible to ensure that the clock cable propagates signals at the same speed as the data cable except over short distances. In the recording case, provision of a separate clock track is impractical at high density because mechanical tolerances cause phase errors between the tracks. The result is the same: timing differences between parallel channels which are known as skew.

The solution is to use a self-clocking waveform, and the generation of this is a further essential function of the coding process. Clearly if data bits are simply clocked serially from a shift register in so-called direct recording or transmission this characteristic will not be obtained. If all the data bits are the same, for example all zeros, there is no clock when they are serialized.

As heads and media cannot know the meaning of the waveforms which they handle, it cannot be the channel which is digital; instead the term describes the way in which the received signals are *interpreted*. When the receiver makes discrete decisions from the input waveform it attempts to reject the uncertainties in voltage and time. The technique of channel coding is one where transmitted waveforms are restricted to those which best allow the receiver to make discrete decisions despite the degradations caused by the analog nature of the channel.

3.2 Types of recording medium

Digital media do not need to have linear transfer functions, nor do they need to be noise-free or continuous. All they need to do is to allow the reproducer to distinguish the presence or absence of replay events, such as the generation of pulses, with reasonable (rather than perfect) reliability. In a magnetic medium, the event will be a flux change from one direction of magnetization to another. In an optical medium, the event must cause the pickup to perceive a change in the intensity of the light falling on the sensor. In the Compact Disc, the apparent contrast is obtained by interference. In some disks it will be through selective absorption of light by dyes. In magneto-optical disks the recording itself is magnetic, but it is made and read using light.

3.3 Magnetism

A magnetic field can be created by passing a current through a solenoid, which is no more than a coil of wire. When the current ceases, the magnetism disappears. However, many materials, some quite common, display a permanent magnetic field with no apparent power source. Magnetism of this kind results from the spin of electrons within atoms. Atomic theory describes atoms as having nuclei around which electrons orbit, spinning as they go. Different orbits can hold a different number of electrons. The distribution of electrons determines

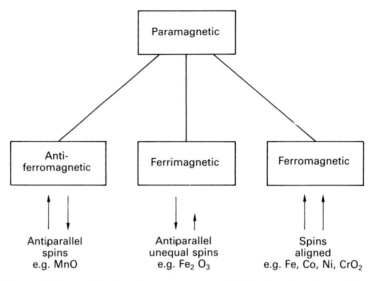

Figure 3.1 The classification of paramagnetic materials. The ferromagnetic materials exhibit the strongest magnetic behaviour.

whether the element is diamagnetic (non-magnetic) or paramagnetic (magnetic characteristics are possible). Diamagnetic materials have an even number of electrons in each orbit, and according to the Pauli exclusion principle half of them spin in each direction. The opposed spins cancel any resultant magnetic moment. Fortunately, there are certain elements, the transition elements, which have an odd number of electrons in certain orbits. The magnetic moment due to electronic spin is not cancelled out in these paramagnetic materials.

Figure 3.1 shows that paramagnetism materials can be classified as antiferromagnetic, ferrimagnetic and ferromagnetic. In some materials alternate atoms are antiparallel and so the magnetic moments are cancelled. In ferrimagnetic materials there is a certain amount of antiparallel cancellation, but a net magnetic moment remains. In ferromagnetic materials such as iron, cobalt or nickel, all of the electron spins can be aligned and as a result the most powerful magnetic behaviour is obtained.

It is not immediately clear how a material in which electron spins are parallel could ever exist in an unmagnetized state or how it could be partially magnetized by a relatively small external field. The theory of magnetic domains has been developed to explain what is observed in practice. Figure 3.2(a) shows a ferromagnetic bar which is demagnetized. It has no net magnetic moment because it is divided into domains or volumes which have equal and opposite moments. Ferromagnetic material divides into domains in order to reduce its magnetostatic energy. Figure 3.2(b) shows a domain wall which is around 0.1 micrometres thick. Within the wall the axis of spin gradually rotates from one state to another. An external field of quite small value is capable of disturbing the equilibrium of the domain wall by favouring one axis of spin over the other. The result is that the domain wall moves and one domain becomes larger at the

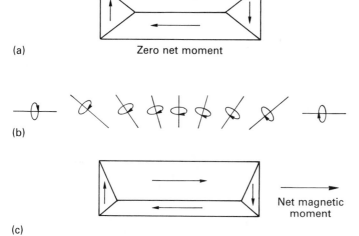

(a)   Zero net moment

(b)

(c)

Net magnetic
moment

Figure 3.2 (a) A magnetic material can have a zero net moment if it is divided into domains as shown here. Domain walls (b) are areas in which the magnetic spin gradually changes from one domain to another. The stresses which result store energy. When some domains dominate, a net magnetic moment can exist as in (c).

expense of another. In this way the net magnetic moment of the bar is no longer zero, as shown in (c).

For small distances, the domain wall motion is linear and reversible if the change in the applied field is reversed. However, larger movements are irreversible because heat is dissipated as the wall jumps to reduce its energy. Following such a domain wall jump, the material remains magnetized after the external field is removed and an opposing external field must be applied which must do further work to bring the domain wall back again. This is a process of hysteresis where work must be done to move each way. Were it not for this non-linear mechanism magnetic recording would be impossible. If magnetic materials were linear, tapes would return to the demagnetized state immediately after leaving the field of the head and this book would have nothing to describe.

Figure 3.3 shows a hysteresis loop which is obtained by plotting the magnetization M when the external field H is swept to and fro. On the macroscopic scale, the loop appears to be a smooth curve, whereas on a small scale it is in fact composed of a large number of small jumps. These were first discovered by Barkhausen. Starting from the unmagnetized state at the origin, as an external field is applied, the response is initially linear and the slope is given by the susceptibility. As the applied field is increased a point is reached where the magnetization ceases to increase. This is the saturation magnetization M_s. If the applied field is removed, the magnetization falls, not to zero, but to the remanent magnetization M_d. This remanence is the magnetic memory mechanism which makes recording possible. The ratio of M_d to M_s is called the squareness ratio. In recording media, squareness is beneficial as it increases the remanent magnetization.

If an increasing external field is applied in the opposite direction, the curve continues to the point where the magnetization is zero. The field required to

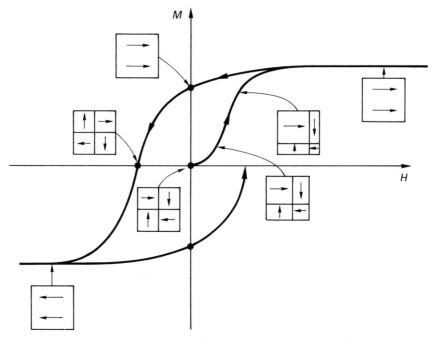

Figure 3.3 A hysteresis loop which comes about because of the non-linear behaviour of magnetic materials. If this characteristic were absent, magnetic recording would not exist.

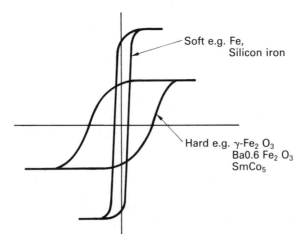

Figure 3.4 The recording medium requires a large loop area (a) whereas the head requires a small loop area (b) to cut losses.

achieve this is called the intrinsic coercive force $_mH_c$. A small increase in the reverse field reaches the point where, if the field where to be removed, the remanent magnetization would become zero. The field required to do this is the remanent coercive force $_dH_c$.

As the external field H is swept to and fro, the magnetization describes a major hysteresis loop. Domain wall transit causes heat to be dissipated on every cycle around the loop and the dissipation is proportional to the loop area. For a recording medium, a large loop is beneficial because the replay signal is a function of the remanence and high coercivity resists erasure. Heating is not an issue. For a device such as a recording head, a small loop is beneficial. Figure 3.4(a) shows the large loop of a hard magnetic material used for recording media and for permanent magnets, and the small loop of a soft magnetic material which is used for recording heads and transformers.

According to the Nyquist noise theorem, anything which dissipates energy when electrical power is supplied must generate a noise voltage when in thermal equilibrium. Thus magnetic recording heads have a noise mechanism which is due to their hysteretic behaviour. The smaller the loop, the less the hysteretic noise. In conventional heads, there are a large number of domains and many small domain wall jumps. In thin-film heads there are fewer domains and the jumps must be larger. The noise this causes is known as Barkhausen noise, but as the same mechanism is responsible it is not possible to say at what point hysteresis noise should be called Barkhausen noise.

3.4 Magnetic recording

Magnetic recording relies on the hysteresis of magnetically hard media, as described above. By definition the transfer function is non-linear, and analog magnetic recorders have to use bias to linearize the process. Digital recorders are not concerned with the non-linearity, and HF bias is unnecessary.

Figure 3.5 shows the construction of a typical digital record head, which is not dissimilar to an analog record head. Heads designed for use with tape work in actual contact with the magnetic coating. The tape is tensioned to pull it against

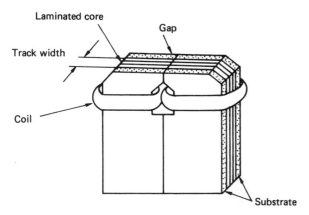

Figure 3.5 A digital record head is similar in principle to an analog head but uses much narrower tracks.

the head. There will be a wear mechanism and need for periodic cleaning. A magnetic circuit carries a coil through which the record current passes and generates flux. A non-magnetic gap forces the flux to leave the magnetic circuit of the head and penetrate the medium. The most efficient recording will be obtained when the reluctance of the magnetic circuit is dominated by that of the gap. This means making the ring structure only just large enough to fit the coil to shorten the magnetic circuit as much as possible. The current through the head must be set to suit the coercivity of the tape, but is less than the current level which would cause saturation of the medium. The amplitude of the current is constant, and recording is performed by reversing the direction of the current with respect to time. As the track passes the head, this is converted to the reversal of the magnetic field left on the tape with respect to distance. The magnetic recording is therefore bipolar. Figure 3.6 shows that the recording is actually made just after the trailing pole of the record head where the flux strength from the gap is falling. As in analog recorders, the width of the gap is generally made

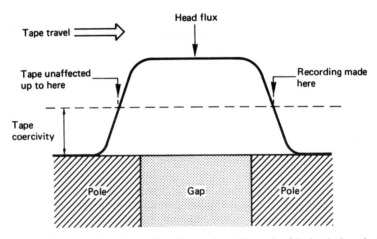

Figure 3.6 The recording is actually made near the trailing pole of the head where the head flux falls below the coercivity of the tape.

quite large to ensure that the full thickness of the magnetic coating is recorded, although this cannot be done if the same head is intended to replay. The record current is selected to be as large as possible without resulting in transition spreading which occurs as saturation is approached. In practice the best value for the record current may be that which minimizes the error rate.

The flux from the head primarily results in a magnetic moment which is longitudinal and the medium will be oriented during manufacture to reflect that. Alternatively the medium may be oriented vertically so that the vertical component of the head flux is emphasized in the recording. Whilst vertical recording has numerous theoretical advantages, such as longer, thinner magnetic regions in the medium which are less prone to self demagnetization, in practice it is difficult to make a vertical recording from one side of a medium because of the need to have a complete magnetic circuit.

3.5 Fixed heads

The construction of a bulk ferrite multitrack head is shown in Figure 3.7, where it will be seen that space must be left between the magnetic circuits to accommodate the windings. Track spacing is improved by putting the windings on alternate sides of the gap. The parallel close-spaced magnetic circuits have considerable mutual inductance, and suffer from crosstalk. This can be compensated when several adjacent tracks record together by cross-connecting antiphase feeds to the record amplifiers.

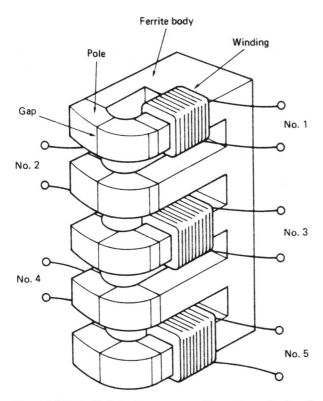

Figure 3.7 Typical bulk ferrite structure used for stationary-head applications. Windings are placed on alternate sides to save space, but parallel magnetic circuits have high crosstalk.

Using thin-film heads, the magnetic circuits and windings are produced by deposition on a substrate at right angles to the tape plane, and as seen in Figure 3.8 they can be made very accurately at small track spacings. Perhaps more importantly, because the magnetic circuits do not have such large parallel areas, mutual inductance and crosstalk are smaller allowing a higher practical track density.

Whereas most replay heads are inductive and generate an output which is the differential of the tape flux, there is another, less common, device known as the magneto-resistive head. In this device, use is made of the Hall effect, where an

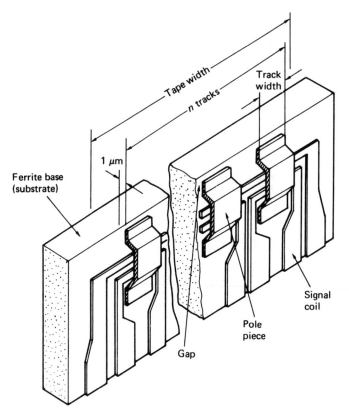

Figure 3.8 The thin-film head shown here can be produced photographically with very small dimensions. Flat structure reduces crosstalk and allows a finer track pitch to be used.

applied magnetic field causes electrons passing down a semiconductor to bunch together so that they experience higher resistance. The strength of flux is measured directly by the head, but it is not sensitive to polarity, and it is usually necessary to incorporate a steady biasing field into the head so that the reversing flux from the tape is converted to a unidirectional changing flux at the sensor. Such heads have a noise advantage over inductive heads at very low tape speeds, but a separate head is required for recording.

3.6 Flying heads in disk drives

Disk drives permanently sacrifice storage density in order to offer rapid access. The use of a flying head with a deliberate air gap between it and the medium is necessary because of the high medium speed, but this causes a severe separation loss which restricts the linear density available. The air gap must be accurately maintained, and consequently the head is of low mass and is mounted flexibly.

Figure 3.9 shows that the aerohydrodynamic part of the head is known as the slipper; it is designed to provide lift from the boundary layer which changes rapidly

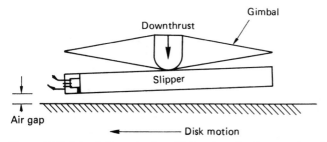

Figure 3.9 Disk head slipper develops lift from boundary layer moving with disk. This reaches equilibrium with the downthrust at the designed flying height. Resultant air gap prevents head wear but restricts storage density.

with changes in flying height. It is not initially obvious that the difficulty with disk heads is not making them fly, but making them fly close enough to the disk surface. The boundary layer travelling at the disk surface has the same speed as the disk, but as height increases, it slows down due to drag from the surrounding air. As the lift is a function of relative air speed, the closer the slipper comes to the disk, the greater the lift will be. The slipper is therefore mounted at the end of a rigid cantilever sprung towards the medium. The force with which the head is pressed towards the disk by the spring is equal to the lift at the designed flying height. Because of the spring, the head may rise and fall over small warps in the disk. It would be virtually impossible to manufacture disks flat enough to dispense with this feature. As the slipper negotiates a warp it will pitch and roll in addition to rising and falling, but it must be prevented from yawing, as this would cause an azimuth error. Downthrust is applied to the aerodynamic centre by a spherical thrust button, and the required degrees of freedom are supplied by a thin, flexible gimbal. The slipper has to bleed away surplus air in order to approach close enough to the disk, and holes or grooves are usually provided for this purpose in the same way that tyres have grooves to take away water on wet roads.

Figure 3.10 shows how disk heads are made. The magnetic circuit of disk heads was originally assembled from discrete magnetic elements. As the gap and flying height became smaller to increase linear recording density, the slipper was made from ferrite, and became part of the magnetic circuit. This was completed by a small C-shaped ferrite piece which carried the coil. In thin-film heads, the magnetic circuit and coil are both formed by deposition on a substrate which becomes the rear of the slipper.

In a moving-head device it is difficult to position separate erase, record and playback heads accurately. Erase is by overwriting, and reading and writing are often carried out by the same head. An exception is where MR read heads are used. As these cannot write, two separate heads must be closely mounted in the same slipper.

The spacing loss of a flying head is a serious drawback and efforts have been made to overcome it. One approach is to apply a thin, low coercivity, high permeability layer over the high coercivity recording layer.[1] Recording takes place normally except that the keeper layer saturates. On reading, the keeper layer would ordinarily shunt the recorded flux away from the read head. However, a small DC bias current flows in the head, and this is sufficient to saturate the keeper layer, locally lowering its permeability dramatically. As a

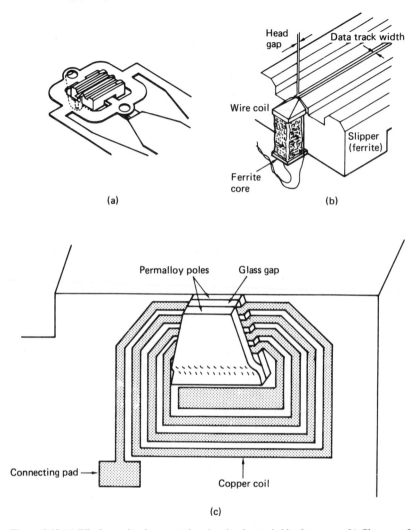

Figure 3.10 (a) Winchester head construction showing large air bleed grooves. (b) Close-up of slipper showing magnetic circuit on trailing edge. (c) Thin-film head is fabricated on the end of the slipper using microcircuit technology.

result, the keeper layer effectively contains a gap and the signal flux is not shunted but passes to the read head. The virtual read gap is in the keeper layer, and is not subject to spacing loss. In fact the virtual gap is slightly smaller than the actual head gap and a further improvement in reading performance results.

3.7 Azimuth recording and rotary heads

Figure 3.11(a) shows that, in azimuth recording, the transitions are laid down at an angle to the track by using a head which is tilted. Machines using azimuth recording must always have an even number of heads, so that adjacent tracks can

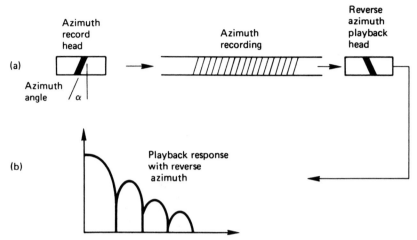

Figure 3.11 In azimuth recording (a), the head gap is tilted. If the track is played with the same head, playback is normal, but the response of the reverse azimuth head is attenuated (b).

be recorded with opposite azimuth angle. The two track types are usually referred to as A and B. Figure 3.11(b) shows the effect of playing a track with the wrong type of head. The playback process suffers from an enormous azimuth error. The effect of azimuth error can be understood by imagining the tape track to be made from many identical parallel strips. In the presence of azimuth error, the strips at one edge of the track are played back with a phase shift relative to strips at the other side. At some wavelengths, the phase shift will be 180 degrees, and there will be no output; at other wavelengths, especially long wavelengths, some output will reappear. The effect is rather like that of a comb filter, and serves to attenuate crosstalk due to adjacent tracks so that no guard bands are required. Since no tape is wasted between the tracks, more efficient use is made of the tape. The term guard-band-less recording is often used instead of, or in addition to, the term azimuth recording. The failure of the azimuth effect at long wavelengths is a characteristic of azimuth recording, and it is necessary to ensure that the spectrum of the signal to be recorded has a small, low-frequency content. The signal will need to pass through a rotary transformer to reach the heads, and cannot therefore contain a DC component.

In recorders such as RDAT there is no separate erase process, and erasure is achieved by overwriting with a new waveform. Overwriting is only successful when there are no long wavelengths in the earlier recording, since these penetrate deeper into the tape, and the short wavelengths in a new recording will not be able to erase them. In this case the ratio between the shortest and longest wavelengths recorded on tape should be limited. Restricting the spectrum of the code to allow erasure by overwrite also eases the design of the rotary transformer.

There are two different approaches to azimuth recording, as shown in Figure 3.12. In the first method, there is no separate erase head, and in order to guarantee that no previous recording can survive a new recording, the recorded tracks can be made rather narrower than the head pole simply by reducing the linear speed

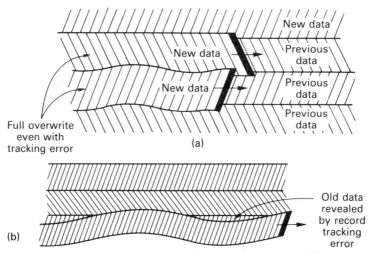

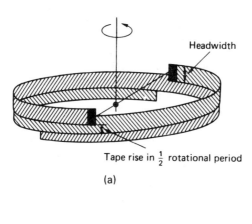

Figure 3.12 In (a) if the azimuth record head is wider than the track, full overwrite is obtained even with misalignment. In (b) if the azimuth record head is the same width as the track, misalignment results in failure to overwrite and an erase head becomes necessary.

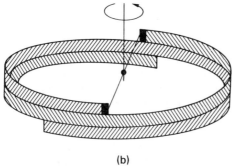

Figure 3.13 With azimuth recording, the record head may be wider than (a) or of the same width as (b) the track.

of the tape so that it does not advance so far between sweeps of the rotary heads. This is shown in Figure 3.13. In RDAT, for example, the head pole is 20.4 μm wide, but the tracks it records are only 13.59 μm wide. Alternatively, the record head can be the same width as the track pitch and cannot guarantee complete overwrite. A separate erase head will be necessary. The advantage of this approach is that insert editing does not leave a seriously narrowed track.

As azimuth recording rejects crosstalk, it is advantageous if the replay head is some 50% wider than the tracks. It can be seen from Figure 3.14 that there will be crosstalk from tracks at both sides of the home track, but this crosstalk is attenuated by azimuth effect. The amount by which the head overlaps the adjacent track determines the spectrum of the crosstalk, since it changes the delay in the azimuth comb-filtering effect. More importantly, the signal-to-crosstalk ratio becomes independent of tracking error over a small range, because as the head moves to one side, the loss of crosstalk from one adjacent track is balanced by the increase of crosstalk from the track on the opposite side. This phenomenon allows for some loss of track straightness and for the residual error which is present in all track-following servo systems.

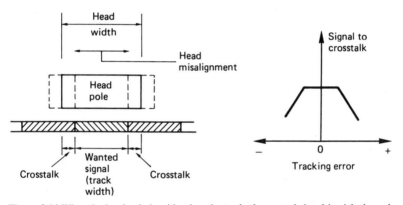

Figure 3.14 When the head pole is wider than the track, the wanted signal is picked up along with crosstalk from the adjacent tracks. If the head is misaligned, the signal-to-crosstalk ratio remains the same until the head fails to register with the whole of the wanted track.

The azimuth angle used has to be chosen with some care. The greater the azimuth angle, the less will be the crosstalk, but the effective writing speed is the head-to-tape speed multiplied by the cosine of the azimuth angle. A further smaller effect is that the tape is anisotropic because of particle orientation. Noise due to the medium, head or amplifier is virtually unaffected by the azimuth angle, and there is no point in reducing crosstalk below the noise. A typical value of ±20 degrees reduces crosstalk to the same order as the noise, with a loss of only 1 dB due to the apparent reduction in writing speed.

3.8 Magnetic playback

Figure 3.15 shows what happens when a conventional inductive head, i.e. one having a normal winding, is used to replay the bipolar track made by reversing

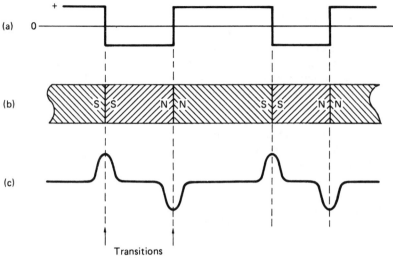

Figure 3.15 Basic digital recording. In (a) the write current in the head is reversed from time to time, leaving a binary magnetization pattern shown in (b). When replayed, the waveform in (c) results because an output is only produced when flux in the head changes. Changes are referred to as transitions.

the record current. The head output is proportional to the rate of change of flux and so only occurs at flux reversals. In other words, the replay head differentiates the flux on the track. The polarity of the resultant pulses alternates as the flux changes and changes back. A circuit is necessary which locates the peaks of the pulses and outputs a signal corresponding to the original record current waveform. There are two ways in which this can be done.

The amplitude of the replay signal is of no consequence and often an AGC system is used to keep the replay signal constant in amplitude. What matters is the time at which the write current, and hence the flux stored on the medium, reverses. This can be determined by locating the peaks of the replay impulses, which can conveniently be done by differentiating the signal and looking for zero crossings. Figure 3.16 shows that this results in noise between the peaks. This problem is overcome by the gated peak detector, where only zero crossings from a pulse which exceeds the threshold will be counted. The AGC system allows the thresholds to be fixed. As an alternative, the record waveform can also be restored by integration, which opposes the differentiation of the head as in Figure 3.17.[2]

A conventional inductive head has a frequency response shown in Figure 3.18. At DC there is no change of flux and no output. As a result inductive heads are at a disadvantage at very low speeds. The output rises with frequency until the rise is halted by the onset of thickness loss. As the frequency rises, the recorded wavelength falls and flux from the shorter magnetic patterns cannot be picked up so far away. At some point, the wavelength becomes so short that flux from the back of the tape coating cannot reach the head and a decreasing thickness of tape contributes to the replay signal.[3] In digital recorders using short wavelengths to obtain high density, there is no point in using thick coatings. As wavelength further reduces, the familiar gap loss occurs, where the head gap is too big to

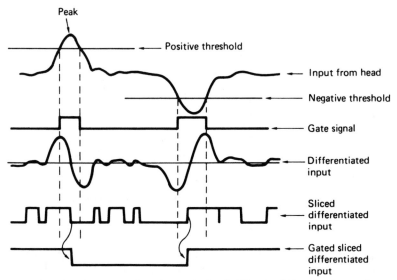

Figure 3.16 Gated peak detection rejects noise by disabling the differentiated output between transitions.

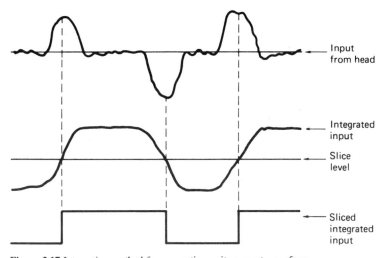

Figure 3.17 Integration method for re-creating write-current waveform.

resolve detail on the track. The construction of the head results in the same action as that of a two-point transversal filter, as the two poles of the head see the tape with a small delay interposed due to the finite gap. As expected, the head response is like a comb filter with the well-known nulls where flux cancellation takes place across the gap. Clearly the smaller the gap the shorter the wavelength of the first null. This contradicts the requirement of the record head to have a large gap. In quality analog audio recorders, it is the norm to have different

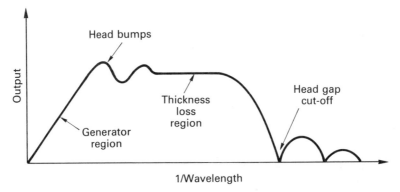

Figure 3.18 The frequency response of a conventional inductive head. See text for details.

record and replay heads for this reason, and the same will be true in digital machines which have separate record and playback heads. Clearly where the same heads are used for record and play, the head gap size will be determined by the playback requirement.

It will also be seen from Figure 3.18 that there are some irregularities in the low-frequency response region which are known as head bumps. These irregularities come about because of interactions between longer wavelengths on the medium and the width of the head poles. Analog audio recorders must use physically wide heads to drive the head bumps down to low frequencies. Unfortunately, large head poles result in low contact pressure. In digital recorders, channel coding can be used to narrow the recorded spectrum, and the heads can be made much smaller with a corresponding increase in contact pressure over the gap. Figure 3.19 shows that thin-film heads necessarily have very small poles, and this results in the head bumps moving up the band. As can be seen, the frequency response is far from ideal, and steps must be taken to

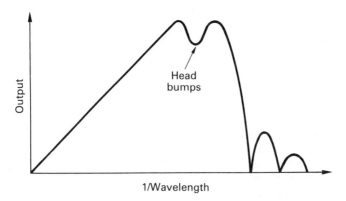

Figure 3.19 In thin-film heads the poles are very short in the direction of media movement and the resultant 'head bumps' move up the passband.

ensure that recorded data waveforms do not contain frequencies which suffer excessive losses.

A more recent development is the magneto-resistive (MR) head. This is a head which measures the flux on the tape rather than using it to generate a signal directly. Flux measurement works down to DC and so offers advantages at low tape speeds. Unfortunately, flux measuring heads are not polarity conscious but sense the modulus of the flux and if used directly they respond to positive and negative flux equally, as shown in Figure 3.20. In some systems this is overcome by using a small extra winding in the head carrying a constant current or by the incorporation of a small permanent magnet into the head. This creates a steady bias field which adds to the flux from the tape. The flux seen by the head is now unipolar and changes between two levels and a more useful output waveform results. Alternatively the output of an unbiased head may be decoded using a variation of peak detection.[4]

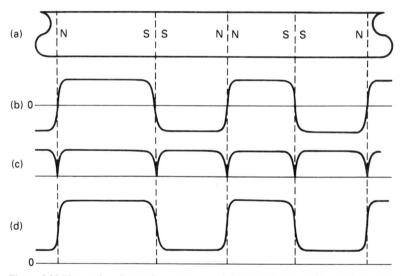

Figure 3.20 The sensing element in a magneto-resistive head is not sensitive to the polarity of the flux, only the magnitude. At (a) the track magnetization is shown and this causes a bidirectional flux variation in the head as at (b), resulting in the magnitude output at (c). However, if the flux in the head due to the track is biased by an additional field, it can be made unipolar as at (d) and the correct output waveform is obtained.

Recorders which have low head-to-medium speed, such as DCC (digital compact cassette) tend to use MR heads, whereas recorders with high speeds, such as DASH (digital audio stationary head), RDAT (rotary-head digital audio tape) and magnetic disk drives tend to use inductive heads.

Digital recorders are sold into a highly competitive market and must operate at high density in order to be commercially viable. As a result the shortest possible wavelengths will be used. Figure 3.21 shows that when two flux changes, or transitions, are recorded close together, they affect each other on

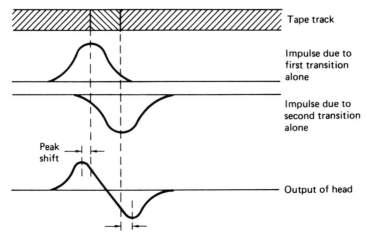

Tape track

Impulse due to
first transition
alone

Impulse due to
second transition
alone

Peak
shift

Output of head

Figure 3.21 Readout pulses from two closely recorded transitions are summed in the head and the effect is that the peaks of the waveform are moved outwards. This is known as peak-shift distortion and equalization is necessary to reduce the effect.

replay. The amplitude of the composite signal is reduced, and the position of the peaks is pushed outwards. This is known as intersymbol interference, or peak-shift distortion, and it occurs in all magnetic media.

The effect is primarily due to high-frequency loss and it can be reduced by equalization on replay, as is done in most tapes, or by pre-compensation on record as is done in hard disks.

3.9 Equalization

The characteristics of most channels are that signal loss occurs which increases with frequency. This has the effect of slowing down rise times and thereby sloping off edges. If a signal with sloping edges is sliced, the time at which the waveform crosses the slicing level will be changed, and this causes jitter. Figure 3.22 shows that slicing a sloping waveform in the presence of baseline wander causes more jitter.

Compensation for peak shift distortion in recording requires equalization of the channel,[5] and this can be done by a network after the replay head, termed an equalizer or pulse sharpener,[6] as in Figure 3.23(a). This technique uses transversal filtering to oppose the inherent transversal effect of the head. As an

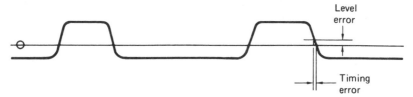

Level
error

Timing
error

Figure 3.22 A DC offset can cause timing errors.

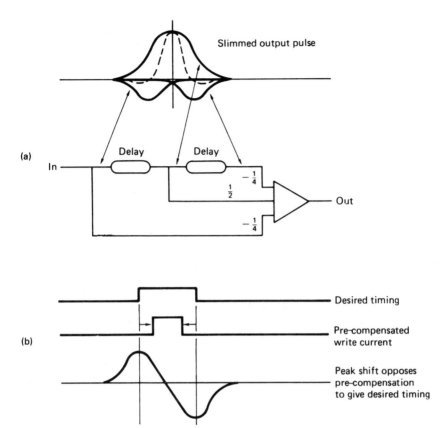

Figure 3.23 Peak-shift distortion is due to the finite width of replay pulses. The effect can be reduced by the pulse slimmer shown in (a) which is basically a transversal filter. The use of a linear operational amplifier emphasizes the analog nature of channels. Instead of replay pulse slimming, transitions can be written with a displacement equal and opposite to the anticipated peak shift as shown in (b).

alternative, pre-compensation in the record stage can be used as shown in Figure 3.23(b). Transitions are written in such a way that the anticipated peak shift will move the readout peaks to the desired timing.

In practice there are difficulties in providing correct equalization at all times. Tape surface asperities and substrate irregularities cause variations in the intimacy of head contact, which changes the response at high frequencies much more than at low frequencies, thereby undermining any fixed equalization. In disk drives, the varying radius of the tracks results in a linear density variation of about two to one. The presence of the air film causes severe separation loss, and peak shift distortion is a major problem. The flying height of the head varies with the radius of the disk track, and it is difficult to provide accurate equalization of the replay channel because of this. The write current is often controlled as a function of track radius so that the changing reluctance of the air gap does not change the resulting record flux. Equalization is used on recording in the form of pre-compensation, which moves recorded transitions in such a way as to oppose the effects of peak shift. As optimum fixed equalization is difficult under dynamic conditions, recent machines may incorporate an adaptive equalizer in the replay channel. The timing errors caused by poor equalization will reflect in the random error rate and this can be used to change the response.

In most of the above, a clearer picture has been obtained by studying the impulse response of devices than from the frequency response, and this follows from the impulsive nature of digital techniques.

3.10 Noise

The signal from the read head in a magnetic recorder contains the wanted component which is a function of the write process, along with unwanted signals which are grouped together under the heading of noise. Noise[7] reduces the information capacity of the channel and in practice results in an increased error rate. Noise has three major subclassifications: noise from the medium, from the read head and from the read electronics. Figure 3.24 shows a typical relationship between the noise power spectra of the three sources. In practical recorders it is normal for the medium noise to predominate, although as mechanisms improve to allow narrower tracks to be followed, head noise may become dominant. In addition to noise, which is generally understood to describe random signals, there is also interference, which consists of non-random signals. These include crosstalk from adjacent tracks, print-through, and external electromagnetic fields which influence the read head and circuitry.

Medium noise results from uncertainty in the position of the magnetic particles. The result for a homogeneous medium is additive noise. However, any inhomogeneity of the medium caused by, for example, particle clustering, will result in modulation of the amplitude of the read signal. This results in sidebands superimposed on the signal. The phenomenon is generally called modulation noise, but this is not a satisfactory term.

Head noise can be subdivided into a number of sources. According to the Nyquist noise theorem, any device capable of dissipating energy when fed power

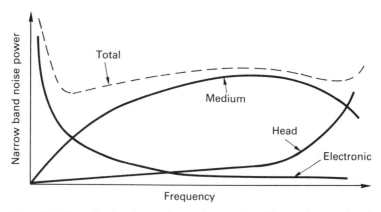

Figure 3.24 The read noise of magnetic recorders consists of three main categories whose spectra are contrasted here.

will generate noise power passively. The head contains two mechanisms which can dissipate power. One is the resistance of the coil, the other is the hysteresis of the magnetic circuit. As hysteresis loss increases with frequency, it follows that head noise will also increase with frequency and this can be seen in Figure 3.24. In thin-film heads, the coil resistance dominates, whereas in ferrite heads the coil resistance is negligible and the hysteresis dominates. Tape heads which are fabricated from magnetostrictive material can also generate noise due to vibrations excited by the rubbing of the passing tape.

Thin-film heads have small dimensions in some axes and this results in domain wall jumps becoming larger. The resulting increased hysteretic noise is called Barkhausen noise in thin-film heads.

Noise from the read electronics is predictably dominated by the noise input of the first amplification stage. Electronic noise should be set below other contributions by design.

3.11 Optical disks

Optical recorders have the advantage that light can be focused at a distance whereas magnetism cannot. This means that there need be no physical contact between the pickup and the medium and no wear mechanism. Non-contact recording also makes the provision of removable media easier as contamination introduced with the medium will not cause mechanical problems.

In the same way that the recorded wavelength of a magnetic recording is limited by the gap in the replay head, the density of optical recording is limited by the size of light spot which can be focused on the medium. This is controlled by the wavelength of the light used and by the aperture of the lens. When the light spot is as small as these limits allow, it is said to be diffraction limited. Chapter 10 explores the recording density limits in detail. The recorded details on the disk are minute, and could easily be obscured by dust particles. In practice the information layer needs to be protected by a thick transparent coating. Light enters the coating well out of focus over a large area so that it can pass around dust particles, and comes to a focus within the thickness of the coating. Although the number of bits per unit area is high in optical recorders the number of bits per unit volume is not as high as that of tape because of the thickness of the coating.

Figure 3.25 shows the principle of readout of the Compact Disc, which is a read-only disk manufactured by pressing. The track consists of raised bumps separated by flat areas. The entire surface of the disk is metallized, and the bumps are one-quarter of a wavelength in height. The player spot is arranged so that half of its light falls on top of a bump, and half on the surrounding surface. Light returning from the flat surface has travelled half a wavelength further than light returning from the top of the bump, and so there is a phase reversal between the two components of the reflection. This causes destructive interference, and light cannot return to the pickup. It must reflect at angles which are outside the aperture of the lens and be lost. Conversely, when light falls on the flat surface between bumps, the majority of it is reflected back to the pickup. The pickup thus sees a disk *apparently* having alternately good or poor reflectivity. The sensor in the pickup responds to the incident intensity and so the replay signal is unipolar and varies between two levels in a manner similar to the output of an MR head.

Some disks can be recorded once, but not subsequently erased or re-recorded. These are known as WORM (write once read many) disks. One type of WORM

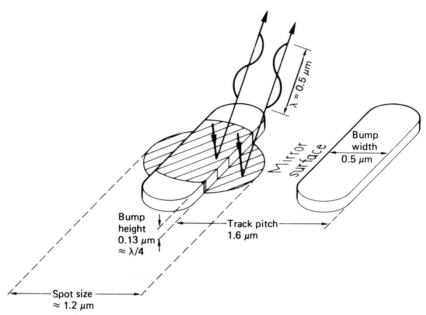

Figure 3.25 CD readout principle and dimensions. The presence of a bump causes destructive interference in the reflected light.

disk uses a thin metal layer which has holes punched in it on recording by heat from a laser. Others rely on the heat raising blisters in a thin metallic layer by decomposing the plastic material beneath. Yet another alternative is a layer of photochemical dye which darkens when struck by the high-powered recording beam. Whatever the recording principle, light from the pickup is reflected more or less, or absorbed more or less, so that the pickup senses a change in reflectivity. Certain WORM disks can be read by conventional CD players and are thus called recordable CDs, or CD-R, whereas others will only work in a particular type of drive.

Certain optical disks can be re-recorded, with or without a separate erase process, depending on the type. Magneto-optical disks are magnetic recordings made and replayed optically, whereas phase-change disks rely on using laser heat to change the state, or phase, of a suitable material between; for example, amorphous and crystalline states having different reflectivities.

All optical disks need mechanisms to keep the pickup following the track and sharply focused on it; these will be discussed in Chapter 10 and need not be treated here.

3.12 Magneto-optical disks

When a magnetic material is heated above its Curie temperature, it becomes demagnetized, and on cooling will assume the magnetization of an applied field which would be too weak to influence it normally. This is the principle of magneto-optical recording. The heat is supplied by a finely focused laser; the field is supplied by a coil which is much larger.

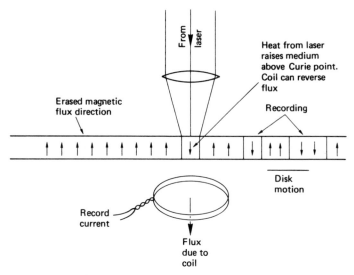

Figure 3.26 The thermomagneto-optical disk uses the heat from a laser to allow magnetic field to record on the disk.

Figure 3.26 shows that the medium is initially magnetized in one direction only. In order to record, the coil is energized with a current in the opposite direction. This is too weak to influence the medium in its normal state, but when it is heated by the recording laser beam the heated area will take on the magnetism from the coil when it cools. Thus a magnetic recording with very small dimensions can be made even though the magnetic circuit involved is quite large in comparison.

Readout is obtained using the Kerr effect or the Faraday effect, which are phenomena whereby the plane of polarization of light can be rotated by a magnetic field. The angle of rotation is very small and needs a sensitive pickup. The pickup contains a polarizing filter before the sensor. Changes in polarization change the ability of the light to get through the polarizing filter and results in an intensity change which once more produces a unipolar output.

The magneto-optic recording can be erased by reversing the current in the coil and operating the laser continuously as it passes along the track. A new recording can then be made on the erased track.

A disadvantage of magneto-optical recording is that all materials having a Curie point low enough to be useful are highly corrodible by air and need to be kept under an effectively sealed protective layer.

The magneto-optical channel has virtually the same frequency response as that of any optical recorder, as it is dominated by the resolution of the optical path.

3.13 Optical theory

Optical recorders are restricted by the wave and quantum nature of light, and depend heavily on certain optical devices such as lasers, polarizers and diffraction gratings. These subjects will be outlined here.

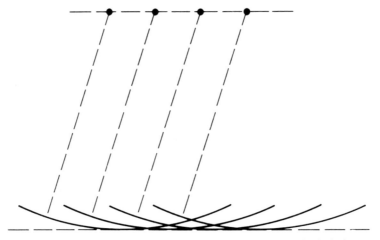

Figure 3.27 Plane-wave propagation considered as infinite numbers of spherical waves.

Wave theory of light suggests that a plane wave advances because an infinite number of point sources can be considered to emit spherical waves which will only add when they are all in the same phase. This can only occur in the plane of the wavefront. Figure 3.27 shows that at all other angles, interference between spherical waves is destructive.

When such a wavefront arrives at an interface with a denser medium, the velocity of propagation is reduced; therefore the wavelength in the medium becomes shorter, causing the wavefront to leave the interface at a different angle

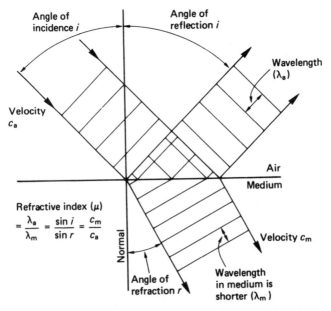

Figure 3.28 Reflection and refraction, showing the effect of the velocity of light in a medium.

(Figure 3.28). This is known as refraction. The ratio of velocity *in vacuo* to velocity in the medium is known as the refractive index of that medium; it determines the relationship between the angles of the incident and refracted wavefronts. Reflected light, however, leaves at the same angle to the normal as the incident light. If the speed of light in the medium varies with wavelength, incident white light will be split into a rainbow spectrum leaving the interface at different angles. Glass used for chandeliers and cut glass is chosen to be highly dispersive, whereas glass for optical instruments is chosen to have a refractive index which is as constant as possible with changing wavelength.

When a wavefront reaches an aperture which is small compared with the wavelength, the aperture acts as a point source, and the process of diffraction can be observed as a spherical wavefront leaving the aperture as in Figure 3.29. Where the wavefront passes through a regular structure, known as a diffraction grating, light on the far side will form new wavefronts wherever radiation is in phase, and Figure 3.30 shows that these will be at an angle to the normal

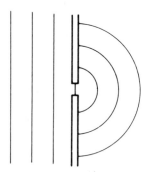

Figure 3.29 Diffraction as a plane wave reaches a small aperture.

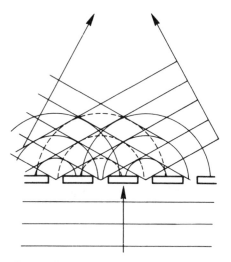

Figure 3.30 In a diffraction grating, constructive interference can take place at more than one angle for a single wavelength.

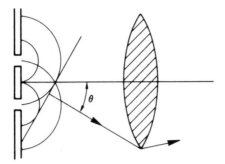

Figure 3.31 Fine detail in an object can only be resolved if the diffracted wavefront due to the highest spatial frequency is collected by the lens. Numerical aperture (NA) = sin θ, and as θ is the diffraction angle it follows that, for a given wavelength, NA determines resolution.

depending on the spacing of the structure and the wavelength of the light. A diffraction grating illuminated by white light will produce a dispersed spectrum at each side of the normal. To obtain a fixed angle of diffraction, monochromatic light is necessary.

For a given wavelength, the greater the spatial frequency of the grating (bars per unit of distance) the greater will be the angle of diffraction. A corollary of this effect is that the more finely detailed an object is, the greater the angle over which light must be collected to see the detail. The light-collecting angle of a lens shown in Figure 3.31 is measured by the numerical aperture (NA), which is the sine of the angle between the optical axis and the wavefront carrying the finest detail in the image. All lenses thus act as spatial filters which cut off at a spatial frequency limited by NA. The response is known as the modulation transfer function (MTF). Light travelling on the axis of a lens is conveying the average brightness of the image, not the detail, as this is conveyed in the more oblique light collected at the rim of the lens. Lenses can fall short of their theoretical MTF because of shortcomings in manufacture. If a lens is made accurately enough, a wavefront which has passed through it will have the same phase over its entire area. Where wavefront aberrations have a variance of less than the square of the wavelength divided by 180, the lens is said to meet the Maréchal criterion, which essentially means that the performance of the lens is as good as it is going to get because it is now diffraction-limited rather than tolerance-limited.

When a diffraction-limited lens is used to focus a point source on a plane, the image will not be a point owing to exclusion of the higher spatial frequencies by the finite numerical aperture. The resulting image is in fact the spatial equivalent of the impulse response of a low-pass filter, and results in a diffraction pattern known as an Airy pattern, after Sir George Airy, who first quantified the intensity function. It is the dimensions of the Airy pattern which limit the density of all optical media, since it controls the minimum size of features that the laser can produce or resolve. The only way a laser disk could hold more data would be if the working wavelength could be reduced, since this would reduce the size of the spot.

By the same argument, it is not much use trying to measure the pit dimensions of a laser disk with an optical microscope. It is necessary to use an electron microscope to make measurements where conventional optics are diffraction-limiting.

3.14 The laser

The semiconductor laser is a relative of the light-emitting diode (LED). Both operate by raising the energy of electrons to move them from one valence band to another conduction band. Electrons which fall back to the valence band emit a quantum of energy as a photon whose frequency is proportional to the energy difference between the bands. The process is described by Planck's law:

Energy difference $E = H \times f$

where H = Planck's constant
$\qquad$ = 6.6262×10^{-34} joules/hertz

For gallium arsenide, the energy difference is about 1.6 eV, where 1 eV is 1.6×10^{-19} joules.

Using Planck's law, the frequency of emission will be:

$$f = \frac{1.6 \times 1.6 \times 10^{-19}}{6.6262 \times 10^{-34}} \text{ Hz}$$

The wavelength will be c/f where:

c = the velocity of light = 3×10^8 m/sec

$$\text{wavelength} = \frac{3 \times 10^8 \times 6.6262 \times 10^{-34}}{2.56 \times 10^{-19}} \text{ m}$$

$$= 780 \text{ nanometres}$$

In the LED, electrons fall back to the valence band randomly, and the light produced is incoherent. In the laser, the ends of the semiconductor are optically flat mirrors, which produce an optically resonant cavity. One photon can bounce

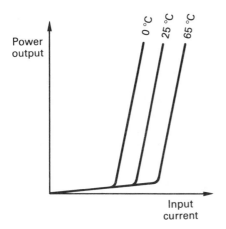

Figure 3.32 The transfer function of a laser shows strong temperature dependency and a threshold.

to and fro, exciting others in synchronism, to produce coherent light. This can result in a runaway condition, where all available energy is used up in one flash. In injection lasers, an equilibrium is reached between energy input and light output, allowing continuous operation. Lasers are basically unstable and need to be modulated with care. Figure 3.32 shows that the transfer function of a laser has a threshold which is strongly temperature dependent. Such devices are usually fed from a current source. To avoid runaway when the temperature increases, a photosensor is often fed back to the current source. Such lasers have a finite life, and become steadily less efficient. The feedback will maintain output, and it is possible to anticipate the failure of the laser by monitoring the drive voltage needed to give the correct output. The laser cannot be modulated with a simple switch. If the drive current is allowed to fall below the threshold, transient oscillation may occur when the current is re-applied. Careful biasing is required, using temperature-dependent feedback from the local photodetector.

The equilibrium of a laser can also be disturbed if some of the output light is allowed to re-enter the cavity. Returning light will trigger off emission in the cavity at a wavelength determined by the return path. This will be of a different frequency from the normal output and the laser may hop between two or more frequencies.

3.15 Polarization

In natural light, the electric-field component will be in many planes. Light is said to be polarized when the electric field direction is constrained. The wave can be considered as made up from two orthogonal components. When these are in phase, the polarization is said to be linear. When there is a phase shift between the components, the polarization is said to be elliptical, with a special case at 90 degrees called circular polarization. These types of polarization are contrasted in Figure 3.33.

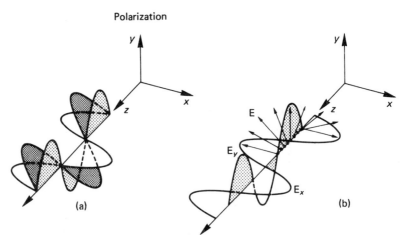

Figure 3.33 (a) Linear polarization: orthogonal components are in phase. (b) Circular polarization: orthogonal components are in phase quadrature.

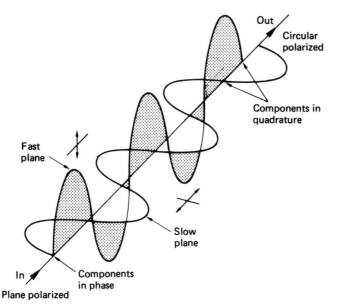

Figure 3.34 Different speed of light in different planes rotates the plane of polarization in a quarter-wave plate to give a circular-polarized output.

In order to create polarized light, anisotropic materials are necessary. Polaroid material, invented by Edwin Land, is vinyl which is made anisotropic by stretching it whilst hot. This causes the long polymer molecules to line up along the axis of stretching. If the material is soaked in iodine, the molecules are rendered conductive, and short out any electric-field component along themselves. Electric fields at right angles are unaffected; thus the transmission plane is at right angles to the stretching axis.

Stretching plastics can also result in anisotropy of refractive index; this effect is known as birefringence. If a linearly polarized wavefront enters such a medium, the two orthogonal components propagate at different velocities, causing a relative phase difference proportional to the distance travelled. The plane of polarization of the light is rotated. Where the thickness of the material is such that a 90 degree phase change is caused, the device is known as a quarter-wave plate. The action of such a device is shown in Figure 3.34. If the plane of polarization of the incident light is at 45 degrees to the planes of greatest and least refractive index, the two orthogonal components of the light will be of equal magnitude, and this results in circular polarization. Similarly, circular-polarized light can be returned to the linear-polarized state by a further quarter-wave plate. Rotation of the plane of polarization is a useful method of separating incident and reflected light in a laser pickup. Using a quarter-wave plate, the plane of polarization of light leaving the pickup will have been turned 45 degrees, and on return it will be rotated a further 45 degrees, so that it is now at right angles to the plane of polarization of light from the source. The two can easily be separated by a polarizing prism, which acts as a transparent block to light in one plane, but as a prism to light in the other plane.

3.16 Optical readout

The information layer of an optical disk is read through the thickness of the disk. Figure 3.35 shows that this approach causes the readout beam to enter and leave the disk surface through the largest possible area. The actual dimensions of CD are shown in the figure as an example. Despite the minute spot size of about 1.2 μm diameter, light enters and leaves through a 0.7 mm diameter circle. As a result, surface debris has to be three orders of magnitude larger than the readout spot before the beam is obscured. The size of the entry circle is a function of the refractive index of the disk material, the numerical aperture of the objective lens and the thickness of the disk. The method of readout through the disk thickness tolerates surface scratches very well. By way of contrast, the label side of CD is actually more vulnerable than the readout side, since the lacquer coating is only 30 μm thick. CD is unique in being single sided. Most optical disks are in fact made from two disks sandwiched together with the two information layers on the inside.

Continuing the example of CD, the specified wavelength of 780 nm and the numerical aperture of 0.45 results in an Airy function where the half-power level is at a diameter of about 1 μm. The first dark ring will be at about 1.9 μm diameter. As the illumination follows an intensity function, it is really meaningless to talk about spot size unless the relative power level is specified. The analogy is quoting frequency response without dB limits.

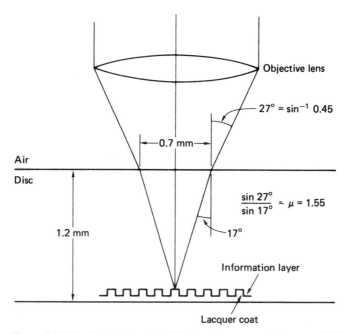

Figure 3.35 The objective lens of a CD pickup has a numerical aperture (NA) of 0.45; thus the outermost rays will be inclined at approximately 27° to the normal. Refraction at the air/disk interface changes this to approximately 17° within the disk. Thus light focused to a spot on the information layer has entered the disk through a 0.7 mm diameter circle, giving good resistance to surface contamination.

Allowable crosstalk between tracks then determines the track pitch. The first ring outside the central disc carries some 7 % of the total power, and limits crosstalk performance. The track spacing is such that with a slightly defocused beam and a slight tracking error, crosstalk due to adjacent tracks is acceptable. Since aberrations in the objective will increase the spot size and crosstalk, the CD specification requires the lens to be within the Maréchal criterion. Clearly the numerical aperture of the lens, the wavelength of the laser, the refractive index and thickness of the disc and the height and size of the bumps must all be simultaneously specified.

The cutter spot size determines the reader spot size, and this in turn determines the shortest wavelength along the track which can be resolved. If the track velocity is specified, the wavelength limit becomes a frequency limit. The optical cut-off frequency is that frequency where the amplitude of modulation replayed from the disk has fallen to zero, and is given by:

$$F_c = \frac{2NA}{wavelength} \times velocity$$

The minimum linear velocity of CD is 1.2 m/s, giving a cut-off frequency of:

$$F_c = \frac{2 \times 0.45 \times 1.2}{780 \times 10^{-9}} = 1.38\,MHz$$

Figure 3.36 shows that the frequency response falls linearly to the cut-off, and that actual measurements are only a little worse than the theory predicts. Clearly, to obtain any noise immunity, the maximum operating frequency must be rather less than the cut-off frequency. The maximum frequency used in CD is 720 kHz, which represents an absolute minimum wavelength of 1.666 μm, or a bump length of 0.833 μm, for the lowest permissible track speed of 1.2 m/s used on the

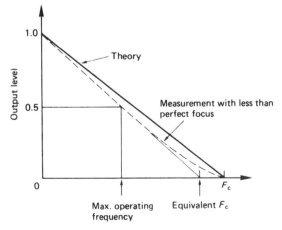

Figure 3.36 Frequency response of laser pickup. Maximum operating frequency is about half of cut-off frequency F_c.

full-length 75 min playing discs. One-hour-playing discs have a minimum bump length of 0.972 μm at a track velocity of 1.4 m/s. The maximum frequency is the same in both cases.

3.17 Structure of laser drive

A typical laser disk drive resembles a magnetic drive in that it has a spindle drive mechanism to revolve the disk, and a positioner to give radial access across the disk surface. The pickup must contain a dynamic focusing mechanism to follow disk warps, and it must be able to keep the laser spot on track despite runout in the disk. The positioner has to carry a collection of lasers, lenses, prisms, gratings and so on, and usually cannot be accelerated as fast as a magnetic-drive positioner. A penalty of the very small track pitch possible in laser disks, which gives the enormous storage capacity, is that very accurate track following is needed, and it takes some time to lock on to a track. For this reason, tracks on laser disks are usually made as a continuous spiral, rather than the concentric rings of magnetic disks. In this way, continuous data transfer involves no more than track following once the beginning of the file is located.

3.18 Data separation

The important step of information recovery at the receiver or replay circuit is known as data separation. The data separator is rather like an analog-to-digital converter because the two processes of sampling and quantizing are both present. In the time domain, the sampling clock is derived from the clock content of the channel waveform. In the voltage domain, the process of *slicing* converts the analog waveform from the channel back into a binary, or sometimes ternary representation. The slicer in the binary case is a quantizer which has only one-bit resolution. The slicing process makes a discrete decision about the voltage of the incoming signal in order to reject noise. The sampler makes discrete decisions along the time axis in order to reject jitter. These two processes will be described in detail.

3.19 Slicing

The slicer is implemented with a comparator which has analog inputs but a binary output. In an inductive magnetic replay system, the replay waveform is differentiated and must first pass through a peak detector (Figure 3.16) or an integrator (Figure 3.17). The signal voltage is compared with the midway voltage, known as the threshold, baseline or slicing level by the comparator. If the signal voltage is above the threshold, the comparator outputs a high level; if below, a low level results.

Figure 3.37 shows some waveforms associated with a slicer. In (a) the transmitted waveform has an uneven duty cycle. The DC component, or average level, of the signal is received with high amplitude, but the pulse amplitude falls as the pulse gets shorter. Eventually the waveform cannot be sliced.

In (b) the opposite duty cycle is shown. The signal level drifts to the opposite polarity and once more slicing is impossible. The phenomenon is called baseline wander and will be observed with any signal whose average voltage is not the same as the slicing level.

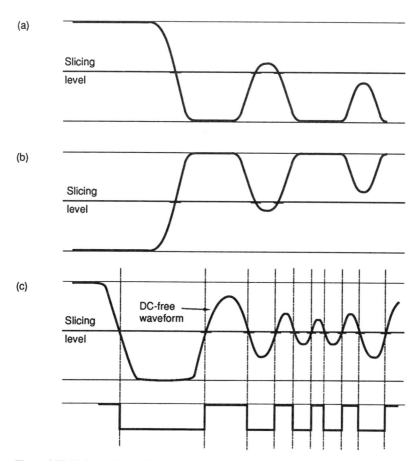

Figure 3.37 Slicing a signal which has suffered losses works well if the duty cycle is even. If the duty cycle is uneven, as in (a), timing errors will become worse until slicing fails. With the opposite duty cycle, the slicing fails in the opposite direction as in (b). If, however, the signal is DC free, correct slicing can continue even in the presence of serious losses, as (c) shows.

In (c) it will be seen that if the transmitted waveform has a relatively constant average voltage, slicing remains possible up to high frequencies even in the presence of serious amplitude loss, because the received waveform remains symmetrical about the baseline.

It is clearly not possible simply to serialize data in a shift register for so-called direct transmission, because successful slicing can only be obtained if the number of ones is equal to the number of zeros; there is little chance of this happening consistently with real data. Instead, a modulation code or channel code is necessary. This converts the data into a waveform which is DC free or nearly so for the purpose of transmission.

The slicing threshold level is naturally zero in a bipolar system such as magnetic inductive replay or a cable. When the amplitude falls it does so symmetrically and slicing continues. The same is not true of MR heads and

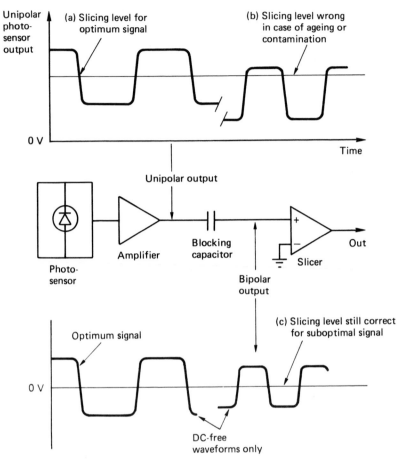

Figure 3.38 (a) Slicing a unipolar signal requires a non-zero threshold. (b) If the signal amplitude changes, the threshold will then be incorrect. (c) If a DC-free code is used, a unipolar waveform can be converted to a bipolar waveform using a series capacitor. A zero threshold can be used and slicing continues with amplitude variations.

optical pickups, which both respond to intensity and therefore produce a unipolar output. If the replay signal is sliced directly, the threshold cannot be zero, but must be some level approximately half the amplitude of the signal as shown in Figure 3.38(a). Unfortunately, when the signal level falls it falls towards zero and not towards the slicing level. The threshold will no longer be appropriate for the signal, as can be seen in (b). This can be overcome by using a DC-free coded waveform. If a series capacitor is connected to the unipolar signal from an optical pickup, the waveform is rendered bipolar because the capacitor blocks any DC component in the signal. The DC-free channel waveform passes through unaltered. If an amplitude loss is suffered, Figure 3.38(c) shows that the resultant bipolar signal now reduces in amplitude about the slicing level and slicing can continue.

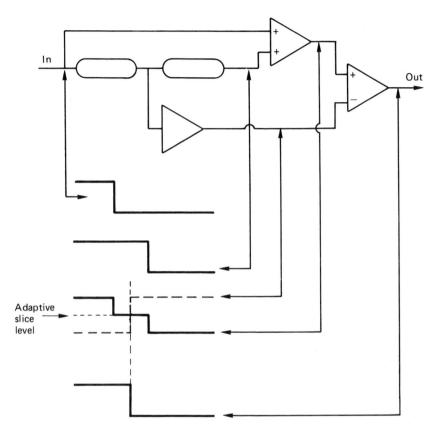

Figure 3.39 An adaptive slicer uses delay lines to produce a threshold from the waveform itself. Correct slicing will then be possible in the presence of baseline wander. Such a slicer can be used with codes which are not DC free.

Whilst a DC-free waveform is ideal, some channel waveforms used in magnetic recording have a reduced DC component, but are not completely DC free. As a result, the received waveform will suffer from baseline wander. If this is moderate, an adaptive slicer which can move its threshold can be used. As Figure 3.39 shows, the adaptive slicer consists of a pair of delays. If the input and output signals are linearly added together with equal weighting, when a transition passes, the resultant waveform has a plateau which is at the half-amplitude level of the signal and can be used as a threshold voltage for the slicer. The coding of the DASH format (see Chapter 7) is not DC free and a slicer of this kind is employed.

3.20 Jitter rejection

The binary waveform at the output of the slicer will be a replica of the transmitted waveform, except for the addition of jitter or time uncertainty in the position of the edges due to noise, baseline wander, intersymbol interference and imperfect equalization.

Binary circuits reject noise by using discrete voltage levels which are spaced further apart than the uncertainty due to noise. In a similar manner, digital coding combats time uncertainty by making the time axis discrete using events, known as transitions, spaced apart at integer multiples of some basic time period, called a detent, which is larger than the typical time uncertainty. Figure 3.40 shows how this jitter-rejection mechanism works. All that matters is to identify the detent in which the transition occurred. Exactly where it occurred within the detent is of no consequence.

As ideal transitions occur at multiples of a basic period, an oscilloscope, which is repeatedly triggered on a channel-coded signal carrying random data, will show an eye pattern if connected to the output of the equalizer. Study of the eye pattern shown in Figure 3.41 reveals how well the coding used suits the channel. In high-density recorders, the harmonics are lost because it is uneconomic to provide bandwidth much beyond the fundamental. This gives the eyes a diamond shape.

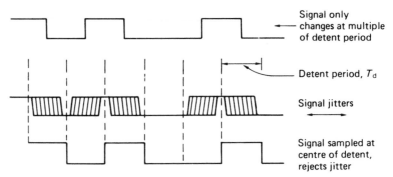

Figure 3.40 A certain amount of jitter can be rejected by changing the signal at multiples of the basic detent period T_d.

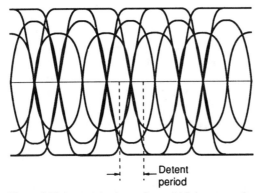

Figure 3.41 A transmitted waveform which is generated according to the principle of Figure 3.40 will appear like this on an oscilloscope as successive parts of the waveform are superimposed on the tube. When the waveform is rounded off by losses, diamond-shaped eyes are left in the centre, spaced apart by the detent period.

Noise closes the eyes in a vertical direction, and jitter closes the eyes in a horizontal direction. If the eyes remain sensibly open, data separation will be possible. Clearly more jitter can be tolerated if there is less noise, and vice versa. If the equalizer is adjustable, the optimum setting will be where the greatest eye opening is obtained.

In the centre of the eyes, the receiver must make binary decisions at the channel bit rate about the state of the signal, high or low, using the slicer output. As stated, the receiver is sampling the output of the slicer, and it needs to have a sampling clock in order to do that. In order to give the best rejection of noise and jitter, the clock edges which operate the sampler must be in the centre of the eyes.

As has been stated, a separate clock is not practicable in recording or transmission. A fixed frequency clock at the receiver is of no use as even if it was sufficiently stable, it would not know what phase to run at.

The only way in which the sampling clock can be obtained is to use a phase-locked loop to regenerate it from the clock content of the self clocking channel-coded waveform. In phase-locked loops, the voltage-controlled oscillator is driven by a phase error measured between the output and some reference, such that the output eventually has the same frequency as the reference. If a divider is placed between the VCO and the phase comparator, as in Figure 3.42, the VCO frequency can be made to be a multiple of the reference. This also has the effect of making the loop more heavily damped. If a channel-coded waveform is used as a reference to a PLL, the loop will be able to make a phase comparison whenever a transition arrives and will run at the channel bit rate. When there are several detents between transitions, the loop will *flywheel* at the last known frequency and phase until it can rephase at a subsequent transition. Thus a continuous clock is re-created from the clock content of the channel waveform. In a recorder, if the speed of the medium should change, the PLL will change frequency to follow. Once the loop is locked, clock edges will be phased with the

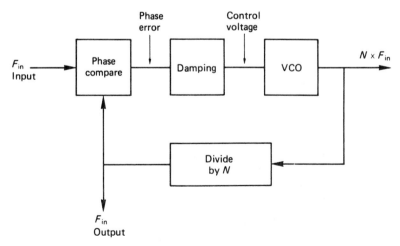

Figure 3.42 A typical phase-locked loop where the VCO is forced to run at a multiple of the input frequency. If the input ceases, the output will continue for a time at the same frequency until it drifts.

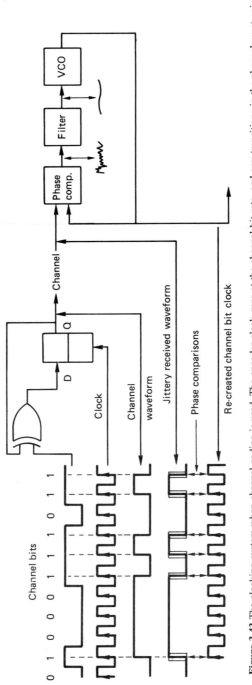

Figure 3.43 The clocking system when channel coding is used. The encoder clock runs at the channel bit rate, and any transitions in the channel must coincide with encoder clock edges. The reason for doing this is that, at the data separator, the PLL can lock to the edges of the channel signal, which represent an intermittent clock, and turn it into a continuous clock. The jitter in the edges of the channel signal causes noise in the phase error of the PLL, but the damping acts as a filter and the PLL runs at the average phase of the channel bits, rejecting the jitter.

average phase of the jittering edges of the input waveform. If, for example, rising edges of the clock are phased to input transitions, then falling edges will be in the centre of the eyes. If these edges are used to clock the sampling process, the maximum jitter and noise can be rejected. The output of the slicer when sampled by the PLL edge at the centre of an eye is the value of a channel bit. Figure 3.43 shows the complete clocking system of a channel code from encoder to data separator. Clearly data cannot be separated if the PLL is not locked, but it cannot be locked until it has seen transitions for a reasonable period. In recorders, which have discontinuous recorded blocks to allow editing, the solution is to precede each data block with a pattern of transitions whose sole purpose is to provide a timing reference for synchronizing the phase-locked loop. This pattern is known as a preamble. In interfaces, the transmission can be continuous and there is no difficulty remaining in lock indefinitely. There will simply be a short delay on first applying the signal before the receiver locks to it.

One potential problem area which is frequently overlooked is to ensure that the VCO in the receiving PLL is correctly centred. If it is not, it will be running with a static phase error and will not sample the received waveform at the centre of the eyes. The sampled bits will be more prone to noise and jitter errors. VCO centring can simply be checked by displaying the control voltage. This should not change significantly when the input is momentarily interrupted.

References

1. GOOCH, B., NIEDERMEYER, R., WOOD, R. and PISHARODY, R., A high resolution flying magnetic disk recording system with zero reproduce spacing loss. *IEE Trans. Magn*, **MAG-27**, 4549–4554 (1991)

2. DEELEY, E.M., Integrating and differentiating channels in digital tape recording. *Radio Electron. Eng.*, **56**, 169–173 (1986)

3. MEE, C.D., *The Physics of Magnetic Recording*. Amsterdam and New York: Elsevier–North-Holland Publishing (1978)

4. SMITH, R.L., Use of unbiased MR sensors in a rigid disk file. *IEE Trans. Magn*, **MAG-27**, 4561–4566 (1991).

5. JACOBY, G.V., Signal equalization in digital magnetic recording. *IEEE Trans. Magn.*, **MAG-11**, 302–305 (1975)

6. SCHNEIDER, R.C., An improved pulse-slimming method for magnetic recording. *IEEE Trans. Magn.*, **MAG-11**, 1240–1241 (1975)

7. MALLINSON, J.C., *The foundations of magnetic recording*, Chapter 7. London: Academic Press (1987)

Chapter 4
Channel coding

Channel coding is an essential stage in data recording as it converts raw data into waveforms having advantageous properties. Much of the progress in recording density has been due to developments in channel coding.

4.1 Introduction

It is not practicable simply to serialize raw data in a shift register for the purpose of recording. Practical systems require the use of a modulation scheme, known as a channel code, which expresses the data as waveforms which are self clocking in order to reject jitter, to separate the received bits and to avoid skew on separate clock lines. The coded waveforms should further be DC free or nearly so to enable slicing in the presence of losses and have a narrower spectrum than the raw data to make equalization possible.

Jitter causes uncertainty about the time at which a particular event occurred. The frequency response of the channel then places an overall limit on the spacing of events in the channel. Particular emphasis must be placed on the interplay of bandwidth, jitter and noise, which will be shown here to be the key to the design of a successful channel code.

Figure 4.1 shows that a channel coder is necessary prior to the record stage, and that a decoder, known as a data separator, is necessary after the replay stage. The output of the channel coder is generally a logic level signal which contains a 'high' state when a transition is to be generated. The waveform generator produces the transitions in a signal whose level and impedance is suitable for driving the medium or channel. The signal may be bipolar or unipolar as appropriate.

Some codes eliminate DC entirely, which is advantageous for optical media and for rotary-head recording. Some codes can reduce the channel bandwidth needed by lowering the upper spectral limit. This permits higher linear density, usually at the expense of jitter rejection. Other codes narrow the spectrum by raising the lower limit. A code with a narrow spectrum has a number of advantages. The reduction in asymmetry will reduce peak shift and data separators can lock more readily because the range of frequencies in the code is smaller. In theory the narrower the spectrum the less noise will be suffered, but this is only achieved if filtering is employed. Filters can easily cause phase errors which will nullify any gain.

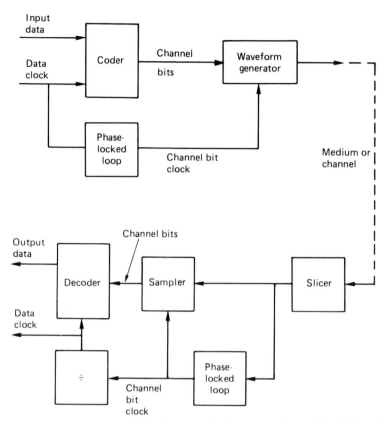

Figure 4.1 The major components of a channel coding system. See text for details.

A convenient definition of a channel code (for there are certainly others) is: 'A method of modulating real data such that they can be reliably received despite the shortcomings of a real channel, whilst making maximum economic use of the channel capacity.'

The basic time periods of a channel-coded waveform are called positions or detents, in which the transmitted voltage will be reversed or stay the same. The symbol used for the units of channel time is T_d.

There are many ways of creating such a waveform, but the most convenient is to convert the raw data bits to a larger number of *channel bits* which are output from a shift register to the waveform generator at the detent rate. The coded waveform will then be high or low according to the state of a channel bit which describes the detent.

Channel coding is the art of converting real data into channel bits. Figure 4.2 shows that there are two conventions in use relating channel bits to the recorded waveform. The most commonly used convention is one in which a channel-bit 1 represents a voltage (or flux) change, whereas a 0 represents no change. This convention is used because it is possible to assemble sequential groups of channel bits together without worrying about whether the polarity of the end of

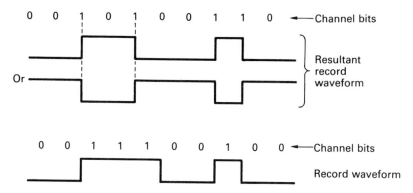

Figure 4.2 The two conventions for channel bit notation. A channel bit 1 most commonly represents a transition, but some codes use the bit status to describe the direction of the record current.

the last group matches the beginning of the next. The polarity is unimportant in most codes and all that matters is the length of time between transitions. Less common is the convention where the channel bit state directly represents the direction of the recording current. Clearly steps then need to be taken to ensure that the boundary between two groups is properly handled. Such an approach is used in the D-3/D-5 formats and in the MIL-STD 2179 instrumentation format. It should be stressed that channel bits are not recorded. They exist only in a circuit technique used to control the waveform generator. In many media, for example CD, the channel bit rate is beyond the frequency response of the channel and so it *cannot* be recorded.

One of the fundamental parameters of a channel code is the density ratio (DR). One definition of density ratio is that it is the worst-case ratio of the number of data bits recorded to the number of transitions in the channel. It can also be thought of as the ratio between the Nyquist rate of the data (one-half the bit rate) and the frequency response required in the channel. The storage density of data recorders has steadily increased due to improvements in medium and transducer technology, but modern storage densities are also a function of improvements in channel coding. Figure 4.3(a) shows how the density ratio has improved as more sophisticated codes have been developed.

As jitter is such an important issue in digital recording and transmission, a parameter has been introduced to quantify the ability of a channel code to reject time instability. This parameter, the jitter margin, also known as the window margin or phase margin (T_w), is defined as the permitted range of time over which a transition can still be received correctly, divided by the data bit-cell period (T).

Since equalization is often difficult in practice, a code which has a large jitter margin will sometimes be used because it resists the effects of intersymbol interference well. Such a code may achieve a better performance in practice than a code with a higher density ratio but poor jitter performance.

A more realistic comparison of code performance will be obtained by taking into account both density ratio and jitter margin. This is the purpose of the figure

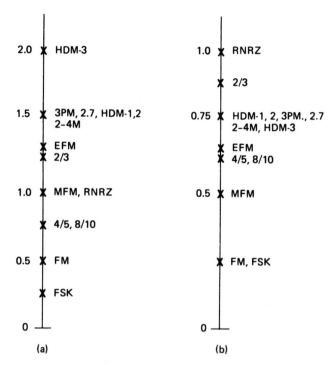

Figure 4.3 (a) Comparison of codes by density ratio; (b) comparison of codes by figure of merit. Note how 4/5, 2/3, 8/10 + RNRZ move up because of good jitter performance; HDM-3 moves down because of jitter sensitivity.

of merit (FoM), which is defined as DR $\times T_w$. Figure 4.3(b) shows a number of codes compared by FoM.

4.2 Recording-oriented codes

Many channel codes are sufficiently versatile that they have been used in recording, electrical or optical cable transmission and radio transmission. Others are more specialized and are intended for only one of these categories. Channel coding has roots in computers, in telemetry and in telex services, but has for some time been considered a single subject. These starting points will be considered here.

In magnetic recording, the first digital recordings were developed for early computers and used very simple techniques. Figure 4.4(a) shows that in return to zero (RZ) recording, the record current has a 0 state between bits and flows in one direction to record a 1 and in the opposite direction to record a 0. Thus every bit contains two flux changes which replay as a pair of pulses, one positive and one negative. The signal is self clocking because pulses always occur. The order in which they occur determines the state of the bit. RZ recording cannot erase by overwrite because there are times when no record current flows. Additionally the signal amplitude is only one-half of what is possible. These problems were

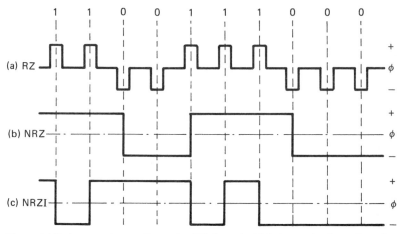

Figure 4.4 Early magnetic recording codes. RZ shown in (a) had poor signal-to-noise ratio and poor overwrite capability. NRZ in (b) overcame these problems but suffered error propagation. NRZI in (c) was the final result where a transition represented a 1. NRZI is not self clocking.

overcome in the non-return to zero code shown in Figure 4.4(b). As the name suggests, the record current does not cease between bits, but flows at all times in one direction or the other dependent on the state of the bit to be recorded. This results in a replay pulse only when the data bits change from one state to another. As a result, if one pulse was missed, the subsequent bits would be inverted. This was avoided by adapting the coding such that the record current would change state or invert whenever a data 1 occurred, leading to the term non-return to zero invert or NRZI shown in Figure 4.4(c). In NRZI a replay pulse occurs whenever there is a data 1. Clearly neither NRZ or NRZI are self clocking, but require a separate clock track. Skew between tracks can only be avoided by working at low density and so the system cannot be used for digital audio. However, virtually all of the codes used for magnetic recording are based on the principle of the reversing the record current to produce a transition.

4.3 Communications-oriented codes

In cable transmission, also known as line signalling, and in telemetry, the starting point was often the speech bandwidth available in existing telephone lines and radio links. There was no DC response, just a range of frequencies available. Figure 4.5(a) shows that a pair of frequencies can be used, one for each state of a data bit. The result is frequency shift keying (FSK) which is the same as would be obtained from an analog frequency modulator fed with a two-level signal. This is exactly what happens when two-level pseudo-video from a digital audio PCM adaptor is fed to a VCR. PCM adaptors have also been used to carry digital audio over a video landline or microwave link. Clearly FSK is DC free and self clocking.

Instead of modulating the frequency of the signal, the phase can be modulated or shifted instead, leading to the generic term of phase shift keying or FSK. This method is highly suited to broadcast as it is easily applied to a radio frequency

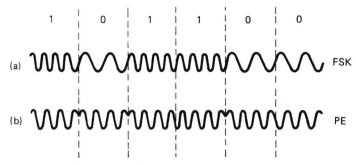

Figure 4.5 Communications-oriented codes: (a) frequency shift keying (FSK); (b) phase encoding.

carrier. The simplest technique is selectively to invert the carrier phase according to the data bit as in Figure 4.5(b). There can be many cycles of carrier in each bit period. This technique is known as phase encoding (PE) and is used in GPS (global positioning system) broadcasts. The receiver in a PE system is a well-damped phase-locked loop which runs at the average phase of the transmission. Phase changes will then result in phase errors in the loop and so the phase error is the demodulated signal.

4.4 General-purpose codes

Despite the different origins of codes, there are many similarities between them.

If the two frequencies in an FSK system are one octave apart, the limiting case in which the highest data rate is obtained is when there is one half cycle of the lower frequency or a whole cycle of the high frequency in one bit period. This gives rise to the term frequency modulation (FM). In the same way, the limiting case of phase encoding is where there is only one cycle of carrier per bit. In recording, this technique is what is meant by the same term. These can be contrasted in Figure 4.6.

The FM code, also known as Manchester code or bi-phase mark code, shown in Figure 4.6(a), was the first practical self clocking binary code and it is suitable for both transmission and recording. It is DC free and very easy to encode and decode. In the field of recording it remains in use today only where density is not of prime importance, for example in SMPTE/EBU timecode for professional audio and video recorders and in low-cost floppy disks.

In FM there is always a transition at the bit-cell boundary which acts as a clock. For a data 1, there is an additional transition at the bit-cell centre. Figure 4.6(a) shows that each data bit can be represented by two channel bits. For a data 0, they will be 10, and for a data 1 they will be 11. Since the first bit is always 1, it conveys no information, and is responsible for the density ratio of only one-half. Since there can be two transitions for each data bit, the jitter margin can only be half a bit, and the resulting FoM is only 0.25. The high clock content of FM does, however, mean that data recovery is possible over a wide range of speeds; hence the use for timecode. The lowest frequency in FM is due to a stream of zeros and is equal to half the bit rate. The highest frequency is due to

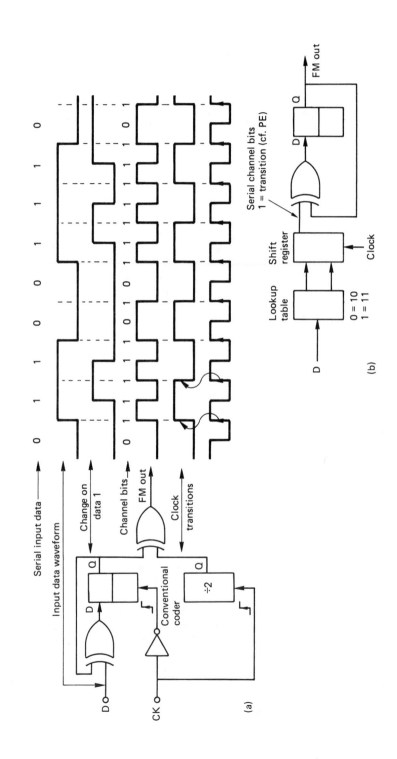

Serial input data →

Input data waveform

Change on data 1

Channel bits

FM out

Clock transitions

D

Q

Conventional coder

CK

÷2

Q

(a)

Serial channel bits
1 = transition (cf. PE)

FM out

Q

D

Lookup table

Shift register

Clock

0 = 10
1 = 11

D

(b)

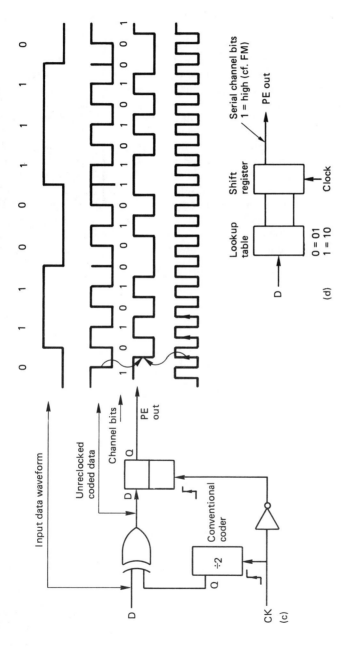

Figure 4.6 FM and PE contrasted. In (a) are the FM waveform and the channel bits which may be used to describe transitions in it. The FM coder is shown in (b). The PE waveform is shown in (c). As PE is polarity conscious, the channel bits must describe the signal level rather than the transitions. The coder is shown in (d).

a stream of ones, and is equal to the bit rate. Thus the fundamentals of FM are within a band of one octave. Effective equalization is generally possible over such a band. FM is not polarity conscious and can be inverted without changing the data.

Figure 4.6(b) shows how an FM coder works. Data words are loaded into the input shift register which is clocked at the data bit rate. Each data bit is converted to two channel bits in the code book or lookup table. These channel bits are loaded into the output register. The output register is clocked twice as fast as the input register because there are twice as many channel bits as data bits. The ratio of the two clocks is called the code rate; in this case it is a rate one-half code. Ones in the serial channel bit output represent transitions whereas zeros represent no change. The channel bits are fed to the waveform generator which is a one-bit delay, clocked at the channel bit rate, and an exclusive OR gate. This changes state when a channel bit 1 is input. The result is a coded FM waveform where there is always a transition at the beginning of the data bit period, and a second optional transition whose presence indicates a 1.

In PE there is always a transition in the centre of the bit but Figure 4.6(c) shows that the transition between bits is dependent on the data values. Although its origins were in line coding, phase encoding can be used for optical and magnetic recording as it is DC free and self clocking. It has the same DR and T_w as FM, and the waveform can also be described using channel bits, but with a different notation. As PE is polarity sensitive, the channel bits determine the level of the encoded signal rather than causing a transition. Figure 4.6(d) shows that the allowable channel bit patterns are now 10 and 01.

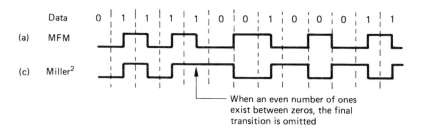

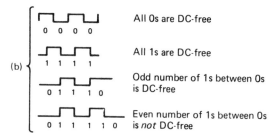

Figure 4.7 MFM or Miller code is generated as shown here. The minimum transition spacing is twice that of FM or PE. MFM is not always DC free as shown in (b). This can be overcome by the modification of (c) which results in the Miller^2 code.

In modified frequency modulation (MFM), also known as Miller code,[1] the highly redundant clock content of FM was reduced by the use of a phase-locked loop in the receiver which could flywheel over missing clock transitions. This technique is implicit in all the more advanced codes. Figure 4.7(a) shows that the bit-cell centre transition on a data 1 was retained, but the bit-cell boundary transition is now only required between successive zeros. There are still two channel bits for every data bit, but adjacent channel bits will never be 1, doubling the minimum time between transitions, and giving a DR of 1. Clearly the coding of the current bit is now influenced by the preceding bit. The maximum number of prior bits which affect the current bit is known as the constraint length L_c, measured in data-bit periods. For MFM $L_c = T$. Another way of considering the constraint length is that it assesses the number of data bits which may be corrupted if the receiver misplaces one transition. If L_c is long, all errors will be burst errors.

MFM doubled the density ratio compared with FM and PE without changing the jitter performance; thus the FoM also doubles, becoming 0.5. It was adopted for many rigid disks at the time of its development, and remains in use on double-density floppy disks. It is not, however, DC free. Figure 4.7(b) shows how MFM can have DC content under certain conditions.

4.5 Miller^2 code

The Miller^2 code is derived from MFM, and Figure 4.7(c) shows that the DC content is eliminated by a slight increase in complexity.[2,3] Wherever an even number of ones occurs between zeros, the transition at the last 1 is omitted. This creates two additional, longer run lengths and increases the T_{max} of the code. The decoder can detect these longer run lengths in order to reinsert the suppressed ones. The FoM of Miller^2 is 0.5 as for MFM. Miller^2 was used in early 3M stationary-head digital audio recorders, in high bit-rate instrumentation recorders and in the D-2 and DCT DVTR format.

4.6 Group codes

Further improvements in coding rely on converting patterns of real data to patterns of channel bits with more desirable characteristics using a conversion table known as a codebook. If a data symbol of m bits is considered, it can have 2^m different combinations. As it is intended to discard undesirable patterns to improve the code, it follows that the number of channel bits n must be greater than m. The number of patterns which can be discarded is:

$$2^n - 2^m$$

One name for the principle is group code recording (GCR), and an important parameter, is the code rate, defined as:

$$R = \frac{m}{n}$$

It will be evident that the jitter margin T_w is numerically equal to the code rate, and so a code rate near to unity is desirable. The choice of patterns which are

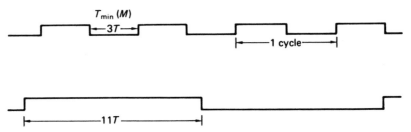

Figure 4.8 A channel code can control its spectrum by placing limits on T_{min} (*M*) and T_{max} which define upper and lower frequencies. The ratio of T_{max}/T_{min} determines the asymmetry of waveform and predicts DC content and peak shift. Example shown is EFM.

used in the codebook will be those which give the desired balance between clock content, bandwidth and DC content.

Figure 4.8 shows that the upper spectral limit can be made to be some fraction of the channel bit rate according to the minimum distance between ones in the channel bits. This is known as T_{min}, also refered to as the minimum transition parameter *M*, and in both cases is measured in data bits *T*. It can be obtained by multiplying the number of channel detent periods between transitions by the code rate. Unfortunately, codes are measured by the number of consecutive zeros in the channel bits, given the symbol *d*, which is always one less than the number of detent periods. In fact T_{min} is numerically equal to the density ratio:

$$T_{min} = M = DR = \frac{(d + 1) \times m}{n}$$

It will be evident that choosing a low code rate could increase the density ratio, but it will impair the jitter margin. The figure of merit is:

$$FoM = DR \times T_w = \frac{(d + 1) \times m^2}{n^2}$$

since

$$T_w = m/n$$

Figure 4.8 also shows that the lower spectral limit is influenced by the maximum distance between transitions T_{max}. This is also obtained by multiplying the maximum number of detent periods between transitions by the code rate. Again, codes are measured by the maximum number of zeros between channel ones, *k*, and so:

$$T_{max} = \frac{(k + 1) \times m}{n}$$

and the maximum/minimum ratio P is:

$$P = \frac{(k + 1)}{(d + 1)}$$

The length of time between channel transitions is known as the *run length*. Another name for this class is the run-length-limited (RLL) codes.[4] Since m data bits are considered as one symbol, the constraint length L_c will be increased in RLL codes to at least m. It is, however, possible for a code to have run-length limits without it being a group code.

In practice, the junction of two adjacent channel symbols may violate run-length limits, and it may be necessary to create a further codebook of symbol size $2n$ which converts violating code pairs to acceptable patterns. This is known as merging and follows the golden rule that the substitute $2n$ symbol must finish with a pattern which eliminates the possibility of a subsequent violation. These patterns must also differ from all other symbols.

Substitution may also be used to different degrees in the same nominal code in order to allow a choice of maximum run length, e.g. 3PM.[5] The maximum number of symbols involved in a substitution is denoted by r.[6,7] There are many RLL codes and the parameters d, k, m, n and r are a way of comparing them.

Sometimes the code rate forms the name of the code, as in 2/3, 8/10 and EFM; at other times the code may be named after the d, k parameters, as in 2,7 code. Various examples of group codes will be given to illustrate the principles involved.

4.7 4/5 code

4/5 code uses 16 out of 32 possible channel symbols to represent the data. The criterion for 4/5 was high clock content to give immunity to jitter without a great sacrifice of DR. The codebook is shown in Figure 4.9. Each one in the code

Data		
Decimal	Binary	Channel bits
0	0000	11001
1	0001	11011
2	0010	10010
3	0011	10011
4	0100	11101
5	0101	10101
6	0110	10110
7	0111	10111
8	1000	11010
9	1001	01001
10	1010	01010
11	1011	01011
12	1100	11110
13	1101	01101
14	1110	01110
15	1111	01111

Figure 4.9 The codebook of 4/5 code. Maximum number of zeros (k) is two; thus T_{max} is $4(k + 1)/5 = 2.4$ bits. Adjacent ones are permitted: thus DR = 4/5.

represents a flux reversal, and there are never more than three channel bits (2.4 data bits) of time between transitions ($k = 2$). This permits simple AGC and clock regeneration. The minimum run length is one channel bit since adjacent ones are permitted in the code ($d = 0$). The code is thus described as 0,1,4,5,1. $L_c = 4T$, and the density ratio is given by:

$$DR = \frac{(d + 1) \times m}{n} = 0.8$$

The spectrum needed is thus 1.25 times that of the data, but there can be no merging violations, and an extremely good window margin T_w of $0.8T$ is obtained, giving an FoM of 0.64.

This code was used in the IBM 6250 BPI tape format and represented an improvement factor of nearly 4 over the 1600 BPI phase-encoded system which preceded it. The FoM improved over that of PE by a factor of more than 2.5, thus reducing the improvements needed to heads and tape.

4.8 2/3 code

Figure 4.10(a) shows the codebook of an optimized code which illustrates one merging technique. This is a 1,7,2,3,2 code known as 2/3. It is designed to have a good jitter window in order to resist peak shift distortion in disk drives, but it also has a good density ratio.[8] In 2/3 code, pairs of data bits create symbols of three channel bits. For bandwidth reduction, codes having adjacent ones are eliminated so that $d = 1$. This halves the upper spectral limit and the DR is improved accordingly:

$$DR = \frac{(d + 1) \times m}{n} = \frac{2 \times 2}{3} = 1.33$$

In Figure 4.10(b) it will be seen that some group combinations cause violations. To avoid this, pairs of three channel bit symbols are replaced with a new six channel bit symbol. L_c is thus $4T$, the same as for the 4/5 code. The jitter window is given by:

$$T_w = \frac{m}{n} = \frac{2}{3} T$$

and the FoM is:

$$\frac{2}{3} \times \frac{4}{3} = \frac{8}{9}$$

Data	Code
0 0	1 0 1
0 1	1 0 0
1 0	0 0 1
1 1	0 1 0

(a)

Data	Illegal code	Substitution
0 0 0 0	1 0 1 1 0 1	1 0 1 0 0 0
0 0 0 1	1 0 1 1 0 0	1 0 0 0 0 0
1 0 0 0	0 0 1 1 0 1	0 0 1 0 0 0
1 0 0 1	0 0 1 1 0 0	0 1 0 0 0 0

(b)

Figure 4.10 2/3 code. In (a) two data bits (m) are expressed as three channel bits (n) without adjacent transitions ($d = 1$). Violations are dealt with by substitution

$$DR = \frac{(d + 1)m}{n} = \frac{2 \times 2}{3} = 1.33$$

Adjacent data pairs can break the encoding rule; in these cases substitutions are made, as shown in (b).

This is an extremely good figure for an RLL code, and is some 10% better than the FoM of 3PM[9] and 2,7, and as a result 2/3 has been highly successful in Winchester disk drives.

4.9 2,7 code

The 2,7 variable length group code[10] has been used extensively in IBM disk drives. The 2,7 of the code name refers to the d and k parameters. With $d = 2$, there are always at least two zero channel bits between ones, dividing the channel bit frequency by three. It will be seen from Figure 4.11 that there are twice as many channel bits as data bits, hence the density ratio is 1.5 and the FoM is 0.75. Encoding a variable-length code is slightly more complex as it is necessary to deserialize the input data stream flexibly according to the data content. The error propagation is limited to the largest group size of four data bits.

Data	Channel bits
1 0	0 1 0 0
1 1	1 0 0 0
0 0 0	0 0 0 1 0 0
0 1 0	1 0 0 1 0 0
0 1 1	0 0 1 0 0 0
0 0 1 0	0 0 1 0 0 1 0 0
0 0 1 1	0 0 0 0 1 0 0 0

Figure 4.11 The 2,7 code is a rate $\frac{1}{2}$ code using variable-length symbols as shown here.

4.10 The 8/10 group code of RDAT

The essential feature of the channel code of RDAT is that it must be able to work well in an azimuth recording system. There are many channel codes available, but few of them are suitable for azimuth recording because of the large amount of crosstalk. The crosstalk cancellation of azimuth recording fails at low frequencies, so a suitable channel code must not only be free of DC, but it must suppress low frequencies as well. A further issue is that erasure is by overwriting, and as the heads are optimized for short-wavelength working, best erasure will be when the ratio between the longest and shortest wavelengths in the recording is small.

In Figure 4.12, some examples from the 8/10 group code of RDAT are shown.[11] Clearly a channel waveform which spends as much time high as low

Eight-bit dataword	Ten-bit codeword	DSV	Alternative codeword	DSV
00010000	1101010010	0		
00010001	0100010010	2	1100010010	−2
00010010	0101010010	0		
00010011	0101110010	0		
00010100	1101110001	2	0101110001	−2
00010101	1101110011	2	0101110011	−2
00010110	1101110110	2	0101110110	−2
00010111	1101110010	0		

Figure 4.12 Some of the 8/10 codebook for non-zero DSV symbols (two entries) and zero DSV symbols (one entry).

has no net DC content, and so all 10 bit patterns which meet this criterion of zero disparity can be found. The term used to measure DC content is called the digital sum value (DSV). For every bit the channel spends high, the DSV will increase by 1; for every bit the channel spends low, the DSV will decrease by 1. As adjacent channel ones are permitted, the window margin and DR will be 0.8, comparing favourably with the figure of 0.5 for MFM, giving an FoM of 0.64. Unfortunately there are not enough DC-free combinations in ten channel bits to provide the 256 patterns necessary to record eight data bits. A further constraint is that it is desirable to restrict the maximum run length to improve overwrite capability and reduce peak shift. In the 8/10 code of RDAT, no more than three channel zeros are permitted between channel ones, which makes the longest wavelength only four times the shortest. There are only 153 10 bit patterns which are within this maximum run length and which have a DSV of zero.

The remaining 103 data combinations are recorded using channel patterns that have non-zero DSV. Two channel patterns are allocated to each of the 103 data patterns. One of these has a DSV of +2, the other has a DSV of −2. For simplicity, the only difference between them is that the first channel bit is inverted. The choice of which channel-bit pattern to use is based on the DSV due to the previous code.

For example, if several bytes have been recorded with some of the 153 DC-free patterns, the DSV of the code will be zero. The first data byte is then found which has no zero disparity pattern. If the +2 DSV pattern is used, the code at the end of the pattern will also become +2 DSV. When the next pattern of this kind is found, the code having the DSV of −2 will automatically be selected to return the channel DSV to zero. In this way the code is kept DC free, but the maximum distance between transitions can be shortened. A code of this kind is known as a low-disparity code.

In order to reduce the complexity of encoding logic, it is usual in large group codes to computer-optimize the relationship between data patterns and code patterns. This has been done for 8/10 so that the conversion can be performed in a programmed logic array. The Boolean expressions for calculating the channel bits from data can be seen in Figure 4.13(a). Only DC-free or DSV = +2 patterns are produced by the logic, since the DSV = −2 pattern can be obtained by reversing the first bit. The assessment of DSV is performed in an interesting manner. If in a pair of channel bits the second bit is 1, the pair must be DC free because each detent has a different value. If the five even channel bits in a 10 bit pattern are checked for parity and the result is 1, the pattern could have a DSV of 0, ±4 or ±8. If the result is zero, the DSV could be ±2, ±6 or ±10. However, the codes used are known to be either zero or +2 DSV, so the state of the parity bit discriminates between them. Figure 4.13(b) shows the encoding circuit. The lower set of XOR gates calculate parity on the latest pattern to be recorded, and store the DSV bit in the latch. The next data byte to be recorded is fed to the PLA, which outputs a 10 bit pattern. If this is a zero disparity code, it passes to the output unchanged. If it is a DSV = +2 code, this will be detected by the upper XOR gates. If the latch is set, this means that a previous pattern had been +2 DSV, and so the first bit of the channel pattern is inverted by the XOR gate in that line, and the latch will be cleared because the DSV of the code has been returned to zero.

Decoding is simpler, because there is a direct relationship between 10 bit codes and 8 bit data.

$a = A + CZ + Y\,(\overline{C} \oplus \overline{F}\,(G + H))$

$b = A\,(B + D\overline{E}) + \overline{A}\,(\overline{B} + \overline{C})$

$c = \overline{A}C + A\,(\overline{D} + E) + BDE$

$d = A\,(C + BD\overline{E}) + CDE + \overline{C}Z + (\overline{A}\,\overline{B} \oplus \overline{F}\,\overline{G}HY)$

$\overline{e} = (AB + \overline{D})\,\overline{E} + \overline{A}BCDE + Y\overline{F}\,(\overline{G} + \overline{H})$

$f = \overline{A}\,\overline{E}\,[C + (B \oplus D)] + [(\overline{D} + C\overline{E}) \oplus F\,(\overline{G} + \overline{H})]$

$\overline{g} = \overline{F}\,\overline{G} + Y + (B + C)\,Z$

$h = FG\overline{H} + \overline{F}\,\overline{Y}$

$i = H + FG + \overline{F}\,Y$ where $Y = \overline{A}\,(\overline{B} + C)\,D\overline{E}$

$j = F\overline{G} + \overline{F}\,Y$ $Z = \overline{A}\,\overline{D}\,\overline{E}\,F\,(\overline{G} + \overline{H})$

(a)

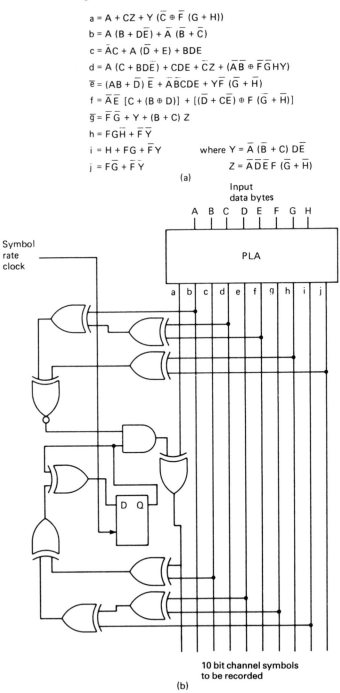

(b)

Figure 4.13 In (a) the truth table of the symbol encoding prior to DSV control. In (b) this circuit controls code disparity by remembering non-zero DSV in the latch and selecting a subsequent symbol with opposite DSV.

4.11 EFM code in D-3/D-5

The ½ inch D-3 and D-5 digital VTR formats use a group code in which $m = 8$ and $n = 14$ so the code rate is 0.57.[12] The code is called 8,14 after the code rate parameters. In group codes the jitter margin T_w is numerically equal to the code rate, and so for jitter resistance a code rate close to unity is preferable. The choice of patterns which are used in the codebook will be those which give the desired balance between clock content, bandwidth and DC content.

The code used in D-3/D-5 uses the convention in which a channel bit 1 represents a high in the recorded waveform. In this convention a flux reversal or transition will be written when the channel bits change.

In Figure 4.14 it is shown that the upper spectral limit is made to be some fraction of the channel bit rate according to the minimum distance between transitions in the channel bits, which in 8,14 is two channel bits. This is known as T_{min}, also referred to as the minimum transition parameter M, and in both cases is measured in data bits T. It can be obtained by multiplying the number of channel detent periods between transitions by the code rate. In fact T_{min} is numerically equal to the density ratio:

$$T_{min} = M = DR = \frac{2 \times 8}{14} = 1.14$$

The figure of merit is:

$$FoM = DR \times T_w = \frac{2 \times 8^2}{14^2} = 0.65$$

since $T_w = \dfrac{m}{n} = \dfrac{8}{14}$

Figure 4.14 also shows that the lower spectral limit is influenced by the maximum distance between transitions T_{max}, which also determines the minimum clock content. This is also obtained by multiplying the maximum number of detent periods between transitions by the code rate. In 8,14 code this is 7 channel bits, and so:

$$T_{max} = \frac{7 \times 8}{14} = 4$$

and the maximum/minimum ratio P is:

$$P = \frac{4}{1.14} = 3.51$$

Since 8 data bits are considered as one symbol, the constraint length L_c will be increased in this code to at least 8 bits. In practice, the junction of some adjacent channel symbols may violate coding rules, and it is necessary to extend the codebook so that the original data can be represented by a number of alternative codes at least one of which will be acceptable. This is known as substitution. Owing to the coding convention used, which generates a transition when the channel bits change, transitions will also be generated at the junction of two channel symbols if the adjacent bits are different.

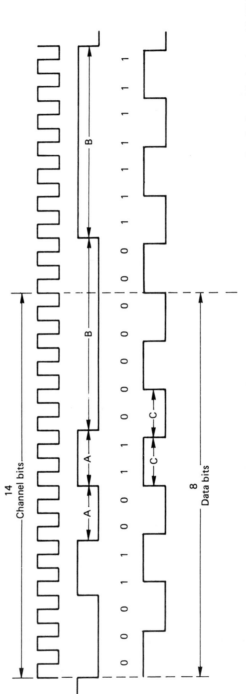

Figure 4.14 In the 8,14 code of D-3, eight data-bit periods are divided into 14 channel-bit periods. However, the shortest run length allowed in the channel is 2 bits, shown at A. This restriction is obtained by selecting 14 bit patterns from those available. The longest run length in the code is seven channel bits. Note that the shortest run length A is 14% longer than the shortest run length in the raw data C. Thus density ratio DR is 1.14. Using this code 14% more data can be recorded with the same wavelength on tape as a simple code.

Data	Code A (begins with 0)	CDS	Code B (begins with 1)	CDS	Code C (begins with 0)	CDS	Code D (begins with 1)	CDS
00								
↑								
42	01100011000111	0	10011100111000	0	01100011000111	0	10011100111000	0
43	01100001111100	0	10011110000011	0	01100001111100	0	10011110000011	0
44	01100001111001	0	10011110000110	0	01100001111001	0	10011110000110	0
45	01100001110011	0	10011110001100	0	01100001110011	0	10011110001100	0
46	01100001100111	0	10011110011000	0	01100001100111	0	10011110011000	0
47	01100000111110	0	10011111000001	0	01100000111110	0	10011111000001	0
48	01100000011111	0	10011111100000	0	01100000011111	0	10011111100000	0
49	01111100000001	−2	10000000110011	−4	01111111001100	4	10000011111110	2
50	01111001100000	−2	10000000111001	−4	01111111000110	4	10000110011111	2
51	01111000110000	−2	10000000111100	−4	01111111000011	4	10000111001111	2
52	01111000011000	−2	10000001100011	−4	01111110011100	4	10000111100111	2
53	01111000001100	−2	10000001100110	−4	01111110011001	4	10000111110011	2
54	01111000000110	−2	10000001110001	−4	01111110001110	4	10000111111001	2
55	01111000000011	−2	10000001111000	−4	01111110000111	4	10000111111100	2
56	01110011100000	−2	10000011000011	−4	01111100111100	4	10001100011111	2
57	01110011000001	−2	10000011000110	−4	01111100111001	4	10001100111110	2
↓								
255								

Figure 4.15 Part of the codebook for D-3 EFM code. For every 8 bit data word (left) there are four possible channel-bit patterns, two of which begin with 0 and two of which begin with 1. This allows successive symbols to avoid violating the minimum run-length limit (A in Figure 4.14) at the junction of the two symbols. See Figures 4.16 and 4.17 for further details.

Figure 4.15 shows part of the 8,14 code (EFM) used in the D-3 format. As stated, eight bit data symbols are represented by 14 bit channel symbols. There are 256 combinations of 8 data bits, whereas 14 bits have 2^{14} or 16 384 combinations. The initial range of possible codes is reduced by the requirements of the maximum and minimum run-length limits and by a requirement that there shall not be more than 5 identical bits in the first 6 bits of the code and not more than 6 in the last 7 bits, as shown in Figure 4.16.

One of the most important parameters of a channel pattern is the code digital sum (CDS) shown in Figure 4.17. This is the number of channel ones minus the

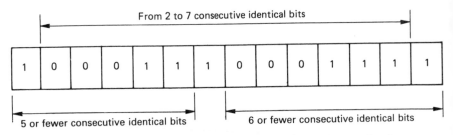

Figure 4.16 The selected 14 bit patterns follow the rules that there cannot be more than five consecutive identical bits at the beginning or more than six at the end. In addition the code digital sum (CDS) cannot exceed 4. See Figure 4.17 for derivation of CDS.

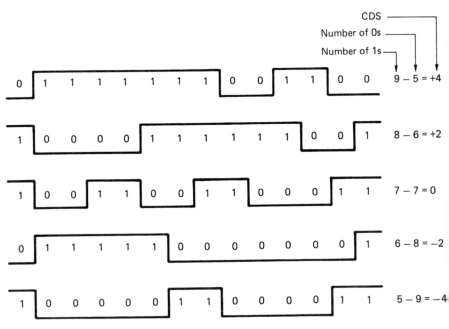

Figure 4.17 Code digital sum (CDS) is the measure of the DC content of a given channel symbol. It is obtained by subtracting the number of zeros in the symbol from the number of ones. Shown above are five actual 14 bit symbols from the D-3 code showing the range of CDS allowed from −4 to +4. Although CDS of zero is optimum, there are not enough patterns with zero CDS to represent all combinations of eight data bits.

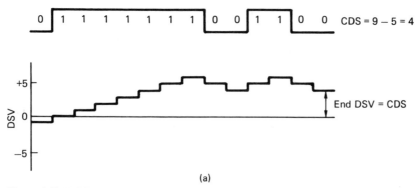

(a)

Figure 4.18 (a) DSV is obtained by subtracting 1 for every zero, and adding 1 for every one which passes during the integration time. Thus DSV changes every channel bit. Note that end DSV = CDS.

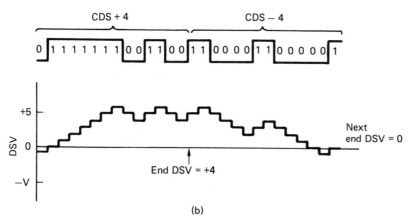

(b)

Figure 4.18 (b) The next end DSV is the current end DSV plus the CDS of the next symbol. Note how the choice of a CDS −4 symbol after a +4 symbol brings DSV back to zero.

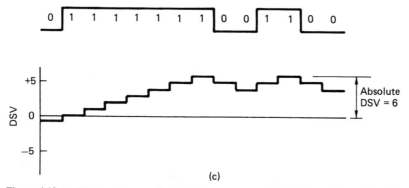

(c)

Figure 4.18 (c) The absolute or peak DSV is the greatest value the DSV can have during the symbol. As shown here, it can be greater than CDS.

number of channel zeros. As the CDS represents the DC content or average voltage of the channel pattern it is to be kept to a minimum.

There are only 118 codes (and 118 inverse codes) which are DC free (CDS = 0) as well as meeting the other constraints. In order to obtain 256 data combinations, codes with non-zero CDS have to be accepted. The actual codes used in 8,14 have CDS of 0, ±2 or ±4.

The CDS is a special case of a more general parameter called the digital sum value (DSV). DSV is a useful way of predicting how an analog channel such as a tape/head system will handle a binary waveform. In a stream of bits, a 1 causes 1 to be added to the DSV whereas a 0 causes 1 to be subtracted. Thus DSV is a form of running discrete integration. Figure 4.18(a) shows how the DSV varies along the time axis. The end DSV is the DSV at the end of a string of channel symbols. Clearly CDS is the end DSV of one code pattern in isolation. The next end DSV is the current one plus the CDS of the next symbol as shown in Figure 4.18(b).

The absolute DSV of a symbol is shown in Figure 4.18(c). This is obtained by finding the peak DSV. Large absolute DSVs are associated with low frequencies and low clock content.

When encoding is performed, each eight bit data symbol selects four locations in the lookup table each of which contains a 14 bit pattern. The recording is made by selecting the most appropriate one of four candidate channel bit patterns. The decoding process is such that any of the four channel patterns will decode to the same data.

The four possible channel symbols for each data byte are classified according to Figure 4.15 into types A, B, C or D. Since 8,14 coding requires alternative inverse symbols, two of the candidates are simply bit inversions of the other two. Where codes are not DC free there may be a pair of +2 CDS candidates and their −2 CDS inverses or a +2 CDS and a +4 CDS candidate and their inverses which will of course have −2 and −4 CDS. In the case of all but two of the DC-free codes the two candidates are one and the same code and the four lookup table locations contain two identical codes and two identical inverse codes. As a result of some of the codes being identical, although there are 1024 locations in the table, only 770 different 14 bit patterns are used, representing 4.7 % of the total.

Code classes are further subdivided into class numbers, which go from 1 to 5 and specify the number of identical channel bits at the beginning of the symbol, and a priority number which only applies to codes of CDS ±2 and is obtained from the channel bit pattern at the end of the code according to Figure 4.19.

Clearly the junction of two channel patterns cannot be allowed to violate the run-length limits. As the next code cannot have more than 5 consecutive identical bits at the beginning, the previous code could end with up to two bits in the same state without exceeding the maximum run-length of 7. If this limit is exceeded by one of the four candidate codes, it will be rejected and one of those having an earlier transition will be chosen instead. Similarly, if the previous code ends in 01 or 10, the first bit of the next code must be the same as the last bit of the previous code or the minimum run-length limit will be violated. The run-length limits can always be met because every code has an inverse, so out of the four possible channel symbols available for a given data byte two of them will begin with 0 and two begin with 1. In some cases, such as where the first code ends in 1100, up to four of the candidates for the next code could meet the run-length limits.

+2 end DSV end pattern of channel bits	−2 end DSV end pattern of channel bits	Priority
. . . xxxxx110	. . . xxxxx001	4
. . . xxxx1100	. . . xxxx0011	1
. . . xxx11000	. . . xxx00111	2
. . . xx110000	. . . xx001111	3
. . . x1100000	. . . x0011111	8
. . . xxxxx001	. . . xxxxx110	10
. . . xxxx0011	. . . xxxx1100	5
. . . xxx00111	. . . xxx11000	6
. . . xx001111	. . . xx110000	7
. . . x0011111	. . . x1100000	9
. . . 00111111	. . . 11000000	11

x: Don't care bit

Figure 4.19 Codes having end DSV of ±2 are prioritized according to the above table as part of the selection process.

In such cases the best candidate will be chosen to optimize some other parameter.

In order to follow how the encoder selects the best channel pattern it is necessary to discuss the criteria that are used. There are a number of these, some of which are compulsory, such as the run-length limits, and others which will be met if possible on a decreasing scale of importance. If a higher criterion cannot be met the decision will still attempt to meet as many of the lower ones as possible.

The overall goal is to meet the run-length limits with a sequence of symbols which has the highest clock content, lowest LF and DC content and the least asymmetry to reduce peak shift. Some channel symbols will be better than others, a phenomenon known as pattern sensitivity. The least optimal patterns are not so bad that they will *cause* errors, but they will be more prone to errors due to other causes. Minimizing the use of sensitive waveforms will enhance the data reliability and is as good as an improvement in the signal-to-noise ratio.

As there are 2^{10} different patterns, there will be 2^{20} different combinations of two patterns. Clearly it is out of the question to create a lookup table to determine how best to merge two patterns. It has to be done algorithmically. The flow chart of the algorithm is shown in Figure 4.20.

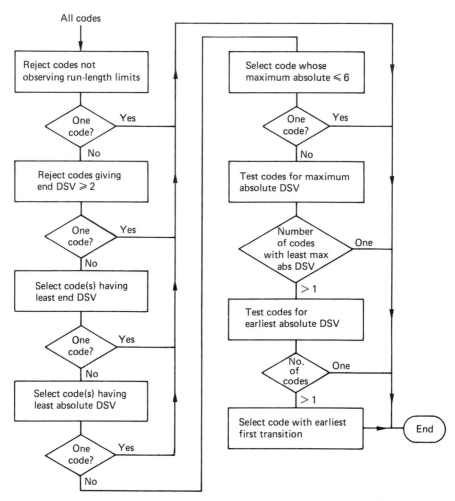

Figure 4.20 The four candidate codes, A, B, C, D, of Figure 4.15 are compared according to this flowchart to locate the single best code which will represent the data byte. Any of the codes will result in the same decode on replay.

The process begins when a data byte selects four candidate channel symbols. Initially tests are made to eliminate unsuitable patterns, and, on some occasions, only one code will emerge from these tests. There are so many combinations, however, that it is possible for several candidate codes to pass the initial tests, and so the flowchart continues to select the best code by further criteria.

The first selection is based on maintaining the run-length limits at the junction between the previous code and the current one and keeping the end DSV as small as possible. If two or more codes give an equal minimum end DSV, the code with the smallest absolute DSV will be selected. If this criterion still results in more than one code being available, a further selection is made to optimize the spectrum due to the junction of the previous and current symbols. The codes are tested to see if any give six or fewer identical channel bits across the junction. If none of the codes has this characteristic, there will be a large run length at the junction and the best code will be one that has a run length of less than six bits later. This criterion will also be applied if more than one code passes the junction run-length test.

If a decision still cannot be made, the remaining candidates could have ±2 end DSV or 0 end DSV. In the former case the priority tables are invoked, and the code(s) with the highest priority is selected. In the latter case, or if two codes emerge equal from the priority test, any code(s) which has a run length of less than six bits at the end is selected. This makes merging with the next symbol easier. It is possible that no code will pass the end run-length test, or that two or more codes are still equal. In this case some of the criteria cannot be met or are equally met, and the final choice reverts to a further selection of the code with minimum absolute DSV. This test was made much earlier, but some codes with equal minimum values could have been rejected in intermediate tests. If two codes still remain, the one whose absolute DSV appears earliest in the bitstream will be selected. If two codes still remain, the one with the earliest transition is selected.

The complexity of the coding rules in 8,14 is such that it could not have been economically implemented until recently. This illustrates the dependence of advanced recorders on LSI technology.

4.12 EFM code in CD

This section is concerned solely with the channel coding of CD. A more comprehensive discussion of how the coding is designed to suit the specific characteristics of an optical disk is given in Chapter 10. Figure 4.21 shows the 8,14 code (EFM) used in the Compact Disc. Here 8 bit symbols are represented by 14 bit channel symbols.[13] There are 256 combinations of eight data bits, whereas 14 bits have 16K combinations. Of these only 267 satisfy the criteria that the maximum run length shall not exceed 11 channel bits (k = 10) nor be less than three channel bits (d = 2). A section of the codebook is shown in the figure. In fact 258 of the 267 possible codes are used because two unique patterns are used to synchronize the subcode blocks. It is not possible to prevent violations between adjacent symbols by substitution, and extra merging bits having no data meaning are placed between the symbols. Two merging bits would be adequate to prevent violations, but in practice three are used because a further task of the merging bits is to control the DC content of the waveform. The merging bits are selected by computing the digital sum value (DSV) of the waveform. The DSV is computed as shown in Figure 4.22(a). A 1 is added to a count for every channel bit period where the waveform is in a high state, and 1 is subtracted for every channel bit period spent in a low state. Figure 4.22(b) shows that if two successive channel symbols have the same sense of DC offset, these can be made to cancel one another by placing an extra transition in the merging period. This has the effect of inverting the second pattern and reversing its DC content. The DC-free code can be high-pass filtered on replay and the lower-frequency signals are then used by the focus and tracking servos without noise due to the DC content of the audio data. Encoding EFM is complex, but was acceptable when CD was

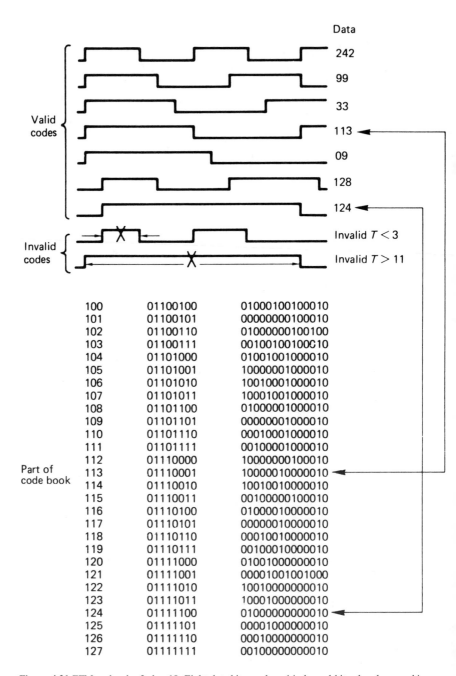

Figure 4.21 EFM code: $d = 2$, $k = 10$. Eight data bits produce 14 channel bits plus three packing bits. Code rate is 8/17. DR = $(3 \times 8)/17 = 1.41$.

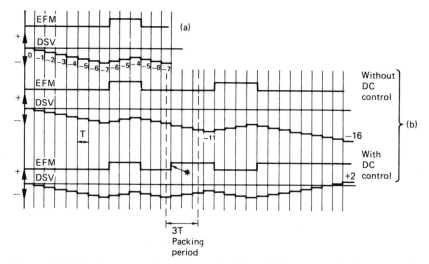

Figure 4.22 (a) Digital sum value example calculated from EFM waveform. (b) Two successive 14T symbols without DC control (upper) give DSV of −16. Additional transition (*) results in DSV of +2, anticipating negative content of next symbol.

launched because only a few encoders are necessary in comparison with the number of players. Decoding is simpler as no DC content decisions are needed and a lookup table can be used. The code book was computer optimized to permit the implementation of a programmable logic array (PLA) decoder with the minimum complexity.

Owing to the inclusion of merging bits, the code rate becomes 8/17, and the density ratio becomes:

$$\frac{3 \times 8}{17} = 1.41$$

and the FoM is:

$$\frac{3 \times 8^2}{17^2} = 0.66$$

The code is thus a 2,10,8,17,r system where r has meaning only in the context of DC control.[14] The constraints d and k can still be met with $r = 1$ because of the merging bits. The figure of merit is less useful for optical media because the straight-line frequency response does not produce peak shift and the rigid, non-contact medium has good speed stability. The density ratio and the freedom from DC are the most important factors.

4.13 Error detection in group codes

In the larger group codes, only a few per cent of the possible channel bit patterns are actually recorded, since the others have undesirable characteristics such as excessive DC content or insufficient clock content. In practice, reading errors will occur which can corrupt some or all of the channel bits in a symbol. Random noise effects or peak shift could result in a tape transition being shifted along the time axis, or in the wrong number of transitions being detected in a symbol. This will change the channel-bit pattern determined by the data separator.

As there are many more channel-bit combinations than those which are actually used, it is probable that a random error will convert a channel symbol into one of the patterns which are not used. Thus it is possible for the lookup table which decodes channel bits back to data bits to perform an error-detecting funtion. When an illegal channel-bit pattern is detected, the lookup table will output an error flag. Clearly this method is not infallible, as it is possible for an error to convert one valid code into a different valid code, which this scheme would not detect. However, the additional detection capability can be used to enhance the power of the error-correction systems which can make use of the error flags produced by the channel decoder.

4.14 Tracking signals in group codes

Many recorders use track-following systems to help keep the head(s) aligned with the narrow tracks used in digital media. These can operate by sensing low-frequency tones which are recorded along with the data. Whilst this can be done by linearly adding the tones to the coder output, it requires a linear record amplifier. An alternative is to use the DC content of group codes. A code is devised where, for each data pattern, several code patterns exist having a range of DC components. By choosing groups with a suitable sequence of DC offsets, a low frequency can be added to the coded signal. This can be filtered from the data waveform on replay.

4.15 Convolutional RLL codes

It has been mentioned that a code can be run-length limited without being a group code. An example of this is the HDM-1 code used in DASH format (digital audio stationary-head recorders). The coding is best described as convolutional, and is rather complex, as Figure 4.23 shows.[15] The DR of 1.5 is achieved by treating the input sequence of 0,1 as a single symbol which has a transition recorded at the centre of the 1. The code then depends upon whether the data continue with ones or revert to zeros. The shorter run lengths are used to describe sequential ones; the longer run lengths describe sequential zeros, up to a maximum run length of $4.5T$, with a constraint length of $5.5T$. In HDM-2, a derivative, the maximum run length is reduced to $4T$ with the penalty that L_c becomes $7.5T$.

The 2/4M code used by the Mitsubishi ProDigi quarter-inch format digital audio recorders[16] is also convolutional, and has an identical density ratio and

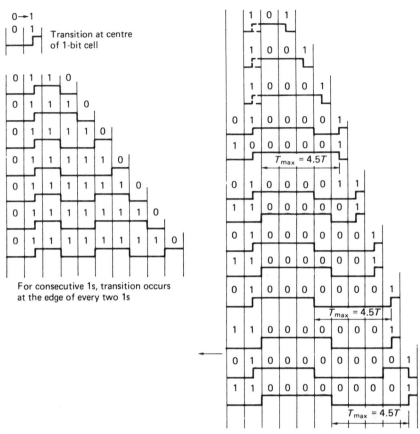

Figure 4.23 HDM-1 code of the DASH format is encoded according to the above rules. Transitions will never be closer than 1.5 bits, nor further apart than 4.5 bits.

window margin to HDM-1. T_{max} is 8 bits. Neither HDM-1 nor 2/4M are DC free, but this is less important in stationary-head recorders and an adaptive slicer can be used. The encoding of 2/4M is just as complex as that of HDM-1 and is shown in Figure 4.24. Two data bits form a group, and result in four channel bits where there are always two channel zeros between ones, to obtain a DR of 1.5. There are numerous exceptions required to the coding to prevent violation of the run-length limits and this requires a running sample of ten data bits to be examined. Thus the code is convolutional although it has many of the features of a substituting group code.

4.16 Graceful degradation

In all of the channel codes described here all data bits are assumed to be equally important and if the characteristics of the channel degrade, there is an equal probability of corruption of any bit. In digital audio samples the bits are not equally important. Loss of a high-order bit causes greater degradation than loss

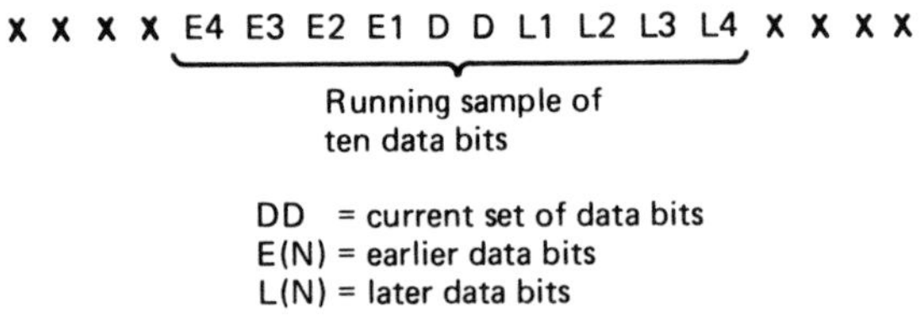

X X X X E4 E3 E2 E1 D D L1 L2 L3 L4 X X X X

Running sample of
ten data bits

DD   = current set of data bits
E(N) = earlier data bits
L(N) = later data bits

(a)

Data bits DD	Channel bits C_1 C_2 C_3 C_4	Exceptions and substitutions
00	0 1 0 0	E4 E3 = 10
	0 0 0 0	E4 E3 $\neq$ 10 and E2 E2 = 10 and L1 L2 $\neq$ 01
		E4 E3 $\neq$ 10 and E2 E1 = 10 and L1 L2 = 01
	0 0 0 1	
01	0 0 1 0	
10	Y 0 0 1	E2 E1 $\neq$ 10 and L1 L2 = 00
	0 1 0 0	E2 E1 = 10 and L1 L2 = 10 and L3 L4 = 00
		E2 E1 = 10 and L1 L2 = 00
	0 0 0 1	E2 E1 = 10 and L1 L2 = 10 and L3 L4 = 00
	0 0 0 0	
11	Y 0 0 0	

Y = XNOR of $C_3 C_4$ of previous DD

(b)

Figure 4.24 Coding rules for 2/4M code. In (a) a running sample is made of two data bits DD and earlier and later bits. In (b) the two data bits become the four channel bits shown except when the substitutions specified are made.

of a low-order bit. For applications where the bandwidth of the channel is unpredictable, or where it may improve as technology matures, a different form of channel coding has been proposed[17] where the probability of corruption of bits is not equal. The channel spectrum is divided in such a way that the least significant bits occupy the highest frequencies and the most significant bits occupy the lower frequencies. When the bandwidth of the channel is reduced, the eye pattern is degraded such that certain eyes are indeterminate, but others remain open, guaranteeing reception and clocking of high-order bits. In PCM audio the result would be sensibly the same waveform but an increased noise level. Any error-correction techniques would need to consider the unequal probability of error possibly by assembling codewords from bits of the same significance.

4.17 Randomizing

NRZ has a DR of 1 and a jitter window of 1 and so has an FoM of 1 which is better than the group codes. It does, however, suffer from an unconstrained spectrum and poor clock content. This can be overcome using randomizing. At

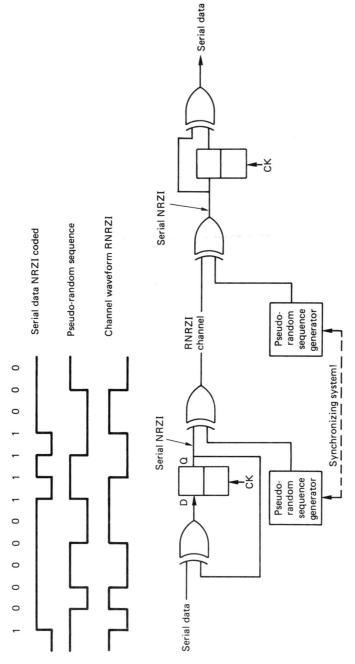

Figure 4.25 When randomizing is used, the same pseudo-random sequence must be provided at both ends of the channel with bit synchronism.

the encoder, a pseudo-random sequence (see Chapter 2) is added modulo-2 to the serial data and the resulting ones generate transitions in the channel. This process drastically reduces T_{max} and reduces DC content. Figure 4.25 shows that at the receiver the transitions are converted back to a serial bit stream to which the same pseudo-random sequence is again added modulo-2. As a result, the random signal cancels itself out to leave only the serial data, provided that the two pseudo-random sequences are synchronized to bit accuracy.

Randomizing with NRZI (RNRZI) is used in the D-1 DVTR. It is also frequently found in conjunction with partial response as in, for example, the Ampex DCRSi instrumentation recorder and the Sony Digital Betacam DVTR. Randomizing can also be used in addition to any other channel coding or modulation scheme. The error-correcting codes of most data recorders are designed to correct a combination of uncorrelated random and burst errors. A large number of random errors will reduce the ability of the system to correct bursts. Most group codes display a phenomenon known as pattern sensitivity, in that not all of the channel-bit groups are precisely DC free, and some of them are asymmetric, resulting in varying amounts of peak shift. In audio recorders, the complexity of the waveform ensures that a wide variety of codes are recorded. However, in computer data, it is possible to encounter lists, tables and arrays where the same byte may be repeated. The same may occur in digital video where flat image areas are to be recorded. In some cases this will select one of the less optimal channel patterns regularly, and the increase in peak shift will reduce the immunity of the system to noise.

This can be overcome by subjecting the data to a randomizing process before recording. This serves to decorrelate adjacent symbols and restores the error rate to that measured with random data. On replay, the same pseudo-random sequence must be generated in synchronism with the symbols off tape in order to recreate the original data. The technique is used in, for example, the D-3/D-5 digital VTR formats and in DDS (the data storage version of RDAT).

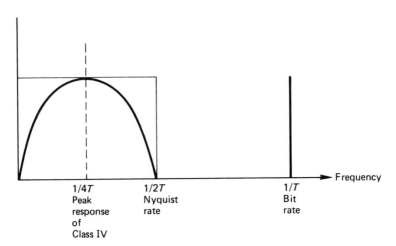

Figure 4.26 Class IV response has spectral nulls at DC and the Nyquist rate, giving a noise advantage, since magnetic replay signal is weak at both frequencies in a high-density channel.

4.18 Partial response and Viterbi detection

It has been stated that a magnetic head acts as a transversal filter, because it has two poles. In addition the output is differentiated, so that the head may be thought of as a $(1 - D)$ impulse response system, where D is the delay which is a function of the tape speed and gap size. It is this delay which results in intersymbol interference. Conventional equalizers attempt to oppose this effect, and succeed in raising the noise level in the process of making the frequency response linear. Figure 4.26 shows that the frequency response necessary to pass data with insignificant peak shift is a bandwidth of half the bit rate, which is the Nyquist rate. In Class IV partial response, the frequency response of the system is made to have nulls at DC and at the Nyquist rate. Such a frequency response is particularly advantageous for rotary-head recorders as it is DC free and the

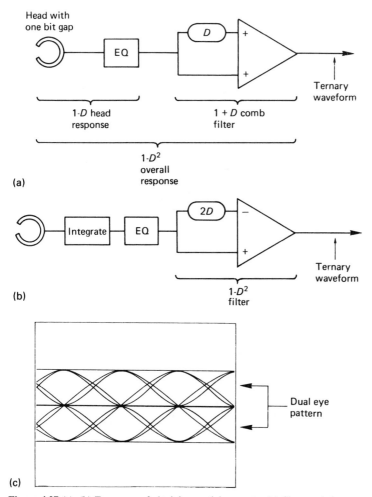

(a)

(b)

(c)

Figure 4.27 (a), (b) Two ways of obtaining partial response. (c) Characteristic eye pattern of ternary signal.

low-frequency content is minimal, hence the use in Digital Betacam. The required response is achieved by an overall impulse response of $(1 - D^2)$, where D is now the bit period. There are a number of ways in which this can be done.

If the head gap is made equal to one bit, the $(1 - D)$ head response may be converted to the desired response by the use of a $(1 + D)$ filter, as in Figure 4.27(a).[18] Alternatively, a head of unspecified gapwidth may be connected to an integrator, and equalized flat to reproduce the record current waveform before being fed to a $(1 - D^2)$ filter as in Figure 4.27(b).[19]

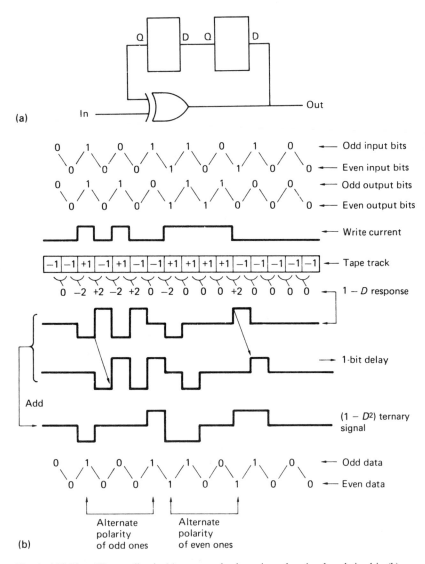

Figure 4.28 Class IV precoding in (a) causes redundancy in replay signal as derived in (b).

The result of both of these techniques is a ternary signal. The eye pattern has two sets of eyes, as in Figure 4.27(c).[20] When slicing such a signal, a smaller amount of noise will cause an error than in the binary case.

The treatment of the signal thus far represents an equalization technique, and not a channel code. However, to take full advantage of Class IV partial response, suitable precoding is necessary prior to recording, which does then constitute a channel-coding technique. This precoding is shown in Figure 4.28(a). Data are added modulo-2 to themselves with a two-bit delay. The effect of this precoding is that the outer levels of the ternary signals, which represent data ones, alternate in polarity on all odd bits and on all even bits. This is because the precoder acts like two interleaved one-bit delay circuits, as in Figure 4.28(b). As this alternation of polarity is a form of redundancy, it can be used to recover the 3 dB SNR loss encountered in slicing a ternary eye pattern. Viterbi decoding[21] can be used for this purpose. In Viterbi decoding, each channel bit is not sliced individually; the slicing decision is made in the context of adjacent decisions. Figure 4.29 shows a replay waveform which is so noisy that, at the decision point, the signal voltage crosses the centre of the eye, and the slicer alone cannot tell whether the correct decision is an inner or an outer level. In this case, the decoder essentially allows both decisions to stand, in order to see what happens. A symbol representing indecision is output. It will be seen from the figure that as subsequent bits are received, one of these decisions will result in an absurd situation, which indicates that the other decision was the right one. The decoder can then locate the undecided symbol and set it to the correct value.

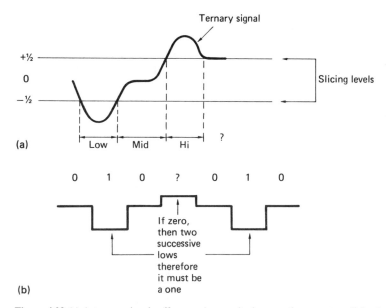

Figure 4.29 (a) A ternary signal suffers a noise penalty because there are two slicing levels. (b) The redundancy is used to determine the bit value in the presence of noise. Here the pulse height has been reduced to make it ambiguous 1/0, but only 1 is valid as zero violates the redundancy rules.

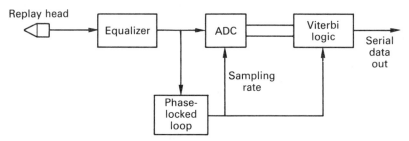

Figure 4.30 A Viterbi decoder is implemented in the digital domain by sampling the replay waveform with a clock locked to the embedded clock of the channel code.

Viterbi decoding requires more information about the signal voltage than a simple binary slicer can discern. Figure 4.30 shows that the replay waveform is sampled and quantized so that it can be processed in digital logic. The sampling rate is obtained from the embedded clock content of the replay waveform. The digital Viterbi processing logic must be able to operate at high speed to handle serial signals from a DVTR head. Its application in Digital Betacam is eased somewhat by the adoption of data reduction which reduces the data rate at the heads by a factor of two.

Clearly a ternary signal having a dual eye pattern is more sensitive than a binary signal, and it is important to keep the maximum run length T_{max} small in order to have accurate AGC. The use of pseudo-random coding along with partial response equalization and precoding is a logical combination.[22] There is then considerable overlap between the channel code and the error-correction system. Viterbi decoding is primarily applicable to channels with random errors due to Gaussian statistics, and such channels cannot cope with burst errors. In a head-noise-limited system, however, the use of a Viterbi detector could increase the power of a separate burst error-correction system by relieving it of the need to correct random errors due to noise. The error-correction system could then concentrate on correcting burst errors unimpaired. This point will become clearer in Chapter 5.

4.19 Synchronizing

Once the PLL in the data separator has locked to the clock content of the transmission, a serial channel bit stream and a channel bit clock will emerge from the sampler. In a group code, it is essential to know where a group of channel bits begins in order to assemble groups for decoding to data bit groups. In a randomizing system it is equally vital to know at what point in the serial data stream the words or samples commence. In serial transmission and in recording, channel bit groups or randomized data words are sent one after the other, one bit at a time, with no spaces in between, so that although the designer knows that a data block contains, say, 128 bytes, the receiver simply finds 1024 bits in a row. If the exact position of the first bit is not known, then it is not possible to put all the bits in the right places in the right bytes; a process known as deserializing. The effect of sync slippage is devastating, because a one-bit disparity between the bit count and the bit stream will corrupt every symbol in the block.[23]

The synchronization of the data separator and the synchronization to the block format are two distinct problems, which are often solved by the same sync pattern. Deserializing requires a shift register which is fed with serial data and read out once per word. The sync detector is simply a set of logic gates which are arranged to recognize a specific pattern in the register. The sync pattern is either identical for every block or has a restricted number of versions and it will be recognized by the replay circuitry and used to reset the bit count through the block. Then by counting channel bits and dividing by the group size, groups can be deserialized and decoded to data groups. In a randomized system, the pseudo-random sequence generator is also reset. Then by counting derandomized bits from the sync pattern and dividing by the wordlength, the replay circuitry can deserialize the data words.

In digital audio the two's complement coding scheme is universal and traditionally no codes have been reserved for synchronizing; they are all available for sample values. It would, in any case, be impossible to reserve all ones or all zeros as these are in the centre of the range in two's complement. The same is true of computer data, in which all bit combinations must be recordable. Even if a specific code were excluded from the recorded data so it could be used for synchronizing, this cannot ensure that the same pattern cannot be falsely created at the junction between two allowable data words. Figure 4.31 shows how false synchronizing can occur due to concatenation. It is thus not generally practical to use a bit pattern which is a data code value in a simple synchronizing recognizer. An exception is in formats such as hard disks in which additional timing information is available from rotation sensors or address marks. These can be used to gate a sync pattern detector when a sync pattern is expected. Upon sync detection the detector is disabled to prevent false detections in the data block.

In run-length-limited codes false detection is not a problem. The sync pattern is no longer a data bit pattern but is a specific waveform. If the sync waveform contains run lengths which violate the normal coding limits, there is no way that these run lengths can occur in encoded data, nor any possibility that they will be interpreted as data. They can, however, be readily detected by the replay circuitry.

In a group code there are many more combinations of channel bits than there are combinations of data bits. Thus after all data bit patterns have been allocated

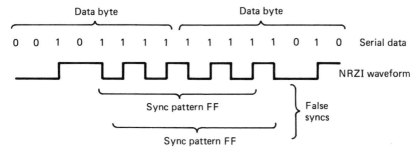

Figure 4.31 Concatenation of two words can result in the accidental generation of a word which is reserved for synchronizing.

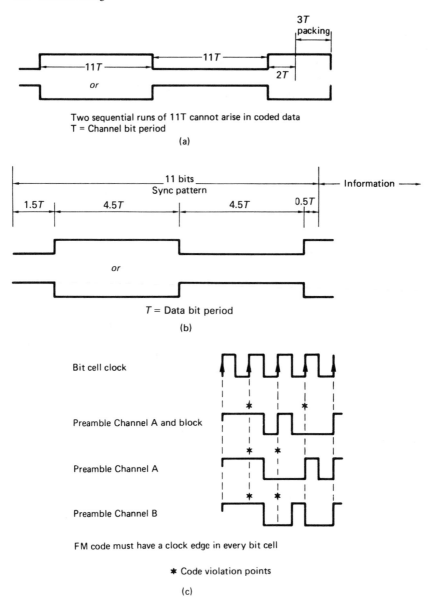

Figure 4.32 Sync patterns in various applications. In (a) the sync pattern of CD violates EFM coding rules, and is uniquely identifiable. In (b) the sync pattern of DASH stays within the run length of HDM-1. (c) The sync patterns of AES/EBU interconnect.

group patterns, there are still many unused group patterns which cannot occur in the data. With care, group patterns can be found which cannot occur due to the concatenation of any pair of groups representing data. These are then unique and can be used for synchronizing.

A similar approach is used in CD, CD-ROM and MiniDisc. Here the sync pattern does not violate a run-length limit, but consists of two sequential maximum run lengths of 11 channel bit periods each as in Figure 4.32. This pattern cannot occur in the data because the data symbols are only 14 channel bits long and the packing bit generator can be programmed to exclude accidental sync pattern generation due to concatenation.

The DASH format uses a similar system, also shown in Figure 4.32, where two sequential maximum run lengths of 4.5 bits are used. In both cases the use of maximum run lengths allows a low frequency to be generated which suffers the least losses. The use of two equal run lengths makes the sync pattern DC free.

References

1. MILLER, A., U.S Patent 3,108,261 (1960)
2. MALLINSON, J.C. and MILLER, J.W., Optimum codes for digital magnetic recording. *Radio and Electron. Eng.*, **47**, 172–176 (1977)
3. MILLER, J.W., DC-free encoding for data transmission system. US Patent 4,027,335 (1977)
4. TANG, D.T., Run-length-limited codes. *IEEE International Symposium on Information Theory* (1969)
5. COHN, M. and JACOBY, G., Run-length reduction of 3PM code via lookahead technique. *IEEE Trans. Magn.*, **18**, 1253–1255 (1982)
6. HORIGUCHI, T. and MORITA, K., On optimization of modulation codes in digital recording. *IEEE Trans. Magn.*, **12**, 740–742 (1976)
7. FRANASZEK, P.A., Sequence state methods for run-length limited coding. *IBM J. Res. Dev.*, **14**, 376–383 (1970)
8. JACOBY, G.V. and KOST, R., Binary two-thirds-rate code with full word lookahead. *IEEE Trans. Magn.*, **20**, 709–714 (1984)
9. JACOBY, G.V., A new lookahead code for increased data density. *IEEE Trans. Magn.*, **13**, 1202–1204 (1977)
10. FRANASZEK, P.A., U.S. Patent 3,689,899 (1972)
11. FUKUDA, S., KOJIMA, Y., SHIMPUKU, Y. and ODAKA, K., 8/10 modulation codes for digital magnetic recording. *IEEE Trans. Magn.*, **MAG-22**, 1194–1196 (1986)
12. UEHARA, T., NAKAYAMA, T., MINAGUCHI, H., SHIBAYA, H., SEKIGUCHI, T. and OBA, Y., A new 8–14 modulation and its application to small format VTR. *SMPTE Tech. Conf.* (1989)
13. OGAWA, H. and SCHOUHAMER IMMINK, K.A., EFM – the modulation method for the Compact Disc digital audio system. In *Digital Audio*, ed. B. Blesser, B. Locanthi and T.G. Stockham Jr., p. 117 New York: Audio Engineering Society (1982)
14. SCHOUHAMER IMMINK, K.A. and GROSS, U., Optimization of low frequency properties of eight-to-fourteen modulation. *Radio Electron. Eng.*, **53**, 63–66 (1983)
15. DOI, T.T., Channel codings for digital audio recordings. *J. Audio Eng. Soc.*, **31**, 224–238 (1983)
16. ANON., PD format for stationary head type 2-channel digital audio recorder. Mitsubishi, January (1986)
17. SCHOUHAMER IMMINK, K.A., Graceful degradation of digital audio transmission systems. Presented at 82nd Audio Engineering Society Convention (London, 1987), preprint 2434(C-3)
18. YOKOYAMA, K., Digital video tape recorder. *NHK Technical Monograph*, No. 31, March (1982)
19. COLEMAN, C.H., *et al.*, High data rate magnetic recording in a single channel. *J. IERE*, **55**, 229–236 (1985)
20. KOBAYASHI, H., Application of partial response channel coding to magnetic recording systems. *IBM J. Res. Dev.*, **14**, 368–375 (1970)
21. FORNEY, G.D. JR., The Viterbi algorithm. *Proc. IEEE*, **61**, 268–278 (1973)
22. WOOD, R.W. and PETERSEN, D.A., Viterbi detection of Class IV partial response on a magnetic recording channel. *IEEE Trans. Commun.*, **34**, 454–461 (1968)
23. GRIFFITHS, F.A., A digital audio recording system. Presented at 65th Audio Engineering Society Convention (London, 1980), preprint 1580(C1)

Chapter 5

Error correction

The subject of error correction is almost always described in mathematical terms by specialists for the benefit of other specialists. Such mathematical approaches are quite inappropriate for a proper understanding of the concepts of error correction and only become necessary to analyse the quantitative behaviour of a system. The description below will use the minimum possible amount of mathematics, and it will then be seen that error correction is, in fact, quite straightforward.

5.1 Sensitivity of message to error

Before attempting to specify any piece of equipment, it is necessary to quantify the problems to be overcome and how effectively they need to be overcome. For a digital recording system the causes of errors must be studied to quantify the problem, and the sensitivity of the destination to errors must be assessed. In audio and video the sensitivity to errors must be subjective. In PCM, the effect of a single bit in error depends upon the significance of the bit. If the least significant bit of a sample is wrong, the chances are that the effect will be lost in the noise. Conversely, if a high-order bit is in error, a massive transient will be added to the analog waveform.

The effect of errors in delta-modulated data is smaller as every bit has the same significance and the information content of each bit is lower. In some applications, a delta-modulated system can be used without error correction when this would be impossible with PCM.

Whilst the exact BER (bit error rate) which can be tolerated will depend on the application, digital audio is less tolerant of errors than digital video and more tolerant than computer data.

As might be expected, when data reduction is used, much of the redundancy is removed from the data and as a result sensitivity to bit errors inevitably increases. In all of these cases, if the maximum error rate which the destination can tolerate is likely to be exceeded by the unaided channel, some form of error handling will be necessary.

There are a number of terms which have idiomatic meanings in error correction. The raw BER is the error rate of the medium, whereas the residual or uncorrected BER is the rate at which the error-correction system fails to detect or miscorrects errors. In practical digital audio systems, the residual BER is negligibly small. If the error correction is turned off, the two figures become the same.

5.2 Error mechanisms

There are many different types of recording and transmission channels and consequently there will be many different mechanisms which may result in errors. As was the case for channel coding, although there are many different applications, the basic principles remain the same.

In magnetic recording, data can be corrupted by mechanical problems such as media dropout and poor tracking or head contact, or noise in media, replay circuits and heads. In optical recording, contamination of the medium interrupts the light beam. Warped disks and birefringent pressings cause defocusing. Inside equipment, data are conveyed on short wires and the noise environment is under the designer's control. With suitable design techniques, errors can be made effectively negligible. In MOS memories the datum is stored in a tiny charge well which acts as a capacitor (see Chapter 2) and natural radioactive decay can cause alpha particles which have enough energy to discharge a well, resulting in a single-bit error. This only happens once every few decades in a single chip, but when large numbers of chips are assembled in computer memories the probability of error rises to one every few minutes.

In Chapter 4 it was seen that when group codes are used, a single defect in a group changes the group symbol and may cause errors up to the size of the group. Single-bit errors are therefore less common in group-coded channels.

Irrespective of the cause, all of these mechanisms cause one of two effects. There are large isolated corruptions, called error bursts, where numerous bits are corrupted all together in an area which is otherwise error free, and there are random errors affecting single bits or symbols. Whatever the mechanism, the result will be that the received data will not be exactly the same as those sent. It is a tremendous advantage of digital audio that the discrete data bits will be each either right or wrong. A bit cannot be off-colour as it can only be interpreted as 0 or 1. Thus the subtle degradations of analog systems are absent from digital recording and transmission channels and will only be found in converters. Equally if a binary digit is known to be wrong, it is only necessary to invert its state and then it must be right and indistinguishable from its original value! Thus error correction itself is trivial; the hard part is working out *which* bits need correcting.

In Chapter 2 the Gaussian nature of noise probability was discussed. Some conclusions can be drawn from the Gaussian distribution of noise.[1] Firstly, it is not possible to make error-free digital recordings, because however high the signal-to-noise ratio of the recording, there is still a small but finite chance that the noise can exceed the signal. Measuring the signal-to-noise ratio of a channel establishes the noise power, which determines the width of the noise distribution curve relative to the signal amplitude. When in a binary system the noise amplitude exceeds the signal amplitude, a bit error will occur. Knowledge of the shape of the Gaussian curve allows the conversion of signal-to-noise ratio into bit error rate (BER). It can be predicted how many bits will fail due to noise in a given recording, but it is not possible to say *which* bits will be affected. Increasing the SNR of the channel will not eliminate errors; it just reduces their probability. The logical solution is to incorporate an error-correction system.

5.3 Basic error correction

Error correction works by adding some bits to the data which are calculated from the data. This creates an entity called a codeword which spans a greater length of time than one bit alone. The statistics of noise means that whilst one bit may be lost in a codeword, the loss of the rest of the codeword because of noise is highly improbable. As will be described later in this chapter, codewords are designed to be able to correct totally a finite number of corrupted bits. The greater the timespan over which the coding is performed, or, on a recording medium, the greater area over which the coding is performed, the greater will be the reliability achieved, although this does mean that an encoding delay will be experienced on recording, and a similar or greater decoding delay on reproduction.

Shannon[2] disclosed that a message can be sent to any desired degree of accuracy provided that it is spread over a sufficient timespan. Engineers have to compromise, because an infinite coding delay in the recovery of an error-free signal is not acceptable.

If error correction is necessary as a practical matter, it is then only a small step to put it to maximum use. All error correction depends on adding bits to the original message, and this of course increases the number of bits to be recorded, although it does not increase the information recorded. It might be imagined that error correction is going to reduce storage capacity, because space has to be found for all the extra bits. Nothing could be further from the truth. Once an error-correction system is used, the signal-to-noise ratio of the channel can be reduced, because the raised BER of the channel will be overcome by the error-correction system. Reduction of the SNR by 3 dB in a magnetic tape track can be achieved by halving the track width, provided that the system is not dominated by head or preamplifier noise. This doubles the recording density, making the storage of the additional bits needed for error correction a trivial matter. In short, error correction is not a nuisance to be tolerated; it is a vital tool needed to maximize the efficiency of recorders. Data recording would not be economically viable without it.

5.4 Error handling

Figure 5.1 shows the broad subdivisions of error handling. The first stage might be called error avoidance and includes such measures as creating bad block files on hard disks or using verified media. The data pass through the channel, which causes whatever corruptions it feels like. On receipt of the data the occurrence of errors is first detected, and this process must be extremely reliable, as it does not matter how effective the correction or how good the concealment algorithm, if it

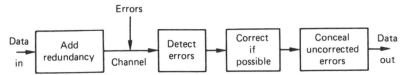

Figure 5.1 The basic stages of an error-correction system. Of these the most critical is the detection stage, since this controls the subsequent actions.

is not known that they are necessary! The detection of an error then results in a course of action being decided.

In most cases of digital audio or video replay, a retry is not possible because the data are required in real time. However, if a computer disk system is transferring to tape for the purpose of backup, real-time operation is not required. If the disk drive detects an error, a retry is easy as the disk is turning at several thousand rpm and will quickly re-present the data. An error due to a dust particle or external interference may not occur on the next revolution. Many magnetic tape systems have *read after write*. During recording, offtape data are immediately checked for errors. If an error is detected, the tape will abort the recording, reverse to the beginning of the current block and erase it. The data from that block are then recorded further down the tape. This is the recording equivalent of a retransmission in a communications system.

5.5 Concealment by interpolation

There are some practical differences between data recording for audio and the computer data recording application. Although audio and video recorders seldom have time for retries, they have the advantage that there is a certain amount of redundancy in the information conveyed. In such systems, if an error cannot be corrected, then it can be concealed. If a sample is lost, it is possible to obtain an approximation to it by interpolating between the samples before and after the missing one. Momentary interpolations are not serious, but sustained use of interpolation can result in aliasing if high frequencies are present in the recording. Clearly concealment of any kind cannot be used with computer data.

If there is too much corruption for concealment, the only course in audio is to mute, as large numbers of uncorrected errors reaching the analog domain cause noise which can be of high level.

In general, if use is to be made of concealment on replay, the data must generally be reordered or shuffled prior to recording. To take a simple example, odd-numbered samples are recorded in a different area of the medium from even-numbered samples. On playback, if a gross error occurs on the tape, depending on its position, the result will be either corrupted odd samples or corrupted even samples, but it is most unlikely that both will be lost. Interpolation is then possible if the power of the correction system is exceeded.

It should be stressed that corrected data are indistinguishable from the original and thus there can be no audible artifacts. In contrast, concealment is only an approximation to the original information and could be audible. In practical equipment, concealment occurs infrequently unless there is a defect requiring attention.

5.6 Parity

The error-detection and error-correction processes are closely related and will be dealt with together here. The actual correction of an error is simplified tremendously by the adoption of binary. As there are only two symbols, 0 and 1, it is enough to know that a symbol is wrong, and the correct value is obvious. Figure 5.2 shows a minimal circuit required for correction once the bit in error has been identified. The XOR (exclusive OR) gate shows up extensively in error correction and the figure also shows the truth table. One way of remembering the

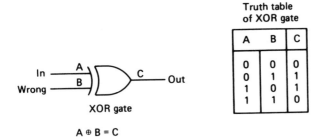

Figure 5.2 Once the position of the error is identified, the correction process in binary is easy.

characteristics of this useful device is that there will be an output when the inputs are different. Inspection of the truth table will show that there is an even number of ones in each row (zero is an even number) and so the device could also be called an even parity gate. The XOR gate is also an adder in modulo-2 (see Chapter 2).

Parity is a fundamental concept in error detection. In Figure 5.3, the example is given of a 4 bit data word which is to be protected. If an extra bit is added to the word which is calculated in such a way that the total number of ones in the 5 bit word is even, this property can be tested on receipt. The generation of the parity bit in Figure 5.3 can be performed by a number of the ubiquitous XOR gates configured into what is known as a parity tree. In the figure, if a bit is corrupted, the received message will be seen no longer to have an even number of ones. If two bits are corrupted, the failure will be undetected. This example can be used to introduce much of the terminology of error correction. The extra bit added to the message carries no information of its own, since it is calculated from the other bits. It is therefore called a *redundant* bit. The addition of the redundant bit gives the message a special property, i.e. the number of ones is even. A message having some special property *irrespective of the actual data content* is called a *codeword*. All error correction relies on adding redundancy to real data to form codewords for transmission. If any corruption occurs, the intention is that the received message will not have the special property; in other words, if the received message is not a codeword there has definitely been an error. The receiver can check for the special property without any prior knowledge of the data content. Thus the same check can be made on all received data. If the received message is a codeword, there probably has not been an error. The word 'probably' must be used because the figure shows that two bits in error will cause the received message to be a codeword, which cannot be discerned from an error-free message. If it is known that generally the only failure mechanism in the channel in question is loss of a single bit, it is *assumed* that receipt of a codeword means that there has been no error. If there is a probability of two error bits, that becomes very nearly the probability of failing to detect an error, since all odd numbers of errors will be detected, and a 4 bit error is much less likely. It is paramount in all error-correction systems that the protection used should be appropriate for the probability of errors to be encountered. An inadequate error-correction system is actually worse than not having any correction. Error correction works by trading probabilities. Error-free performance with a certain error rate is achieved at the expense of performance at higher error rates. Figure 5.4 shows the effect of an error-correction system on the residual BER for a given raw BER. It will be seen that there is a characteristic knee in the graph.

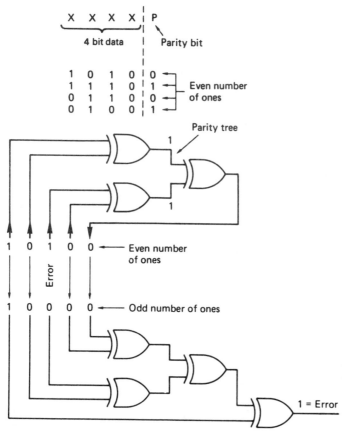

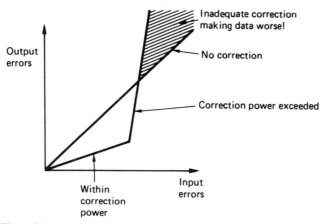

Figure 5.3 Parity checking adds up the number of ones in a word using, in this example, parity trees. One error bit and odd numbers of errors are detected. Even numbers of errors cannot be detected.

Figure 5.4 An error-correction system can only reduce errors at normal error rates at the expense of increasing errors at higher rates. It is most important to keep a system working to the left of the knee in the graph.

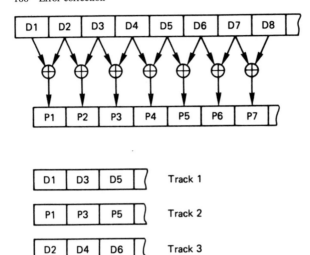

(a)

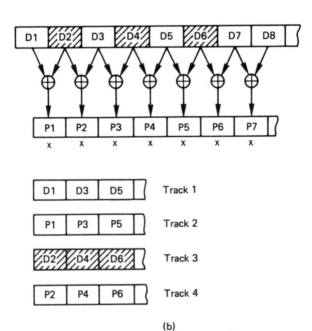

(b)

Figure 5.5 In the Wyner–Ash coding illustrated here, there is 100% overhead due to the additional parity symbols. The data and parity are distributed over the tape tracks, as shown in (a). In (b) a burst error in a data track causes continuous parity errors as shown, and correction can be performed. For example, D2 = D1 $\oplus$ P1, etc. In (c) a burst error in a parity track causes alternate parity errors, which can be ignored.

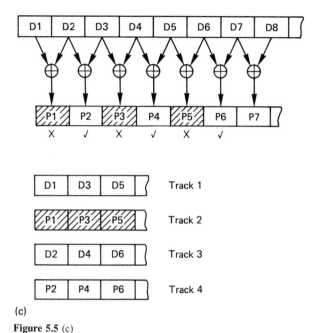

(c)

Figure 5.5 (c)

If the expected raw BER has been misjudged, the consequences can be disastrous. Another result demonstrated by the example is that we can only guarantee to detect the same number of bits in error as there are redundant bits.

5.7 Wyner–Ash code

Despite its simplicity, the principle of parity can be used to make an effective audio error-correcting scheme. Even though the use of parity can only detect errors, correction is still possible if a suitable strategy is used. In the Wyner–Ash code employed in some early BBC recorders,[3] four tape tracks were required to carry one audio channel. This reduced the linear tape speed and the impact of dropouts on a given audio channel. Figure 5.5(a) shows that alternate tracks carried data and parity bits computed from running pairs of data bits. With this mechanism, data track erors always cause an even number of parity failures. Figure 5.5(b) shows how such an error can be corrected. Parity track errors, however, cause single parity failures as shown in Figure 5.5(c). These can be neglected. Whilst successful, this code requires an overhead of 100% which raises tape consumption. Codes which need less overhead are inevitably more complex.

5.8 Block and convolutional codes

Figure 5.6(a) shows an alternative strategy to the Wyner–Ash code which is known as a crossword code, or product code. The data are formed into a two-dimensional array, in which each location can be a single bit or a multibit symbol.

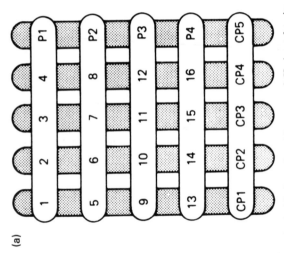

Figure 5.6 A block code is shown in (a). Each location in the block can be a bit or a word. Horizontal parity checks are made by adding P1, P2, etc., and cross-parity or vertical checks are made by adding CP1, CP2, etc. Any symbol in error will be at the intersection of the two failing codewords. In (b) a convolutional coder is shown. Symbols entering are subject to different delays which result in the codewords in (c) being calculated. These have a vertical part and a diagonal part. A symbol in error will be at the intersection of the diagonal part of one code and the vertical part of another.

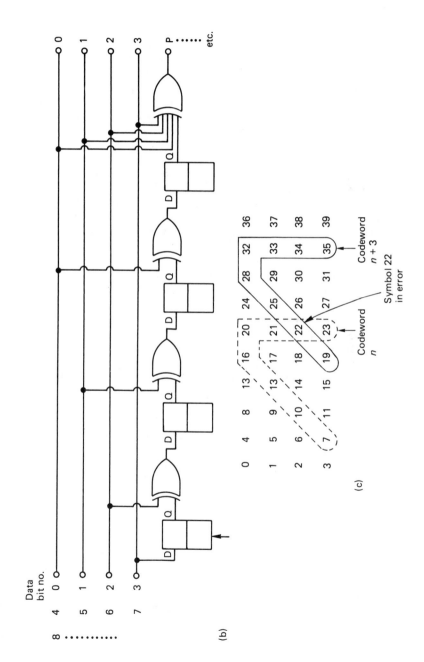

(b)

(c)

Parity is then generated on both rows and columns. If a single bit or symbol fails, one row parity check and one column parity check will fail, and the failure can be located at the intersection of the two failing checks. Although two symbols in error confuse this simple scheme, using more complex coding in a two-dimensional structure is very powerful, and further examples will be given throughout this chapter.

The example of Figure 5.6(a) assembles the data to be coded into a block of finite size and then each codeword is calculated by taking different sets of symbols. This should be contrasted with the operation of the circuit of Figure 5.6(b). Here the data are not in a block, but form an endless stream. A shift register allows four symbols to be available simultaneously to the encoder. The action of the encoder depends upon the delays. When symbol 3 emerges from the first delay, it will be added (modulo-2) to symbol 6. When this sum emerges from the second delay, it will be added to symbol 9 and so on. The codeword produced is shown in Figure 5.6(c) where it will be seen to be bent such that it has a vertical section and a diagonal section. Four symbols later the next codeword will be created one column further over in the data.

This is a convolutional code because the coder always takes parity on the same pattern of symbols which is convolved with the data stream on an endless basis. Figure 5.6(c) also shows that if an error occurs, it can be located because it will cause parity errors in two codewords. The error will be on the diagonal part of one codeword and on the vertical part of the other so that it can be located uniquely at the intersection and corrected by parity.

Comparison with the block code of Figure 5.6(a) will show that the convolutional code needs less redundancy for the same single-symbol location and correction performance as only a single redundant symbol is required for every four data symbols. Convolutional codes are computed on an endless basis which makes them inconvenient in recording applications where editing is anticipated. Here the block code is more appropriate as it allows edit gaps to be created between codes. In the case of uncorrectable errors, the convolutional principle causes the syndromes to be affected for some time afterwards and results in miscorrections of symbols which were not actually in error. This is called error propagation and is a characteristic of convolutional codes. Recording media tend to produce somewhat variant error statistics because media defects and mechanical problems cause errors which do not fit the classical additive noise channel. Convolutional codes can easily be taken beyond their correcting power if used with real recording media.

Convolutional codes are not restricted to the simple parity example given here, but can be used in conjuction with more sophisticated redundancy techniques such as the Reed–Solomon codes.

5.9 Hamming code

In a one-dimensional code, the position of the failing bit can be determined by using more parity checks. In Figure 5.7, the four data bits have been used to compute three redundancy bits, making a 7 bit codeword. The four data bits are examined in turn, and each bit which is a one will cause the corresponding row of a generator matrix to be added to an exclusive OR sum. For example, if the data were 1001, the top and bottom rows of the matrix would be XORed. The matrix used is known as an identity matrix, because the data bits in the codeword

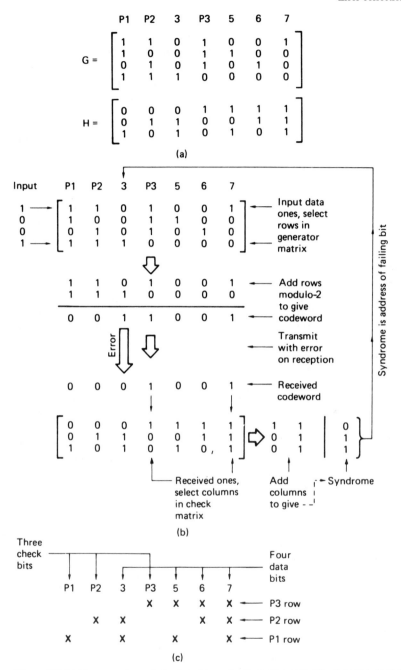

Figure 5.7 (a) The generator and check matrices of a Hamming code. The data and check bits are arranged as shown because this causes the syndrome to be the binary address of the failing bit. (b) An example of Hamming-code generation and error correction. (c) Another way of looking at Hamming code is to say that the rows of crosses in this chart are calculated to have even parity. If bit 3 fails, parity check P3 is not affected, but parity checks P1 and P2 both include bit 3 and will fail.

are identical to the data bits to be conveyed. This is useful because the original data can be stored unmodified, and the check bits are simply attached to the end to make a so-called systematic codeword. Almost all digital recording equipment uses systematic codes. The way in which the redundancy bits are calculated is simply that they do not all use every data bit. If a data bit has not been included in a parity check, it can fail without affecting the outcome of that check. The position of the error is deduced from the pattern of successful and unsuccessful checks in the check matrix. This pattern is known as a syndrome.

In the figure the example of a failing bit is given. Bit 3 fails, and because this bit is included in only two of the checks, there are two ones in the failure pattern, 011. As some care was taken in designing the matrix pattern for the generation of the check bits, the syndrome, 011, is the address of the failing bit. This is the fundamental feature of the Hamming codes due to Richard Hamming.[4] The performance of this 7 bit codeword can be assessed. In seven bits there can be 128 combinations, but in four data bits there are only sixteen combinations. Thus out of 128 possible received messages, only sixteen will be codewords, so if the message is completely trashed by a gross corruption, it will still be possible to detect that this has happened 112 times out of 127, as in these cases the syndrome will be non-zero (the 128th case is the correct data). There is thus only a probability of detecting that all of the message is corrupt. In an idle moment it is possible to work out, in a similar way, the number of false codewords which can result from different numbers of bits being assumed to have failed. For less than three bits, the failure will always be detected, because there are three check bits. Returning to the example, if two bits fail, there will be a non-zero syndrome, but if this is used to point to a bit in error, a miscorrection will result. From these results can be deduced another important feature of error codes. The power of detection is always greater than the power of correction, which is also fortunate, since if the correcting power is exceeded by an error it will at least be a known problem, and steps can be taken to prevent any undesirable consequences.

The efficiency of the example given is not very high because three check bits are needed for every four data bits. Since the failing bit is located with a binary-split mechanism, it is possible to double the code length by adding a single extra check bit. Thus with 4 bit syndromes there are fifteen non-zero codes and so the codeword will be 15 bits long; four bits are redundant and eleven are data. Using five bits of redundancy, the code can be 31 bits long and contain 26 data bits. Thus, provided that the number of errors to be detected stays the same, it is more efficient to use long codewords. Error-correcting memories use typically four or eight data bytes plus redundancy. A drawback of long codes is that if it is desired to change a single memory byte it is necessary to read the entire codeword, modify the desired data byte and re-encode – the so-called read–modify–write process.

The Hamming code shown is limited to single-bit correction, but by addition of another bit of redundancy can be made to correct 1 bit and detect 2 bit errors. This is ideal for error-correcting MOS memories where the SECDED (single-error correcting, double-error detecting) characteristic matches the type of failures experienced.

The correction of one bit is of little use in the presence of burst errors, but a Hamming code can be made to correct burst errors by using interleaving. Figure 5.8 shows that if several codewords are calculated beforehand and woven together as shown before they are sent down the channel, then a burst of errors

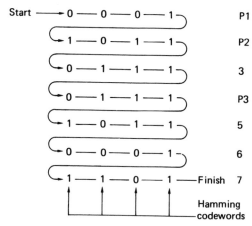

Figure 5.8 The vertical columns of this diagram are all codewords generated by the matrix of Figure 5.7, which can correct a single-bit error. If these words are recorded in the order shown, a burst error of up to 4 bits will result in one single-bit error in each codeword, which is correctable. Interleave requires memory, and causes delay. De-interleave requires the same.

which corrupts several bits will become a number of single-bit errors in separate codewords upon de-interleaving.

Interleaving is used extensively in digital recording and transmission, and will be discussed in greater detail later in this chapter.

5.10 Hamming distance

It is useful at this point to introduce the concept of Hamming distance. It is not a physical distance but is a specific measure of the difference between two binary numbers. Hamming distance is defined in the general case as the number of bit positions in which a pair of words differ. The Hamming distance of a code is defined as the minimum number of bits that must be changed in any codeword in order to turn it into another codeword. This is an important yardstick because if errors convert one codeword into another, it will have the special characteristic of the code and so the corruption will not even be detected.

Figure 5.9 shows Hamming distance diagrammatically. A 3 bit codeword is used with two data bits and one parity bit. With three bits, a received code could have eight combinations, but only four of these will be codewords. The valid codewords are shown in the centre of each of the disks, and these will be seen to be identical to the rows of the truth table in Figure 5.2. At the perimeter of the disks are shown the received words which would result from a single-bit error, i.e. they have a Hamming distance of 1 from codewords. It will be seen that the same received word (on the vertical bars) can be obtained from a different single-bit corruption of any three codewords. It is thus not possible to tell which codeword was corrupted, so although all single-bit errors can be detected, correction is not possible. This diagram should be compared with that of Figure 5.10, which is a Venn diagram where there is a set in which the MSB is 1 (upper circle), a set in which the middle bit is 1 (lower left circle) and a set in which the LSB is 1 (lower right circle). Note that in crossing any boundary only one bit

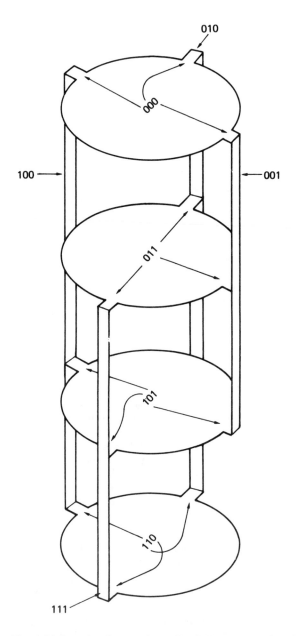

Figure 5.9 Hamming distance of two. The disk centres contain codewords. Corrupting each bit in turn produces the distance 1 values on the vertical members. In order to change one codeword to another, 2 bits must be changed, so the code has a Hamming distance of two.

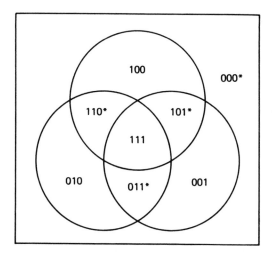

Figure 5.10 Venn diagram shows a 1 bit change crossing any boundary which is a Hamming distance of 1. Compare with Figure 5.9. Codewords marked *.

changes, and so each boundary represents a Hamming distance change of 1. The four codewords of Figure 5.9 are repeated here, and it will be seen that single-bit errors in any codeword produce a non-codeword, and so single-bit errors are always detectable.

Correction is possible if the number of non-codewords is increased by increasing the number of redundant bits. This means that it is possible to spread out the actual codewords in Hamming distance terms.

Figure 5.11(a) shows a distance 2 code, where there is only one redundancy bit, and so half of the possible words will be codewords. There will be non-codewords at distance 1 which can be produced by altering a single bit in either of two codewords. In this case, it is not possible to tell what the original codeword was in the case of a single-bit error.

Figure 5.11(b) shows a distance 3 code, where there will now be at least two non-codewords between codewords. If a single-bit error occurs in a codeword, the resulting non-codeword will be at distance 1 from the original codeword. This same non-codeword could also have been produced by changing *two* bits in a different codeword. If it is known that the failure mechanism is a single bit, it can be *assumed* that the original codeword was the one which is closest in Hamming distance to the received bit pattern, and so correction is possible. If, however, our assumption about the error mechanism proved to be wrong, and in fact a 2 bit error had occurred, this assumption would take us to the wrong codeword, turning the event into a 3 bit error. This is an illustration of the knee in the graph of Figure 5.4, where if the power of the code is exceeded it makes things worse.

Figure 5.11(c) shows a distance 4 code. There are now three non-codewords between codewords, and clearly single-bit errors can still be corrected by choosing the nearest codeword. Double-bit errors will be detected, because they result in non-codewords equidistant in Hamming terms from codewords, but it is not possible to determine what the original codeword was.

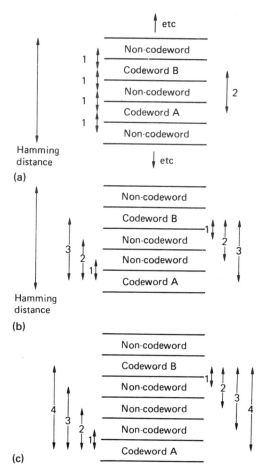

Figure 5.11 (a) Distance 2 code; non-codewords are at distance 1 from two possible codewords so it cannot be deduced what the correct one is. (b) Distance 3 code; non-codewords which have *single-bit errors* can be attributed to the nearest codeword. Breaks down in presence of double-bit errors. (c) Distance 4 code; non-codewords which have single-bit errors can be attributed to the nearest codeword, AND double-bit errors form *different* non-codewords, and can thus be detected but not corrected.

5.11 Cyclic codes

The parallel implementation of a Hamming code can be made very fast using parity trees, which is ideal for memory applications where access time is increased by the correction process. However, in digital audio recording applications, the data are stored serially on a track, and it is desirable to use relatively large data blocks to reduce the amount of the medium devoted to preambles, addressing and synchronizing. Where large data blocks are to be handled, the use of a lookup table or tree has to be abandoned because it would become impossibly large. The principle of codewords having a special characteristic will still be employed, but they will be generated and checked algorithmically by equations. The syndrome will then be converted to the bit(s) in error not by looking them up, but by solving an equation.

Where data can be accessed serially, simpler circuitry can be used because the same gate will be used for many XOR operations. Unfortunately the reduction in component count is only paralleled by an increase in the difficulty of explaining what takes place.

The circuit of Figure 5.12 is a kind of shift register, but with a particular feedback arrangement which leads it to be known as a twisted-ring counter. If seven message bits A–G are applied serially to this circuit, and each one of them is clocked, the outcome can be followed in the diagram. As bit A is presented and the system is clocked, bit A will enter the left-hand latch. When bits B and C are presented, A moves across to the right. Both XOR gates will have A on the upper input from the right-hand latch, the left one has D on the lower input and the right one has B on the lower input. When clocked, the left latch will thus be loaded with the XOR of A and D, and the right one with the XOR of A and B. The remainder of the sequence can be followed, bearing in mind that when the same term appears on both inputs of an XOR gate, it goes out, as the exclusive OR of something with itself is nothing. At the end of the process, the latches contain three different expressions. Essentially, the circuit makes three parity checks through the message, leaving the result of each in the three stages of the register. In the figure, these expressions have been used to draw up a check matrix. The significance of these steps can now be explained. The bits A B C and D are four data bits, and

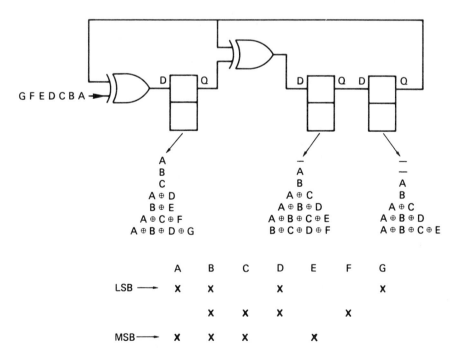

Figure 5.12 When seven successive bits A–G are clocked into this circuit, the contents of the three latches are shown for each clock. The final result is a parity-check matrix.

the bits E F and G are redundancy. When the redundancy is calculated, bit E is chosen so that there is an even number of ones in bits A B C and E; bit F is chosen such that the same applies to bits B C D and F, and similarly for bit G. Thus the four data bits and the three check bits form a 7 bit codeword. If there is no error in the codeword when it is fed into the circuit shown, the result of each of the three parity checks will be zero and every stage of the shift register will be cleared. As the register has eight possible states, and one of them is the error-free condition, then there are seven remaining states, hence the 7 bit codeword. If a bit in the codeword is corrupted, there will be a non-zero result. For example, if bit D fails, the check on bits A B D and G will fail, and a 1 will appear in the left-hand latch. The check on bits B C D F will also fail, and the centre latch will set. The check on bits A B C E will not fail, because D is not involved in it, making the right-hand bit zero. There will be a syndrome of 110 in the register, and this will be seen from the check matrix to correspond to an error in bit D. Whichever bit fails, there will be a different 3 bit syndrome which uniquely identifies the failed bit. As there are only three latches, there can be eight different syndromes. One of these is zero, which is the error-free condition, and so there are seven remaining error syndromes. The length of the codeword cannot exceed 7 bits, or there would not be enough syndromes to correct all of the bits. This can also be made to tie in with the generation of the check matrix. If fourteen bits, A to N, were fed into the circuit shown, the result would be that the check matrix repeated twice, and if a syndrome of 101 were to result, it could not be determined whether bit D or bit K failed. Because the check repeats every seven bits, the code is said to be a cyclic redundancy check (CRC) code.

In Figure 5.7 an example of a Hamming code was given. Comparison of the check matrix of Figure 5.12 with that of Figure 5.7 will show that the only difference is the order of the matrix columns. The two different processes have thus achieved exactly the same results, and the performance of both must be identical. This is not true in general, but a very small cyclic code has been used for simplicity and to allow parallels to be seen. In practice CRC code blocks will be much longer than the blocks used in Hamming codes.

It has been seen that the circuit shown makes a matrix check on a received word to determine if there has been an error, but the same circuit can also be used to generate the check bits. To visualize how this is done, examine what happens if only the data bits A B C and D are known, and the check bits E F and G are set to zero. If this message, ABCD000, is fed into the circuit, the left-hand latch will afterwards contain the XOR of A B C and zero, which is of course what E should be. The centre latch will contain the XOR of B C D and zero, which is what F should be and so on. This process is not quite ideal, however, because it is necessary to wait for three clock periods after entering the data before the check bits are available. Where the data are simultaneously being recorded and fed into the encoder, the delay would prevent the check bits being easily added to the end of the data stream. This problem can be overcome by slightly modifying the encoder circuit as shown in Figure 5.13. By moving the position of the input to the right, the operation of the circuit is advanced so that the check bits are ready after only four clocks. The process can be followed in the diagram for the four data bits A B C and D. On the first clock, bit A enters the left two latches, whereas on the second clock, bit B will appear on the upper input of the left XOR gate, with bit A on the lower input, causing the centre latch to load the XOR of A and B and so on.

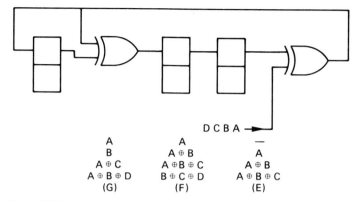

A	A	—
B	A ⊕ B	A
A ⊕ C	A ⊕ B ⊕ C	A ⊕ B
A ⊕ B ⊕ D	B ⊕ C ⊕ D	A ⊕ B ⊕ C
(G)	(F)	(E)

Figure 5.13 By moving the insertion point three places to the right, the calculation of the check bits is completed in only four clock periods and they can follow the data immediately. This is equivalent to premultiplying the data by x^3.

The way in which the cyclic codes work has been described in engineering terms, but it can be described mathematically if analysis is contemplated.

Just as the position of a decimal digit in a number determines the power of ten (whether that digit means one, ten or a hundred), the position of a binary digit determines the power of two (whether it means one, two or four). It is possible to rewrite a binary number so that it is expressed as a list of powers of two. For example, the binary number 1101 means $8 + 4 + 1$, and can be written:

$$2^3 + 2^2 + 2^0$$

In fact, much of the theory of error correction applies to symbols in number bases other than 2, so that the number can also be written more generally as

$$x^3 + x^2 + 1 \ (2^0 = 1)$$

which also looks much more impressive. This expression, containing as it does various powers, is of course a polynomial, and the circuit of Figure 5.12 which has been seen to construct a parity-check matrix on a codeword can also be described as calculating the remainder due to dividing the input by a polynomial using modulo-2 arithmetic. In modulo-2 there are no borrows or carries, and addition and subtraction are replaced by the XOR function, which makes hardware implementation very easy. In Figure 5.14 it will be seen that the circuit of Figure 5.12 actually divides the codeword by a polynomial which is:

$$x^3 + x + 1 \ \text{or} \ 1011$$

This can be deduced from the fact that the right-hand bit is fed into two lower-order stages of the register at once. Once all the bits of the message have been clocked in, the circuit contains the remainder. In mathematical terms, the special property of a codeword is that it is a polynomial which yields a remainder of zero when divided by the generating polynomial. The receiver will make this division, and the result should be zero in the error-free case. Thus the codeword itself disappears from the division. If an error has occurred it is considered that this is due to an error polynomial which has been added to the codeword polynomial.

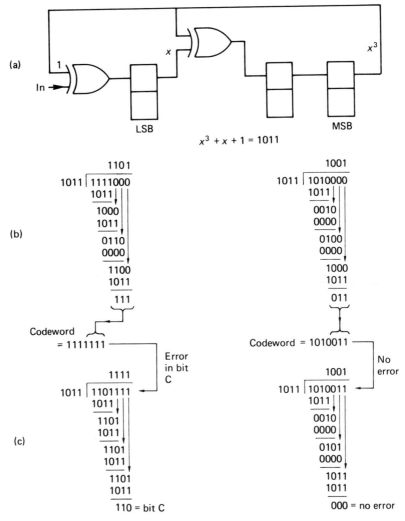

Figure 5.14 (a) Circuit of Figure 5.12 divides by $x^3 + x + 1$ to find remainder. In (b) this is used to calculate check bits. In (c) right, zero syndrome, no error.

If a codeword divided by the check polynomial is zero, a non-zero syndrome must represent the error polynomial divided by the check polynomial. Thus if the syndrome is multiplied by the check polynomial, the latter will be cancelled out and the result will be the error polynomial. If this is added modulo-2 to the received word, it will cancel out the error and leave the corrected data.

Some examples of modulo-2 division are given in Figure 5.14 which can be compared with the parallel computation of parity checks according to the matrix of Figure 5.12.

The process of generating the codeword from the original data can also be described mathematically. If a codeword has to give zero remainder when divided, it follows that the data can be converted to a codeword by adding the remainder when the data are divided. Generally speaking the remainder would have to be subtracted, but in modulo-2 there is no distinction. This process is also illustrated in Figure 5.14. The four data bits have three zeros placed on the right-hand end, to make the wordlength equal to that of a codeword, and this word is then divided by the polynomial to calculate the remainder. The remainder is added to the zero-extended data to form a codeword. The modified circuit of Figure 5.13 can be described as premultiplying the data by x^3 before dividing.

CRC codes are of primary importance for detecting errors, and several have been standardized for use in digital communications. The most common of these are:

$$x^{16} + x^{15} + x^2 + 1 \text{ (CRC-16)}$$

$$x^{16} + x^{12} + x^5 + 1 \text{ (CRC-CCITT)}$$

Figure 5.15 shows one implementation of cyclic codes in which the feedback register can be configured to work backwards if required. The desired polynomial is selected by a 3 bit control code. The code is implemented by switching in a particular feedback configuration stored in ROM. During recording or transmission, the serial data are clocked in whilst the control input CWE (check word enable) is held true. At the end of the serial data, this input is made false and this has the effect of disabling the feedback so that the device becomes a conventional

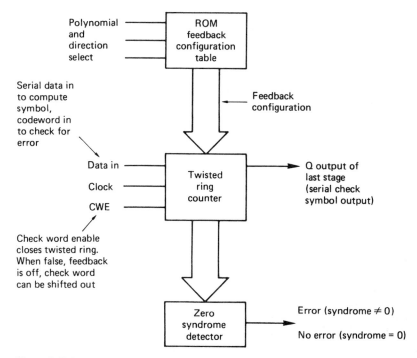

Figure 5.15 Simplified block of CRC chip which can implement several polynomials, and both generate and check redundancy.

shift register and the CRCC is clocked out of the Q output and appended to the data. On playback, the entire message is clocked into the device with CWE once more true. At the end, if the register contains all zeros, the message was a codeword. If not, there has been an error.

5.12 Punctured codes

The 16 bit cyclic codes have codewords of length $2^{16} - 1$ or 65 535 bits long. This may be too long for the application. Another problem with very long codes is that with a given raw BER, the longer the code, the more errors will occur in it. There may be enough errors to exceed the power of the code. The solution in both cases is to shorten or *puncture* the code. Figure 5.16 shows that in a punctured code, only the end of the codeword is used, and the data and

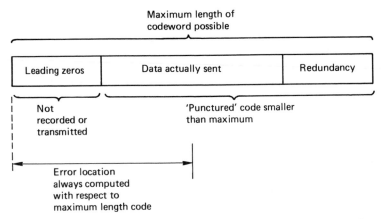

Figure 5.16 Codewords are often shortened, or punctured, which means that only the end of the codeword is actually transmitted. The only precaution to be taken when puncturing codes is that the computed position of an error will be from the beginning of the codeword, not from the beginning of the message.

redundancy are preceded by a string of zeros. It is not necessary to record these zeros, and, of course, errors cannot occur in them. Implementing a punctured code is easy. If a CRC generator starts with the register cleared and is fed with serial zeros: it will not change its state. Thus it is not necessary to provide the zeros, encoding can begin with the first data bit. In the same way, the leading zeros need not be provided during playback. The only precaution needed is that if a syndrome calculates the location of an error, this will be from the beginning of the codeword not from the beginning of the data. Where codes are used for detection only, this is of no consequence.

5.13 Applications of cyclic codes

The Sony PCM-1610/1630 CD mastering recorders use a 16 bit cyclic code for error detection. Figure 5.17 shows that in this system, two sets of three 16 bit audio samples have a CRCC added to form punctured codewords 64 bits long.

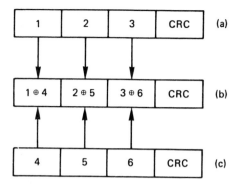

Figure 5.17 The simple crossword code of the PCM-1610/1630 format. Horizontal codewords are cyclic polynomials; vertical codewords are simple parity. Cyclic code detects errors and acts as erasure pointer for parity correction. For example, if word 2 fails, CRC (a) fails, and 1, 2 and 3 are all erased. The correct values are computed from (b) and (c) such that:

$$1 = (1 \oplus 4) \oplus 4$$
$$2 = (2 \oplus 5) \oplus 5$$
$$3 = (3 \oplus 6) \oplus 6$$

The system of Figure 5.15 is used to perform the calculation. Three parity words are formed by taking the XOR of the two sets of samples and a CRCC is added to this also. The three codewords are then recorded. If an error should occur, one of the cyclic codes will have a non-zero remainder, and *all* of the samples in that codeword are deemed to be in error. The samples can be restored by taking the XOR of the remaining two codewords. If the error is in the parity words, no action is necessary. There is 100% redundancy in this unit, but it is designed to work with an existing video cassette recorder whose bandwidth is predetermined and so in this application there is no penalty.

The CRCC simply detects errors and acts as a pointer to a further correction means. This technique is often referred to as correction by erasure. The failing data are set to zero, or erased, since in some correction schemes the erroneous data will interfere with the calculation of the correct values.

5.14 Burst correction

Figure 5.18 lists all of the possible codewords in the code of Figure 5.12. Examination will show that it is necessary to change at least three bits in one codeword before it can be made into another. Thus the code has a Hamming distance of three and cannot detect 3 bit errors. The single-bit error correction limit can also be deduced from the figure. In the example given, the codeword 0101100 suffers a single-bit error marked * which converts it to a non-codeword at a Hamming distance of 1. No other codeword can be turned into this word by a single-bit error; therefore the codeword which is the shortest Hamming distance away must be the correct one. The code can thus reliably correct single-bit errors. However, the codeword 0100111 can be made into the same failure word by a 2 bit error, also marked *, and in this case the original codeword cannot be found by selecting the one which is nearest in Hamming distance. A 2 bit error cannot be corrected and the system will miscorrect if it is attempted.

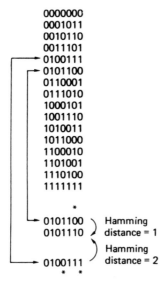

Figure 5.18 All possible codewords of $x^3 + x + 1$ are shown, and the fact that a double error in one codeword can produce the same pattern as a single error in another. Thus double errors cannot be corrected.

The concept of Hamming distance can be extended to explain how more than one bit can be corrected. In Figure 5.19 the example of two bits in error is given. If a codeword four bits long suffers a single-bit error, it could produce one of four different words. If it suffers a 2 bit error, it could produce one of $3 + 2 + 1$ different words as shown in the figure (the error bits are underlined). The total number of possible words of Hamming distance 1 or 2 from a 4 bit codeword is thus:

$$4 + 3 + 2 + 1 = 10$$

If the 2 bit error is to be correctable, no other codeword can be allowed to become one of this number of error patterns because of a 2 bit error of its own. Thus every codeword requires space for itself plus all possible error patterns of Hamming distance 2 or 1, which is eleven patterns in this example. Clearly there are only sixteen patterns available in a 4 bit code, and thus no data can be conveyed if 2 bit protection is necessary.

The number of different patterns possible in a word of n bits is:

$$1 + n + (n - 1) + (n - 2) + (n - 3) + \ldots$$

and this pattern range has to be shared between the ranges of each codeword without overlap. For example an 8 bit codeword could result in $1 + 8 + 7 + 6 + 5 + 4 + 3 + 2 + 1 = 37$ patterns.

As there are only 256 patterns in eight bits, it follows that only 256/37 pieces of information can be conveyed. The nearest integer below is six, and the nearest power of two below is four, which corresponds to two data bits and six check bits in the 8 bit word. The amount of redundancy necessary to correct *any* two bits in error is large, and as the number of bits to be corrected grows, the redundancy

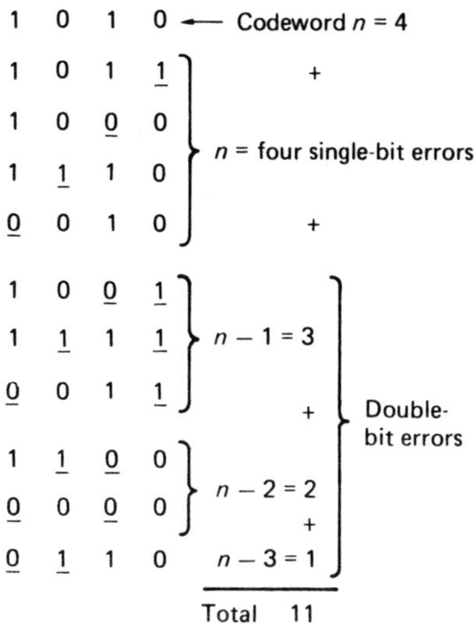

1 0 1 0 ◄── Codeword $n = 4$

```
1  0  1  1  ⎤      +
1  0  0  0  ⎥
           ⎬ n = four single-bit errors
1  1  1  0  ⎥
0  0  1  0  ⎦      +

1  0  0  1  ⎤
1  1  1  1  ⎬ n − 1 = 3
0  0  1  1  ⎦      +            Double-
                               bit errors
1  1  0  0  ⎤
           ⎬ n − 2 = 2
0  0  0  0  ⎦      +
0  1  1  0    n − 3 = 1
```

Total   11

Figure 5.19 Where double-bit errors occur, the number of patterns necessary is $(n - 1) + (n - 2) + (n - 3) + \ldots$. Total necessary is $1 + n + (n - 1) + (n - 2) + (n - 3) + \ldots$. Example here is of 4 bits, and all possible patterns up to a Hamming distance of 2 are shown (errors underlined).

necessary becomes enormous and impractical. A further problem is that the more redundancy is added, the greater the probability of an error in a codeword. Fortunately, in practice errors occur in bursts, as has already been described, and it is a happy consequence that the number of patterns that result from the corruption of a codeword by *adjacent* 2 bit errors is much smaller.

It can be deduced that the number of redundant bits necessary to correct a burst error is twice the number of bits in the burst for a perfect code. This is done by working out the number of received messages which could result from corruption of the codeword by bursts of from 1 bit up to the largest burst size allowed, and then making sure that there are enough redundant bits to allow that number of combinations in the received message.

Some codes, such as the Fire code due to Philip Fire,[5] are designed to correct single bursts, whereas later codes such as the B-adjacent code due to Bossen[6] could correct two bursts. The Reed–Solomon codes (Irving Reed and Gustave Solomon[7]) have the advantage that an arbitrary number of bursts can be corrected by choosing the appropriate amount of redundancy at the design stage.

5.15 Fire code

The operation of the Fire code will now be illustrated. Figure 5.20 shows a data block which has deliberately been made small for simplicity. The matrix for generating parity on the data is shown beneath. In each row of the matrix, the presence of a cross means that the data bit in that column has been included in a parity check. The five rows result in five parity bits which are appended to the data. The simple circuit needed to generate this check serially is also shown. The codeword corrupted by three errors is shown in (a). Certain of the parity checks

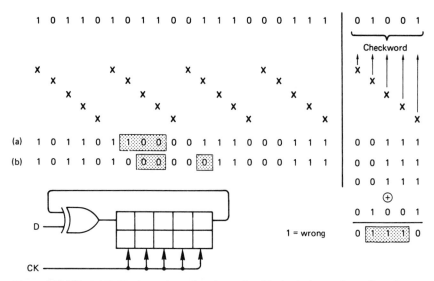

Figure 5.20 This matrix develops a burst-detecting code with circuit shown. On reading, the same encoding process is used, and the two checkwords are XOR-gated. Two examples of error bursts shown (a, b) give the same syndrome; this ambiguity is resolved by the technique of Figure 5.21.

will now fail, and the failure pattern is the syndrome as was the case for the Hamming code in Figure 5.7. However, (b) shows that an alternative error condition can give the same syndrome. This ambiguity is resolved in a manner which is fundamental to the operation of the Fire codes and which will be explained here.

The definition of a burst error of length b bits is that the first and last bits must be wrong, but the intervening bits may or may not be wrong. In the worst case, only the end bits of the burst are wrong. As a bit error results in a 1 in the syndrome, then in the worst case there will be $b - 2$ zeros between the ones. If the number of check bits used to correct a burst of length b is increased to $2b - 1$, then a burst of length b can be unambiguously defined by shifting the syndrome and looking for $b - 1$ successive zeros. Since the burst cannot contain more than $b - 2$ zeros, the $b - 1$ zeros must lie outside the burst. Figure 5.21 shows an example of the process and shows that the number of shifts necessary to put the $b - 1$ zeros at the left-hand side of the register is equal to the distance of the burst edge from the previous $n \times (2b - 1)$th bit boundary. The b right-hand bits will be the burst pattern, and if the received bits are inverted wherever a 1 appears in this pattern, correction will be achieved. Clearly if the burst exceeds b bits long, the $b - 1$ zeros might be found within it and miscorrection could occur.

Using this approach alone, it is impossible to deduce what the value of n is. The burst has been defined, but its location is not known. Location of the burst requires a cyclic polynomial as discussed earlier. A burst-correcting Fire code is made by combining the expression for the burst-defining code with the expression for a locating polynomial. If the burst-locating polynomial appends an

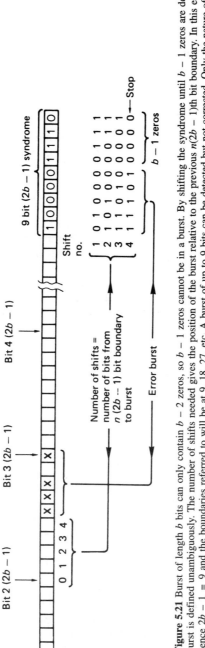

Figure 5.21 Burst of length b bits can only contain $b - 2$ zeros, so $b - 1$ zeros cannot be in a burst. By shifting the syndrome until $b - 1$ zeros are detected, the burst is defined unambiguously. The number of shifts needed gives the position of the burst relative to the previous $n(2b - 1)$th bit boundary. In this example $b = 5$, hence $2b - 1 = 9$ and the boundaries referred to will be at 9, 18, 27, etc. A burst of up to 9 bits can be detected but not corrected. Only the nature of the burst is defined by this process; its position has to be determined independently.

m bit remainder to the data, the redundancy will consist of $m + 2b - 1$ bits and the codeword length becomes:

$$n = (2^m - 1) \times (2b - 1) \text{ bits}$$

Figure 5.22 shows the synthesis of a Fire code from the two parts, with the mathematical expressions shown for comparison with the hardware necessary. During writing, k serial data bits are shifted into the circuit and $n - k$ redundancy bits are shifted out to produce a codeword of length n. On readout, the bits are shifted into the same circuit and if a syndrome of all zeros is obtained, it is assumed that there has been no error. The codeword gives zero remainder, and if a non-zero syndrome is obtained, this must be due to the error polynomial which has been shifted an unknown number of times (see Figure 5.23). The error burst is one state of a Galois field (see Chapter 2) and the syndrome is another. Any state of the Galois field can be reached from any other by shifting with no input. If the syndrome is shifted, sooner or later the burst pattern will be obtained. It is not clear how it will be recognized. The only ones in the correct state are those describing the burst, and they will be confined to the last b stages of the register. All other stages will be zero. Owing to the highly non-sequential nature of the Galois field, there is no possibility that $n - k - b$ contiguous zeros will be found in any other state. The number of shifts needed to obtain this condition is counted because it represents the distance from the beginning of the message to the burst. In most Fire code applications, b will be chosen to exceed the anticipated burst size and m will be chosen to achieve the desired probability of detection of larger errors. This usually results in a codeword which is far longer than the data blocks used in most recorders, and puncturing will be used.

The Fire code used in many IBM disk drives at one time used the following polynomial:

$$(x^{21} + 1)(x^{11} + x^2 + 1)$$

which has a codeword of length

$$(2^{11} - 1) \times 21 = 42\,987 \text{ bits of which } 42\,955 \text{ are data bits.}$$

As was shown in Section 5.12, puncturing is easy, and all that is necessary is to subtract the number of leading zeros from the error position in the codeword to give the error position in the block. Figure 5.24 shows one way in which this can be done. An additional shift counter is provided, which is designed to count up to the number of leading zeros before overflowing. When it does so, it will enable a second shift counter which counts with respect to the beginning of the data block rather than the beginning of the codeword. The zero detection stops the count, and the position count and the error pattern are then available to the system.

An alternative is to reconfigure the twisted-ring counter to run backwards as this will be much quicker with punctured codes. A faster correction still is to use the so-called Chinese remainder theorem. Instead of dividing the codeword by the full polynomial, it is simultaneously divided by the factors. The burst pattern register is shifted first to locate the error at the end. The other registers are then shifted until their contents are the same as the burst pattern. The number of shifts needed in each case can be used to find the location of the burst.

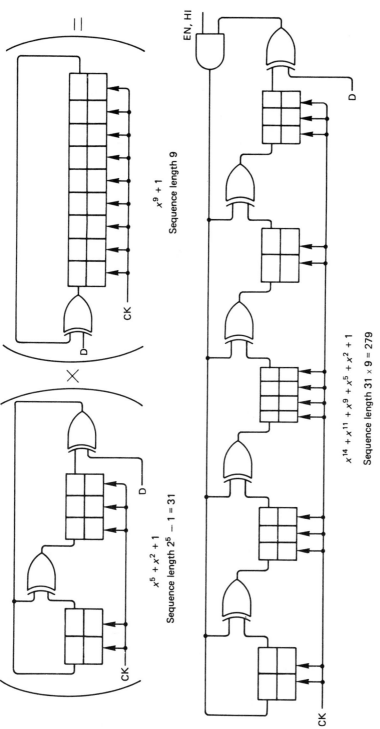

Figure 5.22 Derivation of Fire code from two fundamental expressions, together with encoding circuits. From the codeword length of 279 bits, 14 are check bits, making this a (279, 265) code.

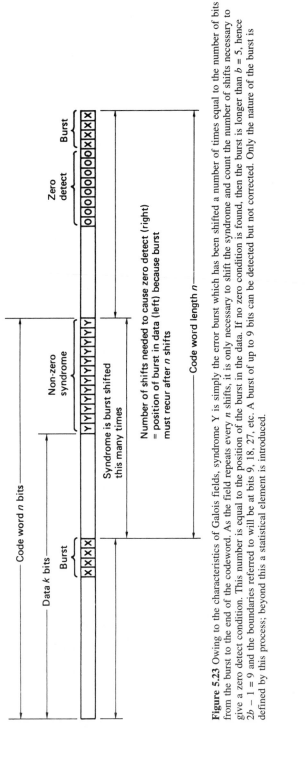

Figure 5.23 Owing to the characteristics of Galois fields, syndrome Y is simply the error burst which has been shifted a number of times equal to the number of bits from the burst to the end of the codeword. As the field repeats every n shifts, it is only necessary to shift the syndrome and count the number of shifts necessary to give a zero detect condition. This number is equal to the position of the burst in the data. If no zero condition is found, then the burst is longer than $b = 5$, hence $2b - 1 = 9$ and the boundaries referred to will be at bits 9, 18, 27, etc. A burst of up to 9 bits can be detected but not corrected. Only the nature of the burst is defined by this process; beyond this a statistical element is introduced.

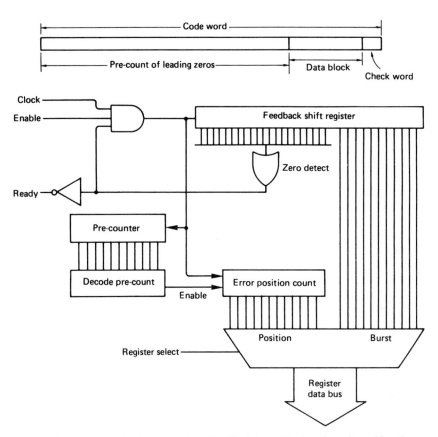

Figure 5.24 Error-correction hardware where data block is smaller than the codeword length. When a non-zero syndrome is detected after a read, the leading zeros in the codeword which precede the data are counted by the pre-counter. When the pre-count satisfies the decoder, error-position counter is enabled, which gives error position relative to the start of data when zero condition is detected. This disables the shifting and raises the ready bit.

Whilst the Fire code was discovered at about the same time as the superior Reed–Solomon codes, it was dominant in disk drives for a long time because it was so much easier to implement. As has been seen, a handful of latches, XOR gates and counters are sufficient, or, more recently, one chip.

5.16 Introduction to the Reed–Solomon codes

The Reed–Solomon codes (Irving Reed and Gustave Solomon) are inherently burst correcting[7] because they work on multibit symbols rather than individual bits. The R–S codes are also extremely flexible in use. One code may be used both to detect and to correct errors and the number of bursts which are correctable can be chosen at the design stage by the amount of redundancy. A further advantage of the R–S codes is that they can be used in conjunction with a separate error-detection mechanism, in which case they perform only the correction by erasure. R–S codes operate at the theoretical limit of correcting efficiency. In other words, no more efficient code can be found.

In the simple CRC system described in Section 5.11, the effect of the error is detected by ensuring that the codeword can be divided by a polynomial. The CRC codeword was created by adding a redundant symbol to the data. In the Reed–Solomon codes, several errors can be isolated by ensuring that the codeword will divide by a number of polynomials. Clearly if the codeword must divide by, say, two polynomials, it must have two redundant symbols. This is the minimum case of an R–S code. On receiving an R–S coded message there will be two syndromes following the division. In the error-free case, these will both be zero. If both are not zero, there is an error.

It has been stated that the effect of an error is to add an error polynomial to the message polynomial. The number of terms in the error polynomial is the same as the number of errors in the codeword. The codeword divides to zero and the syndromes are a function of the error only. There are two syndromes and two equations. By solving these simultaneous equations it is possible to obtain two unknowns. One of these is the position of the error, known as the *locator*, and the other is the error bit pattern, known as the *corrector*. As the locator is the same size as the code symbol, the length of the codeword is determined by the size of the symbol. A symbol size of eight bits is commonly used because it fits in conveniently with both 16 bit audio samples and byte-oriented computers. An 8 bit syndrome results in a locator of the same wordlength. Eight bits have 2^8 combinations, but one of these is the error-free condition, and so the locator can specify one of only 255 symbols. As each symbol contains 8 bits, the codeword will be $255 \times 8 = 2040$ bits long.

As further examples, 5 bit symbols could be used to form a codeword 31 symbols long, and 3 bit symbols would form a codeword seven symbols long. This latter size is small enough to permit some worked examples, and will be used further here. Figure 5.25 shows that in the seven-symbol codeword, five symbols of three bits each, A–E, are the data, and P and Q are the two redundant symbols. This simple example will locate and correct a single symbol in error. It does not matter, however, how many bits in the symbol are in error.

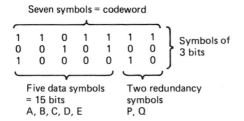

Figure 5.25 A Reed–Solomon codeword. As the symbols are of 3 bits, there can only be eight possible syndrome values. One of these is all zeros, the error-free case, and so it is only possible to point to seven errors; hence the codeword length of seven symbols. Two of these are redundant, leaving five data symbols.

The two check symbols are solutions to the following equations:

$$A \oplus B \oplus C \oplus D \oplus E \oplus P \oplus Q = 0$$

$$a^7A \oplus a^6B \oplus a^5C \oplus a^4D \oplus a^3E \oplus a^2P \oplus aQ = 0$$

where a is a constant. The original data A–E followed by the redundancy P and Q pass through the channel.

The receiver makes two checks on the message to see if it is a codeword. This is done by calculating syndromes using the following expressions, where the prime ($'$) implies the received symbol which is not necessarily correct:

$$S_0 = A' \oplus B' \oplus C' \oplus D' \oplus E' \oplus P' \oplus Q'$$

(This is in fact a simple parity check)

$$S_1 = a^7A' \oplus a^6B' \oplus a^5C' \oplus a^4D' \oplus a^3E' \oplus a^2P' \oplus aQ'$$

If two syndromes of all zeros are not obtained, there has been an error. The information carried in the syndromes will be used to correct the error. For the purpose of illustration, let it be considered that D$'$ has been corrupted before moving to the general case. D$'$ can be considered to be the result of adding an error of value E to the original value D such that:

$$D' = D \oplus E$$

As:

$$A \oplus B \oplus C \oplus D \oplus E \oplus P \oplus Q = 0$$

then

$$A \oplus B \oplus C \oplus (D \oplus E) + E + P + Q = E = S_0$$

As D$'$ = D $\oplus$ E, then:

$$D = D' \oplus E = D' \oplus S_0$$

Thus the value of the corrector is known immediately because it is the same as the parity syndrome S_0. The corrected data symbol is obtained simply by adding S_0 to the incorrect symbol.

At this stage, however, the corrupted symbol has not yet been identified, but this is equally straightforward.

As:

$$a^7A \oplus a^6B \oplus a^5C \oplus a^4D \oplus a^3E \oplus a^2P \oplus aQ = 0$$

then:

$$a^7A \oplus a^6B \oplus a^5C \oplus a^4(D \oplus E) \oplus a^3E \oplus a^2P \oplus aQ = a^4E = S_1$$

Thus the syndrome S_1 is the error bit pattern E, but it has been raised to a power of a which is a function of the position of the error symbol in the block. If the position of the error is in symbol k, then k is the locator value and:

$$S_0 \times a^k = S_1$$

Hence:

$$a^k = \frac{S_1}{S_0}$$

The value of k can be found by multiplying S_0 by various powers of a until the product is the same as S_1. Then the power of a necessary is equal to k. The use of the descending powers of a in the codeword calculation is now clear because the error is then multiplied by a different power of a dependent upon its position. S_1 is known as the locator, because it gives the position of the error. The process of finding the error position by experiment is known as a Chien search.[8]

5.17 R–S calculations

Whilst the expressions above show that the values of P and Q are such that the two syndrome expressions sum to zero, it is not yet clear how P and Q are calculated from the data. Expressions for P and Q can be found by solving the two R–S equations simultaneously. This has been done in Appendix 5.1. The following expressions must be used to calculate P and Q from the data in order to satisfy the codeword equations. These are:

$$P = a^6A \oplus aB \oplus a^2C \oplus a^5D \oplus a^3E$$

$$Q = a^2A \oplus a^3B \oplus a^6C \oplus a^4D \oplus aE$$

In both the calulation of the redundancy shown here and the calculation of the corrector and the locator it is necessary to perform numerous multiplications and raising to powers. This appears to present a formidable calculation problem at both the encoder and the decoder. This would be the case if the calculations involved were conventionally executed. However, the calculations can be simplified by using logarithms. Instead of multiplying two numbers, their logarithms are added. In order to find the cube of a number, its logarithm is added three times. Division is performed by subtracting the logarithms. Thus all of the multiplications necessary can be achieved with addition or subtraction, which is straightforward in logic circuits.

The success of this approach depends upon simple implementation of log tables. As was seen in Chapter 2, raising a constant, a, known as the *primitive element*, to successively higher powers in modulo-2 gives rise to a Galois field. Each element of the field represents a different power n of a. It is a fundamental of the R–S codes that all of the symbols used for data, redundancy and syndromes are considered to be elements of a Galois field. The number of bits in the symbol determines the size of the Galois field, and hence the number of symbols in the codeword.

Figure 5.26 repeats a Galois field deduced in Chapter 2. The binary values of the elements are shown alongside the power of a they represent. In the R–S codes, symbols are no longer considered simply as binary numbers, but also as equivalent powers of a. In Reed–Solomon coding and decoding, each symbol will be multiplied by some power of a. Thus if the symbol is also known as a power of a it is only necessary to add the two powers. For example, if it is necessary to multiply the data symbol 100 by a^3, the calculation proceeds as follows, referring to Figure 5.26:

$$100 = a^2 \text{ so } 100 \times a^3 = a^{(2+3)} = a^5 = 111$$

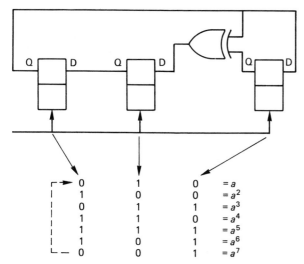

Figure 5.26 The bit patterns of a Galois field expressed as powers of the primitive element *a*. This diagram can be used as a form of log table in order to multiply binary numbers. Instead of an actual multiplication, the appropriate powers of *a* are simply added.

Note that the results of a Galois multiplication are quite different from binary multiplication. Because all products must be elements of the field, sums of powers which exceed 7 wrap around by having 7 subtracted. For example:

$$a^5 \times a^6 = a^{11} = a^4 = 110$$

Figure 5.27 shows some examples of circuits which will perform this kind of multiplication. Note that they require a minimum amount of logic.

Figure 5.28 shows an example of the Reed–Solomon encoding process. The Galois field shown in Figure 5.26 has been used, having the primitive element a = 010. At the beginning of the calculation of P, the symbol A is multiplied by a^6. This is done by converting A to a power of a. According to Figure 5.26, 101 = a^6 and so the product will be $a^{(6 + 6)} = a^{12} = a^5 = 111$. In the same way, B is multiplied by a, and so on, and the products are added modulo-2. A similar process is used to calculate Q.

Figure 5.29 shows a circuit which can calculate P or Q. The symbols A–E are presented in succession, and the circuit is clocked for each one. On the first clock, a^6A is stored in the left-hand latch. If B is now provided at the input, the second GF multiplier produces aB and this is added to the output of the first latch and when clocked will be stored in the second latch which now contains a^6A + aB. The process continues in this fashion until the complete expression for P is available in the right-hand latch. The intermediate contents of the right-hand latch are ignored.

The entire codeword now exists, and can be recorded or transmitted. Figure 5.28 also demonstrates that the codeword satisfies the checking equations. The modulo-2 sum of the seven symbols, S_0, is 000 because each column has an even number of ones. The calculation of S_1 requires multiplication by descending

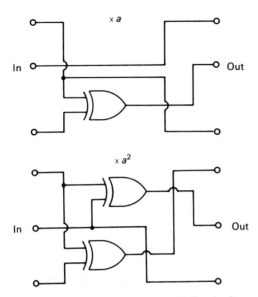

Figure 5.27 Some examples of GF multiplier circuits.

Input data	A	101	a^6A = 111	a^2A = 010
	B	100	a B = 011	a^3B = 111
	C	010	a^2C = 011	a^6C = 001
	D	100	a^5D = 001	a^4D = 101
	E	111	a^3E = 010	a E = 101
Check symbols	P	100 ◄───────── 100		
	Q	100 ◄────────────────── 100		

Codeword	A	101	a^7A = 101
	B	100	a^6B = 010
	C	010	a^5C = 101
	D	100	a^4D = 101
	E	111	a^3E = 010
	P	100	a^2P = 110
	Q	100	a Q = 011
	$S_0 = \overline{000}$		$S_1 = \overline{000}$ ◄─────Both syndromes zero

Figure 5.28 Five data symbols A–E are used as terms in the generator polynomials derived in Appendix 5.1 to calculate two redundant symbols P and Q. An example is shown at the top. Below is the result of using the codeword symbols A–Q as terms in the checking polynomials. As there is no error, both syndromes are zero.

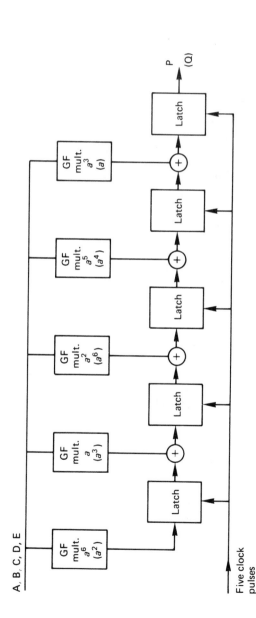

Figure 5.29 If the five data symbols of Figure 5.28 are supplied to this circuit in sequence, after five clocks one of the check symbols will appear at the output. Terms without brackets will calculate P, bracketed terms calculate Q.

powers of a. The modulo-2 sum of the products is again zero. These calculations confirm that the redundancy calculation was properly carried out.

Figure 5.30 gives three examples of error correction based on this codeword. The erroneous symbol is marked with a dash. As there has been an error, the syndromes S_0 and S_1 will not be zero.

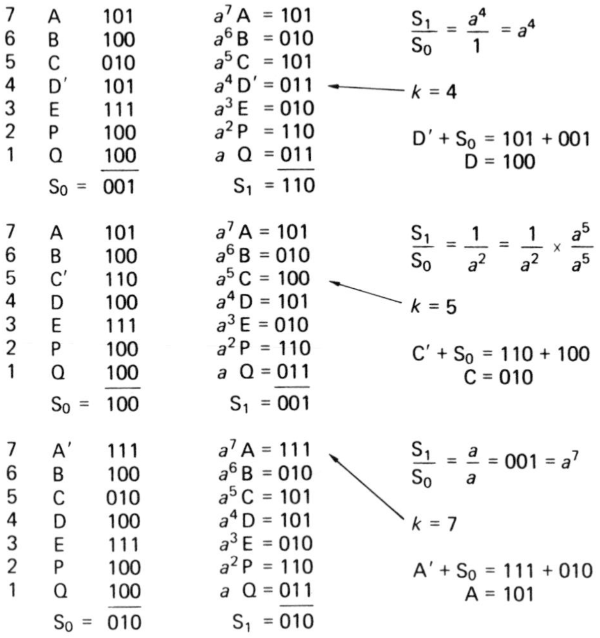

7	A	101	$a^7 A = 101$	
6	B	100	$a^6 B = 010$	
5	C	010	$a^5 C = 101$	
4	D'	101	$a^4 D' = 011$	
3	E	111	$a^3 E = 010$	
2	P	100	$a^2 P = 110$	
1	Q	100	$a\ Q = 011$	
	$S_0 =$	$\overline{001}$	$S_1 = \overline{110}$	

$$\frac{S_1}{S_0} = \frac{a^4}{1} = a^4$$

$k = 4$

$D' + S_0 = 101 + 001$
$D = 100$

7	A	101	$a^7 A = 101$
6	B	100	$a^6 B = 010$
5	C'	110	$a^5 C = 100$
4	D	100	$a^4 D = 101$
3	E	111	$a^3 E = 010$
2	P	100	$a^2 P = 110$
1	Q	100	$a\ Q = 011$
	$S_0 =$	$\overline{100}$	$S_1 = \overline{001}$

$$\frac{S_1}{S_0} = \frac{1}{a^2} = \frac{1}{a^2} \times \frac{a^5}{a^5} = a^5$$

$k = 5$

$C' + S_0 = 110 + 100$
$C = 010$

7	A'	111	$a^7 A = 111$
6	B	100	$a^6 B = 010$
5	C	010	$a^5 C = 101$
4	D	100	$a^4 D = 101$
3	E	111	$a^3 E = 010$
2	P	100	$a^2 P = 110$
1	Q	100	$a\ Q = 011$
	$S_0 =$	$\overline{010}$	$S_1 = \overline{010}$

$$\frac{S_1}{S_0} = \frac{a}{a} = 001 = a^7$$

$k = 7$

$A' + S_0 = 111 + 010$
$A = 101$

Figure 5.30 Three examples of error location and correction. The number of bits in error in a symbol is irrelevant; if all three were wrong, S_0 would be 111, but correction is still possible.

Figure 5.31 shows circuits suitable for parallel calculation of the two syndromes at the receiver. The S_0 circuit is a simple parity checker which accumulates the modulo-2 sum of all symbols fed to it. The S_1 circuit is more subtle, because it contains a Galois field (GF) multiplier in a feedback loop, such that early symbols fed in are raised to higher powers than later symbols because they have been recirculated through the GF multiplier more often. It is possible to compare the operation of these circuits with the example of Figure 5.30 and with subsequent examples to confirm that the same results are obtained.

5.18 Correction by erasure

In the examples of Figure 5.30, two redundant symbols P and Q have been used to locate and correct one error symbol. If the positions of errors are known by some separate mechanism (see product codes, Section 5.21), the locator need not be calculated. The simultaneous equations may instead be solved for two correctors. In this case, the number of symbols which can be corrected is equal

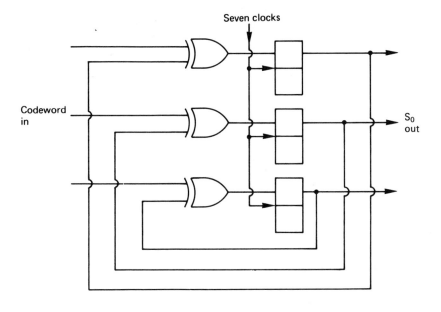

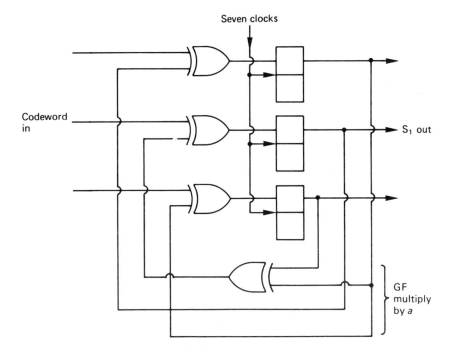

Figure 5.31 Circuits for parallel calculation of syndromes S_0, S_1. S_0 is a simple parity check. S_1 has a GF multiplication by a in the feedback, so that A is multiplied by a^7, B is multiplied by a^6, etc., and all are summed to give S_1.

to the number of redundant symbols. In Figure 5.32(a) two errors have taken place, and it is known that they are in symbols C and D. Since S_0 is a simple parity check, it will reflect the modulo-2 sum of the two errors. Hence:

$$S_0 = E_C + E_D$$

A		101	$a^7 A =$		101
B		100	$a^6 B =$		010
$(C \oplus E_C)$		001	$a^5 (C \oplus E_C)$		111
$(D \oplus E_D)$		010	$a^4 (D \oplus E_D)$		111
E		111	$a^3 E =$		010
P		100	$a^2 P =$		110
Q		100	$a\ Q =$		011
S_1	=	101	S_1 =		000

$$S_0 = E_C \oplus E_D \qquad S_1 = a^5 E_C \oplus a^4 E_D$$

$$S_1 = a^5 E_C \oplus a^4 (S_0 \oplus E_C)$$

$$= a^5 E_C \oplus a^4 S_0 \oplus a^4 E_C$$

$$\therefore E_C = \frac{S_1 \oplus a^4 S_0}{a^5 \oplus a^4} = \frac{000 \oplus 011}{001} = 011$$

$$C = (C \oplus E_C) \oplus E_C = 001 \oplus 011 = 010$$

$$S_1 = a^5 (S_0 \oplus E_D) \oplus a^4 E_D$$

$$= a^5 S_0 \oplus a^5 E_D \oplus a^4 E_D$$

$$\therefore E_D = \frac{S_1 \oplus a^5 S_0}{a^5 \oplus a^4} = \frac{000 \oplus 110}{001} = 110$$

$$D = (D \oplus E_D) + E_D = 010 \oplus 110 = 100$$

(a)

A		101	$a^7 A$	=	101	
B		100	$a^6 B$	=	010	$S_0 = C \oplus D$
C		000	$a^5 C$	=	000	
D		000	$a^4 D$	=	000	$S_1 = a^5 C \oplus a^4 D$
E		111	$a^3 E$	=	010	
P		100	$a^2 P$	=	110	
Q		100	$a\ Q$	=	011	
S_0	=100		S_1	=	000	

$$S_1 = a^5 S_0 \oplus a^5 D \oplus a^4 D = a^5 S_0 \oplus D$$

$$\therefore D = S_1 \oplus a^5 S_0 = 000 \oplus 100 = 100$$

$$S_1 = a^5 C \oplus a^4 C \oplus a^4 S_0 = C \oplus a^4 S_0$$

$$\therefore C = S_1 \oplus a^4 S_0 = 000 \oplus 010 = 010$$

(b)

Figure 5.32 If the location of errors is known, then the syndromes are a known function of the two errors as shown in (a). It is, however, much simpler to set the incorrect symbols to zero, i.e. to *erase* them as in (b). Then the syndromes are a function of the wanted symbols and correction is easier.

The two errors will have been multiplied by different powers in S_1, such that:

$$S_1 = a^5 E_C \oplus a^4 E_D$$

These two equations can be solved, as shown in the figure, to find E_C and E_D, and the correct value of the symbols will be obtained by adding these correctors to the erroneous values. It is, however, easier to set the values of the symbols in error to zero. In this way, the nature of the error is rendered irrelevant and it does not enter the calculation. This setting of symbols to zero gives rise to the term erasure. In this case:

$$S_0 = C \oplus D$$
$$S_1 = a^5C + a^4D$$

Erasing the symbols in error makes the errors equal to the correct symbol values and these are found more simply as shown in Figure 5.32(b).

Practical systems will be designed to correct more symbols in error than in the simple examples given here. If it is proposed to correct by erasure an arbitrary number of symbols in error given by t, the codeword must be divisible by t different polynomials. Alternatively if the errors must be located and corrected, $2t$ polynomials will be needed. These will be of the form $(x + a^n)$ where n takes all values up to t or $2t$. a is the primitive element discussed in Chapter 2.

Where four symbols are to be corrected by erasure, or two symbols are to be located and corrected, four redundant symbols are necessary, and the codeword polynomial must then be divisible by:

$$(x + a^0)(x + a^1)(x + a^2)(x + a^3)$$

Upon receipt of the message, four syndromes must be calculated, and the four correctors or the two error patterns and their positions are determined by solving four simultaneous equations. This generally requires an iterative procedure, and a number of algorithms have been developed for the purpose.[9-11] Modern digital audio formats such as CD and RDAT, and all of the DVTR formats, use 8 bit R–S codes and erasure extensively. The primitive polynomial commonly used with GF(256) is:

$$x^8 + x^4 + x^3 + x^2 + 1$$

The codeword will be 255 bytes long but will often be shortened by puncturing. The larger Galois fields require less redundancy, but the computational problem increases. LSI chips have been developed specifically for R–S decoding in many high-volume formats.[12,13] As an alternative to dedicated circuitry, it is also possible to perform Reed–Solomon calculations in software using general-purpose processors.[14] This may be more economical in small-volume products.

5.19 B-adjacent code

The B-adjacent code is used in digital audio PCM adaptors conforming to the EIAJ standard, such as the PCM-F1. This is a code which can correct two bursts by erasure using two simultaneous equations in a manner similar to the R–S codes. Six symbols of fourteen bits A–F are made into a codeword by the addition of two redundancy symbols P and Q. The redundancy symbols are calculated as follows:

$$P = A \oplus B \oplus C \oplus D \oplus E \oplus F$$

$$Q = T^6A \oplus T^5B \oplus T^4C \oplus T^3D \oplus T^2E \oplus TF$$

where T is a matrix transform. The calculation of P requires a 14 bit version of Figure 5.31(a). The calculation of Q is shown in Figure 5.33. The logic circuit is supplied with the data symbols in turn and clocked, so that after six clocks the register contains Q. It will be seen by comparing the expressions here with those in Section 5.16 that a similar process is taking place to that employed in the R–S codes. The difference is that the B-adjacent code uses descending powers in the *encoding* process whereas the R–S codes use them in the *decoding* process. The symbols A–F, P and Q are recorded. On replay, the following expressions are used to calculate the syndromes:

$$S_P = A \oplus B \oplus C \oplus D \oplus E \oplus F \oplus P$$

$$S_Q = T^6A \oplus T^5B \oplus T^4C \oplus T^3D \oplus T^2E \oplus TF \oplus Q$$

An external CRC mechanism locates the errors. For the purpose of illustration, let it be assumed that words A and C are in error and that these symbols have been erased. In this case, the following must be true:

$$S_P = A \oplus C$$

$$S_Q = T^6A \oplus T^4C$$

Dividing the second equation by T^4 gives:

$$T^{-4}S_Q = T^2A \oplus C$$

Adding S_P to both sides:

$$S_P \oplus T^{-4}S_Q = S_P + T^2A \oplus C$$

but $S_P = A \oplus C$, therefore:

$$S_P \oplus T^{-4}S_Q = T^2A \oplus C \oplus A \oplus C = T^2A \oplus A$$
$$= (1 \oplus T)^2A$$

Therefore:

$$A = \frac{S_P \oplus T^{-4}S_Q}{1 \oplus T^2}$$

and C follows from the first equation.

Thus it is only necessary to process the syndromes according to the erasure flags in order to correct both errors.

5.20 Interleaving

The concept of bit interleaving was introduced in connection with a single-bit correcting code to allow it to correct small bursts. With burst-correcting codes such as Reed–Solomon, bit interleave is unnecessary. In most channels, particularly high-density recording channels on tape, the burst size due to

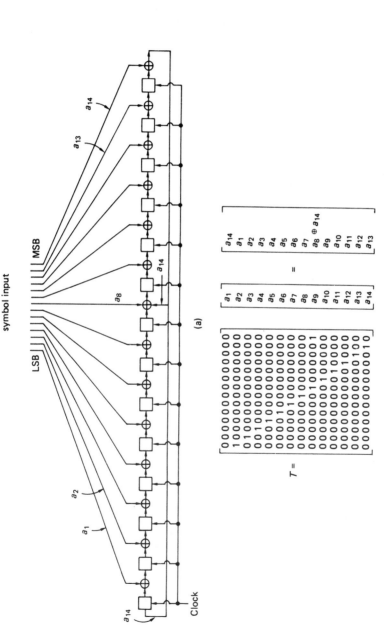

Figure 5.33 B-adjacent encoding; the circuit in (a) is presented with the input symbols sequentially, and each one is clocked. The feedback connections cause the circuit to execute the transform T shown in (b) at each clock. After several clocks, the register will contain the sum of each symbol multiplied by successively higher powers of T.

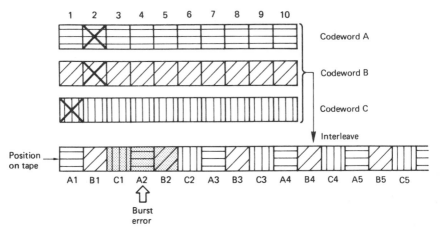

Figure 5.34 The interleave controls the size of burst errors in individual codewords.

dropouts may be many bytes rather than bits, and to rely on a code alone to correct such errors would require a lot of redundancy. The solution in this case is to employ symbol interleaving, as shown in Figure 5.34. Several codewords are encoded from input data, but these are not recorded in the order they were input, but are physically reordered in the channel, so that a real burst error is split into smaller bursts in several codewords. The size of the burst seen by each codeword is now determined primarily by the parameters of the interleave, and Figure 5.35 shows that the probability of occurrence of bursts with respect to the

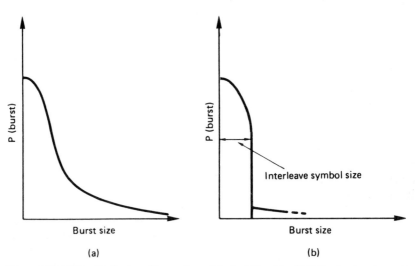

Figure 5.35 (a) The distribution of burst sizes might look like this. (b) Following interleave, the burst size within a codeword is controlled to that of the interleave symbol size, except for gross errors which have low probability.

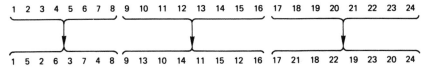

Figure 5.36 In block interleaving, data are scrambled within blocks which are themselves in the correct order.

burst length in a given codeword is modified. The number of bits in the interleave word can be made equal to the burst-correcting ability of the code in the knowledge that it will be exceeded only very infrequently.

There are a number of different ways in which interleaving can be performed. Figure 5.36 shows that in block interleaving, words are reordered within blocks which are themselves in the correct order. This approach is attractive for rotary-head recorders, because the scanning process naturally divides the tape up into blocks. The block interleave is achieved by writing samples into a memory in sequential address locations from a counter, and reading the memory with non-sequential addresses from a sequencer. The effect is to convert a one-dimensional sequence of samples into a two-dimensional structure having rows and columns.

Rotary-head recorders naturally interleave spatially on the tape. Figure 5.37 shows that a single, large tape defect becomes a series of small defects owing to the geometry of helical scanning.

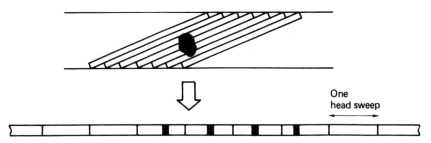

One head sweep

Figure 5.37 Helical-scan recorders produce a form of mechanical interleaving, because one large defect on the medium becomes distributed over several head sweeps.

The alternative to block interleaving is convolutional interleaving where the interleave process is endless. In Figure 5.38 symbols are assembled into short blocks and then delayed by an amount proportional to the position in the block. It will be seen from the figure that the delays have the effect of shearing the symbols so that columns on the left side of the diagram become diagonals on the right. When the columns on the right are read, the convolutional interleave will be obtained. Convolutional interleave works well with stationary-head tape recorders where there is no natural track break and with CD where the track is a continuous spiral. Convolutional interleave has the advantage of requiring less memory to implement than a block code. This is because a block code requires the entire block to be written into the memory before it can be read, whereas a

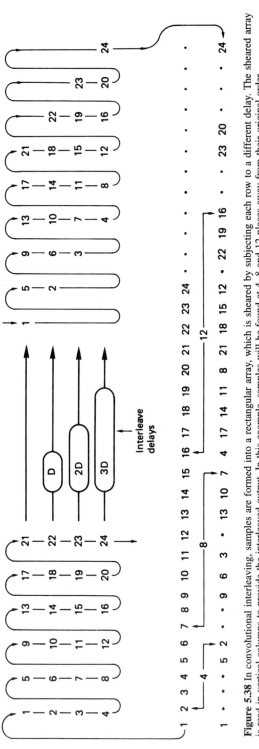

Figure 5.38 In convolutional interleaving, samples are formed into a rectangular array, which is sheared by subjecting each row to a different delay. The sheared array is read in vertical columns to provide the interleaved output. In this example, samples will be found at 4, 8 and 12 places away from their original order.

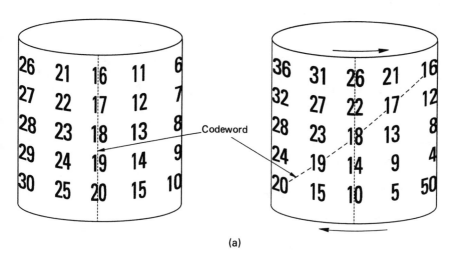

(a)

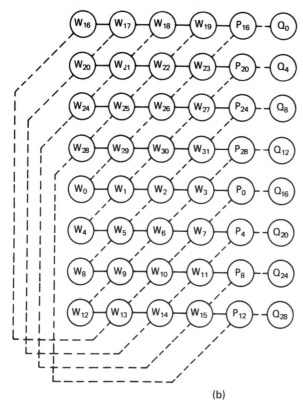

(b)

Figure 5.39 A block-completed convolutional interleave can be considered to be the result of shearing a cylinder as in (a). This results in horizontal and diagonal codewords as shown in (b).

convolutional code requires only enough memory to cause the required delays. Now that RAM is relatively inexpensive, convolutional interleave is less popular.

It is possible to make a convolutional code of finite size by making a loop. Figure 5.39(a) shows that symbols are written in columns on the outside of a cylinder. The cylinder is then sheared or twisted, and the columns are read. The result is a block-completed convolutional interleave shown in (b). This technique is used in the audio blocks of the Video-8 format.

5.21 Product codes

In the presence of burst errors alone, the system of interleaving works very well, but it is known that in most practical channels there are also uncorrelated errors of a few bits due to noise. Figure 5.40 shows an interleaving system where a dropout-induced burst error has occurred which is at the maximum correctable size. All three codewords involved are working at their limit of one symbol. A random error due to noise in the vicinity of a burst error will cause the correction power of the code to be exceeded. Thus a random error of a single bit causes a further entire symbol to fail. This is a weakness of an interleave solely designed to handle dropout-induced bursts. Practical high-density equipment must address the problem of noise-induced or random errors and burst errors occurring at the same time. This is done by forming codewords both before and after the interleave process. In block interleaving, this results in a *product code*, whereas in the case of convolutional interleave the result is called *cross-interleaving*.[15]

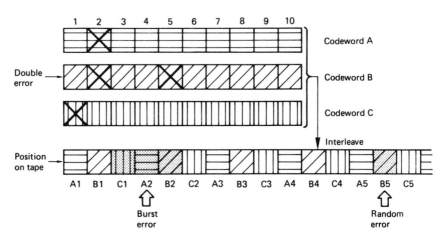

Figure 5.40 The interleave system falls down when a random error occurs adjacent to a burst.

Figure 5.41 shows that in a product code the redundancy calculated first and checked last is called the outer code, and the redundancy calculated second and checked first is called the inner code. The inner code is formed along tracks on the medium. Random errors due to noise are corrected by the inner code and do not impair the burst-correcting power of the outer code. Burst errors are declared

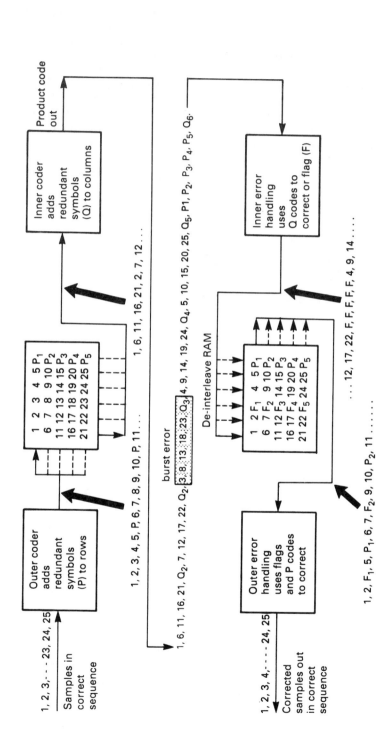

Figure 5.41 In addition to the redundancy P on rows, inner redundancy Q is also generated on columns. On replay, the Q code checker will pass on flags F if it finds an error too large to handle itself. The flags pass through the de-interleave process and are used by the outer error correction to identify which symbol in the row needs correcting with P redundancy. The concept of crossing two codes in this way is called a product code.

uncorrectable by the inner code which flags the bad samples on the way into the de-interleave memory. The outer code reads the error flags in order to correct the flagged symbols by erasure. The error flags are also known as erasure flags. As it does not have to compute the error locations, the outer code needs half as much redundancy for the same correction power. Thus the inner code redundancy does not raise the code overhead. The combination of codewords with interleaving in several dimensions yields an error-protection strategy which is truly synergistic, in that the end result is more powerful than the sum of the parts. Needless to say, the technique is used extensively in all of the DVTR formats, in DCRS, RDAT and DCC. The error-correction strategy of RDAT is treated in the next section as a representative example of a modern product code. Product codes are less suitable for magnetic disk drives because they can map out media defects. Furthermore, the delay inherent in assembling and de-interleaving product codes adds to the access time.

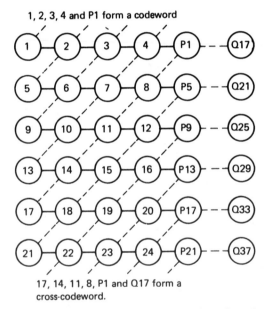

Figure 5.42 In cross-interleaving, codewords are formed on data before interleaving (1, 2, 3, 4, P1) and after convolutional interleaving (21, 18, 15, 12, P5, Q21).

An alternative to the product block code is the convolutional cross-interleave, shown in Figure 5.42. In this system, the data are formed into an endless array and the code words are produced on columns and diagonals. The Compact Disc, MiniDisc and DASH formats use such a system. The original advantage of the cross-interleave is that it needed less memory than a product code. This advantage is no longer so significant now that memory prices have fallen so much. It has the disadvantage that editing is more complicated. The error-correction systems of CD and MiniDisc are discussed in detail in Chapter 10 and that of the DASH format in Chapter 7.

5.22 Introduction to error correction in RDAT

The interleave and error-correction systems of RDAT will now be discussed. Figure 5.43 is a conceptual block diagram of the system which shows that RDAT uses a product code formed by producing Reed–Solomon codewords at right angles across an array. The array is formed in a memory, and the layout used in the case of 48 kHz sampling can be seen in Figure 5.44.

There are two recorded tracks for each drum revolution and incoming samples for that period of time are routed to a pair of memory areas of 4 kbytes capacity, one for each track. These memories are structured as 128 columns of 32 bytes each. The error correction works with 8 bit symbols, and so each sample is divided into high byte and low byte and occupies two locations in memory. Figure 5.44 shows only one of the two memories. Incoming samples are written across the memory in rows, with the exception of an area in the centre, 24 bytes wide. Each row of data in the RAM is used as the input to the Reed–Solomon encoder for the outer code. The encoder starts at the left-hand column, and then takes a byte from every fourth column, finishing at column 124 with a total of 26 bytes. Six bytes of redundancy are calculated to make a 32 byte outer codeword. The redundant bytes are placed at the top of columns 52, 56, 60, etc. The encoder then makes a second pass through the memory, starting in the second column and taking a byte from every fourth column finishing at column 125. A further six bytes of redundancy are calculated and put into the top of columns 53, 57, 61, and so on. This process is performed four times for each row in the memory, except for the last eight rows where only two passes are necessary because odd-numbered columns have sample bytes only down to row 23. The total number of outer codewords produced is 112.

In order to encode the inner codewords to be recorded, the memory is read in columns. Figure 5.45 shows that, starting at top left, bytes from the sixteen even-numbered rows of the first column, and from the first twelve even-numbered rows of the second column, are assembled and fed to the inner encoder. This produces four bytes of redundancy which are written into the memory in the areas marked P1. Four bytes P1, when added to the 28 bytes of data, make an inner codeword 32 bytes long. The second inner code is encoded by making a second pass through the first two columns of the memory to read the samples on odd-numbered rows. Four bytes of redundancy are placed in memory in locations marked P2. Each column of memory is then read completely and becomes one sync block on tape. Two sync blocks contain two interleaved inner codes such that the inner redundancy for both is at the end of the second sync block. The effect is that adjacent symbols in a sync block are not in the same codeword. The process then repeats down the next two columns in the memory and so on until 128 blocks have been written to the tape.

Upon replay, the sync blocks will suffer from a combination of random errors and burst errors. The effect of interleaving is that the burst errors will be converted to many single-symbol errors in different outer codewords.

As there are four bytes of redundancy in each inner codeword, a theoretical maximum of two bytes can be corrected. The probability of miscorrection in the inner code is minute for a single-byte error, because all four syndromes will agree on the nature of the error, but the probability of miscorrection on a double-byte error is much higher. The inner code logic is exposed to random noise during dropout and mistracking conditions, and the probability of noise

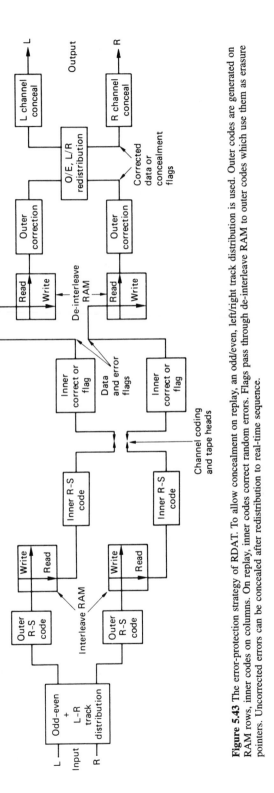

Figure 5.43 The error-protection strategy of RDAT. To allow concealment on replay, an odd/even, left/right track distribution is used. Outer codes are generated on RAM rows, inner codes on columns. On replay, inner codes correct random errors. Flags pass through de-interleave RAM to outer codes which use them as erasure pointers. Uncorrected errors can be concealed after redistribution to real-time sequence.

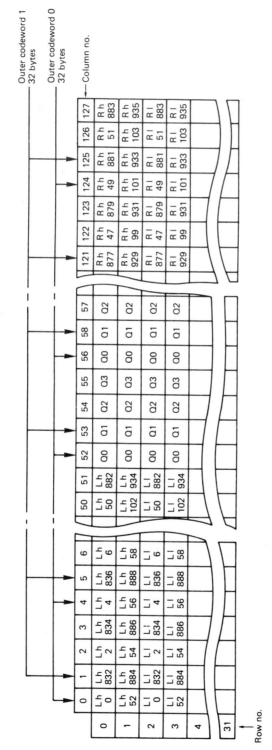

Figure 5.44 Left even/right odd interleave memory. Incoming samples are split into high byte (h) and low byte (l), and written across the memory rows using first the even columns for L 0–830 and R 1–831, and then the odd columns for L 832–1438 and R 833–1439. For 44.1 kHz working, the number of samples is reduced from 1440 to 1323, and fewer locations are filled.

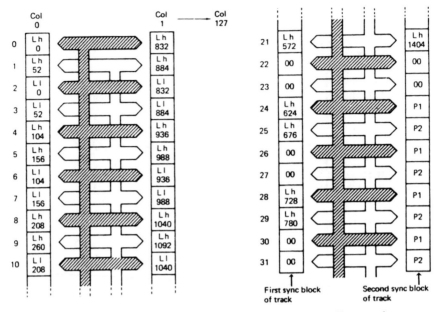

Figure 5.45 The columns of memory are read out to form inner codewords. First, even bytes from the first two columns make one codeword and then odd bytes from the first two columns. As there are 128 columns, there will be 128 sync blocks in one audio segment.

producing what appears to be only a two-symbol error is too great. If more than one byte is in error in an inner code, it is more reliable to declare all bytes bad by attaching flags to them as they enter the de-interleave memory. The interleave of the inner codes over two sync blocks is necessary because of the use of a group code. In the 8/10 code described in Chapter 4, a single mispositioned transition will change one 10 bit group into another, potentially corrupting up to eight data bits. A small disturbance at the boundary between two groups could corrupt up to sixteen bits. By interleaving the inner codes at symbol level, the worst case of a disturbance at the boundary of two groups is to produce a single-symbol error in two different inner codes. Without the inner code interleave, the entire contents of an inner code could be caused to be flagged bad by a single small defect. The inner code interleave halves the error propagation of the group code, which increases the chances of random errors being corrected by the inner codes instead of impairing the burst-error correction of the outer codes.

After de-interleave, any uncorrectable inner codewords will show up as single-byte errors in many different outer codewords accompanied by error flags. To guard against miscorrections in the inner code, the outer code will calculate syndromes even if no error flags are received from the inner code. If two bytes or less in error are detected, the outer code will correct them even though they were due to inner code miscorrections. This can be done with high reliability because the outer code has 3 byte detecting and correcting power which is never used to the full. If more than two bytes are in error in the outer codeword, the correction process uses the error flags from the inner code to correct up to six bytes in error.

The reasons behind the complex interleaving process now become clearer. Because of the four-way interleave of the outer code, four entire sync blocks can be destroyed, but only one byte will be corrupted in a given outer codeword. As an outer codeword can correct up to six bytes in error by erasure, it follows that a burst error of up to 24 sync blocks could be corrected. This corresponds to a length of track of just over 2.5 mm, and is more than enough to cover the tenting effect due to a particle of debris lifting the tape away from the head. In practice the interleave process is a little more complicated than this description would suggest, owing to the requirement to produce recognizable sound in shuttle.

5.23 Editing interleaved recordings

The interleave, de-interleave, time-compression and timebase correction processes cause substantial delay. Confidence replay in audio and video recorders takes place later than the distance between record and replay heads would indicate. In DASH-format recorders, confidence replay is about one-tenth of a second behind the input. Processes such as editing and synchronous recording require new techniques to overcome the effect of the delays.

In analog recording, there is a direct relationship between the distance down the track and the time through the recording and it is possible to mark and cut the tape at a particular time. A further consequence of interleaving in digital recorders is that the reordering of samples means that this relationship is lost.

Editing must be undertaken with care. In a block-based interleave, edits can be made at block boundaries so that coded blocks are not damaged, but these blocks are usually too large for accurate audio editing. In a convolutional interleave, there are no blocks and an edit or splice will damage diagonal codewords over a constraint length near the edit as shown in Figure 5.46.

The only way in which audio can be edited satisfactorily in the presence of interleave is to use a read–modify–write approach, where an entire frame is read into memory and de-interleaved to the real-time sample sequence. Any desired part of the frame can be replaced with new material before it is re-interleaved and re-recorded. In recorders which can only record or play at one time, an edit of this kind would take a long time because of all of the tape repositioning needed. With extra heads read–modify–write editing can be performed dynamically. The

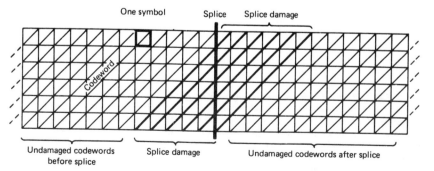

Figure 5.46 Although interleave is a powerful weapon against burst errors, it causes greater data loss when tape is spliced because many codewords are replayed in two unrelated halves.

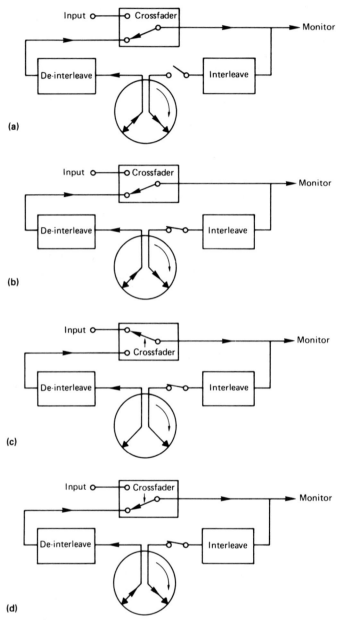

(a)

(b)

(c)

(d)

Figure 5.47 In the most sophisticated version of editing, there are advanced replay heads on the scanner, which allow editing to be performed on de-interleaved data. An insert sequence is shown. In (a) the replay-head signal is decoded and fed to the encoder which, after some time, will produce an output representing what is already on the tape. In (b), at a sector boundary, the write circuits are turned on, and the machine begins to re-record. In (c) the crossfade is made to the insert material. In (d) the insert ends with a crossfade back to the signal from the advanced replay heads. After this, the write heads will once again be recording what is already on the tape, and the write circuits can be disabled at a sector boundary. An assemble edit consists of the first three of these steps only.

sequence is shown in Figure 5.47 for a rotary-head machine but is equally applicable to stationary-head transports. The replay head plays back the existing recording, and this is de-interleaved to the normal sample sequence, a process which introduces a delay. The sample stream now passes through a crossfader which at this stage will be set to accept only the off tape signal. The output of the crossfader is then fed to the record interleave stage which introduces further delay. This signal passes to the record heads which must be positioned so that the original recording on the tape reaches them at the same time that the re-encoded signal arrives, despite the encode and decode delays. In a rotary-head recorder this can be done by positioning the record heads at a different height to the replay heads so that they reach the same tracks on different revolutions. With this arrangement it is possible to enable the record heads at the beginning of a frame, and they will then re-record what is already on the tape. Next the crossfader can be operated to fade across to new material, at any desired crossfade speed. Following the interleave stage, the new recording will update only the new samples in the frame and re-record those which do not need changing. After a short time, the recording will only be a function of the new input. If the edit is an insert, it is possible to end the process by crossfading back to the replay signal and allowing the replay data to be re-recorded. Once this re-recording has taken place for a short time, the record process can be terminated at the end of a frame. There is no limit to the crossfade periods which can be employed in this operating technique; in fact the crossfade can be manually operated so that it can be halted at a suitable point to allow, for example, a commentary to be superimposed upon a recording.

One important point to appreciate about read–modify–write editing is that the physical frames at which the insert begins and ends are independent of the in- and out-points of the edit, simply because the former are in areas where re-recording of the existing data takes place.

Appendix 5.1 Calculation of Reed–Solomon generator polynomials

For a Reed–Solomon codeword over $GF(2^3)$, there will be seven 3 bit symbols. For location and correction of one symbol, there must be two redundant symbols P and Q, leaving A–E for data.

The following expressions must be true, where a is the primitive element of $x^3 \oplus x \oplus 1$ and $\oplus$ is XOR throughout:

$$A \oplus B \oplus C \oplus D \oplus E \oplus P \oplus Q = 0 \tag{1}$$

$$a^7A \oplus a^6B \oplus a^5C \oplus a^4D \oplus a^3E \oplus a^2P \oplus aQ = 0 \tag{2}$$

Dividing Eqn (2) by a:

$$a^6A \oplus a^5B \oplus a^4C \oplus a^3D \oplus a^2E \oplus aP \oplus Q = 0$$
$$= A \oplus B \oplus C \oplus D \oplus E \oplus P \oplus Q$$

Cancelling Q, and collecting terms:

$$(a^6 \oplus 1)A \oplus (a^5 \oplus 1)B \oplus (a^4 \oplus 1)C \oplus (a^3 \oplus 1)D \oplus (a^2 \oplus 1)E$$
$$= (a \oplus 1)P$$

Using Figure 5.26 to calculate $(a^n \oplus 1)$, e.g. $a^6 \oplus 1 = 101 \oplus 001 = 100 = a^2$:

$$a^2A \oplus a^4B \oplus a^5C \oplus aD \oplus a^6E = a^3P$$

$$a^6A \oplus aB \oplus a^2C \oplus a^5D \oplus a^3E = P \tag{3}$$

Multiply Eqn (1) by a^2 and equating to (2):

$$a^2A \oplus a^2B \oplus a^2C \oplus a^2D \oplus a^2E \oplus a^2P \oplus a^2Q = 0$$
$$= a^7A \oplus a^6B \oplus a^5C \oplus a^4D \oplus a^3E \oplus a^2P \oplus aQ$$

Cancelling terms a^2P and collecting terms (remember $a^2 \oplus a^2 = 0$):

$$(a^7 \oplus a^2)A \oplus (a^6 \oplus a^2)B \oplus (a^5 \oplus a^2)C \oplus (a^4 \oplus a^2)D \oplus (a^3 \oplus a^2)E$$
$$= (a^2 \oplus a)Q$$

Adding powers according to Figure 5.26, e.g. $a^7 + a^2 = 001 \oplus 100 = 101 = a^6$:

$$a^6A \oplus B \oplus a^3C \oplus aD \oplus a^5E = a^4Q$$

$$a^2A \oplus a^3B \oplus a^6C \oplus a^4D \oplus aE = Q$$

References

1. MICHAELS, S.R., Is it Gaussian? *Electronics World and Wireless World*, January, 72–73 (1993)
2. SHANNON, C.E., A mathematical theory of communication. *Bell System Tech. J.*, **27**, 379 (1948)
3. BELLIS, F.S., A multichannel digital sound recorder. Presented at the Video and Data Recording Conference, Birmingham, England. *IERE Conf. Proc.*, No. 35, 123–126 (1976)
4. HAMMING, R.W., Error-detecting and error-correcting codes. *Bell System Tech. J.*, **26**, 147–160 (1950)
5. FIRE, P., A class of multiple-error correcting codes for non-independent errors. *Sylvania Reconnaissance Systems Lab. Report.* RSL-E-2 (1959)
6. BOSSEN, D.C., B-adjacent error correction. *IBM J. Res. Dev.*, **14**, 402–408 (1970)
7. REED, I.S. and SOLOMON, G., Polynomial codes over certain finite fields. *J. Soc. Indust. Appl. Math.*, **8**, 300–304 (1960)
8. CHIEN, R.T., CUNNINGHAM, B.D. and OLDHAM, I.B., Hybrid methods for finding roots of a polynomial – with application to BCH decoding. *IEEE Trans. Inf. Theory.*, **IT-15**, 329–334 (1969)
9. BERLEKAMP, E.R., *Algebraic Coding Theory.* New York: McGraw-Hill (1967). Reprint edition: Laguna Hills, CA: Aegean Park Press (1983)
10. SUGIYAMA, Y. *et al.*, An erasures and errors decoding algorithm for Goppa codes. *IEEE Trans. Inf. Theory*, **IT-22** (1976)
11. PETERSON, W.W. and WELDON, E.J., *Error Correcting Codes*, 2nd edn. Cambridge, MA: MIT Press (1972)
12. ONISHI, K., SUGIYAMA, K., ISHIDA, Y., KUSONOKI, Y. and YAMAGUCHI, T., An LSI for Reed–Solomon encoder/decoder. Presented at 80th Audio Engineering Society Convention (Montreux, 1986), preprint 2316(A–4)
13. ANON. *Digital Audio Tape Deck Operation Manual.* Sony Corporation (1987)
14. VAN KOMMER, R., Reed–Solomon coding and decoding by digital signal processors. Presented at 84th Audio Engineering Society Convention (Paris, 1988), preprint 2587(D-7)
15. DOI, T.T., ODAKA, K., FUKUDA, G. and FURUKAWA, S., Crossinterleave code for error correction of digital audio systems. *J. Audio Eng. Soc.*, **27**, 1028 (1979)

Chapter 6

Servos

A servo is any device which is capable of producing controlled movement of a mechanism from a low-powered control signal. The key word here is 'controlled'; thus a motor alone is not a servo. Put simply, servos must contain brains as well as brawn. The field of data recording relies heavily on servo technology, and the servos used are among the most rapid and precise known. This chapter treats the subject generally, as each type of recorder will have its own application which will be dealt with in later chapters.

6.1 Introduction to servos

The signal channel of a modern data recorder contains some highly sophisticated processes and circuitry, but these can only operate correctly if the conditions within the channel are maintained within close tolerances. Many of the channel conditions are dependent on the accuracy of some mechanical process. Tape speed and acceleration, head-to-tape contact pressure, laser disk focus, tracking accuracy, access time, readout timing and rate are all dependent on mechanical systems and if sufficient accuracy is not obtained by purely mechanical means then a servo will be required. In many cases the application of a servo is intended to increase storage density, as was the case with the servo surface disk drive and the tracking servo of RDAT. Figure 6.1 shows some applications of servos in data recorders. Most servos in recorders are designed to control either position or velocity. Figure 6.2 shows a conceptual position servo. The input is an electrical signal of low power which controls the amount of motion required. The output is a mechanical movement, generally rotary or linear, where the necessary effort is provided by some form of motor. The actual mechanical movement is measured by some kind of transducer, and the control system uses the signals from the transducer and the input to decide how much power to feed to the motor.

6.2 Types of motor

Many different principles have been used in data recorders. Early disk drives had quite low recording density by today's standards, and as a result were quite large. The head assemblies were correspondingly large and heavy and hydraulic power was used to position them at high speed. Whilst successful, hydraulic power is messy and only suited to applications needing large thrusts. In modern high-density recorders hydraulic actuation has died out.

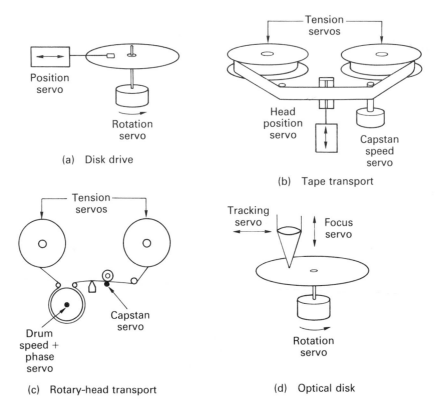

(a)   Disk drive

(b)   Tape transport

(c)   Rotary-head transport

(d)   Optical disk

Figure 6.1 Servo applications in recorders. In (a) a hard disk needs servos for disk rotational speed and head positioning. Multitrack tape transport in (b) uses a track-following servo to counteract tape weave and/or select tape tracks. Rotary-head recorder (c) needs a drum and capstan servos to enable rotating heads to trace recorded tracks. Optical disk (d) has spindle speed, positioner, focus and tracking servos.

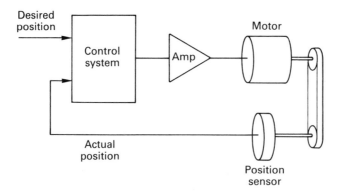

Figure 6.2 A simple position servo. The actual position is measured by a transducer and compared with the desired position. The difference is processed by the control system which drives the positioner motor.

The electric motor is in extensive use, spinning disks and driving capstans, rotary heads and tape reels. The basic principle is simple: a current flowing across a magnetic field develops a force. For continuous rotary operation, a DC motor needs a commutation system which feeds current only to the windings which have the correct orientation with respect to the field. In simple motors this is mechanical, but more sophisticated motors use electronic commutation. These so-called brushless motors are considered in more detail in Section 6.3.

Some applications require linear motion and the moving-coil motor, also known as an electromagnetic actuator or EMA, has the advantage that the moving part is very light. Figure 6.3(a) shows that a moving-coil linear motor resembles a loudspeaker in general construction. An alternative form of moving-coil motor uses a flat construction which is more suitable for low profile devices. Figure 6.3(b) shows that the drive current flows in a loop and two opposite sides

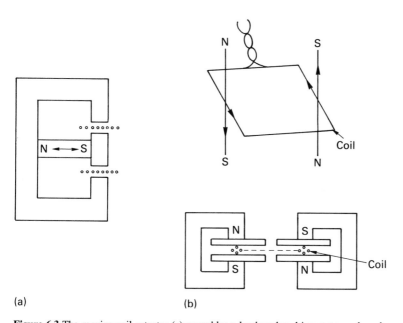

(a)   (b)

Figure 6.3 The moving-coil actuator (a) resembles a loudspeaker drive motor and produces pure linear motion with minimal moving mass. In low profile units an alternative flat construction (b) can be used.

of the loop are subject to magnetic fields of opposite direction. The result is that the forces developed on the two sides of the loop add together. These motors can be linear or rotary.

The piezoelectric actuator is shown in Figure 6.4(a). Piezoelectric materials are crystals, such as barium titanate, which have the characteristic that an applied voltage causes dimensional change or vice versa. When a drive voltage is applied, the material physically shrinks. Although the amount of movement is quite small, a large amount of force can be produced in a small space.

Magnetostriction is the term used to describe a dimensional change due to an applied magnetic field. It is considered a nuisance in many applications and is responsible for the buzz which power transformers make. However, the principle can be harnessed for actuation as shown in Figure 6.4(b). Materials such as Terfenol,[1] an alloy of terbium, dysprosium and iron, have been developed in which the magnetostrictive effect is enhanced. Like piezoelectric actuators, magnetostrictive actuators can provide only a short travel, but produce extremely high thrust and can be controlled very accurately.

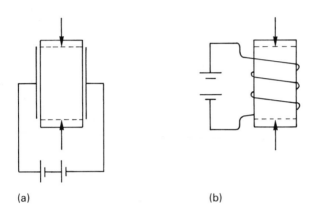

(a)   (b)

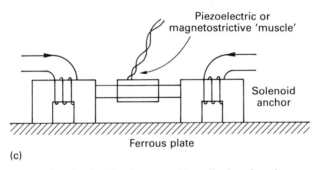

(c)

Figure 6.4 In the piezoelectric actuator (a), application of a voltage causes shrinking, whereas in the magnetostrictive actuator (b) it is an applied magnetic field from a solenoid which causes shrinking. These actuators have a very short travel which can be extended using the 'inchworm' principle shown in (c).

Although piezoelectric and magnetostrictive actuators are restricted to short travel, continuous motion can be obtained using the 'inchworm' or 'caterpillar' principle shown in Figure 6.4(c). The two ends of the caterpillar are alternately anchored to the baseplate by solenoids so that the repeated dimensional changes in the 'muscle' result in linear motion. Alternatively the principle can be used with a disk for a baseplate to obtain endless rotation. The speed which can be obtained depends on the frequency with which the various elements can be made to operate; several kilohertz have been achieved in practice.

6.3 Brushless DC motors

The reliability of recorder circuitry is of little consequence if a breakdown is caused by the failure of an associated mechanical component. Data recorders are a complex alliance of mechanical, magnetic and electronic technology, and the electronic complexity has to be matched by some pretty good mechanical engineering. As the cost of electronics falls, it becomes possible to replace certain mechanical devices cost-effectively, and there is an impetus to do this if a wear mechanism can be eliminated. The brushless motor is one such device. The conventional DC brush motor is ubiquitous, and life would be infinitely less convenient without it, for it allows high efficiency, a wide speed range, reversing and relatively compact size. The weak point of all motors of this kind is the brush/commutator system, which serves to distribute current to the windings which are in the best position relative to the field to generate torque. There is a physical wear mechanism, and the best brush material developed will still produce a conductive powder which will be distributed far and wide by the need to have airflow through the motor for cooling. The interruption of current in an inductive circuit results in sparking, which can cause electrical interference and erosion of the brushes and commutator. The brushless motor allows all of the benefits of the DC motor, without the drawbacks of commutation.

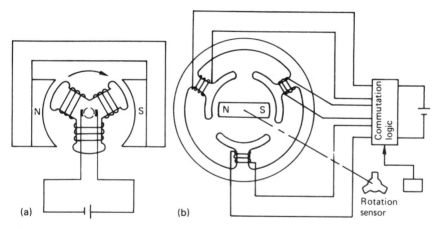

Figure 6.5 In (a) a conventional brush motor has rotating windings. Current is fed through stationary bushes and commutation is automatic. In (b) the motor has been turned inside out: the magnet revolves and the windings are now stationary, so they can be directly connected to an electronic commutating circuit. The rotation sensor on the magnet shaft tells the commutator when to switch.

Figure 6.5 shows that a brushless motor is not unlike a normal motor turned inside out. In a normal motor, the field magnet is stationary, and the windings rotate. In a brushless motor, the windings are stationary, and the magnet rotates. The stationary windings eliminate the need to supply current to the rotor, and with it the need for brushes. The commutating action is replaced by electronic switches. These need to be told the rotational angle of the shaft, a function which is intrinsic in the conventional commutator. A rotation sensor performs this function.

Figure 6.6 shows the circuit of a typical brushless motor. The three-phase winding is driven by six switching devices, usually power FETs. By switching these on in various combinations, it is possible to produce six resultant field directions in the windings. The switching is synchronized to the rotation of the magnet, such that the magnetic field of the rotor always finds itself at right angles to the field from the windings, and so produces the most torque. In this condition the motor will produce the most back-EMF, and the normal way of adjusting the rotation sensor is to allow the motor to run on no load and to mechanically adjust the angular sensor position until the motor consumes minimum current.

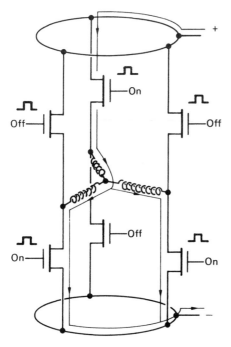

Figure 6.6 Circuit of a brushless DC motor is basically a three-phase bridge. Six different flux directions can be obtained by switching combinations of FETs. One example is shown.

The rotating magnet has to be sufficiently powerful to provide the necessary field, and in early brushless motors was heavy, which gave the motor a high inertial time constant. Whilst this was of no consequence in steady-speed applications such as disk motors, it caused problems in servos. The brushless servo motor was basically waiting for high-energy permanent magnets, which could produce the necessary field without excessive mass. These rare-earth magnets are currently more expensive than the common ferrite magnet, and so the first applications of brushless motors were in machines where the motor cost was a relatively small proportion of the high overall cost, and where reliability was paramount.

The development of the power FET also facilitated brushless motors, since all DC motors regenerate, which is to say that when the torque opposes the direction of rotation, the current reverses. FETs are not perturbed by current direction, whereas bipolar devices were at best inefficient or would at worst fail in the presence of reverse current. Power FETs have a very low 'on' resistance and can handle currents which would destroy brush gear, and so large transient accelerations are easily obtained, overcoming the inertia of the rotating magnet.

A typical brushless motor appears to the drive amplifier just like a normal DC motor. It has only two power terminals, has back-EMF, and will regenerate. The only major difference is the way that reversing is achieved. Brush motors reverse by reversing drive polarity, whereas brushless motors reverse by changing the phase of the commutation.

The number of motor poles directly influences the complexity of the switching circuitry, and brushless motors tend to have relatively few poles. Conventional motors suffer from cogging, or a cyclic variation in torque, and those with few poles suffer most. Whilst it is of little consequence in a disk motor, which runs at high speed and has the inertia of the disk pack to smooth out rotation, it can be important in direct-drive capstan motors, which turn at low speed and have low inertia.

Many transports retain multipole brush motors for the capstan, but it is possible to construct a cogging-free motor. The commutation circuit is no longer switching, but consists of a number of analog amplifiers which will feed the motor with sinusoidal waveforms in fixed phase relationships. In the case of a two-phase motor, this will be two waveforms at 90 degrees; for a three-phase motor, it will be three waveforms at 120 degrees.

The drive signals for the amplifiers are produced by a number of rotation sensors, which directly produce analog sinusoids. Figure 6.7 shows that these can

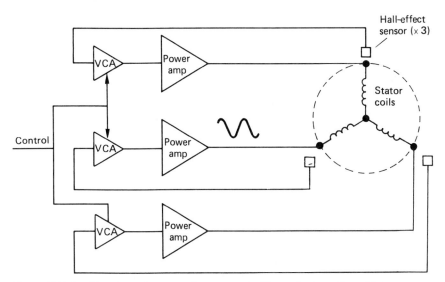

Figure 6.7 A brushless three-phase motor is constructed with a stationary coil set, driving a rotating magnet which produces three feedback sinusoids at 120° phase from Hall-effect magnetic sensors. These signals drive *analog* amplifiers to generate the power waveforms for the motor coils. Motor torque is controlled with VCAs (voltage controlled amplifiers). The three-phase system makes the motor torque independent of shaft angle, and reduces cogging.

conveniently be Hall-effect sensors which detect the fields from rotating magnets. The motor torque is controlled by changing the gain of the sine wave generation. This is conveniently done by changing the bias of the Hall-effect sensors.

6.4 Switched-mode motor amplifiers

The switched-mode motor amplifier has much in common with the switched-mode power supply, since both have the same objectives, namely an increase in electrical efficiency through reduced dissipation, and reduction in size and weight. In fixed applications reduced dissipation will help to increase reliability, whereas in portable recorders it is the efficiency which is paramount since existing battery technology is still a handicap.

The linear amplifier must act as a variable resistance, and so current flowing through it will cause heat to be developed. Linear amplifiers are particularly inefficient for driving tape-reel motors, since to obtain fast shuttle speed, the supply voltage must be high. This means that when the machine plays, the reels are turning slowly and the motor voltage will be very small, so that most of the power supply voltage has to be dropped by the amplifier, which is extremely inefficient. The same is true of a moving coil disk actuator, which requires high current when positioning, but only small currents to maintain position. As an alternative to a switching amplifier, some drives using linear motor amplifiers will program a switched-mode power supply to provide just enough voltage for the instantaneous requirements, helping to raise efficiency.

The principle of a switched-mode amplifier is quite simple. The current is controlled by an electronic switch which is either fully on or fully off. In both cases dissipation in the switch is minimal. The only difficulty consists of providing a variable output despite the binary switching. This will be done by a combination of duty-cycle control and filtering.

Figure 6.8 shows a typical switched-mode motor amplifier. It consists of a normal bridge configuration with a number of additional components, a pair of inductors and a current sense resistor in series with the motor, and a number of reverse connected flywheel diodes.

If it is desired to make current flow through the motor from left to right, then field-effect transistors T_1 and T_4 will be turned fully on. Owing to the presence of the inductors, the current through the motor increases gradually, and when the desired current is reached, transistor T_1 is switched off. The current flowing in the inductive circuit must continue flowing, and it will do so through D_3, as shown in (b). Greater efficiency will be obtained if T_3 is then switched on, as the forward drop of the diode is then bypassed. Transistor T_4 is then switched off, and the current loop will be blocked, causing the flux in the inductors to decay, and raising their terminal voltage. This will result in current flowing through D_2 back to the power supply. Greater efficiency will be obtained if T_2 is turned on. The current is now being opposed by the power supply, and will decay; and after a short time, transistor T_2 must be switched off, and transistor T_4 will be switched on again. In this way, the current rises and falls about the desired value. If the switching rate is made high, the variations in current will be small with respect to the average current. The inertia of the motor will in any case prevent any mechanical response at the switching frequency. It will be noted that during this process current flowed in reverse through two of the transistors, requiring the use of field-effect devices.

Clearly if current flowing from right to left is required, the bridge switching will change over, but the principle remains the same.

The torque generated by the motor (or the thrust in the case of a linear motor) is proportional to the current, and torque can be applied with or against motion. For example, when a tape transport is in play mode, the take-up motor is turning in the same direction as its torque, whereas the supply motor is providing back-tension, and is turning against its torque. In this case, the motor EMF will cause current to flow in the flywheel circuit, and the switching will take energy out of the current flywheel back to the power supply. This is the principle of regenerative braking. If the motor is being turned by the tape, it will generate, and a current will flow as shown in (c). The current will rise gradually owing to the presence of the inductors. When the current reaches the value needed to give the correct back-tension, T_3 will be switched off, and the flywheel current will find itself blocked. The result will be a flux collapse causing the inductors to raise their terminal voltage until a current path is found. When the voltage exceeds the power supply voltage, current will flow in D_1, back to the supply. Again greater efficiency will be obtained if T_1 is switched on, since the diode drop is bypassed. Since the power supply voltage is opposing the motor EMF, the current will fall; when it has fallen sufficiently, T_1 will be switched off, and T_3 will be switched on again.

The switching sequence of the transistors is important, since turning on the wrong pair will short out the power supply! One method of controlling the switching is to produce a current error by comparing the current sensed with the desired current. The current error then changes the DC level of a triangle wave, which is compared with four thresholds, each of which controls one of the transistors. Figure 6.9 shows the switching sequence which results. Note that when the current error is zero, the system alternates equally between opposing and assisting the current, and so there is no change.

A motor which is producing back-tension will return power to the supply, which will be used by the motor which is taking up, and by the drum motor. If the machine is braking from a high shuttle speed, both reel motors may together produce more power than the rest of the machine can use, and the power supply voltage will rise. In AC-powered machines, it is necessary to shunt the supply with a resistor in this condition, whereas in battery-powered machines the regenerative current simply recharges the battery. Clearly a power failure in shuttle is no problem, for as long as the reels are being decelerated, power is available.

6.5 Feedback and feedforward

These two concepts are vital to the provision of accurate servos and are often employed together, although it is possible to describe them individually.

Figure 6.10(a) shows a simple position feedback servo which might be used, for example, to keep a disk head on track. The transducer measures the actual position and the input signal specifies the desired position. The difference between the actual and desired positions is called the position error. The error is amplified by a factor A and used to drive the positioner motor and hence accelerate the load in such a direction that the error will be cancelled. In practice

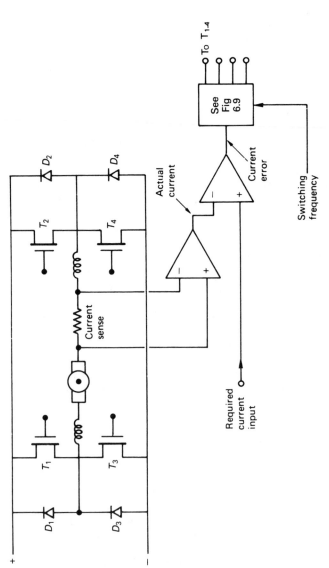

Figure 6.8 General arrangement of switched-mode power amplifier. Devices T_1–T_4 are power FETs which are on or off. Inductors in series with motor inductance limit rate of change of current.

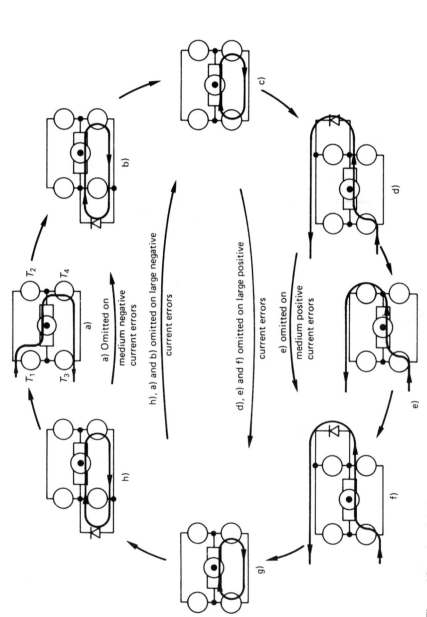

Figure 6.8 continued Switching sequence begins at (a) with current building up, a transitional phase (b) a flywheel phase (c) transitional phase (d) and at (e) the system regenerates, or opposes the power supply. This causes current to fall. System then passes through remaining phases back to (a). To increase current, system spends more time in phase (a), whereas to reduce current, system spends more time in phase (e). Figure 6.9 shows how this is done.

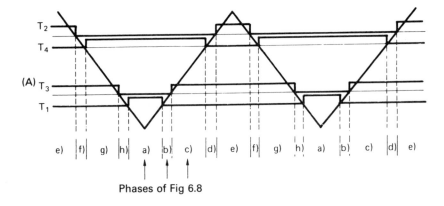

Phases of Fig 6.8

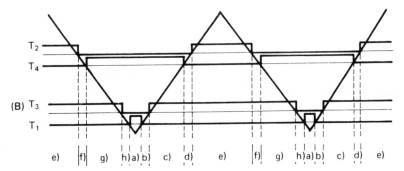

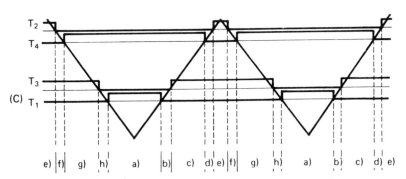

Figure 6.9 The power FETs of Figure 6.8 are switched by comparing the current error with a sawtooth signal produced from the switching frequency. Four offset voltages are added to the current error, and four comparators are used, one for each power device. The offsets are constant, so all four current errors move together.

In (A) above, the current error is zero, so the switching is symmetrical because time period (a) has the same length as time period (e) and the current is neither increased nor reduced. In (B) the current error is negative, and phase (a) is very short whereas phase (e) is much longer; thus current reduces because the motor is regenerating. In (C) the current error is positive and phase (a) is now longer than phase (e), so current increases. If the current error increases further, some phases will no longer take place. An inverse of the error in (C) will result in phase (e) disappearing since (d) and (f) are identical. Further increase will cause (d), (e) and (f) to disappear giving the sequence a, b, c, g, h, . . .

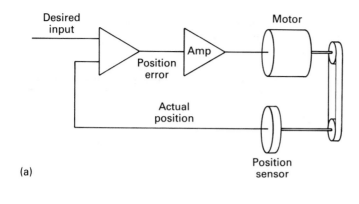

(a)

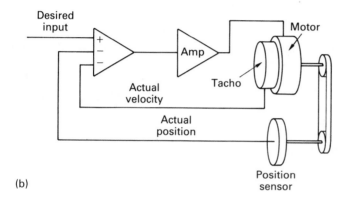

(b)

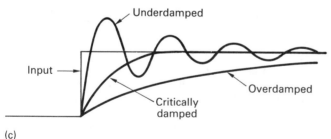

(c)

Figure 6.10 In a simple feedback servo (a), there is oscillation because of load inertia. The addition of velocity sensing (b) allows the oscillation to be damped out. The damping factor affects the response to an input. Various responses are shown in (c).

this simple servo is unusable because when the load is brought back to the correct place it will arrive at speed as it has been accelerated continuously by the position error. When the position error falls to zero, the drive to the motor will disappear. However, the load does not stop because of its inertia but overshoots. The result is oscillation where the load repeatedly overshoots every time it is brought back to the correct place.

The solution is to add damping to the system so that the load is actively slowed down as it returns to the correct place. Figure 6.10(b) shows how damping is added by using a separate velocity transducer, or tachometer, or by differentiating the position error. The sense of the velocity signal is such that it opposes the position error. In this way as the load returns to the correct place and the position error approaches zero, the velocity signal will have the opposite sense and the positioner drive will actually reverse and slow down the load. The amount of velocity feedback controls the damping factor and the response of the system to a sudden input step. Figure 6.10(c) shows the result of various damping factors. If an oscillation or overshoot occurs, the system is said to be underdamped, whereas if the response is excessively slowed down, the system is overdamped. In between there is a damping factor which brings the system to rest in the shortest time without overshooting. This is called a critically damped system. In practice systems err on the underdamped side as a useful increase in speed can be obtained if a small overshoot is acceptable.

It will be seen that feedback systems are error driven: no drive to the load can be obtained without a position error. If the input is constant, but an external force attempts to disturb the load position, it will succeed in doing so only until a position error is created which results in a restoring force equal to the disturbing force. The larger the gain A, the smaller will be the position error required to produce a given restoring force. The system acts like a spring, and the ratio of the restoring force to the load displacement is called the stiffness. The stiffness is proportional to the gain A. Figure 6.11(a) shows that a high feedback loop gain makes the servo more accurate as external forces are more readily rejected.

Unfortunately it is not possible to increase the gain indefinitely. All practical servo systems are made from components which are not infinitely stiff. For example the connection between the motor and the load has a finite stiffness and will flex as it carries forces needed to cause acceleration. Figure 6.11(b) shows that flexure results in phase lags between the drive waveform and the load response. The amplitude falls, but the phase lag will increase with frequency and inevitably at some frequency the lag will become 180 degrees. When this occurs, the negative feedback has become positive feedback. If the loop gain exceeds unity at that frequency, there will be oscillation. Thus the gain has to be restricted to a value which prevents instability. An increase in gain can be obtained by fitting a frequency-dependent network in the feedback loop. The network is designed to have the opposite phase response to the rest of the loop. Use of such a network is known as compensation.

Feedback systems are restricted in the accuracy they can achieve because the output drive results from amplifying an error. There must be an error to obtain any drive.

Figure 6.12(a) shows that, in a feedforward system, the input signal is converted to a drive signal in a predictor unit which effectively models the characteristics of the mechanical system and opposes them. For example, if the system response is non-linear, an opposing non-linearity may be incorporated in the model. If the frequency response of the system falls prematurely, the predictor incorporates a suitable boost. The accuracy of a feedforward system depends upon how closely the predictor models the actual system. As there is no feedback, the predictor can only use typical values, and it cannot compensate for external loads.

Feedforward is seldom used alone, but it is advantageous when combined with a feedback system. When combined in this way, the amplified feedback signal is

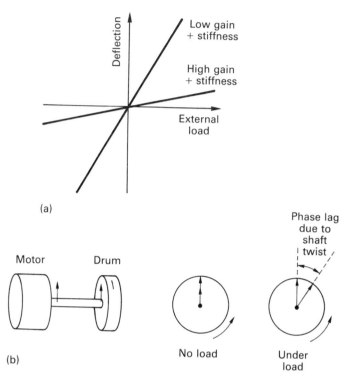

Figure 6.11 As feedback servos require an error to obtain drive to the load, it follows that increasing the gain will reduce the error. The deflection obtained by an external force (a) is a measure of the stiffness of the servo. In all servos there are phase lags caused by mechanical flexure. (b) shows how the shaft between motor and drum in a rotary-head recorder acts as a torsion spring. If there is net loop gain when the phase lag reaches 180°, there will be oscillation.

added to the predictor signal as shown in Figure 6.12(b). The predictor is responsible for most of the drive to the load. The feedback system only has to correct for the difference between the predicted drive signal and the actual displacement measured by the transducer. As this correction signal will be smaller than the main drive signal the error required to produce it will be smaller and so the system is more accurate.

One of the fundamental drawbacks of feedforward is that it is insensitive to changes in operating parameters. Adaptive servos overcome this problem by using the error in the feedback loop to improve the accuracy of the predictive model. Adaptive servos are complex, and can only be practically implemented in the digital domain.

6.6 Microprocessor-based servos

Accurate analog servos are inevitably complex, requiring filters, differentiators, summing, etc. If advanced techniques such as feedforward and adaptation are used, analog implementations become unwieldy. If signals from transducers are

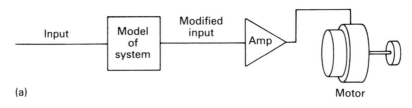

(a)

Motor

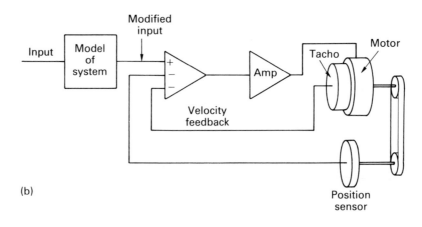

(b)

Position
sensor

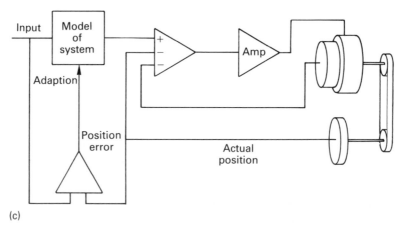

(c)

Figure 6.12 (a) In feedforward, the drive signal is processed by a predictor to drive the load. There is no compensation if the load changes. If feedback and feedforward are combined, (b), the feedback only has to cancel the prediction error and so the total error will be smaller. In adaptive servos (c), the error and input signals are analysed to dynamically optimize the predictor model.

converted to the digital domain, all of the necessary processes can be performed numerically. Arbitrary transfer functions, which are difficult to produce with analog techniques, are easily obtained from digital lookup tables.

The microprocessor is a highly cost-effective tool for implementation of servos. Operating speed is not generally an issue, and the functionality of the servo is largely independent of the hardware configuration. Circuit boards can be designed and built before the servo design is complete because final design details affect only the firmware which controls the system. The physical size of circuitry is heavily constrained in certain applications, particularly in peripherals for personal computers where standard sized envelopes are required.

It is not intended here to repeat any explanations of microprocessor operation as such treatments are readily available. Figure 6.13 shows a generic microprocessor-based servo. The microprocessor obtains instructions from ROM, and dynamic data are stored in RAM. Input parameters from transducers are obtained via ports connected to ADCs and, similarly, DAC ports are provided for analog outputs to motors. As many servo functions are inherently real-time, a number of programmable timers are incorporated. These will provide an interrupt after a software-determined time from loading has elapsed. One of these may be used to determine the sampling rate of the analog inputs. Another may be used to control the repetition rate of the main servo algorithm.

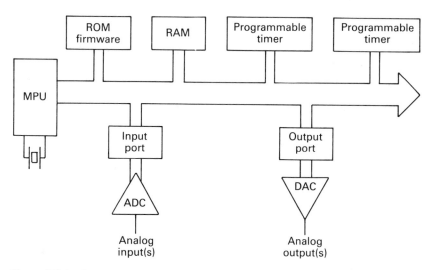

Figure 6.13 A microprocessor-based servo. Analog inputs drive ADC ports, and output DACs drive motors, or stepping motors can be driven directly. A number of programmable counters are needed to establish time constants and sampling rates in real time. The operation of the servo is entirely program controlled and can be changed without hardware redesign.

Figure 6.14 shows how a microprocessor can be used to implement an adaptive servo for a high-density floppy disk drive.[6] Floppy disks are anisotropic (see Chapter 9) and temperature changes result in the track distorting from an ideal circle to a complex shape. A track-following head can be made to follow more accurately if the system can learn the shape of the track and provide feedforward to the positioner. The offset needed by the positioner is built up in RAM by the following mechanism. The timing of the system is locked to the rotation of the disk. Every time the head passes a tracking pattern, a tracking error is produced, and this drives the feedback loop of the servo as normal. However, the polarity of the feedback error is used to increment or decrement a

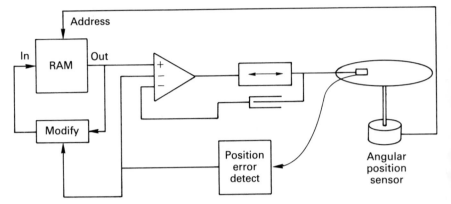

Figure 6.14 An adaptive track-following servo 'learns' the track shape by adapting the feedforward incrementally from the feedback polarity. As the feedforward adapts more closely, the feedback error reduces.

feedforward parameter for that angular position of the disk. It will be seen from the figure that on the next revolution the feedforward parameter will have changed so that the feedback error is made smaller. After a few revolutions a 'map' of the disk track offset will exist in memory such that the correct head offset is provided from memory at each sector. Interpolation in the control algorithm can be used to move the head smoothly between tracking patterns.

6.7 Controlling motor speed

In various modes of operation, the capstan and/or the drum will need to have accurate control of their rotational speed. During crash record (a mode in which no attempt is made to lock to a previous recording on the tape) the capstan must run at an exact and constant speed. When the drum is first started, it must be brought to the correct speed before phase lock can be attempted. The principle of speed control commonly used will be examined here.

Figure 6.15(a) shows that the motor whose speed is to be controlled is fitted with a toothed wheel or slotted disk. For convenience, the number of slots will usually be some power of two. A sensor, magnetic or optical, will produce one pulse per slot, and these will be counted by a binary divider. A similar counter is driven by a reference frequency. This may often be derived by multiplying the input video field rate in a phase-locked loop.

The outputs of the two counters are taken to a full adder, whose output drives a DAC which in turn drives the motor. The bias of the motor amplifier is arranged so that a DAC code of one-half of the quantizing range results in zero drive to the motor, and smaller or larger codes will result in forward or reverse drive.

If the count in the tacho divider lags the count in the reference divider, the motor will receive increased power, whereas if the count in the tacho divider leads the count in the reference divider, the motor will experience reverse drive, which slows it down. The result is that the speed of the motor is exactly proportional to the reference frequency. In principle the system is a phase-locked loop, where the voltage-controlled oscillator has been replaced by a motor and a frequency generating (FG) wheel.

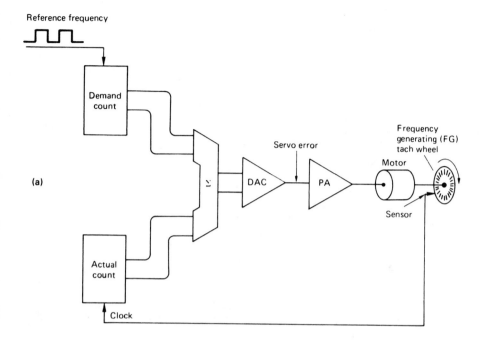

(a)

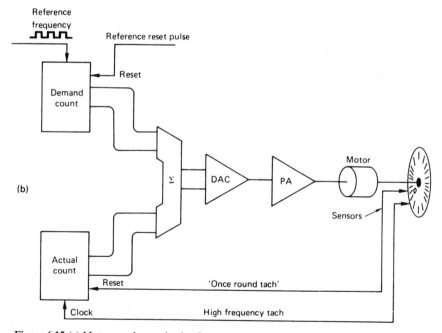

(b)

Figure 6.15 (a) Motor speed control using frequency generator on motor shaft. Pulses from FG are compared with pulses from reference to derive servo error. (b) An additional sensor resets the actual count once per revolution, so it counts motor phase angle. Demand count is reset by reference timing. Thus motor phase is locked to reference.

6.8 Phase-locked servos

In a rotary-head recorder, the rotational phase of the drum and capstan must be accurately controlled. In the case of the drum, the phase must be controlled so that the heads reach the beginning of a track at a time which has a constant relationship to signals from the master timing generator controlling the record or replay process.

A slightly more complex version of the speed control system of Figure 6.15(a) is required, as will be seen in Figure 6.15(b). In addition to a toothed wheel or slotted disk, the motor carries a reference slot which produces a rotational phase reference commonly called *once-round tach*. This reference presets the tach divider, so that the tach count becomes an accurate binary representation of the actual angle of rotation.

A similar divider is fed by a reference clock as before, and preset at appropriate intervals. The reference clock has the same frequency as the tooth-passing frequency of the tacho at normal speed. In a segmented DVTR which needs two drum rotations per field, the counter will need to be preset twice per field. Alternatively, and more elegantly, the counter will have an additional high-order bit which does not go to the adder, and then it can be preset once per field, since disconnection of the upper bit will cause two repeated counts of half a field duration each, with an overflow between.

The adder output will increase or decrease the motor drive until the once-round tach occurs exactly opposite the reference preset pulse, because in this condition the sum of the two inputs to the adder is always zero.

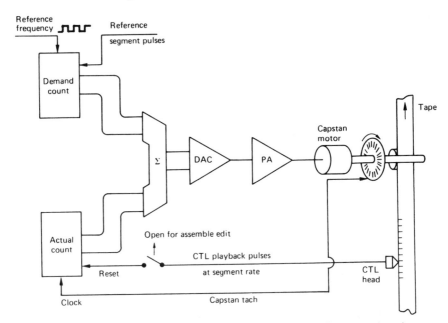

Figure 6.16 If the encoder counter is reset by CTL pulses, it will count linear tape phase, i.e. distance between CTL pulses. Controlling demand counter from reference segment pulses phase locks tape CTL track to segment rate resulting in correct tracking. At an assemble edit the reset is disabled and the capstan servo makes a smooth transition to the velocity control mode of Figure 6.15(a).

The binary count of the tach counter can be used to address a rotation phase PROM. This will be programmed to generate signals which enable the different sectors of the recorded format to be put in the correct place on the track. For example, if it is desired to edit one audio channel without changing any other part of a recording, the record head must be enabled for a short period at precisely the correct drum angle. The drum phase PROM will provide the timing information needed.

When the tape is playing, the phase of the control track must be locked to reference segment phase in order to achieve accurate tracking.

Figure 6.16 shows that a similar configuration to the drum servo is used, but there is no once-round tach on the capstan wheel. Instead, the tach counter is reset by the segment pulses obtained by replaying the control track. Since the speed of the control track is proportional to the capstan speed, resetting the tach count in this way results in a count of control track phase. The reference counter is reset by segment rate pulses, which can be obtained from the drum, and so the capstan motor will be driven in such a way that the phase error between control track pulses and reference pulses is minimized. In this way, the rotary heads will accurately track the diagonal tracks.

During an assemble edit, the capstan will phase-lock to control track during the pre-roll, but must revert to constant speed mode at the in-point, since the control track will be recorded from that point. This transition can be obtained by simply disabling the capstan tach counter reset, which causes the system to revert to the speed control servo of Figure 6.15.

6.9 Tension servos

It will be seen in Chapter 8 that tape tension control is critical in helical scan machines, primarily to ensure interchange and the correct head contact. Tension control will also be necessary for shuttle to ensure correct tape packing.

Figure 6.17 shows a typical back-tension control system. A swinging guide called a tension arm is mounted on a position sensor which can be optical or magnetic. A spring applies a force to the tension arm in a direction which would make the tape path longer. The position sensor output is connected to the supply reel motor amplifier which is biased in such a way that when the sensor is in the centre of its travel the motor will receive no drive. The polarity of the system is arranged so that the reel motor will be driven in reverse when the spring contracts. The result is that the reel motor will apply a reverse torque which will extend the spring as it attempts to return the tension arm to the neutral position. If the system is given adequate loop gain, a minute deflection of the arm will result in full motor torque, so the arm will be kept in an essentially constant position. This means that the spring will have a constant length, and so the tape tension will be constant. Different tensions can be obtained by switching offsets into the feedback loop, which result in the system null being at a different extension of the spring.

The error in the servo will only be small if the reel can accelerate fast enough to follow tape motion. In a machine with permanent capstan engagement, the capstan can accelerate much faster than the reels can. If not controlled, this would lead to the tension arm moving to one or other end of its travel, resulting in tape stretch, or a slack loop which will subsequently snatch tight with the same results. A fixed acceleration limit on the capstan servo would prevent the

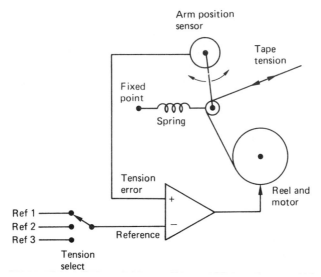

Figure 6.17 Tension servo controls reel motor current so that motor extends sprung arm. Sensor determines extension of spring and thus tape tension.

problem, but it would have to be set to allow a full reel on a large-size cassette to keep up. The motion of a small cassette with vastly reduced inertia would be made artificially ponderous. The solution is to feed back the displacement of the tension sensors to the capstan servo. If the magnitude of the tension error from either tension arm is excessive, the capstan acceleration is cut back. In this way the reels are accelerated as fast as possible without the tension becoming incorrect.

In a cassette-based recorder, the tension arms usually need to be motorized so that they can fit into the mouth of the cassette for loading, and pull tape out into the threaded position. It is possible to replace the spring which provides tape tension with a steady current through the arm motor. By controlling this current, the tape tension can be programmed.

6.10 Tape remaining sensing

It is most important in a cassette to prevent the tape running out at speed. The tape is spliced to a heavy leader at each end, and this leader is firmly attached to the reel hub. In an audio cassette, there is sufficient length of this leader to reach to the other reel, and so the impact of a run-off can be withstood. This approach cannot be used with a video cassette, because the heavy leader cannot be allowed to enter the drum, as it would damage the rotating heads.

The transport must compute the tape remaining in order to prevent running off at speed. This may be done by measuring the linear speed of the tape and comparing it with the rotational speed of the reel. The linear speed will be the capstan speed in a permanent capstan drive transport; a timer roller will be necessary in a pinch-roller-type transport. Alternatively, tape remaining may be computed by comparing the speed of the two reels. The rotational speed of the reels will be obtained from a frequency generator on the reel motors. Figure 6.18 shows a simple method of computing the tape remaining. Pulses from the capstan FG cause a counter to increment. When a reel FG pulse occurs, the count will be transferred to a latch, and the counter will be reset. When the reel is full, there will be many capstan FG pulses between reel FG pulses, but as the radius of the tape pack falls, the count transferred to the latch will also fall. It will be possible to determine the limit count from a knowledge of the capstan and reel hub diameters, and the number of teeth on their generators. The latch count is not quite the pack radius, because if the tension arm is moving due to an acceleration,

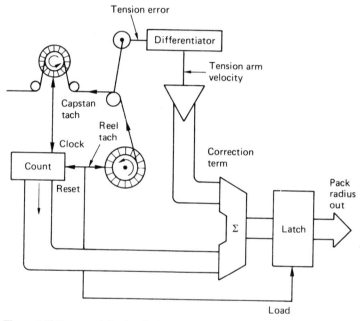

Figure 6.18 Tape remaining is calculated by comparing capstan tach with reel tach. If tension arm is moving, tape speed at reel and capstan will be different, so correction term from tension arm sensor is added.

Pinch-roller-type transports disengage the capstan in shuttle, and so the timer roller tacho would be used instead.

the linear speed of the tape at the capstan will not be the same as the linear speed at the reel. To prevent false shutdowns when accelerating near the end of the tape, the tension arm signal may be differentiated to give an arm velocity signal, and this can be digitized and used to produce a correction factor for the radius parameter.

To prevent runoffs, the reel pack radius of the reel which is unwinding profiles the allowable shuttle speed so that, as the pack radius falls, the tape speed falls with it. Thus when the tape finally runs out, it will be travelling at very low speed, and the photoelectric sensor which detects the leader will be able to halt the transport without damage.

Chapter 7

Stationary-head tape recorders

Stationary-head digital recorders are direct descendants of analog tape recorders and early machines resembled their ancestors closely. Storage density lagged behind that of rotary-head machines, but the development of thin-film and magnetoresistive heads has helped to redress the balance. Tape-based data recorders are used for three main applications: computer data, high bit-rate instrumentation data and digital audio. Although it is possible to record and replay digital video on a stationary-head transport such machines are unable to provide picture-in-shuttle, and digital VTRs universally employ rotary heads (see Chapter 8).

7.1 Computer data recorders

In computer data use, tape decks are used for storage of variable-length blocks which are discrete. In most cases the tape transport comes to a halt between blocks and a so-called inter-record gap (IRG) is provided to allow the transport space to stop and start. The use of variable-length blocks allows more efficient use of the medium than the fixed-length blocks of disk drives and helps to reduce the cost per bit. Variable-length blocks do, however, make updating or editing of blocks in the middle of a tape (so-called update-in-place) impossible. The solution is to divide the tape into two independent areas or partitions, separated by a unique marker as shown in Figure 7.1. The partition near the beginning of the tape (BOT) is quite small and is used to store an index or directory of the contents of the second partition and the physical position of the files. If it is required to edit a file, it is read from the second partition into host memory and altered. Upon rewriting to tape, the new version is appended to the end of the previous files. The first partition is then rewritten to reflect the new state of the

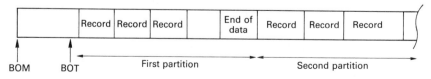

Figure 7.1 In order to maintain a directory near the head of a tape, two partitions are used with a unique marker pattern between them.

265

files. If the updated file is required, the updated index will automatically direct the retrieval process to the new version of the file. Early magtapes were extremely simple and the access method ponderous. Upon loading a tape it would advance to BOT, stop and assert 'ready'. The commands were restricted to read, write, skip forwards, skip reverse and rewind to BOT. In order to locate a file, the tape deck would be given a skip command and it would then advance tape until the next IRG when it would stop and assert 'ready'. The skip command would be repeated by the host until the correct file was located. If commanded to read, the transport would transfer data until the next IRG.

Such systems were simple and cheap, but as storage density increased the number of files on a tape would increase with it. The impact of the skip/ready/ skip/ready sequence on the processor became unacceptable. This led to the development of the file mark (FM), a record placed between two IRGs and which the transport could identify. A new command, search to file mark, was introduced. Figure 7.2(a) shows how the use of filemarks reduces the number of interrupts needed to access a file. Ultimately even filemarks were not sufficient, and the hierarchically superior save set mark (SSM) was introduced. Figure 7.2(b) shows how the SSM functions.

7.2 Computer tape formats

Early recorders used seven, later nine, tracks on half-inch open-reel tape. One of the tracks was a parity track, not just to detect errors, but also to allow the use of NRZI channel coding. As Chapter 4 showed, in NRZI when successive zeros are recorded, there is no bit clock. This was overcome by using odd parity across the tape tracks. With odd parity, it is impossible to have a bit cell without at least one transition somewhere across the tape. Thus a guaranteed bit clock could be obtained by using an OR function of all of the tracks.

As tape drives often have to be able to read existing tapes, new formats have to be backwards compatible with existing formats. This led to the nine-track layout persisting for some time, during which density improvements were confined to increasing the linear density. The first machines used 200 bits per inch (bpi) rising to 800 bpi. This represented the limit for reliable crosstrack clocking. At higher densities, skew between head gaps introduced intertrack phase differences and self clocking independent tracks were then needed.

The later NRZI formats had a single CRC character at the end of each record,[1] followed by a longitudinal parity symbol (LRC). The LRC served to ensure that every record contained an even number of transitions so that the record current returned to the same direction as the erase current at the end of every block. This prevented the generation of spurious transitions when the write current was turned on and off. The CRCC could identify the track containing errors and the crosstrack or vertical parity could correct the error on re-reading the block. At such low densities single-track correction was acceptable, especially as read-after-write was employed to check the integrity of recordings. The block length was in fact limited by the codeword length of the CRCC polynomial (see Chapter 5).

Later transports adopted phase encoding (PE, see Chapter 4) which was self clocking. As PE always has a mid-bit transition, the lack of a transition indicates an error. Thus with a CRCC to check integrity, a PE-equipped transport could correct one entire track in error on-the-fly using crosstrack parity. PE allowed 1600 bpi, later 3200 bpi.

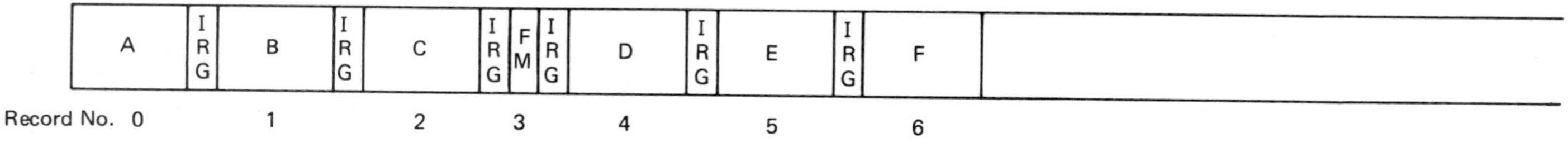

A	I R G	B	I R G	C	I F R G / M	D	I R G	E	I R G	F

Record No.   0   1   2   3   4   5   6

Figure 7.2(a) Simple magtapes locate records by separating them with inter-record gaps (IRGs). A record can be skipped by searching for the next IRG. This process is eased by introducing the filemark (FM) which must, however, be counted as a record because this is how a simple magtape would treat it.

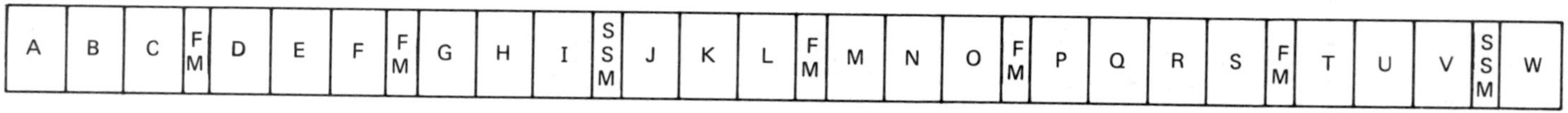

A	B	C	F M	D	E	F	F M	G	H	I	S S M	J	K	L	F M / M	M	N	O	F M / M	P	Q	R	S	F M / M	T	U	V	S S M / M	W

Figure 7.2(b) The save set mark (SSM) is hierarchically superior to the filemark, and saves operations in high-capacity recorders. For example, locating record M in a simple machine would require 16 record skips. With FM handling it would require three FM skips; with SSM handling it requires one SSM skip, one FM skip.

Further linear density increases were obtained with the use of group codes. 6250 bpi was reached with a 4/5 code and the correction power was necessarily doubled to allow double-track on-the-fly correction. Later the number of tracks was doubled to 18 and a linear density of 22 kbpi was reached with an 8/9 code. The error-correction capacity went up to four tracks.

The development of the Winchester disk drive led to a requirement for high-speed tapes for backup. The requirement to stop in an IRG and accelerate up to speed again put severe constraints on the transport. The streaming drive was designed to overcome the problem by recording non-stop. The standard tape format was laid down so that it could be read by non-streaming drives, but the transport would continue running through the IRG and continue writing if data were continuously available. The transport need then only be capable of transporting at high speed, without having the acceleration to reach that speed in an IRG. In order to begin writing, host data would be ready in a buffer, and the drive would back up into the end of the previous block in order to take a run or pre-roll. The correct tape speed would be reached by the end of the previous block and recording would commence. The recording process could continue for as long as the host computer could furnish data. In the event of an underflow, the transport would have to abort the current block, then back up into the end of the previous block in order to take a run up to speed when data became available again.

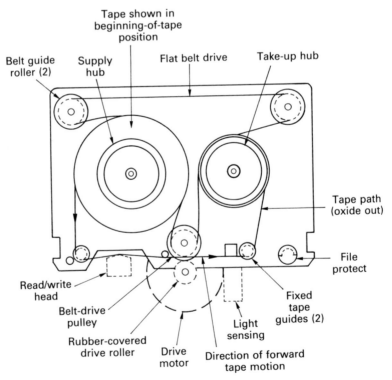

Figure 7.3 In the QIC (quarter-inch cassette), tape is transported entirely by an elastomeric belt which wraps the reel packs. A single drive motor engages the centre belt pulley.

In addition to increasing the access speed and transfer rate of tapes, efforts were also made to produce lower cost, smaller products. These used cassettes or cartridges with typically $\frac{1}{4}$ inch tape. In a cassette, there are two hubs and the tape is permanently attached to both whereas in a cartridge there is only one hub and the free end of the tape is automatically threaded onto a second hub which is part of the drive. In order to reduce cost, instead of a multitrack head some drives had a single-track head which was mechanically indexed across the tape. By reversing the tape and indexing the head in a sequence a serpentine recording can be made.

Figure 7.3 shows a quarter-inch cassette (QIC).[2] This consists of a rigid metal baseplate and a plastic cover. Within the cover are two coplanar tape reels. Separate reel and capstan drives are dispensed with by employing an elastomeric belt which wraps around both reels and a drive pulley which engages with a motor in the drive. Tape drive is handled entirely by the belt which is capable of keeping the tape loop between the reels under tension. The cassette geometry is such that the belt tension is higher around the hub which is taking up tape. The cross section of the belt will be reduced by the tension and so its effective radius is reduced whereas on the supply hub the radius will be increased. There will thus be a slight differential drive speed which keeps the tape under tension.

As the cost of implementing logic circuitry continued to fall, the complexity which was initially only available on mainframe drives, such as group codes and Reed–Solomon codes, filtered down to smaller formats and increased their performance.

7.3 Computer tape drives

The computer tape deck was originally designed for start/stop operation. The IRG was $\frac{1}{2}$ inch long and this allowed half that distance in which to stop, half in which to accelerate. Figure 7.4 shows how a capstan drive amplifier operates. When running at speed it is a feedback-controlled velocity servo, typically using a tachogenerator to measure the actual speed. However, when fed with a step input, the velocity error is large enough to saturate the drive amplifier and the acceleration is uncontrolled. In order to obtain a smooth acceleration ramp up to speed, a current limiter is used. Whenever the set current is exceeded the velocity error is shunted. As the motor torque is proportional to the current, a constant current provides a linear acceleration ramp.

The tape reels cannot be accelerated as quickly as the capstan. Even if sufficient power were available, extreme reel acceleration would result in the tape layers slipping over one another. The tape reels were initially decoupled from the tape in the area of the capstan and heads by tension arms. Figure 7.5 shows a tension-arm transport. The tape motion is determined entirely by the capstan. The tension arms drive the reel motors, as was described in Chapter 6, in order to keep the arm position constant and will take up or pay out tape automatically. The arms are biased by springs and if the arm position is constant the tape tension is constant. Tape tension is used to obtain grip between the tape and the capstan and to provide contact pressure against the heads. Sudden capstan acceleration is absorbed by movement of the tension arms until the reels can be accelerated. During this time the spring extension and thus the tape tension must vary.

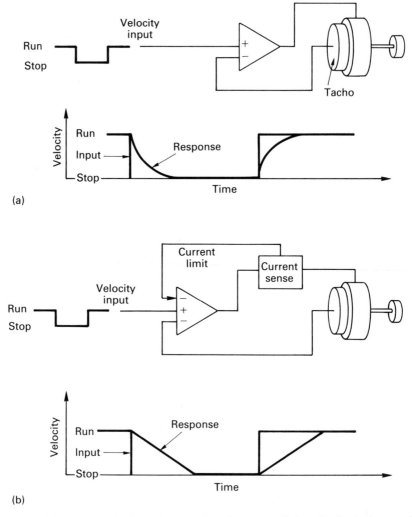

Figure 7.4 Simple velocity feedback capstan in (a) has uncontrolled acceleration in the case of an input step. Addition of current limiting in (b) results in linear velocity ramp during IRG.

There is constant pressure to improve the access time and the transfer rate of magtapes. This can be done by increasing the tape speed, but requires greater acceleration to reach that speed in the same IRG. The force required to accelerate the tension arms is transmitted by the tape, and the strength of the tape places a limit on the acceleration possible. The mass to be accelerated can be dramatically reduced by adopting vacuum columns. Figure 7.6 shows that between the reels and the capstan/head assembly the tape is buffered by forming loops in vacuum chambers. The tape tension is created by the action of atmospheric pressure on the loops. Photoelectric sensors or pressure transducers are distributed along the columns and drive the reel motors in order to return the tape loops to the centres of the columns. The advantages of the vacuum-column approach are twofold.

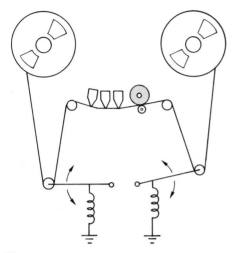

Figure 7.5 Tension-arm-type computer transport allows tape acceleration to be decoupled from heavy reels. Acceleration is limited by tape tension needed to accelerate tension-arm mass.

Firstly, the system acts like a massless tension arm, and extremely rapid accelerations can be obtained without exceeding the elastic limit of the tape. Secondly, the tape tension is provided by a constant-pressure differential and is independent of the position of the loop. When the tape accelerates, the position of the loop moves until the reel catches up, but, unlike a sprung arm, there is no

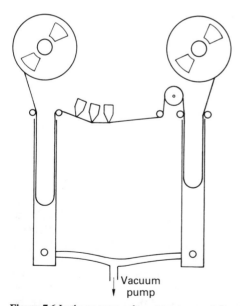

Figure 7.6 In the vacuum-column tape transport the tension arms are replaced by atmospheric pressure which acts as a massless constant-tension spring. Reel servos try to keep the loops centred in the columns.

tension variation due to this motion. The drawbacks of vacuum-column transports are that they are noisy and consume a lot of power.

In high-speed transports the acceleration may be restricted by slip between the capstan and the tape. This can be eliminated by drilling the capstan surface and applying suction from the vacuum pump. Vacuum-column drives have been built which subject the tape to accelerations of up to $500\,g$. Inevitably tape which has to endure such conditions needs to be much stronger, and hence thicker, than tape used in audio and instrumentation applications. The tape tension used is correspondingly high, and the crushing force on the reels due to many layers of tape under tension led to the adoption of metal hubs.

The head block contains erase, record and replay heads and may be preceded by a vacuum-operated tape cleaner. A pair of photoelectric cells are installed to detect metallic BOT and EOT markers. The EOT marker is positioned some distance before the physical end of the tape so that if EOT is detected during writing the data block can be completed. The transport cannot begin to record after EOT. The head arrangement is shown in Figure 7.7. The erase head erases

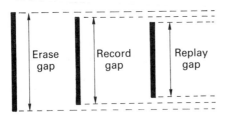

Figure 7.7 A stationary-head transport erases a wider track than is recorded and in turn plays a narrower track in order to ensure interchange between different machines.

a wider track than the record head in order to ensure that no part of a previous recording remains in the presence of misalignments. Similarly the replay head reads a narrower track than the record head. When writing, the replay head operates in read-after-write mode. This was intended to detect errors due to tape defects which would exceed the correcting power of the replay system. In order to increase the confidence level of the read-after-write process the thresholds in the replay peak detectors (see Chapter 4) could be raised during writing.

7.4 Error-correction strategies

Figure 7.8(a) shows the simple arrangement of an 800 bpi NRZI record having vertical parity, longitudinal parity and a CRC character. The CRCC turns the recorded data into a codeword. If, on reading a block, the syndrome was non-zero due to errors in a single track (due possibly to a dirty head), the track in error could be determined from the CRC. It would then be necessary to reverse to the beginning of the block and re-read the block with one track disabled. The missing bits are computed using parity.

The 1600 and 3200 bpi phase-encoded tapes used the same arrangement, but the phase encoding code itself is capable of error detection and single-track correction by erasure is possible without a re-read.

In the 6250 bpi format using a 4/5 group code, the error-correction strategy was based on the Reed–Solomon code.[1] Seven data bytes have one redundancy byte computed in one dimension to form an 8 byte block. The second redundancy byte is computed orthogonally to the first to make 9 byte codewords which repeat throughout the data block. The ninth tape track carries conventional vertical parity. One track in error can be detected and corrected, whereas if the tracks in error are known, two tracks can be corrected by erasure.

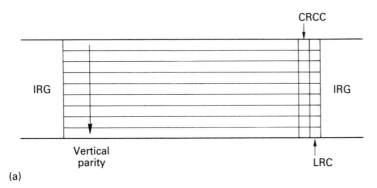

(a)

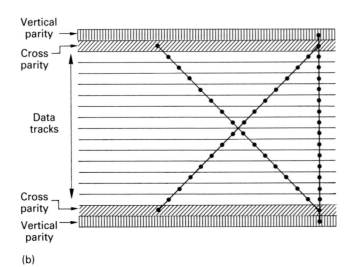

(b)

Figure 7.8 (a) The simple format of 800 bpi tapes. (b) The cross parity of the IBM 18 track tape format. See text for details.

In the 18 track format of the IBM 3480 which uses an 8/9 group code, a cross-interleaving system (see Chapter 5) known as adaptive cross parity is used,[1] having some similarity to the approach used in the DASH digital audio format. Figure 7.8(b) shows that parity is calculated convolutionally on two opposed diagonals across 16 tracks. Although the block must begin with values which are forced to zero, once the convolution is under way the check bytes from earlier diagonals are protected in the codewords formed on the opposite diagonals. In addition to the diagonal parity, vertical crosstrack parity is computed. The tracks are divided into two sets and vertical parity is computed for each set to produce characters which are recorded in two additional tracks. The track positions in Figure 7.8(b) are symbolic and the tracks of the two sets are mechanically interleaved on tape. Location of the failing symbol is performed geometrically as it must be at the intersection of vertical and diagonal codewords. As with all convolutional interleaves, the decoding is iterative. One failing track can be located and corrected in each set. Using erasure, two tracks in each set can be corrected. As the diagonal codewords embrace all data tracks, using erasure three tracks in one set can be corrected.

7.5 Digital audio recorders

Professional digital stationary-head audio recorders are specifically designed for record production and mastering, and have to be able to offer all the features of an analog multitrack. It could be said that many digital multitracks mimic analog machines so exactly that they can be installed in otherwise analog studios with the minimum of fuss. When the stationary-head formats were first developed, the necessary functions of a professional machine were: independent control of which tracks record and play, synchronous recording, punch-in/punch-out editing, tape-cut editing, variable-speed playback, offtape monitoring in record, various tape speeds and bandwidths, autolocation and the facilities to synchronize several machines. This is a much more rigorous set of constraints than those for a digital computer recorder although the requirement for stop/start recording is absent and thinner tape can be employed. Digital audio recorders must work in real time, and retries are not possible. However, audio recorders can use concealment and a larger interleave and can accept a residual error rate which is much higher than computer data can tolerate.

In both theory and practice a rotary-head recorder can achieve a higher storage density than a stationary-head recorder, thus using less tape. When multitrack digital audio recorders were first proposed, the adoption of rotary heads had to be ruled out because the requirement for individual track recording could not be met without control logic complexity which was then unacceptable. In addition rotary recorders then lacked the necessary bandwidth. For example, a 24 track machine requires about 20 megabits per second. A further difficulty is that helical-scan recorders were not designed to handle tape-cut edits. Accordingly, multitrack digital audio recorders have evolved with stationary heads and open reels; they look like analog recorders, but offer sufficient bandwidth for digital recording and support splicing, although some early multitrack machines were built which did not support tape-cut editing. These had to be supplied in pairs so that editing could be performed by assembling from one machine to the other. Now that the digital video recorder has become economic, with a prodigious bit-rate which may be put to other purposes, a rotary-head 48 track machine based on a video cassette is perfectly feasible.

7.6 Outline of digital audio recorder

A stationary-head digital audio recorder is basically quite simple, as the block diagram of Figure 7.9 shows. The transport is not dissimilar to that of an analog recorder. The tape substrate used in professional analog recording is quite thick

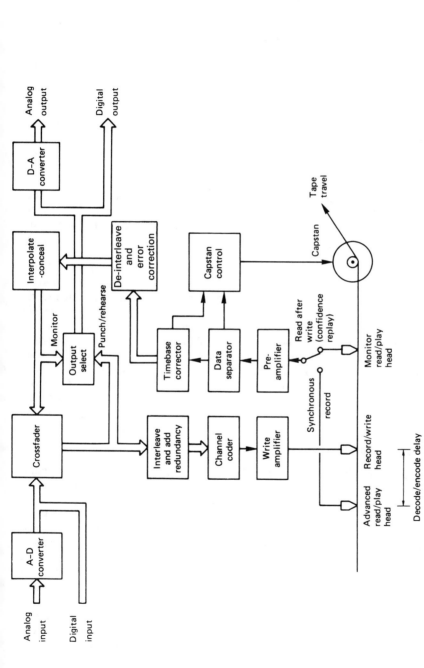

Figure 7.9 Block diagram of typical open-reel digital audio recorder. Note advanced head for synchronous recording, and capstan controlled by replay circuits.

to reduce print-through, whereas in digital recording the tape is very thin, rather like videotape, to allow it to conform closely to the heads for short-wavelength working. The tape tension is correspondingly low. Print-through is not an issue in digital recording. The roughness of the backcoat has to be restricted in digital tape to prevent it embossing the magnetic layer of the adjacent turn when on the reel, since this would nullify the efforts made to provide a smooth surface finish for good head contact. The roughness of the backcoat allows the boundary layer to bleed away between turns when the tape is spooled, and so low-tension digital audio recorders do not spool as quickly as analog recorders. They cannot afford to risk the edge damage which results from storing a poor tape pack. The digital transport has rather better tension and reel-speed control than an analog machine. Some transports offer a slow-wind mode to achieve an excellent pack on a tape prior to storage.

Control of the capstan is rather different too, being more like that of a video recorder. The capstan turns at constant speed when a virgin tape is being recorded, but for replay it will be controlled to run at whatever speed is necessary to make the off tape sample rate equal to the reference rate. In this way, several machines can be kept in exact synchronism by feeding them with a common reference. Variable-speed replay can be achieved by changing the reference frequency. It should be emphasized that, when variable speed is used, the output sampling rate changes. This may not be of any consequence if the samples are returned to the analog domain, but it prevents direct connection to a digital mixer, since these usually have fixed sampling rates.

The major items in the block diagram have been discussed in the relevant chapters. Samples are interleaved, redundancy is added, and the bits are converted into a suitable channel code. In stationary-head recorders, the frequencies in each head are low, and complex coding is not difficult. The lack of the rotary transformer of the rotary-head machine means that DC content is a less important issue. The codes used generally try to emphasize density ratio, which keeps down the linear tape speed, and the jitter window, since this helps to reject the inevitable crosstalk between the closely spaced heads. DC content in the code is handled using adaptive slicers as detailed in Chapter 4. On replay there are the usual data separators, timebase correctors and error-correction circuits.

7.7 The DASH format

The DASH (digital audio stationary head)[3] format is not one format as such, but a family of like formats, and thus supports a number of different track layouts. With ferrite-head technology, it was possible to obtain adequate channel SNR with 24 tracks on ½ in tape, one for each audio channel. This gave rise to the single-density family of formats known as DASH I. The most frequently found member of this family is the Sony PCM-3324.

The dimensions of the 24 track tape layout are shown in Figure 7.10. The analog tracks are placed at the edges where they act as guard bands for the digital tracks, protecting them from edge lifting. Additionally there is a large separation between the analog tracks and the digital tracks. This prevents the bias from the analog heads from having an excessive erasing effect on the adjacent digital tracks. For the same reason AC erase may have to be ruled out. One alternative mechanism for erasure of the analog tracks is to use two DC heads in tandem.

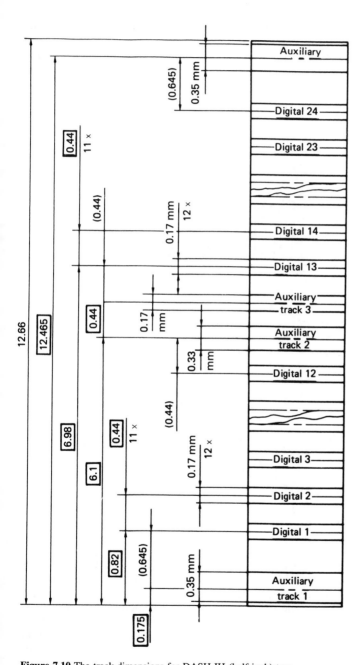

Figure 7.10 The track dimensions for DASH IH (half-inch) tape.

The first erases the tape by saturating it, and the second is wound in the opposite sense, and carries less current, to return the tape to a near-demagnetized state. The timecode and control tracks are placed at the centre of the tape, where they suffer less skew with respect to the digital tracks.

The construction of a bulk ferrite multitrack head is shown in Figure 7.11, where it will be seen that space must be left between the magnetic circuits to accommodate the windings. Track spacing is improved by putting the windings on alternate sides of the gap. The parallel close-spaced magnetic circuits have

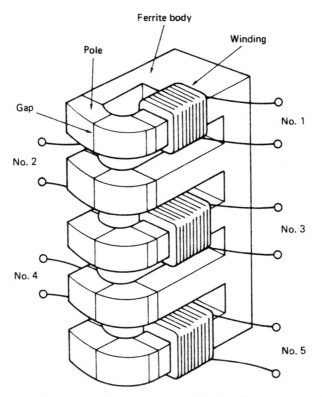

Figure 7.11 A typical ferrite head used for DASH I. Windings are placed on alternate sides to save space, but parallel magnetic circuits have high crosstalk.

considerable mutual inductance, and suffer from crosstalk. This can be compensated when several adjacent tracks record together by cross-connecting antiphase feeds to the record amplifiers.

Using thin-film heads, the magnetic circuits and windings are produced by deposition on a substrate at right angles to the tape plane, and as seen in Figure 7.12 they can be made very accurately at small track spacings. Perhaps more importantly, because the magnetic circuits do not have such large parallel areas, mutual inductance and crosstalk are smaller allowing a higher practical track density.

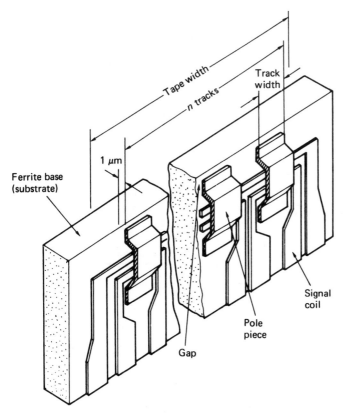

Figure 7.12 The thin-film head shown here can be produced photographically with very small dimensions. Flat structure reduces crosstalk. This type of head is suitable for DASH II which has twice as many tracks as DASH I.

The so-called double-density version, known as DASH II, uses such thin-film heads to obtain 48 digital tracks on ½ in tape and 16 tracks on ¼ in tape. The 48 track version of DASH II is shown in Figure 7.13 where it will be seen that the dimensions allow 24 of the replay head gaps on a DASH II machine to align with and play tapes recorded on a DASH I machine. In fact the 48 track machines can take 24 track tapes and record a further 24 tracks on them.

The DASH format supports three sampling rates and the tape speed is normalized to 30 in/s at the highest rate. The three rates are 32 kHz, 44.1 kHz and 48 kHz. This last frequency was originally 50.4 kHz, which had a simple fractional relationship to 44.1 kHz, but this was dropped in favour of 48 kHz when arbitrary sampling rate conversion was shown to be feasible. In fact most stationary-head recorders will record at any reasonable sampling rate just by supplying them with an external reference, or word clock, at the appropriate frequency. Under these conditions, the sampling-rate switch on the machine only controls the status bits in the recording which set the default playback rate.

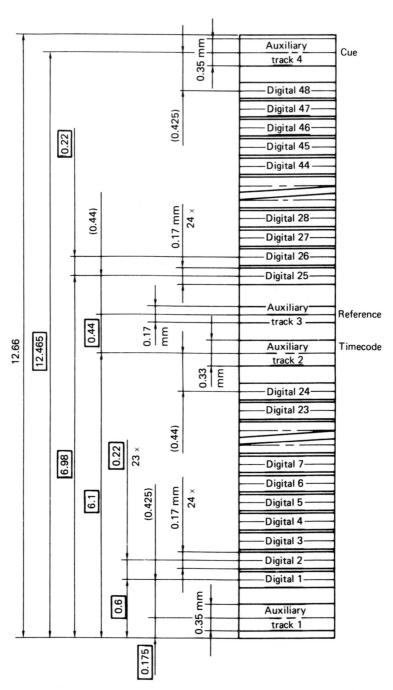

Figure 7.13 The track dimensions for DASH II H (half inch). Comparison with Figure 7.10 will show that half of the tracks align with the single-density format allowing backwards compatibility.

7.8 DASH control and cue tracks

The control track of DASH has a discrete block structure, where each record is referred to as a sector, a term borrowed from disk-drive technology. The length of a sector is equal to four data blocks on a digital audio track. As each data block contains twelve audio samples, one sector corresponds to 48 samples along a track, so at 48 kHz sampling rate, the sector will last 1 ms with DASH-F.

Part of the control-track block is a status word which specifies the type of format and the sampling rate in use, since these must be common for all tracks across the tape. The sector also contains a unique 28 bit binary sector address which will be used by the absolute autolocator and for synchronization between several machines.

The control track must be capable of reading over a wide speed range, and so it uses low density and a simple FM channel code (see Chapter 4). To help with variable-speed operation, a synchronizing pattern precedes the sector data. At the end of the sector, a CRCC detects whether the status bits or the sector address have been corrupted. Normally the sector address counts up, and at an assemble edit, the sector addresses will continue contiguously. Thus if a control track CRC error ocurs, the logic simply adds 1 to the previous sector address. If the tape is spliced, there will be a sector address jump.

The cue tracks of DASH are at the extreme edges of the tape. As most digital audio recorders mute if the speed is more than 25% out, the cue tracks are important to locate edit points over a wide speed range. Sony use biased analog recording for the cue tracks. As the digital headstacks are optimized for short-wavelength recording, their analog performance is poor, and separate heads are used for the analog tracks. These are placed one decode delay downtape from the

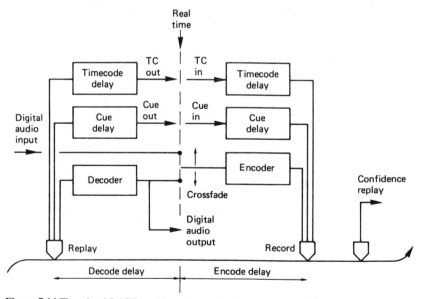

Figure 7.14 Three-head DASH machine with synchronous record capability and time-aligned cue and timecode using CCD delays. The same delay circuits could be used for record or reproduce. Similarly, decoder stages could be shared between replay and confidence.

digital replay head, and one encode delay uptape from the synchronous record head in order to maintain sync. This head also records timecode. Studer take the view that the cue tracks should use a form of modulation suited to short wavelengths which operates over a wide speed range, so that the digital headstacks can be used.[4] Figure 7.14 shows how a three-head DASH machine could be constructed using CCD delays to time-align the cue and timecode signals with the digital audio channels which are subject to interleave delays.

7.9 Redundancy in DASH

The error-correction strategy of DASH is to form codewords which are confined to single tape tracks. DASH uses cross-interleaving and erasure correction, which were described in principle in Chapter 5. In all practical recorders measures have to be taken for the rare cases when the error correction is overwhelmed by gross corruption. In open-reel stationary-head recorders, one obvious mechanism is the act of splicing the tape and the resultant contamination due to fingerprints.

The use of interleaving is essential to handle burst errors; unfortunately it conflicts with the requirements of tape-cut editing. Figure 7.15 shows that a splice in cross-interleave destroys codewords for the entire constraint length of the interleave. The longer the constraint length, the greater the resistance to burst errors, but the more damage is done by a splice.

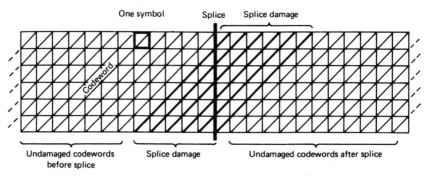

Figure 7.15 Although interleave is a powerful weapon against burst errors, it causes greater data loss when tape is spliced because many codewords are replayed in two unrelated halves.

In order to handle dropouts or splices, samples from the converter or direct digital input are first sorted into odd and even. The odd/even distance has to be greater than the cross-interleave constraint length. In DASH, the constraint length is 119 blocks, or 1428 samples, and the odd/even delay is 204 blocks, or 2448 samples. In the case of a severe dropout, after the replay de-interleave process, the effect will be to cause two separate error bursts, first in the odd samples, then in the even samples. The odd samples can be interpolated from the even and vice versa in order to conceal the dropout. In the case of a splice, samples are destroyed for the constraint length, but Figure 7.16 shows that this occurs at different times for the odd and even samples. Using interpolation, it is possible to obtain simultaneously the end of the old recording and the beginning of the new one. A digital crossfade is made between the old and new recordings.

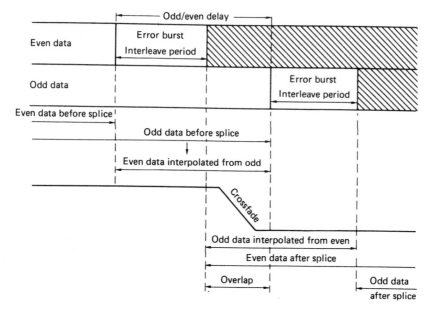

Figure 7.16 Following de-interleave, the effect of a splice is to cause odd and even data to be lost at different times. Interpolation is used to provide the missing samples, and a crossfade is made when both recordings are available in the central overlap.

The interpolation during concealment and splices causes a momentary reduction in frequency response which may result in aliasing if there is significant audio energy above one-quarter of the sampling rate.

Following the odd/even shuffle, the cross-interleave process is performed. As there are twelve samples in each block, the odd and even samples are assembled

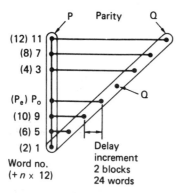

Figure 7.17 The cross-interleave of DASH is achieved with a system of different delays. Data are formed into two arrays of six samples each, one odd numbered and one even numbered. The odd samples are shifted relative to even by 2448. Parity P is generated, followed by the delays shown here to produce parity Q. The remaining interleave is shown in Figure 7.19.

P codeword   Q codeword

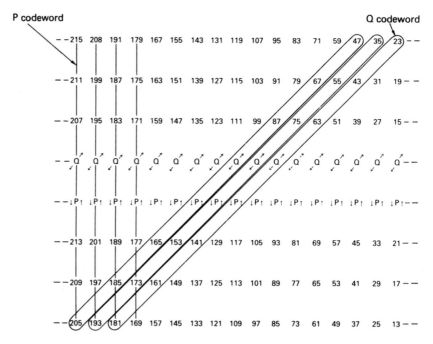

Figure 7.18 The system of Figure 7.17 results in P and Q codewords passing in two directions through the array. The CRC codeword passes in a third direction and will be recorded in that sequence. The example shows only odd samples.

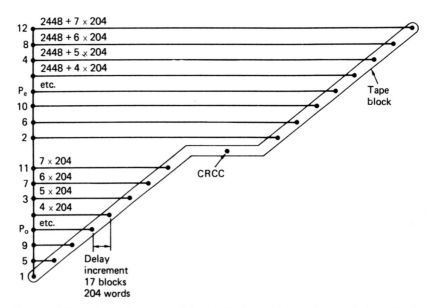

Figure 7.19 Following the interleave of Figure 7.17, further delays produce the final data block and its CRCC.

into groups of six each, and reordered. Thus samples 1, 3, 5, 7, 9 and 11 become 1, 5, 9, 3, 7 and 11. This reordering produces the maximum distance between adjacent samples on tape after interleave. For example, samples 1 and 3 will be three times further apart on tape than they would be without reordering. In the case of gross error, samples 1 and 3 will be used to interpolate sample 2. The wide separation between them increases the probability that both will be correct or correctable.

The six odd samples and the six even samples produce redundancy words P_o and P_e by simple parity. Placing the parity symbols in the centre of the reordered samples further increases the distance between adjacent samples on tape. Figure 7.17 shows that the samples and P words are then interleaved so that adjacent symbols appear two blocks apart. This is achieved by inserting delays which are a function of the position in the block. Following this interleave, Q parity words are generated.

Figure 7.18 shows the resultant structure for odd samples for the DASH cross-interleave. The P redundancy is on vertical columns, the Q redundancy is on diagonals. The data cannot be recorded in the Q diagonal sequence, since bursts would damage multiple symbols, and parity has no way of determining the position of random errors. A further interleave is necessary. Figure 7.19 shows that this is achieved by further stages of delay, where the delay period is again a function of position in the block. Note the difference of 2448 words between odd and even samples.

7.10 Block contents

The contents of a block are shown in Figure 7.20. There is a sync word necessary to synchronize the phase-locked loop in the data separators, some control bits, twelve samples, four parity words and a CRCC. The samples and the parity words are highly non-contiguous, due to the use of cross-interleave of Figure 7.19. A CRCC is calculated from the output of the final interleave, and this covers the samples, and P and Q words, as well as the status word in the block. This is the only polynomial calculation in DASH since all other redundancy is simple parity. The presence of the CRCC makes a block into a codeword and can be used to detect a read error in the block and to generate erasure flags for the correction stage.

When a new recording is to be made in the presence of an existing recording, the new recording will begin at a block boundary. In practice it is difficult physically to position the tape, and the last block of the previous recording may be corrupted by the beginning of the new one. The error-correction system is designed to cope with this.

The control bits identify the use of pre-emphasis prior to the ADC, and there is a sector-position count. Since there are four data blocks to every sector, a 2 bit binary code is sufficient to identify the block within the sector.

The channel code of DASH is known as HDM-1 which is a run-length-limited code with a high density ratio to minimize the linear tape speed necessary.

7.11 How error correction works in DASH

The error-correction mechanism works as follows. If a block CRC check fails, then the error could be in any or all of the samples in the block. No attempt is

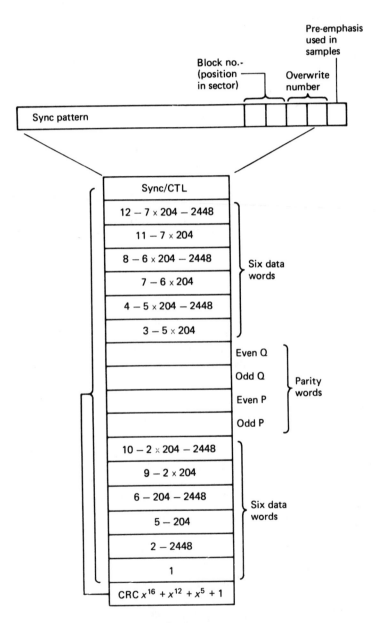

Figure 7.20 Contents of one data block. The samples are highly non-contiguous according to the interleave expressions shown. The CRC codeword extends over the control bits but not the sync pattern. If the check fails, all samples are assumed bad.

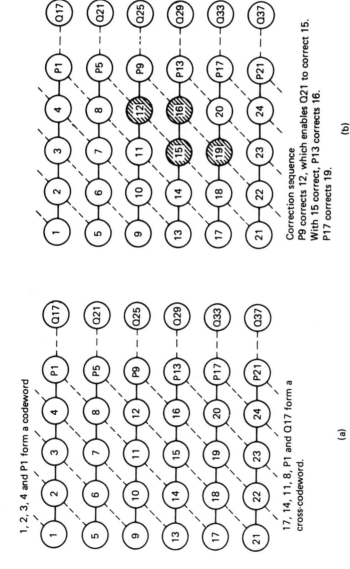

Figure 7.21 (a) In cross-interleaving, codewords are formed on data before interleaving (1, 2, 3, 4, P1), and after convolutional interleaving (21, 18, 15, 12, P5, Q21). (b) Multiple errors in one codeword will become single errors in another. If the sequence shown is followed, then all the errors can be corrected.

made to determine which, because the simple CRCC used has no locating power. All the samples in the block are declared bad by attaching an error flag to them. After de-interleave, single-error-flagged samples will be found in several different P codewords, and these can be corrected by erasure (see Chapter 5) using the parity symbols and the flags, which are then reset.

The presence of a random error in the vicinity of a burst can result in two error flags appearing in one P codeword, which the simple parity system cannot correct. Samples are then re-interleaved to time-align symbols in a Q codeword. As can be seen in the simplified example of Figure 7.21, if two samples are in error in a P word then, in most cases, only one will be in error in two different Q words and vice versa. The Q parity symbol and the error flags will again correct single faulty samples, and the error flags will again be reset. Samples must be de-interleaved again following this stage. A final stage of correction is then possible using P parity, but this is often omitted and interpolation is used to conceal samples which leave the de-interleave process with error flags still set.

Figure 7.22 shows the total interleave timing through a DASH machine. The apparently complex interleaving process is achieved using a RAM. Samples are written into the RAM in address sequence, but are read out using a sequencer.

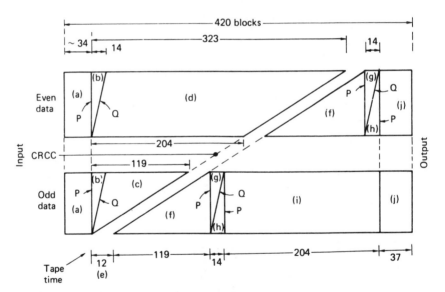

Figure 7.22 Encode/decode delays through PCM-3324 (all numbers are blocks = 12 words). (a) Data written into interleave RAM waits for read page. (b) Cross-interleave of P (vertical) and Q (diagonal) parity is formed. Note this step has no effect on encode period. (c) Odd data are delayed by multiples of 17 blocks up to maximum of 119 blocks. (d) Even data are delayed from 204 blocks up to 323 blocks by multiples of 17 blocks. CRC is formed and block is written. (e) Replay process begins with data separator delay and TBC delay of 12 blocks. (f) Data are re-interleaved to P and flags are used to correct single errors. (g) Data are re-interleaved to Q and double P errors become single Q errors which are corrected. (h) Data are de-interleaved to P and remaining errors are corrected. (i) Odd data are delayed 204 blocks. (j) Data written into de-interleave. RAM waits for read page. Average encode delay is 34 + 323/2 = approx. 196 blocks. Average decode delay is 12 + 37 + 14 + 323/2 = approx. 224 blocks.

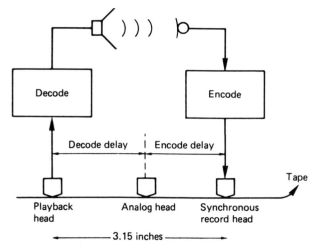

Figure 7.23 Synchronous recording requires displaced heads, separated by the decode/encode delay. In DASH this is about 3.15 in or 420 blocks.

De-interleave on playback is achieved using an equal and opposite process. Both interleave and de-interleave processes cause a delay in the sample stream, but the re-interleave on replay means that the decode delay is longer than the encode delay. This is only of any consequence when using a multitrack recorder to perform synchronous recording. Analog machines play back using the record head in this mode to eliminate tape-path delay, but clearly this will not work with digital machines owing to the encode/decode delays. The solution is to add another head downstream for synchronous recording, as in Figure 7.23. The head has to be displaced from the replay head by exactly the distance travelled by the tape in one encode/decode period, or the length of 420 tape blocks. As there are twelve samples in a block, at a sampling rate of 48 kHz the block rate will be 4 kHz. As the tape speed will be 30 in/s, the necessary distance will be:

$$\frac{30}{4000} \times 420\,\text{in} = 3.15\,\text{in}$$

If a synchronous record head has to be replaced on a stationary-head machine, an adjustment will be necessary to set this distance accurately.

7.12 Splice handling in DASH

A tape splice will result in a random jump of control track phase of $\pm\frac{1}{2}$ sector. In replay, the capstan is controlled by comparing the data rate off tape with a reference, and this is sometimes done by a phase comparison between sector sync from tape and a reference-derived sector-rate signal. The effect of a splice will be to cause a sudden phase step which disturbs the capstan. In order to reduce this disturbance, one solution is to control the capstan using block phase, since a block is one-quarter the size of a sector. This results in rapid locking, but

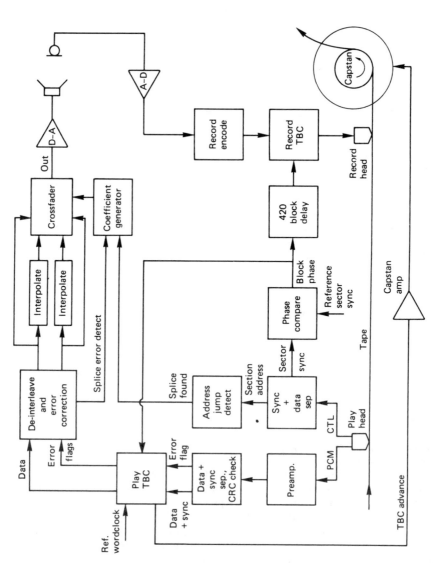

Figure 7.24 Splice-handling DASH recorder requires interpolators and a crossfader after error-correction unit, and a block phase delay for synchronous recording over an earlier splice. In twin DASH, the interpolators would not be necessary, and would be replaced by a multiplexer selecting correct data from the two recordings.

produces four relationships between block phase and sector phase. In order to restore the correct relationship between the block and sector phase, the delay of replay data in the timebase corrector will be changed by 12 or 24 samples. This process is important because synchronism between machines is achieved by sector lock; thus samples must have a fixed relationship to sector timing, and tape splicing always operates in sector steps, however the tape is cut. As there are 1000 sectors in 30 in, there is no point in attempting to cut the tape more accurately than 0.03 in, which represents 1 ms.

When a synchronous recording is made over a splice, it is necessary to duplicate exactly the change in block to sector phase. Thus a timebase corrector is necessary in the record channel also, which will experience a timing change of 12 or 24 samples at the instant the splice passes the record head. When a synchronous recording is made, the recording takes place 420 blocks after the replay. The replay-TBC delay change is made the instant the splice passes the playback head, whereas the record-TBC must change its delay by the same amount when the splice passes the synchronous record head. The delay change parameter must be stored for 420 blocks to ensure that this is so.[5]

Clearly a crossfade is neither necessary nor desirable in a synchronous recording made over a splice. Thus the decision to operate the crossfade mechanism must be made on a channel-by-channel basis. The presence of a splice causes a sector-address jump in the control track. There can be no other cause, since an assemble results in sector addresses which are contiguous.

A synchronous recording made over a splice will suffer a relatively small number of errors which will be correctable. A splice between two different recordings will result in uncorrectable errors and cause interpolation. Accordingly, any track which is not interpolating continuously in the presence of a sector address jump will not need to crossfade. Figure 7.24 shows the essentials of a DASH splice handling system, which supports synchronous recording over splices.

Some DASH recorders control the capstan in replay by examining the average delay in the timebase correctors, which means that the control track is not necessary for normal replay, and control-track dropout ceases to be a problem. It is still necessary to retain the control track because it contains the sector addresses necessary for absolute autolocation and synchronizing. This led to the control track being renamed the reference track.

7.13 DCC – digital compact cassette

DCC is a stationary-head format in which the tape transport is designed to play existing analog compact cassettes in addition to making and playing digital recordings. This backward compatibility means that an existing compact cassette collection can still be played whilst newly made or purchased recordings will be digital.[6] To achieve this compatibility, DCC tape is the same width as analog compact cassette tape (3.81 mm) and travels at the same speed (1⅞ in/sec or 4.76 cm/sec). The formulation of the DCC tape is different; it resembles conventional chrome video tape, but the principle of playing one 'side' of the tape in one direction and then playing the other side in the opposite direction is retained.

Although the DCC cassette has similar dimensions to the compact cassette so that both can be loaded in the same transport, the DCC cassette is of radically

Table 7.1 Tape playing time (minutes)

Hole	45	60	75	90	105	120	U
3	*		*		*		
4		*	*			*	
5				*	*	*	

* = hole present, U = undefined

different construction. The DCC cassette only fits in the machine one way; it cannot be physically turned over as it only has hub-drive apertures on one side. The head access bulge has gone and the cassette has a uniform rectangular cross-section, taking up less space in storage. The transparent windows have also been deleted as the amount of tape remaining is displayed on the panel of the player. This approach has the advantage that labelling artwork can cover almost the entire top surface. As the cassette cannot be turned over, all transports must be capable of playing in both directions. Thus DCC is an auto-reverse format. In addition to a record lockout plug, the cassette body carries identification holes. Combinations of these specify six different playing times from 45 min to 120 min as in Table 7.1.

The apertures for hub drive, capstans, pinch rollers and heads are covered by a sliding cover formed from metal plate. The cover plate is automatically slid aside when the cassette enters the transport. The cover plate also operates hub brakes when it closes and so the cassette can be left out of its container. The container fits the cassette like a sleeve and has space for an information booklet.

DCC uses a form of data reduction which Philips call precision adaptive sub-band coding (PASC). PASC was described in detail in Chapter 2 and its use allows the recorded data rate to be about one-quarter that of the original PCM

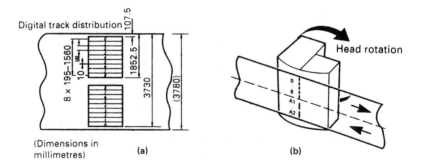

(a)   (b)

Figure 7.25 In DCC audio and auxiliary data are recorded on nine parallel tracks along each side of the tape as shown in (a). The replay head shown in (b) carries magnetic poles which register with one set of nine tracks. At the end of the tape, the replay head rotates 180° and plays a further nine tracks on the other side of the tape. The replay head also contains a pair of analog audio magnetic circuits which will be swung into place if an analog cassette is to be played.

audio. This allows for conventional chromium tape to be used with a minimum wavelength of about 1 μm instead of the more expensive high-coercivity tapes normally required for use with shorter wavelengths. The advantage of the conventional approach with linear tracks is that tape duplication can be carried out at high speed. This makes DCC attractive to record companies. Even with data reduction, the only way in which the bit rate can be accommodated is to use many tracks in parallel.

Figure 7.25 shows that in DCC audio data are distributed over eight parallel tracks along with a subcode track which together occupy half the width of the tape. At the end of the tape the head rotates about an axis perpendicular to the tape and plays the remaining tracks in reverse. The other half of the head is fitted with magnetic circuits sized for analog tracks and so the head rotation can also select the head type which is in use for a given tape direction.

However, reducing the data rate to one-quarter and then distributing it over eight tracks means that the frequency recorded on each track is only 96 kbits/sec or about one-sixteenth that of a PCM machine recording a single audio channel with a single head. The linear tape speed is incredibly low by stationary-head digital standards in order to obtain the desired playing time. The rate of change of flux in the replay head is very small due to the low tape speed, and conventional inductive heads are at a severe disadvantage because their self-noise drowns the signal. Magnetoresistive heads are necessary

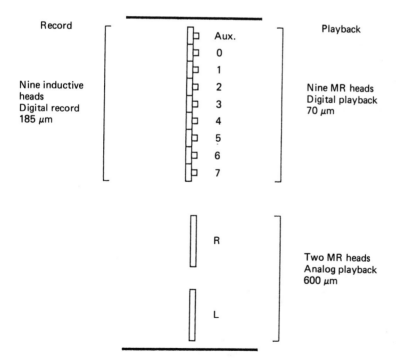

Figure 7.26 The head arrangement used in DCC. There are nine record heads which leave tracks wider than the MR replay heads to allow for misregistration. Two MR analog heads allow compact cassette replay.

because they do not have a derivative action, and so the signal is independent of speed. A magnetoresistive head uses an element whose resistance is influenced by the strength of flux from the tape; its operation was discussed in Chapter 4.

Magnetoresistive (MR) heads are unable to record, and so separate record heads are necessary. Figure 7.26 shows a schematic outline of a DCC head. There are nine inductive record heads for the digital tracks, and these are recorded with a width of 185 μm and a pitch of 195 μm. Alongside the record head are nine MR replay gaps. These operate on a 70 μm band of the tape which is nominally in the centre of the recorded track. There are two reasons for this large disparity between the record and replay track widths. Firstly, replay signal quality is unaffected by a lateral alignment error of ±57 μm and this ensures tracking compatibility between machines. Secondly, the loss due to incorrect azimuth is proportional to track width and the narrower replay track is thus less sensitive to the state of azimuth adjustment. In addition to the digital replay gaps, a further two analog MR head gaps are present in the replay stack. These are aligned with the two tracks of a stereo pair in a compact cassette.

The 20 gap head could not be made economically by conventional techniques. Instead it is made lithographically using thin-film technology.

Tape guidance is achieved by a combination of guides on the head block and pins in the cassette. Figure 7.27 shows that at each side of the head is fitted a C-shaped tape guide. This guide is slightly narrower than the nominal tape width.

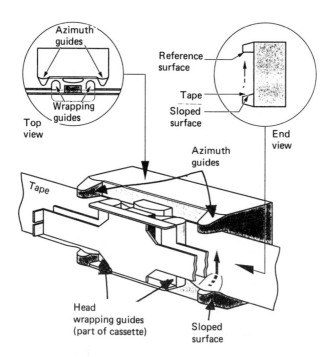

Figure 7.27 The tape guidance of DCC uses a pair of shaped guides on both sides of the head. See text for details.

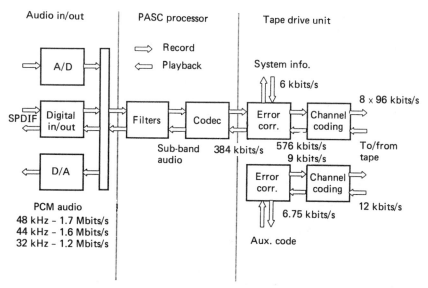

Figure 7.28 Block diagram of DCC machine. This is basically similar to any stationary-head recorder except for the data reduction (PASC) unit between the converters and the transport.

The reference edge of the tape runs against a surface which is at right angles to the guide, whereas the non-reference edge runs against a sloping surface. Tape tension tends to force the tape towards the reference edge. As there is such a guide at both sides of the head, the tape cannot wander in the azimuth plane. The tape wrap around the head stack and around the azimuth guides is achieved by a pair of pins behind the tape which are part of the cassette. Between the pins is a conventional sprung pressure pad and screen.

Figure 7.28 shows a block diagram of a DCC machine. The audio interface contains converters which allow use in analog systems. The digital interface may be used as an alternative. DCC supports 48, 44.1 and 32 kHz sampling rates, offering audio bandwidths of 22, 20 and 14.5 kHz respectively with 18 bit dynamic range. Between the interface and the tape subsystem is the PASC coder. The tape subsystem requires error correction and channel coding systems not only for the audio data, but also for the auxiliary data on the ninth track.

7.14 Outline of DCC format

The format of DCC uses Reed–Solomon product codes with a block completed interleave. Codewords along the tracks act as error detectors for codewords distributed across the tracks which correct by erasure. The recordings on tape are divided into main data frames separated by edit gaps. Figure 7.29(a) shows a data frame which contains 8192 bytes of PASC data, 128 bytes of system data and approximately 40% redundancy for error correction. Each data frame is logically subdivided into 16 product codes and so has a three-dimensional structure. Figure 7.29(b) shows that each product code consists of 32 byte outer

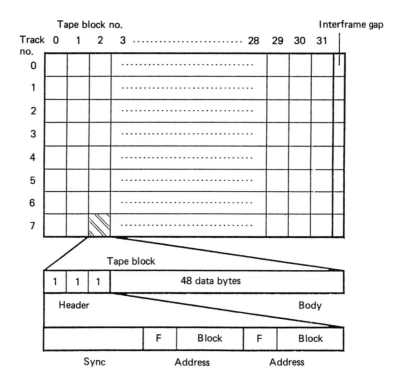

(a) Data frame extending over eight tape tracks

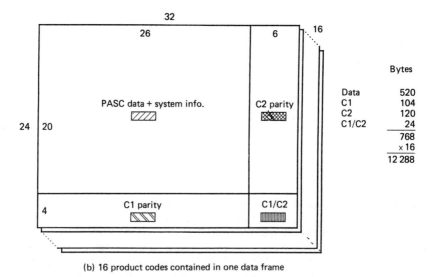

(b) 16 product codes contained in one data frame

Figure 7.29 In (a) the contents of a tape frame are shown. In (b) the frame consists of 16 interleaved product codes.

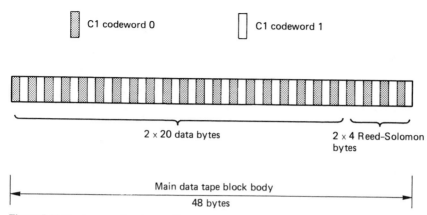

Figure 7.30 The two-way interleave of inner codes in one sync block.

code words and 24 byte inner codes. The inner codes are recorded along the tracks. In each of the eight tracks there are 32 sync blocks. Figure 7.30 shows that the sync blocks have a two-way interleave similar to that of RDAT and CD. Two inner or C1 error-correction codewords, from two different product codes, each consisting of 20 data bytes and four Reed–Solomon redundancy bytes occupy one sync block on a byte-interleaved basis. In this way an error at the boundary of 2 bytes appears as a single error in two different codewords. Each sync block begins with a 3 byte header of which the first byte is a sync pattern to lock the data separator. The remaining bytes carry the address of the frame along the tape and the address of the sync block within the frame. The entire sync block is thus 51 bytes long. The sync blocks are recorded using the 8/10 channel code described in Chapter 4, where eight data bits are recorded with selected 10 bit patterns. The interframe gap is recorded with the channel bit frequency in order to keep the phase-locked loop in the data separator locked to the channel bit rate.

In actual use, the inner or C1 code is exposed to large dropouts which can result in the replay of little more than random noise. In this case, the risk of miscorrection is too great to allow the full 2 byte correction power of each codeword to be used. Instead each codeword corrects a single byte in error with much greater reliability because all four redundancy symbols are used in the correction. If all four equations do not agree on the error, the codeword is declared uncorrectable and erasure flags are attached to the memory input to allow the outer or C2 code to perform the correction after de-interleave.

Figure 7.31 shows how the outer code interleave is arranged. The outer codes contain 32 bytes, of which 6 are Reed–Solomon redundancy. Adjacent symbols in the codeword are non-adjacent on tape and are spread over eight tracks and along the length of each frame. The figure shows the sync blocks in which the C2 symbols of the first product code can be found.

When sync blocks are written, each is formed by taking a column from two product codes and interleaving them on a byte basis. The next sync block will use the same columns from the next two product codes and so on until a column from all 16 product codes has been written in eight sync blocks. In the next sync block

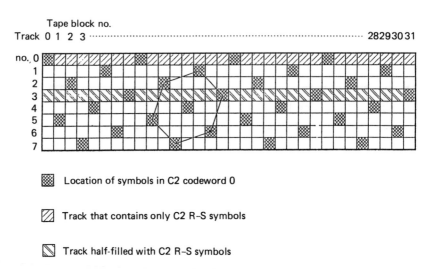

Figure 7.31 The offset in the product code address from one track to the next results in the honeycomb-like interleave structure shown here. The hexagon shows the correction limit for a single circular defect.

the next column from the first and second product codes is taken. The track continues until, in 32 sync blocks, 64 inner codes have been recorded, corresponding to four columns from 16 different product codes.

All eight tracks write to the tape in parallel, each one starting at a different column. Thus if each track writes four columns from each product code, eight tracks will be able to write all 32 columns. The block-completed interleave is obtained by offsetting the product code address by 6 multiplied by the track address. Thus track 1 starts the frame at product code 6, track 2 starts at product code 12, track 3 starts at product code 18, which overflows to 2 and so on. In this way the two-dimensional interleave is arranged such that bytes

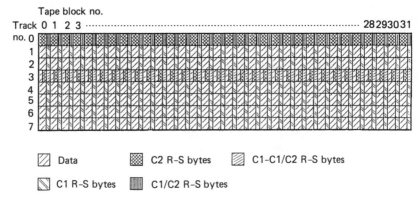

Figure 7.32 The redundancy in DCC is laid out according to this diagram. Note that track 0 and half of track 3 are needed to record the outer redundancy.

in the same outer codeword appear on tape in a honeycomb-like pattern. Since each outer code can correct six bytes by erasure, this determines the size of a hole which may appear in the tape coating and yet be fully correctable. This is shown by the hexagon in Figure 7.31 and corresponds to a defect of 1.45 mm diameter.

As there are six columns of C2 redundancy in each product code and one track can write four columns, it follows that 1½ tracks are needed to write all of the outer redundancy. Track 0 is filled with C2 redundancy and track 3 is half filled with redundancy and half with data. Figure 7.32 shows the position of inner and outer redundancy in each track.

7.15 Auxiliary track

Track 8 is used for auxiliary data. As there can be no cross-track interleave, the auxiliary track is harder to protect against errors. In compensation, the data rate is reduced to one-eighth of the audio track rate. Thus in each frame there are only four sync blocks in the auxiliary track alongside 32 sync blocks in each audio track. A one-dimensional Reed–Solomon code protects the auxiliary data. In order to locate tracks in shuttle without reading the auxiliary data, the auxiliary track at the beginning of each piece on the tape is recorded only with alternate sync blocks. In between the tape is unrecorded and the alternating RF signal can be detected at high speed.

7.16 Instrumentation recording

The stationary-head approach allows extremely high bit rates to be obtained by combining a high linear tape speed with a large number of tracks across the tape.[7] In order to obtain a reasonable recording time at speeds of 8 m/s, very thin tape is used and a vacuum column transport is used, not for rapid acceleration but because of its gentle tape handling when the acceleration is more modest. As multitrack headstacks cannot be made with close-track spacing, it is necessary to interleave the tracks with multiple headstacks. Figure 7.33 shows a four-way interleave. This can be used in two ways. If a single-headstack is used, mounted on a positioner, a serpentine recording can be made in four passes. If all four headstacks are installed, a single-pass recording can be made at four times the data rate.

At high tape speeds a boundary layer film of air is entrapped at the take-up reel. This allows the top tape layer to float on the pack and causes irregular packing. A solution is to make the spacing between the reel flanges only slightly more than the tape width so that the freedom of lateral movement is removed. The reel flanges must be extremely stiff as any flexing would cause tape damage and glass flanges are used.

Whereas computer and audio recorders generally only operate at one data rate, instrumentation recorders are often required to replay at a much slower rate than when recording because the data analysis equipment cannot operate in real time. An open-reel transport can easily be made to work over a wide range of speeds, but there are some difficulties in the replay electronics. The impulse response of the replay head is spatial, and thus its frequency response is speed dependent. As

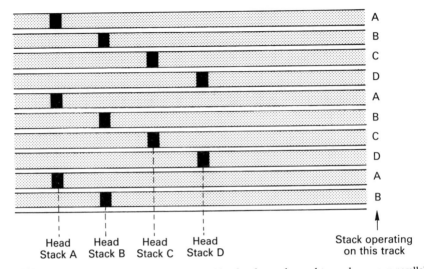

Figure 7.33 In multitrack recorders interleaved headstacks can be used to produce many parallel tracks at once. A four-way interleave is shown here. Alternatively, a single headstack of the type shown here could be indexed to four locations across the tape making a serpentine recording with four tape passes.

a result speed-controlled or adaptive equalizers are needed in each replay channel. The phase-locked loops in the data separators will need to have their centre frequencies programmed by the tape speed to prevent phase errors and false locking to harmonics. The result is a complex and expensive machine.

References

1. MEE, C.D. and DANIEL, E.D. (eds), *Magnetic Recording, Vol. II*, Chapter 5. New York: McGraw-Hill (1987)
2. CUTLER, D.S., Quarter and half inch streaming tape drives. *IERE Conf. Publ. No. 67*, pp. 95–111 (1986)
3. DOI, T.T., TSUCHIYA, Y., TANAKA, M. and WATANABE, N., A format of stationary-head digital audio recorder covering wide range of applications. Presented at 67th Audio Engineering Society Convention (New York, 1980), preprint 1677(H6)
4. LAGADEC, R., Current status in digital audio. Presented at IERE Video and Data Recording Conf. (Southampton, 1984)
5. WATKINSON, J.R., Splice-handling mechanisms in DASH format. Presented at 77th Audio Engineering Society Convention (Hamburg, 1985), preprint 2199(A-2)
6. LOKHOFF, G.C.P., DCC: Digital compact cassette. *IEEE Trans. Consum. Electron.*, **CE-37**, 702–706 (1991)
7. HINTEREGGER, H.F. *et al.*, A high data rate recorder for astronomy. *IEEE Trans. Magn.*, **27**, No. 3 (1991)

Chapter 8

Rotary-head data recording

Although the electronic circuitry in a rotary-head data recorder is complex, it also depends heavily on mechanical engineering of the highest quality, and on several extraordinarily accurate servo systems. This chapter looks at the different types of transports and tracking systems which have been developed and the supporting control and signal systems. Examples are given from contrasting applications.

8.1 Why rotary heads?

When head and tape technology was less advanced than it is today, wavelengths on tape were long, and the only way that high frequencies could be accommodated was to use high speeds. High speed can be achieved in two ways: the head can remain fixed and the tape can be transported rapidly, with obvious consequences; or the tape can travel relatively slowly and the head can be moved. The latter is the principle of the rotary-head recorder. Figure 8.1 shows the general arrangement of the two major categories of rotary-head recorder. In transverse-scan recorders, relatively short tracks are recorded almost at right angles to the direction of tape motion by a rotating headwheel containing, typically, four or six heads. In helical-scan recorders, the tape is wrapped around the drum in such a way that it enters and leaves in two different planes. This causes the rotating heads to record long, slanting tracks. In both approaches, the width of the space between tracks is determined by the linear tape speed, not by multitrack head technology. The track pitch can easily be made much smaller than in stationary-head recorders. Chapter 3 showed how rotary-head machines make better use of the tape area, particularly if azimuth recording is used. The high head speed raises the frequency of offtape signals, and since output is proportional to frequency in inductive heads, playback signals are raised above head noise even with very narrow tracks. The development of rotary heads was instrumental in the success of the first video recorders. As video signals consist of discrete lines and frames, it was possible to conceal the interruptions in the tracks of a rotary-head machine by making them coincident with the time when the CRT was blanked during flyback. The wide bandwidth of rotary-head video recorders led them to be adapted for data-recording purposes. At the same time continued development in video recording led to the digital video recorder. In data recorders time compression can be

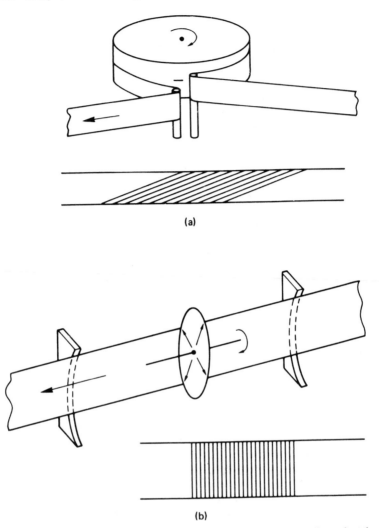

(a)

(b)

Figure 8.1 Types of rotary-head recorder. (a) Helical scan records long diagonal tracks. (b) Transverse scan records short tracks across the tape.

used to accommodate any head-changeover period. The transverse and helical scan approaches have quite different characteristics and the most appropriate choice depends upon the application.

8.2 Transverse-scan geometry

The head drum axis is parallel to the tape path in a transverse-scan recorder. Figure 8.2 shows that the width of the tape is formed into a segment of a circle because it passes between the headwheel and a guide. The transition area from flat tape to segment and back again is known colloquially as the canoe which stretches from the entry guide to the exit guide. Head-to-tape contact pressure is

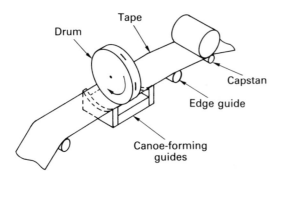

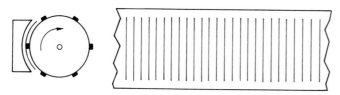

Figure 8.2 In a transverse-scan recorder the tape is formed into a transverse curve by a cupped guide.

obtained by the profile of the guide, which carries a recess into which the tape is deflected by the heads. The diameter of the headwheel and the number of heads are generally designed so that as one head reaches the end of a track the next one is at the beginning of the next track, although with time compression this is not essential. A multichannel rotary transformer is fitted on the face of the headwheel in order to couple the rotating heads to the stationary circuitry. A tracking mechanism is necessary to ensure that the heads pass accurately down the tracks on replay. In a basic transport a linear control track is provided which operates in conjunction with a stationary head. The transverse heads actually pass across the linear tracks, but they will not be recording at those times. One pulse is recorded in the linear track for every transverse track. The phase of the pulses is compared with the rotational phase of the headwheel and used to drive the capstan so that the tracks are correctly followed on replay. Section 8.10 considers tracking in more detail. As a result of the linear tape motion the transverse tracks are not quite perpendicular to the edge of the tape. When azimuth recording is used, the head pole width and the track width are not necessarily equal. The tape speed is often made deliberately slow so that part of the previous track is trimmed by the next. In this case the track width is determined by the tape speed, not by the head design.

The guidance of the tape is extremely positive in a transverse-scan transport. Both edges of the tape are restrained by flanges on the headwheel guide, and the track geometry and head contact are relatively insensitive to tape tension variations.

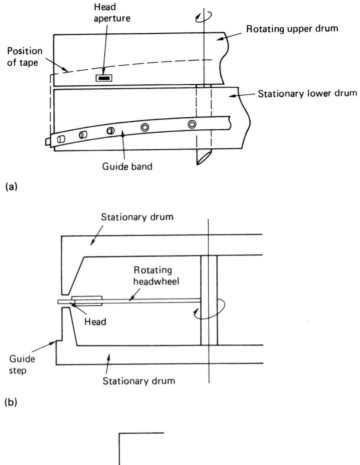

(a)

(b)

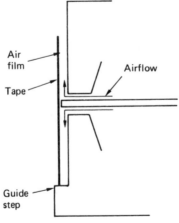

(c)

Figure 8.3 (a) Rotating-top-type scanner. The upper drum is slightly smaller than the lower drum due to the air film it develops. Helical band guides lower edge of tape. (b) Stationary-top scanner, where headwheel rotates in a slot between upper and lower drums. (c) Airflow in stationary-top scanner. Headwheel acts as a centrifugal pump, producing air film between tape and drums.

8.3 Helical-scan geometry

Helical-scan transports wrap the tape around a cylindrical drum, also known as a scanner. Figure 8.3 shows the two fundamental approaches to drum design. In the rotating upper drum system, one or more heads are mounted on the periphery of the revolving section of the drum. The fixed base of the drum carries a helical ramp in the form of a step or, for greater wear resistance, a hardened band which is suitably attached. Alternatively, both top and bottom of the drum are fixed, and the headwheel turns in a slot between them. Both approaches have advantages and disadvantages. The rotating upper drum approach is simpler to manufacture than the fixed upper drum, because the latter requires to be rigidly and accurately cantilevered out over the headwheel. The rotating part of the drum will produce an air film, which raises its effective diameter. The rotor will thus need to be made a slightly different diameter to the lower drum, so that the tape sees a constant diameter as it rises up the drum. There will be plenty of space inside the rotor to install individually replaceable heads.

The fixed upper drum approach requires less power, since there is less air resistance. The headwheel acts as a centrifugal pump, and supplies air to the periphery of the slot where it lubricates both upper and lower drums, which are of the same diameter. The airflow may also be used to cool circuitry inside the drum. It is claimed that the fixed upper drum approach gives head contact which is more consistent over the length of the track, but it makes the provision of replaceable heads more difficult, and it is generally necessary to replace the entire headwheel as an assembly.

The presence of the air film means that the tape surface is not normally in contact with the cylindrical surface of the drum. Many drums have a matt etched finish, which does not become polished in service because there is no contact. The thickness of the air film is that where the pumping effect of the rotating drum reaches equilibrium with the tape tension. It will be clear that helical-scan transports rely on aerodynamic principles and their operation can be affected by ambient pressure. Another characteristic of rotary-head recorders is that in condensing humidity conditions (high relative humidity coupled with falling temperature) it is possible for the tape to become stuck to the rotating drum by surface tension. The drum drive amplifier usually has an overcurrent cut-out to prevent damage.

Figure 8.4 shows that the heads project out of the drum by a distance which must exceed the air film thickness in order to deform the tape slightly. In the absence of such a deformation there would be no contact pressure. It will be clear

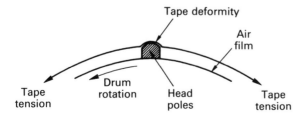

Figure 8.4 The tape is supported on an air film and the heads must project by a greater distance to achieve contact pressure.

that the tape tension must be maintained accurately if the desired head contact pressure is to be obtained.

The creation and collapse of the deformities in the tape results in appreciable acoustic output, in the form of an irritating buzz. The production of a deformity in the tape due to head impact results in the propagation of a wave motion down the tape. This has a finite velocity and the velocity of the head must always be slower or it will produce a shock wave resulting in tremendous contact forces and rapid wear. In practice excessive head-to-tape speeds are avoided by using several heads in parallel.

The presence of the air film means that the tape is only located around the drum by one edge. It must be arranged to follow the helical step without drifting away from it. Two sets of fixed guides, known as the entry and exit guides, lead the tape to and from the ramp. Figure 8.5 shows the tape path around the drum as if it had been unrolled into a plane. It will be seen that the step on the drum acts as a single flanged guide. The two fixed guides are arranged to contact only one edge of the tape each. The height and angle of the tape is set by the drum step and the lower flange of the outer guide. The tape is prevented from leaving that path by the upper flange of the inner guide. The reference flanges are fixed, and will be made of some wear-resistant material such as ceramic. The other flanges may be spring-loaded to accommodate slight variations in tape width. Like the transverse-scan transport, a basic helical-scan machine will need a linear control track and fixed head driving the capstan in order to line up the tape tracks with the replay head scan.

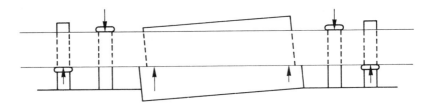

Figure 8.5 The head drum is shown here as if it had been unrolled to make the tape straight. It can then be seen that the drum step acts as a single flanged guide. The entry and exit guides work in conjunction with the drum step to locate the tape accurately.

The tape may wrap around the drum by various amounts. Some early analog machines used a complete circuit around the drum which led the tape to cross itself in the so-called alpha wrap. The C-format used almost a complete circuit of the drum where the tape turns sharply around the entrance and exit guides in the shape of an omega. These techniques were necessary to allow the use of a single head, which avoided banding in analog recording, but the result is a machine which is difficult to lace and cannot use a cassette. In DVTRs and most data recorders the tape passes between half-way and three-quarters of the way around the drum. The total angle of drum rotation for which the heads touch the tape is called the *mechanical wrap angle* or the *head contact angle*. The angle over which a useful recorded track is laid down is always somewhat shorter than the mechanical wrap angle. This is not only to allow the head/tape contact to settle after the initial impact, but also to allow the entire track to be read when any

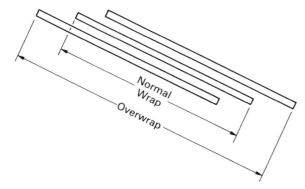

Figure 8.6 In helical-scan recordings, successive tracks start at a different distance along the tape. These appear displaced around the drum and so an overwrap is needed to allow the whole track to be read by a deflected head.

track-following heads are deflected. Figure 8.6 shows that successive tracks start at a different distance along the tape. Deflecting a head to follow a different track results in that track being read earlier or later than normal, and an extended wrap is necessary to guarantee head contact with a deflected head.

It will be evident that as the tape is caused to travel along the drum axis by the ramp, it actually takes on the path of a helix. The head rotates in a circular path, and so will record diagonal tracks across the width of the tape. So it is not really the scanning which is helical, it is the tape path.

In practical machines the tape may, in normal forward motion, travel up the ramp (e.g. D-2) or down the ramp (e.g. D-3). This reverses the slant angle of the tracks. In addition, the drum can rotate either with (e.g. D-3) or against (e.g. D-2) the direction of linear tape motion.

If the tape is stationary, as in Figure 8.7(a) the head will constantly retrace the same track, and the angle of the track can be calculated by measuring the rise of the tape along the drum axis, and the circumferential distance over which this rise takes place. The latter can be obtained from the diameter of the drum and the wrap angle. The tangent of the *helix angle* is given by the rise over the distance. It can also be obtained by measuring the distance along the ramp corresponding to the wrap angle. In conjunction with the rise, this dimension will give the sine of the helix angle. In some helical-scan computer data recorders, the tape is stationary during data transfer so that retries are facilitated. The *track angle* and the helix angle are the same. The linear tape motion is incremental. In all other applications, the linear tape motion is constant.

When the tape moves, the angle between the tracks and the edge of the tape will not be the helix angle. Figure 8.7(b) shows an example in which tape climbs up the drum which rotates against the direction of tape travel (e.g. D-2). When the head contact commences, the tape will be at a given location, but when the head contact ceases, the tape will have moved a certain linear distance and the resultant track will be longer. Figure 8.7(c) shows what happens when the tape moves down the drum in the same direction as head rotation. In this case the track is shorter.

In order to obtain the track angle it is necessary to take into account the tape motion. The length of the track resulting from scanning a stationary tape, which will be at the helix angle, can be resolved into two distances at right angles as shown in Figure 8.7. One of these is across the tape width, the other is along the length of the tape. The tangent of the helix angle will be the ratio of these lengths. If the length along the tape is corrected by adding or subtracting the distance the tape moves during one scan, depending upon whether tape motion aids or opposes drum rotation, the new ratio of the lengths will be the tangent of the track angle. In practice this process will often be reversed, because it is the track

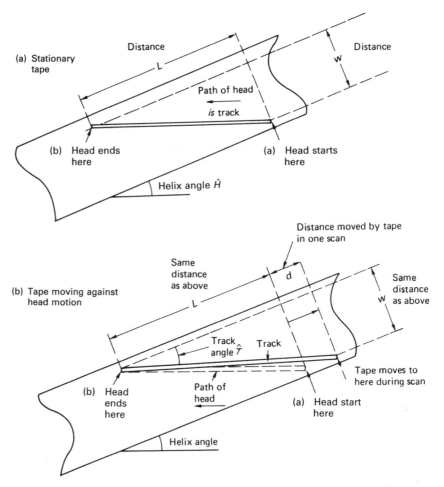

Figure 8.7 When the tape is moving the track laid down will be at an angle which is different from the helix angle, because the tape is in a different place at the end of the scan than at the beginning. Track length can be considered as two components L and w for stationary case, and $L + d$ and w for moving case. Hence:

$$\frac{w}{L} = \tan \hat{H} \text{ and } \frac{w}{L + d} = \hat{T}.$$

In (b) tape moves against head motion and track angle is less than helix angle. In (c) tape moves with the head motion and track angle is greater than helix angle.

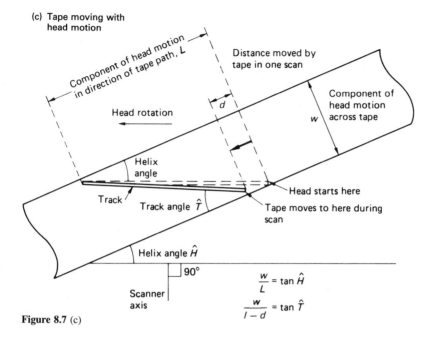

Figure 8.7 (c)

angle which is standardized in a given format, and the transport designer has to find a helix angle which will produce it.

It can also be seen from Figure 8.7 that when a normally recorded tape is stopped, the head must be deflected by a triangular waveform or ramp in order to follow the track. A further consequence of the track angle being different from the helix angle is that, when azimuth recording is used, the azimuth angles at which the heads are mounted in the drum are not the same as the angles between the transitions and the edge of the track. One of the angles is slightly increased and one is slightly reduced. In the D-3 DVTR, for example, the difference is 0.017 degrees.

The relative direction of drum and tape motion is unimportant, as both configurations work equally well. Often the direction is left undefined until many other parameters have been settled. If the segmentation and coding scheme proposed results in the wavelengths on tape being on the short side, opposite rotation will be chosen, as this lengthens the tracks and with it the wavelength. Sometimes the direction of rotation is a given; in Digital Betacam, playback of analog tapes was a requirement, so the rotation direction had to be the same as in analog Betacam.

Provided that the tape linear speed and drum speed remain the same, the theoretical track angle will remain the same. In practice this will only be the case if the tape tension is constant. Figure 8.8 shows that if the back-tension changes, the effective length of the tape will also change, and with it the track angle. It will be evident that the result is a tracking error which increases towards the ends of the track. In addition the changed track length will alter the signal timing, advancing it at one end of the track whilst delaying it at the other, a phenomenon known as *skew*. As shown above, tension errors also affect the air-film thickness

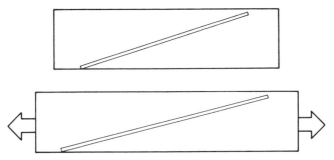

Figure 8.8 Tape is flexible, so change of tension will result in change of length. This causes a change in track angle known as skew, shown exaggerated here.

and head contact pressure. All digital rotary-head recorders need some form of tape tension servo to maintain the tape tension around the drum constant irrespective of the size of the pack on the supply hub. In practice tension servos can only control the tension of the tape entering the drum. Since there will be friction between the edge of tape and the drum step, the tape tension will gradually increase between the entrance and exit guides, and so the tape will be extended more towards the exit guide. When the tape subsequently relaxes, it will be found that the track is actually curved. The ramp can be made to deviate from a theoretical helix to counteract this effect, or all drums can be built to the same design, so that effectively the track curvature becomes part of the format. Another possibility is to use some form of embedded track-following system, or a system like azimuth recording which tolerates residual tracking errors.

When the tape direction reverses, the sense of the friction in the drum will also reverse, so the back-tension has to increase to keep the mid-span tension the same as when going forward.

When verifying the track angle produced by a new design, it is usual to develop a tape which it has recorded with magnetic fluid, and take measurements under a travelling microscope. With the very small track widths of digital recorders, it is usually necessary to compensate for skew by applying standard tension to the tape when it is being measured, or by computing a correction factor for the track angle from the modulus of elasticity of the tape.

8.4 Transverse scan versus helical scan

The first (analog) video recorders developed by Ampex used the transverse-scan approach, with four evenly spaced heads on the rotor: hence the name quadruplex which was given to this system. The tracks were a little shorter than the two-inch width of the tape, and several sweeps were necessary to build up a video frame.

Variable-speed operation in rotary-head video recorders is obtained by deflecting the playback heads along the drum axis to follow the tape tracks. Periodically the heads will need to jump in order to omit or repeat a field. In transverse scan the number of tracks needed to accommodate one field is high, and the head deflection required to jump fields was virtually impossible to achieve. The headwheel is quite small and there is insufficient space to

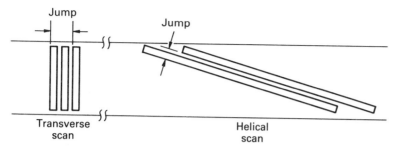

Figure 8.9 Helical scan results in longer tracks so a shorter distance needs to be jumped to miss out or repeat a field.

accommodate a head-deflection mechanism. The short tracks of a transverse-scan machine result in a higher number of tracks per unit time for a given data rate. This causes the head-impact noise to be higher in pitch than that of a helical machine and some kind of acoustic treatment is usually needed.

In helical scanning the tracks are longer, so fewer of them are needed to accommodate a field. Figure 8.9 shows that the head displacement needed for field jumping is then reduced. The drum is larger in helical scan, making space for deflecting heads.

Thus, for video recording, helical scan has distinct advantages. For professional use, the quadruplex format gave way to one-inch analog C-format, which used helical scan and an almost total wrap to fit an entire field into a slant track about 15 in (380 mm) long. The change-over between tracks was then made in the vertical interval. Field jumps could then be made with a head displacement of single track. The advantages of helical scan also apply to digital VTRs. In such machines the analog-to-digital conversion process represents the video signal in a form which requires a much smaller signal-to-noise ratio but with a much higher bandwidth. As a result, tracks on the tape are required to be narrower but longer. A single track containing an entire digital field would be impractically long and in practice fields are inevitably segmented into between six (NTSC D-2, Digital Betacam) and sixteen (D-5) tracks, but as the tracks are so much narrower in digital recorders the head displacement required for variable speed is of the same order as on analog machines.

For instrumentation recording the requirements are quite different, particularly for airborne or other adverse environment operation.[1] With transverse-scan the headwheel is physically small and it is possible to build a transport which is little bigger than the cassette. With helical scan the transport has to be at least twice the size of the cassette. The small headwheel of the transverse-scan transport has a moment of inertia which is only a few percent of that of a helical-scan drum, and it can reach operating speed very rapidly. The low inertia also makes it possible to keep the scanner servo locked whilst subject to disturbances. Transverse-scan machines are particularly suited to incremental operation in which the transport is in standby mode until an input buffer fills with data and enters record mode to commit the buffer contents to tape. In standby mode the transverse-scan machine has the drum running at speed, but out of contact with the tape. The machine can go from standby to record in milliseconds simply by driving the cupped guide towards the drum with a solenoid. A helical-scan transport cannot do this.

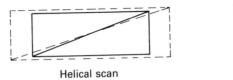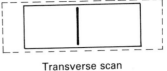

Helical scan   Transverse scan

Figure 8.10 Tape is anisotropic and humidity and temperature changes result in different expansions lengthways and transversely. This results in a change of track angle in helical scan but has a negligible effect in transverse scan.

In transverse scan, the unsupported length of tape is negligible, whereas in helical-scan recorders the tape is supported by one side only around the drum. Tape is anisotropic and its coefficient of linear expansion is different along its length and transversely. The expansion of tape due to moisture absorption is also anisotropic. Figure 8.10 shows that with anisotropic tape a transverse-scan recorder suffers second-order effects which can be neglected. Helical-scan recorders are at a disadvantage because the track angle actually changes with temperature, humidity and tape tension.

In high-g adverse environments transverse-scan machines offer greater resistance to track distortion and higher confidence in interchange with ground replay machines. The compact transport is less affected by ambient pressure changes and is easier to provide with an environmental housing. For airborne work these housings are sealed, pressurized and thermostatically heated.

A further advantage of transverse-scan is that the tape is naturally wide to obtain tracks of reasonable length. For a given recording density, the same data can be recorded on a shorter tape if it is wider. This allows quicker access.

8.5 Track and head geometry

The *track pitch* is the distance, measured at right angles to the tracks, from a given place on one track to the same place on the next. In transverse-scan recorders, it is easy to deduce that the track pitch is a function of the linear tape

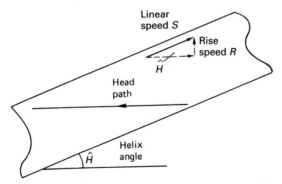

Figure 8.11 The linear speed of the tape S can be resolved into the speed of the tape along the scanner axis which is the rise speed R. $R = S \sin \hat{H}$. Dividing the rise speed by the head passing frequency gives the track pitch. Head-passing frequency is simply the number of heads multiplied by the scanner rotational frequency. Thus track pitch is proportional to tape speed

(a)

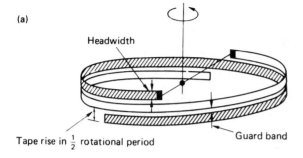

Headwidth

Tape rise in $\frac{1}{2}$ rotational period

Guard band

(b)

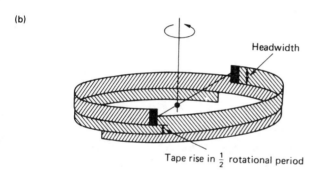

Headwidth

Tape rise in $\frac{1}{2}$ rotational period

(c)

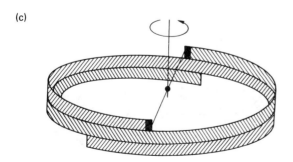

Figure 8.12 (a) Where tape rise is more than head width, a guard band between the tracks results. (b) Where tape rise is less than head width, overwrite takes place and the tracks are narrower than the heads. Shown here for two-headed scanner, the minimum configuration for azimuth recording. In the absence of azimuth recording, guard bands (a) must be left between the tracks. With azimuth recording, the record head may be wider than (b) or of the same width as (c) the track.

speed and the head-passing frequency because the tape moves along the headwheel axis. In helical-scan recorders the track pitch is further affected by the helix angle. It can be seen in Figure 8.11 that the linear speed and the helix angle determine the rise rate (or fall rate) with respect to the drum axis, and the knowledge of the rotational period of the drum will allow the travel in one revolution to be calculated. If the travel is divided by the number of active heads on the drum, the result will be the track pitch. If everything else remains equal, the track pitch is proportional to the linear tape speed. Note that the track angle will also change with tape speed.

Figure 8.12(a) shows that in guard-band recording, the track pitch is equal to the width of the track plus the width of the guard band. The track width is

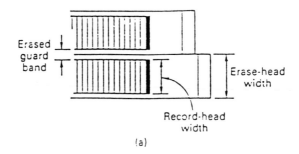

Erased guard band

Erase-head width

Record-head width

(a)

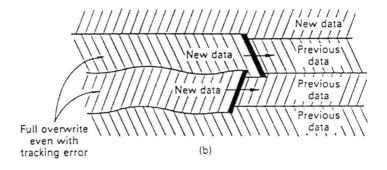

New data

New data

Previous data

New data

Previous data

Previous data

Full overwrite even with tracking error

(b)

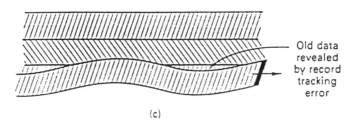

Old data revealed by record tracking error

(c)

Figure 8.13 (a) The erase head is wider than the record head in guard-band recording. In (b) If the azimuth record head is wider than the track, full overwrite is obtained even with misalignment. In (c) if the azimuth record head is the same width as the track, misalignment results in failure to overwrite and an erase head becomes necessary.

determined by the width of the head poles, and the linear tape speed will be high enough so that the desired guard-band is obtained. In guard-band recording, the erase head is wider than the record head, which in turn is wider than the replay head, as shown in Figure 8.13(a). This ensures that despite inevitable misalignments, the entire area to be recorded is erased and the playback head is entirely over a recorded track.

In azimuth recording the situation is different, depending upon whether it is proposed to use flying erase heads. In Figure 8.12(b) the head width is greater than the track pitch, so that the tape does not rise far enough for one track to clear the previous one. Part of the previous track will be overwritten, so that the track width and the track pitch become identical. As Figure 8.13(b) shows, this approach guarantees that, when re-recording, previous tracks are fully overwritten as the overlapping heads cover the entire tape area at least once, and in places twice. For some purposes, flying erase heads are not then necessary.

The alternative shown in Figure 8.12(c) is for the track width to be exactly the same as the track pitch so there is no overlapping. In this case misalignment during re-recording can allow a thin strip of a previous track to survive unless a flying erase head is used. This is shown in Figure 8.13(c).

8.6 Helical head configurations

There is some freedom in positioning of heads in the drum. Figure 8.14(a) shows a drum which carries four heads spaced evenly around the periphery. All of the heads are at the same height on the drum axis, which means that they would all pass the same point in space as the drum rotates.

One revolution of such a drum would lay down four evenly spaced tracks on the tape, and would play them back equally well. With a wrap angle of 180 degrees, two heads would be in contact with the tape at any one time, and so the data rate of an individual head will be half the total.

If it is necessary to use track-following actuators, each of the heads will need to deflect on its own actuator, and will need to be individually controlled, so the cost of implementation will be rather high. An alternative approach is shown in Figure 8.14(b) where the heads are mounted in pairs at 180 degrees. The same tape format can be recorded, provided that the heads in each pair are mounted in different planes. The separation between the head planes depends on the track pitch and the angular separation between the heads. If this geometry is correct, the same format will result, but the time at which the various tracks are laid down will be different, as the figure shows. The tracks are effectively written in pairs, known as *segments*. No problem will arise provided that the record and reproduce electronics are designed to expect to transfer data at the appropriate time. The main advantage of this approach is that there is now only a requirement for two head positioners, which is a great simplification of the drum and servo circuitry.

The physical stagger between the heads is necessary whether the heads are intended for azimuth recording or guard-band recording. In both cases the head is much wider than the track it writes, due to the poles being milled away in the area of the gap. It is not possible to put the heads side by side without a large

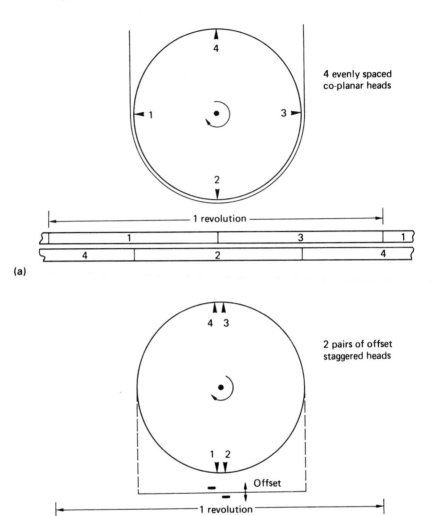

Figure 8.14 (a) Evenly spaced heads in a single plane require actuators for variable speed. (b) Two of the heads are slid along the tape track to give pairs of offset staggered heads. Same tape format results if signal timing to heads is suitably modified.

guard band resulting. Figure 8.15 shows that staggering the heads allows the guard band to be any size, even negative in azimuth applications.

The heads in the segment are staggered and if the recording waveforms in the two heads are synchronous, diagonal tracks will begin in slightly different places along the tape as is evident in the D-2 format. Alternatively, it is possible to delay the record signal to one of the heads so that both tracks begin and end in the same

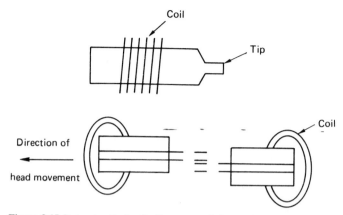

Figure 8.15 Staggering the heads allows any relative track spacing to be used.

place. This is done in D-3/D-5, for example, and as a result the edit gaps between sectors line up in adjacent tracks allowing the use of a single flying erase head shared between the tracks. The bit error rate from the trailing head of a staggered head pair is generally slightly worse than that of the leading head because it is working in the shockwave pattern set up by the first head, and flies over particles of debris which the first head loosens.

The stagger is necessary to allow the two heads physically to overlap, but it also means that the transverse displacement between the two heads is not equal to the track pitch. Figure 8.16 shows that the longitudinal offset between the heads must take into account the fact that the tape is moving down the drum as the heads pass. By the time the trailing head has reached a given point on a track made by the leading head, that track will be lower on the drum than it was when it was written, and so the trailing head must be positioned lower on the drum to put the next track in the correct place.

It is easy to calculate the adjustment necessary, and an example is given here using the D-3 DVTR format. In both PAL and NTSC versions, the tape falls by

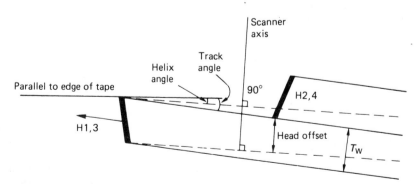

Figure 8.16 The movement of the tape causes the track angle to be different from the helix angle of the scanner. Thus the track width T_w is not the same as the head offset. The necessary adjustment to the head spacing along the scanner axis is derived in the text.

two track widths in half a rotation of the drum. The correction is obtained by calculating the fall which takes place between the passing of the two heads, or in 6.789 degrees of rotation, which is as follows:

(a) for PAL:

$$\text{tape rise} = \frac{18 \times 2 \times 6.789}{180} \ \mu\text{m} = 1.36 \,\mu\text{m}$$

(b) for NTSC:

$$\text{tape rise} = \frac{20 \times 2 \times 6.789}{180} \ \mu\text{m} = 1.51 \,\mu\text{m}$$

Subtracting these correction factors from the track pitch results in the head displacement along the drum axis which is necessary to produce the standard format. The displacement is 16.7 μm for PAL and 18.5 μm for NTSC.

DVTRs vary considerably in the number of heads installed in the drum. Digital VTRs often implement read–modify–write or pre-read in which the tape tracks are read by heads prior to the record heads for editing purposes. In many cases, such as D-2 and D-3, the pre-read function is obtained by deflecting the track following playback heads so that they precede the record heads. Clearly there is then no confidence replay (read-after-write) in this editing mode.

In formats which use data reduction, the compression and expansion processes introduce significant additional delay into the read-modify-write loop and the pre-read head must then be physically further advanced. The additional distance required may be beyond the deflection range of the track following actuator and extra heads will be necessary. Extra heads do, however, mean that confidence replay is always available.

Figure 8.17(a) shows an early D-2 drum in which two pairs of record heads are mounted opposite one another so that they function alternately with a 180 degree wrap. The replay heads pairs are mounted at 90 degrees on track-following actuators.

Figure 8.17(b) shows a D-3 drum which has a pair of flying erase heads in addition to the record and play heads. In D-3 the two tracks in the segment are aligned by delaying the record signals, so one flying erase head functions for two tracks.

The D-5 format is backward compatible with D-3 tapes, but can also record the higher data rate of component digital video by doubling the data throughput of the drum. This is done by having four parallel tracks per segment, requiring four heads on each base. To play a D-3 tape, only two of the heads are used. In order to work in components, the drum speed is unchanged, but the tape linear speed is doubled. Figure 8.17(c) shows a D-5 drum in which the general arrangement is the same as for D-3, but each base is fitted with four heads.

Figure 8.17(d) shows the drum of an analog-compatible Digital Betacam. The two tracks in each segment are aligned by delays so that double-width flying erase heads can be used. The erase, record A and record B heads corresponding to one segment can be seen to the bottom right of the diagram, with the same configuration diametrically opposite. Fixed confidence replay heads are arranged

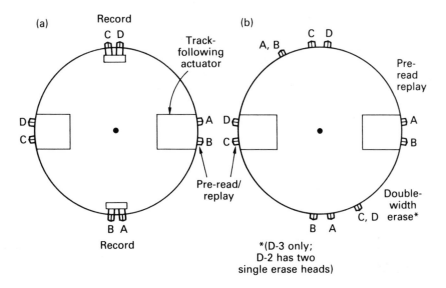

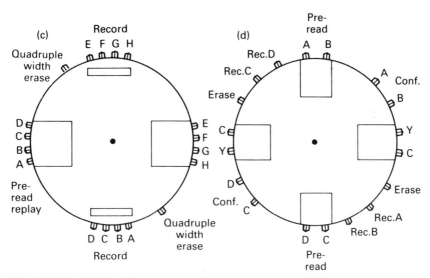

Figure 8.17 (a–d) Various drum configurations contrasted. In (a) early D-2 recorders had no flying erase. In (b) later D-2 and D-3 drums have flying erase. In (c) D-5 uses four tracks per segment. Two heads of D-5 head base will register with D-3 segments. In (d) analog-compatible digital Betacam has separate confidence replay heads as well as track-following analog heads.

nearly at right angles to the record heads. These heads trace the tracks which have just been recorded. At the top and bottom of the diagram can be seen the advanced playback heads which are also used for track following. Finally there are two more track-following actuators which carry pairs of heads which suit the width of tracks on analog Betacam tapes.

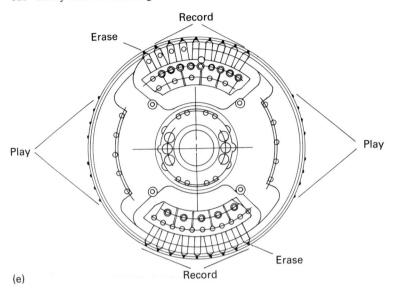

(e)

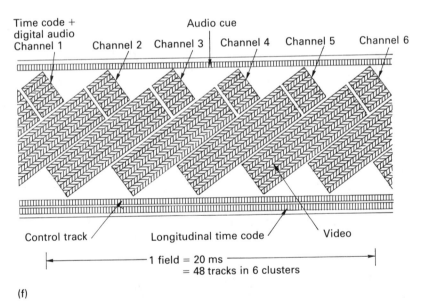

(f)

Figure 8.17 (e) and (f) (e) The head configuration of an eight-channel HD recorder with single flying erase. (f) The track pattern of the drum in (e). Delays are used to line up the tracks written by the staggered heads.

High-definition recording requires extremely high data rates and this is accommodated by using many heads in parallel. Figure 8.17(e) shows the head arrangement of a DVTR built by BTS[2] in which eight heads are required in one segment. Although the heads are distributed around the perimeter of the drum, the record signals are subject to differing delays such that all tracks in a segment start in the same place and a single erase head a little over eight tracks wide can be used. The resultant track pattern is shown in Figure 8.17(f).

8.7 Time compression

The length of the track laid on the tape is a function of the drum diameter and the wrap angle. Figure 8.17 shows a number of ways in which the same length of track can be put on the tape.

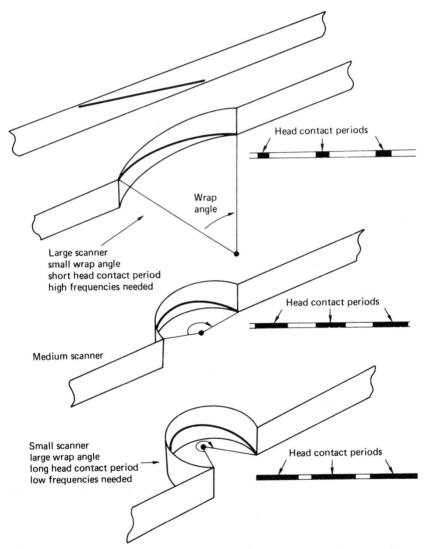

Figure 8.18 A standard track can be put on tape with a variety of scanners. A large wrap allows the lowest frequencies at the head but increases complexity of threading mechanism and increases tape path friction. The helix angle will be different in each case in order to match the tape rise speed to the head peripheral speed – giving the same track angle.

A small drum with a large wrap angle works just as well as a large drum with a small wrap angle. If the tape speed, and hence the track rate, is constant, and for the purposes of this comparison the number of heads on the drum remains constant, the heads on the smaller drum will take a longer time to traverse the track than the heads on the larger drum. This has the effect of lowering the frequencies seen by the heads, and is responsible for the 270 degree wrap of the Sony D-1 recorders.

Changing the wrap angle also means that the helix angle will need to be different so that the same track angle is achieved in all cases. In practice, a larger drum can be used to mount more heads which work in turn, so that the drum speed will then be less than before. Alternatively the space inside the larger drum may be used to incorporate track-following heads. Another advantage of the large drum is that the reduced wrap angle is easier to thread up. A small drum is attractive for a portable machine since it is compact and requires less power. The greater wrap angle has to be accepted. Most RDAT transports use a 30 mm diameter scanner with 90 degree wrap. Miniaturized machines use 15 mm diameter scanners with 180 degree wrap.

The different drum sizes in the example of Figure 8.18 traced standard tracks in different periods of time, as shown in the diagram. In analog video recorders, the time period had to be one television field so that the television waveform could be directly fed to the heads, and design of the drum was extremely inflexible.

In the digital VTR there is more freedom. The video field is expressed by a given number of samples, and as long as these appear on replay in the right sequence, their actual position in the recording or the exact time at which they were recorded is of no consequence. Clearly the record and replay processes must complement one another.

8.8 Track layout and segmentation in DVTRs

The number of bits to be recorded for one field will be a direct result of the sampling scheme chosen. The minimum wavelength which can be reliably recorded will then determine the length of track that is necessary.

The recording density used in DVTRs is such that a track length of up to one metre would be needed for one field. Clearly no one in their right mind is going to design a scanner large enough to put the whole of one field on one track. A further consideration is that with current head technology it is difficult to pass all the data through one head. Eddy current losses in the head get worse at high frequencies. Even if it were possible to record all of the data with one head, this would not be desirable from a practical standpoint, since if that head became clogged there would be nothing to be done. Sharing the data between a number of heads allows concealment to be used should one of them clog.

The solution to both problems is *segmentation*, where the data for one field are recorded in a number of head sweeps. With segmentation it is easy to share the data between more than one head. In DVTRs, two or four heads working simultaneously are necessary.

With segmentation, the contents of a field can be divided into convenient-sized pieces for recording. This allows the width of the tape to be chosen. If the tape is wide, then tracks of a given length can be placed at a greater angle to the edge of the tape, and so the tape will move more slowly for a given track rate. This means that the effective rewinding time will be reduced because a given recording will occupy a shorter length of tape. Taken to extremes, this would result in very wide tape on small reels.

This is not the only criterion, however. A wide tape needs a physically larger scanner assembly, and requires greater precision in guidance. It is seldom possible to engineer a tape transport with total precision, so the tape will always be expected to accommodate small inaccuracies by flexing. The stiffness of the tape against bending in its own plane is proportional to the moment of inertia of its cross-section. This rises disproportionately with tape width. The selection of a narrower tape will ease transport accuracy requirements slightly. Another factor to be considered is the recording density. A high-density recording requires less tape area per unit time, and so the effective rewinding speed will be proportional to the recording density.

Having chosen the tape width, the number of segments per field can be established. A large number of short, steep tracks will give the same overall track length as a smaller number of long, shallow tracks. For normal speed operation, there is little difference between the two approaches, but in video recorders, the smaller the number of segments the better, since the magnitude of head jumps will be reduced. Where two different television standards have to be recorded, the number of segments will be chosen so that a whole number results in both standards.

8.9 The basic helical-scan transport

Figure 8.19 shows the important components of a rotary-head helical-scan tape transport. There are four servo systems which must correctly interact to obtain all modes of operation: two reel servos, the scanner servo and the capstan servo. The

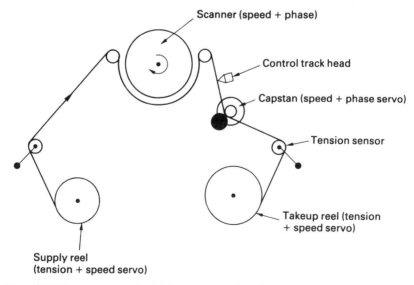

Figure 8.19 The four servos essential for proper operation of a helical-scan DVTR. Cassette-based units will also require loading and threading servos, and for variable speed a track-following servo will be necessary.

capstan and reel servos together move the tape, and the scanner servo moves the heads. The servos act according to the principles discussed in Chapter 6. For track following a further servo system will be necessary to deflect the heads.

The tape is held against the capstan by pressure from a resilient pinch roller which is normally pulled toward the capstan by a solenoid. The capstan only drives the tape over a narrow speed range, generally the range in which broadcastable pictures are required. Outside this range, the pinch roller retracts, the tape will be driven by reel motors alone, and the reel motors will need to change their operating mode.

The capstan motor must be free from cogging, so a multipole ironless rotor pancake-type brush motor or a sinusoidal drive brushless motor can be used.

The simplest operating mode to consider is the first recording on a blank tape. In this mode, the capstan will rotate at constant speed, and drive the tape at the linear speed specified for the format. The drum must rotate at a precisely determined speed, so that the correct number of tracks per unit distance will be laid down on the tape. Since in a segmented recording each track will be a constant fraction of a television field, the scanner speed must ultimately be determined by the incoming video signal to be recorded. To take the example of a PAL D-3 recorder having two record head pairs, eight tracks or four segments will be necessary to record one field, and so the scanner must make exactly two complete revolutions in one field period, requiring it to run at 100 Hz. In the case of NTSC D-3, there are six tracks or three segments per field, and so the scanner must turn at one and a half times field rate, or a little under 90 Hz. The phase of the scanner depends upon the time delay necessary to shuffle and interleave the video samples. This will typically be one field.

8.10 Tracking systems

All rotary-head machines need some kind of active tracking system to register the recorded tracks with the replay heads. Tracking systems vary considerably in complexity. Figure 8.20 shows the most basic system which uses a linear control track. The rotary head carries a pulse generator which produces a pulse every time a head begins a sweep across the tape. On recording, these pulses are sent to the control-track head so that one linear track pulse is recorded for each data track. On playback, the control track is replayed, and the phase of the control-track pulses is compared with the phase of the pulses from the rotary head. The phase error is used to drive the capstan in such a way that the error is cancelled.

All transports must be aligned to have the same mechanical spacing between the rotary heads and the control-track head gap, otherwise tracking errors occur on interchange. One solution is to place an operator-adjustable delay in series with the control-track head replay signal. This can compensate for misalignment because adjusting the delay has the same effect as physically moving the head and thus forms an effective tracking control. All consumer VCRs have a control which works in this way.

An operator tracking control is subject to misadjustment and as tracks become narrower the adjustment becomes critical. In the RDAT/DDS format the tracking system dispensed with the control-track head and measured a tracking error from tones recorded on the slant tracks themselves in order to control the capstan. This system is described in Section 8.11. In the Ampex DCRS, tracking tones are also

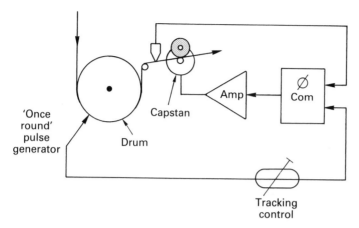

Figure 8.20 In a simple rotary-head tracking system, pulses from the headwheel are phase-compared with pulses from a fixed-control track head. The phase error drives the capstan. A tracking control varies a delay in one of the inputs to the phase comparator.

present in the data tracks but the tracking error from these is used in conjunction with a control track as described in Section 8.12.

The above tracking systems move the tape bodily and can only control the average alignment of a track. They can do nothing about tracks having curvature or incorrect angles due to temperature or tension variation. In order to accommodate alignment errors within the track capstan control is not enough and the rotary heads must be made to deflect along the axis of rotation. In data recorders this technique can be used to increase recording density in the same way as is done in hard disks. In digital video recorders the technique is extended to allow tracks to be followed even with the tape moving at the wrong speed. Tracking systems of this kind are considered in Section 8.13.

For replay only, it is possible to dispense with the drum and tracking servos in some applications. No control track is necessary. The drum free-runs at approximately twice normal speed, whilst the capstan continues to run at the correct speed. The rotary heads cross tracks randomly, but because of the increased speed, virtually every sync block is recovered, many of them twice. The increased drum speed requires a higher clock frequency in the data separator.

Each sync block on tape contains error-correcting codewords, and those which are found to be error free or which contain correctable random errors can be used. Each sync block also contains an ID pattern and this is used to put the data in the correct place in the product block. If a second copy of any sync block is recovered it is discarded at this stage.

Once the product code memory is full, the de-interleave and error-correction process can occur as normal. Any blocks which are not recovered due to track crossing will be treated as dropouts by the error-correction system, as will genuine dropouts.

An advantage is that alignment of the scanner is not necessary during manufacture, and tapes which are recorded on misaligned machines can still be played. Mistracking resulting from shock and vibration has no effect since the system is mistracking all the time. The Sony NT (non-tracking) format recorder works on this principle. The NT format is a subminature rotary-head audio recorder using data reduction and postage-stamp-sized cassettes.

8.11 The tracking system of RDAT

The traditional control track is adequate for the wide tracks of analog video recorders, but errors in the mounting of the fixed head and variations in tape tension rule it out for high-density use. In any case the control-track head adds undesirable mechanical complexity. In RDAT, the tracking is achieved by reading special alignment patterns on the tape tracks themselves, and by using the information contained in them to control the capstan.

RDAT uses a technique called area-divided track following (ATF) in which separate parts of the track are set aside for track-following purposes. Figure 8.21 shows the basic way in which a tracking error is derived. The tracks at each side of the home track have bursts of pilot tone recorded in two different places. The

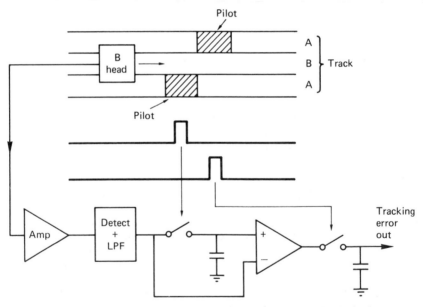

Figure 8.21 In the track-following system of RDAT, the signal picked up by the head comes from pilot tones recorded in adjacent tracks at different positions. These pilot tones have low frequency, and are unaffected by azimuth effect. The system samples the amplitude of the pilot tones, and subtracts them.

frequency of the pilot tone is 130 kHz, which has been chosen to be relatively low so that it is not affected by azimuth loss. In this way an A head following an A track will be able to detect the pilot tone from the adjacent B tracks.

In Figure 8.22(a) the case of a correctly tracking head is shown. The amount of side-reading pilot tone from the two adjacent B tracks is identical. If the head is off track for some reason, as shown in Figure 8.22(b), the amplitude of the

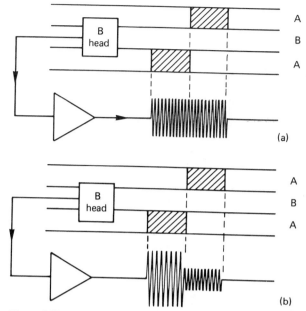

A

B

A

(a)

A

B

A

(b)

Figure 8.22 (a) A correctly tracking head produces pilot-tone bursts of identical amplitude. (b) The head is off track, and the first pilot burst becomes larger, whereas the second becomes smaller. This produces the tracking error in the circuit of Figure 8.21.

pilot tone from one of the adjacent tracks will increase, and the other will decrease. The tracking error is derived by sampling the amplitude of each pilot-tone burst as it occurs, and by holding the result so the relative amplitudes can be compared.

There are some practical considerations to be overcome in implementing this simple system, which result in some added complication. The pattern of pilot tones must be such that they occur at different times on each side of every track. To achieve this there must be a burst of pilot tone in every track, although the pilot tone in the home track does not contribute to the development of the tracking error. Additionally there must be some timing signals in the tracks to determine when the samples of pilot tone should be made. The final issue is to prevent the false locking which could occur if the tape happened to run at twice normal speed.

Figure 8.23 shows how the actual track-following pattern of RDAT is laid out.[3] The pilot burst is early on A tracks and late on B tracks. Although the pilot bursts have a two-track cycle, the pattern is made to repeat over four tracks by changing the period of the sync patterns which control the pilot sampling. This can be used to prevent false locking. When an A head enters the track, it finds the home pilot burst first, followed by pilot from the B track above, then pilot from the B track below. The tracking error is derived from the latter two. When a B head enters the track, it sees pilot from the A track above first, A track below next, and finally home pilot. The tracking error in this case is derived from the former two. The machine can easily tell which processing mode to use because the sync signals have a different frequency depending on whether they are in

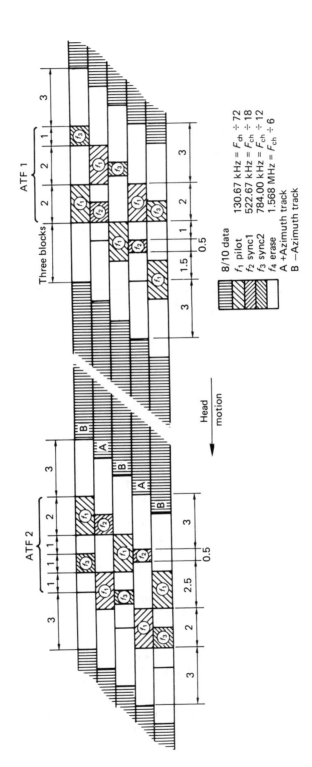

Figure 8.23 The area-divided track-following (ATF) patterns of RDAT. To ease generation of patterns on recording, the pattern lengths are related to the data-block dimensions and the frequencies used are obtained by dividing down the channel bit clock F_{ch}. The sync signals are used to control the timing with which the pilot amplitude is sampled.

8/10 data

f_1 pilot   130.67 kHz $= F_{ch} \div 72$
f_2 sync1   522.67 kHz $= F_{ch} \div 18$
f_3 sync2   784.00 kHz $= F_{ch} \div 12$
f_4 erase   1.568 MHz $= F_{ch} \div 6$

A +Azimuth track
B −Azimuth track

A tracks (522 kHz) or B tracks (784 kHz). The remaining areas are recorded with the inter-block gap frequency of 1.56 MHz which serves no purpose except to erase earlier recordings. Although these pilot and synchronizing frequencies appear strange, they are chosen so that they can be simply obtained by dividing down the master channel-bit-rate clock by simple factors. The channel-bit-rate clock, F_{ch}, is 9.408 MHz; pilot, the two sync frequencies and erase are obtained by dividing it by 72, 18, 12 and 6 respectively. The time at which the pilot amplitude in adjacent tracks should be sampled is determined by the detection of the synchronizing frequencies. As the head sees part of three tracks at all times, the sync detection in the home track has to take place in the presence of unwanted signals. On one side of the home sync signal will be the inter-block gap frequency, which is high enough to be attenuated by azimuth. On the other side is pilot, which is unaffected by azimuth. This means that sync detection is easier in the tracking-error direction away from pilot than in the direction towards it. There is an effective working range of about +4 and −5 μm due to this asymmetry, with a dead band of 4 μm between tracks. Since the track-following servo is designed to minimize the tracking error, once lock is achieved the presence of the dead zone becomes academic. The differential amplitude of the pilot tones produces the tracking error, and so the gain of the servo loop is proportional to the playback gain, which can fluctuate as a result of head-contact variations and head tolerance. This problem is overcome by using AGC in the servo system. In addition to subtracting the pilot amplitudes to develop the tracking error, the circuitry also adds them to develop an AGC voltage. Two sample and hold stages are provided which store the AGC parameter for each head separately. The heads can thus be of different sensitivities without upsetting the servo. This condition could arise from manufacturing tolerances, or if one of the heads became contaminated.

8.12 The tracking system of DCRSi

The Ampex DCRSi machines are transverse-scan instrumentation recorders using a headwheel fitted with six or twelve heads. An active track-following system is used. In contrast with RDAT, which uses an area-divided tracking system, in DCRSi the tracking tones are continuous and are added to the data. When a recording is made a tracking tone is linearly added to the waveform from the channel coder. The record amplifier is actually an analog device which contains pre-emphasis to compensate for record-head losses and so the addition of a tracking tone is quite easy.

The tracking-tone frequency is quite low for several reasons: (a) The azimuth effect fails at low frequencies and this allows the tracking system to detect signals not only from the correct track but also from adjacent tracks having opposite azimuth. (b) Interference between the tracking tone and data is minimized. (c) Phase errors due to jitter are proportional to frequency so a low-frequency tone will be immune to jitter.

Figure 8.24 shows that the frequency of the tracking tone is carefully selected and locked to the headwheel speed so that the phase shifts by 90 degrees from one track to the next.[4] There are four fixed-phase relationships between the tracking tone and the sync pattern at the beginning of the data track. The tracking signal detected by the replay head will be the sum of three contributions: that from the home track and those due to crosstalk from the two adjacent tracks. In

+90°   0°   −90°

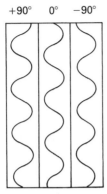

Figure 8.24 In DCRS the tracking tone is carefully phased by 90 degrees from one track to the next. On replay the signals from tracks adjacent to the home track should cancel, but mistracking results in a net phase shift which is detected to drive the capstan.

the case of a correctly tracking head the amplitudes of the crosstalk signals from adjacent tracks will be equal, and there will be cancellation because of the phase inversion over two tracks.

In the case of a tracking error, the amplitude of one crosstalk signal will increase but the other will reduce. The replay signal will then contain the sum of the signal from the home track and a quadrature signal from the crosstalk. The result is that the phase changes proportionally with the tracking error. The phase, and hence the tracking error, is measured by a synchronous rectifier whose reference frequency is locked to the sync patterns. The tracking error is added to the error in the existing control-track loop so that it effectively eliminates the manual tracking adjustment.

8.13 Track following in DVTRs

The variable speed range first achieved by the C-format analog machines has essentially become the yardstick by which later formats are measured. It is important for the success of a DVTR that at least an equal speed range is available and the means to obtain this will be discussed here. Although the problem of variable speed is defined by the format, the solutions adopted by various manufacturers are quite different and will be contrasted.

It was seen in Section 8.3 that the movement of the tape results in the tracks having an angle different from the helix angle. The rotary head will only be able to follow the track properly if the tape travels at the correct speed. At all other speeds, the head will move at an angle to the tracks. If the head is able to move along the drum axis as it turns, it will be possible to follow whole tracks at certain tape speeds by moving the head as a function of the rotational angle of the drum. The necessary function can be appreciated by considering the situation when the tape is stopped. The tape track will, of course, be at the track angle, but the head will rotate at the helix angle. The head can be made to follow a stationary track by deflecting it at constant rate by one segment pitch per sweep. In other words, a ramp or triangle waveform is necessary to deflect the head. The slope of the ramp is proportional to the speed *difference*, since at normal speed the difference is zero and no deflection is needed. Clearly the deflection cannot continue to grow forever, because the head will run out of travel, and it must then jump to miss out some tracks and reduce the deflection.

There are a number of issues to be addressed in providing a track-following system. The use of segmented formats means that head jumps necessary to omit or repeat one or more fields must jump over several segments. This requires a mechanical head-positioning system which has the necessary travel and will work reliably despite the enormous acceleration experienced at the perimeter of the drum. As there are generally two head bases, two such systems are needed, and they must be independently controlled since they are mounted in opposition on the drum and contact the tape alternately. In addition a control system is required which will ensure that jumps only take place at the end of a field to prevent a picture from two different fields being displayed.

The degree of accuracy required is much higher than in analog formats because the tracks are much narrower.

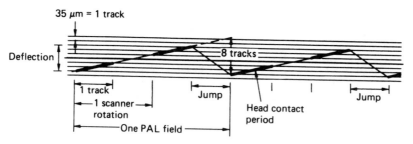

Figure 8.25 Head deflection waveform for PAL D-3 at +3× normal speed. This requires a jump of two fields between every field played, and this corresponds to eight tracks. Since head pairs trace the tape alternately, the head has half a revolution in which to jump, so the actual jump is only six tracks. However, the vertical position of the above waveform is subject to an uncertainty of plus or minus two tracks because capstan phase is random during variable speed.

When the tape speed is close to three times normal, most of the time a two-field jump will be necessary at the end of every field. Figure 8.25 shows the resulting ramp deflection waveform (for one head pair only). Since the control track phase is random, an offset of up to ±½ field will be superimposed on the deflection, so that for a two-field jump always to be possible, a total deflection of three fields must be available. This, along with the segmentation employed, determines the mechanical travel of the heads.

8.14 The actuator

In Sony and Panasonic machines, the actuator used for head deflection is based on piezoelectric elements as used in numerous previous products. Figure 8.26 shows the construction of the Sony dynamic tracking head. A pair of parallel piezoelectric bimorphs is used, to ensure that head zenith is affected as little as possible by deflection. The basic principle of the actuator is that an applied voltage causes the barium titanate crystal to shrink. If two thin plates are bonded together to create a bimorph, the shrinkage of one of them will result in bending.

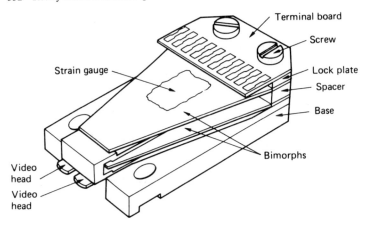

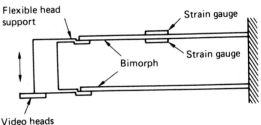

Figure 8.26 The dynamic tracking head of a Sony D-2 transport uses a pair of parallel bimorphs to maintain head zenith angle. Note use of strain gauges for feedback. (Courtesy Sony Broadcast)

A stale sandwich displays the same effect. Application of voltage to one or other of the elements allows deflection in either direction, although care must be taken to prevent reverse voltage being applied to an element since this will destroy the inherent electric field. In view of the high-g environment, which attempts to restore the actuator to the neutral position, high deflection voltages are necessary. The deflection amplifiers are usually static, and feed the drum via slip rings which are often fitted on the top of the drum. When worn, these can spark and increase the error rate. Piezoelectric actuators display hysteresis, and some form of position feedback is necessary to allow a linear system. This is obtained by strain gauges which are attached to one of the bimorphs, and can be seen in the figure. When power is first applied to the transport, the actuator is supplied with a gradually decaying sinusoidal drive signal, which removes any unwanted set from the bimorph.

In Ampex D-2 and DCT machines, the piezoelectric actuator was not considered adequate for the larger travel demanded in a segmented format,[5] and a moving-coil actuator has been developed. These had been used experimentally in certain analog recorders, but gave way to piezoelectric actuators in the C-format. Now that rare-earth magnets are available, which offer high field strength with low mass, the moving-coil actuator becomes attractive again, because it allows a low-mass cantilever which has higher resonant frequencies and requires less force to deflect. The moving coil is inherently a low-impedance

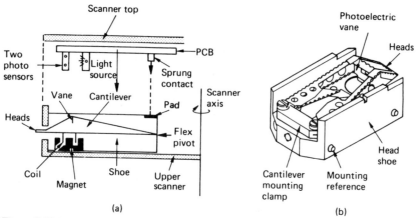

Figure 8.27 (a) Showing the concept of moving-coil head deflection. The cantilever is flexurally pivoted at the opposite end to the heads, and position feedback is obtained from a vane on the cantilever which differentially varies the light falling on two photosensors. (b) The appearance of an actual replaceable AST head assembly. (Courtesy Ampex)

device requiring a current drive which is easier to provide than the high voltages needed by piezoelectric devices.

Figure 8.27(a) shows the concept of the moving-coil head and Figure 8.27(b) shows the appearance of the actual unit used in D-2. The cantilever is folded from thin sheet metal which is perforated to assist the folding process. The resulting structure is basically a torsion box supported on a wide flexural pivot. This means that it can bend up and down, but it cannot twist, since twisting would introduce unwanted azimuth errors. The cantilever carries the actuator coil, and is supported in a metal shoe which carries the magnet.

Positional feedback of the cantilever deflection is obtained by a photoelectric system. This has one light source and two sensors between which moves a blade which is integral with the cantilever. When the cantilever deflects, a differential signal results from the sensors. The photoelectric sensor is mounted inside the top of the drum, and automatically aligns with the moving blade when the top is fitted.

For the DCT format a similar actuator was developed, but having a parallel action to maintain constant head zenith angle.

Whichever of these actuators is used, the combination of actuator, drive amplifier and position feedback gives a subassembly which will deflect the head in proportion to an applied voltage. It is then necessary to provide suitable drive signals to ensure that the deflection makes the head follow the track.

8.15 Detecting the tracking error

Track following is a means of actively controlling the relationship between the replay head and the track so that the track is traced more accurately than it would be by purely mechanical means. This can be applied to systems operating at normal speed, in order to allow interchange in adverse conditions as is done in

Digital Betacam, but in many formats track following is an option, and satisfactory interchange can be achieved without it.

The tracking error will be used on two different levels. Firstly, the DC component of the tracking error will be used to set the average elevation of the head about which the ramp deflection will take place. Secondly, variations of tracking error during the track can be used to compensate for tracks which are not straight, due to some relative misalignment between the machine which recorded the tape and the player. The tracking-error detection systems differ between manufacturers and these differences will be noted.

Figure 8.28 shows three relationships of the head to the track, and corresponding signal output. The waveforms in Figure 8.28 correspond to the RF envelope of the channel-coded signal. Case (a) and case (c) display the same output, although the tracking error has the opposite sense. Simple processing of the RF level only gives the magnitude of the error, not the sense.

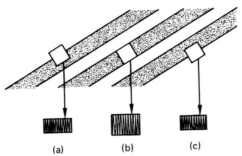

(a)   (b)   (c)

Figure 8.28 Effect of tracking error on playback signal. Signal amplitude in (a) and (c) is identical, despite sense of tracking error. Maximum signal occurs with correct alignment as in (b).

In order to extract the sense of the tracking error, it is necessary to move the tracking head, to see if the error becomes greater or smaller. The process of manually tuning an AM radio is very similar.

In Sony D-2 machines, the head elevation is changed by small steps between segments, and if the steps cause the average RF level to fall, the direction of the steps is reversed. This process is known colloquially as 'bump and look', and was originally developed for the Betacam products.

In the Ampex machines, the head is subject to a sinusoidal oscillation or dither, as was done in C-format machines. One field scan contains many cycles of dither. The effect on the RF envelope, as shown in Figure 8.29, is an amplitude modulation of the carrier, which has little effect on the video, owing to the insensitivity of the digital recording system to amplitude effects. Figure 8.29(a) shows that the effect of dither on a correctly aligned head is a frequency doubling in the RF envelope. Figures 8.29(b) and (c) show the effect of the head off track. Both cases appear similar, but the phase of the envelope modulation is different, and can be used to extract the sense of the tracking error.

Each cantilever carries two heads, one of each azimuth type, and the RF levels from the two heads are averaged together. This gives a 3 dB improvement in signal-to-noise ratio, as well as accommodating manufacturing tolerances in the

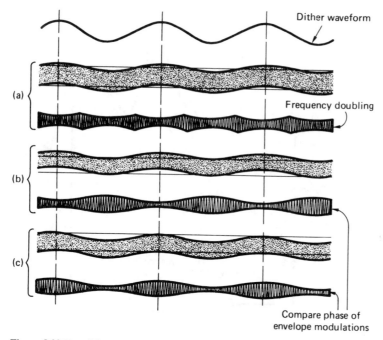

Figure 8.29 Top, dither waveform which causes head to oscillate across track. In (a) is optimum alignment, showing frequency doubling in RF envelope. With head above track centre, as in (b), RF amplitude increases as head reaches lowest point, whereas reverse applies in case (c).

elevation of the video tips. Only one detector or synchronous rectifier is then required per cantilever.

Dither cannot be used with analog VTRs employing azimuth recording because the transverse head motion interacts with the azimuth angle to give the effect of rising and falling head-to-tape speed. In FM recording, this introduces an unwanted signal into the video, which is why Sony developed the bump and look system for Betacam. The effect is still present in a digital recorder, but the result is that the instantaneous offtape data rate rises and falls slightly. This is accommodated by the phase-locked loop in the data separator, and has no effect on the data. A harmless dither component will be observed in the VCO control voltage, and the speed variation in the discrete data is completely removed in the timebase correction.

In Figure 8.30 the RF is detected to obtain a level, which is fed to a phase-sensitive rectifier, whose reference is the dither drive signal. The output of the phase-sensitive rectifier is a tracking-error signal which contains both magnitude and sense and rather a lot of harmonics of dither. Careful choice of the dither frequency allows easier cancelling of the dither harmonics. In the VPR-300, there are five and a half cycles of dither per segment, or eleven cycles per revolution. Both heads are dithered by the same waveform, which means that the dither on odd segments will be phase reversed with respect to even segments. A dither frequency of 1100 Hz results in PAL, whereas in NTSC it is 990 Hz.

The tracking error is averaged over a pair of segments to cancel the harmonics and to produce an elevation error. The tracking error will also be sampled at

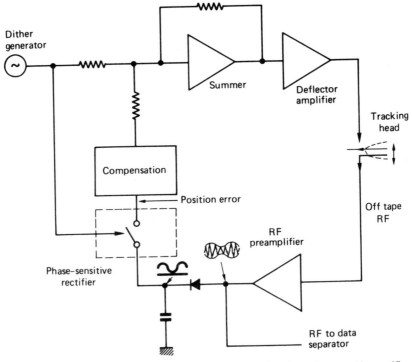

Figure 8.30 The tracking error is extracted from the RF envelope by a phase-sensitive rectifier.

several points down the track to see if there is a consistent curvature in the tracking. This can be reduced by adding a correction curve to the deflection waveform which will adjust itself until the best envelope is obtained over the whole track length.

A different approach to measuring track curvature is used in Sony D-2 and Panasonic transports. As has been stated, deflecting a head which uses azimuth recording causes timing changes. If a pair of heads of opposite azimuth are tracing the appropriate tracks, tracking error will result in differential timing changes. This can be measured by comparing the time at which sync patterns are detected in the two channels. Figure 8.31 illustrates the principle. This system will detect tracking errors due to track distortion. Unfortunately, manufacturing tolerances in the physical stagger between the heads on both the machine which made the recording and the player will combine to put a permanent offset in the tracking error derived using this principle. It is necessary to calibrate the system each time it is used. The bump-and-look system maximizes the RF level at the beginning of the track, and the control system then inserts a changing offset into the sync timing comparator until it too gives zero tracking error at the beginning of the track. The offset is then held at that value. This process removes the static deflection and allows the tracking error to be used to deflect the heads within the track.

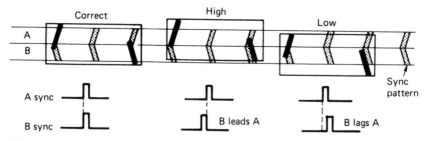

Figure 8.31 In the Sony D-2 DT system the tracking error is detected by comparing the times at which sync patterns are detected by the two heads on each arm. Owing to the use of azimuth recording a component of transverse movement results in a movement of the effective position of the head along the track.

The Digital Betacam format is unique in that it contains tracking tones in the slant tracks which are part of the format. These tracking tones are intended to eliminate manual tracking adjustments in normal play and cannot measure tracking errors which change along the track.

8.16 The ramp generator

The positional feedback generated by the observation of the dithered RF envelope or the sync pattern phase is not sufficiently accurate to follow the tracks unassisted except at normal speed where it can be used as an interchange aid. In variable speed the deflection of the head is predicted to produce a feedforward signal which adds to the head deflection. The feedback then only has to correct for the difference between the feedforward and the actuality. When the tape travels at the wrong speed, the track angle changes, and so the head needs to deflect by a distance proportional to the angle it has rotated in order to follow the track. The deflection signal will be in the form of a ramp, which becomes steeper as the tape speed deviates more from normal. The actual speed of the capstan can be used to generate the slope of the ramp. One possible implementation of this is shown in Figure 8.32. A counter has count-up and count-down inputs. The first of these is driven by the capstan tacho disk, and the second is driven by a clock whose frequency is exactly equal to that generated by the capstan tacho at normal speed. When the capstan runs at normal speed, the counter receives as many up clocks as down clocks, and remains unchanged. However, if the capstan speed is raised, the counter will begin to count up at a rate proportional to the speed difference. The counter drives a DAC which produces the deflection ramp. The RF amplitude detector will generate pulses which are also fed into the counter so that the elevation correction can be made. It is also possible to predict the average or static deflection of the heads from the control-track phase. The capstan frequency generator can be used to measure control-track phase. The capstan FG wheel will be designed so that a known number of FG pulses is generated when the capstan transports the tape by the distance between control-track segment pulses. The FG pulses are fed to a counter which is reset by segment pulses from the control-track head. The counter then produces control-track phase which can be used to establish head elevation.

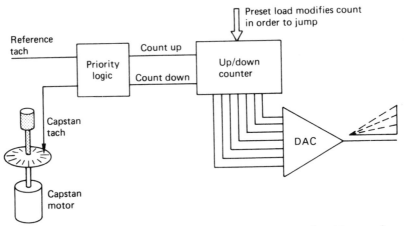

Figure 8.32 An up/down counter is fed with pulses from the capstan tach and from a reference whose frequency is precisely that of capstan tach at normal speed. The counter will thus integrate speed deviation from unity, and the DAC will produce a ramp whose slope is proportional to speed difference. This is the feedforward signal which drives the head deflection system.

The same deflection ramp slope will be fed to both head pairs so that they will read alternate segments for an entire field. At some point it will be necessary to jump the heads to reduce the deflection, and this requires some care. The heads are 180 degrees opposed, and contact the tape alternately. The jump takes place whilst the head is out of contact with the tape. The two head pairs will have to jump at different times, half a drum revolution apart. Clearly if one head jumps, the second head must also jump, otherwise the resulting picture will have come from two fields. As the jumps are half a revolution apart, it follows that the decision to jump must be made half a drum revolution *before* the end of the current field. The decision is made by extrapolating the deflection ramp forward to see what the deflection *will be* when the end of the field is reached. If the deflection will exceed half a field, it can be reduced by jumping one field. If the deflection will exceed one field, it can be reduced by jumping two fields. The jump can be executed by adding or subtracting a number of pulses in the ramp counter.

Tape tension changes can cause the track width to vary minutely. This is normally of no consequence, but when taken over all of the tracks in a segment the error may be significant. It is possible to compare the tracking error before and after a jump, and if the error becomes greater, the jump distance was inappropriate for the tape being played. It is possible to modify the distance jumped simply by changing the number of pulses fed to the ramp counter during the jump command. In this way the jump distance can optimize itself for the tape being played.

Figure 8.33(a) shows the ramping action for the two moving heads in PAL D-2 or D-3 with the tape moving at twice normal speed. It will be seen that when one head jumps, the other one will also jump, so both heads always play the same field. The timing shift due to the heads being separated by half a revolution can be seen. As there are four segments per field in PAL, corresponding to two drum revolutions, all fields will contain the same sequence. Figure 8.33(b) shows the

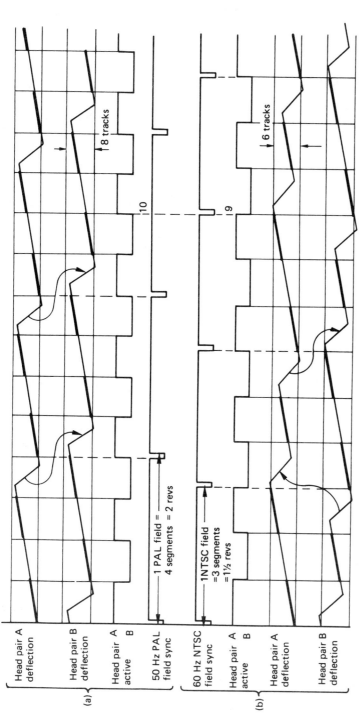

Figure 8.33 The timing and deflections necessary at a speed of +2× in D-2 for (a) PAL and (b) NTSC. Note the segment ratio of 9:10 between the two formats, which is also the ratio of scanner speeds. In order to play entire fields, jumps must take place about the field boundary, so that if one head pair jumps, the other must follow (serpentine arrow). In NTSC there are three segments per field, so the jumping follows a two-field sequence, where the head fails to jump in one field, but jumps twice in the next.

equivalent sequence of events for NTSC. As there are three segments per field and two moving heads, the action differs between odd fields and even fields. During one field, a given head may jump twice, but in the next field it will not jump at all.

8.17 Track-following block diagram

Figure 8.34 shows an Ampex D-2/DCT track-following system. There is an inner feedback loop which consists of the head actuator, the position feedback sensor and an amplifier. This loop is a position servo which makes the head deflection proportional to the input voltage. Like any position servo it is provided with compensation to prevent oscillation and maximize frequency response. The inner loop is driven by the sum of four signals. These are:

(1) The dither signal, which is a sinusoid designed to wobble the head either side of its average elevation.

(2) The elevation correction obtained by averaging the tracking error over the entire track.

(3) The track-curvature compensation, which is a segment rate curve obtained by sampling the tracking error at several points along the track.

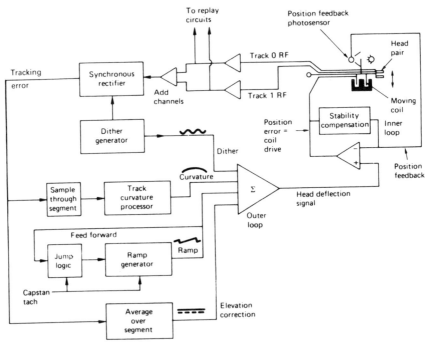

Figure 8.34 Ampex D-2 track-following system. Position feedback in an inner loop around the head positioner linearizes and damps positioner so that mechanical deflection is proportional to head deflection signal from outer loop. Dither generator wobbles the head and drives synchronous receiver to obtain tracking error which is used to correct the head elevation and to compensate for track curvature. Feedforward system generates ramps.

(4) The feedforward ramp and jump signal. The slope is obtained from capstan speed difference and the jumps are initiated by analysing the deflection.

Figure 8.35 shows the track-following system used by Sony and Panasonic. The capstan FG and control track are used together for elevation prediction, and capstan FG is used alone for ramp slope prediction. The bump-and-look system is controlled by the RF detector, which is also used to calibrate the differential sync pattern timing detector.

In both types of machine, there are two moving heads and so two of these systems are necessary. They are largely independent except for a common jump-control system which ensures that when one head jumps during the last segment of a field the other head will follow once it has played that segment.

When a head jumps, it will move to a track which began at a different place along the tape, and so the timing in that track will not be the same as in the track

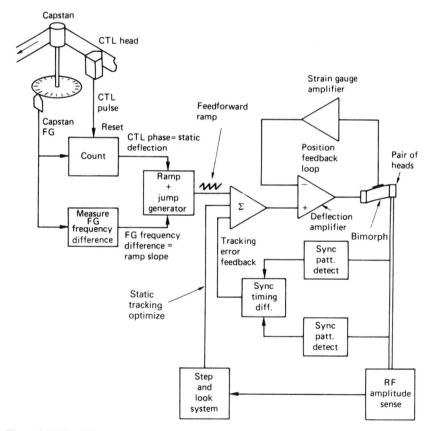

Figure 8.35 The DT system used by Sony D-2 machines combines ramp feedforward from the capstan speed and control track with tracking feedback from the differential sync detection of Figure 8.32. In addition the bump-and-look system slightly offsets the heads by a different amount each scan and assesses the RF amplitude to find an optimum static deflection. This is really a slow dither process. Note that this is a conceptual diagram. In practice many of these stages are carried out by microprocessor.

342 Rotary-head data recording

which the head left. In a segmented format, the effect is magnified by the number of tracks in a field. To support a speed range from $-1 \times$ to $+3 \times$, it has been seen that an overall head travel of three fields is necessary. From the start of a given segment to the start of the same segment three fields away is nearly 8 mm in PAL D-2, and over 6.5 mm in NTSC D-2. The wrap of the scanner must be extended to allow tape contact over a greater angle, and the replay circuitry must be able to accommodate the timing uncertainty which amounts to about 5% of the segment period. Clearly the timing error can be eliminated by the timebase correction processes within the playback system.

8.18 Digital tape cassettes

The D-1/2179 and D-2/DD-2 formats use the same mechanical parts and dimensions in their respective ¾ inch cassettes, even though the kind of tape and the track pattern are completely different. The Ampex DCT cassette is the same as a D-2 cassette. The Ampex DCRS uses a 1 inch cassette which is specially designed for use with a transverse-scan transport. D-3 and D-5 use the same ½ inch cassette, and Digital Betacam uses a ½ inch cassette which is identical mechanically to the analog Betacam cassette, but contains different tape. RDAT/DDS uses a 3.81 mm cassette.

The main advantages of a cassette are that the medium is better protected from contamination whilst out of the transport, and that an unskilled operator or a mechanical elevator can load the tape. It is not true that cassettes offer any advantage for storage except for the ease of handling. In fact a cassette takes up more space than a tape reel, because it must contain two such reels, only one of which will be full at any one time. In some cases it is possible to reduce the space needed by using flangeless hubs and guiding liner sheets as is done in RDAT/DDS, or pairs of hubs with flanges on opposite sides, as in U-matic. Whilst such approaches are acceptable for consumer and industrial products, they are inappropriate for professional units which will be expected to wind at high speeds or work in poor environments. Accordingly, most digital cassettes contain two fully flanged reels side by side. The centre of each hub is fitted with a thrust pad and when the cassette is not in the drive a spring acts on this pad and presses the lower flange of each reel firmly against the body of the cassette to exclude dust. When the cassette is in the machine the relative heights of the reel turntables and the cassette supports are such that the reels seat on the turntables before the cassette comes to rest. This opens a clearance space between the reel flanges and the cassette body by compressing the springs. This should be borne in mind if a machine is being tested without the cassette elevator as a suitable weight must be placed on the cassette in order to compress the springs.

The use of a cassette means that it is not as easy to provide a range of sizes as it is with open reels. Simply putting smaller reels in a cassette with the same hub spacing does not produce a significantly smaller cassette. The only solution is to specify different hub spacings for different sizes of cassette. This gives the best volumetric efficiency for storage, but it does mean that the transport must be able to reposition the reel-drive motors if it is to play more than one size of cassette.

Most digital-VTR-based formats offer three cassette sizes. If the small, medium and large digital video cassettes are placed in a stack with their throats and tape guides in a vertical line, the centres of the hubs will be seen to fall on

	D-1	D-2	D-3	D-5	DCT	Digital Betacam
Track pitch (μm)	45	35	18	18	35	26
Tape speed (mm/s)	286·9	131·7	83·2	167·2	131·7	96·7
Play time (min) S	14/11	32	64/50	32/25	32	40
Play time (min) M	50/37	104	125/95	62/47	104	–
Play time (min) L	101/75	208	245/185	123/92	208	124
Data rate (mbits/s)	216	142	142	288	113	126
Density (mbits/cm²)	4	5·8	13	13	5·8	10

Figure 8.36 The D-1/D-2, D-3/D-5, DCT and Digital Betacam tape sizes and playing times contrasted.

a pair of diagonal lines going outwards and backwards. This arrangement was chosen to allow the reel motors to travel along a linear track in machines which accept more than one size. The D-1 format has very low recording density by modern standards and is somewhat pushed to get long playing time. The large size cassette was the largest size which could be accommodated in a transport which would still fit in a 19 inch rack. Figure 8.36 compares the sizes and capacities of the various digital cassettes.

8.19 The D-1/D-2/DCT/2179 cassette

All three sizes of cassette have basically the same structure, and detail differences will be noted. The cassette has a double-door arrangement shown in Figure 8.37. When the cassette is removed, both sides of the tape in the throat are covered. The inner door is guided by a curved track. The door extends to the edges of the small and medium cassettes, but this is unnecessary on the large cassette. The door has a lock which prevents accidental opening, and this is released by a pin when the cassette enters the transport. The lock release mechanism is as near the edge of the small cassette as possible, but it cannot be in the same place on the medium cassette, as it would foul the tape path to the larger reel. Three lock release pins are needed, one for each size, and the larger cassettes need dummy slots which clear the pins used by the smaller sizes.

The cassettes also have hub locks which prevent unwanted rotation in storage or transit. On the larger two sizes, the lock is released by a lever operated by the act of opening the door. There is insufficient room for this mechanism on the small cassette, and so the brake is released by a central post in the transport.

The cassettes are designed for front- or side-loading, and so have guiding slots running at right angles. Most studio recorders are front-loading, whereas most

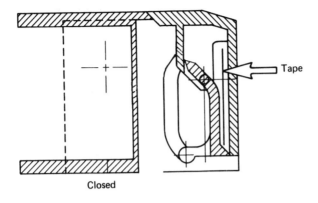

Closed

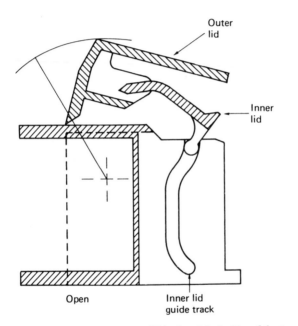

Open

Figure 8.37 When the cassette lid is closed, both sides of the tape are protected by covers. As the outer lid swings up on a pivot, the inner lid is guided around the back of the tape by a curved track.

automated machines use side-loading. The front-loading guide groove is centrally positioned and the threading throat forms a lead-in to it, helping to centralize the smaller cassettes in a loading slot which will accept a large cassette.

A number of identification holes are provided in the cassettes which are sensed by switches on the transport. Four of these are coding holes which are in the form of break-off tabs which will be set when the cassette is made, and four of them are resettable user holes, which can be controlled with a screwdriver. Table 8.1 shows the significance of the coding and user holes.

Table 8.1 (a) Manufacturers' coding holes (0 = tab removed). (b) User holes (0 = tab removed)

(a) Holes 1 and 2 shall be used in combination to indicate tape thickness according to the following logic table:

Hole Number: 1 2
0 0 = 16 µm tape
0 1 = 13 µm tape
1 0 = Undefined/reserved
1 1 = Undefined/reserved

Holes 3 and 4 shall be used to indicate the coercivity of the magnetic recording tape.

Hole number: 3 4
0 0 = Class 850
0 1 = Undefined/reserved
1 0 = Undefined/reserved
1 1 = Undefined/reserved

(b) When a '0' state exists, the user holes shall identify the following conditions:

1. Total record lockout (audio/video/cue/time code/control track)
2. Reserved and undefined
3. Reserved and undefined
4. Reserved and undefined

Areas are specified for the positioning of labels, and these are recessed to prevent fouling of elevators or guides. Automated machines will use the end location for a bar code which can be read by the elevator whilst the cassette is stacked.

8.20 The D-3/D-5 cassette

All three sizes of cassette have basically the same structure, and detail differences will be noted. The cassette has a double-door arrangement shown in Figure 8.38. The inner door hinges in the top of the outer door. When the cassette is removed, both sides of the tape in the throat are covered. The inner door is guided by a curved track. The door extends to the edges of the S and M cassettes only. The door has a lock which prevents accidental opening, and this is released by a pin when the cassette enters the transport. The lock release mechanism is at the edge of the S and M cassettes, and slightly inset on the L cassette. Three lock release pins are needed, one for each size, and the larger cassettes need dummy slots which clear the release pins used by the smaller sizes.

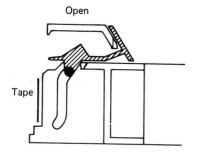
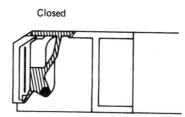

Figure 8.38 The D-3 cassette has a double door which protects both sides of the front tape run when closed. The inner door (shaded) carries guide pins which run in serpentine tracks in the ends of the cassette. These guide the door around the back of the tape as the cassette closes.

The cassettes also have hub locks which prevent unwanted rotation in storage or transit. On all sizes, the lock is released by a rounded post on the deckplate which enters the cassette as it is lowered. This post contains a light source for the BOT/EOT sensors. Light from the post travels across the cassette on a path nearly parallel to the door and, if allowed to pass, by the transparent leader tape, emerges through a hole in each end of the cassette which is only revealed when the cassette door is open.

The cassettes are designed for front- or side-loading, and so have guiding slots running at right angles. The front-loading groove is centrally positioned, whereas the side-loading groove runs across the cassette on the opposite side to the door.

A number of identification holes are provided in the cassettes, sensed by switches on the transport. Three of these are coding holes which are in the form of break-off tabs which will be set when the cassette is made, and three of them are resettable user holes, which can be controlled with a screwdriver. Table 8.2 shows the significance of the coding and user holes. It will be seen that the hub diameter of the cassette can be conveyed in the coding holes. The hub of the L cassette is larger in diameter than that of the other sizes. The tape-remaining computation needs to know the hub diameter as well as the tape thickness to

Table 8.2 The cassette has two sets of coding holes. The first of these, labelled 1.2.3, is for cassette recognition. The second, labelled a,b,c, is for user record lockout. Hole significance is shown in the tables below. Holes 1, 2 and 3 shall be used in combination to indicate tape thickness and diameter of hub according to the following logic table.

Hole numbers:

(1) = 0 low coercivity
(1) = 1 high coercivity

(2)	(3)	
0	0	11 μm tape, small-diameter hub
0	1	11 μm tape, large-diameter hub
1	0	14 μm tape, small-diameter hub
1	1	14 μm tape, large-diameter hub

A '1' in the above table indicates that the indicator tab is removed or open, an undetected state by the record/player sensor mechanism.

When a '0' state exists, the user holes shall identify the following conditions:

(a) Total record lockout (audio/video/cue/timecode/control track)
(b) Video and control-track record lockout
(c) Reserved and undefined

work out the remaining time from the reel FGs. It is possible to mix hub sizes and cassette sizes. A large-size hub may be used in a small cassette to increase shuttle speed, reducing access time with the penalty of reduced playing time.

The first user hole is a total record lockout, whereas the second only prevents video and control-track recording, and thus allows audio editing. The third user hole is undefined. Two of the user holes are used to align the cassette in the transport. The transport registration pins are fitted with switches.

8.21 The RDAT/DDS cassette

The general appearance of the RDAT cassette is shown in Figure 8.39. The overall dimensions are only 73 mm × 54 mm × 10.5 mm, which is rather smaller than the Compact Cassette. The design of the cassette incorporates some

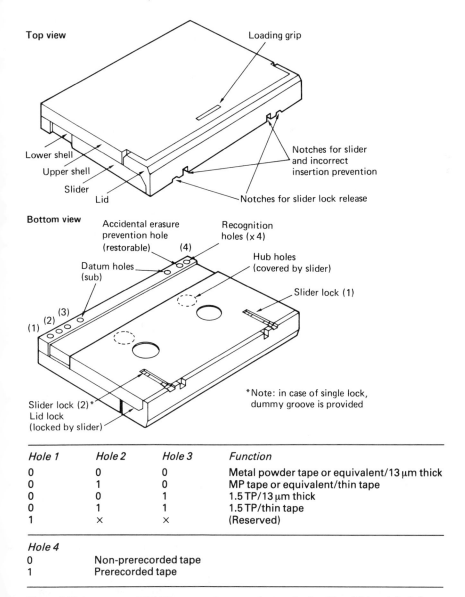

Hole 1	Hole 2	Hole 3	Function
0	0	0	Metal powder tape or equivalent/13 μm thick
0	1	0	MP tape or equivalent/thin tape
0	0	1	1.5 TP/13 μm thick
0	1	1	1.5 TP/thin tape
1	×	×	(Reserved)

Hole 4		
0	Non-prerecorded tape	
1	Prerecorded tape	

Figure 8.39 Appearance of RDAT cassette. Access to the tape is via a hinged lid, and the hub drive holes are covered by a sliding panel, affording maximum protection to the tape. Recognition holes 1, 2 and 3 form a coded pattern, whereas hole 4 is independent; see tables (1 = hole present, 0 = hole blanked off). (Courtesy TDK)

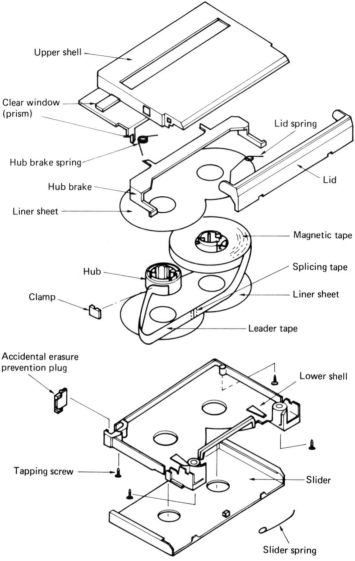

Upper shell

Clear window
(prism)

Lid spring

Hub brake spring

Hub brake

Liner sheet

Lid

Magnetic tape

Splicing tape

Hub

Clamp

Liner sheet

Leader tape

Accidental erasure
prevention plug

Lower shell

Tapping screw

Slider

Slider spring

Figure 8.40 Exploded view of RDAT cassette showing intricate construction. When the lid opens, it pulls the ears on the brake plate, releasing the hubs. Note the EOT/BOT sensor prism moulded into the corners of the clear window. (Courtesy TDK)

improvements over its analog ancestor.[6] As shown in Figure 8.40, the apertures through which the heads access the tape are closed by a hinged door, and the hub drive openings are covered by a sliding panel which also locks the door when the cassette is not in the transport. The act of closing the door operates brakes which act on the reel hubs. This results in a cassette which is well sealed against contamination due to handling or storage. The short wavelengths used in digital recording make it more sensitive to spacing loss caused by contamination. As in the Compact Cassette, the tape hubs are flangeless, and the edge guidance of the tape pack is achieved by liner sheets. The flangeless approach allows the hub centres to be closer together for a given length of tape. The cassette has recognition holes in four standard places so that players can automatically determine what type of cassette has been inserted. In addition there is a write-protect (record-lockout) mechanism which is actuated by a small plastic plug sliding between the cassette halves. The end-of-tape condition is detected optically and the leader tape is transparent. There is some freedom in the design of the EOT sensor. As can be seen in Figure 8.41, transmitted-light sensing can be used across the corner of the cassette, or reflected-light sensing can be used,

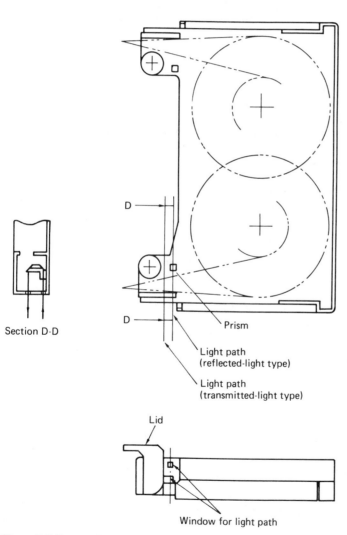

Section D-D

Prism

Light path
(reflected-light type)

Light path
(transmitted-light type)

Lid

Window for light path

Figure 8.41 Tape sensing can either be by transmission across the corner of the cassette, or by reflection through an integral prism. In both cases, the apertures are sealed when the lid closes. (Courtesy TDK)

because the cassette incorporates a prism which reflects light around the back of the tape. Study of Figure 8.40 will reveal that the prisms are moulded integrally with the corners of the transparent insert used for the cassette window.

The high coercivity (typically 1480 Oe) metal powder tape is 3.81 mm wide, the same width as Compact Cassette tape. The standard overall thickness is 13 μm. A striking feature of the metal tape is that the magnetic coating is so thin, at about 3 μm, that the tape appears translucent. The maximum capacity of the cassette is about 60 m.

When the cassette is placed in the transport, the slider is moved back as it engages. This releases the lid lock. Continued movement into the transport pushes the slider right back, revealing the hub openings. The cassette is then lowered onto the hub-drive spindles and tape guides, and the door is fully opened to allow access to the tape.

8.22 Loading the cassette

The sequence of operations when a cassette is inserted in the machine will be followed. In most transports, all cassette sizes can be used without any adjustment. The operator simply pushes the cassette into the aperture in the machine and the cassette is lowered onto the transport by an elevator. The smaller sizes are located at the centre of the aperture by sprung guides which are pushed aside when a large-size cassette is used. The presence of the cassette is sensed optically, or by switches, and by the same means the machine can decide which size of cassette has been inserted. The cassette fits into a cage or compartment which is driven by a toothed rack so that it can move inwards and down. Alternatively the cassette may be driven by rubber belts. In portable machines and camcorders only the small cassette will be accommodated and the cassette compartment will be closed by hand.

As the hub spacing differs between cassette sizes, the transport automatically moves the sliding reel motors to the correct position. The final part of horizontal travel unlocks the cassette door. The cassette elevator is then driven downwards and the door is opened. The opened cassette is then lowered onto the reel motors, and locating dowels on the transport register the cassette body. The hub brakes are released either by a post entering the cassette as it is lowered or by the act of opening the door. The identification tabs on the cassette operate the sensor switches on the deckplate. The several guides and tension arms and the pinch roller, where applicable, are positioned so that the throat of the cassette drops over them with the front run of tape between them and the head drum.

In some transports the elevator can be manually operated by turning a slotted socket on the motor shaft with a screwdriver inserted through an aperture in the front of the machine below the control panel. This is useful in the case of a power failure if the cassette must be retrieved. In some designs, the transport can still operate with the elevator removed. This allows a great deal more space to work on the transport. The cassette must be loaded by hand with the door already opened. In the absence of the sensors on the elevator it will be necessary to move the reel motors to the correct spacing by entering an appropriate software routine. The system software will also have to be told the elevator is missing or it will interpret the condition as an error.

Instrumentation recorders such as DCRS do not have cassette elevators as these take up too much room and add unnecessary weight. In DCRS the cassette is loaded manually over a guide post which releases the brakes. A lever on the transport operates a positive cassette-retaining clamp system which ensures that the cassette is firmly seated under high-g loading.

8.23 Threading the tape

In transverse-scan recorders threading the tape is almost trivial. Upon loading the cassette the front run of tape passes between the headwheel and the curved

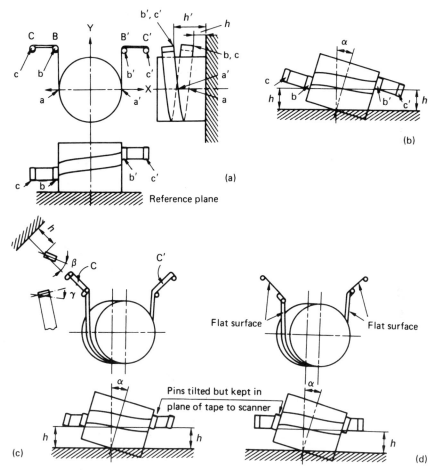

Figure 8.42 In (a) the scanner has a vertical axis which results in a height difference and a twist between the entrance plane BC and the exit plane B′C′.

In (b) the scanner has been tilted through an angle α such that points b and b′ are both at height h.

In (c) the wrap angle on the guides nearest the scanner is reduced until the edge of the tape lies in the reference plane. The tape in planes C and C′ remains flat. The pins now incline at angle β to the reference surface.

In (d) the outer pins can be made vertical if the plane of C and C′ is brought perpendicular to the reference surface. This is done by tilting the inner pins but keeping them in the plane of the tape from inner pin to scanner. Tape entry and exit is now coplanar. (Based on drawings courtesy of Sony Broadcast)

guide which is retracted. It is only necessary to bring the headwheel up to speed, activate the reel-tension servos and engage the guide with the headwheel and the tape is ready to play. A standby mode is possible in which the guide is retracted so there is no headwheel-to-tape contact. The tension servos are active and the headwheel is maintained at speed. The machine can remain in standby indefinitely without head wear, but can resume data transfer simply by engaging the curved guide with a solenoid. This rapid transition from standby to operation is a strength of transverse-scan transports which helical scan cannot match.

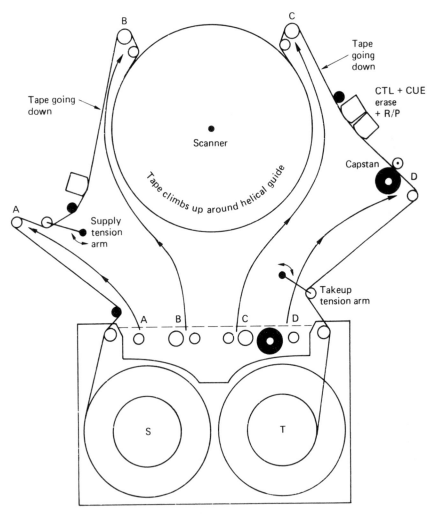

Figure 8.43 In the Sony D-1 transport an extended wrap is used, and guides move on both sides of the scanner to create the wrap. Tape begins the helix below the cassette plane and ends the scan above it. This contrasts with the Ampex approach where the tape begins the helix far below the cassette plane and ends in the cassette plane.

It is inherent in helical-scan recorders that the tape enters and leaves the head drum at different heights. In open-reel recorders, the reels are simply mounted at different heights, but in a cassette this is not practicable. The tape must be geometrically manipulated in some way. There are several approaches to the geometrical problem:

(1) The drum can be inclined so that the height of the tape is the same at entry and exit.

(2) The drum can be vertical and the tape is manipulated out of the plane of the cassette on both entry and exit sides.

(3) The tape enters the drum in the plane of the cassette and is manipulated on the exit side only.

(4) The tape leaves the drum in the plane of the cassette and is manipulated on the entry side only.

In the Sony D-2 transports, the first approach is taken to the tape guidance. Figure 8.42(a) shows tape wrapping a drum, with the usual elevation difference between entrance and exit. In (b) the drum has been tilted so that entrance and exit guides are at the same height. The tape now approaches in the wrong plane. It will be found that if the wrap angle on the entry and exit guides is reduced, an angle can be found where the edge of the tape enters and leaves in the plane of the cassette, as shown in (c). At this stage the tape edge is in the cassette plane, but its surface is not at right angles to that plane: it is leaning over. The entry and exit guides are now tilted in the plane of the tape tangential to the drum until the tape feeding them is at right angles to the cassette plane, as in (d). In this way, the tape is not subjected to any twisting as it always remains planar. The same approach is used in the RDAT transports built by Sony. The coplanar approach allows a very shallow transport construction which is highly suitable for portable operation.

Figure 8.43 shows the second approach used in the Sony D-1 transport. This uses an extended wrap angle in order to reduce the frequencies at the heads. The previous approach is difficult to use with an extended wrap. The drum axis is vertical and tape is led down from the supply reel to the drum entrance. Tape then climbs up the drum ramp, and is led down once more to the cassette plane.

Figure 8.44 shows the arrangement of the Panasonic D-3 and D-5 machines, which use the third method. Digital Betacam adopts the same technique. Tape stays in the plane of the cassette on the supply side and the drum is angled to receive it. Tape leaving the drum is manipulated back to the cassette plane.

Figure 8.45 shows arrangement (d) which is used in Ampex D-2 and DCT transports. Here the drum is angled so that tape leaves it in the plane of the take-up reel. All manipulation is then done between the supply reel and the drum entry.

Various methods exist for achieving the helical displacement of the tape. Some VTR transports have used conical posts, but these have the disadvantages that there is a considerable lateral force against the edge of the tape, and that they cannot be allowed to revolve or the tape would climb off them. Angled pins do not suffer side force, but again cannot be allowed to revolve. The friction caused by non-rotating pins can be reduced by air lubrication from a compressor, as used

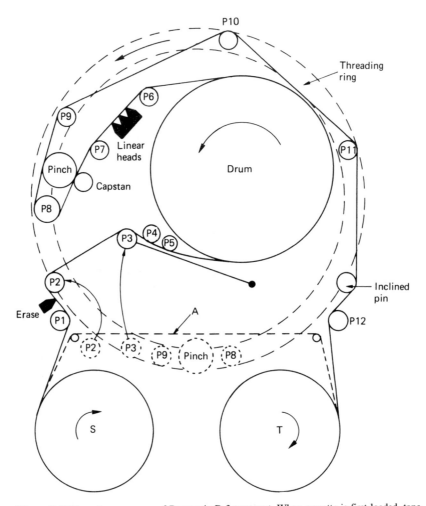

Figure 8.44 Threading sequence of Panasonic D-3 transport. When cassette is first loaded, tape runs straight between the cassette pins (dotted line shown at A) in front of the moving guide pins P2, P3, P9, P8 and the pinch roller. Guides P2 and P3 wrap the entry side by swinging on arms. P3 is in fact the tension arm. The pinch roller and its guides travel anticlockwise on the large threading ring. As the ring rotates P10 and P11 guide the return loop. The inclined pin hinges over the edge of the tape and does not need to be in the cassette mouth at threading start.

in Ampex transports, or by vibrating them ultrasonically with a piezoelectric actuator, as is done in certain Sony transports.

In the Ampex D-2 and DCT transports, the tape in the plane of the cassette is slightly twisted on a long run, and then passes around a conventional guide which causes it to leave the cassette plane at an angle. The twist is too small to approach the elastic limit of the tape, which is quite unharmed. A second guide set at the same angle as the drum axis passes the tape to the drum.[7] Figure 8.46 contrasts the tape-twist and angled-guide methods.

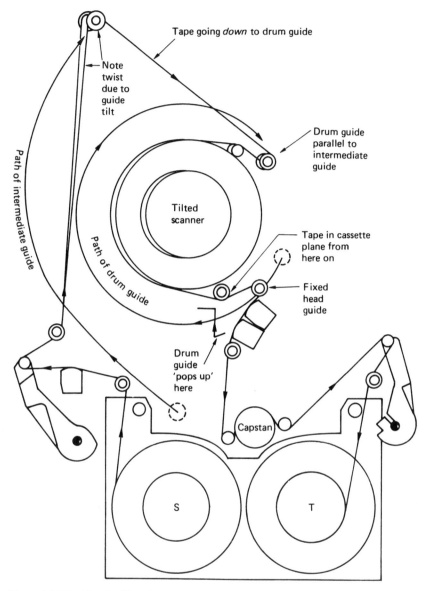

Figure 8.45 Fixed head guide swings out, and capstan guides swing in. Tension arms extend. Then drum and intermediate guides complete scanner wrap.

If the scanner guides are not operated, tape can be transported past stationary heads for timecode striping or pre-positioning tape without scanner wear.

The threading process will be considered using two different transports as examples.

In the Panasonic D-3/D-5 transports, as with any VCR, the guides start inside the cassette, and move to various positions as threading proceeds. The sequence

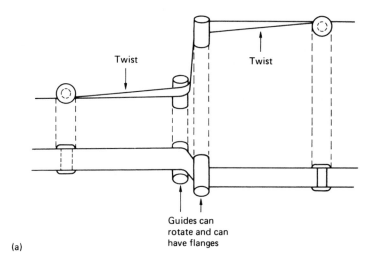

Twist

Twist

Guides can
rotate and can
have flanges

(a)

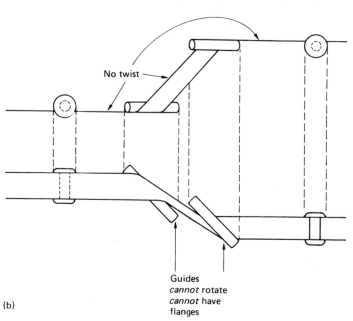

No twist

Guides
cannot rotate
cannot have
flanges

(b)

Figure 8.46 The contradictions of shifting the tape plane in helical scan. If the tape is twisted, the guides can rotate. If it is not, they cannot. Long, gentle twist is good, but not compact enough for portable use.

can be followed in Figure 8.44. The entry-side threading is performed by guide P2 which swings anticlockwise on an arm to wrap the tape onto fixed guide P1 and the full-width erase head and by the tension arm guide P3 which swings clockwise to bring the tape across the drum entry guides P4 and P5. The drum-wrapping and exit-side threading is performed by guides which move in a circular path on a threading ring, which rotates around the drum and capstan. When the cassette is initially lowered, guide P8, the pinch roller and guide P9 are inside the front run of tape. As the threading ring turns anticlockwise, these guides take a loop of tape from the cassette and begin to wrap it around the drum. As the threading ring proceeds further, guide P10 and then guide P11 come into contact with the return loop, and the leading guide completes the wrap of the drum and wraps fixed exit guide P6, the fixed heads, fixed capstan guide P7 and the capstan. The pinch roller completes its travel by locating in a cage which is operated by the pinch solenoid. It is no longer supported by the threading ring.

The Ampex $\frac{3}{4}$ inch transport is designed for rapid threading and unthreading without tape damage, and particular care was taken to ensure that the tape path geometry is perfect not just when threaded, but at all times during the threading process. The threading sequence can be followed in Figure 8.47 and Figure 8.43.

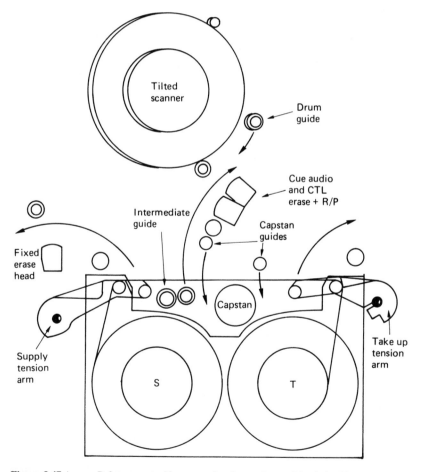

Figure 8.47 Ampex D-2 transport with cassette just lowered onto drive hubs. Note permanently engaged capstan in cassette throat.

The permanently engaged capstan fits inside the cassette throat. A short movement of the tape guides allows the tape to wrap the capstan and the stationary timecode/erase head. This is known as coplanar mode, which means that the tape path is still entirely in the plane of the tape reels. In this mode tape can be shuttled at high speed, and it is possible to erase and timecode stripe without causing wear to the rotary-head assembly. Timecode can also be read to position a tape without rotary-head wear.

For functions involving the rotary heads, the threading process proceeds further. There are two guides which primarily control threading the tape around the drum. The drum guide moves in a circular path on a threading ring, which rotates concentric with the drum. This guide begins its motion on the wrong side of the tape but, as the threading ring turns, the guide pops up and engages the back of the tape. Then as the threading ring rotates further, the guide is slowly lowered along the drum axis at the correct rate by a cam, such that the tape is laid onto the drum at the helix angle. When the drum guide reaches the end of its travel, its supporting shaft comes up against a fixed vee-block which repeatably positions it. It is held in contact with the block by a solenoid.

The intermediate guide is designed to move away from the cassette as the drum guide proceeds around the threading ring, and the tilt angle of this guide, which imparts the tape twist, is changed as it moves so that a cylindrical wrap is always maintained. This guide is mounted on three vee-shaped rollers which are pre-loaded outwards and ride in a matching slot in the deck plate. The tilt of the guide is controlled by a spherical roller on an extension of the guide shaft, which bears against a cam profile below the guide track. The principle is shown in Figure 8.48. All of the cam profiles which achieve these operations were computer generated.

Since the total guide wrap angle of cassette transports inevitably amounts to several revolutions, tension buildup is often a problem. In this transport, all tape guides are lubricated by compressed air, except for the tilting threading guide,

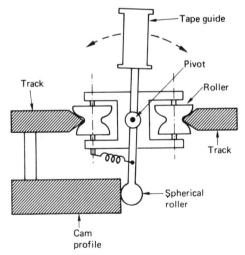

Figure 8.48 The spherical roller and cam profile tilt the tape guide axis to the correct angle as threading proceeds. Tape geometry can then be perfect at all points in the threading.

which is a roller. The drum guide has to travel a long distance, and it is difficult to provide a permanent air supply. The air feed is through the solenoid locking arm, so that air supply becomes available when the tape is fully threaded.

The threading technique used in RDAT is significantly different because the transport uses time compression and a partial wrap.

In portable machines, the first stage of cassette loading is often manual in order to save power. The operator places the cassette into the aperture in the loading elevator, and then pushes the elevator down into the machine.

In larger machines, the cassette is placed in a drawer which is pulled into the machine horizontally by motor. During the final part of horizontal travel, ramps on the transport disengage the locking pins on the sliding base and prevent the base from moving as the cassette carries on forwards. This slides open the cassette base, revealing the hub splines and unlocking the cassette door. The cassette elevator is then driven downwards. The door encounters a projection on the deck and is opened, releasing the hub brakes. The opened cassette is lowered onto the reel motors, and four locating dowels on the transport register the cassette body. The pinch roller, several guides and the tension arm are positioned so that the throat of the cassette drops over them with the front run of tape between them and the drum. At this stage the EOT and BOT sensors will be aligned with the windows in the ends of the cassette, and the identification switches will have been operated as the cassette descended. The cassette-compartment motor is stopped by a limit switch at this point.

The tape-guiding technique universally adopted in RDAT transports is to tilt the scanner to put both the entrance and exit in the cassette plane; the tape is then manipulated on both sides of the drum to overcome the angular discrepancy. Angled pins are necessary to guide the tape to and from the scanner.

The pair of guides necessary on each side of the scanner are mounted on die-cast blocks which can slide in slots in the deckplate. The guides are driven by a threading motor which turns a pair of large contra-rotating gears under the scanner. Links connected to the periphery of the gears pull the guide blocks towards fixed vee-blocks adjacent to the scanner. The links are telescopic and contain tension springs, so that the threading gears can overrun. The guide blocks will then be held firmly against the vee-blocks by spring tension. The same motor also swings the pinch roller out from the cassette mouth. The scanner guides reach the end of their travel somewhat before the pinch roller reaches the capstan. Using the overtravel springs, the threading motor can double as the pinch-roller engagement motor. The tape can be driven by the capstan with full travel of the motor, but if the motor is driven slightly in the unthread direction, the pinch roller will disengage, allowing the tape reels to shuttle the tape, whilst the scanner guides are held in place by the springs. The two detenting positions for the threading motor are determined by a shaft encoder.

8.24 Aligning for interchange

One of the most important aspects of rotary-head transport maintenance is to ensure that tapes made on a particular machine meet the specifications laid down in the format. If they do, then it will be possible to play those tapes on any other properly aligned machine. In this section the important steps necessary to achieve interchange between transports will be outlined. Regular cleaning, particularly of the drum step, is necessary to maintain interchange and no interchange adjustment should be attempted until it has been verified that the machine is clean.

When the cassette is lowered into the transport it seats on pillars which hold it level. The tape hubs seat on the reel turntables. The first step in aligning the transport is to ensure that the reel hubs and all of the guides the tape runs past on its way to and from the drum are at the correct height. The guides are generally threaded so that they can be screwed up and down. In the correct position, the tape will stay in the cassette plane and distortion will be avoided. The height of the cassette pillars can be adjusted to ensure that the spools inside the cassette are lifted free of the cassette body at the end of the elevator travel. If this is not done the spools will rub against the cassette body, causing debris and tension errors.

Once the tape can be passed through the machine without damage, the basic transport functions can be checked. Since tape tension affects the track angle and the head-contact pressure, verifying the correct tension is essential before attempting any adjustments at the drum. This is done with a tape tension gauge. Many tension gauges change their reading as a result of tape motion and it may be necessary to calibrate the gauge whilst moving the tape and calibration weight at approximately the correct speed for the format. The tension can then be checked in various transport and shuttle modes. Since the drum friction is in the opposite sense when the tape is reversed, the back-tension must be higher than for forward mode to keep the average drum tension constant. In some transports the tension-sensing arm is not statically balanced, and the tape tension becomes a function of the orientation of the machine. In this case the adjustment must be made with the machine in the attitude in which it is to be used.

The track spacing on record is determined by the capstan speed, which must be checked. As the capstan speed will be controlled by a frequency-generating wheel on the capstan shaft, it is generally only necessary to check that the capstan FG frequency is correct in record mode. A scratch tape will be used for this check.

Helical interchange can now be considered. Tape passing around the drum is guided in three ways. On the approach, the tape is steered by the entrance guides, which continue to affect the first part of the drum wrap. The centre part of the drum wrap is guided by the machined step on the drum base. Finally the last part of the wrap is steered by the exit guides. Helical interchange is obtained by adjusting the entrance- and exit-guide heights so that the tape passes smoothly between the three regions.

As tape is flexible, it will distort as it passes round the drum if the entrance and exit guides are not correctly set. The state of alignment can be assessed by working out the effect of misalignments on the ability of the replay head to follow tape tracks. Figure 8.49(a) shows an example of the entrance guide being too low. The tape is forced to climb up to reach the drum step, and then it has to bend down again to run along the step. If straight tracks were originally recorded on the tape, they will no longer be straight when the tape is distorted in this way. Figure 8.49(b) shows what happens to the track. Since in an azimuth-recording machine the head is larger than the track, small distortions of this kind will be undetectable. It is necessary to offset the tracking deliberately so that the effect of the misalignment can be seen. If the head is offset upwards, then the effect will be that the RF signal grows in level briefly at the beginning of the track, giving the envelope an onion-like

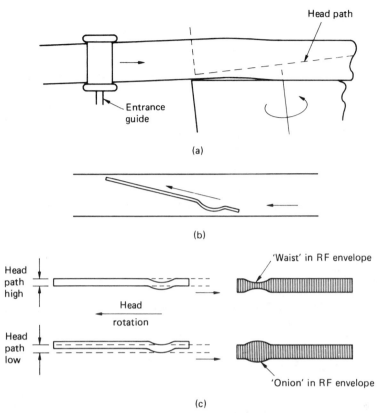

Figure 8.49 The effects of guide misalignment shown exaggerated for clarity. In (a) the entrance guide is too low and forces the tape to flex as it enters the scanner. In (b) the tape relaxes to produce a bent track. In (c) an alignment tape is being played and the transport has bent the tracks. The RF envelope will show different disturbances as the tracking is offset above or below optimum. A correctly aligned transport has an envelope which collapses uniformly as the tracking is offset.

appearance on an oscilloscope. If the head is offset downwards, the distortion will take the track away from the head path and the RF envelope will be waisted. If the misalignment is in the exit guide, then the envelope disturbances will appear at the right-hand end of the RF envelope. The height of both the entrance and exit guides is adjusted until no disturbance of the RF envelope rectangularity is apparent whatever tracking error is applied. A rough alignment can be performed with a tape previously recorded on a trustworthy machine, but final alignment requires the use of a reference tape.

Once the mechanical geometry of the drum is set up, straight tracks on tape will appear straight to the drum, and it is then possible to set up the tracking. This requires adjustment of the position of the control-track head along the tape path. This is done by observing the RF level of a test tape on playback. If the machine has a front panel tracking adjustment, it should be set to zero whilst the mechanical adjustment is made.

The final interchange adjustment is to ensure that the drum timing is correct. Even with correct geometry, the tracks can be laid down at the correct angle and spacing, but at the wrong height on the tape, as Figure 8.50 shows. A recording made with this adjustment incorrect may still play, but would cause serious difficulty if insert editing is attempted, particularly of the audio blocks.

The point where recording commences is determined by the sensor which generates a pulse once per revolution of the drum. The correct timing can be obtained either by physically moving the sensor around the drum axis, or by adjusting a variable delay in series with an artificially early fixed sensor. A timing reference tape is necessary that has an observable event in the RF waveform. The tape is played, and the sensor or delay is adjusted to give the specified relative timing between the event on the reference tape and the sensor pulse. When this is correct, the machine will record tracks in the right place along the helical sweep.

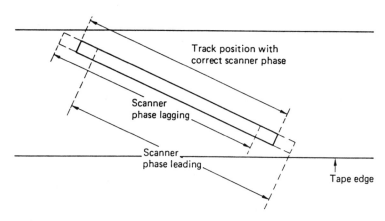

Figure 8.50 Even with correct tape path geometry, a machine can record data in the wrong place along the track if the scanner phase is misadjusted. The scanner pulse generator signal is rephased or delayed in order to make the adjustment.

In transverse-scan recorders, the interchange procedure has much in common with that for helical scan. The cassette-support and reel-hub heights, the tape speed and tension, the control-track head position and the drum-phase adjustment are all made in the same way. The tape stays in the plane of the cassette in a transverse transport, and so there is little room for misalignment in the entry to and the exit from the scanner. Figure 8.51 shows that the main interchange adjustment in a transverse transport consists of ensuring that the cupped guide is symmetrically disposed about the head-tip path and that the entry and exit guides of the canoe are symmetrical about the cupped guide. When this symmetry exists all tape flexure due to cupping cancels out about the head path and straight tracks are recorded. Any asymmetry results is distorted tracks as shown.[8]

The cupped guide is actually a double guide with a central channel. The head-contact pressure is obtained because the head-tip radius is greater than the guide

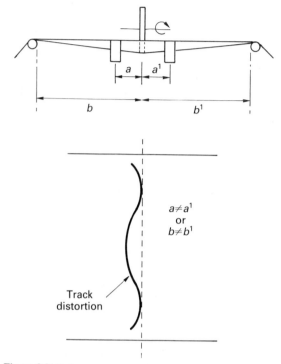

Figure 8.51 In transverse scan, symmetry of the entry and exit guides and of the cupped guide about the headwheel results in straight tracks because the flexing due to the cupping of the tape cancels out in the centre of the canoe. If this condition is not met, the tracks are distorted as shown.

radius and the head deforms the tape into the channel. Stable contact pressure requires that the centre of curvature of the guide should coincide with the drum axis.

8.25 Head replacement

In modern machines, head replacement generally requires the replacement of the entire rotating disk or wafer, which contains factory-adjusted heads. The exception is the approach taken by Ampex in helical-scan machines where individual head bases are replaceable. These are pre-aligned and no mechanical adjustment is necessary.

When heads are replaced, certain electronic adjustments are necessary. Replay heads require equalization to compensate for high-frequency loss, and this varies with head wear. When a head is replaced the equalization will no longer be correct. Equalization is adjusted manually by playing a test tape and minimizing the error rate. Some machines are able to adjust their own replay equalization in service. Record heads need to have the record current set. If this is too low then the replay-error rate will be excessive due to noise, whereas if it is too high peak shift distortion will result and difficulties may be experienced in overwriting recordings. Some machines can automatically optimize the record current by analysing the error rate from the confidence-replay heads.

Track-following heads mounted on actuators will display some spread in their resonant frequency and mechanical damping factor, and it will be necessary to adjust the drive circuitry to suit.

In transverse-scan machines, the drum motor and headwheel assembly is very compact and is replaced as a unit. On replacement it is necessary to ensure that the new assembly is correctly registered against locating dowels on the transport baseplate. The secondary of the rotary transformer remains on the baseplate when the heads are replaced and it may be necessary to reset the air gap in the transformer afterwards.

8.26 Cart machines

The cart machine began life as a broadcast device which was designed to automatically assemble commercial breaks from a library of video cassettes. Improvements in storage density have led the concept to be extended to a point where the entire playout of a TV station comes from a mechanized library. With the advent of digital VTRs, a cart machine has essentially become a digital storage device which, by computer standards, has a truly phenomenal capacity. A one-hour component digital video cassette holds about 80 gigabytes of data and a moderately sized cart machine can hold 256 cassettes, giving an overall capacity of nearly 20 terabytes (a terabyte is a million megabytes). Modifications to broadcast machines for computer data use primarily require an additional layer of error correction to improve the residual bit error rate and a file access structure.

A cart machine consists of a storage area for cassettes, a number of transports and a simple signal switcher, a robotic arm which moves cassettes, and a computerized control system.

The storage area consists of compartments to hold cassettes in the library. This is often modular so that different sizes can be constructed. Most libraries store cassettes on a rectangular grid, but as an alternative the library may be a large cylinder which can rotate as part of the access mechanism.

The robotic arm is capable of traversing the entire area of the library and the transports with an XY motion. The arm is equipped with a bar-code reader so that it can identify cassettes, and a gripper which can move forward to grasp the selected cassette. The control of the robot must be extremely accurate as damage can be caused if a cassette is pushed into a transport or a library compartment when there is a misalignment. In addition to high accuracy, the robot must move at high speed so that the machine can assemble programs from short spots on different cassettes. The robot will be driven by powerful motors through toothed belts or steel cables so that a library several metres long can be traversed in a second or so. Interlocks are necessary to cut the power if someone opens the machine, as a traversing robot can cause injury. The motion of the robot is controlled by velocity and position feedback so that a traverse can begin and end with smooth acceleration. In large libraries it is impossible to assemble the modules accurately, and the library will not be an exact rectangular grid. Before use, the robot learns the position of every compartment by successively accessing each one and locating its precise position from a reference point.

Early broadcast cart machines were analog and were restricted to storing one spot or *event* on each cassette. This allows any sequence of playout to be obtained. As storage density improved, it became wasteful to have only one event per cassette, and control systems were developed which could handle multiple events on each. A problem arises where a playlist requires two events in different places on the same cassette to be assembled. This is overcome by dubbing one of the events to a spare caching cassette which is kept in the library for that purpose. In the digital domain such dubbing causes no loss of quality, whereas an analog machine would have suffered generation loss. Long programs such as feature films can be automatically split into several cassettes for playout.

Many cart machines can store hundreds of hours of material and are designed to work unattended for long periods. Often there are more tape transports fitted than necessary so that in the case of a failure one can be de-assigned and the work is reallocated to the remainder. Transports can usually be withdrawn on rails for servicing whilst the remainder of the machine continues to operate. Some machines have two robots. If one fails it will be de-activated and the remaining robot will push it out of the way.

8.27 The DVTR signal system

The signal system of a DVTR lies between the signal input/output connectors and the heads, and in production machines is divided into separate record and replay sections so that both processes can take place at the same time.

The data to be recorded are subject to some variation, as Figure 8.52 shows. The input may be composite or component, and data reduction may or may not

Standard	Lines/field	Pixels/line	Pixels/field	Bit rate
4:2:2 50 Hz	300	720 Y 360 C_r 360 C_b	432 000	173 M bits/s (8 bit) 216 M bits/s (10 bit)
4:2:2 60 Hz	250	720 Y 360 C_r 360 C_b	360 000	173 M bits/s (8 bit) 216 M bits/s (10 bit)
16:9 50 Hz	300	960 Y 480 C_r 480 C_b	576 000	230 M bits/s (8 bit) 288 M bits/s (10 bit)
16:9 60 Hz	250	960 Y 480 C_r 480 C_b	480 000	230 M bits/s (8 bit) 288 M bits/s (10 bit)
$4F_{sc}$ PAL	304	948	288 192	115 M bits/s (8 bit) 144 M bits/s (10 bit)
$4F_{sc}$ NTSC	255	768	195 840	94 M bits/s (8 bit) 117 M bits/s (10 bit)

Figure 8.52 The data to be recorded in DVTR formats are subject to a great deal of variation as shown here.

be employed. The various DVTR formats largely employ the same processing stages, but there are considerable differences in the order in which these are applied. It is proposed first to define here the processes and then to contrast the formats by the way in which they are applied.

Distribution is shown in Figure 8.53(a). This is a process of sharing the input bit rate over two or more signal paths so that the bit rate recorded in each is reduced. The data are subsequently recombined on playback. Each signal path requires its own tape track and head. The parallel tracks which result form a *segment*.

Segmentation is shown in Figure 8.53(b). This is the process of sharing the data resulting from one video field over several segments. The replay system must have some means of ensuring that associated segments are reassembled into the original field. This is generally a function of the control track.

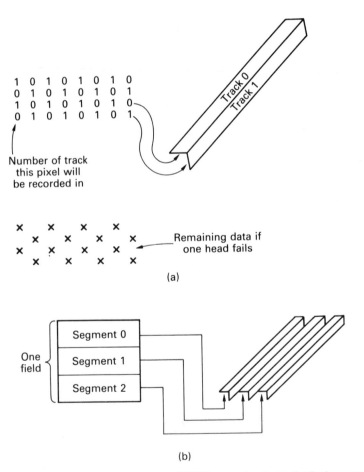

Figure 8.53 The fundamental stages of DVTR processing. In (a) distribution spreads data over more than one track to make concealment easier and to reduce the data rate per head. In (b) segmentation breaks video fields into manageable track lengths. Product codes (c) correct mixture of random and burst errors. Correction failure requires concealment which may be in three dimensions as shown in (d). Irregular shuffle (e) makes concealments less visible.

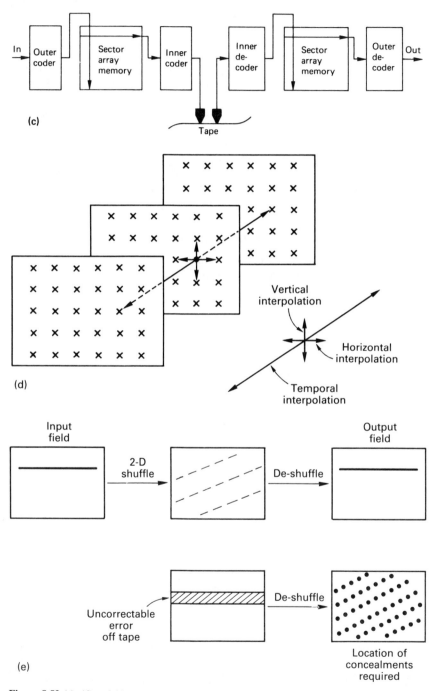

Figure 8.53 (c), (d) and (e)

Figure 8.53(c) shows a product code. Data to be recorded are protected by two error-correcting codeword systems at right angles; the inner code and the outer code (see Chapter 5). When it is working within its capacity the error-correction system returns corrupt data to its original value and its operation is undetectable.

If errors are too great for the correction system, concealment will be employed. Concealment is the *estimation* of missing data values from surviving data nearby. Nearby means data on vertical, horizontal or time axes as shown in Figure 8.53(d). Concealment relies upon distribution, as all tracks of a segment are unlikely to be simultaneously lost, and upon the *shuffle* shown in Figure 8.53(e). Shuffling re-orders the pixels prior to recording and is reversed on replay. The result is that uncorrectable errors due to dropouts are not concentrated, but are spread out by the de-shuffle, making concealment easier. A different approach is required where data reduction is used because the data recorded are not pixels representing a point, but coefficients representing an area of the image. In this case it is the DCT blocks (typically eight pixels across) which must be shuffled.

8.28 Product codes and segmentation

There are two approaches to error correction in segmented recordings. In D-1 and D-2 the approach shown in Figure 8.54(a) is used. Here, following distribution

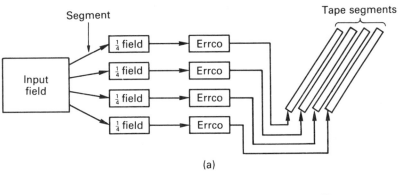

(a)

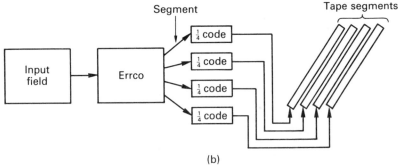

(b)

Figure 8.54 Early formats would segment data before producing product codes as in (a). Later formats perform product coding first, and then segment for recording as in (b). This gives more robust performance.

the input field is segmented first, then each segment becomes an independent shuffled product code. This requires less RAM to implement, but it means that from an error-correction standpoint each tape track is self contained and must deal alone with any errors encountered.

Later formats, beginning with D-3, use the approach shown in Figure 8.54(b). Here, following distribution the entire field is used to produce one large shuffled product code in each channel. The product code is then segmented for recording on tape. Although more RAM is required to assemble the large product code, the result is that outer codewords on tape spread across several tracks and redundancy in one track can compensate for errors in another. The result is that size of a single burst error which can be fully corrected is increased. As RAM is now cheaper than when the first formats were designed, this approach is becoming more common.

8.29 The data to be recorded

The input data rate of a component digital machine can be directly deduced from the CCIR-601 standard. In every active line, 720 luminance samples and 360 of each type of colour difference sample are produced, making a total of 1440 samples per line. In 625/50, lines 11–310 and lines 324–623 are recorded, making 300 lines per field, or 1500 lines per second. The D-1 and D-5 formats record these data directly. In 525/60, lines 14–263 and lines 276–525 are recorded, making 250 lines per field, which results in the same data rate of 1500 lines per second.

In both cases the video data rate will be 1500×1440 samples/sec, or 2.16 million samples/sec. If 18 MHz sampling is used, the data rate will be correspondingly higher.

The actual bit rate recorded will be in excess of the video data rate to take into account the redundancy, the audio and identification codes. Further track space will be required to accommodate preambles and synchronizing patterns.

As the fields in the two line standards contain 300 and 250 lines, it makes a good deal of sense for each segment or track pair to record the highest common multiple, 50 lines, such that a field will comprise either 6 or 5 segments. The segment rate will then be 300 Hz in both standards, and since the scanner in a typical transport has two pairs of heads, it will turn at 150 revolutions per second. The transport can be mechanically identical in the two line standards. It should be appreciated that in fact the field rate of the 525 line system is 59.94 Hz, and so the scanner speed (and hence the capstan speed) will be 0.1% slower in the 525 line version. This is of no real consequence to the format, except for some very small dimensional changes, and for simplicity will not be mentioned again in this chapter.

In composite formats the situation becomes more complex. In both line standards, the sampling clock is precisely derived from subcarrier. The very existence of the samples indicates the phase of subcarrier, and so it is not necessary to record the burst. The subcarrier has a mathematical relationship with sync, which can readily be reconstructed on replay, and so it is not necessary to record syncs either.

Accordingly, D-2 and D-3 only record the active line, along with sufficient positioning information so that syncs and burst can be regenerated on replay. Both D-2 and D-3 in PAL record 948 samples symmetrically disposed around the unblanked active line, and in NTSC record 768 samples similarly. In each case, sample zero is defined as the first sample to be recorded in each line. Since not all of the line period is recorded, it then becomes important to ensure that sampling commences in a consistent place on each line of each frame, and that the first sample has a consistent relationship to subcarrier. Clearly the position of the first sample in a line must be on one cycle or another of the sampling clock, and, as has been seen, this is derived from input burst. The edge of the picture is, however, defined by the sync pulse leading edge, and the input stage has to resolve the conflict of sampling at a fixed relationship to H-sync in order to keep the edge of the picture straight with the need to sample coherently with

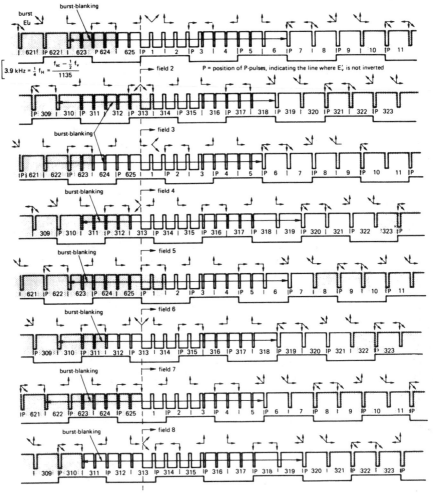

Figure 8.55 (a) Each field recorded contains 304 lines in PAL D-2, but the actual lines recorded change from field to field so that the fields always begin with the same line type in the PAL sequence. This eases the production of picture-in-shuttle since the colour processor then only needs to know the position in the field, since all fields offtape appear identical.

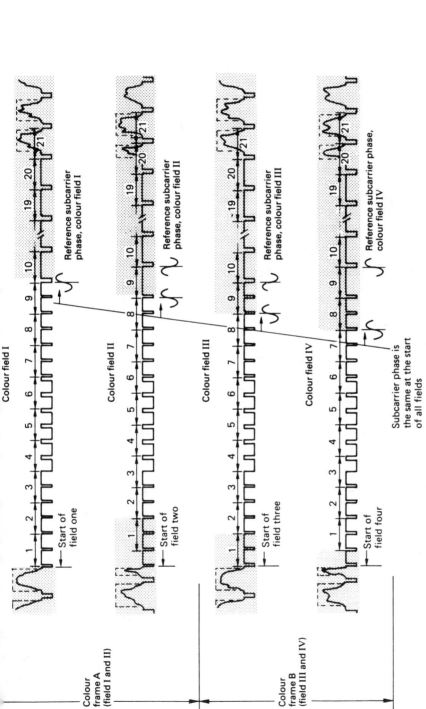

Figure 8.55(b) The recorded lines in NTSC D-2 are shown shaded here. The starting point in each field is chosen so that the subcarrier-phase is the same at the beginning of all fields on tape.

subcarrier. In NTSC this is relatively easy, owing to the simple relationship between subcarrier and sync. It is only necessary to wait a fixed number of sample periods after sync, and the first sample of the active line will be consistently located.

In the PAL system it becomes more complex because of the 25 Hz component of subcarrier. In the absence of 25 Hz, there would be exactly 283¾ cycles per line and exactly 1135 sample clocks per line. Instead, there will be an additional four sample clocks in one frame period. Not all lines of the field are recorded, and in fact the lines which are recorded vary from one field to the next. This is necessary to allow picture-in-shuttle. The recording is composite and contains an embedded chroma signal. Colour processing is necessary in shuttle to change the phase of the offtape signal to that of reference. When tracks are crossed in shuttle, sync blocks are picked up at random, and a frame store is updated by information which has come from several different fields. This is only possible if samples offtape can be colour processed. The necessary interleave and shuffle processes in a DVTR mean that each sync block contains samples which have come from various places within a field segment. When a frame store is updated in shuttle, successive samples in a given line could have come from a different colour line type, and they would no longer represent the modulation of a continuous subcarrier. The colour processor would not be able to operate.

The solution adopted in D-2 is to record more lines than necessary, so that the first line of each field recorded can change over a four or eight field sequence as shown in Figure 8.55. The choice of the first line to be recorded is made by the input colour framer. This ensures that all fields on tape have the same chroma phase at the same line number, and (in PAL only) to change the position of the first sample recorded in those lines. The choice of the first sample in a field to be recorded is made by the input colour framer. In NTSC, there is only the subcarrier inversion from line to line to consider, and so sampling will begin one line later in alternate frames.

At normal speed and in slow motion, the recorded lines are put back into the correct position in the reference fields, and the normal chroma sequences result; in shuttle, however, the colour processor now only needs to know the line number of recovered pixels and they can be correctly processed without knowing the number of the field from which they came. The offset of the line start causes a loss of vertical resolution in shuttle (four lines in PAL, two in NTSC).

D-3 uses the same technique in NTSC, but achieves the same goal in a slightly different way in PAL. Instead of moving the starting line over four lines, a range of two lines is used to handle changes in V-switch in conjunction with a 2 pixel horizontal shift which opposes the subcarrier inversion between line pairs. Figure 8.56(a) shows how the sampling structure results in every field beginning with a $(U-V)$ sample.

The offset of the line start causes a loss of vertical resolution in shuttle of two lines in NTSC and PAL along with a loss of horizontal resolution of two pixels in PAL only, but this is acceptable since resolution falls in shuttle anyway due to movement in the picture.

The raw video data rate which must be sustained by a composite digital recorder can now be derived. For PAL, 948 samples in 304 lines at 50 Hz results in 14 409 600 samples per second, whereas for NTSC, 768 samples in 255 lines at 59.94 Hz results in 9 976 089.6 samples per second. Each sample is of 8 bit resolution in D-2 and D-3.

Field number	(a) PAL	(b) NTSC
1	Line 8 Sample 1133	Line 9 Sample 0
2	Line 320 Sample 0	Line 8 Sample 0
3	Line 7 Sample 1133	Line 9 Sample 2
4	Line 321 Sample 1133	Line 8 Sample 2
5	Line 8 Sample 0	
6	Line 320 Sample 1133	
7	Line 7 Sample 0	
8	Line 321 Sample 0	

Figure 8.56 Composite sampling requires the first recorded sample to move from field to field to enable picture-in-shuttle with constant colour framing off tape.

In (a) combinations of two sample shifts to invert chroma and one line shift to reverse V-switch allow every field on tape to begin with U–V sample in PAL.

In (b) NTSC requires only two sample shifts to compensate for inversion of subcarrier from line to line.

In practice, these figures will need to be increased somewhat to allow for an error correction overhead, the presence of addressing or identification codes and for the recording of four audio channels. Additionally, a proportion of each track will be used up with the preambles and sync patterns necessary to the operation of the channel coding, and tolerance gaps needed to allow independent editing of audio and video.

8.30 Distribution

Component formats require three signal components to be recorded in parallel. These components must be distributed between the number of signal channels used. In D-1 and D-5 no data reduction is employed and four signal channels are required. The distribution strategy is based on the requirement for concealment of uncorrected errors. This requires samples from all three video components to be distributed over all four recording channels. If this is done the loss of a channel causes an equal loss to each video component rather than a greater loss concentrated in one component.

Figure 8.57(a) shows the distribution strategy of D-1 in which the data are distributed over four channels.[9] The distribution is complicated by the fact that the video data consist of pixels which are alternately co-sited Y, C_r, C_b samples and Y-only samples. The goal of the distribution strategy is to permit the best concealment possible in the case of lost sectors, and Figure 8.57(b) also shows the samples which will be lost if one sector is unrecoverable. Horizontal or vertical interpolation is possible to conceal the missing samples. Figure 8.57(c) shows the result if two sectors are lost. Samples of both luminance and colour

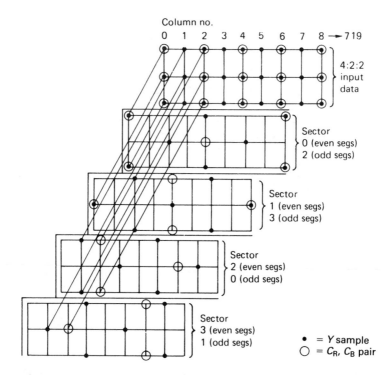

Figure 8.57(a) Distribution of the input 4:2:2 data over four parallel channels is performed as shown here. The criterion is the best concealment ability in case of the loss of one or more channels.

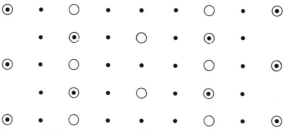

Figure 8.57(b) The result of combining the channels when data from sector 1 are lost. Spatial interpolation can be used to restore picture content.

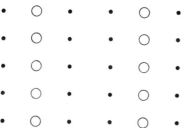

Figure 8.57(c) When sectors 0 and 1 are both lost both Y and C_R, C_B are still available at half the normal sampling rate and so effective concealment is still possible.

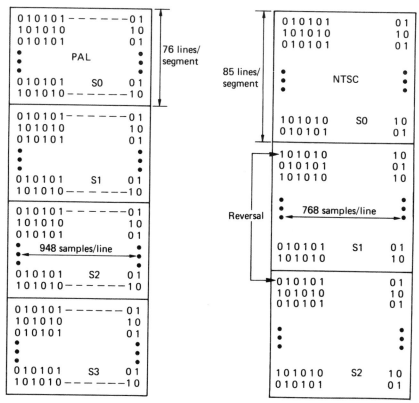

Figure 8.58 D-2 distribution, showing the track number (0 or 1) in which a given sample will be recorded. In PAL (left) there is an even number of lines in the segment so they are all the same. In NTSC there is an odd number, so the distribution reverses from segment to segment in order to maintain the pattern across segment boundaries.

difference are still available at one-half of the original sampling rates of each, and so a reduced bandwidth picture can still be produced.

In composite digital formats, data to be recorded are distributed between the two heads which are active at any one time. Figure 8.58 shows the segmented distribution scheme for D-2 and Figure 8.59 shows the same scheme applied to D-3 but over entire fields. In both cases the distribution ensures that, in both rows and columns of a field, alternate samples are recorded by a different head. If samples from a given head are lost for any reason, each lost sample is surrounded on four sides by samples from the other head. In the case of complete loss of signal from one head, due perhaps to clogging, it is still possible to produce a picture of reasonable quality from the remaining head because the quality will be as if the picture had originally been sampled at $2 \times F_{sc}$.

Where data reduction is employed, the reduction process takes place directly on the input signal and produces blocks of coefficients. It is these blocks which enter the distribution process. The contents of the DCT blocks cannot be divided because of the requirement of picture-in-shuttle. When a single sync block is recovered in shuttle, it must contain all of the coefficients of the DCT blocks it

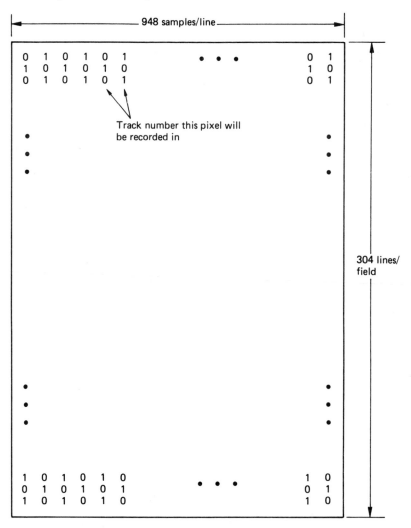

Figure 8.59 Distribution scheme for PAL D-3 (NTSC similar) shows that alternate pixels in two dimensions are recorded by alternate heads. Loss of one head signal allows interpolation from the remaining data.

contains otherwise the pixel data cannot be recreated in that screen area. Thus the distribution and shuffle processes take the DCT block as the minimum unit of data.

8.31 The shuffle strategy

Error correction in DVTRs is more complex than in other forms of recording because of the number of conflicting requirements. Chapter 5 showed that interleave is necessary to break up burst errors, and that a product code gives an efficient and reliable system. Unfortunately the product code produces a regular structure of rows and columns, and, if such a system is overwhelmed, regular patterns of uncorrected errors are produced and the effectiveness of concealment is reduced because the eye can still perceive the regular structure.

An irregular interleave, or *shuffle*, can be designed to disperse contiguous errors on the tape track over two dimensions on the screen, and the concealment is then more effective. For the best concealment, the shuffle should work over the entire field and this will also help the provision of a picture-in-shuttle.

In shuttle the track-following process breaks down, and the heads cross tracks randomly so that the recovery of entire segments is impossible. A picture of some sort is needed in shuttle, in order to assist in the location of wanted material, but the quality does not need to be as high as in other modes.

Figure 8.60 shows that, in shuttle, the path of the head crosses tape tracks obliquely. The use of azimuth recording allows the replay head to be about 50% wider than the track, and so a useful replay signal results for a reasonable proportion of the head path, at the times where the head is near the centreline of a track of the same azimuth type, interrupted by noise when the heads cross tracks of the wrong azimuth type. The sectors are broken into short elements called *sync blocks* which are smaller than the length of track which can be recovered at typical shuttle speeds. Each sync block contains a Reed–Solomon codeword, and so it is possible to tell if the sync block was correctly recovered or not, without reference to any other part of the recording.

If a sync block is read properly, it is used to update a framestore which refreshes the picture monitor. Sync blocks which are not read correctly will not update the framestore, and so if concealment cannot be used, data from an earlier field will be used to refresh the display.

Using this mechanism, the picture-in-shuttle is composed of data from different segments of many offtape fields. A problem with segmented recordings is that at certain tape speeds beating occurs between the passage of tracks and the scanner rotation so that some parts of the segments are never recovered and the picture has to be refreshed with stale data which are no longer representative of the recording. There are two solutions to the problem. The use of a field-based

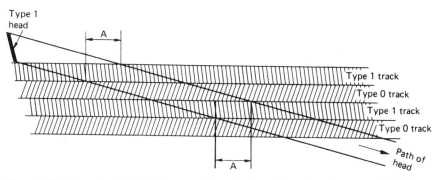

Figure 8.60 During shuttle, the heads cross tracks randomly as shown here (exaggerated). Owing to the use of azimuth recording, a head can only play a track of its own type (0 or 1) but as the head is typically 50% wider than the track it is possible to recover normal signal for the periods above marked A. If sync blocks are shorter than this period, they can be picked up intact. In fact a slightly longer pickup will be possible because the replay system may tolerate a less-than-perfect signal. In any case the final decision is made by checking that the sync block recovered contains valid or correctable codewords.

shuffle helps because one offtape sync block then contains samples from all over the screen. A field-based shuffle is complex to implement and D-3 was the first format to use it. In the earlier D-1 and D-2 formats the shuffle was restricted to operate only over one segment of the field.

The beating effect is mechanical, and results in certain parts of a track being inaccessible. If the data within successive tracks are ordered differently, beating will cause loss from all over the picture once more. Thus in a segment-based shuffle, each track in the field will use a different shuffle. In a field-based shuffle the two channels will use different shuffles. In composite formats the data in successive fields of the colour-frame sequence may be rotated by differing amounts.

Obtaining a shuttle picture is easier if the shuffle is random, but a random shuffle is less effective for concealment because it can result in variable density of uncorrected errors, which are harder to conceal than the constant error density resulting from a maximum-distance shuffle.

Essentially the field of data to be shuffled is considered to be a two-dimensional memory, and the shuffle is achieved by address mapping in each dimension. The address generator used should not be unnecessarily complicated and it will be simpler if the rows and columns of the memory are mapped in turn. Clearly the shuffle process on recording has to be exactly reversed on replay.

In address mapping, samples in each channel of a segment are at addresses which are initially sequential. The samples are selected non-sequentially by generating a suitable address sequence. When data reduction is used, individual pixels cannot be shuffled, but instead it is the addresses of DCT blocks which are mapped.

Address A	A × 11		A × 11 mod 16
0	0		0
1	11		11
2	22	(−16)	6
3	33	(−32)	1
4	44	(−32)	12
5	55	(−48)	7
6	66	(−64)	2
7	77	(−64)	13
8	88	(−80)	8
9	99	(−96)	3
10	110	(−96)	14
11	121	(−112)	9
12	132	(−128)	4
13	143	(−128)	15
14	154	(−144)	10
15	165	(−160)	5

Figure 8.61 (a) The permuted addresses for a shuffle can be obtained by multiplication of the addresses by a number relatively prime to the modulo base.

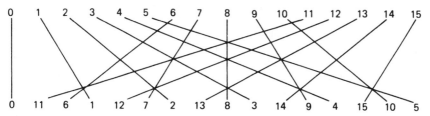

Figure 8.61 (b) The shuffle which results from the calculation in Figure 8.61(a).

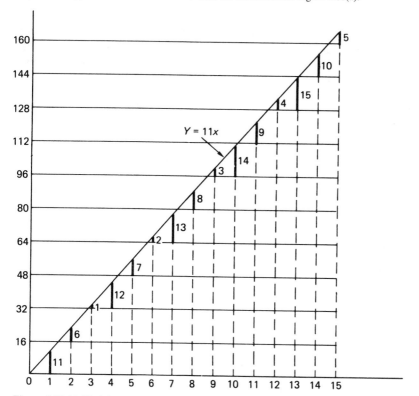

Figure 8.61 (c) Modulo arithmetic is rather similar to quantizing. The results of Figure 8.61(a) can be obtained by quantizing the graph of $y = 11x$ with the quantizing intervals of 16 units.

In principle, the address sequence could be arbitrarily generated from a lookup table, but the memory arrays are large, and this approach would be extremely expensive to implement. It is desirable that the address generation should be algorithmic to reduce cost, but an algorithm must be found which gives irregular results.

The solution adopted in DVTR formats is to obtain a pseudo-random address sequence by using address multiplication by a prime number in modulo arithmetic for one of the mapping axes. This is easier than it sounds, as the simple example of Figure 8.61(a) shows. In this example, 16 pixels are to be shuffled. The pixel addresses are multiplied by 11, which is relatively prime to 16, and the result is expressed modulo-16, which is to say that if the product equals or exceeds an integer multiple of 16, that integer multiple is subtracted. It will be seen from Figure 8.61(b) that an effective shuffle is created. Modulo arithmetic has a similar effect to quantizing; in fact a number expressed modulo is the quantizing error due to quantizing in steps equal to the modulo base, as Figure 8.61(c) shows. When the input has a large range, the quantizing error becomes random.

Generating a randomizing effect with modulo arithmetic depends upon the terms in the expression being relatively prime so that repeats are not found in the resulting shuffle, and this constrains the dimensions which can be used for the codewords.

A calculation of the type described will shuffle samples or DCT blocks in a pseudo-random manner in one dimension, but in the other dimension of the memory a pseudo-random shuffle is undesirable as this would result in a variable-distance shuffle. A straightforward interleave is used in the other

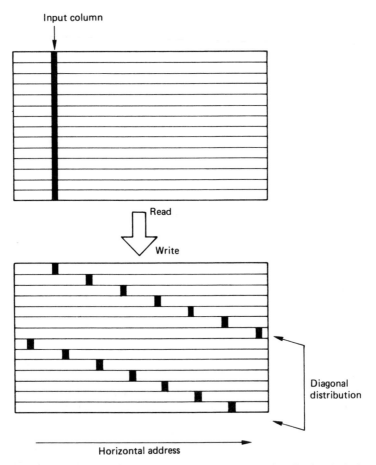

Figure 8.62 The second dimension of the shuffle is obtained by offsetting the horizontal address during transfer from one array to another. This results in a diagonal shuffle if the offset increases by a constant from one line to the next.

dimension to give a maximum-distance shuffle. Figure 8.62 shows a conceptual example. When samples are read in rows for recording they retain the same horizontal sequence but there is an offset in the starting address which is a simple function of the row number. This turns a column into a series of diagonals. The combination of these two processes results in the two-dimensional shuffle. The effect of the shuffle can be seen by turning off the correction and concealment circuits on a machine and searching for a large dropout with the jog control. This will reveal the irregular diagonal structure.

8.32 The product code

The product code of a DVTR may extend over a segment, as in D-1 and D-2, or over the entire field as in D-3. Figure 8.63(a) shows the field array of D-3 PAL, and Figure 8.63(b) shows the equivalent in NTSC. Outer codes are vertical columns and three of these are necessary to contain the samples from one TV line after distribution. Data are recorded on tape by passing horizontally across the array to form inner codewords which are placed sequentially along the track. The inner code word will correct random errors, but if its correction power is exceeded the inner code declares the entire block bad, and the outer code must correct by erasure. If the inner code were too large, this would effectively magnify burst errors to the size of the codeword. A further consideration is that if each sector were to be one long data block, loss of synchronization in the data separator due to a dropout would result in the loss of the rest of the sector, again magnifying the error.

Instead, one row of the segment array is made into 12 inner code blocks in PAL and 9 in NTSC, and this reduces error magnification due to small bursts. Each array will be recorded on four different tracks for PAL, three for NTSC. Two arrays are needed to record one field. Each array is recorded in tracks of the same azimuth type. The outer redundancy is distributed evenly over the tracks. Since the outer codes contain eight redundancy symbols, each can correct eight symbols by erasure. This corresponds to eight bytes per column of the field array. The largest data loss which can be handled will be when this damage is experienced in every column of the array, so the maximum correctable burst error size is given by multiplying the number of columns in the sector array by eight. The resulting figures are $912 \times 8 = 7296$ data bytes for PAL and $765 \times 8 = 6120$ data bytes for NTSC. These figures are for video data only; the actual size of the burst will be larger because the length of the track involved also contains sync and ID patterns and inner redundancy.

As the field array in D-3 is spread over several tracks, the length of a correctable tape defect along the track depends upon the number of tracks over which the defect spreads. Figure 8.64 shows that if the error is due to a helical scratch or a particle of debris passing under the head, it will be restricted to one track only and the correctable track length will be a maximum. If the defect is a linear tape scratch affecting all tracks, the correctable length of the defect is given by dividing the field-array correction power by the number of tracks in which the array is recorded (3 or 4). Note that this is only possible because the product code spreads over the whole field.

The maximum correctable single-track burst corresponds to about 19 mm of track length, or a longitudinal tape scratch of about 1.6 mm width.

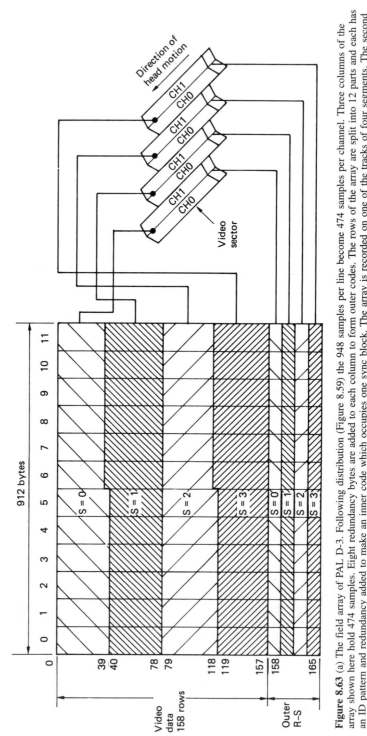

Figure 8.63 (a) The field array of PAL D-3. Following distribution (Figure 8.59) the 948 samples per line become 474 samples per channel. Three columns of the array shown here hold 474 samples. Eight redundancy bytes are added to each column to form outer codes. The rows of the array are split into 12 parts and each has an ID pattern and redundancy added to make an inner code which occupies one sync block. The array is recorded on one of the tracks of four segments. The second array is recorded on the other tracks. Outer redundancy is recorded first in each track.

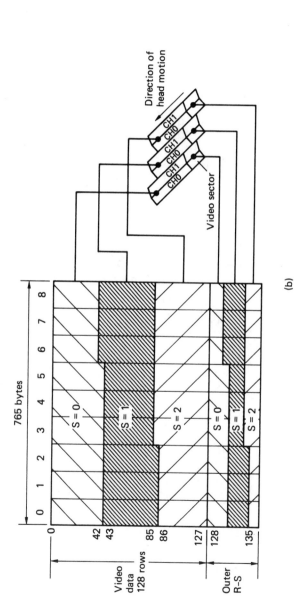

Figure 8.63 (b) The field array of NTSC D-3. Following distribution (Figure 8.59) the 768 samples per line become 384 samples per channel. Three columns of the array shown here hold 384 samples. Eight redundancy bytes are added to each column to form outer codes. The rows of the array are split into nine parts and each has an ID pattern and redundancy added to make an inner code which occupies one sync block. The array is recorded in one of the tracks of three segments. Outer redundancy is recorded first in each track.

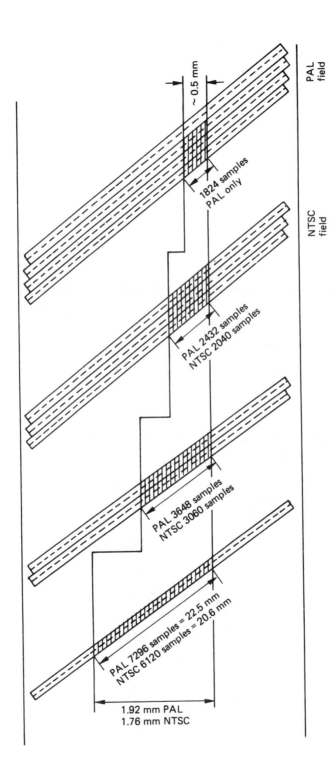

Figure 8.64 Error-correcting performance of D-3. For a single-segment helical scratch, reference to Figure 8.63 shows that eight rows can be corrected in each track by outer codes. This corresponds to 8 × 912 = 7296 samples (PAL) or 8 × 765 = 6120 samples (NTSC). In the case of a scratch along the tape, the maximum correction per field array must be divided by the number of tracks affected. In NTSC there are six tracks per field so a sustained scratch of 2040 samples can be corrected. In PAL there are eight tracks per field so a sustained scratch of 1824 samples can be corrected. This could be up to about 0.5 mm wide.

If these conditions are exceeded, total correction is no longer possible, and rows of flagged erroneous data will appear in the field array. Concealment will become necessary and the concealment patterns are made irregular by using shuffling.

In shuttle, sync blocks will be recovered at random, and the shuffle means that when a sync block is successfully read, the pixels it contains are spread over the field, so the frame store will be updated all over instead of just in certain areas. The twinkling effect on the picture-in-shuttle is caused by the shuffle.

8.33 The sync block

The inner codes in product codes are designed to correct random errors and to detect the presence of burst errors by declaring the whole inner block bad. There is an optimum size for an inner code: too small and the redundancy factor rises; too large and burst errors are magnified, as are errors due to losing sync.

When the product code becomes large, one row will be too long to be one inner code, and so in D-3, for example, it is split into 12 or 9 inner code blocks.

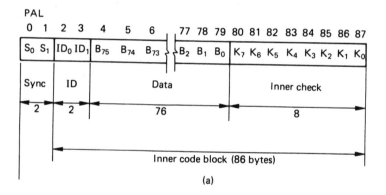

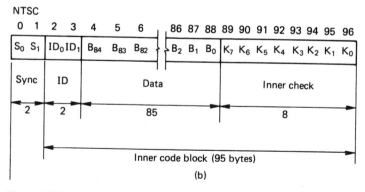

Figure 8.65 D-3 sync blocks (a) PAL and (b) NTSC. Each begins with the sync pattern 97F1 which is not randomized. The 2 byte ID, the data and the 8 bytes of inner check symbols are all randomized prior to EFM coding. The same block structure is used in both audio and video sectors.

The dimensions of these are chosen to give adequate correction performance. One sync block contains one inner codeword and an ID code. 12 or 9 sync blocks then form one complete row of the sector array.

Figure 8.65(a) shows a PAL D-3 sync block. A 2 byte synchronizing pattern serves to phase the data separator and the deserializer. Following this is a 2 byte ID code which uniquely identifies this sync block in an eight-field sequence. The data block of 76 bytes then follows, and the 8 bytes of inner redundancy are calculated over the ID code as well as the data, so a random error in the ID can be corrected. The codeword is thus 86 bytes long. The entire sync block occupies about a quarter of a millimetre of track.

Figure 8.65(b) shows an NTSC D-3 sync block. A 2 byte synchronizing pattern serves to phase the data seperator and the deserializer. Following this is a 2 byte ID code which uniquely identifies this sync block in a four-field sequence. The data block of 85 bytes then follows, and the 8 bytes of inner redundancy are calculated over the ID code as well as the data, so a random error in the ID can be corrected. The codeword is thus 95 bytes long.

Whilst the size of the inner codeword is related to correction power, it is not essential for each inner code to have its own ID. In fact, individually identifying each inner code would raise the recording overheads. In shuttle, a geometric calculation reveals the shortest length of track which will be recovered at maximum tape speed, and this determines that in D-2, for example, it is not necessary to identify every inner codeword. Accordingly one sync block contains two inner codewords, but only one ID code. Three sync blocks then form one complete row of the sector array.

Figure 8.66(a) shows a PAL D-2 sync block. A 2 byte synchronizing pattern serves to phase the data separator and the deserializer. Following this is a 2 byte

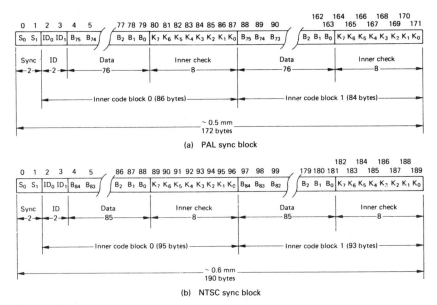

(a) PAL sync block

(b) NTSC sync block

Figure 8.66 The sync blocks of D-2 contain two codewords but only one ID code which forms part of the first codeword. As a result, the first code block is 2 bytes longer than the second.

ID code which uniquely identifies this sync block in an eight-field sequence. The first data block of 76 bytes then follows, and the 8 bytes of inner redundancy are calculated over the ID code as well as the data, so a random error in the ID can be corrected. The first codeword is thus 86 bytes long. The second inner code block is 2 bytes shorter because it contains no ID. The entire sync block occupies just over half a millimetre of track.

Figure 8.66(b) shows an NTSC D-2 sync block. A 2 byte synchronizing pattern serves to phase the data separator and the deserializer. Following this is a 2 byte ID code which uniquely identifies this sync block in a four-field sequence. The first data block of 85 bytes then follows, and the 8 bytes of inner redundancy are calculated over the ID code as well as the data, so a random error in the ID can be corrected. The first codeword is thus 95 bytes long. The second inner code block is 2 bytes shorter because it contains no ID. The entire sync block occupies nearly two-thirds of a millimetre of track.

8.34 Synchronization and identification

Each sync block contains one or two inner codewords, depending on the format, and is the smallest quantum of data on the track with which the playback channel can synchronize independently. Synchronization takes place on three levels: to the bit, to the symbol and to the sync block.

The recording density in DVTRs is such that it is not possible to mechanically position the heads with sufficient accuracy to locate an individual bit. The heads are rotated with reasonable accuracy, and the replay signal is accepted as and when it arrives. A phase-locked loop in the data separator must lock to the bit rate and phase of the recording. At the beginning of the track a reference for the phase-locked loop known as a track preamble is recorded. This serves to set the frequency of the PLL the same as the offtape bit rate. Once the loop is locked, it can stay in synchronism by phase-comparing the data transitions with its own. However, if synchronism is lost due to a dropout, it cannot be regained until the next synchronizing pattern is seen. This is one reason why the tracks are broken into short sync blocks.

Once bit synchronism has been achieved at the preamble, the serial data has to be correctly divided up into symbols, or deserialized, in order to decode the original samples. This requires word synchronization, and is achieved by the unique pattern which occurs at the beginning of every sync block. Detection of this pattern resets the counter which deserializes the data by dividing by the wordlength. If randomizing is used, as in D-1, D-3/5 and Digital Betacam, sync detection will also be used to preset the derandomizer to the correct starting value. The sync pattern should differ from itself shifted by as many bits as possible to reduce the possibility of false sync generation. Within a sector, sync patterns occur at regular spacing, so it is possible for the replay circuitry to predict the arrival of the sync pattern in a time window.

Once symbol synchronizing is achieved, it is then possible to read the inner code blocks, particularly the two bytes which contain the ID code as this reveals which sync block has been recovered. In normal play this will be the one after the previous one, but in shuttle the sequence will be unpredictable.

In shuttle, samples from any sync block properly recovered can be put in the correct place in a frame store by reference to the ID code.

Figure 8.67(a) shows the ID structure of D-3, which is very similar to that of D-2. The information recorded in the ID code is split into two parts. The first byte and bit 0 of the second is the 9 bit sync block number in the track; the remaining seven bits of the second byte identifies the sector. The V/A bit specifies whether the block is audio or video. The segment bits determine which segment out of four for PAL and three for NTSC is present, and the field bits specify the position in the eight- or four-field sequences to help colour framing.

Figure 8.67(b) shows the sync block numbering within the segment for PAL, and Figure 8.67(c) shows the equivalent for NTSC.

8.35 Gaps, preambles and postambles

Each slant track is subdivided into sectors. In D-1, D-5, DCT and Digital Betacam there is a video sector at each end and four audio sectors in the middle. In D-2 and D-3 there are two audio sectors at each end, and one video sector in the centre. It is necessary to be able to edit any or all of the audio channels independently of the video. For this reason short spaces are left between the sectors to allow write current to turn on and off away from wanted data. Since the write current can only turn off at the end of a sector, it follows that the smallest quantum of data which can be written in the track at one time is a whole sector, although the smallest quantum which can be read is a sync block.

A preamble is necessary before the first sync block in a sector to allow the phase-locked loop in the data separator to lock. The preamble also contains a sync pattern and ID code so that the machine can confirm the position of the head before entering the sector proper. At the end of the sector a postamble containing

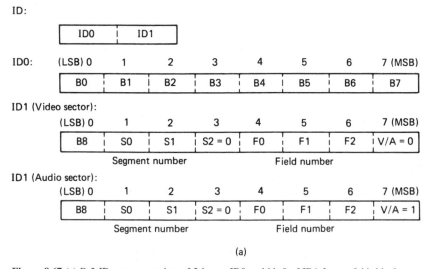

(a)

Figure 8.67 (a) D-3 ID pattern consists of 2 bytes. ID0 and bit 0 of ID1 form a 9 bit block address. Bit 7 of ID1 is the video/audio flag and determines the type of sector. Remainder of the data carries field number (0–3 NTSC, 0–7 PAL) and segment number (0–2 NTSC, 0–3 PAL). Audio segment number requires only 2 bit code; thus S2 = 0.

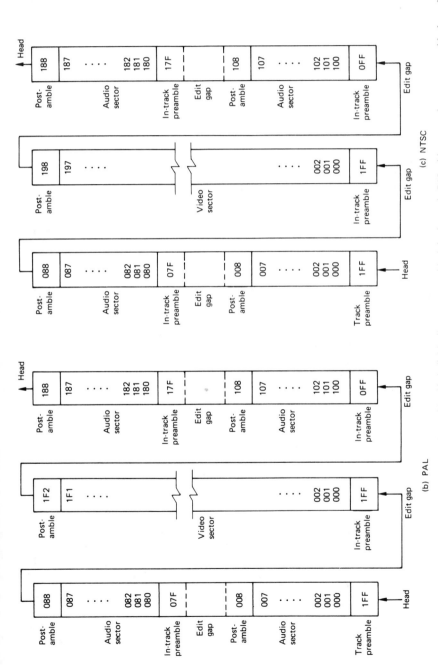

Figure 8.67 (b) and (c) Showing ID code numbering to identify individually every sync block in the track. PAL video sector has more sync blocks and reaches higher count than that of NTSC in (c).

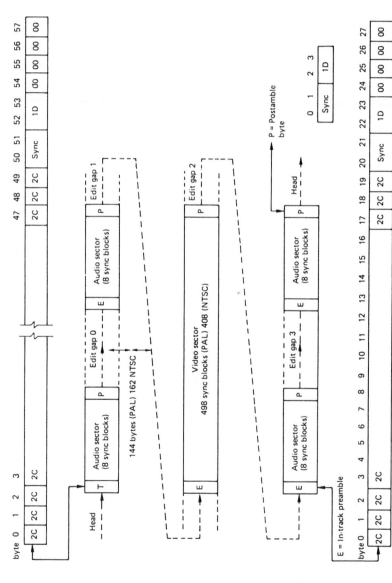

Figure 8.68 All separately recordable areas begin with a preamble E except for the first sector which has a longer track preamble T. Edit gaps are the same size as two sync blocks and begin with the postamble P of the previous sector and end with the preamble E of the next sector.

an ID code is written before the write current is turned off. The pre- and postamble details of D-3 can be seen in Figure 8.68.

The space between two adjacent sectors is known as an edit gap, and it will be seen in Figure 8.68 to begin with the postamble of the previous sector and end with the preamble of the next sector. Editing may result in a discontinuity nominally in the middle of the gap. There is some latitude, but the new recording must not begin so early that the postamble at the end of the previous sector is damaged, and at least 20 bytes of preamble must be written before the sync pattern at the beginning of the next sector, because it will not be possible to maintain continuity of bit phase at an edit, and the PLL must re-synchronize.

In practice the length of the postamble, gap and preamble combined will be made exactly equal to the length of one or two sync blocks according to the format. This simplifies the design of the sequencer which controls the track recording.

8.36 Digital Betacam

Digital Betacam (DB) is a component format which accepts 8 or 10 bit 4:2:2 data with 720 luminance samples per active line and four channels of 48 KHz digital audio having up to 20 bit wordlength. Video data reduction based on discrete cosine transform is employed, with a compression factor of almost two to one (assuming 8 bit input). The audio data are uncompressed. The cassette shell of the half-inch analog Betacam format is retained, but contains fourteen micrometre metal-particle tape. The digital cassette contains an identification hole which allows the transport to identify the tape type. Unlike the other digital formats, only two cassette sizes are available. The large cassette offers 124 minutes of playing time; the small cassette plays for 40 minutes.

Owing to the tradeoff between SNR and bandwidth which is a characteristic of digital recording, the tracks must be longer than in the analog Betacam format, but narrower. The drum diameter of the DB transport is 81.4 mm, which is designed to produce tracks of the required length for digital recording. The helix angle of the digital drum is designed such that when an analog Betacam tape is driven past at the correct speed, the track angle is correct. Certain DB machines are fitted with analog heads which can trace the tracks of an analog tape. As the drum size is different, the analog playback signal is time-compressed by about 9%, but this is easily dealt with in the timebase correction process.[10] The fixed heads are compatible with the analog Betacam positioning. The reverse compatibility is for playback only; the digital machine cannot record on analog cassettes.

Figure 8.69 shows the track patterns for 525/60 and 625/50 Digital Betacam. The four digital audio channels are recorded in separate sectors of the slant tracks, and so one of the linear audio channels of the analog format is dispensed with, leaving one linear audio track for cueing.

Azimuth recording is employed, with two tracks being recorded simultaneously by adjacent heads. Electronic delays are used to align the position of the edit gaps in the two tracks of a segment, allowing double-width flying erase heads to be used. Three segments are needed to record one field, requiring one and a half drum revolutions. Thus the drum speed is three times that of the analog format. However, the track pitch is less than one-third that of the analog format so the linear speed of the digital tape is actually slower. In 625/50, track width

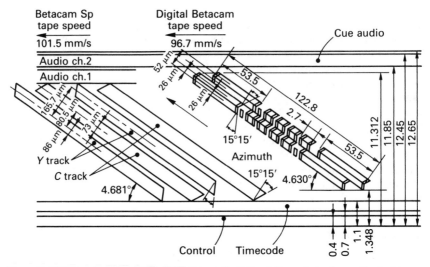

Figure 8.69 The track pattern of Digital Betacam. Control and timecode tracks are identical in location to the analog format, as is the single analog audio cue track. Note the use of a small guard band between segments.

is 24 micrometres, with a 4 micrometre guard band between segments making the effective track pitch 26 micrometres, whereas in 525/60 the track width is 20 micrometres with a 3.4 micrometre guard band between segments making an effective track pitch of 21.7 micrometres. These figures should be compared with 18 micrometres for D-3/D-5 and 39 micrometres for D-2/DCT.

There is a linear timecode track whose structure is identical to the analog Betacam timecode, and a control track shown in Figure 8.70 having a fundamental frequency of 50 Hz. Ordinarily the duty cycle is 50%, but this changes to 65/35 in field 1 and 35/65 in field 5. The rising edge of the CTL signal coincides with the first segment of a field, and the duty-cycle variations allow four- or eight-field colour framing if decoded composite sources are used. As the drum speed is 75 Hz, CTL and drum phase coincides every three revolutions.

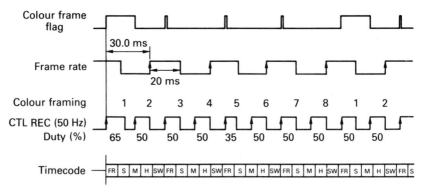

Figure 8.70 The control track of Digital Betacam uses duty cycle modulation for colour framing purposes.

Figure 8.71 shows the track layout in more detail. Unlike other digital formats, DB incorporates tracking pilot tones recorded between the audio and video sectors. The first tone has a frequency of approximately 4 MHz and appears once per drum revolution. The second is recorded at approximately 400 KHz and appears twice per drum revolution. The pilot tones are recorded when a recording is first made on a blank tape, and will be re-recorded following an assemble edit, but during an insert edit the tracking pilots are not re-recorded, but used as a guide to the insertion of the new tracks.

The amplitude of the pilot signal is a function of the head tracking. The replay heads are somewhat wider than the tracks, and so a considerable tracking error will have to be present before a loss of amplitude is noted. This is partly offset by the use of a very long wavelength pilot tone in which fringing fields increase the effective track width. The low-frequency tones are used for automatic playback tracking.

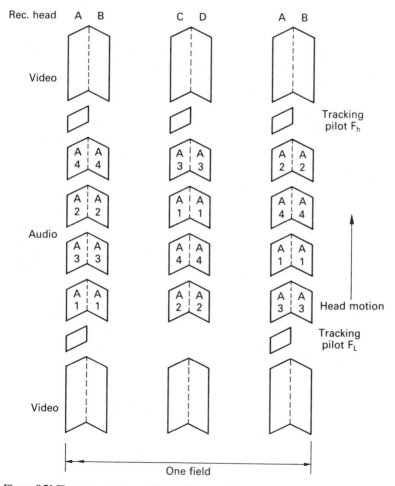

Figure 8.71 The sector structure of Digital Betacam. Note the tracking tones between the audio and video sectors which are played back for alignment purposes during insert edits.

With the tape moving at normal speed, the capstan phase is changed by steps in one direction then the other as the pilot tone amplitude is monitored. The phase which results in the largest amplitude will be retained. During the edit pre-roll the record heads play back the high-frequency pilot tone and capstan phase is set for largest amplitude. The record heads are the same width as the tracks and a short-wavelength pilot tone is used such that any mistracking will cause immediate amplitude loss. This is an edit optimize process and results in new tracks being inserted in the same location as the originals. As the pilot tones are played back in insert editing, there will be no tolerance buildup in the case of multiple inserts.

The data reduction of DB[11] works on an intra-field basis to allow complete editing freedom and uses processes described in Chapter 2.

8.37 Block diagram of Digital Betacam

Figure 8.72 shows a block diagram of the record section of DB. Analog component inputs are sampled at 13.5 and 6.75 MHz. Alternatively the input may be SDI at 270 Mbits/sec which is deserialized and demultiplexed to separate components. The raster scan input is first converted to blocks which are 8 pixels wide by 4 pixels high in the luminance channel and 4 pixels by 4 in the two colour-difference channels. When two fields are combined on the screen, the result is effectively an interlaced 8×8 luminance block with colour-difference pixels having twice the horizontal luminance pixel spacing. The pixel blocks are then subject to a field shuffle. A shuffle based on individual pixels is impossible because it would raise the high-frequency content of the image and destroy the power of the data-reduction process. Instead the block shuffle helps the data reduction by making the average entropy of the image more constant. This happens because the shuffle exchanges blocks from flat areas of the image with blocks from highly detailed areas. The shuffle algorithm also has to consider the requirements of picture-in-shuttle. The blocking and shuffle take place when the read addresses of the input memory are permuted with respect to the write addresses.

Following the input shuffle the blocks are associated into sets of ten in each component and are then subject to the discrete cosine transform. The resulting coefficients are then subject to an iterative requantizing process followed by variable-length coding. The iteration adjusts the size of the quantizing step until the overall length of the ten coefficient sets is equal to the constant capacity of an entropy block which is 364 bytes. Within that entropy block the amount of data representing each individual DCT block may vary considerably, but the overall block size stays the same.

The DCT process results in coefficients whose wordlength exceeds the input wordlength. As a result it does not matter if the input wordlength is eight bits or ten bits; the requantizer simply adapts to make the output data rate constant. Thus the compression is greater with 10 bit input, corresponding to about 2.4 to 1.

The next step is the generation of product codes as shown in Figure 8.73(a). Each entropy block is divided into two halves of 162 bytes each and loaded into the rows of the outer code RAM which holds 114 such rows, corresponding to one-twelfth of a field. When the RAM is full, it is read in columns by address mapping and 12 bytes of outer Reed–Solomon redundancy are added to every column, increasing the number of rows to 126.

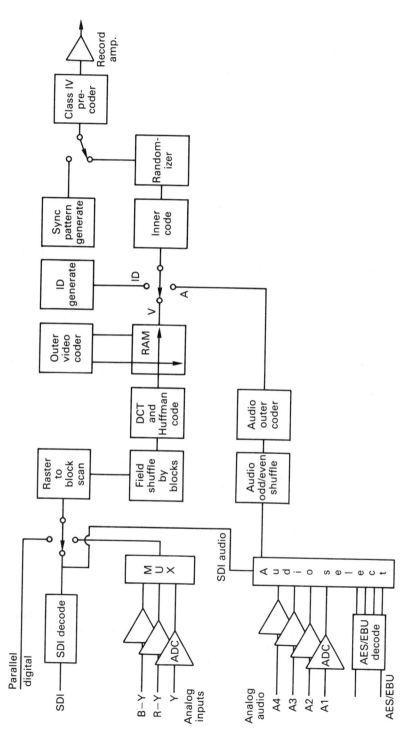

Figure 8.72 Block diagram of Digital Betacam record channel. Note that the use of data reduction makes this rather different to the block layout of full-bit formats.

(a) Video . . . 12 ECC blocks/field (2 ECC blocks/track)

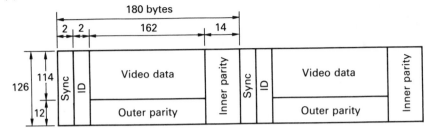

(b) Audio . . . 2 ECC blocks/ (CH. × field)

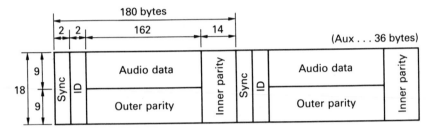

(c) Sync block

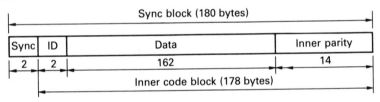

Figure 8.73 Video product codes of Digital Betacam are shown in (a); 12 of these are needed to record one field. Audio product codes are shown in (b); two of these record samples correspond to one field period. Sync blocks are common to audio and video as shown in (c). The ID code discriminates between video and audio channels.

The outer-code RAM is read out in rows once more, but this time all 126 rows are read in turn. To the contents of each row is added a 2 byte ID code and then the data plus ID bytes are turned into an inner code by the addition of 14 bytes of Reed–Solomon redundancy.

Inner codewords pass through the randomizer and are then converted to serial form for Class IV partial-response precoding. With the addition of a sync pattern of two bytes, each inner codeword becomes a sync block as shown in Figure 8.73(c). Each video block contains 126 sync blocks, preceded by a preamble and followed by a postamble. One field of video data requires twelve such blocks. Pairs of blocks are recorded simultaneously by the parallel heads of a segment. Two video blocks are recorded at the beginning of the track, and two more are recorded after the audio and tracking tones.

The audio data for each channel are separated into odd and even samples for concealment purposes and assembled in RAM into two blocks corresponding to one field period. Two 20 bit samples are stored in 5 bytes. Figure 8.73(b) shows that each block consists of 1458 bytes including auxiliary data from the AES/EBU interface, arranged as a block of 162 × 9 bytes. 100% outer code redundancy is obtained by adding 9 bytes of Reed–Solomon check bytes to each column of the blocks.

The inner codes for the audio blocks are produced by the same circuitry as the video inner codes on a time-shared basis. The resulting sync blocks are identical in size and differ only in the provision of different ID codes. The randomizer and precoder are also shared. It will be seen from Figure 8.71 that there are three segments in a field and that the position of an audio sector corresponding to a particular audio channel is different in each segment. This means that damage due to a linear tape scratch is distributed over three audio channels instead of being concentrated in one.

Each audio product block results in 18 sync blocks. These are accommodated in audio sectors of six sync blocks each in three segments. The audio sectors are preceded by preambles and followed by postambles. Between these are edit gaps which allow each audio channel to be independently edited.

By spreading the outer codes over three different audio sectors the correction power is much improved because data from two sectors can be used to correct errors in the third.

Figure 8.74 shows the replay channel of DB. The RF signal picked up by the replay head passes first to the Class IV partial-response playback circuit in which it becomes a three-level signal as was shown in Chapter 4. The three-level signal is passed to an ADC which converts it into a digitally represented form so that the Viterbi detection can be carried out in logic circuitry. The sync detector identifies the synchronizing pattern at the beginning of each sync block and resets the block bit count. This allows the entire inner codeword of the sync block to deserialized into bytes and passed to the inner error-checker. Random errors will be corrected here, whereas burst errors will result in the block being flagged as in error.

Sync blocks are written into the de-interleave RAM with error flags where appropriate. At the end of each video sector the product code RAM will be filled, and outer code correction can be performed by reading the RAM at right angles and using the error flags to initiate correction by erasure. Following outer-code correction the RAM will contain corrected data or uncorrectable error flags which will later be used to initiate concealment.

The sync blocks can now be read from memory and assembled in pairs into entropy blocks. The entropy block is of fixed size, but contains coefficient blocks of variable length. The next step is to identify the individual coefficients and separate the luminance and colour-difference coefficients by decoding the Huffman-coded sequence. Following the assembly of coefficient sets the inverse DCT will result in pixel blocks in three components once more.

The pixel blocks are de-shuffled by mapping the write address of a field memory. When all of the tracks of a field have been decoded, the memory will contain a de-shuffled field containing either correct sample data or correction flags. By reading the memory without address mapping the de-shuffled data are then passed through the concealment circuit where flagged data are concealed by data from nearby in the same field or from a previous field. The memory readout process is buffered from the offtape timing by the RAM and as a result the timebase correction stage is inherent in the replay process. Following

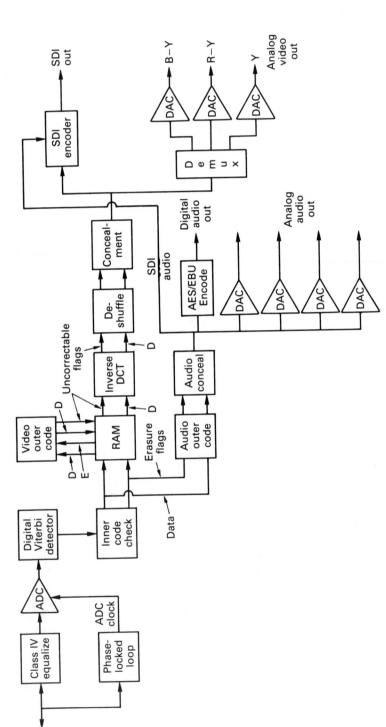

Figure 8.74 The replay channel of Digital Betacam. This differs from a full-bit system primarily in the requirement to deserialize variable-length coefficient blocks prior to the inverse DCT.

concealment the data can be output as conventional raster scan video either formatted to parallel or serial digital standards or converted to analog components.

8.38 Outline of an RDAT machine

As its name suggests, the system uses rotary heads, but there is only limited similarity to video recorders. In video recorders, each diagonal tape track stores one television field, and the switch from one track to the next takes place during the vertical interval. In a recorder with two heads, one at each side of the drum, it is necessary to wrap the tape a little more than 180 degrees around the drum so that one head begins a new track just before the previous head finishes. This constraint means that the threading mechanism of VCRs is quite complex. In RDAT, threading is simplified because the digital recording does not need to be continuous. RDAT uses the technique of time compression to squeeze continuous audio samples into intermittent recorded bursts. Blocks of samples to be recorded are written into a memory at the sampling rate, and are read out at a much faster rate when they are to be recorded. In this way the memory contents can be recorded in less time. Figure 8.75 shows that when the samples are time-compressed, recording is no longer continuous, but is interrupted by long pauses.

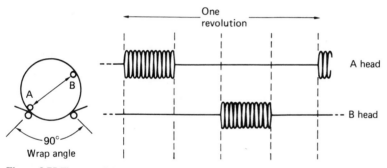

Figure 8.75 The use of time compression reduces the wrap angle necessary, at the expense of raising the frequencies in the channel.

During the pauses in recording, it is not actually necessary for the head to be in contact with the tape, and so the angle of wrap of the tape around the drum can be reduced, which makes threading easier. In RDAT the wrap angle is only 90 degrees on the commonest drum size. As the heads are 180 degrees apart, this means that for half the time neither head is in contact with the tape. The partial-wrap concept allows the threading mechanism to be very simple indeed. As the cassette is lowered into the transport, the pinch roller and several guide pins pass behind the tape. These then simply move towards the capstan and drum and threading is complete. A further advantage of partial wrap is that the friction between the tape and drum is reduced, allowing power saving in portable applications, and allowing the tape to be shuttled at high speed without the partial unthreading needed by video cassettes. In this way the player can read subcode during shuttle to facilitate rapid track access.

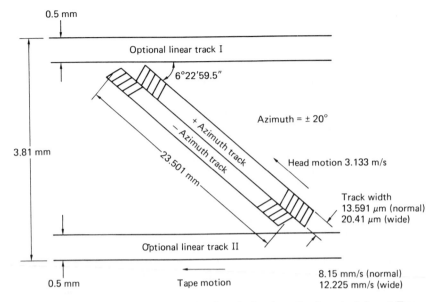

Figure 8.76 The two heads of opposite azimuth angles lay down the above track format. Tape linear speed determines track pitch.

The track pattern laid down by the rotary heads is shown in Figure 8.76. The heads rotate at 2000 rev/min in the same direction as tape motion, but because the drum axis is tilted, diagonal tracks 23.5 mm long result at an angle of just over 6 degrees to the edge. The diameter of the scanner needed is not specified, because it is the track pattern geometry which ensures interchange compatibility. For portable machines, a small scanner is desirable, whereas for professional use, a larger scanner allows additional heads to be fitted for confidence replay and editing.

There are two linear tracks, one at each edge of the tape, where they act as protection for the diagonal tracks against edge damage. Owing to the low linear tape speed the use of these edge tracks is somewhat limited.

Figure 8.77 shows a block diagram of a typical RDAT recorder, which will be used to introduce most of the major topics to be described. In order to make a recording, an analog signal is fed to an input ADC, or a direct digital input is taken from a standard interface. The incoming samples are subject to interleaving to reduce the effects of error bursts. Reading the memory at a higher rate than it was written performs the necessary time compression. Additional bytes of redundancy computed from the samples are added to the data stream to permit subsequent error correction. Subcode information is added, and the parallel-byte structure is converted to serial form and fed to the channel encoder, which combines a bit clock with the data and produces a recording signal known as a 10/8 code which is free of DC (see Chapter 4). This signal is fed to the heads via a rotary transformer to make the binary recording, which leaves the tape track with a pattern of transitions between the two magnetic states.

On replay, the transitions on the tape track induce pulses in the head, which are used to re-create the record current waveform. This is fed to the 10/8 decoder

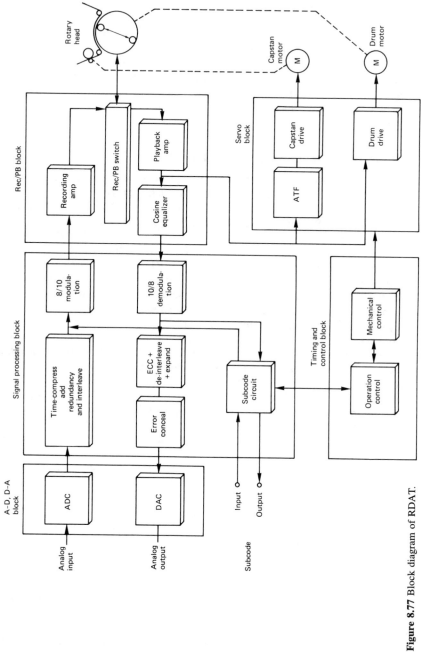

Figure 8.77 Block diagram of RDAT.

which converts it to a serial bit stream and a separate clock. The subcode data are routed to the subcode output, and the audio samples are fed into a de-interleave memory which, in addition to time-expanding the recording, functions to remove any wow or flutter due to head-to-tape speed variations. Error correction is performed partially before and partially after de-interleave. The subject of error correction is discussed in Chapter 5. The corrected output samples can be fed to DACs or to a direct digital output.

In order to keep the rotary heads following the very narrow slant tracks, alignment patterns are recorded as well as the data. The automatic track-following system processes the playback signals from these patterns to control the drum and capstan motors. Section 8.11 described the operation of the tracking system. The subcode and ID information can be used by the control logic to drive the tape to any desired location specified by the user.

8.39 Data-integrity measures for DDS

A number of measures have been devised to increase the data integrity of the basic RDAT system to make it appropriate for data storage.[2, 12]

The existing frame-based error-correction strategy of RDAT is incorporated in DDS, so that the LSI chips developed for the purpose can be used. As was shown in Chapter 5, the C1, C2 error correction can correct a defect stretching over a 2.5 mm length of track, and so the normal RDAT error correction will only fail if this limit is exceeded. The C1 and C2 codes of RDAT were designed to correct a combination of uncorrelated random and burst errors. A large number of random errors will reduce the ability of the system to correct bursts. As was noted in Chapter 4, the 8/10 channel code of RDAT shows a slight pattern sensitivity, in that not all of the channel-bit groups are DC free, and some of them are asymmetric, resulting in peak shift. In computer data, it is possible to encounter lists, tables and arrays where the same byte may be repeated. In some cases this will select one of the less optimal channel patterns regularly, and the increase in peak shift will reduce the immunity of the system to noise. In DDS the same channel coding as RDAT is used, but the data are subjected to a randomizing process before recording as was shown in Chapter 4. Randomizing is compulsory in DDS; the remaining strategies are optional. As a further data-integrity measure, DDS calculates a checksum for the data content of every track and records it in the subcode area for that track.

All error-correction systems distort the relationship between raw, or offtape, error rate and output, or residual, error rate. At low raw-error rates, the residual error rate is less. However, at some point, the performance of the error-correction system is exceeded, and the graph bends, entering a region where the residual errors can become greater than the raw errors. Clearly the system must be prevented from entering this region.

Figure 8.78 shows the correcting power of the existing RDAT system. The coding in each track can correct a burst error of 792 symbols or 6336 bits, which corresponds to a track length of 2.64 mm. Figure 8.79 shows that this corresponds to a horizontal error pattern (due to a scratch) 0.3 mm wide, and a vertical error pattern (due to excessive capstan acceleration) 2.6 mm wide. In RDAT, the main reason for errors exceeding the capacity of the existing C1, C2 system is infrequent media defects. Measurements on actual media show that

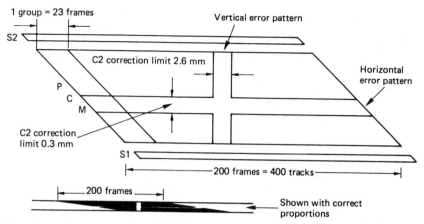

Figure 8.78 The correcting power of the C1, C2 codes of RDAT. The maximum correctable burst error length in 792 symbols (6336 bits). Since the linear recording density of DAT is 61 000 bits/inch, this is equal to 2.64 mm along a helical track. The horizontal correctable error width is 2.64 × sin 6.35° ≈ 0.3 mm, and the vertical correctable error width is 2.64 × cos 6.35° ≈ 2.6 mm. The physical defects are shown conceptually in the upper diagram, and to scale in the lower diagram.

defects tend to be roughly circular, so that if a defect is large enough to exceed the error-correction power of one frame, then it will probably affect a large number of adjacent frames, so that an additional, C3 error-correcting code working across frames would be unable to correct it. A defect of this magnitude will, however, be easily detected by read-after-write. In this case the failing frame can be recorded elsewhere until it is successfully written. The system must be able to handle groups in which the number of physical or absolute frames exceeds the logical frame count of 22. Owing to the use of azimuth recording, there has to be a physical spacing between write and read heads so that a track is not checked until after it has been side-trimmed by the next track. As a result, a defective frame will not necessarily be identified until several more have been written. In this case, it is possible to repeat the faulty frame and all of the frames which were recorded before it was decided to repeat, up to a maximum of five frames. Although this appears to be wasteful of tape, in fact it is not, because a defect large enough to cause a read-after-write failure will probably extend over several frames.

The repeated recordings are handled by an addressing system. The header at the beginning of the data area of each frame contains a logical frame number which will be correct even if some frames are repeated. The system will simply use any copy of a frame which is correctable until it has identified enough different logical frames to assemble the group. One way in which this can be done is for the system to read ahead by up to six frames after an uncorrectable frame is found, to see if it repeats, and then to resume reading.

In practice the read-after-write process can be very simply implemented. As it is only large dropouts which are being detected, it is not actually necessary to decode the replay data; a simple check of replay RF amplitude is adequate. It is obviously necessary to have extra heads on the scanner if read-after-write is to be implemented. In low-cost products based on consumer RDAT transports, these may not be available, and alternative strategies must be devised.

The next optional data-integrity strategy is N-group writing. When this is used, each group is written contiguously several times, up to a maximum of eight. The repeated groups are identical except for the absolute frame count and group count values. There is a 2 bit repeat flag in the subcode, where 1 bit set denotes that a previous group is identical to this one, and the other bit set denotes that the next group is identical. Clearly N-group writing decreases tape capacity in proportion to N, but provides protection against gross events which can be expected in uncontrolled environments, and against certain transport defects.

A third option for increasing data integrity is the use of additional redundancy. Following the 22 data/index frames in a group, an additional frame is recorded which produces codewords across the frames. Every byte in a given position in each track is used to calculate the two redundancy bytes in the same positions in the C3 tracks. If any two tracks in a group become uncorrectable by the usual C1, C2 correction, then this condition can be used as a pointer(s) to correct those tracks by erasure. Since only one frame can be corrected in this fashion, protection is provided against helical scratches caused by debris trapped on the head. Clearly the C3 redundancy is inadequate to counter two-dimensional defects; this is the job of read-after-write.

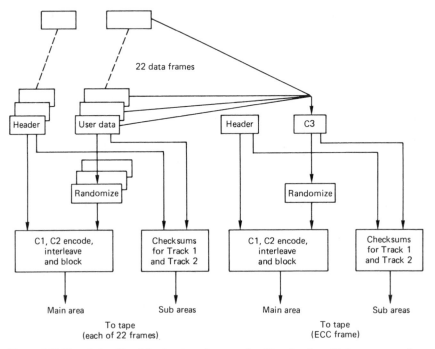

Figure 8.79 The relationship of the data-integrity strategies. User data from 22 frames are used to compute C3 redundancy. C3 and user data are randomized. Header and data checksums are recorded in the subcode area to guard against C1, C2 miscorrection.

Since there are three error-protection strategies, which are optional in any combination, there are eight ways in which a tape might have been recorded. In fact the recording strategy may change along the length of the tape. A DDS system is only considered to comply with the standard if it can read all combinations, although it is only necessary to be able to record one of the combinations to be considered standard. Figure 8.79 shows how the various data-integrity strategies interrelate.

8.40 The DCRSi format

DCRSi (Digital Cassette Recording System – incremental) is a transverse-scan rotary-head instrumentation recorder using a unique one inch cassette. The system has a transport which runs at one speed only, but the incorporation of a large RAM buffer means that any data rate from zero up to maximum can be accommodated using incremental transport operation. The transverse-scan transport is ideally suited to incremental operation as the tape can remain out of contact with the rotating heads until data transfer is required.

The 1.5 inch headwheel is fitted with six heads or twelve heads, depending on the data rate required, which are set to ±15 degrees of azimuth. The track pitch is slightly smaller than the track width to ensure overwrite. Figure 8.80 shows the

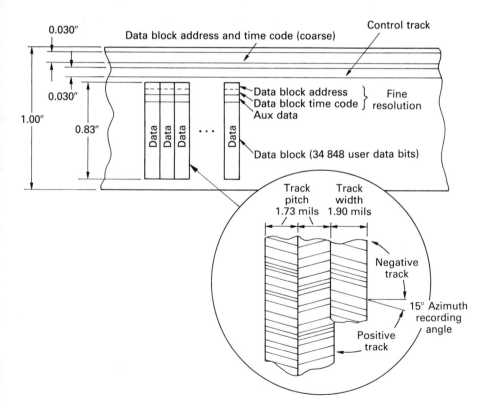

Figure 8.80 The track layout of DCRSi includes a block address track so that individual transverse tracks can be located. Note the use of azimuth recording.

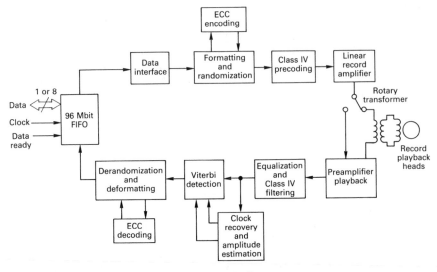

Figure 8.81 Block diagram of DCRSi. See text for details.

tape track layout. In addition to the control track needed by the transport there is a data block address track which enables individual transverse tracks to be located on replay. The track also records a form of timecode so that data may be located by time.

Figure 8.81 shows a block diagram of the system. A product code is not used; instead the system relies on very large interleave. Each 81 bytes of user data is formed into an R–S codeword by the addition of four redundancy bytes. 54 such codewords are interleaved to form one track. The data are randomized and then subject to a Class IV partial-response precoding step prior to recording. The record amplifier is linear and has pre-emphasis to counteract recording-head losses. Tracking signals according to Section 8.12 are added to the record waveform.

On replay the Class IV equalization step is performed, resulting in a three-level eye pattern. The three-level signal is sampled by a clock recovered from the channel and quantized for digital Viterbi detection. Data are derandomized prior to error correction.

Cassette	Tape thickness (μm)	Tape length (m)	Play time (min)
Small	16	190	8
	13	225	9
Medium	16	587	24
	13	708	29
Large	16	1311	55
	13	1622	68

Figure 8.82 Recording times available in MIL-2179 at 240 Mbits/sec.

8.41 MIL-STD 2179

MIL-STD 2179 is an instrumentation recording format based on the technology of the D-1 DVTR. The cassettes are standard D-1 using 850 oersted tape and the format is designed to achieve a user data rate of up to 240 Mbits/sec. Various recording times are available according to the size of cassette and tape thickness; these are shown in Figure 8.82.

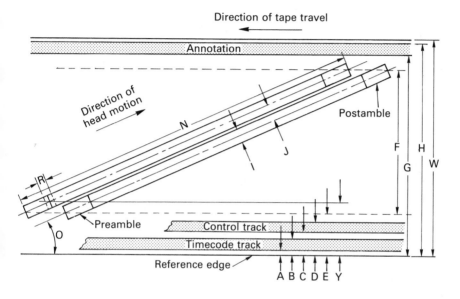

		Dimensions (mm)	
		Nominal	Tolerance
A	Timecode track lower edge	0.2	(+0.1)
B	Timecode track upper edge	0.7	(+0.1)
C	Control track lower edge	1.0	(+0.1)
D	Control track upper edge	1.5	(+0.1)
E	Digital data area lower edge	1.8	(derived)
F	Digital data area width	16	(derived)
G	Auxiliary track lower edge	18.1	(+0.15)
H	Auxiliary track upper edge	18.8	(+0.2)
I	Helical track width	0.04	(+0/−0.005)
J	Helical track pitch	0.045	basic
N	Helical track total length	170	(derived)
P	Servo control head location	−92.3 to +118.7	(+0.1)
R	Sector-recording tolerance		(±0.1)
T	Longitudinal track sync tolerance		(±0.1)
O	Track angle	(5.4005°)	(basic)
W	Tape width	19.01	(+0.015)
Y	Reference point	1.81	(basic)

Figure 8.83 Track layout of MIL-2179 format. Transport design is not specified.

Figure 8.83 shows the tape track layout. There is a control track, a timecode track and annotation track. Unlike the DVTR formats, 2179 specifies the IRIG timecode format. The format specifies only the tape track dimensions and contents, leaving manufacturers to use any drum design which meets the specifications. A 240 Mbit/sec machine will need the data to be distributed over

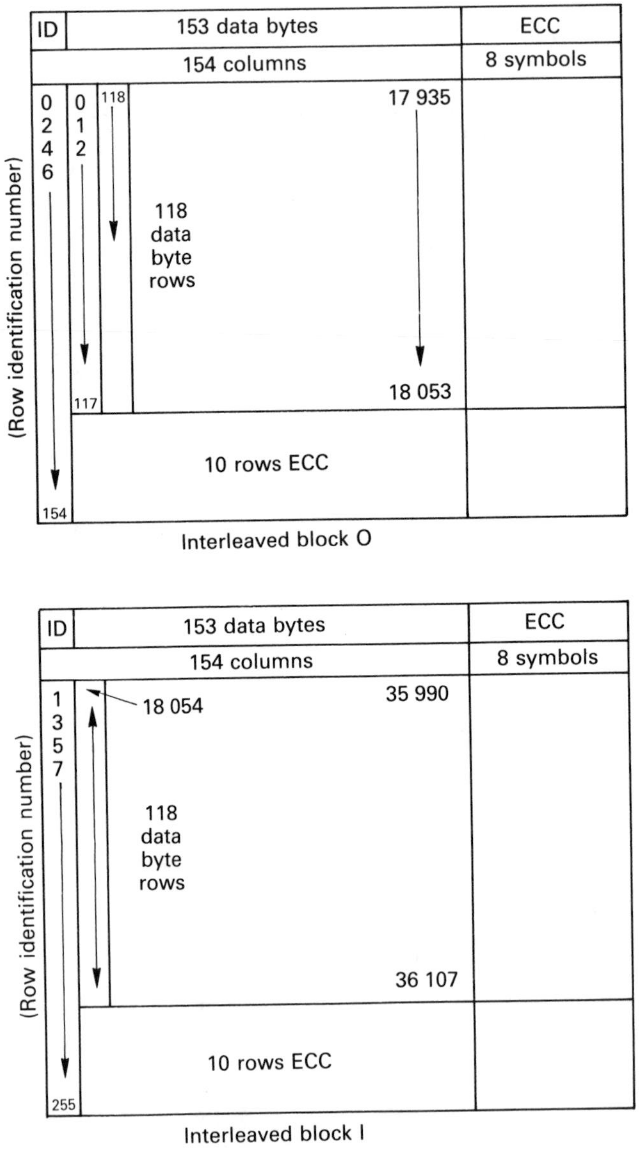

Interleaved block O

Interleaved block I

Note: Input data bytes are sequential from 0 to 36 107
and are read into the arrays in columns

Figure 8.84 The product codes of MIL-2179. See text.

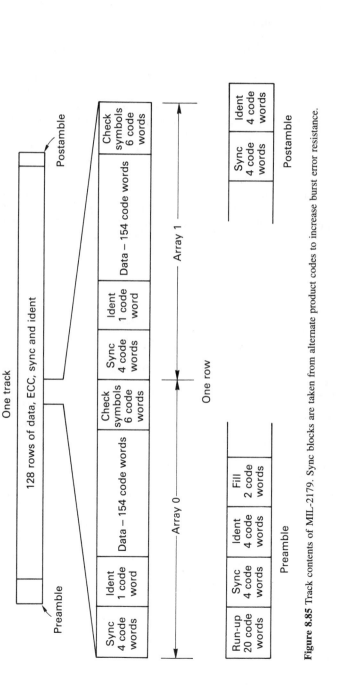

Figure 8.85 Track contents of MIL-2179. Sync blocks are taken from alternate product codes to increase burst error resistance.

four heads in order to meet the bandwidth requirement. However, data rates of half or a quarter of that figure could be supported using drums having two heads or one head. Changing the tape linear speed in proportion to the data rate will require different helix angles to meet the track-angle specification. However, this approach means that a standard tape can be played on any machine at a data rate determined by the machine. Data are not shuffled between tracks; each track contains a contiguous period of input data.

Input data corresponding to one track are formed into a pair of product codes as shown in Figure 8.84. Outer codes consist of 118 data bytes and 10 bytes of R–S redundancy. Inner codes consist of 154 bytes of data/outer redundancy and 6 bytes of R–S redundancy. On reading the product arrays to tape, successive inner codes are taken from alternate product blocks in order to interleave them. Figure 8.85 shows that a sync pattern and ident symbol are appended to each inner code to form a sync block. There are 256 such sync blocks in each track, with track preambles and postambles as shown. The two-way interleave means that a burst error twenty sync blocks long in each track is fully correctable. This corresponds to over 3000 bytes of data.

The data are recorded using a low-disparity 8/9 group code which is designed to control channel DC content. There are 70 DC-free patterns, but the remainder of the 256 data combinations can be represented by one of two candidate codes having opposite CDS (see Chapter 4), the candidates are chosen to maintain the smallest code DSV. Synchronization is achieved using channel bit patterns which are not in the code book.

References

1. WATKINSON, J.R., The technology of the Ampex DCRSi. *IERE Conf. Publ. No. 79*, pp. 159–166 (1988)
2. LÜTZELER, J., An experimental HDTV cassette recorder. *18th ITS Symposium Record*, pp. 302–316 (Montreux, 1993)
3. HITOMI, A. and TAKI, T., Servo technology of R-DAT. *IEEE Trans. Consum. Electron.*, **CE-32**, 425–432 (1986)
4. COLEMAN, C.C., U.S. Patent No. 4,432,026 (1981)
5. OLDERSHAW, R., Design of an automatic scan tracking system for a D-2 recorder. *IEE Conf. Pub. No. 293*, pp. 395–398 (1988)
6. ITOH, F., SHIBA, H., HAYAMA, M. and SATOH, T., Magnetic tape and cartridge of R-DAT. *IEEE Trans. Consum. Electron.*, **CE-32**, 442–452 (1986)
7. RYAN, D.M., Mechanical considerations in the design of a digital video cassette recorder. Presented at International Broadcasting Convention, Brighton, 1988 *IEE Conf. Pub. 293*, pp. 387–390 (1988)
8. ROBINSON, J.F., *Videotape recording*, Chapter 8. Oxford: Focal Press (1978)
9. BRUSH, R., Video data shuffling for the 4:2:2 DVTR. Presented at 20th SMPTE Television Conf. (Chicago 1986). *SMPTE J.*, **95**, 1009–1016 (1986)
10. HUCKFIELD, D., SATO, N. and SATO, I., Digital Betacam – The application of state of the art technology to the development of an affordable component DVTR. *Record of 18th ITS*, pp. 180–199 (Montreux, 1993)
11. CREED, D. and KAMINAGA, K., Digital compression strategies for video tape recorders in studio applications. *Record of 18th ITS*, pp. 291–301 (Montreux, 1993)
12. ODAKA, K., TAN, E.T. and VERMEULEN, B., Designing a data storage format for digital audio tape (DAT). Hewlett-Packard Ltd (1988)

Chapter 9

Magnetic disk drives

Disk drives came into being as random-access file-storage devices for digital computers. They were prominent in early experiments with digital audio, but their cost at that time was too great in comparison with emerging tape technology. However, the explosion in personal computers has fuelled demand for low-cost high-density magnetic disk drives and the rapid access offered is increasingly finding applications in digital audio and video. Magneto-optic (MO) disks are considered in Chapter 10.

9.1 Types of disk drive

Once the operating speed of computers began to take strides forward, it became evident that a single processor could be made to jump between several different programs so fast that they all appeared to be executing simultaneously, a process known as multiprogramming. Computer memory remains more expensive than other types of mass storage, and so it has never been practicable to store every program or data file necessary within the computer memory. In practice some kind of storage medium is necessary where only programs which are running or are about to run are in the memory, and the remainder are stored on the medium. Punched cards, paper tape and magnetic tape are all computer media, but suffer from the same disadvantage of slow access. A derivative of the rotating drum,[1] the disk drive was developed specifically to offer rapid random access by storing data on a circular track. In floppy disks, the magnetic medium is flexible, and the head touches it. This restricts the rotational speed. In hard-disk drives, the disk is rigid and rotates at several thousand rev/min so that the head-to-disk speed is of the order of 100 miles per hour. At this speed no contact can be tolerated, and it was shown in Section 3.6 that the head flies on a boundary layer of air turning with the disk at a height measured in micro-inches. The longest time it is necessary to wait to access a given data block is a few milliseconds. To increase the storage capacity of the drive without a proportional increase in cost, many concentric tracks are recorded on the disk surface, and the head is mounted on a positioner which can rapidly bring the head to any desired track. Such a machine is termed a moving-head disk drive. The positioner was usually designed so that it could remove the heads away from the disk completely, which could thus be exchanged. The exchangeable-pack moving-head disk drive became the standard for mainframe and minicomputers for a long time, and usually at least two were furnished so that important data could be 'backed up' or copied to a second disk for safe keeping.

Later came the so-called Winchester technology disks, where the disk and positioner formed a sealed unit which allowed increased storage capacity but precluded exchange of the disk pack. This led to the development of high-speed tape drives which could be used as security backup storage.

Disk-drive development has been phenomenally rapid. The first flying-head disks were about three feet across.[2] Subsequently disk sizes of 14, 8, 5¼, 3½ inches and smaller were developed.[3] Despite the reduction in size, the storage capacity is not compromised because the recording density has increased and continues to increase. In fact there is an advantage in making a drive smaller because the moving parts are then lighter and travel a shorter distance, improving access time.

9.2 Disk terminology

In all technologies there are specialist terms, and those relating to disks will be explained here. Figure 9.1 shows a typical multiplatter disk pack in conceptual

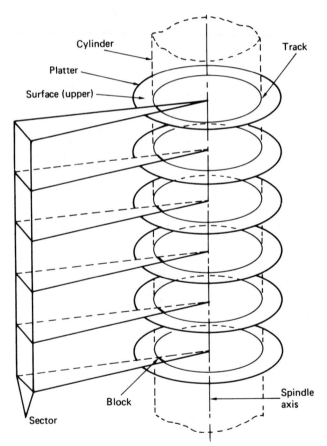

Figure 9.1 Disk terminology. Surface: one side of a platter. Track: path described on a surface by a fixed head. Cylinder: imaginary shape intersecting all surfaces at tracks of the same radius. Sector: angular subdivision of pack. Block: that part of a track within one sector. Each block has a unique cylinder, head and sector address.

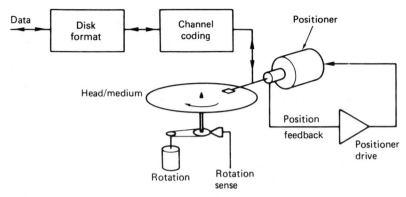

Figure 9.2 The main subsystems of a typical disk drive.

form. Given a particular set of coordinates (cylinder, head, sector), known as a disk physical address, one unique data block is defined. A common block capacity is 512 bytes. The subdivision into sectors is sometimes omitted for special applications. Figure 9.2 introduces the essential subsystems of a disk drive which will be discussed.

9.3 Structure of disk

The floppy disk is actually made using tape technology, and will be discussed later. Rigid disks are made from aluminium alloy. Magnetic oxide types use an aluminium oxide substrate, or undercoat, giving a flat surface to which the oxide binder can adhere. Later metallic disks are electroplated with the magnetic medium. In both cases the surface finish must be extremely good owing to the very small flying height of the head. Figure 9.3 shows a cross-section of a typical multiplatter disk pack. As the head-to-disk speed and recording density are functions of track radius, the data are confined to the outer areas of the disks to minimize the change in these parameters. As a result, the centre of the pack is often an empty well. In fixed (i.e. non-interchangeable) disks the drive motor is often installed in the centre well. Removable packs usually seat on a taper to ensure concentricity and elaborate fixing mechanisms are needed on large packs to prevent the pack from working loose in operation. Smaller packs are held to the spindle by a permanent magnet, and a lever mechanism is incorporated in the cartridge to assist their removal.

9.4 Reading and writing

Chapter 3 showed how disk heads are made. The presence of the air film between head and disk causes severe separation loss, and peak shift distortion is a major problem. The flying height of the head varies with the radius of the disk track, and it is difficult to provide accurate equalization of the replay channel because of this. The write current is often controlled as a function of track radius so that the changing reluctance of the air gap does not change the resulting record flux. Automatic gain control (AGC) is used on replay to compensate for changes in signal amplitude from the head.

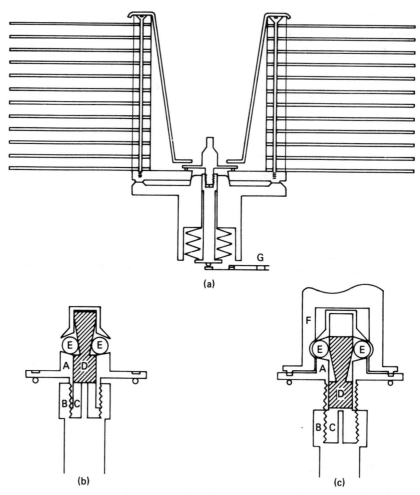

Figure 9.3 (a) Typical construction of multiplatter exchangeable pack. The pack weighs about 20 lb (9 kg) and turns at up to 3600 rpm. The hold-down mechanism must be faultlessly reliable, to resist the forces involved, and must centre the pack precisely to allow proper track alignment and balance. In (b) the hold-down screw A is fully engaged with the lockshaft B, and the pin C lifts the ramp D, retracting the balls E. In (c) the hold-down screw is withdrawn from the lockshaft, which retracts, causing the ramp to force the balls into engagement with the cover F. The lockshaft often operates a switch to inform the logic that a pack is present (G).

Equalization may be used on recording in the form of pre-compensation, which moves recorded transitions in such a way as to oppose the effects of peak shift in addition to any replay equalization used. This was discussed in Chapter 3.

Early disks used FM coding, which was easy to decode, but had a poor density ratio. The invention of MFM revolutionized hard disks, and was at one time universal. Further progress led to run-length-limited codes such as 2/3 and 2/7 which had a high density ratio without sacrificing the large jitter window

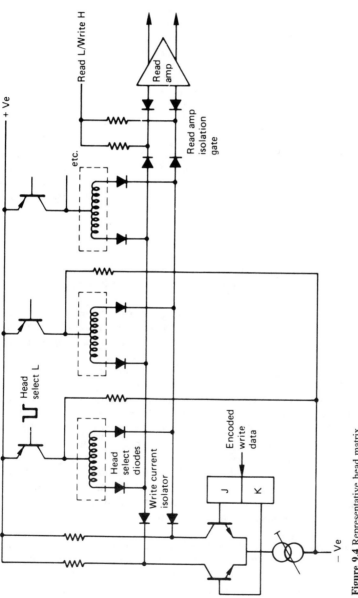

Figure 9.4 Representative head matrix.

necessary to reject peak shift distortion. Partial response is also suited to disks, but is not yet in common use.

Typical drives have several heads, but with the exception of special-purpose parallel-transfer machines for digital video or instrumentation work, only one head will be active at any one time, which means that the read and write circuitry can be shared between the heads. Figure 9.4 shows that in one approach the centre-tapped heads are isolated by connecting the centre tap to a negative voltage, which reverse-biases the matrix diodes. The centre tap of the selected head is made positive. When reading, a small current flows through both halves of the head winding, as the diodes are forward-biased. Opposing currents in the head cancel, but read signals due to transitions on the medium can pass through the forward-biased diodes to become differential signals on the matrix bus. During writing, the current from the write generator passes alternately through the two halves of the head coil. Further isolation is necessary to prevent the write-current-induced voltages from destroying the read preamplifier input. Alternatively, FET analog switches may be used for head selection.

The read channel usually incorporates AGC, which will be overridden by the control logic between data blocks in order to search for address marks, which are short unmodulated areas of track. As a block preamble is entered, the AGC will be enabled to allow a rapid gain adjustment.

The high bit rates of disk drives, due to the speed of the medium, mean that peak detection in the replay channel is usually by differentiation. The detected peaks are then fed to the data separator.

9.5 Moving the heads

The servo system required to move the heads rapidly between tracks, and yet hold them in place accurately for data transfer, is a fascinating and complex piece of engineering.

In exchangeable-pack drives, the disk positioner moves on a straight axis which passes through the spindle. The head carriage will usually have preloaded ball races which run on rails mounted on the bed of the machine, although some drives use plain sintered bushes sliding on polished rods.

Motive power on early disk drives was hydraulic, but this soon gave way to moving-coil drive, because of the small moving mass which this technique permits. Lower-cost units use a conventional electric motor, as shown in Figure 9.5, which drives the carriage through steel wires wound around it, or via a split metal band which is shaped to allow both ends to be fixed to the carriage despite the centre making a full turn around the motor shaft. The final possibility is a coarse-threaded shaft or leadscrew which engages with a nut on the carriage. In very low-cost drives, the motor will be a stepping motor, and the positions of the tracks will be determined by the natural detents of the stepping motor. This has an advantage for portable drives, because a stepping motor will remain detented without power. Moving-coil actuators require power to stay on track.

When a drive is track-following, it is said to be detented, in fine mode or in linear mode depending on the manufacturer. When a drive is seeking from one track to another, it can be described as being in coarse mode or velocity mode. These are the two major operating modes of the servo.

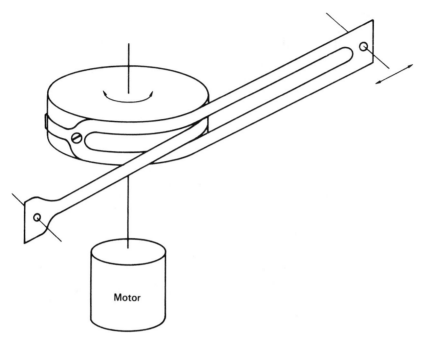

Figure 9.5 A low-cost linear positioner can be obtained using a drum and split-band drive, shown here, or with flexible wire. The ends of the band are fixed to the carriage.

With the exception of stepping-motor-driven carriages, the servo system needs positional feedback from a transducer of some kind. The purpose of the transducer will be one or more of the following:

(1) To count the number of cylinders crossed during a seek.
(2) To generate a signal proportional to carriage velocity.
(3) To generate a position error proportional to the distance from the centre of the desired track.

Sometimes the same transducer is used for all of these, and so transducers are best classified by their operating principle rather than by their function in a particular drive.

The simplest transducer is the magnetic moving-coil type, with its complementary equivalent the moving-magnet type. Both generate a voltage proportional to velocity, and can give no positional information, but no precise alignment other than a working clearance is necessary. These devices are usually called tachos.

Optical transducers consist of gratings, one fixed on the machine base and one on the carriage. The relative position of the two controls the amount of light which can shine through onto a sensor. Reference to Figure 9.6 will show that there are basically two categories of grating transducer, the moiré-fringe device and the parallel-bar type.

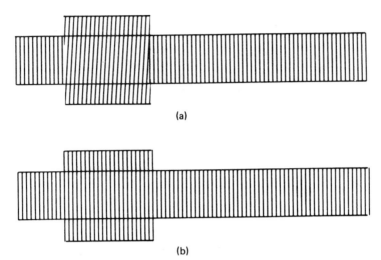

(a)

(b)

Figure 9.6 Glass-grating transducers work by modulating a light beam with the interaction of moving and stationary bars. It is vital that these units are correctly adjusted both mechanically and electrically, and this is often a time-consuming process. (a) Moiré-grating transducer has non-parallel bars, and the resulting fringe patterns generate a sinusoidal output. (b) Parallel-bar grating transducer generates triangular waveform.

In a moiré-fringe transducer, the two sets of bars are not parallel, and relative movement causes a fringe pattern which travels at right angles to the direction of carriage motion. This results in sinusoidal modulation of the light beam. In the parallel-bar type, the moving grating acts as a simple shutter, and the output is a triangle wave. In both types, the spacing between the two parts of the grating is critical. Both types give the same performance for counting cylinder crossings, as the waveform is not of any consequence for that application. The choice of which type to use is determined by whether positional information for track following or velocity feedback for seeking is needed. The slope of a sine wave is steeper in the zero region than an equivalent triangle wave, and so the moiré type is preferable for position sensing. Conversely, the constant slope of the triangle wave is easier to differentiate to give a velocity signal.

As the differential of a triangle wave changes sign twice per cycle, a two-phase optical system is often used to give a continuous output. The stationary grating has two sets of bars with a 90 degree phase relationship, and the resultant two output signals are invariably called sin and cos even if they are triangular waves. Figure 9.7 shows that the two waveforms and their complements are differentiated, and then the four differentials are selected at times when they have no sign change. This process of commutation is achieved by analog switches controlled by comparators looking for points where the input waveforms cross. The result is a clean signal proportional to carriage velocity.

Where one transducer has to generate all three signals, the moiré type is better as the position sensing is more important, and ripple on the velocity signal has to be accepted.

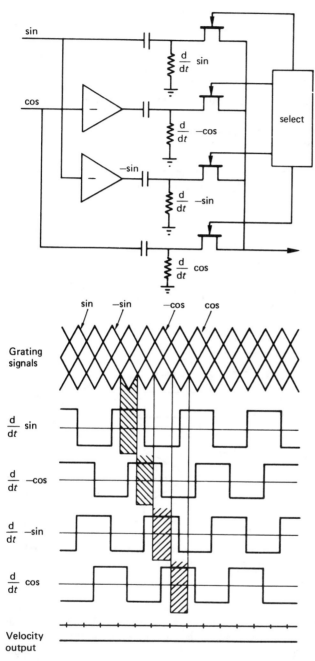

Figure 9.7 Optical velocity transducer. Four quadrature signals are produced from the two-phase transducer. Each of these is differentiated, and the four derivatives are selected one at a time by analog switches. This process results in a continuous analog output voltage proportional to the slope of the transducer waveform, which is itself proportional to carriage velocity. In some drives one of the transducer signals may also be used to count cylinder crossings during a seek and to provide a position error for detenting.

Optical transducers usually contain additional light paths to aid carriage-travel limit detection and to provide an absolute reference to the incremental counting.

9.6 Controlling a seek

A seek is a process where the positioner moves from one cylinder to another. The speed with which a seek can be completed is a major factor in determining the access time of the drive. The main parameter controlling the carriage during a seek is the cylinder difference, which is obtained by subtracting the current cylinder address from the desired cylinder address. The cylinder difference will be a signed binary number representing the number of cylinders to be crossed to reach the target, direction being indicated by the sign. The cylinder difference is loaded into a counter which is decremented each time a cylinder is crossed. The counter drives a DAC which generates an analog voltage proportional to the cylinder difference. As Figure 9.8 shows, this voltage, known as the scheduled velocity, is compared with the output of the carriage-velocity tacho. Any difference between the two results in a velocity error which drives the carriage to cancel the error. As the carriage approaches the target cylinder, the cylinder difference becomes smaller, with the result that the run-in to the target is critically damped to eliminate overshoot.

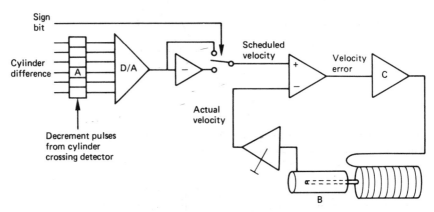

Figure 9.8 Control of carriage velocity by cylinder difference. The cylinder difference is loaded into the difference counter A. A digital-to-analog converter generates an analog voltage from the cylinder difference, known as the scheduled velocity. This is compared with the actual velocity from the transducer B in order to generate the velocity error which drives the servo amplifier C.

Figure 9.9(a) shows graphs of scheduled velocity, actual velocity and motor current with respect to cylinder difference during a seek. In the first half of the seek, the actual velocity is less than the scheduled velocity, causing a large velocity error which saturates the amplifier and provides maximum carriage acceleration. In the second half of the graphs, the scheduled velocity is falling below the actual velocity, generating a negative velocity error which drives a reverse current through the motor to slow the carriage down. The scheduled deceleration slope can clearly not be steeper than the saturated acceleration slope.

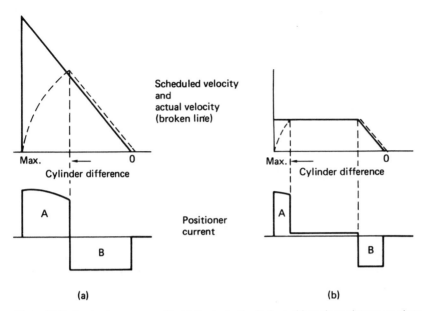

Figure 9.9 In the simple arrangement in (a) the dissipation in the positioner is continuous, causing a heating problem. The effect of limiting the scheduled velocity above a certain cylinder difference is apparent in (b) where heavy positioner current only flows during acceleration and deceleration. During the plateau of the velocity profile, only enough current to overcome friction is necessary. The curvature of the acceleration slope is due to the back-EMF of the positioner motor.

Areas A and B on the graph will be about equal, as the kinetic energy put into the carriage has to be taken out. The current through the motor is continuous, and would result in a heating problem, so to counter this the DAC is made non-linear so that above a certain cylinder difference no increase in scheduled velocity will occur. This results in the graph of Figure 9.9(b). The actual velocity graph is called a velocity profile. It consists of three regions: acceleration, where the system is saturated; a constant velocity plateau, where the only power needed is to overcome friction; and the scheduled run-in to the desired cylinder. Dissipation is only significant in the first and last regions.

A consequence of the critically damped run-in to the target cylinder is that short seeks are slow. Sometimes further non-linearity is introduced into the velocity scheduler to speed up short seeks. The velocity profile becomes a piecewise linear approximation to a curve by using non-linear feedback. Figure 9.10 shows the principle of an analog shaper or profile generator. Later machines will compute the curve in microprocessor sofware or use a PROM lookup table.

In small disk drives the amplifier may be linear in all modes of operation, resembling an audio power amplifier. Larger units may employ pulse-width-modulated drive to reduce dissipation, or even switched-mode amplifiers with inductive flywheel circuits (see Chapter 6). These switching systems can generate appreciable electromagnetic radiation, but this is of no consequence as they are only active during a seek. In track-following mode, the amplifier reverts to linear mode; hence the use of the term linear to mean track-following mode.

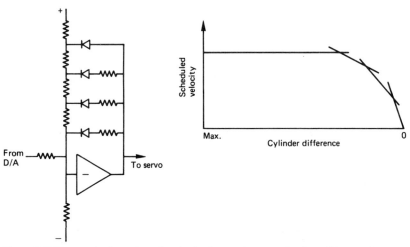

Figure 9.10 The use of voltage-dependent feedback around an operational amplifier permits a piecewise linear approximation to a curved velocity profile. This has the effect of speeding up short seeks without causing a dissipation problem on long seeks. The circuit is referred to as a shaper.

The input of the servo amplifier normally has a number of analog switches which select the appropriate signals according to the mode of the servo. As the output of the position transducer is a triangle or sine wave, the sense of the position feedback has to be inverted on odd-numbered cylinders to allow detenting on the negative slope. Sometimes a separate transducer is used for head retraction only. A typical analog system is shown in Figure 9.11.

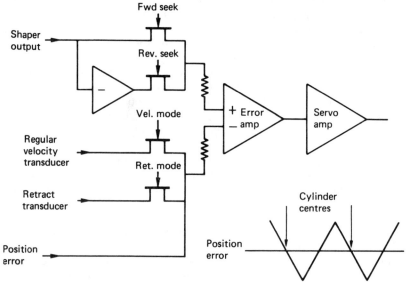

Figure 9.11 A typical servo amplifier input stage. In velocity mode the shaper and the velocity transducer drive the error amp. In track-following mode the position error is the only input.

9.7 Rotation

The rotation subsystems of disk drives will now be covered. The track-following accuracy of a drive positioner will be impaired if there is bearing runout, and so the spindle bearings are made to a high degree of precision. On larger drives, squirrel-cage induction motors are used to drive the spindle through a belt. The different motor speeds resulting from 50 Hz and 60 Hz supplies are accommodated by changing the relative sizes of the pulleys. As recording density increases, the size of drives has come down, and the smaller units incorporate brushless DC motors with integral speed control. In exchangeable-pack drives, some form of braking is usually provided to slow down the pack rapidly for convenient removal. This can be done by feeding DC to an AC motor, which causes it to act as an eddy-current brake. In battery-powered equipment, regenerative braking of disk packs can be used to return some of the kinetic energy of the disk to the battery.

In order to control reading and writing, the drive control circuitry needs to know which cylinder the heads are on, and which sector is currently under the head. Sector information is often obtained from a sensor which detects slots cut in the hub of the disk. These can be optical, variable-reluctance or eddy-current devices. Pulses from the transducer increment the sector counter, which is reset by a double slot once per revolution. The desired sector address is loaded into a register, which is compared with the sector counter. When the two match, the desired sector has been found. This process is referred to as a search, and usually takes place after a seek. Having found the correct physical place on the disk, the next step is to read the header associated with the data block to confirm that the disk address contained there is the same as the desired address.

9.8 Cooling and filtration

Rotation of a disk pack at speed results in heat build-up through air resistance. This heat must be carried away. A further important factor with exchangeable pack drives is to keep the disk area free from contaminants which might lodge between the head and the disk and cause the destructive phenomenon known as a head crash, where debris builds up on the head until it ploughs the disk surface.

The cooling and filtration systems are usually combined. Air is drawn through an absolute filter, passed around the disk, and exhausted, sometimes cooling the positioner motor and circuitry on the way. This full-flow system is fine for environmentally controlled computer rooms, but for the office or studio environment, a closed-circuit filtration system can be used, where the same air goes round the pack and through the blower and filter endlessly. This results in extended filter life in adverse environments, but requires a heat exchanger in the loop to carry away the heat developed by disk rotation. In many drives, particularly the smaller units, the disk rotation itself is used as the source of airflow.

9.9 Servo-surface disks

One of the major problems to be overcome in the development of high-density disk drives was that of keeping the heads on track despite changes of temperature. The very narrow tracks used in digital recording have similar dimensions to the amount a disk will expand as it warms up. The cantilevers and the drive base all expand and contract, conspiring with thermal drift in the

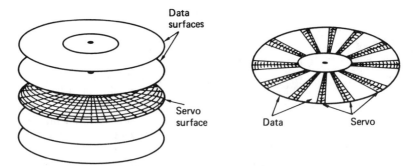

Figure 9.12 In a multiplatter disk pack, one surface is dedicated to servo information. In a single platter, the servo information is embedded in the data on the same surfaces.

cylinder transducer to limit track pitch. The breakthrough in disk density came with the introduction of the servo-surface drive. The position error in a servo-surface drive is derived from a head reading the disk itself. This virtually eliminates thermal effects on head positioning and allows great increases in storage density.

In a multiplatter drive, one surface of the pack holds servo information which is read by the servo head. In a ten-platter pack this means that 5% of the medium area is lost, but this is unimportant since the increase in density allowed is enormous. Using one side of a single-platter cartridge for servo information would be unacceptable as it represents 50% of the medium area, so in this case the servo information can be interleaved with sectors on the data surfaces. This is known as an embedded-servo technique. These two approaches are contrasted in Figure 9.12.

The servo surface is written at the time of disk-pack manufacture, and the disk drive can only read it. Writing the servo surface has nothing to do with disk formatting, which affects the data storage areas only.

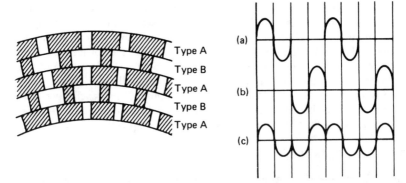

Figure 9.13 The servo surface is divided into two types of track, A and B, which are out of phase by 180 degrees and are recorded with reverse polarity with respect to one another. Waveform (a) results when the servo head is entirely above a type A track, and waveform (b) results from reading solely a type B track. When the servo head is correctly positioned with one-half of its magnetic circuit over each track, waveform (c) results.

The key to the operation of the servo surface is the special magnetic pattern recorded on it. In a typical servo surface, recorded pairs of transitions, known as dibits, are separated by a space. Figure 9.13 shows that there are two kinds of track. On an A track, the first transition of the pair will cause a positive pulse on reading, whereas on a B track, the first pulse will be negative. In addition the A-track dibits are shifted by one half cycle with respect to the B-track dibits. The width of the magnetic circuit in the servo head is equal to the width of a servo track. During track following, the correct position for the servo head is with half of each type of track beneath it. The read/write heads will then be centred on their respective data tracks. Figure 9.14 illustrates this relationship.

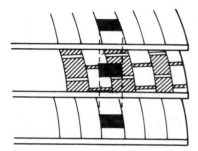

Figure 9.14 When the servo head is straddling two servo tracks, the data heads are correctly aligned with their respective tracks.

The amplitude of dibits from A tracks with respect to the amplitude of dibits from B tracks depends on the relative areas of the servo head which are exposed to the respective tracks. As the servo head has only one magnetic circuit, it will generate a composite signal whose components will change differentially as the position of the servo head changes. Figure 9.15 shows several composite waveforms obtained at different positions of the servo head. The composite waveform is processed by using the first positive and negative pulses to generate a clock. From this clock are derived sampling signals which permit only the second positive and second negative pulses to pass. The resultant waveform has a DC component which after filtering gives a voltage proportional to the distance from the centre of the data tracks. The position error reaches a maximum when the servo head is entirely above one type of servo track, and further movement causes it to fall. The next time the position error falls to zero will be at the centre line of the adjacent cylinder.

Cylinders with even addresses (LSB = 0) will be those where the servo head is detented between an A track and a B track. Cylinders with odd addresses will be those where the head is between a B track and an A track. It can be seen from Figure 9.15 that the sense of the position error becomes reversed on every other cylinder. Accordingly, an inverter has to be switched into the track-following feedback loop in order to detent on odd cylinders. This inversion is controlled by the LSB of the desired cylinder address supplied at the beginning of a seek, such that the sense of the feedback will be correct when the heads arrive at the target cylinder.

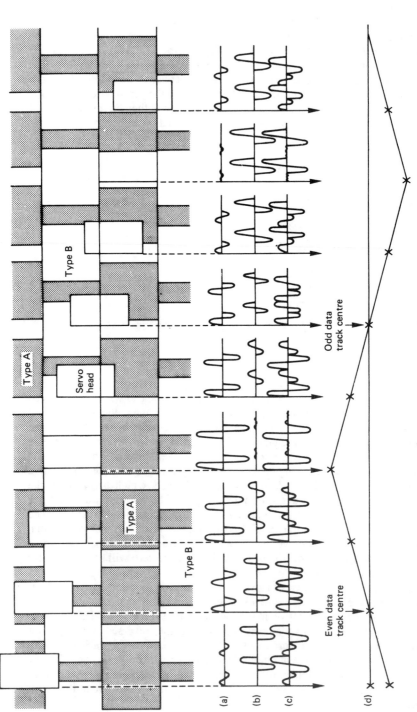

Figure 9.15 Waveforms resulting from several positions of the servo head with respect to the disk. In (a) and (b) are the two components of the waveforms, whose relative amplitudes are controlled by the relative areas of the servo head exposed to the two types of servo track. Because the servo head has only one magnetic circuit, these waveforms are not observed in practice, but are summed together, resulting in the composite waveforms shown in (c). By comparing the magnitudes of the second positive and second negative peaks in the composite waveforms, a position error signal is generated, as shown in (d).

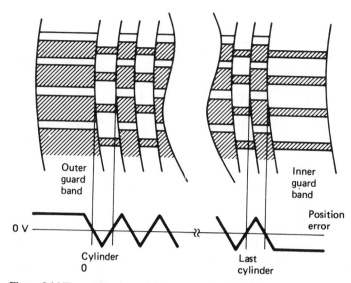

Figure 9.16 The working area of the servo surface is defined by the inner and outer guard bands, in which the position error reaches its maximum value.

Seeking across the servo surface results in the position-error signal rising and falling in a sawtooth. This waveform can be used to count down the cylinder difference counter which controls the seek. As with any cyclic transducer there is the problem of finding the absolute position. This difficulty is overcome by making all servo tracks outside cylinder 0 type A, and all servo tracks inside the innermost cylinder type B. These areas of identical track are called guard bands, and Figure 9.16 shows the relationship between the position error and the guard bands. During a head load, the servo head generates a constant maximum positive position error in the outer guard band. This drives the carriage forward until the position error first falls to zero. This, by definition, is cylinder zero. Some drives, however, load by driving the heads across the surface until the inner guard band is found, and then perform a full-length reverse seek to cylinder zero.

9.10 Soft sectoring

It has been seen that a position error and a cylinder count can be derived from the servo surface, eliminating the cylinder transducer. The carriage velocity could also be derived from the slope of the position error, but there would then be no velocity feedback in the guard bands or during retraction, and so some form of velocity transducer is still necessary.

As there are exactly the same number of dibits or tribits on every track, it is possible to describe the rotational position of the disk simply by counting them. All that is needed is a unique pattern of missing dibits once per revolution to act as an index point, and the sector transducer can also be eliminated.

Unlike the read-data circuits, the servo-head circuits are active during a seek as well as when track following, and have to be protected against interference from switched-mode positioner drivers. The main problem is detecting index, where noise could cause a 'missing' dibit to be masked. There are two solutions available: a preamplifier can be built into the servo-head cantilever, or driver switching can be inhibited when index is expected.

The advantage of deriving the sector count from the servo surface is that the number of sectors on the disk can be varied. Any number of sectors can be accommodated by feeding the dibit-rate signal through a programmable divider, so the same disk and drive can be used in numerous different applications.

In a non-servo-surface disk, the write clock is usually derived from a crystal oscillator. As the disk speed can vary owing to supply fluctuations, a tolerance gap has to be left at the end of each block to cater for the highest anticipated speed, to prevent overrun into the next block on a write. In a servo-surface drive, the write clock is obtained by multiplying the dibit-rate signal with a phase-locked loop. The write clock is then always proportional to disk speed, and recording density will be constant.

Most servo-surface drives have an offset facility, where a register written by the controller drives a DAC which injects a small voltage into the track-following loop. The action of the servo is such that the heads move off track until the position error is equal and opposite to the injected voltage. The position of the heads above the track can thus be program controlled. Offset is only employed on reading if it is suspected that the pack in the drive has been written by a different drive with non-standard alignment. A write function will cancel the offset.

9.11 Embedded-servo drives

In drives with a small number of platters, the use of an entire surface for servo information gives an excessive loss of data-recording area. In the embedded-servo drive, servo information is interleaved with data on the same surface, causing a smaller loss of storage area.

The embedded-servo drive heads will be reading data at some times and alignment information at others as the disk rotates. A sector transducer is required to generate a pulse which is true when the head is over servo information. Figures 9.17 and 9.18 show the principle. On all disk drives, the

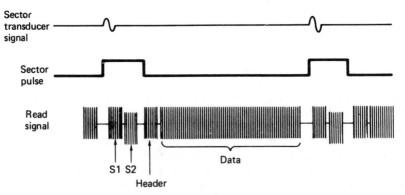

Figure 9.17 The same head is used on the embedded servo drive for both servo information and read/write data. During a sector pulse, the read signal is treated as servo information.

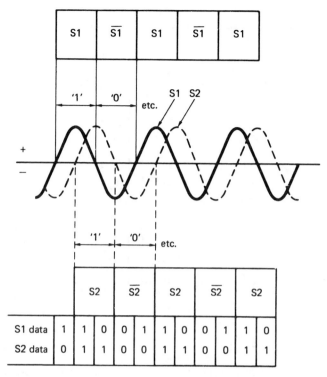

Figure 9.18 There are two basic types of servo track, S1 and S2, but these are recorded at two different places, in a staggered fashion. During S1 time, a position error is generated from the relative areas of the two types of track under the head as in the conventional servo surface drive. This position error is maintained with sample-and-hold circuitry. For track counting, the position error is compared with 0 V to generate a data bit. At S2 time another position error and another data bit are generated. The four possible combinations of the 2 bits are shown here in relation to the two position errors.

width of the head pole is less than the track pitch to prevent crosstalk. As the servo head is also the read/write head in an embedded-servo drive, it is slightly narrower than the servo-information pitch. This has the harmless effect of rounding off the peaks of the position-error waveform. During the pulse from the sector transducer, the head sees alignment information, and develops a position error in much the same way as any servo drive. Within the servo area are two sets of patterns, the second giving a position error of zero when the first is a maximum, i.e. there is a 90 degree phase shift between them. The two bursts of information are known as S1 and S2. Sample-and-hold circuitry is used to carry over the position errors whilst the head is reading and writing in the data area.

The discontinuous nature of the servo information means that cylinder crossings cannot be counted directly during a seek as the positioner is fast enough to cross several tracks between bursts. With reference to Figure 9.19, this problem is overcome as follows. During the S1 period, the position error is compared with zero volts to produce a single data bit, whose state depends upon whether the head was inside or outside the track centre. A similar process takes

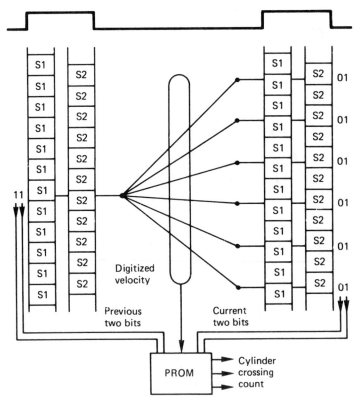

Figure 9.19 For the same initial and subsequent data bits, there can be several possible head trajectories. The ambiguity is resolved by using the carriage velocity in digital form.

place for the S2 period, and the position of the head relative to the track centre is then described to the accuracy of one-quarter of the track pitch by the two bits. These bits are stored, and at the next servo burst, two further bits are computed, describing the new position of the head. Figure 9.19 shows that there can be many cases which satisfy the same initial and final conditions. The only difference between the cases is the carriage velocity, so the output of the velocity transducer is digitized and used to resolve the ambiguity. At every sector pulse, two bits from the previous burst, two bits from the current burst and the digitized velocity are fed into a ROM which is preprogrammed to return the number of cylinders which must have been crossed for all combinations of inputs. This number is then subtracted from the cylinder-difference counter which is controlling the seek. The calculation will only be valid for one disk rotational speed, and so the disk motor requires close control. This is conveniently done by counting cycles of a reference clock between sector pulses to produce a speed error. As the cylinder count is deductive, there will be the odd occasion where the count is in error and the positioner comes to the wrong cylinder. In a conventional disk drive this would result in a mispositioning error which would warrant maintenance. In the embedded-servo drive, however, the condition is handled differently. Figure 9.20 shows a flowchart for control of the drive, which

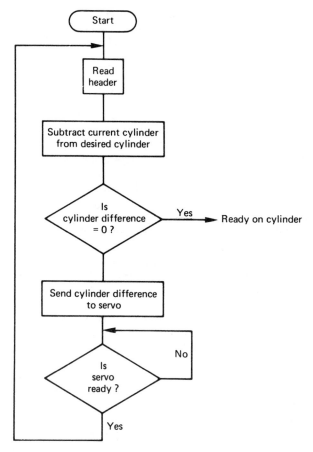

Figure 9.20 Flowchart for the control of an embedded-servo positioner. All seeks are relative, and seek errors are transparent, as they simply cause an extra execution of the loop.

has no absolute cylinder-address register, and in which all seeks are relative. The system only knows where the heads are by reading headers. In order to reach a particular cylinder, the program has to read the first header it sees on the current cylinder, and calculate the cylinder difference needed. This is used to perform a deductive seek. When this is complete, a further header will be read. Most of the time this will indicate the correct cylinder, but in the occasional condition where the positioning was in error, the program simply loops and calculates a new cylinder difference until the correct cylinder is finally reached.

Since each surface has its own alignment information, some exchangeable-pack drives using this principle need no head alignment during manufacture at all. When switching between heads, a repositioning cycle will be necessary because all of the heads will not necessarily be on the same cylinder. In fact the definition of a cylinder is indistinct in such drives.

Alternatively a multiplatter disk may combine a servo surface with embedded servos on each of the data surfaces. The servo surface provides write clock, sector timing and tacho functions, along with coarse positioning during a seek, and the embedded servo allows the individual heads to track accurately despite discrepancies in temperature and adjustment of the individual platters and heads in the stack.

9.12 Winchester technology

In order to offer extremely high capacity per spindle, which reduces the cost per bit, a disk drive must have very narrow tracks placed close together, and must use very short recorded wavelengths, which implies that the flying height of the heads must be small. The so-called Winchester technology is one approach to high storage density. The technology was developed by IBM, and the name came about because the model number of the development drive was the same as that of the famous rifle.

Reduction in flying height magnifies the problem of providing a contaminant-free environment. A conventional disk is well protected whilst inside the drive, but outside the drive the effects of contamination become intolerable.

In exchangeable-pack drives, there is a real limit to the track pitch that can be achieved because of the difficulty or cost of engineering head-alignment mechanisms to make the necessary minute adjustments to give interchange compatibility.

The essence of Winchester technology is that each disk pack has its own set of read/write and servo heads, with an integral positioner. The whole is protected by a dust-free enclosure, and the unit is referred to as a head disk assembly, or HDA.

As the HDA contains its own heads, compatibility problems do not exist, and no head alignment is necessary or provided for. It is thus possible to reduce track pitch considerably compared with exchangeable-pack drives. The sealed environment ensures complete cleanliness which permits a reduction in flying height without loss of reliability, and hence leads to an increased linear density. If the rotational speed is maintained, this can also result in an increase in data transfer rate.

The HDA is completely sealed, but some have a small filtered port to equalize pressure. Into this sealed volume of air, the drive motor delivers the majority of its power output. The resulting heat is dissipated by fins on the HDA casing. Some larger HDAs are filled with helium which significantly reduces drag and heat build-up.

An exchangeable-pack drive must retract the heads to facilitate pack removal. With Winchester technology this is not necessary. An area of the disk surface is reserved as a landing strip for the heads. The disk surface is lubricated, and the heads are designed to withstand landing and take-off without damage. Winchester heads have very large air-bleed grooves to allow low flying height with a much smaller downthrust from the cantilever, and so they exert less force on the disk surface during contact. When the term *parking* is used in the context of Winchester technology, it refers to the positioning of the heads over the landing area.

Disk rotation must be started and stopped quickly to minimize the length of time the heads slide over the medium. A powerful motor will accelerate the pack quickly. Eddy-current braking cannot be used with AC motors, since a power failure would allow the unbraked disk to stop only after a prolonged head-contact

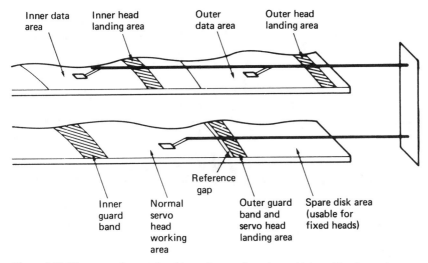

Inner data area | Inner head landing area | Outer data area | Outer head landing area

Reference gap

Inner guard band | Normal servo head working area | Outer guard band and servo head landing area | Spare disk area (usable for fixed heads)

Figure 9.21 When more than one head is used per surface, the positioner still only requires one servo head. This is often arranged to be equidistant from the read/write heads for thermal stability.

period. One solution is a failsafe mechanical brake, which is applied by a spring and released with a solenoid. Alternatively regenerative braking can be applied to DC motors.

A major advantage of contact start/stop is that more than one head can be used on each surface if retraction is not needed. This leads to two gains: firstly, the travel of the positioner is reduced in proportion to the number of heads per surface, reducing access time; and, secondly, more data can be transferred at a given detented carriage position before a seek to the next cylinder becomes necessary. This increases the speed of long transfers. Figure 9.21 illustrates the relationships of the heads in such a system.

9.13 Servo-surface Winchester drives

With contact start/stop, the servo head is always on the servo surface, and it can be used for all of the transducer functions needed by the drive. Figure 9.22 shows the position-error signal during a seek. The signal rises and falls as servo tracks are crossed, and the slope of the signal is proportional to positioner velocity. The position-error signal is differentiated and rectified to give a velocity feedback signal. Owing to the cyclic nature of the position-error signal, the velocity signal derived from it has troughs where the derivative becomes zero at the peaks. These cannot be filtered out, as the signal is in a servo loop, and the filter would introduce an additional lag. The troughs would, however, be interpreted by the servo driver as massive momentary velocity errors which might overload the amplifier. The solution which can be adopted is to use a signal obtained by integrating the positioner-motor current which is selected when there is a trough in the differentiated position-error signal.

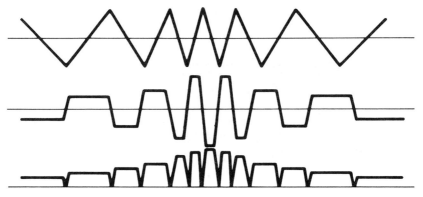

Figure 9.22 To generate a velocity signal, the position error from the servo head is differentiated and rectified.

In order to make velocity feedback available over the entire servo surface, the conventional guard-band approach cannot be used since it results in steady position errors in the guard bands. In contact start/stop drives, the servo head must be capable of detenting in a guard band for the purpose of landing on shutdown.

A modification to the usual servo surface is used in Winchester drives, one implementation of which is shown in Figure 9.23, where it will be seen that there are extra transitions, identical in both types of track, along with the familiar dibits. The repeating set of transitions is known as a frame, in which the first dibit is used for synchronization, and a phase-locked oscillator is made to run at a multiple of the sync signal rate. The PLO is used as a reference for the write clock, as well as to generate sampling pulses to extract a position error from the composite waveform and to provide a window for the second dibit in the frame, which may or may not be present. Each frame thus contains one data bit, and successive frames are read to build up a pattern in a shift register. The parallel output of the shift register is examined by a decoder which recognizes a number of unique patterns. In the guard bands, the decoder will repeatedly recognize the guard-band code as the disk revolves. An index is generated in the same way, by recognizing a different pattern. In a contact start/stop drive, the frequency of index detection is used to monitor pack speed in order to dispense with a separate transducer. This does mean, however, that it must be possible to detect index everywhere, and for this reason, index is still recorded in the guard bands by replacing the guard-band code with index code once per revolution.

A consequence of deriving velocity information from the servo surface is that the location of cylinder zero is made more difficult, as there is no longer a continuous maximum position error in the guard band. A common solution is to adopt a much smaller area of continuous position error known as a reference gap; this is typically three servo tracks wide. In the reference gap and for several tracks outside it, there is a unique reference gap code recorded in the frame data bits. Figure 9.24 shows the position error which is generated as the positioner crosses this area of the disk, and shows the plateau in the position-error signal due to the reference gap. During head loading, which in this context means

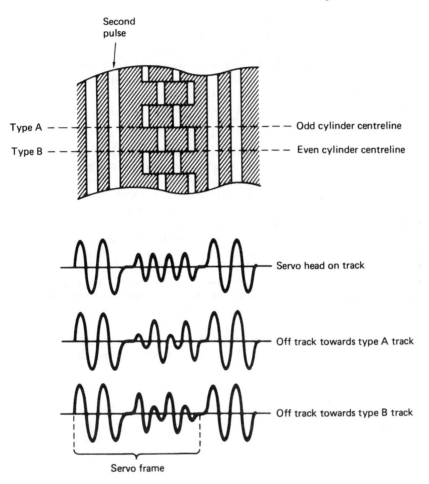

Figure 9.23 This type of servo surface pattern has a second pulse which may be omitted to act as a data bit. This is used to detect the guard bands and index.

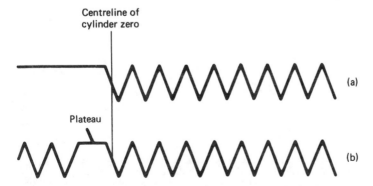

Figure 9.24 (a) Conventional guard band. (b) Winchester guard band, showing the plateau in the position error, known as the reference gap, which is used to locate cylinder 0.

positioning from the parking area to cylinder zero, the heads move slowly inwards. When the reference code is detected, positioner velocity is reduced, and the position error is sampled. When successive position-error samples are the same, the head must be on the position-error plateau, and if the servo is put into track-following mode, it will automatically detent on cylinder zero, since this is the first place that the position error falls to zero.

9.14 Rotary positioners

Figure 9.25 shows that rotary positioners are feasible in Winchester drives; they cannot be used in exchangeable-pack drives because of interchange problems. There are some advantages to a rotary positioner. It can be placed in the corner of a compact HDA allowing smaller overall size. The manufacturing cost will be less than a linear positioner because fewer bearings and precision bars are needed. Significantly, a rotary positioner can be made faster since its inertia is smaller. With a linear positioner all parts move at the same speed. In a rotary positioner, only the heads move at full speed, as the parts closer to the shaft must move more slowly. Figure 9.26 shows a typical HDA with a rotary positioner. The principle of many rotary positioners is exactly that of a moving-coil ammeter, where current is converted directly into torque. Alternatively various configurations of electric motor or stepping motor can be used with band or wire drive.

One disadvantage of rotary positioners is that there is a component of windage on the heads which tends to pull the positioner in towards the spindle. In linear

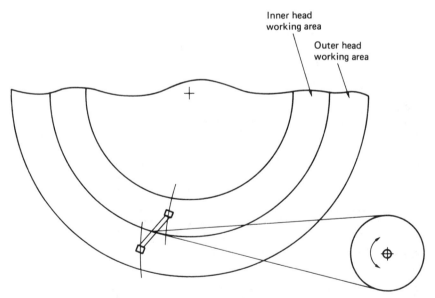

Figure 9.25 A rotary positioner with two heads per surface. The tolerances involved in the spacing between the heads and the axis of rotation mean that each arm records data in a unique position. Those data can only be read back by the same heads, which rules out the use of a rotary positioner in exchangeable-pack drives. In a head disk assembly the problem of compatibility does not arise.

Breather filter

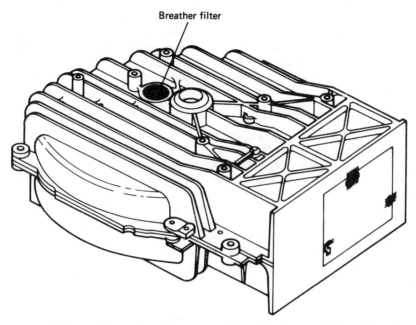

Figure 9.26 Head disk assembly with a rotary positioner. The adoption of this technique allows a very compact structure.

positioners windage is at right angles to motion and can be neglected. Windage can be overcome in rotary positioners by feeding the current cylinder address to a ROM which sends a code to a DAC. This produces an offset voltage which is fed to the positioner driver to generate a feedforward torque which balances the windage whatever the position of the heads.

When extremely small track spacing is contemplated, it cannot be assumed that all the heads will track the servo head due to temperature gradients. In this case the embedded-servo approach must be used, where each head has its own alignment patterns. The servo surface is often retained in such drives to allow coarse positioning, velocity feedback and index and write-clock generation, in addition to locating the guard bands for landing the heads.

Winchester drives have been made with massive capacity, but the problem of backup is then magnified, and the general trend has been for the physical size of the drive to come down as the storage density increases in order to improve access time. Very small Winchester disk drives are now available which plug into standard integrated circuit sockets. These are competing with RAM for memory applications where non-volatility is important.

9.15 Floppy disks

Floppy disks are the result of a search for a fast yet cheap non-volatile memory for the programmable control store of a processor under development at IBM in the late 1960s. Both magnetic tape and hard disk were ruled out on grounds of cost since only intermittent duty was required. The device designed to fulfil these requirements – the floppy disk drive – incorporated both magnetic-tape and disk technologies.

The floppy concept was so cost effective that it transcended its original application to become a standard in industry as an online data-storage device. The original floppy disk, or diskette as it is sometimes called, was 8 in in diameter, but a 5¼ in diameter disk was launched to suit more compact applications. More recently Sony introduced the 3½ in floppy disk which has a rigid shell with sliding covers over the head access holes to reduce the likelihood of contamination.

Strictly speaking the floppy is a disk, since it rotates and repeatedly presents the data on any track to the heads, and it has a positioner to give fast two-dimensional access, but it also resembles a tape drive in that the magnetic medium is carried on a flexible substrate which deforms when the read/write head is pressed against it.

Floppy disks are stamped from wide, thick tape, and are anisotropic, because the oxide becomes oriented during manufacture. On many disks this can be seen by the eye as parallel striations on the disk surface. A more serious symptom is the presence of sinusoidal amplitude modulation of the replay signal at twice the rotational frequency of the disk, as illustrated in Figure 9.27.

One-quarter revolution

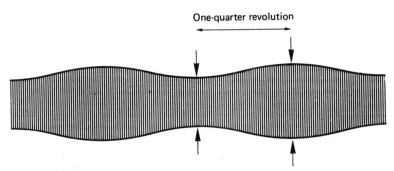

Figure 9.27 Sinusoidal amplitude modulation of floppy disk output due to anisotropy of medium.

Eight inch and 5¼ in floppy disks have radial apertures in their protective envelopes to allow access by the head. A further aperture allows a photoelectric index sensor to detect a small hole in the disk once per revolution. The protective envelopes are also flexible. In the 3½ in disk the envelope is rigid and includes a sliding shutter which covers the head access apertures when the disk is not in the drive. The disk envelopes are lined with a soft, non-woven fabric which wipes the disk clean as it rotates and prevents it contacting the envelope.

Figure 9.28 shows that the disk is inserted into the drive edge-first, and slides between an upper and a lower hub assembly. One of these has a fixed bearing which transmits the drive; the other is spring-loaded and mates with the drive hub when the door is closed, causing the disk to be centred and gripped firmly. The moving hub is usually tapered to assist centring. In the 3½ in disk, there is a metal hub which is attracted to a magnetic drive spindle. There is an arrangement which ensures repeatable centring of the disk on the

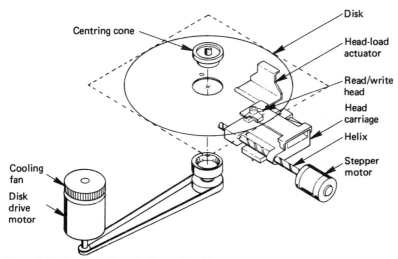

Figure 9.28 The mechanism of a floppy disk drive.

spindle.[4] It will be seen from Figure 9.29 that the disk hub has two apertures, one central and one offset. When the disk is first installed, the spindle centre pin engages loosely with the centre hole. When the drive spindle first rotates, a spring-loaded pin in the spindle engages the offset disk-hub hole and forces the spindle shaft firmly into one corner of the centre disk-hub hole.

To avoid frictional heating and prolong life, the spindle speed of floppy disks is restricted when compared with that of hard disks. Recent drives almost universally use direct-drive brushless DC motors. Since the rotational latency is so great, there is little point in providing a fast positioner, and the use of leadscrews or split bands driven by a stepping motor is extremely common. The permanent magnets in the stepping motor provide the necessary detenting, and to seek it is only necessary to provide a suitable number of drive pulses to the motor. As the drive is incremental, some form of reference is needed to determine the position of cylinder zero. At the rearward limit of carriage travel, a light beam is interrupted which resets the cylinder count. Upon power-up, the drive has to

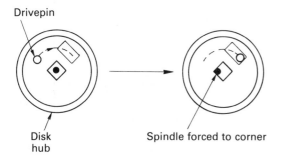

Figure 9.29 In the 3½ in floppy disk the hub is metal and carries two holes. As will be seen here, as the spindle rotates a sprung pin engages with the offset hole with the result that the drive spindle is positively located in the centre hole.

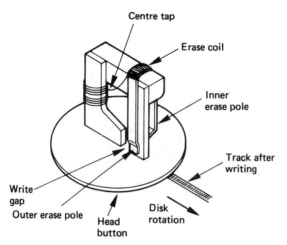

Figure 9.30 The poor dimensional stability of the plastic diskette means that tunnel erase or side trim has to be used. The extra erase poles can be seen here.

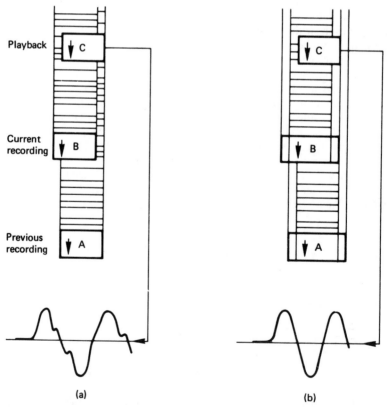

Figure 9.31 The effect of side trim is to prevent the traces of a previous recording from interfering with the latest recording: (a) without side trim; (b) with side trim.

reverse-seek until this limit is found in order to calibrate the positioner. The grinding noise this makes is a characteristic of most PCs on power-up.

One of the less endearing features of plastics materials is a lack of dimensional stability. Temperature and humidity changes affect plastics much more than metals. The effect on the anisotropic disk substrate is to distort the circular tracks into a shape resembling a dog bone. For this reason, the track width and pitch have to be generous.

The read/write head of a single-sided floppy disk operates on the lower surface only, and is rigidly fixed to the carriage. Contact with the medium is achieved with the help of a spring-loaded pressure pad applied to the top surface of the disk opposite the head. Early drives retracted the pressure pad with a solenoid when not actually transferring data; later drives simply stop the disk. In double-sided drives, the pressure pad is replaced by a second sprung head. There is an offset between the upper and lower magnetic circuits to prevent magnetic coupling through the disk.

Because of the indifferent stability of the medium, side trim or tunnel erasing is used, because it can withstand considerable misregistration.

Figure 9.30 shows the construction of a typical side-trimming head, which has erase poles at each side of the magnetic circuit. When such a head writes, the erase poles are energized and erase a narrow strip of the disk either side of the new data track. If the recording is made with misregistration, the side trim prevents traces of the previous recording from being played back as well (Figure 9.31).

As the floppy disk drive was intended to be a low-cost item, sophisticated channel codes were not used on early models.

Single-density drives used FM and double-density drives used MFM. With the maturing of the floppy disk as a PC storage device, pressure to increase capacity led to the use of RLL codes in recent products. As the recording density becomes higher at the inner tracks, the write current is sometimes programmed to reduce with inward positioner travel. The capacity of floppy disks is in the range of hundreds of kilobytes to a few megabytes. Higher capacities have been reported experimentally in units which use embedded tracking signals and adaptive servos.[5]

9.16 Bernoulli disks

The rotational speed of a conventional floppy disk is limited by friction with the liner, which causes heating. The Bernoulli disk[6] is an approach which combines the economy of plastics media with the speed of a hard drive. Figure 9.32 shows

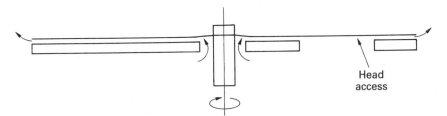

Figure 9.32 In the Bernoulli disk an air film is created between the floppy disk and the smooth backing plate which stabilizes the rotation.

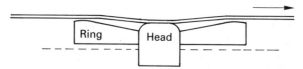

Figure 9.33 In order to improve head contact, a ring surrounding the head may be used to create a local low-pressure zone.

the principle of the Bernoulli drive. A flexible disk is rotated at speed adjacent to a smooth, flat surface. The relative motion creates a radial/tangential pumping action in the air between the disk and the plate. This draws the disk close to the plate, but, as the spacing falls, the pumping action is impaired by the small separation. As a result a stable condition is created where the disk flies over the plate at a constant height. The rigidity of the plate is largely transferred to the disk and speeds of 1500 rpm and higher can be used. A slot in the plate allows head access. Conventional floppy disk heads are no use at these speeds as they will suffer excessive spacing loss. Slotted heads have been used to allow the air pressure to bleed away. Alternatively, the disk can be drawn towards a fixed head by aerodynamically reduced local pressure. Figure 9.33 shows that a rounded ring surrounds the head. The ring is slightly tilted so that the leading edge is closer to the disk than the trailing edge. This causes a reduction in pressure inside the ring which draws the disk into contact with the head.

9.17 Defect handling

The protection of data recorded on disks differs considerably from the approach used on other media in digital audio. This has much to do with the intolerance of data processors to errors when compared with audio. In particular, it is not possible to interpolate to conceal errors in a computer program or a data file.

In the same way that magnetic tape is subject to dropouts, magnetic disks suffer from surface defects whose effect is to corrupt data. The shorter wavelengths employed as disk densities increase are affected more by a given size of defect. Attempting to make a perfect disk is subject to a law of diminishing returns, and eventually a state is reached where it becomes more cost effective to invest in a defect-handling system.

There are four main methods of handling media defects in magnetic media, and further techniques needed in WORM laser disks (see Chapter 10), whose common goal is to make their presence transparent to the data. These methods vary in complexity and cost of implementation, and can often be combined in a particular system.

9.18 Bad-block files

In the construction of bad-block files, a brand new disk is tested by the operating system. Known patterns are written everywhere on the disk, and these are read back and verified. Following this the system gives the disk a volume name, and creates on it a directory structure which keeps records of the position and size of every file subsequently written. The physical disk address of every block which fails to verify is allocated to a file which has an entry in the disk directory. In this way, when genuine data files come to be written, the bad blocks appear to the

	1	1	1	1	1	1	1	1	1	1	1	0	0	0	0	0	A
A	0	0	0	0	0	0	1	1	1	1	1	1	1	1	1	1	
	1	1	1	1	1	1	1	1	1	1	1	1	1	1	1	1	
	1	1	1	1	1	1	1	0	0	0	0	1	0	0	0	0	B
	0	0	1	1	1	1	1	1	1	1	1	1	1	0	0	0	
	0	0	0	0	0	0	0	0	e	tc.							

Figure 9.34 A disk-block-usage bit map in 16 bit memory for a cluster size of 11 blocks. Before writing on the disk, the system searches the bit map for contiguous free space equal to or larger than the cluster size. The first available space is unusable because the presence of a bad block B destroys the contiguity of the cluster. Thus one bad block causes the loss of a cluster.

system to be in use storing a fictitious file, and no attempt will be made to write there. Some disks have dedicated tracks where defect information can be written during manufacture or by subsequent verification programs, and these permit a speedy construction of the system bad-block file.

In association with the bad-block file, many drives allocate bits in each header to indicate that the associated block is bad. If a data transfer is attempted at such a block, the presence of these bits causes the function to be aborted. The bad-block file system gives very reliable protection against defects, but can result in a lot of disk space being wasted. Systems often use several disk blocks to store convenient units of data called clusters, which will all be written or read together. Figure 9.34 shows how a bit map is searched to find free space, and illustrates how the presence of one bad block can write off a whole cluster.

9.19 Sector skipping

In sector skipping, space is made at the end of every track for a spare data block, which is not normally accessible to the system. Where a track is found to contain a defect, the affected block becomes a skip sector. In this block, the regular defect flags will be set, but in addition, a bit known as the skip-sector flag is set in this and every subsequent block in the track. When the skip-sector flag is encountered, the effect is to add one to the desired sector address for the rest of the track, as in Figure 9.35. In this way the bad block is unused, and the track

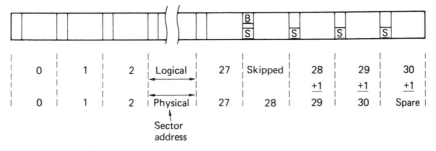

Figure 9.35 Skip sectoring. The bad block in this example has a physical sector address of 28. By setting the skip-sector flags in the header, this and subsequent logical blocks have 1 added to their sector addresses, and the spare block is brought into use.

format following the bad block is effectively slid along by one block to bring into use the spare block at the end of the track. Using this approach, the presence of single bad blocks does not cause the loss of clusters, but requires slightly greater control complexity. If two bad blocks exist in a track, the second will be added to the bad-block file as usual.

9.20 Defect skipping

The two techniques described so far have treated the block as the smallest element. In practice, the effect of a typical defect is to corrupt only a few bytes. The principle of defect skipping is that media defects can be skipped over within the block so that a block containing a defect is made usable. The header of each block contains the location of the first defect in bytes away from the end of the header, and the number of bytes from the first defect to the second defect, and so on up to the maximum of four shown in the example of Figure 9.36. Each defect is overwritten with a fixed number of bytes of preamble code and a sync pattern. The skip is positioned so that there is sufficient undamaged preamble after the defect for the data separator to regain lock. Each defect lengthens the block, causing the format of the track to slip round. A space is left at the end of each track to allow a reasonable number of skips to be accommodated. Often a track descriptor is written at the beginning of each track which contains the physical position of defects relative to index. The disk format needed for a particular system can then be rapidly arrived at

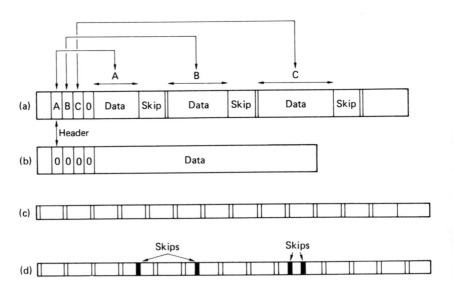

Figure 9.36 Defect skipping. (a) A block containing three defects. The header contains up to four parameters which specify how much data is to be written before each skip. In this example only three entries are needed. (b) An error-free block for comparison with (a); the presence of the skips lengthens the block. To allow for this lengthening, the track contains spare space at the end, as shown in (c), which is an error-free track. (d) A track containing the maximum of four skips, which have caused the spare space to be used up.

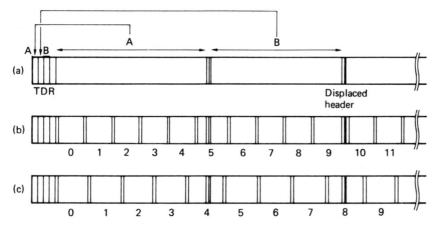

Figure 9.37 The purpose of the track descriptor record (TDR) is to keep a record of defects independent of disk format. The positions of the defects stored in the TDR (a) are used by the formatter to establish the positions relative to the format used. With the format (b), the first defect appears in sector 5, but the same defect would be in sector 4 for format (c). The second defect falls where a header would be written in (b) so the header is displaced for sector 10. The same defect falls in the data area of sector 8 in (c).

by reading the descriptor, and translating the physical defect locations into locations relative to the chosen sector format. Figure 9.37 shows how a soft-sectoring drive can have two different formats around the same defects using this principle.

In the case where there are too many defects in a track for the skipping to handle, the system bad-block file will be used. This is rarely necessary in practice, and the disk appears to be contiguous, error-free logical and physical space. Defect skipping requires fast processing to deal with events in real time as the disk rotates. Bit-slice microsequencers are one approach, as a typical microprocessor would be too slow.

9.21 Revectoring

A refinement of sector skipping which permits the handling of more than one bad block per track without the loss of a cluster is revectoring. A bad block caused by a surface defect may only have a few defective bytes, so it is possible to record highly redundant information in the bad block. On a revectored disk, a bad block will contain in the data area repeated records pointing to the address where data displaced by the defect can be found. The spare block at the end of the track will be the first such place, and can be read within the same disk revolution, but out of sequence, which puts extra demands on the controller. In the less frequent case of more than one defect in a track, the second and subsequent bad blocks revector to spare blocks available in an area dedicated to that purpose. The principle is illustrated in Figure 9.38. In this case a seek will be necessary to locate the replacement block. The low probability of this means that access time is not significantly affected.

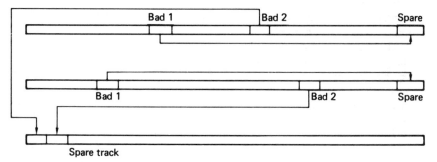

Figure 9.38 Revectoring. The first bad block in each track is revectored to the spare block at the end of the track. Unlike skip sectoring, subsequent good blocks are unaffected, and the replacement block is read out of sequence. The second bad block on any one track is revectored to one of a number of spare tracks kept on the disk for this purpose.

9.22 Error correction

The steps outlined above are the first line of defence against errors in disk drives, and serve to ensure that, by and large, the errors due to obvious surface defects are eliminated. There are other error mechanisms in action, such as noise and jitter, which can result in random errors, and it is necessary to protect disk data against these also. The error-correction mechanisms described in Chapter 5 will be employed. In general each data block is made into a codeword by the addition of redundancy at the end. The error-correcting code used in disks was, for a long time, Fire code, because it allowed correction with the minimum circuit complexity. It could, however, only correct one error burst per block, and it had a probability of miscorrection which was marginal for some applications. The advances in complex logic chips meant that the adoption of a Reed–Solomon code was a logical step, since these have the ability to correct multiple error bursts. As the larger burst errors in disk drives are taken care of by verifying the medium, interleaving in the error-correction sense and product codes are not generally needed, especially as such techniques introduce delay into the system, which adds to the access time. When interleaving is used in the context of disks, it usually means that the sector addresses along a track are interleaved so that reading them in numerical order requires two revolutions. This will slow down the data transfer rate where the drive is too fast for the associated circuitry.

In some systems, the occurrence of errors is monitored to see if they are truly random, or if an error persistently occurs in the same physical block. If this is the case, and the error is small, and well within the correction power of the code, the block will continue in use. If, however, the error is larger than some threshold, the data will be read, corrected and rewritten elsewhere, and the block will then be added to the bad-block file so that it will not be used again.

9.23 The disk controller

A disk controller is a unit which is interposed between the drives and the rest of the system. It consists of two main parts: that which issues control signals to and obtains status from the drives, and that which handles the data to be stored and retrieved. Both parts are synchronized by the control sequencer. The essentials of a disk controller are determined by the characteristics of drives and the functions needed, and so they do not vary greatly. Disk drives are generally built to interface to a standard controller interface, such as the SCSI bus.

The execution of a function by a disk subsystem requires a complex series of steps, and decisions must be made between the steps to decide what the next will be. There is a parallel with computation, where the function is the equivalent of an instruction, and the sequencer steps needed are the equivalent of the micro-instructions needed to execute the instruction. The major failing in this analogy is that the sequence in a disk drive must be accurately synchronized to the rotation of the disk.

Most disk controllers use direct memory access, which means that they have the ability to transfer disk data in and out of the associated memory without the assistance of the processor. In order to cause an audio-file transfer, the disk controller must be told the physical disk address (cylinder, sector, track), the physical memory address where the audio file begins, the size of the file and the direction of transfer (read or write). The controller will then position the disk heads, address the memory and transfer the samples. One disk transfer may consist of many contiguous disk blocks, and the controller will automatically increment the disk-address registers as each block is completed. As the disk turns, the sector address increases until the end of the track is reached. The track or head address will then be incremented and the sector address reset so that transfer continues at the beginning of the next track. This process continues until all of the heads have been used in turn. In this case both the head address and sector address will be reset, and the cylinder address will be incremented, which causes a seek. A seek which takes place because of a data transfer is called an implied seek, because it is not necessary formally to instruct the system to perform it. As disk drives are block-structured devices, and the error correction is codeword-based, the controller will always complete a block even if the size of the file is less than a whole number of blocks. This is done by packing the last block with zeros.

The status system allows the controller to find out about the operation of the drive, both as a feedback mechanism for the control process, and to handle any errors. Upon completion of a function, it is the status system which interrupts the control processor to tell it that another function can be undertaken.

In a system where there are several drives connected to the controller via a common bus, it is possible for non-data-transfer functions such as seeks to take place in some drives simultaneously with a data transfer in another.

Before a data transfer can take place, the selected drive must physically access the desired block, and confirm this by reading the block header. Following a seek to the required cylinder, the positioner will confirm that the heads are on track and settled. The desired head will be selected, and then a search for the correct sector begins. This is done by comparing the desired sector with the current sector register, which is typically incremented by dividing down servo-surface pulses. When the two counts are equal, the head is about to enter the desired block. Figure 9.39 shows the structure of a typical disk track. In between blocks are placed address marks, which are areas without transitions which the read circuits can detect. Following detection of the address mark, the sequencer is roughly synchronized to begin handling the block. As the block is entered, the data separator locks to the preamble, and in due course the sync pattern will be found. This sets to zero a counter which divides the data-bit rate by eight, allowing the serial recording to be correctly assembled into bytes, and also

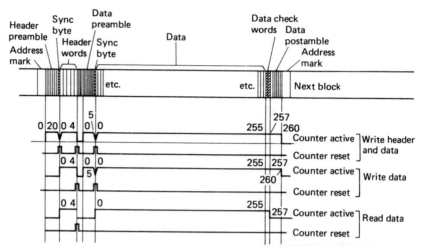

Figure 9.39 The format of a typical disk block related to the count process which is used to establish where in the block the head is at any time. During a read the count is derived from the actual data read, but during a write, the count is derived from the write clock.

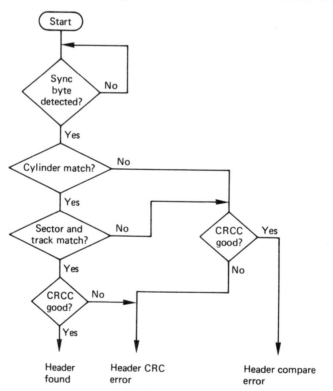

Figure 9.40 The vital process of position confirmation is carried out in accordance with the above flowchart. The appropriate words from the header are compared in turn with the contents of the disk-address registers in the subsystem. Only if the correct header has been found and read properly will the data transfer take place.

allowing the sequencer to count the position of the head through the block in order to perform all the necessary steps at the right time.

The first header word is usually the cylinder address, and this is compared with the contents of the desired cylinder register. The second header word will contain the sector and track address of the block, and these will also be compared with the desired addresses. There may also be bad-block flags and/or defect-skipping information. At the end of the header is a CRCC which will be used to ensure that the header was read correctly. Figure 9.40 shows a flowchart of the position verification, after which a data transfer can proceed. The header reading is completely automatic. The only time it is necessary formally to command a header to be read is when checking that a disk has been formatted correctly.

During the read of a data block, the sequencer is employed again. The sync pattern at the beginning of the data is detected as before, following which the actual data arrive. These bits are converted to byte or sample parallel, and sent to the memory by DMA. When the sequencer has counted the last data byte off the track, the redundancy for the error-correction system will be following.

During a write function, the header-check function will also take place as it is perhaps even more important not to write in the wrong place on a disk. Once the header has been checked and found to be correct, the write process for the associated data block can begin. The preambles, sync pattern, data block, redundancy and postamble have all to be written contiguously. This is taken care of by the sequencer, which is obtaining timing information from the servo surface to lock the block structure to the angular position of the disk. This should be contrasted with the read function, where the timing comes directly from the data.

9.24 Command queueing

In the disk controller described above, only one command can be accepted at time. Once a command is issued, the subsystem status will be set to 'busy' and

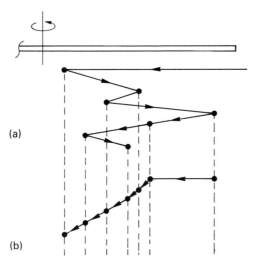

Figure 9.41 Positioner movement for sequentially executed commands is shown at (a). If the controller can queue and reorder commands, the more efficient sequence (b) can be implemented.

no further commands can be accepted until the current command is completed. Whilst this approach is adequate for small PCs, in central disk systems used for shared databases or in multiprogramming mainframe computers it slows down access. Figure 9.41(a) shows what happens. The host computer generates a number of different commands to transfer data at widely differing physical addresses. If these are exectuted in the order they are issued, the total travel of the positioner is greater than necessary. Figure 9.41(b) shows what happens if the disk controller is capable of stacking commands and re-ordering them. Commands can then be executed in the order which allows the shortest total positioner travel. The average access time then falls and the throughput of the system is increased.

When one controller is connected to several disk drives, only one data transfer can take place at a time, but any number of drives can be commanded to seek at once. With command reordering the disk controller can use the data path to transfer data on the first drive to reach the correct physical address.

9.25 RAID technology

Large databases are traditionally serviced by large, high-capacity, Winchester disk drives. As has been stated, Winchester disk drives are sealed units, and a failure can permanently lose all stored data. With the traditional approach, frequent backup to tape is needed, a process which requires a proportion of the available system access. Another factor is that the mass market for PCs has resulted in greater efforts being expended in improving the performance of physically small drives with the result that their cost per bit is lower than in larger products. Redundant arrays of inexpensive disks (RAID) can be used to advantage in large database applications.[7]

In a simple application, shown in Figure 9.42, host data are distributed over several drives to increase system capacity. The system is rendered safe against a single permanent drive failure by recording redundancy on one drive. The controller calculates redundancy from the host data on writing and checks it on reading. In the case of a single drive failure, all host data can be recovered by error correction from the remaining disks. The redundant drive raises the cost per bit of the system by the redundancy factor, but this will still be lower than that of a single drive of equivalent capacity. In the system described above the positioners move together and the effect is that of a single, large disk drive with powerful error correction.

In order to take full advantage of the technique, the data are rearranged so that the multiple drive positioners in the array can access data independently. In most databases, reading takes place far more often than writing and there is a distribution of block sizes read. A system block size is selected which caters for typically 80% of accesses and this becomes the block size of a single drive.

Figure 9.42 Simple RAID system stores redundancy on one drive and acts as a single, large, failsafe drive.

Sector	Drive 1	Drive 2	Drive 3	Drive 4	Drive 5
0	Parity	Block 0	Block 1	Block 2	Block 3
1	Block 4	Parity	Block 5	Block 6	Block 7
2	Block 8	Block 9	Parity	Block 10	Block 11
3	Block 12	Block 13	Block 14	Parity	Block 15
4	Block 16	Block 17	Block 18	Block 19	Parity
5	Parity				

Figure 9.43 Command queueing RAID system rotates redundancy through all drives so that parallel drive reading can take place.

Multiple drive blocks are then associated for the purpose of calculating a block of redundancy. If it is required to update a single block, a read–modify–write process is necessary to update the redundancy, but as writing is less frequent this does not cause difficulty. If the array controller can queue commands, those which require a single disk block can be handled by a single drive and several accesses can take place simultaneously. The system now acts almost like a large drive with multiple positioners and the throughput of typical accesses is increased. If all of the redundancy is held on one drive, it cannot contribute to multiple accesses. However, if the redundancy is rotated through the drives as shown in Figure 9.43 then all of the drives contain data and there can be as many parallel accesses as there are drives.

It is important to the success of a RAID system of this kind that the block size is well matched to typical accesses. A host access which requires more than one block will require two drives to service it, halving the command execution rate.

References

1. HAGEN, G.E., Air-floating: a new principle in magnetic recording of information. *Computers and Automation*, **2**, 23–25 (1953)
2. NOYES, T. and DICKINSON, W.E., Engineering design of a magnetic disk random access memory. *Proc. Western Joint Computer Conf.*, pp. 42–44 (San Francisco, 1956)
3. HARKER, J.M. *et al.*, A quarter century of disk file innovation. *IBM J. Res. Dev.*, **25**, 677 (1981)
4. TAKAHASHI, S., *The latest floppy disc drives and their application know-how* (In Japanese). Tokyo: CQ Publishing Co. (1984)
5. MATSUKAWA, S. and TANIMURA, T., An advanced sector servo using a learning estimating and oversampling method for a 3.5" 28 Mbyte FDD. *IEE Trans. Magn.*, **27**, 4484–4489 (1991)
6. TRIPATHI, K.C., Development of removable mass information storage through Bernoulli principle. *IEE Conf. Publ. No. 319*, 79–83 (1990)
7. PATTERSON, D., GIBSON, D. and KATZ, R., A case for redundant arrays of inexpensive disks (RAIDs). *ACM SIGMOD Conf. Proc.*, pp. 109–116 (Chicago, 1988)

Chapter 10

Optical and magneto-optical disks

Optical disks are becoming increasingly important to data recording as the technology is refined. Optical disks result from the marriage of many disciplines, including laser optics, servomechanisms, error correction and both analog and digital circuitry in VLSI form. The technology will be explained here, along with examples of actual practice.

10.1 Types of optical disk

There are numerous types of optical disk, which have different characteristics.[1] There are, however, three broad groups, shown in Figure 10.1, which can be usefully compared.

(1) The Compact Disc, its data derivative CD-ROM and the prerecorded MiniDisc and its data equivalent are read-only laser disks, which are designed for mass duplication by stamping. They cannot be recorded.

(2) Some laser disks can be recorded, but once a recording has been made, it cannot be changed or erased. These are usually referred to as write-once-read-many (WORM) disks. Recordable CDs work on this principle.

(3) Erasable optical disks have essentially the same characteristic as magnetic disks, in that new and different recordings can be made in the same track indefinitely. Sometimes a separate erase process is necessary before rewriting.

The Compact Disc, generally abbreviated to CD, is a consumer digital audio recording which is intended for mass replication. When optical recording was in its infancy, many companies were experimenting with a variety of optical media. In most cases the goal was to make an optical recorder where the same piece of apparatus could record and immediately reproduce information. This would be essential for most computer data applications and for use in audio or video production. This was not, however, the case in the consumer music industry, where the majority of listening was, and still is, to prerecorded music. The vinyl disk could not be recorded in the home, yet it sold by the million. Individual vinyl disks were not recorded as such by the manufacturer as they were replicated by pressing, or moulding, molten plastic between two surfaces known as stampers which were themselves made from a master disk produced on a cutting lathe. This master disk was the recording.

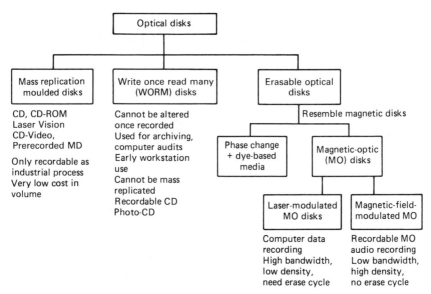

Figure 10.1 The various types of optical disk. See text for details.

Philips' approach was to invent an optical medium which would have the same characteristics as the vinyl disk in that it could be mass replicated by moulding or stamping with no requirement for it to be recordable by the user. The information on it is carried in the shape of flat-topped physical deformities in a layer of plastic, and as a result the medium has no photographic, magnetic or electronic properties, but is simply a relief structure. Such relief structures lack contrast and are notoriously difficult to study with conventional optics, but in 1934 Zernike[2] described a Nobel Prize-winning technique called phase contrast microscopy which allowed an apparent contrast to be obtained from such a structure using optical interference. This principle is used to read relief recordings.

Figure 10.2(a) shows that the information layer of CD, CD-ROM and the prerecorded MiniDisc is an optically flat mirror upon which microscopic bumps are raised. A thin coating of aluminium renders the layer reflective. When a small spot of light is focused on the information layer, the presence of the bumps affects the way in which the light is reflected back, and variations in the reflected light are detected in order to read the disk. Figure 10.2 also illustrates the very small dimensions which are common to both disks. For comparison, some sixty tracks can be accommodated in the groove pitch of a vinyl LP. These dimensions demand the utmost cleanliness in manufacture.

Figure 10.2(b) shows that there are two main types of WORM disks. In the first, the disk contains a thin layer of metal; on recording, a powerful laser melts spots on the layer. Surface tension causes a hole to form in the metal, with a thickened rim around the hole. Subsequently a low-power laser can read the disk because the metal reflects light, but the hole passes it through. Computer WORM disks work on this principle. In the second, the layer of metal is extremely thin,

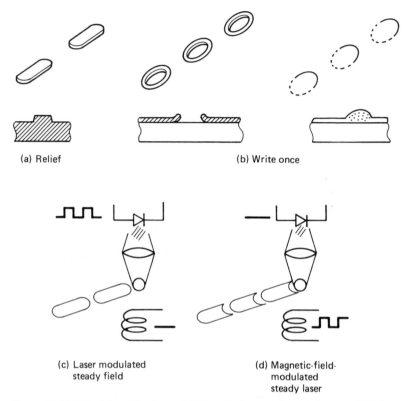

(a) Relief   (b) Write once

(c) Laser modulated   (d) Magnetic-field-
    steady field   modulated
                                    steady laser

Figure 10.2 (a) The information layer of CD is reflective and uses interference. (b) Write-once disks may burn holes or raise blisters in the information layer. (c) High data rate MO disks modulate the laser and use a constant magnetic field. (d) At low data rates the laser can run continuously and the magnetic field is modulated.

and the heat from the laser heats the material below it to the point of decomposition. This causes gassing which raises a blister or bubble in the metal layer. Recordable CDs may use this principle as the relief structure can be read like a normal CD. Clearly once such a pattern of holes or blisters has been made, it is permanent.

Re-recordable or erasable optical disks rely on magneto-optics,[3] also known more fully as thermomagneto-optics. Writing in such a device makes use of a thermomagnetic property possessed by all magnetic materials, which is that above a certain temperature, known as the Curie temperature, their coercive force becomes zero. This means that they become magnetically very soft, and take on the flux direction of any externally applied field. On cooling, this field orientation will be frozen in the material, and the coercivity will oppose attempts to change it. Although many materials possess this property, there are relatively few which have a suitably low Curie temperature. Compounds of terbium and gadolinium have been used, and one of the major problems to be overcome is that almost all suitable materials from a magnetic viewpoint corrode very quickly in air.

There are two ways in which magneto-optic (MO) disks can be written. Figure 10.2(c) shows the first system, in which the intensity of laser is modulated with the waveform to be recorded. If the disk is considered to be initially magnetized along its axis of rotation with the north pole upwards, it is rotated in a field of the opposite sense, produced by a steady current flowing in a coil which is weaker than the room-temperature coercivity of the medium. The field will therefore have no effect. A laser beam is focused on the medium as it turns, and a pulse from the laser will momentarily heat a very small area of the medium past its Curie temperature, whereby it will take on a reversed flux due to the presence of the field coils. This reversed-flux direction will be retained indefinitely as the medium cools.

Alternatively the waveform to be recorded modulates the magnetic field from the coils as shown in Figure 10.2(d). In this approach, the laser is operating continuously in order to raise the track beneath the beam above the Curie temperature, but the magnetic field recorded is determined by the current in the coil at the instant the track cools. Magnetic field modulation is used in the recordable MiniDisc.

In both of these cases, the storage medium is clearly magnetic, but the writing mechanism is the heat produced by light from a laser; hence the term thermomagneto-optics. The advantage of this writing mechanism is that there is no physical contact between the writing head and the medium. The distance can be several millimetres, some of which is taken up with a protective layer to prevent corrosion. In prototypes, this layer is glass, but commercially available disks use plastics.

The laser beam will supply a relatively high power for writing, since it is supplying heat energy. For reading, the laser power is reduced, such that it cannot heat the medium past the Curie temperature, and it is left on continuously. Readout depends on the so-called Kerr effect, which describes a rotation of the plane of polarization of light due to a magnetic field. The magnetic areas written on the disk will rotate the plane of polarization of incident polarized light to two different planes, and it is possible to detect the change in rotation with a suitable pickup.

In phase-change disks, the two states of a binary recording can be represented by two phases of a compound such as crystalline and amorphous. These will have different reflectivities and can be read optically. Recording is performed using laser heat where the laser intensity will affect the phase which results on cooling.

10.2 CD and MD contrasted

CD and MD have a great deal in common. Both use a laser of the same wavelength which creates a spot of the same size on the disk. The track pitch and speed are the same and both offer the same playing time. The channel code and error-correction strategy are the same.

CD carries 44.1 kHz 16 bit PCM audio and is intended to be played in a continuous spiral like a vinyl disk. MD begins with the same PCM data, but uses a form of data reduction known as ATRAC (see Chapter 2) having a compression factor of 0.2. After the addition of subcode and housekeeping data MD has an average data rate which is 0.225 that of CD. However, MD has the same recording density and track speed as CD, so the data rate from the disk is greatly in excess of that needed by the audio decoders. The difference is absorbed in RAM which, in a typical player, is capable of buffering about 3 seconds of audio. When the RAM is full, the disk drive stops transferring data but keeps turning. As the RAM empties into the decoders, the disk drive will top it up in bursts. As the drive need not transfer data for over three-quarters of the time, it can re-position between transfers and so it is capable of editing in the same way as a magnetic hard disk. A further advantage of the RAM buffer is that if the pickup is knocked off track by an external shock the RAM continues to provide data to the audio decoders and provided the pickup can get back to the correct track before the RAM is exhausted there will be no audible effect.

When recording an MO disk, the MiniDisc drive also uses the RAM buffer to allow repositioning so that a continuous recording can be made on a disk which has become chequerboarded through selective erasing. The full total playing time is then always available irrespective of how the disk is divided into different recordings.

10.3 CD and MD – disk construction

Figure 10.3 shows the mechanical specification of CD and CD-ROM. Within an overall diameter of 120 mm the program area occupies a band 33 mm wide between the diameters of 50 and 116 mm. Lead-in and lead-out areas increase the width of this band to 35.5 mm. As the track pitch is a constant 1.6 μm, there will be:

$$\frac{35.6 \times 1000}{1.6} = 22\,188$$

tracks crossing a radius of the disk. As the track is a continuous spiral, the track length will be given by the above figure multiplied by the average circumference:

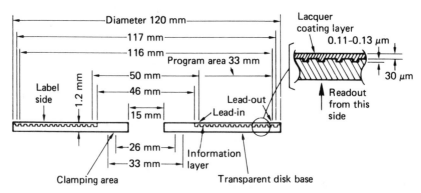

Figure 10.3 Mechanical specification of CD. Between diameters of 46 and 117 mm is a spiral track 5.7 km long.

$$\text{Length} = 2 \times \pi \times \frac{58.5 + 23}{2} \times 22\,188 = 5.7\,\text{km}$$

These figures give a good impression of the precision involved in CD manufacture. The CD case is for protection in storage and the CD has to be taken out of its case and placed in the player. The disk has a plain centre hole and most players clamp the disk onto the spindle from both sides. There are some CD transports which require the standard CD to be placed into a special cassette. The CD can then be played inside the cassette.

Figure 10.4 shows the mechanical specification of prerecorded MiniDisc. Within an overall diameter of 64 mm the lead-in area begins at a diameter of 29 mm and the program area begins at 32 mm. The track pitch is exactly the same as in CD, but the MiniDisc can be smaller than CD without any sacrifice of

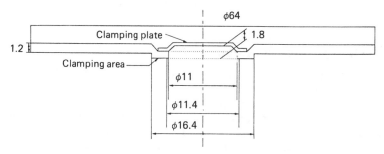

Figure 10.4 The mechanical dimensions of MiniDisc.

playing time because of the use of data reduction. For ease of handling, MiniDisc is permanently enclosed in a shuttered plastic cartridge which is $72 \times 68 \times 5$ mm. The cartridge resembles a smaller version of a 3½ inch floppy disk, but, unlike a floppy, it is slotted into the drive with the shutter at the side. An arrow is moulded into the cartridge body to indicate this.

In the pre-recorded MiniDisc, it was a requirement that the whole of one side of the cartridge should be available for graphics. Thus the disk is designed to be secured to the spindle from one side only. The centre of the disk is fitted with a ferrous clamping plate and the spindle is magnetic. When the disk is lowered into the drive it simply sticks to the spindle. The ferrous disk is only there to provide the clamping force. The disk is still located by the moulded hole in the plastic component. In this way the ferrous component needs no special alignment accuracy when it is fitted in manufacture. The back of the cartridge has a centre opening for the hub and a sliding shutter to allow access by the optical pickup.

The recordable MiniDisc and cartridge has the same dimensions as the prerecorded MiniDisc, but access to both sides of the disk is needed for recording. Thus the recordable MiniDisc has a shutter which opens on both sides of the cartridge, rather like a double-sided floppy disk. The opening on the front allows access by the magnetic head needed for MO recording, leaving a smaller label area.

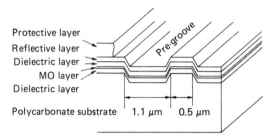

Protective layer
Reflective layer
Dielectric layer
MO layer
Dielectric layer
Polycarbonate substrate   1.1 μm   0.5 μm

Pre-groove

Figure 10.5 The construction of the MO recordable MiniDisc.

Figure 10.5 shows the construction of the MO MiniDisc. The 1.1 μm wide tracks are separated by grooves which can be optically tracked. Once again the track pitch is the same as in CD. The MO layer is sandwiched between protective layers.

10.4 Rejecting surface contamination

A fundamental characteristic of optical disks is that they are removable and no special working environment or handling skill is required. High-density recording implies short wavelengths. Using a laser focused on the disk from a distance allows short-wavelength recordings to be played back without physical contact, whereas conventional magnetic recording requires intimate contact and implies a wear mechanism, the need for periodic cleaning, and susceptibility to contamination.

The information layer of CD and MD is read through the thickness of the disk. Figure 10.6 shows that this approach causes the readout beam to enter and leave the disk surface through the largest possible area. The actual dimensions involved are shown in the figure. Despite the minute spot size of about 1.2 μm diameter, light enters and leaves through a 0.7 mm diameter circle. As a result, surface debris has to be three orders of magnitude larger than the readout spot before the beam is obscured. This approach has the further advantage in MO drives that the magnetic head, on the opposite side to the laser pickup, is then closer to the magnetic layer in the disk.

The size of the entry circle in Figure 10.6 is a function of the refractive index of the disk material, the numerical aperture of the objective lens and the thickness of the disk. MiniDiscs are permanently enclosed in a cartridge, and scratching is unlikely. This is not so for CD, but fortunately the method of readout through the disk thickness tolerates surface scratches very well. In extreme cases of damage, a scratch can often be successfully removed with metal polish. By way of contrast, the label side is actually more vulnerable than the readout side, since the lacquer coating is only 30 μm thick. For this reason, writing on the label side of CD is not recommended. Pressure from a ballpoint pen could distort the information layer, and solvents from marker pens have been known to penetrate the lacquer and cause corruption. The common party-piece of writing on the readout surface of CD with a felt pen to show off the error-correction system is quite harmless, since the disk base material is impervious to most solvents.

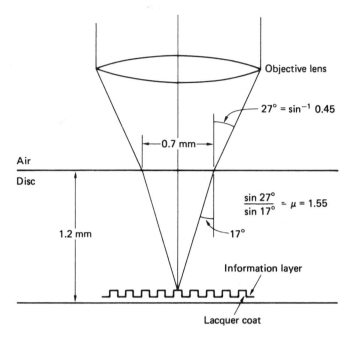

Figure 10.6 The objective lens of a CD pickup has a numerical aperture (NA) of 0.45; thus the outermost rays will be inclined at approximately 27° to the normal. Refraction at the air/disk interface changes this to approximately 17° within the disk. Thus light focused to a spot on the information layer has entered the disk through a 0.7 mm diameter circle, giving good resistance to surface contamination.

The base material is in fact a polycarbonate plastic produced by (among others) Bayer under the trade name of Makrolon. It has excellent mechanical and optical stability over a wide temperature range, and lends itself to precision moulding and metallization. It is often used for automotive indicator clusters for the same reasons. An alternative material is polymethyl methacrylate (PMMA), one of the first optical plastics, known by such trade names as Perspex and Plexiglas, and widely used for illuminated signs and aircraft canopies. Polycarbonate is preferred by some manufacturers since it is less hygroscopic than PMMA. The differential change in dimensions of the lacquer coat and the base material can cause warping in a hygroscopic material. CD and MD are too small for this to be a problem, but the larger analog video disks are actually two disks glued together back-to-back to prevent this warpage.

10.5 Playing optical disks

A typical laser disk drive resembles a magnetic drive in that it has a spindle drive mechanism to revolve the disk, and a positioner to give radial access across the disk surface. The positioner has to carry a collection of lasers, lenses, prisms, gratings and so on, and cannot be accelerated as fast as a magnetic-drive positioner. In some drives the reaction due to accelerating the pickup is cancelled by accelerating a balance weight in the opposite direction. This is easily done with a band and pulley system. A penalty of the very small track pitch possible in laser disks, which gives the enormous storage capacity, is that very accurate track following is needed, and it takes some time to lock on to a track. For this reason tracks on laser disks are often made as a continuous spiral, rather than the concentric rings of magnetic disks. In this way, a continuous data transfer involves no more than track following once the beginning of the file is located.

In order to record MO disks or replay any optical disk, a source of monochromatic light is required. The light source must have low noise otherwise the variations in intensity due to the noise of the source will mask the variations due to reading the disk. The requirement for a low-noise monochromatic light source is economically met using a semiconductor laser as described in Chapter 3.

Some of the light reflected back from the disk re-enters the aperture of the objective lens. The pickup must be capable of separating the reflected light from the incident light. Figure 10.7 shows two systems. In (a) an intensity beamsplitter consisting of a semisilvered mirror is inserted in the optical path and reflects some of the returning light into the photosensor. This is not very efficient, as half of the replay signal is lost by transmission straight on. In the example in (b) separation is by polarization.

Rotation of the plane of polarization is a useful method of separating incident and reflected light in a laser pickup. Using a quarter-wave plate, the plane of polarization of light leaving the pickup will have been turned 45 degrees, and on return it will be rotated a further 45 degrees, so that it is now at right angles to the plane of polarization of light from the source. The two can easily be separated by a polarizing prism, which acts as a transparent block to light in one plane, but as a prism to light in the other plane, such that reflected light is directed towards the sensor.

In pickups used for CD, WORM or phase-change disks, the sensor is concerned only with the intensity of the light falling on it. When playing MO

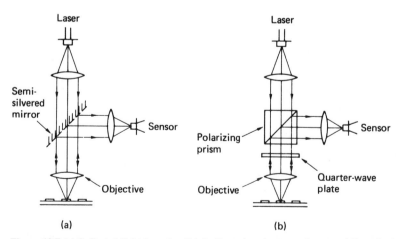

Figure 10.7 (a) Reflected light from the disk is directed to the sensor by a semisilvered mirror. (b) A combination of polarizing prism and quarter-wave plate separates incident and reflected light.

disks, the intensity does not change, but the magnetic recording on the disk rotates the plane of polarization one way or the other depending on the direction of the vertical magnetization. MO disks cannot be read with circular-polarized light. Light incident on the medium must be plane polarized and so the quarter-wave plate of the CD pickup cannot be used. Figure 10.8(a) shows that a polarising prism is still required to linearly polarize the light from the laser on its way to the disk. Light returning from the disk has had its plane of polarization rotated by approximately ±1 degree. This is an extremely small rotation. Figure 10.8(b) shows that the returning rotated light can be considered to be comprised of two orthogonal components. R_x is the component which is in the same plane as the illumination and is called the *ordinary* component and R_y is the component due to the Kerr-effect rotation and is known as the *magneto-optic* component. A polarizing beam splitter mounted squarely would reflect the magneto-optic component R_y very well because it is at right angles to the transmission plane of the prism, but the ordinary component would pass straight on in the direction of

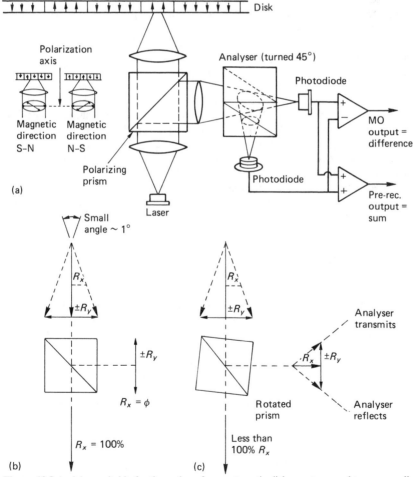

Figure 10.8 A pickup suitable for the replay of magneto-optic disks must respond to very small rotations of the plane of polarization.

the laser. By rotating the prism slightly a small amount of the ordinary component is also reflected. Figure 10.8(c) shows that when combined with the magneto-optic component, the angle of rotation has increased.[4] Detecting this rotation requires a further polarizing prism or analyser, as shown in Figure 10.8. The prism is twisted such that the transmission plane is at 45 degrees to the planes of R_x and R_y. Thus with an unmagnetized disk, half of the light is transmitted by the prism and half is reflected. If the magnetic field of the disk turns the plane of polarization towards the transmission plane of the prism, more light is transmitted and less is reflected. Conversely if the plane of polarization is rotated away from the transmission plane, less light is transmitted and more is reflected. If two sensors are used, one for transmitted light and one for reflected light, the difference between the two sensor outputs will be a waveform representing the angle of polarization and thus the recording on the disk. This differential analyser eliminates common mode noise in the reflected beam.[5] As Figure 10.8 shows, the output of the two sensors is summed as well as subtracted in a MiniDisc player. When playing MO disks, the difference signal is used. When playing prerecorded disks, the sum signal is used and the effect of the second polarizing prism is disabled.

10.6 Focus systems

In all types of optical disk drive the frequency response of the laser pickup and the amount of crosstalk are both a function of the spot size and care must be taken to keep the beam focused on the information layer. If the spot on the disk becomes too large, it will be unable to discern the smaller features of the track, and can also be affected by the adjacent track. Disk warp and thickness irregularities will cause focal-plane movement beyond the depth of focus of the optical system, and a focus servo system will be needed. The depth of field is related to the numerical aperture, which is defined, and the accuracy of the servo must be sufficient to keep the focal plane within that depth, which is typically ± 1 µm.

The focus servo moves a lens along the optical axis in order to keep the spot in focus. Since dynamic focus changes are largely due to warps, the focus system must have a frequency response in excess of the rotational speed. A moving-coil actuator is often used owing to the small moving mass which this permits. Figure 10.9 shows that a cylindrical magnet assembly almost identical to that of a loudspeaker can be used, coaxial with the light beam. Alternatively a moving-magnet design can be used. A rare-earth magnet allows a sufficiently strong magnetic field without excessive weight.

A focus-error system is necessary to drive the lens. There are a number of ways in which this can be derived, the most common of which will be described here.

In Figure 10.10 a cylindrical lens is installed between the beam splitter and the photosensor. The effect of this lens is that the beam has no focal point on the sensor. In one plane, the cylindrical lens appears parallel-sided, and has negligible effect on the focal length of the main system, whereas in the other plane, the lens shortens the focal length. The image will be an ellipse whose aspect ratio changes as a function of the state of focus. Between the two foci, the image will be circular. The aspect ratio of the ellipse, and hence the focus error,

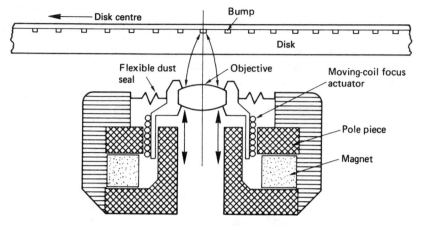

Figure 10.9 Moving-coil-focus servo can be coaxial with the light beam as shown.

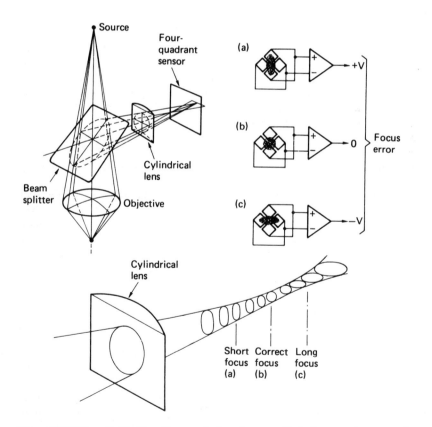

Figure 10.10 The cylindrical lens focus method produces an elliptical spot on the sensor whose aspect ratio is detected by a four-quadrant sensor to produce a focus error.

can be found by dividing the sensor into quadrants. When these are connected as shown, the focus-error signal is generated. The data readout signal is the sum of the quadrant outputs.

Figure 10.11 shows the knife-edge method of determining focus. A split sensor is also required. In (a) the focal point is coincident with the knife edge, so it has little effect on the beam. In (b) the focal point is to the right of the knife edge, and rising rays are interrupted, reducing the output of the upper sensor. In (c) the focal point is to the left of the knife edge, and descending rays are interrupted,

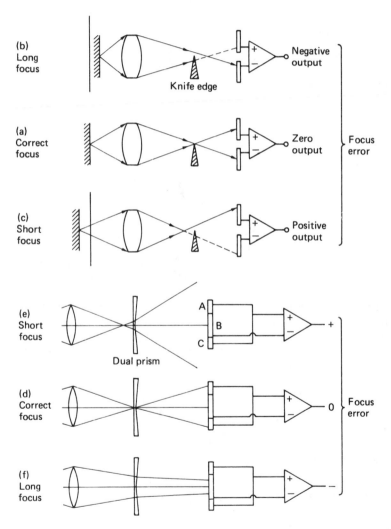

Figure 10.11 (a)–(c) Knife-edge focus method requires only two sensors, but is critically dependent on knife-edge position. (d)–(f) Twin-prism method requires three sensors (A, B, C), where focus error is (A + C) – B. Prism alignment reduces sensitivity without causing focus offset.

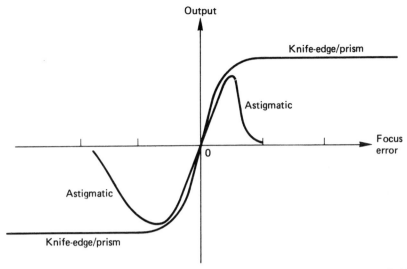

Figure 10.12 Comparison of captive range of knife-edge/prism method and astigmatic (cylindrical lens) system. Knife edge may have a range of 1 mm, whereas astigmatic may only have a range of 40 μm, requiring a focus-search mechanism.

reducing the output of the lower sensor. The focus error is derived by comparing the outputs of the two halves of the sensor. A drawback of the knife-edge system is that the lateral position of the knife edge is critical, and adjustment is necessary. To overcome this problem, the knife edge can be replaced by a pair of prisms, as shown in Figure 10.11(d)–(f). Mechanical tolerances then only affect the sensitivity, without causing a focus offset.

The cylindrical-lens method is compared with the knife-edge/prism method in Figure 10.12, which shows that the cylindrical-lens method has a much smaller capture range. A focus-search mechanism will be required, which moves the focus servo over its entire travel, looking for a zero crossing. At this time the feedback loop will be completed, and the sensor will remain on the linear part of its characteristic. The spiral track of many optical disks starts at the inside and works outwards. This was deliberately arranged because there is less vertical runout near the hub, and initial focusing will be easier.

10.7 Tracking systems

The track pitch of optical disks is of the order of 1 μm, and this is much smaller than the accuracy to which the player chuck or the disk centre hole can be made; on a typical drive, runout will swing several tracks past a fixed pickup. The non-contact readout means that there is no inherent mechanical guidance of the pickup. In addition, a warped disk will not present its surface at 90 degrees to the beam, but will constantly change the angle of incidence during two whole cycles per revolution. Owing to the change of refractive index at the disk surface, the tilt

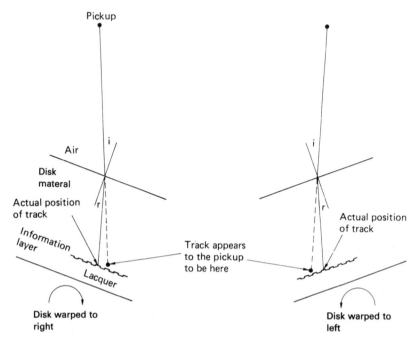

Figure 10.13 Owing to refraction, the angle of incidence (i) is greater than the angle of refraction (r). Disk warp causes the apparent position of the track (dashed line) to move, requiring the tracking servo to correct.

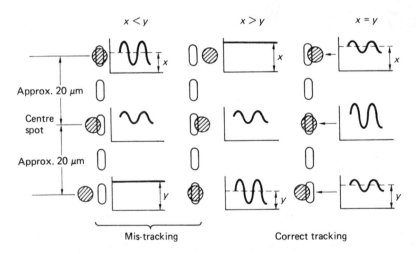

Figure 10.14 Three-spot method of producing tracking error compares average level of side-spot signals. Side spots are produced by a diffraction grating and require their own sensors.

will change the apparent position of the track to the pickup, and Figure 10.13 shows that this makes it appear wavy. Warp also results in coma of the readout spot. The disk format specifies a maximum warp amplitude to keep these effects under control. Finally, vibrations induced in the player from outside will tend to disturb tracking. A track-following servo is necessary to keep the spot centralized on the track in the presence of these difficulties. There are several ways in which a tracking error can be derived.

In the three-spot method, two additional light beams are focused on the disk track, one offset to each side of the track centre-line. Figure 10.14 shows that, as one side spot moves away from the track into the mirror area, there is less destructive interference and more reflection. This causes the average amplitude of the side spots to change differentially with tracking error. The laser head contains a diffraction grating which produces the side spots, and two extra photosensors onto which the reflections of the side spots will fall. The side spots feed a differential amplifier, which has a low-pass filter to reject the channel-coded information and retain the average brightness difference. Some drives use a delay line in one of the side-spot signals whose period is equal to the time taken for the disk to travel between the side spots. This helps the differential amplifier to cancel the channel-coded signal.

An alternative approach to tracking-error detection is to analyse the diffraction pattern of the reflected beam. The effect of an off-centre spot is to rotate the radial diffraction pattern about an axis along the track. Figure 10.15 shows that, if a split sensor is used, one half will see greater modulation than the other when off track. Such a system may be prone to develop an offset due either to drift or to contamination of the optics, although the capture range is large.

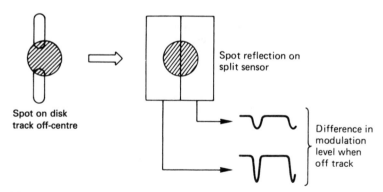

Figure 10.15 Split-sensor method of producing tracking error focuses image of spot onto sensor. One side of spot will have more modulation when off track.

Figure 10.16 shows a dither- or wobble-based system in which a sinusoidal drive is fed to the tracking servo, causing a radial oscillation of spot position of about ±50 nm. This results in modulation of the envelope of the readout signal, which can be synchronously detected to obtain the sense of the error. The dither can be produced by vibrating a mirror in the light path, which enables a high

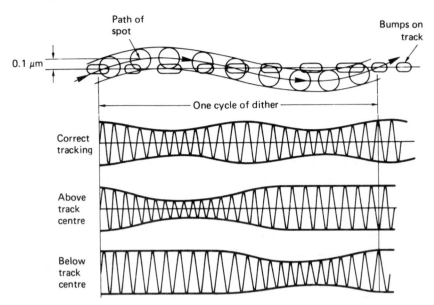

Figure 10.16 Dither applied to readout spot modulates the readout envelope. A tracking error can be derived.

frequency to be used, or by oscillating the whole pickup at a lower frequency. Alternatively the disk is made with such a spot wobble in the mastering cutter so that it has a wobbling track. No wobble is then needed in the reader. An advantage of track wobble is that the wobble frequency is proportional to the speed of the track and so it can be used for spindle-speed control. The wobble may also be modulated by addressing codes.

10.8 Typical pickups

It is interesting to compare different designs of laser pickup. Figure 10.17 shows a Philips laser head.[6] The dual-prism focus method is used, which combines the output of two split sensors to produce a focus error. The focus amplifier drives the objective lens which is mounted on a parallel motion formed by two flexural arms. The capture range of the focus system is sufficient to accommodate normal tolerances without assistance. A radial differential tracking signal is extracted from the sensors as shown in the figure. Additionally, a dither frequency of 600 Hz produces envelope modulation which is synchronously rectified to produce a drift-free tracking error. Both errors are combined to drive the tracking system. As only a single spot is used, the pickup is relatively insensitive to angular errors, and a rotary positioner can be used, driven by a moving coil. The assembly is statically balanced to give good resistance to lateral shock.

Figure 10.18 shows a Sony laser head used in consumer players. The cylindrical-lens focus method is used, requiring a four-quadrant sensor. Since

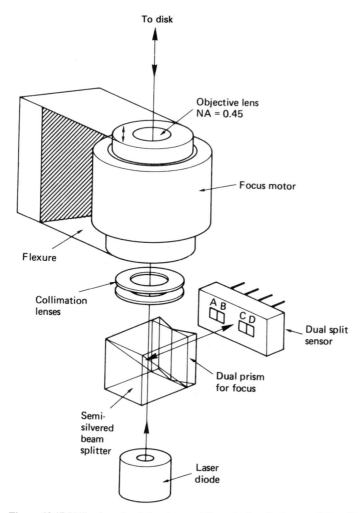

Figure 10.17 Philips laser head showing semisilvered prism for beam splitting. Focus error is derived from dual-prism method using split sensors. Focus error $(A + D) - (B + C)$ is used to drive focus motor which moves objective lens on parallel action flexure. Radial differential tracking error is derived from split sensor $(A + B) - (C + D)$. Tracking error drives entire pickup on radial arm driven by moving coil. Signal output is $(A + B + C + D)$. System includes 600 Hz dither for tracking. (Courtesy *Philips Technical Review*)

this method has a small capture range, a focus-search mechanism is necessary. When a disk is loaded, the objective lens is ramped up and down looking for a zero crossing in the focus error. The three-spot method is used for tracking. The necessary diffraction grating can be seen adjacent to the laser diode. Tracking error is derived from side-spot sensors (E, F). Since the side-spot system is sensitive to angular error, a parallel-tracking laser head traversing a disk radius is essential. A cost-effective linear motion is obtained by using a

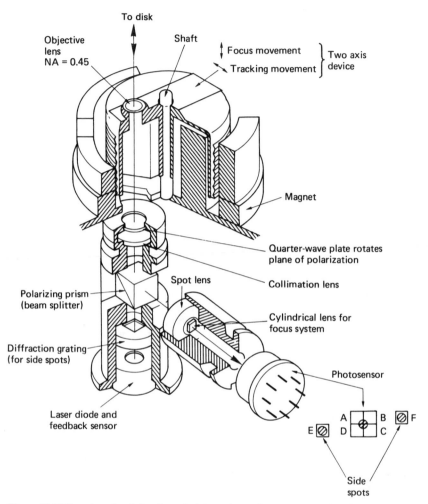

Figure 10.18 Sony laser head showing polarizing prism and quarter-wave plate for beam splitting, and diffraction grating for production of side spots for tracking. The cylindrical lens system is used for focus, with a four-quadrant sensor (A, B, C, D) and two extra sensors E, F for the side spots. Tracking error is E − F; focus error is (A + C) − (B + D). Signal output is (A + B + C + D). The focus and tracking errors drive the two-axis device. (Courtesy *Sony Broadcast*)

rack-and-pinion drive for slow, coarse movements, and a laterally moving lens in the light path for fine, rapid movements. The same lens will be moved up and down for focus by the so-called two-axis device, which is a dual-moving coil mechanism. In some players this device is not statically balanced, making the unit sensitive to shock, but this was overcome on later heads designed for portable players. Figure 10.19 shows a later Sony design having a prism which reduces the height of the pickup above the disk.

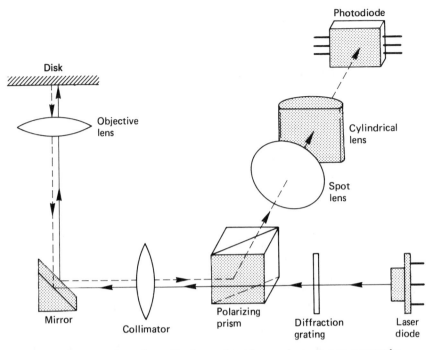

Figure 10.19 For automotive and portable players, the pickup can be made more compact by incorporating a mirror, which allows most of the elements to be parallel to the disk instead of at right angles.

10.9 CD readout in detail

The CD medium is designed to be read with a phase-contrast microscope, and so it is correct to describe the deformities on the information layer as a phase structure. The original LaserVision disk patent[7] contains a variety of approaches, but in the embodiment used in CD it consists of two parallel planes separated by a distance which is constant and specifically related to the wavelength of the light which will be used to read it. The phase structure is created with deformities which depart from the first of the planes and whose extremities are in the second plane. These deformities are called pits when the second plane is below the first and bumps when the second plane is above the first.

Whilst a phase structure can be read by transmission or reflection, commercial designs based the Philips medium, such as LaserVision,[8] CD, CD-Video, CD-ROM and prerecorded MiniDisc, use reflective readout exclusively.

Optical physicists characterize materials by their reflectivity, transmissivity and absorption. Light energy cannot disappear, so when light is incident on some object, the amounts of light transmitted, absorbed and reflected must add up to the original incident amount. When no light is absorbed, the incident light is divided between that transmitted and that reflected. When light is absorbed, the transmitted and reflected amounts of light are both reduced. A medium such as a photograph contains pigments which absorb light more in the dark areas and less in the light areas. Thus the amount of light reflected varies. A medium such as a transparency also contains such pigments but in this case it is primarily the amount of light transmitted which varies. Such a variation in transmitted or reflected light from place to place is known as contrast.

Figure 10.2 showed that, in CD, the information layer consists of an optically flat surface above which flat-topped bumps project. The entire surface of the phase structure is metallized to render it reflective. This metallization of the entire information layer means that little light is transmitted or absorbed, and as a result virtually all incident light must be reflected. The information layer of CD does not have conventional contrast. Contrast is in any case unnecessary as interference is used for readout, and this works better with a totally reflecting structure. Returning to Figure 10.2 it will be seen that a spot of light is focused onto the phase structure such that it straddles a bump. Ideally half the light energy should be incident on the top of the bump and half on the surrounding mirror surface. The height of the bump is ideally one-quarter the wavelength of the light in a reflective system and as a result light which has reflected from the mirror surface has travelled one-half a wavelength further than light which has reflected from the mirror surface. Consequently, along the normal, there are two components of light of almost equal energy, but they are in phase opposition, and destructive interference occurs such that no wavefront can form in that direction. As light energy cannot disappear, wavefronts will leave the phase structure at any oblique angle at which constructive interference between the components can be achieved, creating a diffraction pattern. In the case of the light beam straddling the centre of a long bump the diffraction pattern will be in a plane which is normal to the disk surface and which intersects a disk radius. It is thus called a radial diffraction pattern. The zeroth order radiation (that along the normal) will be heavily attenuated, and most of the incident energy will be concentrated in the first- and second-order wavefronts.

Some treatments use the word scattering to describe the effect of the interaction of the readout beam with the relief structure. This is technically incorrect as scattering is a random phenomenon which is independent of wavelength. The diffraction pattern is totally predictable and strongly wavelength dependent.

When the light spot is focused on a plain part of the mirror surface, known as a land, clearly most of the energy is simply reflected back whence it came. Thus when a bump is present, light is diffracted away from the normal, whereas in the absence of a bump it returns along the normal. Although all incident light is reflected at all times, the effect of diffraction is that the direction in which wavefronts leave the phase structure is changed by the presence of the bump. What then happens is a function of the optical system being used. In a conventional CD player the angle to the normal of the first diffracted order in the radial diffraction pattern due to a long bump will be sufficiently oblique that it passes outside the aperture of the objective and does not return to the photosensor. Thus the bumps appear dark to the photosensor and the lands appear bright. Although all light is reflected at all times and there is no conventional contrast, inside the pickup there are variations in the light falling on the photosensor, a phenomenon called phase contrast.

The phase-contrast technique described will only work for a given wavelength and with an appropriate aperture and lens design, and so the CD must be read with monochromatic light. Whilst the ideal case is where the two components of light are equal to give exact cancellation, in practice this ideal is not met but instead there is a substantial reduction in the light returning to the pickup.

Some treatments of CD refer to a 'beam' of light returning from the disk to the pickup, but this is incorrect. What leaves the disk is a hemispherical diffraction pattern, certain orders of which enter the aperture of the pickup. The destructive interference effect can be seen with the naked eye by examining any CD under a conventional incandescent lamp. The data surface of a CD has many parallel tracks and works somewhat like a diffraction grating by dispersing the incident white light into a spectrum. However, the resultant spectrum is not at all like that produced by a conventional diffraction grating or by a prism. These latter produce a spectrum in which the relative brightness of the colours is like that of a rainbow, i.e. the green in the centre is brightest, the red at one end is less bright and the blue at the other end is fainter still. This is due to the unequal response of the eye to various colours, where equal red, green and blue stimuli produce responses in approximately the proportions 2:5:1 respectively. In the diffracted spectrum from a CD, however, the blue component appears as strong or stronger than the other colours. This is because the relief structure of CD is designed not to reflect infrared light of 780 nm wavelength. This relief structure will, however, reflect perfectly ultraviolet light of half that wavelength as the zeroth-order light reflected from the top of the bumps will be in phase with light reflected from the land. Thus a CD reflects visible blue light much more strongly than longer wavelength colours.

Figure 10.2 was simplified only to the extent that the light spot was depicted as having a distinct edge of a given diameter. In reality such a neat spot cannot be obtained. It is essential to the commercial success of optical disks that a high recording density should be obtained. It follows that the smaller the spot of light which can be created, the smaller can be the deformities carrying the information, and so more information per unit area (the superficial recording density) can be stored. Development of a successful high-density optical recorder requires an intimate knowledge of the behaviour of light focused into small spots. If it is attempted to focus a uniform beam of light to an infinitely small spot on a surface normal to the optical axis, it will be found that it is not possible. This is probably just as well as an infinitely small spot would have infinite intensity and any matter it fell on would not survive. Instead the result of such an attempt is a distribution of light in the area of the focal point which has no sharply defined boundary. This is called the Airy distribution[9] (sometimes pattern or disk) after Lord Airy (1835), the then astronomer royal. If a line is considered to pass across the focal plane, through the theoretical focal point, and the intensity of the light is plotted on a graph as a function of the distance along that line, the result is the intensity function shown in Figure 10.20. It will be seen that this contains a central sloping peak surrounded by alternating dark rings and light rings of diminishing intensity. These rings will in theory reach to infinity before their intensity becomes zero. The intensity distribution or function described by Airy is due to diffraction effects across the finite aperture of the objective. For a given wavelength, as the aperture of the objective is increased, so the diameter of the features of the Airy pattern reduces. The Airy pattern vanishes to a singularity of infinite intensity with a lens of infinite aperture, which of course cannot be made. The approximation of geometric optics is quite unable to predict the occurrence of the Airy pattern.

An intensity function does not have a diameter, but for practical purposes an effective diameter typically quoted is that at which the intensity has fallen to

some convenient fraction of that at the peak. Thus one could state, for example, the half-power diameter.

Since light paths in optical instruments are generally reversible, it is possible to see an interesting corollary which gives a useful insight into the readout principle of optical disks. Considering light radiating from a phase structure, as in Figure 10.21, the more closely spaced the features of the phase structure, i.e. the higher the spatial frequency, the more oblique the direction of the wavefronts in the diffraction pattern which results and the larger the aperture of the lens needed to collect the light if the resolution is not to be lost. The corollary of this is that the smaller the Airy distribution it is wished to create, the larger must be the aperture of the lens. Spatial frequency is measured in lines per millimetre and, as it increases, the wavefronts of the resultant diffraction pattern become more oblique. In the case of a CD, the smaller the bumps and the spaces between them along the track, the higher the spatial frequency, and the more oblique the diffraction pattern becomes in a plane tangential to the track. With a fixed objective aperture, as the tangential diffraction pattern becomes more oblique, less light passes the aperture and the depth of modulation transmitted by the lens falls. At some spatial frequency, all of the diffracted light falls outside the aperture and the modulation depth transmitted by the lens falls to zero. This is known as the spatial cut-off frequency. Thus a graph of depth of modulation versus spatial frequency can be drawn and is known as the modulation transfer function (MTF). This is a straight line commencing at unity at zero spatial frequency (no detail) and falling to zero at the cut-off spatial frequency (finest detail). Thus one could describe a lens of finite aperture as a form of spatial low-pass filter. The Airy function is no more than the spatial impulse response of the lens, and the concentric rings of the Airy function are the spatial analogue of the symmetrical ringing in a phase-linear electrical filter. The Airy function and the triangular frequency response form a transform pair.[10]

When an objective lens is used in a conventional microscope, the MTF will allow the resolution to be predicted in lines per millimetre. However, in a scanning microscope the spatial frequency of the detail in the object is multiplied by the scanning velocity to give a temporal frequency measured in Hertz. Thus lines per millimetre multiplied by millimetres per second gives lines per second. Instead of a straight-line MTF falling to the spatial cut-off frequency, a scanning microscope has a temporal frequency response falling to zero at the optical cut-off frequency. Put more technically, the frequency response of an optical recorder is the Fourier transform of the Airy distribution of the readout spot multiplied by the track velocity.

In magnetic recorders and vinyl disk recorders there is at least a frequency band where the response is reasonably flat. In scanning microscopes, Figure 10.22 shows that the frequency response falls progressively from DC to the optical cut-off frequency which is given by:

$$F_c = \frac{2NA}{\text{wavelength}} \times \text{velocity}$$

For example, the minimum linear velocity of CD is 1.2 m/s, giving a cut-off frequency of:

$$F_c = \frac{2 \times 0.45 \times 1.2}{780 \times 10^{-9}} = 1.38\,\text{MHz}$$

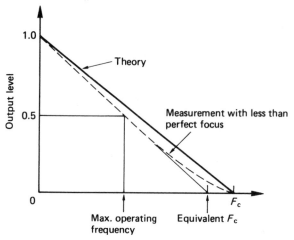

Figure 10.22 Frequency response of laser pickup. Maximum operating frequency is about half of cut-off frequency F_c.

Actual measurements reveal that the optical response is only a little worse than the theory predicts. This characteristic has a large bearing on the type of modulation schemes which can be successfully employed. Clearly, to obtain any noise immunity, the maximum operating frequency must be rather less than the cut-off frequency. The maximum frequency used in CD is 720 kHz, which represents an absolute minimum wavelength of 1.666 μm, or a bump length of 0.833 μm, for the lowest permissible track speed of 1.2 m/s used on the full-length 75 min-playing discs. One-hour-playing discs have a minimum bump length of 0.972 μm at a track velocity of 1.4 m/s. The maximum frequency is the same in both cases. This maximum frequency should not be confused with the bit rate of CD since this is different owing to the channel code used. Figure 10.20 showed a maximum-frequency recording, and the physical relationship of the intensity function to the track dimensions.

In an optical drive, the source of light is a laser, and this does not produce a beam of uniform intensity. It is more intense in the centre than it is at the edges, and this has the effect of slightly increasing the half-power diameter of the intensity function. The effect is analogous to the effect of window functions in FIR filters. The intensity function can also be enlarged if the lens used suffers from optical aberrations. This was studied by Maréchal[11] who established criteria for the accuracy to which the optical surfaces of the lens should be made to allow the ideal Airy distribution to be obtained. CD player lenses must meet the Maréchal criterion. With such a lens, the diameter of the distribution function is determined solely by the combination of numerical aperture (NA) and the wavelength. When the size of the spot is as small as the NA and wavelength allow, the optical system is said to be diffraction limited. Figure 10.21 showed how numerical aperture is defined, and illustrates that the smaller the spot needed, the larger must be the NA. Unfortunately the larger the NA the more obliquely to the normal the light arrives at the focal plane and the smaller the depth of focus will be. This was investigated by Hopkins,[12] who established the depth of focus available for a given NA. Most optical recorders use an NA of around 0.45 which is a compromise between a small spot and an impossibly small depth of focus.[13]

The intensity function will also be distorted and grossly enlarged if the optical axis is not normal to the medium. The initial effect is that the energy in the first bright ring increases strongly in one place and results in a secondary peak adjacent to the central peak. This is known as coma and its effect is extremely serious as the enlargement of the spot restricts the recording density. The larger the NA the smaller becomes the allowable tilt of the optical axis with respect to the medium before coma becomes a problem. With a typical NA this angle is less than 1 degree.[13]

Numerical aperture is defined as the cosine of the angle between the optical axis and rays converging from the perimeter of the lens. It will be apparent that there are many combinations of lens diameter and focal length which will have the same NA. As the difficulty of manufacture, and consequently the cost, of a lens meeting the Maréchal criterion increases disproportionately with size, it is advantageous to use a small lens of short focal length, mounted close to the medium and held precisely perpendicular to the medium to prevent coma. As the lens needs to be driven along its axis by a servo to maintain focus, the smaller lens will facilitate the design of the servo by reducing the mass to be driven. It is extremely difficult to make a lens which meets the Maréchal criterion over a range of wavelengths because of dispersion. The use of monochromatic light eases the lens design as it has only to be correct for one wavelength.

At the high recording density of optical disks, there is literally only one scanning mechanism with which all of the optical criteria can be met and this is the approach known from the scanning microscope. The optical pickup is mounted in a carriage which can move it parallel to the medium in such a way that the optical axis remains at all times parallel to the axis of rotation of the medium. The latter rotates as the pickup is driven away from the axis of rotation in such a way that a spiral track on the disk is followed. The pickup contains a short focal length lens of small diameter which must therefore be close to the disk surface to allow a large NA. All high-density optical recorders operate on this principle in which the readout of the carrier is optical but the scanning is actually mechanical.

10.10 How optical disks are made

The steps used in the production of CDs and CD-ROM will next be outlined. Prerecorded MiniDiscs are made in an identical fashion except for detail differences which will be noted. MO disks need to be grooved so that the track-following system will work. The grooved substrate is produced in a similar way to a CD master, except that the laser is on continuously instead of being modulated with a signal to be recorded. The MO groove must also wobble, and means are provided to deflect the cutter beam. As stated, CD is replicated by moulding, and the first step is to produce a suitable mould. This mould must carry deformities of the correct depth for the standard wavelength to be used for reading, and as a practical matter these deformities must have slightly sloping sides so that it is possible to release the CD from the mould.

The major steps in CD manufacture are shown in Figure 10.23. The mastering process commences with an optically flat glass disk about 220 mm in diameter and 6 mm thick. The blank is washed first with an alkaline solution, then with a fluorocarbon solvent, and spun dry prior to polishing to optical flatness. A critical cleaning process is then undertaken using a mixture of de-ionized water and isopropyl alcohol in the presence of ultrasonic vibration, with a final fluorocarbon wash. The blank must now be inspected for any surface irregularities which would cause data errors. This is done by using a laser beam and monitoring the reflection as the blank rotates. Rejected blanks return to the

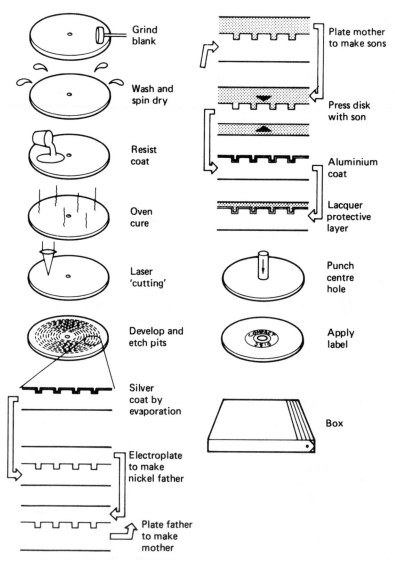

Figure 10.23 The many stages of CD manufacture, most of which require the utmost cleanliness.

polishing process; those which pass move on, and an adhesive layer is applied followed by a coating of positive photoresist. This is a chemical substance which softens when exposed to an appropriate intensity of light of a certain wavelength, typically ultraviolet. Upon being thus exposed, the softened resist will be washed away by a developing solution down to the glass to form flat-bottomed pits whose depth is equal to the thickness of the undeveloped resist. During development the master is illuminated with laser light of a wavelength to which it is insensitive. The diffraction pattern changes as the pits are formed. Development is arrested when the appropriate diffraction pattern is obtained.[14] The thickness of the resist layer must be accurately controlled, since it affects the height of the bumps on the finished disk, and an optical scanner is used to check that there are no resist defects which would cause data errors or tracking problems in the end product. Blanks which pass this test are oven cured, and are ready for cutting. Failed blanks can be stripped of the resist coating and used again.

The cutting process is shown in simplified form in Figure 10.24. A continuously operating helium–cadmium[15] or argon-ion[16] laser is focused on the resist coating as the blank revolves. Focus is achieved by a separate helium–neon laser sharing the same optics. The resist is insensitive to the wavelength of the

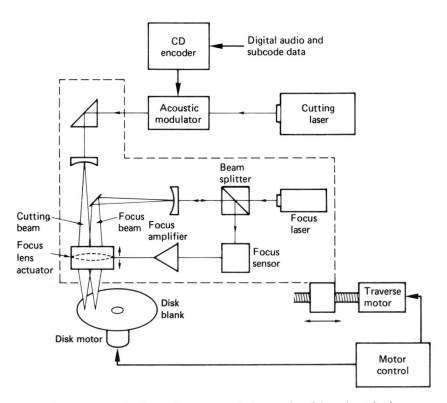

Figure 10.24 CD cutter. The focus subsystem controls the spot size of the main cutting laser on the photosensitive blank. Disk and traverse motors are coordinated to give constant track pitch and velocity. Note that the power of the focus laser is insufficient to expose the photoresist.

He–Ne laser. The laser intensity is controlled by a device known as an acousto-optic modulator which is driven by the encoder. When the device is in a relaxed state, light can pass through it, but when the surface is excited by high-frequency vibrations, light is scattered. Information is carried in the lengths of time for which the modulator remains on or remains off. As a result the deformities in the resist produced as the disk turns when the modulator allows light to pass are separated by areas unaffected by light when the modulator is shut off. Information is carried solely in the variations of the lengths of these two areas.

The laser makes its way from the inside to the outside as the blank revolves. As the radius of the track increases, the rotational speed is proportionately reduced so that the velocity of the beam over the disk remains constant. This constant linear velocity (CLV) results in rather longer playing time than would be obtained with a constant speed of rotation. Owing to the minute dimensions of the track structure, the cutter has to be constructed to extremely high accuracy. Air bearings are used in the spindle and the laser head, and the whole machine is resiliently supported to prevent vibrations from the building from affecting the track pattern.

As the player is a phase-contrast microscope, it must produce an intensity function which straddles the deformities. As a consequence the intensity function which produces the deformities in the photoresist must be smaller in diameter than that in the reader. This is conveniently achieved by using a shorter wavelength of 400–500 nm from a helium–cadmium or argon-ion laser combined with a larger lens aperture of 0.9. These are expensive, but are only needed for the mastering process.

It is a characteristic of photoresist that its development rate is not linearly proportional to the intensity of light. This non-linearity is known as 'gamma'. As a result there are two intensities of importance when scanning photoresist: the lower sensitivity, or threshold, below which no development takes place, and the upper threshold above which there is full development. As the laser light falling on the resist is an intensity function, it follows that the two thresholds will be reached at different diameters of the function. It can be seen in Figure 10.25 that advantage is taken of this effect to produce tapering sides to the pits formed in the resist. In the centre, the light is intense enough to fully develop the resist right down to the glass. This gives the deformity a flat bottom. At the edge, the intensity falls and as some light is absorbed by the resist, the diameter of the resist which can be developed falls with depth in the resist. By controlling the intensity of the laser, and the development time, the slope of the sides of the pits can be controlled.

In summary, the resist thickness controls the depth of the pits, the cutter laser wavelength and the NA of the objective together control the width of the pits in the radial direction, and the laser intensity and sensitivity of the resist together with the development time control the slope. The length of the pits in the tangential direction, i.e. along the track, is controlled by the speed of the disk past the objective and the length of time for which the modulator allows light to pass. The space between the pits along the track is controlled by the speed of the disk past the objective and the length of time for which the modulator blocks the laser light. In practice all of these values are constant for a given cutting process except for the times for which the modulator turns on or off. As a result pits of constant depth and cross-section are formed, and only their length and the space between them along the track is changed in order to carry information.

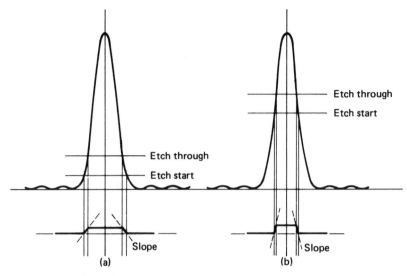

Figure 10.25 The two levels of exposure sensitivity of the resist determine the size and edge slope of the bumps in the CD. (a) Large exposure results in large bump with gentle slope; (b) less exposure results in smaller bump with steeper sloped sides.

The specified wavelength of 780 nm and the numerical aperture of 0.45 used for playback results in an Airy function where the half-power level is at a diameter of about 1 μm. The first dark ring will be at about 1.9 μm diameter. As the illumination follows an intensity function, it is really meaningless to talk about spot size unless the relative power level is specified. The analogy is quoting frequency response without dB limits. Allowable crosstalk between tracks then determines the track pitch. The first ring outside the central disk carries some 7% of the total power, and limits crosstalk performance. The track spacing is such that with a slightly defocused beam and a slight tracking error, crosstalk due to adjacent tracks is acceptable. Since aberrations in the objective will increase the spot size and crosstalk, the CD specification requires the lens to be within the Maréchal criterion. Clearly the numerical aperture of the lens, the wavelength of the laser, the refractive index and thickness of the disk and the height and size of the bumps must all be simultaneously specified.

The master recording process has produced a phase structure in relatively delicate resist, and this cannot be used for moulding directly. Instead a thin metallic silver layer is sprayed onto the resist to render it electrically conductive so that electroplating can be used to make robust copies of the relief structure. This conductive layer then makes the resist optically reflective and it is possible to 'play' the resist master for testing purposes.

The electrically conductive resist master is then used as the cathode of an electroplating process where a first layer of metal is laid down over the resist, conforming in every detail to the relief structure thereon. This metal layer can then be separated from the glass, the resist dissolved away and the silver recovered leaving a laterally inverted phase structure on the surface of the metal, in which the pits in the photoresist have become bumps in the metal. From this point on, the production of CD is virtually identical to the replication process used for vinyl disks, save only that a good deal more precision and cleanliness is needed.

This first metal layer could itself be used to mould disks, or it could be used as a robust submaster from which many stampers could be made by pairs of plating steps. The first metal phase structure can itself be used as a cathode in a further electroplating process in which a second metal layer is formed having a mirror image of the first. A third such plating step results in a stamper. The decision to use the master or substampers will be based on the number of disks and the production rate required.

The master is placed in a moulding machine, opposite a flat plate. A suitable quantity of molten plastic is injected between, and the plate and the master are forced together. The flat plate renders one side of the disk smooth, and the bumps in the metal stamper produce pits in the other surface of the disk. The surface containing the pits is next metallized, with any good electrically conductive material, typically aluminium. This metallization is then covered with a lacquer for protection. In the case of CD, the label is printed on the lacquer. In the case of a prerecorded MiniDisc, the ferrous hub needs to be applied prior to fitting the cartridge around the disk.

As CD and prerecorded MDs are simply data disks, they do not need to be mastered in real time. Raising the speed of the mastering process increases the throughput of the expensive equipment. The U-matic-based PCM-1630 CD mastering recorder is incapable of working faster than real time, and pressing plants have been using computer tape streamers in order to supply the cutter with higher data rates. The Sony MO mastering disk drive is designed to operate at up to 2.5 times real time to support high-speed mastering.

10.11 MiniDisc read/write in detail

MiniDisc has to operate under a number of constraints which largely determine how the read/write pickup operates. A prerecorded MiniDisc has exactly the same track dimensions as CD so that it can be mastered on similar equipment. When playing a prerecorded disk, the MiniDisc player pickup has to act in the same way as a CD pickup. This determines the laser wavelength, the NA of the objective and the effective spot diameter on the disk. This spot diameter must also be used when the pickup is operating with an MO disk.

Figure 10.26(a) shows to scale a CD track being played by a standard pickup. The readout spot straddles the track so that two antiphase components of reflected light can be obtained. As was explained in Section 10.10, the CD mastering cutter must use a shorter wavelength and larger NA than the subsequent player in order to 'cut' the small pits in the resist. Figure 10.26(b) shows that the cutting process convolves the laser enabling pulse with the spot profile so that the pit is actually longer than the pulse duration by a spot diameter. The effect is relatively small in CD because of the small spot used in the cutter.

When using an MO disk, the tracks recorded will be equal in width to the spot diameter and so will be wider than CD tracks, as Figure 10.26(c) shows. MO writing can be performed in two ways. The conventional method used in computer disks is to apply a steady current to the coil and to modulate the laser. This is because the coil has to be some distance from the magnetic layer of the

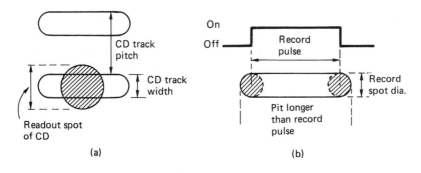

(a)   (b)

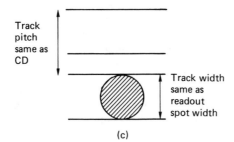

(c)

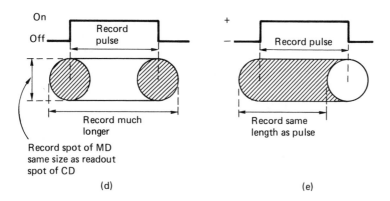

(d)   (e)

Figure 10.26 (a) A CD track and readout spot to scale. (b) The CD track is cut by a smaller spot, but the process results in pits which are longer than the pulse duration. (c) An MO track and readout spot to scale. If this spot is pulsed for writing, the magnetized areas are much larger than the pulse period and density is compromised as in (d). If, however, the magnetic field is modulated, as in (e), the recording is made at the trailing edge of the spot and short wavelengths can be used.

disk and must be quite large. The inductance of the coil is too great to allow it to be driven at the data frequency in computer applications.

Figure 10.26(d) shows what would happen if MD used laser modulation. The spot profile is convolved with the modulation pulse as for a CD cutter, but the spot is the same size as a replay spot. As a result the magnetized area is considerably longer than the modulation pulse. The shortest wavelengths of a recording could not be reproduced by this system, and it would be necessary to increase the track speed, reducing the playing time.

The data rate of MiniDisc is considerably lower than is the case for computer disks, and it is possible to use magnetic field modulation instead of laser modulation. The laser is then on continuously, and the spot profile is no longer convolved with the modulation. The recording is actually made at the instant the magnetic layer cools below the Curie temperature of about 180 degrees C just after the spot has passed. The state of the magnetic field at this instant is preserved on the disk. Figure 10.26(e) shows that the recorded wavelength can be much shorter because the recording is effectively made by the trailing edge of the spot. This makes the ends of the recorded flux patterns somewhat crescent shaped. Thus a spot the same size as a CD readout spot can be made to record flux patterns as short as the pits made by the smaller spot of a cutter. The recordable MiniDisc can thus have the same playing time as a prerecorded disk. The optical pickup is simplified because no laser modulator is needed.

The magnetic layer of MO disks should show a large Kerr rotation angle in order to give an acceptable SNR on replay. A high Curie temperature requires a high recording power, but allows greater readout power to be used without fear of demagnetization. This increases the readout signal with respect to the photodiode noise. As a result the Curie temperature is a compromise. Magnetic layers with practical Curie temperatures are made from proprietary alloys of iron, cobalt, platinum, terbium, gadolinium and various other rare earths. These are all highly susceptible to corrosion in air and are also incompatible with the plastics

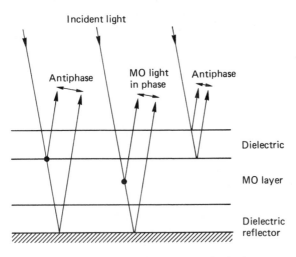

Figure 10.27 In MO disks the dielectric and reflective layers are as important as the magneto-optic layer itself.

used for moulded substrates. The magnetic layer must be protected by sandwiching it between layers of material which require to be impervious to corrosive ions but which must be optically transmissive. Thus only dielectrics such as silicon dioxide or aluminium nitride can be used.

The disk pickup is concerned with analysing light which has returned from within the MO layer as only this will have the Kerr rotation. Reflection from the interface between the MO layer and the dielectric overlayer will have no Kerr rotation. The optical characteristics of the dielectric layers can be used to enhance readout by reducing the latter reflection. Figure 10.27 shows that the MO disks have an optically reflective layer behind the sandwiched MO layer. The thickness of the dielectric between the MO layer and the reflector is selected such that light from the reflector is antiphase with light from the overlayer/MO layer interface, and instead of being reflected back to the pickup is absorbed in the MO layer. Conversely, light originating in the MO layer and leaving in the direction of the pickup experiences constructive interference with reflected components of that light. These components which contain Kerr rotation are readily able to exit the disk. These measures enhance the ratio of the magneto-optic component to ordinary light at the pickup.

10.12 How recordable MO disks are made

MO disks make the recording as flux patterns in a magnetic layer. However, the disks need to be pre-grooved so that the tracking systems described in Section 10.7 can operate. In MiniDisc the grooves have the same pitch as CD and the prerecorded MD, but the tracks are the same width as the laser spot: about 1.1 μm. The grooves are not a perfect spiral, but have a sinusoidal waviness at a fixed wavelength. Like CD, MD uses constant track linear velocity, not constant speed of rotation. When recording on a blank disk, the recorder needs to know how fast to turn the spindle to get the track speed correct. The wavy grooves will be followed by the tracking servo and the frequency of the tracking error will be proportional to the disk speed. The recorder simply turns the spindle at a speed which makes the grooves wave at the correct frequency. The groove frequency is 75 Hz; the same as the data sector rate. Thus a zero crossing in the groove signal can also be used to indicate where to start recording. The grooves are particularly important when a chequerboarded recording is being replayed. On a CLV disk, every seek to a new track radius results in a different track speed. The wavy grooves allow the track velocity to be monitored as soon as a new track is reached.

The pre-grooves are moulded into the plastics body of the disk when it is made. The mould is made in a similar manner to a prerecorded disk master, except that the laser is not modulated and the spot is larger. The track velocity is held constant by slowing down the resist master as the radius increases, and the waviness is created by injecting 75 Hz into the lens radial positioner. The master is developed and electroplated as normal in order to make stampers. The stampers make pre-grooved disks which are then coated by vacuum deposition with the MO layer, sandwiched between dielectric layers. The MO layer can be made less susceptible to corrosion if it is smooth and homogeneous. Layers which contain voids, asperities or residual gases from the coating process present a larger surface area for attack. The life of an MO disk is affected more by the manufacturing process than by the precise composition of the alloy.

Above the sandwich an optically reflective layer is applied, followed by a protective lacquer layer. The ferrous clamping plate is applied to the centre of the disk, which is then fitted in the cartridge. The recordable cartridge has a double-sided shutter to allow the magnetic head access to the back of the disk.

10.13 Channel code of CD and MiniDisc

CD and MiniDisc use the same channel code. This was optimized for the optical readout of CD and prerecorded MiniDisc, but is also used for the recordable version of MiniDisc for simplicity.

The frequency response falling to the optical cut-off frequency is only one of the constraints within which the modulation scheme has to work. There are a number of others. In all players the tracking and focus servos operate by analysing the average amount of light returning to the pickup. If the average amount of light returning to the pickup is affected by the content of the recorded data, then the recording will interfere with the operation of the servos. Debris on the disk surface affects the light intensity and means must be found to prevent this reducing the signal quality excessively.

Optical disks are serial media which produce on replay only a single voltage varying with time. If it is attempted simply to serialize raw data, a process known as direct recording, it is not difficult to see what will happen in the case where the data contain runs of zeros. Upon serializing, the zeros code waveform is simply a steady logical low level and in the absence of a separate clock it is impossible to tell how many zeros were present, nor in the case of CD will there be a track to follow. A similar problem would be experienced if all ones occur in the data except that a steady high logic level results in a continuous bump. In digital logic circuits it is common to have signal lines and separate clock lines to overcome this problem, but with a single signal the separate clock is not possible. A further problem with direct optical recording is that the average brightness of the track is a function of the relative proportion of ones and zeros. Focus and

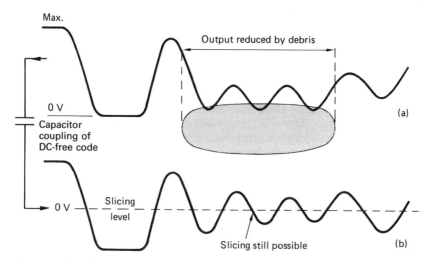

Figure 10.28 A DC-free code allows signal amplitude variations due to debris to be rejected.

tracking servos cannot be used with direct recordings because the data determine the average brightness and confuses the servos. Chapter 4 discussed modulation schemes known as DC-free codes. If such a code is used, the average brightness of the track is constant and independent of the data bits. Figure 10.28(a) shows the replay signal from the pickup being compared with a threshold voltage in order to recover a binary waveform from the analog pickup waveform, a process known as slicing. If the light beam is partially obstructed by debris, the pickup signal level falls, and the slicing level is no longer correct and errors occur. If, however, the code is DC free, the waveform from the pickup can be passed through a high-pass filter (e.g. a series capacitor) and Figure 10.28(b) shows that this rejects the falling level and converts it to a reduction in amplitude about the slicing level so that the slicer still works properly. This step cannot be performed unless a DC-free code is used.

As the frequency response on replay falls linearly to the cut-off frequency determined by the aperture of the lens and the wavelength of light used, the shorter bumps and lands produce less modulation than longer ones. Figure 10.29(a) shows what happens to the replay waveform as a bump between two long lands is made shorter. At some point the replayed signal no longer crosses the slicing level and readout is impossible. Figure 10.29(b) shows that the same effect occurs as a land between two long bumps is made shorter. In these cases recorded frequencies have to be restricted to those which produce wavelengths long enough for the player to register. Using direct recording where, for example, lands represent a 1 and bumps represent a 0, it is clear that the length of track corresponding to a 1 or a 0 would have to be greater than the limit at which the slicing in the player failed and this would restrict the playing time.

Figure 10.29(c) shows that if the recorded waveform is restricted to one which is DC free, as the length of bumps and lands falls with rising density, the replay waveform simply falls in amplitude but the average voltage remains the same and so the slicer still operates correctly. It will be clear that by using a DC-free code correct slicing remains possible with much shorter bumps and lands than with direct recording. Thus in practical high-density optical disk players, a DC-free code must be used. The output of the pickup passes to two filters. A low-pass filter removes the DC-free modulation and leaves a signal which can be used for tracking, and the high-pass filter removes the effect of debris and allows the slicer to continue to function properly. Clearly direct recording of serial data from a shift register cannot be DC free and so it cannot be read at high density, it will not be self clocking and it will not be resistant to errors caused by debris, and it will interfere with the operation of the servos. The solution to all of these problems is to use a suitable channel code. The concepts of channel coding were discussed in Chapter 4, in which frequency shift keying (FSK) was described. In FSK it is possible to use a larger number of different discrete frequencies; for example, four frequencies allow all combinations of two bits to be conveyed, eight frequencies allow all combinations of three bits to be conveyed and so on. The channel code of CD is similar in that it is the minimal case of multitone FSK where only a half cycle of each of nine different frequencies is used. These frequencies are 196, 216, 240, 270, 308, 360, 430, 540 and 720 kilohertz and are obtained by dividing a master clock of 2.16 megahertz by 11, 10, 9, 8, 7, 6, 5, 4 and 3. There are therefore nine different periods or run lengths in the CD signal, and it does not matter whether the period is the length of a land or the length of a bump. In fact the signal from a CD pickup could be inverted without making

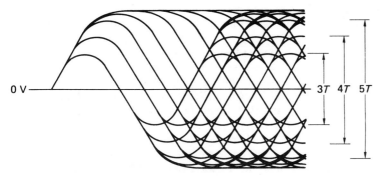

Figure 10.30 The characteristic eye pattern of EFM observed by oscilloscope. Note the reduction in amplitude of the higher-frequency components. The only information of interest is the time when the signal crosses zero.

megahertz, and so it will be evident that the master clock frequency of 2.16 megahertz cannot be recorded or reproduced. This is of no consequence in CD as it does not need to be recorded. 1.4 megahertz is the frequency at which the depth of modulation has fallen to zero. As stated, the highest frequency which can be reliably recorded is about one-half of the optical cut-off frequency. Frequencies above this replay with an amplitude so small that they have inadequate signal-to-noise ratio. It will be seen that the highest frequency in CD is 720 kilohertz, which is about half of 1.4 megahertz. Although frequencies lower than 196 kHz can be replayed easily, the clock content of lower frequencies is considered inadequate.

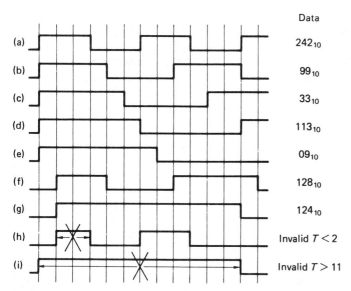

	Data
(a)	242_{10}
(b)	99_{10}
(c)	33_{10}
(d)	113_{10}
(e)	09_{10}
(f)	128_{10}
(g)	124_{10}
(h)	Invalid $T < 2$
(i)	Invalid $T > 11$

Figure 10.31 (a–g) Part of the codebook for EFM code showing examples of various run lengths from $3T$ to $11T$. (h, i) Invalid patterns which violate the run-length limits.

CD uses a coding scheme where combinations of the data bits to be recorded are represented by unique waveforms. These waveforms are created by combining various run lengths from $3T$ to $11T$ together to give a channel pattern which is $14T$ long.[17] Within the run-length limits of $3T$ to $11T$, a waveform $14T$ long can have 267 different patterns. This is slightly more than the 256 combinations of 8 data bits and so 8 bits are represented by a waveform lasting $14T$. Some of these patterns are shown in Figure 10.31. As stated, these patterns are not polarity conscious and they could be inverted without changing the meaning.

Not all of the $14T$ patterns used are DC free; some spend more time in one state than the other. The overall DC content of the recorded waveform is rendered DC free by inserting an extra portion of waveform, known as a packing period, between the $14T$ channel patterns. This packing period is $3T$ long and may or may not contain a transition, which if it is present can be in one of three places. The packing period contains no information, but serves to control the DC content of the overall waveform.[18] The packing waveform is generated in such a way that in the long term the amount of time the channel signal spends in one state is equal to the time it spends in the other state. A packing period is placed between every pair of channel patterns and so the overall length of time needed to record eight bits is $17T$. Packing periods were discussed in Chapter 4.

CD is recorded using such patterns where the lengths of bumps and lands are modulated in ideally discrete steps. The simplest way in which such patterns can be generated is to use a lookup table which converts the data bits to a control code for a programmable waveform generator. As stated, the polarity of the CD waveform is irrelevant. What matters on the disk is the lengths of the bumps or lands. The change of state in the signal sent to the cutter laser is called a transition. Clearly if a bump is being cut, it will be terminated by interrupting the light beam. If a land is being recorded, it will be terminated by allowing through the light beam. Both of these are classified as a transition, and therefore it is logical for the control code to cause transitions rather than to control the waveform level as it is not concerned with the polarity of the waveform. This is conveniently achieved by controlling the cutter laser with the output waveform of a JK-type bistable as shown in Figure 10.32. A bistable of this kind can be configured to have a data input and a clock input. If the data input is 0, there is no effect on the output when the clock edge arrives, whereas if the data input is 1

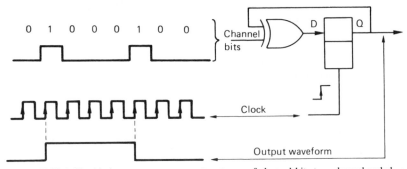

Figure 10.32 A bistable is necessary to convert a stream of channel bits to a channel-coded waveform. It is the waveform which is recorded, not the channel bits.

the output changes state when the clock edge arrives. The change of state causes a transition on the disk. If the clock has a period of T, at each channel time period or detent the output waveform will contain a transition if the control code is 1 or not if it is 0.

The control code is a binary word having fourteen bits which are known in the art as channel bits or binits. Thus a group of eight data bits is represented by a code of fourteen channel bits, hence the name of eight-to-fourteen modulation (EFM). The use of groups gives rise to the generic name of group code recording (GCR). It is a common misconception that the channel bits of a group code are recorded; in fact they are simply a convenient but not essential way of synthesizing a coded waveform having uniform time steps. It should be clear that channel bits cannot be recorded as they have a rate of 4.3 megabits per second whereas the optical cut-off frequency of CD is only 1.4 megahertz.

Another common misconception is that channel bits are data. If channel bits were data, all combinations of 14 bits, or 16 384 different values could be used. In fact only 267 combinations produce waveforms which can be recorded.

In a practical CD modulator, the eight bit data symbols to be recorded are used as the address of a lookup table which outputs a fourteen bit channel bit pattern. As the highest frequency which can be used in CD is 720 kHz, transitions cannot be closer together than $3T$ and so successive ones in the channel bit stream must have two or more zeros between them. Similarly transitions cannot be further apart than $11T$ or there will be insufficient clock content. Thus there cannot be more than ten zeros between channel ones. Whilst the lookup table can be programmed to prevent code violations within the $14T$ pattern, they could occur at the junction of two successive patterns. Thus a further function of the packing period is to prevent violation of the run-length limits. If the previous pattern ends with a transition and the next begins with one, there will be no packing transition and so the $3T$ minimum requirement can be met. If the patterns either side have long run lengths, the sum of the two might exceed $11T$ unless the packing period contained a transition. In fact the minimum run-length limit could be met with $2T$ of packing, but the requirement for DC control dictated $3T$ of packing.

The coding of CD may appear complex, but this is because it was designed to offer the required playing time on a disk of restricted size. It does this by reducing the frequency of the recorded signal compared with the data frequency. Eight data bits are represented by a length of track corresponding to $17T$. The shortest run length in a conventional recording code such as MFM would be the length of one bit, and as 8 bits require $17T$ of track, the length of one bit would be $17/8T$ or $2.125T$. Using the CD code the shortest run length is $3T$. Thus the highest frequency in the CD code is less than that of an MFM recording, so a density improvement of $3/2.125$ or 1.41 is obtained. Thus CD can record 41% more using EFM than if it used MFM. A CD can play for 75 minutes maximum. Using MFM a CD would only play for 53 minutes.

The high-pass-filtered DC-free signal from the CD pickup can be readily sliced back to a binary signal having transitions at the zero crossings. A group-coded waveform needs a suitably designed data separator to decode and deserialize the replay signal. When the disk is initially scanned, the data separator simply sees a single voltage varying with time, and it has no other information to go on whatsoever. The scanning of the disk will not necessarily be at the correct speed, and the transitions recovered will suffer from jitter. The jitter comes from two main sources. The first of these is variations in the thickness of the disk. Everyone is familiar with the illusion that the bottom of a shallow pond is moving when there are ripples in the water. In the same way, ripples in the disk thickness make the track appear to vary in speed. The second source is simply in the production tolerance to which bump edges can be made. The replication process from master to stamper will cause some slight migration of edge position, and stampers can wear in service. In order to interpret the replay waveform in the presence of jitter, use is made of the fact that transitions ideally occur at integer multiples of T. When a real transition occurs at a time other than an exact multiple of T, it can be attributed to the nearest multiple if the jitter is not too serious, and the jitter will be completely rejected. If, however, the jitter is too great, the wrongly timed transition will be attributed to the incorrect detent, and the wrong pattern will be identified.

A phase-locked loop is an essential part of a practical high-density data separator. If the input is a group-coded signal, it will contain transitions at certain multiples of the basic time period T, but not at every cycle owing to the run-length limits. The reason for the use of multiples of a basic time period in group codes is simply that a phase-locked loop can lock to such a waveform. When a transition occurs, a phase comparison can be made, but when no transition occurs, there is no phase comparison but the VCO will continue to run at the same frequency like a flywheel. The maximum run-length limit of $11T$ in CD is to ensure that the VCO does not have to run for too long between phase corrections. As a result, the VCO re-creates a continuous clock from the intermittent clock content of the channel-coded signal. In a group-coded system, the VCO re-creates the channel bit rate. In CD this is the only way in which the channel bit rate can be reproduced, as the disk itself cannot record the channel bit rate.

Jitter in the transition timing is handled by inserting a low-pass or averaging filter between the phase detector and the VCO and/or by increasing the division ratio in the feedback. Both of these steps increase the flywheel inertia. The VCO then runs at the average frequency obtained from many channel transitions and the jitter is substantially removed from the re-created clock. With a jitter-free continuous clock available from the VCO, the actual time at which a transition occurs can differ from the ideal by a considerable amount. When the recording was made, the transitions were intended to be spaced at multiples of the channel bit period, and the run lengths in the code ideally should be discrete. In practice the analog nature of the channel causes the run lengths to vary. A certain amount of variation can be rejected in a properly engineered channel code. The VCO is used to create windows called detents along the time axis of the replay signal. An ideal jitter-free signal would have a transition in the centre of the window, but real transitions may occur before or after the centre. As long as the variation is within the window, it is rejected, but if the jitter were so large that a transition crossed into an adjacent window, an error would occur. It was shown in Chapter 4 that the jitter window of EFM is $8/17$ of a data bit. Transitions on a CD replay signal can be up to $\pm 4/17$ of a data bit period out of time before errors are caused. The jitter rejection mechanism allows considerable production tolerances to be absorbed so that disks can be mass produced.

The length of a deformity on a CD master is affected not only by the duration of the record pulse, which can be as accurate as necessary, but also by the sensitivity of the resist and the intensity function of the laser. The pit which is formed in the resist is the result of the convolution of the rectangular pulse operating the modulator with the Airy function. Thus the pit will be longer than the period of the pulse would suggest. The pit edge is then subject to further position tolerance as a result of electroplating mothers and sons to create a large number of stampers. The stampers themselves will wear in service. The position of a transition is now subject to the tolerance of the cutting laser intensity function and state of focus, resist sensitivity, electroplating accuracy and wear, so the actual disk will be non-ideal.

The shortest deformity in CD is nominally $3T$ long or $3 \times 8/17$ data bits long. This can suffer nearly $\pm 4/17$ data bit periods of jitter at each end before it cannot be read properly. Thus in the worst case, where the leading edge was early and the trailing edge late, the deformity could be almost 30% longer than the ideal. In typical production disks, the edge position is held a little more accurately than this theoretical limit in order to allow extra jitter in the replay process due to thickness ripple, coma due to warped disks or out-of-focus conditions.

Once the phase-locked loop has reached the lock condition, it outputs a clock whose frequency is proportional to the speed of the track. If the track speed is correct it will have the same frequency as the channel bit clock in the cutter. This clock can then be used to sample the sliced analog signal from the pickup. As can be seen from Figure 10.33, transitions nominally occur in the centre of a T period. If the samples are taken on the edge of every T period, a transition will be reliably detected as the difference between two successive samples even if it has positional jitter approaching $\pm T/2$. Thus the output of the sampler is a jitter-free replica of the replay signal, and in the absence of errors it will be identical to the output of the JK bistable in the cutter. The sampling clock runs at the average phase of a large number of transitions from the track. Every transition conveys not only part of the waveform representing data, but also allows the phase of the clock to be updated and so every transition can also be considered to have a synchronizing function. The $11T$ maximum run-length limit is necessary to ensure that synchronizing information for the VCO is regularly available in the replay waveform.

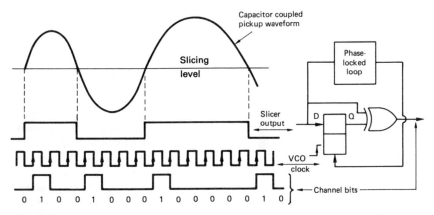

Figure 10.33 The output of the slicer is sampled at the boundary of every T period. Where successive samples differ, a channel bit 1 is generated.

The information in the CD replay waveform is carried in the timing of the transitions, not in the polarity. It is thus necessary to create a polarity-independent signal from the sliced de-jittered replay waveform. This is done by differentiating the sampler output. Figure 10.33 shows that this can be achieved by a D-type latch and an exclusive OR gate. The latch is clocked at the channel bit rate, and so acts as a 1 bit delay. The gate compares the input and output of the delay. When they are the same, there is no transition and the gate outputs 0. When a transition passes through, the input and output of the latch will be different and the gate outputs 1. Thus some distance through the replay circuitry from the pickup, the channel bits reappear, just as they disappeared before reaching the cutter laser.

10.14 Deserialization

Decoding the stream of channel bits into data requires that the boundaries between successive $17T$ periods are identified. This is the process of deserialization. On the disk one $17T$ period runs straight into the next; there are no dividing marks. Symbol separation is performed by counting channel bit periods and dividing them by 17 from a known reference point. The three packing periods are discarded and the remaining $14T$ symbol is decoded to eight data bits. The reference point is provided by the synchronizing pattern which is given that name because its detection synchronizes the deserialization counter to the replay waveform.

Synchronization has to be as reliable as possible because if it is incorrect all of the data will be corrupted up to the next sync pattern. Synchronization is achieved by the detection of a unique waveform periodically recorded on the track with regular spacing. It must be unique in the strict sense in that nothing else can give rise to it, because the detection of a false sync is just as damaging as failure to detect a correct one. Clearly the sync pattern cannot be a data code value in CD as there would then be a Catch 22 situation. It would not be possible to deserialize the EFM symbols in order to decode them until the sync pattern had been detected, but if the sync pattern were a data code value, it could not be detected until the deserialization of the EFM waveform had been synchronized. Thus in a group code recording a data code value simply cannot be used for synchronizing. In any case it is undesirable and unnecessary to restrict the data code values which can be recorded; CD requires all 256 combinations of the 8 bit symbols recorded.

In practice CD synchronizes deserialization with a waveform which is unique in that it is different from any of the 256 waveforms which represent data. For reliability, the sync pattern should have the best signal-to-noise ratio possible, and this is obtained by making it one complete cycle of the lowest frequency ($11T$ plus $11T$) which gives it the largest amplitude and also makes it DC free. Upon detection of the $2 \times T_{max}$ waveform, the deserialization counter which divides the channel bit count by 17 is reset. This occurs on the next system clock, which is the reason for the 0 in the sync pattern after the third 1 and before the merging bits. CD therefore uses forward synchronization and correctly deserialized data are available immediately after the first sync pattern is detected. The sync pattern is longer than the data symbols, and so clearly no data code value can create it, although it would be possible for certain adjacent data symbols to create a false sync pattern by concatenation were it not for the presence of the packing period.

It is a further job of the packing period to prevent false sync patterns being generated at the junction of two channel symbols.

Each data block or frame in CD and MD, shown in Figure 10.34, consists of 33 symbols 17*T* each following the preamble, making a total of 588*T* or 136 μs. Each symbol represents eight data bits. The first symbol in the block is used for subcode, and the remaining 32 bytes represent 24 audio sample bytes and 8 bytes of redundancy for the error-correction system. The subcode byte forms part of a subcode block which is built up over 98 successive data frames.

The channel bits which are re-created by sampling and differentiating the sliced replay waveform in time to the restored clock from the VCO are conveniently converted to parallel format for decoding in a shift register which need only have 14 stages. The bit counter which is synchronized to the serial replay waveform by the detection of the sync pattern will output a pulse every 17*T* when a complete 14*T* pattern of channel bits is in the register. This pattern can then be transferred in parallel to the decoder which will identify the channel pattern and output the data code value.

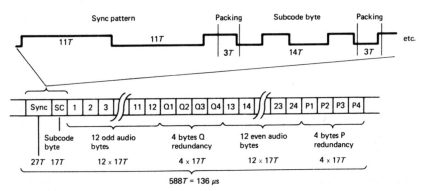

Figure 10.34 One CD data block begins with a unique sync pattern, and one subcode byte, followed by 24 audio bytes and eight redundancy bytes. Note that each byte requires 14*T* in EFM, with 3*T* packing between symbols, making 17*T*.

Detection of sync in CD is simply a matter of identifying a complete cycle of the lowest recorded frequency. In practical players the sync pattern will be sliced, sampled and differentiated to channel bits along with the rest of the replay waveform. As a shift register is already present it is a matter of convenience to extend it to 23 stages so that the sync pattern can be detected by continuously examining the parallel output as the patterns from the track shift by. The pattern will be detected by a combination of logic gates which will only output a 'true' value when the shift register contains 10000000000100000000001 in the correct place.

This is not a bit pattern which exists on the disk; the disk merely contains two maximum run lengths in series and it does not matter whether these are a bump followed by a land or a land followed by a bump. The sliced replay waveform cannot be sampled at the correct frequency until the VCO has locked and this requires the *T* rate synchronizing information from a prior length of data track.

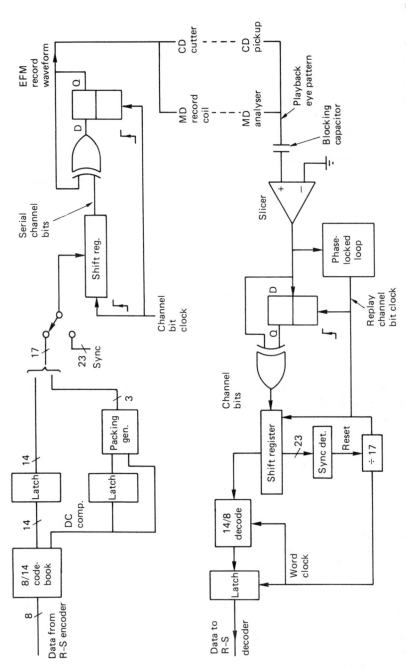

Figure 10.35 Overall block diagram of the EFM encode/decode process. A MiniDisc will contain both. A CD player only has the decoder; the encoding is in the mastering cutter.

If the VCO were not locked, the sync waveform would be sampled into the wrong number of periods and would not be detected. Following sampling, the replay signal is differentiated so that transitions of either direction produce a channel bit 1.

Figure 10.35 shows an overall block diagram of the record modulation scheme used in CD mastering and the corresponding replay system or data separator. The input to the record channel coder consists of 16 bit audio samples which are divided in two to make symbols of 8 bits. These symbols are used in the error correction system which interleaves them and adds redundant symbols. For every twelve audio symbols, there are four symbols of redundancy, but the channel coder is not concerned with the sequence or significance of the symbols and simply records their binary code values.

Symbols are provided to the coder in eight bit parallel format, with a symbol clock. The symbol clock is obtained by dividing down the 4.3218 megahertz T rate clock by a factor of 17. Each symbol is used to address the lookup table which outputs a corresponding 14 channel bit pattern in parallel into a shift register. The T rate clock then shifts the channel bits along the register. The lookup table also outputs data corresponding to the digital sum value (DSV) of the 14 bit symbol to the packing generator. The packing generator determines if action is needed between symbols to control DC content. The packing generator checks for run-length violations and potential false sync patterns. As a result of all the criteria, the packing generator loads three channel bits into the space between the symbols, such that the register then contains 14 bit symbols with 3 bits of packing between them. At the beginning of each frame, the sync pattern is loaded into the register just before the first symbol is looked up in such a way that the packing bits are correctly calculated between the sync pattern and the first symbol.

A channel bit 1 indicates that a transition should be generated, and so the serial output of the shift register is fed to the JK bistable along with the T rate clock. The output of the JK bistable is the ideal channel-coded waveform containing transitions separated by $3T$ to $11T$. It is a self-clocking, run-length-limited waveform. The channel bits and the T rate clock have done their job of changing the state of the JK bistable and do not pass further on. At the output of the JK the sync pattern is simply two $11T$ run lengths in series.

At this stage the run-length-limited waveform is used to control the acousto-optic modulator in the cutter. This actually results in pits which are slightly too long and lands which are too short because of the convolution of the record waveform with the Airy function which was mentioned above. As the cutter spot is about $0.4\,\mu m$ across, the pit edges in the resist are moved slightly. Thus although the ideal waveform is created in the encoding circuitry, having integer multiples of T between transitions, the pit structure is non-ideal and pit edges are not located at exact multiples of a basic distance. The duty cycle of the pits and lands is not exactly 50% and the replay waveform will have a DC offset. This is of no consequence in CD as the channel code is known to be DC free and an equivalent offset can be generated in the slicing level of the player such that the duty cycle of the slicer output becomes 50%.

The resist master is developed and used to create stampers. The resulting disks can then be replayed. The track velocity of a given CD is constant, but the rotational speed depends upon the radius. In order to get into lock, the disk must be spun at roughly the right track speed. This is done using the run-length limits

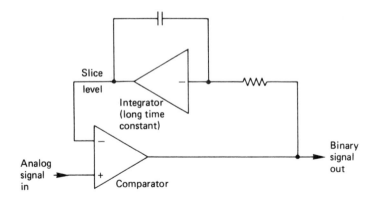

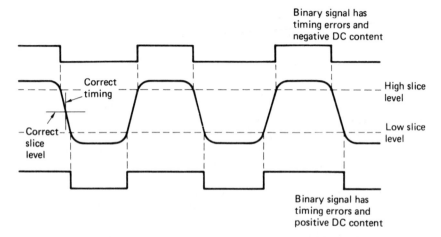

Figure 10.36 Self-slicing a DC-free channel code. Since the channel code signal from the disk is band limited, it has finite rise times, and slicing at the wrong level (as shown here) results in timing errors, which cause the data separator to be less reliable. As the channel code is DC free, the binary signal when correctly sliced should integrate to zero. An incorrect slice level gives the binary output a DC content and, as shown here, this can be fed back to modify the slice level automatically.

of the recording. The pickup is focused and the tracking is enabled. The replay waveform from the pickup is passed through a high-pass filter to remove level variations due to contamination and sliced to return it to a binary waveform. The slicing level is self adapting as Figure 10.36 shows so that a 50% duty cycle is obtained. The slicer output is then sampled by the unlocked VCO running at approximately T rate. If the disk is running too slowly, the longest run length on the disk will appear as more than $11T$, whereas if the disk is running too fast, the shortest run length will appear as less than $3T$. As a result the disk speed can be brought to approximately the right speed and the VCO will then be able to lock to the clock content of the EFM waveform from the slicer. Once the VCO is locked, it will be possible to sample the replay waveform at the correct T rate. The output of the sampler is then differentiated and the channel bits reappear and

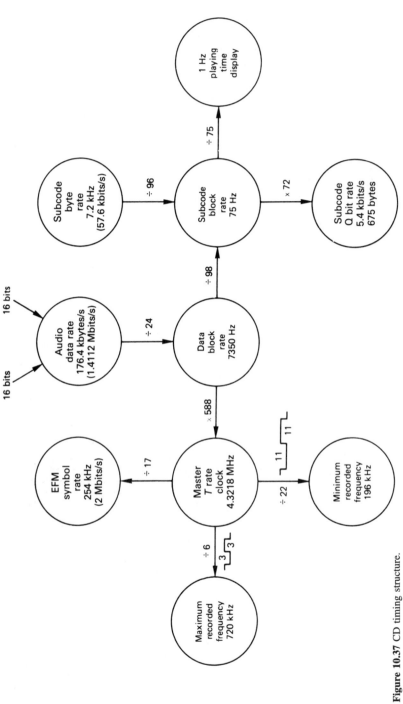

Figure 10.37 CD timing structure.

are fed into the shift register. The sync pattern detector will then function to reset the deserialization counter which allows the $14T$ symbols to be identified. The $14T$ symbols are then decoded to 8 bits in the reverse coding table.

Figure 10.37 reveals the timing relationships of the CD format. The sampling rate of 44.1 kHz with 16 bit words in left and right channels results in an audio data rate of 176.4 kbits/s (k = 1000 here, not 1024). Since there are 24 audio bytes in a data frame, the frame rate will be:

$$\frac{176.4}{24}\,\text{kHz} = 7.35\,\text{kHz}$$

If this frame rate is divided by 98, the number of frames in a subcode block, the subcode block or sector rate of 75 Hz results. This frequency can be divided down to provide a running-time display in the player. Note that this is the frequency of the wavy grooves in recordable MDs.

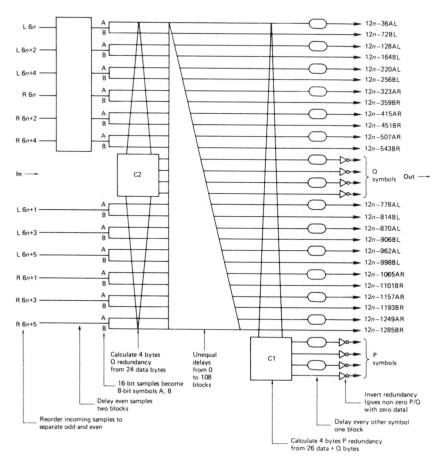

Figure 10.38 CD interleave structure.

If the frame rate is multiplied by 588, the number of channel bits in a frame, the master clock rate of 4.3218 MHz results. From this the maximum and minimum frequencies in the channel, 720 kHz and 196 kHz, can be obtained using the run-length limits of EFM.

10.15 Error-correction strategy

This section discusses the track structure of CD in detail. The track structure of MiniDisc is based on that of CD and the differences will be noted in the next section.

Each sync block was seen in Figure 10.34 to contain 24 audio bytes, but these are non-contiguous owing to the extensive interleave.[19-21] There are a number of interleaves used in CD, each of which has a specific purpose. The full interleave structure is shown in Figure 10.38. The first stage of interleave is to introduce a delay between odd and even samples. The effect is that uncorrectable errors cause odd samples and even samples to be destroyed at different times, so that interpolation can be used to conceal the errors, with a reduction in audio bandwidth and a risk of aliasing. The odd/even interleave is performed first in the encoder, since concealment is the last function in the decoder. Figure 10.39

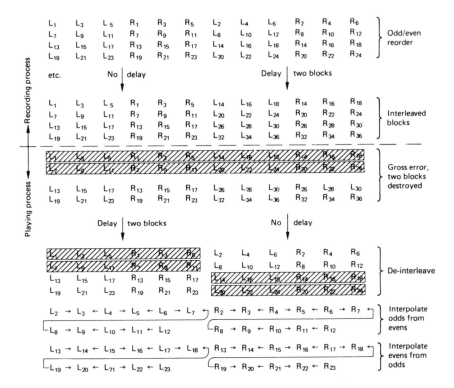

Figure 10.39 Odd/even interleave permits the use of interpolation to conceal uncorrectable errors.

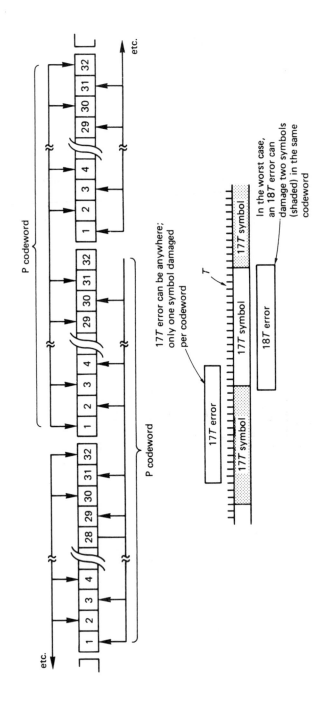

Figure 10.40 The final interleave of the CD format spreads P codewords over two blocks. Thus any small random error can only destroy one symbol in one codeword, even if two adjacent symbols in one block are destroyed. Since the P code is optimized for single-symbol error correction, random errors will always be corrected by the C1 process, maximizing the burst-correcting power of the C2 process after de-interleave.

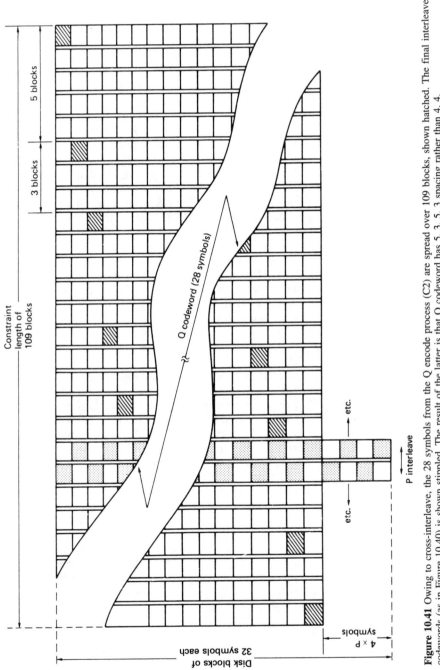

Figure 10.41 Owing to cross-interleave, the 28 symbols from the Q encode process (C2) are spread over 109 blocks, shown hatched. The final interleave of P codewords (as in Figure 10.40) is shown stippled. The result of the latter is that Q codeword has 5, 3, 5, 3 spacing rather than 4, 4.

shows that an odd/even delay of two blocks permits interpolation in the case where two uncorrectable blocks leave the error-correction system.

Left and right samples from the same instant form a sample set. As the samples are 16 bits, each sample set consists of four bytes, AL, BL, AR, BR. Six sample sets form a 24 byte parallel word, and the C2 encoder produces four bytes of redundancy Q. By placing the Q symbols in the centre of the block, the odd/even distance is increased, permitting interpolation over the largest possible error burst. The 28 bytes are now subjected to differing delays, which are integer multiples of four blocks. This produces a convolutional interleave, where one C2 codeword is stored in 28 different blocks, spread over a distance of 109 blocks.

At one instant, the C2 encoder will be presented with 28 bytes which have come from 28 different codewords. The C1 encoder produces a further four bytes of redundancy P. Thus the C1 and C2 codewords are produced by crossing an array in two directions. This is known as cross-interleaving.

The final interleave is an odd/even output symbol delay, which causes P codewords to be spread over two blocks on the disk as shown in Figure 10.40. This mechanism prevents small random errors destroying more than one symbol in a P codeword. The choice of 8 bit symbols in EFM assists this strategy. The expressions in Figure 10.38 determine how the interleave is calculated. Figure 10.41 shows an example of the use of these expressions to calculate the contents of a block and to demonstrate the cross-interleave.

The calculation of the P and Q redundancy symbols is made using Reed–Solomon polynomial division. The P redundancy symbols are primarily for detecting errors, to act as pointers or error flags for the Q system. The P system can, however, correct single-symbol errors.

10.16 Track layout of MD

MD uses the same channel code and error-correction interleave as CD for simplicity and the sectors are exactly the same size. The interleave of CD is convolutional, which is not a drawback in a continuous recording. However, MD uses random access and the recording is discontinuous. Figure 10.42 shows that the convolutional interleave causes codewords to run between sectors. Re-recording a sector would prevent error correction in the area of the edit. The solution is to use a buffering zone in the area of an edit where the convolution can begin and end. This is the job of the link sectors. Figure 10.43 shows the layout of data on a recordable MD. In each cluster of 36 sectors, 32 are used for encoded audio data. One is used for subcode and the remaining three are link sectors. The cluster is the minimum data quantum which can be recorded and represents just over two seconds of decoded audio. The cluster must be recorded continuously because of the convolutional interleave. Effectively the link sectors form an edit gap which is large enough to absorb both mechanical tolerances and the interleave overrun when a cluster is rewritten. One or more clusters will be assembled in memory before writing to the disk is attempted.

Prerecorded MDs are recorded at one time, and need no link sectors. In order to keep the format consistent between the two types of MiniDisc, three extra subcode sectors are made available. As a result it is not possible to record the entire audio and subcode of a prerecorded MD onto a recordable MD because the link sectors cannot be used to record data.

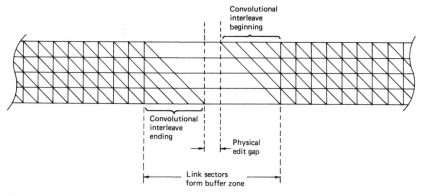

Figure 10.42 The convolutional interleave of CD is retained in MD, but buffer zones are needed to allow the convolution to finish before a new one begins, otherwise editing is impossible.

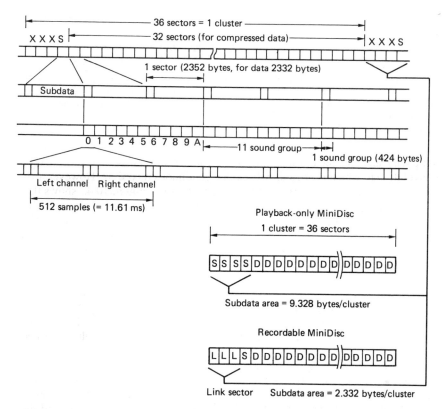

Figure 10.43 Format of MD uses clusters of sectors including link sectors for editing. Prerecorded MDs do not need link sectors, so more subcode capacity is available. The ATRAC coder of MD produces the sound groups shown here.

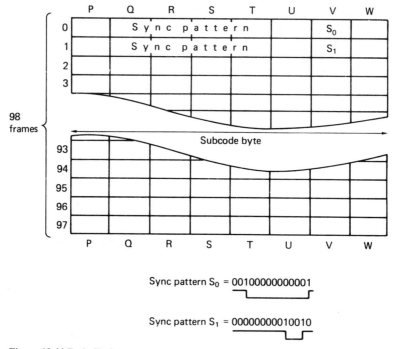

Sync pattern S_0 = 00100000000001

Sync pattern S_1 = 00000000010010

Figure 10.44 Each CD frame contains one subcode byte. Afer 98 frames, the structure above will repeat. Each subcode byte contains 1 bit from eight 96 bit words following the two synchronizing patterns. These patterns cannot be expressed as a byte, because they are 14 bit EFM patterns additional to those which describe the 256 combinations of eight data bits.

The ATRAC coder produces data blocks which are known as sound groups. Figure 10.44 shows that these contain 212 bytes for each of the two audio channels and are the equivalent of 11.6 milliseconds of real-time audio. Eleven of these sound groups will fit into two standard CD sectors with 20 bytes to spare. The 32 audio data sectors in a cluster thus contain a total of $16 \times 11 = 176$ sound groups.

References

1. BOUWHUIS, G. *et al., Principles of optical disc systems.* Bristol: Adam Hilger (1985)
2. ZERNIKE, F., Beugungstheorie des schneidenverfahrens und seiner verbesserten form, der phasenkontrastmethode. *Physica*, **1**, 689 (1934)
3. MEE, C.D. and DANIEL, E.D. (eds), *Magnetic Recording Vol. III*, Chapter 6. New York: McGraw-Hill (1987)
4. CONNELL, G.A.N. *et al.*, Signal to noise ratio for magneto-optic readout from quadrilayer structures. *Appl. Phys. Lett.*, **42**, 742 (1983)
5. GOLDBERG, N., A high density magneto-optic memory. *IEEE Trans. Magn.*, **MAG-3**, 605 (1967)
6. Various authors, *Philips Tech. Rev.*, **40**, 149–180 (1982)
7. German Patent No. 2,208,379
8. Various authors, Video long-play systems. *Appl. Opt.*, **17**, 1993–2036 (1978)
9. AIRY, G.B., *Trans. Camb. Phil. Soc.*, **5**, 283 (1835)

10. RAY, S.F., *Applied photographic optics*, Chapter 17. Oxford: Focal Press (1988)
11. MARÉCHAL, A., *Rev. d'Optique*, **26**, 257 (1947)
12. HOPKINS, H.H., Diffraction theory of laser read-out systems for optical video discs. *J. Opt. Soc. Am.*, **69**, 4 (1979)
13. BOUWHUIS, G. *et al.*, op cit. Ch. 2
14. PASMAN, J.H.T., Optical diffraction methods for analysis and control of pit geometry on optical discs. *J. Audio Eng. Soc.*, **41**, 19–31 (1993)
15. VERKAIK, W., Compact Disc (CD) mastering – an industrial process. In *Digital Audio*, ed. B.A. Blesser, B. Locanthi and T.G. Stockham Jr, pp. 189–195. New York: Audio Engineering Society 189 (1983)
16. MIYAOKA, S., Manufacturing technology of the Compact Disc. In *Digital Audio*, op. cit., pp. 196–201
17. OGAWA, H. and SCHOUHAMER IMMINK, K.A., EFM – the modulation system for the Compact Disc digital audio system. In *Digital Audio*, op. cit., pp. 117–124
18. SCHOUHAMER IMMINK, K.A. and GROSS, U., Optimization of low-frequency properties of eight-to-fourteen modulation. *Radio Electron. Eng.*, **53**, 63–66 (1983)
19. PEEK, J.B.H., Communications aspects of the Compact Disc digital audio system. *IEEE Commun. Mag.*, **23**, 7–15 (1985)
20. VRIES, L.B. *et al.*, The digital Compact Disc – modulation and error correction. Presented at 67th Audio Engineering Society Convention (New York, 1980), preprint 1674
21. VRIES, L.B. and ODAKA, K., CIRC – the error correcting code for the Compact Disc digital audio system. In *Digital Audio*, op. cit., pp. 178–186

Index